"Novakovic provides a welcome and long-anticipated contribution to the Baylor Handbook on the Greek New Testament series. Tackling the deceptive simplicity of John's language, Novakovic deftly untangles John's subtlety and takes up grammatical questions too often overlooked in commentaries or dismissed by those too focused on John's 'elementary Greek.' Her insights not only guide readers just beginning to learn more about Greek syntax but also engage seasoned scholars by offering detailed interpretations with ranging interpretive and theological possibilities."

—**Alicia Myers**, *Associate Professor of New Testament & Greek, Divinity School, Campbell University*

"Because grammar and syntax are the foundations for interpretation, this handbook is a valuable resource for serious students of the Gospel of John. In the introduction Novakovic briefly summarizes distinctive characteristics of the Gospel's vocabulary and style, repetition and variation, tenses and verbal aspect, and word order. The translation provides a fresh, literal rendering of the Greek text, which is itself often a guide to interpretation. While this is not a commentary, the annotations on well-known cruxes of interpretation are remarkably insightful. These are volumes you will want to keep on your desk!"

—**R. Alan Culpepper**, *Dean and Professor of New Testament Emeritus, McAfee School of Theology, Mercer University*

"The aim of this series is to supplement standard New Testament commentaries with an 'accessible and succinct' guide to the dynamics of the Greek text, and in these volumes Lidija Novakovic does this for the Fourth Gospel with precision, care, and clarity. Her methodological assumptions are crafted with considered sensitivity to scholarly discussion on Johannine style. Her glossary furnishes a ready means for entering the kind of discourse required by syntactical and text-critical issues. Her analysis, itself, while comprehensive, is consciously pitched to the problems most challenging for interpretation."

—**Michael A. Daise**, *Walter G. Mason Professor, College of William & Mary*

BHGNT

Baylor Handbook on the Greek New Testament
Lidija Novakovic
General Editor

OTHER BOOKS IN THIS SERIES

John 1–10	Lidija Novakovic
Matthew 1–14	Wesley G. Olmstead
Matthew 15–28	Wesley G. Olmstead
Mark 1–8	Rodney J. Decker
Mark 9–16	Rodney J. Decker
Luke	Martin M. Culy, Mikeal C. Parsons, and Joshua J. Stigall
Acts	Martin M. Culy and Mikeal C. Parsons
1 Corinthians 1–9	Timothy A. Brookins and Bruce W. Longenecker
1 Corinthians 10–16	Timothy A. Brookins and Bruce W. Longenecker
2 Corinthians	Fredrick J. Long
Galatians	David A. deSilva
Ephesians	William J. Larkin
Colossians and Philemon	Constantine R. Campbell
The Pastoral Letters	Larry J. Perkins
James	A. K. M. Adam
1 Peter	Mark Dubis
2 Peter and Jude	Peter H. Davids
1, 2, 3 John	Martin M. Culy
Revelation	David L. Mathewson

JOHN 11–21

A Handbook on the Greek Text

Lidija Novakovic

BAYLOR UNIVERSITY PRESS

© 2020 by Baylor University Press
Waco, Texas 76798

All Rights Reserved. No part of this publication may be reproduced, stored in a retrieval system, or transmitted, in any form or by any means, electronic, mechanical, photocopying, recording, or otherwise, without the prior permission in writing of Baylor University Press.

Typesetting by Scribe Inc.
Cover design by Pamela Poll

The Library of Congress has cataloged this book under the
ISBN 978-1-4813-1214-1.

CONTENTS

Series Introduction	ix
Preface	xv
Abbreviations	xvii
Introduction	xxi
John 11:1-10	1
John 11:11-16	9
John 11:17-27	13
John 11:28-37	20
John 11:38-44	27
John 11:45-54	33
John 11:55-57	40
John 12:1-8	42
John 12:9-11	49
John 12:12-19	50
John 12:20-26	57
John 12:27-33	63
John 12:34-36	67
John 12:37-43	70
John 12:44-50	76

John 13:1-11	81
John 13:12-17	91
John 13:18-20	96
John 13:21-30	98
John 13:31-35	106
John 13:36-38	111
John 14:1-7	113
John 14:8-14	119
John 14:15-21	126
John 14:22-26	132
John 14:27-31	137
John 15:1-8	141
John 15:9-17	149
John 15:18-27	156
John 16:1-15	164
John 16:16-24	175
John 16:25-33	183
John 17:1-5	190
John 17:6-8	194
John 17:9-19	197
John 17:20-26	206
John 18:1-11	214
John 18:12-14	222
John 18:15-18	224
John 18:19-24	227
John 18:25-27	231
John 18:28-40	233

John 19:1-16a	245
John 19:16b-30	259
John 19:31-37	272
John 19:38-42	277
John 20:1-10	281
John 20:11-18	290
John 20:19-23	298
John 20:24-29	303
John 20:30-31	309
John 21:1-14	313
John 21:15-19	325
John 21:20-23	331
John 21:24-25	335
Glossary	339
Works Cited	349
Author Index	359
Grammar Index	365

SERIES INTRODUCTION

The Baylor Handbook on the Greek New Testament (BHGNT) is designed to guide new readers and seasoned scholars alike through the intricacies of the Greek text. Each handbook provides a verse-by-verse treatment of the biblical text. Unlike traditional commentaries, however, the BHGNT makes no attempt to expound on the theological meaning or significance of the document under consideration. Instead, the handbooks serve as supplements to commentary proper. Readers of traditional commentaries are sometimes dismayed by the fact that even those that are labeled "exegetical" or "critical" frequently have little to say about the mechanics of the Greek text and all too often completely ignore the more perplexing grammatical issues. In contrast, the BHGNT offers an accessible and comprehensive, though not exhaustive, treatment of the Greek New Testament, with particular attention given to the grammar of the text. In order to make the handbooks more user friendly, authors have only selectively interacted with secondary literature. Where there is significant debate on an issue, the handbooks provide a representative sample of scholars espousing each position; when authors adopt a less known stance on the text, they generally list any other scholars who have embraced that position.

The BHGNT, however, is more than a reliable guide to the Greek text of the New Testament. Each author brings unique strengths to the task of preparing the handbook, such as textual criticism, lexical semantics, discourse analysis, or other areas. As a result, students and scholars alike will at times be introduced to ways of looking at the Greek language that they have not encountered before. This feature makes the handbooks valuable not only for intermediate and advanced Greek courses, but also for students and scholars who no longer have the luxury of increasing their Greek proficiency within a classroom context. While handbook authors do not consider modern linguistic theory to be a panacea for all questions exegetical, the BHGNT does aim both to help move linguistic insights into the mainstream of New Testament reference works and, at the same time, to help weed out some of the myths about the Greek language that continue to appear in both scholarly and popular treatments of the New Testament.

Using the Baylor Handbook on the Greek New Testament

Each handbook consists of the following features. The introduction draws readers' attention to some of the distinctive characteristics of the New Testament document under consideration and treats some of the broader issues relating to the text as a whole in a more thorough fashion. In the handbook proper, the biblical text is divided into sections, each of which is introduced with a translation that illustrates how the insights gleaned from the analysis that follows may be expressed in modern English. Following the translation is the heart of the handbook, an extensive analysis of the Greek text. Here, the Greek text of each verse is followed by comments on grammatical, lexical, and text-critical issues. Every verb is parsed for the sake of pedagogical expediency, while nouns are parsed only when the form is unusual or requires additional explanation. Handbook authors may also make use of other features, such as passage overviews between the translation and notes.

Each page of the handbook includes a header to help readers quickly locate comments on a particular passage. Terminology used in the comments that is potentially unfamiliar is included in a glossary in the back of the handbook and/or cross-referenced with the first occurrence of the expression, where an explanation may be found. This is followed by a bibliography of works cited, providing helpful guidance in identifying resources for further research on the Greek text. Each volume concludes with a grammar index and an author index. The list of grammatical phenomena occurring in the biblical text provides a valuable resource for students of Greek wanting to study a particular construction more carefully or Greek instructors needing to develop illustrations, exercises, or exams.

The handbooks assume that users will possess a minimal level of competence with Greek morphology and syntax. Series authors generally utilize traditional labels such as those found in Daniel Wallace's *Greek Grammar beyond the Basics*. Labels that are drawn from the broader field of modern linguistics are explained at their first occurrence and included in the glossary. Common labels that users may be unfamiliar with are also included in the glossary.

The primary exception to the broad adoption of traditional syntactic labels relates to verb tenses. Most New Testament Greek grammars describe the tense system as being formally fairly simple (only six tenses) but functionally complex. The aorist tense, it is frequently said, can function in a wide variety of ways that are associated with labels such as "ingressive," "gnomic," "constative," "epistolary," "proleptic," and so forth. Similar functional complexity is posited for the other tenses. Positing such functions, however, typically stems not from a careful analysis of Greek syntax but rather from grappling with the challenges of translating Greek verbs into English. When we carefully examine the Greek verb tenses, we find that the tense forms do not themselves denote semantic features such as ingressive, iterative, or conative; at best they may allow for ingressive, iterative, or conative translations. In addition, the tense labels have frequently led to exegetical claims that go beyond the syntax. For this reason, handbook authors do not generally utilize these labels but seek to express nuances typically associated with them in the translation.

Avoidance of traditional tense labels is based on the insights gained from the discussions about verbal aspect theory over the past three decades, which distinguish *Aktionsart* (kind of action) from aspect (subjective portrayal of an action). Many contributors to the BHGNT series agree with the basic premise of verbal aspect theory that tense forms do not grammaticalize time and adopt a three-aspect paradigm that differentiates between perfective aspect, imperfective aspect, and stative aspect. Some authors also concur with Stanley Porter's (1989; 1994) claim about different levels of semantic density or markedness, i.e., the concept of the perfective aspect as the least marked (background), the imperfective aspect as more marked (foreground), and the stative aspect as the most marked aspect (frontground). There is, however, still significant scholarly disagreement concerning the nature of verbal aspects and their semantic functions. Constantine Campbell (2008), for example, identifies the Greek perfect not with stative aspect, like Porter and others, but with imperfective aspect with heightened remoteness, which he describes as a dynamic action in progress. Steven Runge (2014), conversely, challenges the foundational idea of Porter's verbal aspect theory that Greek tense forms do not have temporal references and argues for a mixed time-aspect system. Handbook authors are encouraged to interact with these and other discussions about verbal aspect and incorporate their insights in the analysis of the Greek text.

Deponency

Although series authors will vary in the theoretical approaches they bring to the text, the BHGNT has adopted the same general approach on one important issue: deponency. Traditionally, the label "deponent" has been applied to verbs with middle, passive, or middle/passive morphology that are thought to be "active" in meaning. Introductory grammars tend to put a significant number of middle verbs in the New Testament in this category, despite the fact that some of the standard reference grammars have questioned the validity of the label. Archibald Robertson (332), for example, argues that the label "should not be used at all."

In recent years, a number of scholars have taken up Robertson's quiet call to abandon this label. Carl Conrad's posts on the B-Greek Internet discussion list (beginning in 1997) and his subsequent formalization of those concerns in unpublished papers available on his website have helped flesh out the concerns raised by earlier scholars. In his essay, "New Observations on Voice in the Ancient Greek Verb," Conrad argues that the Greek voice system is not built upon trichotomy (active, middle, and passive) but upon a bipolar basis (active and middle/passive). He further claims that the verbs that have been traditionally termed "deponent" are by their nature subject focused, like the forms that are regarded as genuine middle, and suggests that "both term and concept of 'Deponency' should be eliminated forever from formal categories and thinking about ancient Greek voice" (11). Similar conclusions are reached by Jonathan Pennington (60–64), who helpfully summarizes the rationale for dispensing with the label, maintaining that widespread use of the term "deponent" stems from two key factors: (1) the tendency to analyze Greek syntax through reference to English translation—if a workable translation of a middle form appears "active" in English, we conclude that the verb must be active in meaning even though it is middle in form; and (2) the imposition of Latin categories on Greek grammar. Pennington concludes, "Most if not all verbs that are considered 'deponent' are in fact truly middle in meaning" (61).

The questions that have been raised regarding deponency as a syntactic category, then, are not simply issues that interest a few Greek scholars and linguists without much bearing on how one understands the text. Rather, the notion of deponency has, at least in some cases, effectively obscured the semantic significance of the middle voice, leading to imprecise readings of the text (see also Bakker; Taylor). It is not only middle-voice verbs, however, that are the focus of attention in this debate. Conrad, Pennington, and others also maintain that deponency is an invalid category for passive verbs that have traditionally been placed in this category. To account for putative passive deponent verbs, these scholars have turned to the evolution of voice morphology in the Greek language. They draw attention to the fact that middle morphology was being replaced by passive morphology (the θη morpheme) during the Koine period (see esp. Conrad, 3, 5–6; cf. Pennington, 68; Taylor, 175; Caragounis, 153). Consequently, in the Common Era we find "an increasing number of passive forms without a distinctive passive idea . . . replacing older middle forms" (Pennington, 68). This diachronic argument leads Conrad (5) to conclude that the θη morpheme should be treated as a middle/passive rather than a passive morpheme. Such arguments have a sound linguistic foundation and raise serious questions about the legitimacy of the notion "passive deponent."

Should, then, the label "deponent" be abandoned altogether? While more research needs to be done to account for middle/passive morphology in Koine Greek fully, the arguments are both compelling and exegetically significant. Consequently, users of the BHGNT will discover that verbs that are typically labeled "deponent," including some with θη morphology, tend to be listed as "middle" or "middle/passive."

In recognizing that so-called deponent verbs should be viewed as true middles, users of the BHGNT should not fall into the trap of concluding that the middle form emphasizes the subject's involvement in the action of the verb. At times, the middle voice appears simply to be a morphological flag indicating that the verb is intransitive. More frequently, the middle morphology tends to be driven by the "middle" semantics of the verb itself. In other words, the middle voice is sometimes used with the verb not in order to place a focus on the subject's involvement in the action, but precisely because the sense of the lexical form itself involves subject focus.

It is the hope of Baylor University Press, the series editors, and each of the authors that these handbooks will help advance our understanding of the Greek New Testament, be used to equip further pastors and other church leaders for the work of ministry, and fan into flame a love for the Greek New Testament among a new generation of students and scholars.

Martin M. Culy
Founding Series Editor

Lidija Novakovic
Series Editor

PREFACE

I would like to thank Carey Newman, director of Baylor University Press, who in 2015 invited me to serve as editor of the BHGNT series, which gave me the opportunity to refine my editorial skills before I undertook the task of writing one of the handbooks myself. I am also grateful to the Baylor Arts & Sciences Research Leave Committee for awarding me a research leave in the spring of 2018, which allowed me to complete the greater part of this project. Special thanks are due to my graduate assistants Jeremiah Bailey, who did the initial parsing of most of the verbs, and Daniel Glover, who helped with proofreading. Above all, I am indebted to John Genter, who not only proofread the entire manuscript but also prepared the abbreviations list and the glossary. I also wish to thank my husband, Ivo Novakovic, and my children, Andreja and Matthew. I could not have finished this project, which required countless hours of painstaking work, without their continuous support.

I wish to dedicate this handbook to the memory of Claus Meister, my first Greek teacher at the Baptist Theological Seminary, Rüschlikon, whose ingenious explanations of grammatical intricacies instilled in me a deep love for the Greek language. It was his textbook with selected readings that gave me a chance to read my first sentence in Greek: Ἐν ἀρχῇ ἦν ὁ λόγος, καὶ ὁ λόγος ἦν πρὸς τὸν θεόν, καὶ θεὸς ἦν ὁ λόγος (John 1:1).

ABBREVIATIONS

1st	first person
2nd	second person
2 Pet	2 Peter
3rd	third person
acc	accusative
act	active
aor	aorist
ASV	American Standard Version
BCE	Before the Common Era
BDAG	Danker, *A Greek-English Lexicon of the New Testament*, 2000
BDB	Brown, Driver, Briggs, *A Hebrew and English Lexicon of the Old Testament*
BDF	Blass, Debrunner, Funk, *A Greek Grammar of the New Testament*
CEB	Common English Bible
ch.	chapter
cf.	compare (*confer*)
CJB	Complete Jewish Bible
dat	dative
DBY	The Darby Bible
e.g.	for example (*exempli gratia*)
ESV	English Standard Version

et al.	and others (*et alii*)
fem	feminine
FG	Fourth Gospel
fut	future
gen	genitive
GNT	Good News Translation
GW	God's Word
HCSB	Holman Christian Standard Bible
HP	historical present
i.e.	that is (*id est*)
impf	imperfect
impv	imperative
ind	indicative
inf	infinitive
JB	Jerusalem Bible
J.W.	*Bellum judaicum* (*Jewish War*)
KJV	King James Version
LEB	The Lexham English Bible
lit.	literally
LN	Louw and Nida, *Greek-English Lexicon*
LSJ	Liddell, Scott, Jones, *A Greek-English Lexicon*
LXX	Septuagint
masc	masculine
MHT	Moulton, Howard, Turner, *A Grammar of New Testament Greek*, 4 vols.
mid	middle
MSG	The Message
MSS/mss	manuscripts
MT	Masoretic Text
n.	note
NA[28]	Nestle-Aland, *Novum Testamentum Graece*, 28th ed.
NAB	New American Bible

NASB	New American Standard Bible
NCV	New Century Version
NEB	New English Bible
NET	New English Translation
neut	neuter
NIV	New International Version
NKJV	New King James Version
NLT	New Living Translation
nom	nominative
NRSV	New Revised Standard Version
NT	New Testament
NWT	New World Translation
opt	optative
OT	Old Testament
pace	with deference to
pass	passive
pl	plural
plprf	pluperfect
PN	predicate nominative
PP	prepositional phrase
pres	present
prf	perfect
ptc	participle
REB	Revised English Bible
RHE	Douay-Rheims Catholic Bible (English translation of the Vulgate)
RSV	Revised Standard Version
SBLGNT	The SBL Greek New Testament
sg	singular
subj	subjunctive
TCNT	Twentieth Century New Testament
TDNT	Kittel, *Theological Dictionary of the New Testament*, 10 vols.

TSKS	article-substantive-καί-substantive (relating to Granville Sharp's rule)
UBS[5]	The United Bible Societies' Greek New Testament, 5th ed.
v./vv.	verse/verses
voc	vocative
WBT	Webster Bible
WYC	Wycliffe Bible

INTRODUCTION

The Gospel of John, habitually called the Fourth Gospel because of its placement in the New Testament canon, is sometimes described as "a book in which a child can wade and an elephant can swim" (Barackman, 63). Indeed, the profound theology of the Fourth Gospel is expressed through one of the most accessible Greek texts. Consisting of twenty-one chapters, 879 verses, and 15,635 words, the Gospel of John employs only 1,011 different words. Compared with 1,345 different words used by Mark, 1,691 different words used by Matthew, and 2,055 different words used by Luke, John's vocabulary is quite limited. Barrett rightly notes, however, that "[i]n spite of the small vocabulary the reader never receives the impression of an ill-equipped writer at a loss for the right word" (7). The syntax of John's sentences is also less complicated than that of the Synoptic Gospels. Individual clauses are typically linked by καί (parataxis) rather than by subordinating conjunctions and participles, or they are laid side by side without the use of any coordinating conjunctions (asyndeton).

Yet the apparent simplicity of John's language and syntax could be deceptive. As I methodically worked through the text of the Fourth Gospel, I encountered numerous convoluted constructions that are only sporadically explained in standard grammars and commentaries. The purpose of this handbook is to help students, pastors, and interested scholars better understand the grammar and syntax of the Greek text of John's Gospel. I wish to emphasize that this is not a commentary but a prequel or a supplement to a commentary. The questions of authorship, sociohistorical context, compositional history, structure, and theology of the Fourth Gospel are not addressed here. Rather, I seek to explain the syntactical role of individual words, phrases, and clauses in the canonical version of the Gospel of John. I have also provided comments on major text-critical issues in the Greek text, using the critical apparatus in the 28th edition of Nestle-Aland, *Novum Testamentum Graece*. My translations correspond to my grammatical explanations, seeking to approximate the syntax—even when it is cumbersome or runs counter to the default English word order—and function of the Greek text as much as possible for educational purposes. I have used square brackets in the translations to indicate that the English words within them do not have equivalents in the Greek text.

John's Style

In addition to the use of parataxis and asyndeton mentioned above, one of the distinguishing characteristics of the style of the Fourth Gospel is the numerous repetitions of words, phrases, or clauses. For example, the prepositional phrases μετὰ τοῦτο (2:12; 11:7, 11; 19:28) and μετὰ ταῦτα (3:22; 5:1, 14; 6:1; 7:1; 13:7; 21:1) are routinely used to indicate a transition to a new scene or to a new section. The formulaic clause ἀμὴν λέγω ὑμῖν/σοι introduces Jesus' declarations twenty-five times (1:51; 3:3, 5, 11; 5:19, 24, 25; 6:26, 32, 47, 53; 8:34, 51, 58; 10:1, 7; 12:24; 13:16, 20, 21, 38; 14:12; 16:20, 23; 21:18). The ἐγώ εἰμι saying is repeatedly used as an absolute statement (6:20; 8:24, 28, 58; 13:19; 18:5, 6, 8) or is followed by a predicate that metaphorically describes what Jesus is: "the bread of life" (6:35, 48, 51), "the light of the world" (8:12; 9:5), "the door for the sheep" (10:7, 9), "the good shepherd" (10:11, 14), "the resurrection and the life" (11:25), "the way, the truth, and the life" (14:6), and "the true vineyard" (15:1, 5). The evangelist sometimes repeats entire clauses verbatim: ἔμπροσθέν μου γέγονεν, ὅτι πρῶτός μου ἦ (1:15 and 1:30), κἀγὼ οὐκ ᾔδειν αὐτόν (1:31 and 1:33), Ἐγώ εἰμι ὁ ἄρτος τῆς ζωῆς (6:35 and 6:48), ἐγὼ ἐν τῷ πατρὶ καὶ ὁ πατὴρ ἐν ἐμοί (14:10 and 14:11), οὐκ ἔστιν δοῦλος μείζων τοῦ κυρίου αὐτοῦ (13:16 and 15:20), ἐν τῷ ὀνόματί σου ᾧ δέδωκάς μοι (17:11 and 17:12), οὐκ εἰσὶν ἐκ τοῦ κόσμου καθὼς ἐγὼ οὐκ εἰμὶ ἐκ τοῦ κόσμου (17:14 and 17:16), Ἦν δὲ Σίμων Πέτρος ἑστὼς καὶ θερμαινόμενος (18:18 and 18:25), μὴ καὶ σὺ ἐκ τῶν μαθητῶν αὐτοῦ εἶ (18:17 and 18:25), σημαίνων ποίῳ θανάτῳ ἤμελλεν ἀποθνῄσκειν (12:33 and 18:32), ἦραν τὸν κύριον ἐκ τοῦ μνημείου καὶ οὐκ οἴδαμεν ποῦ ἔθηκαν αὐτόν (20:2 and 20:13), and γύναι, τί κλαίεις (20:13 and 20:15). There is a growing recognition among Johannine scholars that "to speak about repetition and variation is to speak about the style of John's Gospel. Style in the last analysis consists of the eternal repetition and variation of an otherwise limited vocabulary" (Van Belle, 31). In his study of the relationship between repetition and functionality in the Fourth Gospel, van der Watt concludes that "repetition and variation are *inter alia* functionally employed to develop a particular concept, reminding the implied reader of a concept in relation to others, linking different contexts together aiming at developing the relationship between the concepts mentioned in those contexts" (2009, 108).

Other distinguishing markers of John's peculiar style include his frequent use of οὖν as a transitional particle rather than as an inferential conjunction and of ἐκεῖνος as a third-person personal pronoun rather than as a demonstrative pronoun. The prepositional phrase ἐκ + genitive is used in place of the partitive genitive fifty-two times. The subordinate conjunction ἵνα introduces not only purpose clauses but also epexegetical clauses (eighteen times). The Fourth Evangelist is also fond of various point/counterpoint sets, such as οὐκ/μὴ . . . ἀλλά (thirty times) and οὐκ/οὐδεὶς . . . εἰ μή (eight times). He also likes to use words or phrases that are open to two interpretations (double entendre), such as κατέλαβεν (1:5), ὁ ζῆλος (2:17), ἄνωθεν (3:3, 7), ὕδωρ ζῶν (4:10), δοξάζω (7:39; 12:16, 23; 13:31, 32; 17:1), ὑπάγω (8:21), κεκοίμηται (11:11), and ἀναστήσεται (11:23).

John's limited vocabulary and distinctive literary style, especially the use of parataxis, asyndeton, and the epexegetical ἵνα clauses, are usually explained by presuming some Semitic influence on the Greek text, although most scholars today reject the idea, proposed by Burney and Torrey in the early twentieth century, that the Fourth Gospel is a Greek translation of a lost Aramaic original. The most evident influence is the appearance of various Aramaic words that are transliterated and then translated into Greek, such as ῥαββί, ὃ λέγεται μεθερμηνευόμενον διδάσκαλε (1:38; cf. 20:16), τὸν Μεσσίαν, ὅ ἐστιν μεθερμηνευόμενον χριστός (1:41; cf. 4:25), Κηφᾶς, ὃ ἑρμηνεύεται Πέτρος (1:42), or Θωμᾶς ὁ λεγόμενος Δίδυμος (11:16; 21:2), as well as the frequent use of the pleonastic clause καὶ εἶπαν/εἶπεν αὐτῷ/αὐτῇ/αὐτοῖς (thirty times).

Verbal Aspect

This handbook incorporates major insights of verbal aspect theory advanced by McKay, Porter, Fanning, and Campbell. It presumes that a speaker or writer grammaticalizes a view of a particular situation by selecting a particular verb form in the verbal system: the aorist tense if the situation is viewed as a complete event without regard for its progress (perfective aspect), the present or imperfect tense if the situation is viewed as in progress without regard for its beginning and end (imperfective aspect), and the perfect or pluperfect tense if a writer depicts a state of affairs that exists with no reference to any progress (stative aspect). Although I do not agree with Campbell's view that the perfect tense grammaticalizes imperfective aspect, I find his suggestion that the distinguishing semantic quality of the perfect tense is heightened proximity with intensive implicature (2007, 195–201) applicable to some contexts (e.g., the intensive rendering of ἕστηκεν in 1:26 or πεπιστεύκαμεν in 6:69).

Regarding the contentious question of whether Greek tenses carry any temporal references, I side with scholars who think that in the indicative mood Greek verbs do encode time. I am not persuaded by Porter's (1989, 75–83) test of contrastive substitution, i.e., the reasoning that if different tense forms could be used in the same context or, conversely, if the identical tense form could be used in different temporal contexts, we must conclude that Greek verbs do not grammaticalize time (Porter 1993, 32; for a critique of Porter's argument, see Runge 2014, 154–73). To expect that a verb tense must always have the same temporal reference is to create an absolute category into which no language could fit. Runge rightly points out that "[e]ven a highly time-oriented verbal system like English does not grammaticalize uncancelable, absolute temporal references" (167). Another observation that supports the idea that in the indicative mood Greek verbs encode time is the existence of two tense forms (the present and the imperfect) that convey imperfective aspect and two tense forms (the perfect and the pluperfect) that convey stative aspect. In a recent article that examines cross-linguistic evidence for polysemous past tenses, Fresch concludes that "there is substantial reason to regard +PFV [perfective aspect] and +PAST [past-temporal reference] as semantic components of the aorist indicative," though he adds that, "in a perfective past verb form, such as the aorist, perfective aspect will typically be the dominant component and the past-temporal reference will be secondary" (410).

Although my analysis of the Fourth Gospel is informed by the above understanding of the semantics of Greek verbs, my task in this handbook is pragmatic: to interpret aspect and the temporal dimension of verbs as they are used in specific passages. Since I do not understand temporal information grammaticalized by the indicative mood absolutely, I have paid attention to various contextual features and asked how they inform the meaning and function of individual verbs.

The aorist indicative is the default tense form in the Fourth Gospel (used 836 times), which is not surprising given its narrative genre. It is primarily used to portray the events that constitute the main story line. The imperfect tense occurs 289 times. Its less frequent use in the narrative, however, is not a sufficient reason to regard it as a tense that carries more prominence than the aorist, as Porter (1989, 92–93) claims. The primary function of the imperfect is "to provide background details about events, persons and other features of the mainline narrative. These expressions, which are generally short and often parenthetic, typically appear anywhere inside the body of the episode" (du Toit, 222). Levinsohn (2000, 174) claims that the imperfective aspect of the imperfect makes it especially suitable to convey the information that is of less importance than the information conveyed through the aorist in the main storyline. This does not mean, however, that every imperfect verb is less prominent than the aorist. The particular function of the imperfect depends on a correlation between its imperfective aspect and the specific background information it conveys. For example, the likely effect of using the imperfect ἔλεγεν in 8:31 is foregrounding because it does not describe an event that can be viewed as being in progress (cf. Levinsohn 2000, 175; 2016, 169–70).

The perfect indicative plays an important role in the Fourth Gospel because it allows the evangelist to emphasize the ongoing relevance of God's and Jesus' acts in relation to each other and to believers. Of 206 perfect indicatives in John, 198 (96 percent) occur within indirect discourse. In most of these occurrences, the semantic weight of the perfect tense corresponds to its prominence in the text or, to use Porter's term, the perfect tense is frontgrounded (1989, 92–93). Frey is therefore right to conclude that "the use of the perfect here results from an authorial choice of the linguistic expression. It characterizes the Johannine style and expresses, beyond this, the constitutive relatedness of the post-Easter community to the enduringly valid word and work of Christ and his connection back to the initiative of the Father, who sent and authorized him" (2018, 81). The perfect tense is particularly prominent in connection with specific lexemes such as δίδωμι, ἀποστέλλω, ὁράω, and λαλέω. The perfect tense of δίδωμι conveys the idea "that what the Father 'has given' to the Son . . . is definitively in his hand," of ἀποστέλλω that "the sending of Jesus . . . is regarded not only as an act of the past but as the enduring foundation of the sending of the disciples," of ὁράω "that what the Son 'has seen' . . . stays enduringly before his eyes," and of λαλέω that what Jesus "'has spoken' . . . is enduringly valid revelation" (81).

The distribution of the historical presents in the Fourth Gospel is uneven, occurring mostly in chapters 1, 4, 13, 20, and 21. One of its main functions is to indicate structural or thematic prominence, i.e., to help the readers/hearers discern the themes to which they should pay attention. The use of the historical present with the verbs of speaking, which is by far the most frequent use of the historical present in John's Gospel (119 forms of λέγω out of 164 historical presents), however, is not to mark the action of speaking for prominence. Rather, as Runge explains, "attention is drawn prospectively to the speech that the quotative frame introduces" (2010, 137 n. 45).

Word Order

I have frequently called attention to word order that differs from the default order of a Greek clause in which the finite verb is placed in the initial position (Levinsohn 2000, 38). When other elements of a clause are placed before the verb, i.e., when they are "fronted," they receive more prominence, but the pragmatic effect of such a departure from the standard word order could be varied. I have adopted Runge's view that "[p]lacing nonfocal information in [the] clause-initial position has the effect of establishing an explicit frame of reference for the clause that follows. It does not result in emphasis. By definition, emphasis refers to taking what was already most important in a clause and placing it ... at the beginning of the clause" (2010, 224). Similarly, when the verb is placed at the end of a clause, the most likely pragmatic effect is that the verb becomes the focal point of a clause. My comments on the specific functions of clausal elements that depart from the default word order are generally informed by the *Lexham Discourse Greek New Testament*.

I have also adopted Runge's suggestion that various cleft constructions should be interpreted linguistically as dislocations. I have identified forty-four left-dislocations, "where the new entity is dislocated to the beginning of the clause and then resumed in the main clause through the use of a pronominal trace" (2010, 289), and eleven right-dislocations, which entail "referring to a participant in the midst of a clause using a pronoun or generic phrase and then adding more information about the same participant at the end of the clause" (317), in the Fourth Gospel. The categories of left- and right-dislocations allow us to understand various detachment constructions, which are typical for John's syntax, not as cumbersome structures due to the evangelist's limited linguistic skills but as convenient rhetorical devices that are frequently more effective in introducing new entities, especially when they are complex, than the more conventional methods. To approximate the structure of the Greek sentence in the translation without sacrificing clarity, I have frequently used the em dash (—) to indicate the end of the left-dislocation and the beginning of the main clause.

A HANDBOOK ON THE GREEK TEXT OF
JOHN 11-21

John 11:1-10

¹Now a certain man was sick, Lazarus from Bethany, from the village of Mary and Martha, her sister. ²Mary, whose brother Lazarus was sick, was the one who anointed the Lord with perfume and wiped his feet with her hair. ³The sisters therefore sent a message to him, saying, "Lord, behold, the one whom you love is sick." ⁴When Jesus heard this, he said, "This illness is not to end in death, but it is for God's glory, in order that the Son of God may be glorified through it." ⁵Now Jesus loved Martha and her sister and Lazarus. ⁶So when he heard that he was sick, he then stayed in the place where he was two more days. ⁷Then after this he said to the disciples, "Let us go back to Judea." ⁸The disciples said to him, "Rabbi, just now the Jews were seeking to stone you, and are you going there again?" ⁹Jesus answered, "Are there not twelve hours of daylight? If someone walks during the day, he does not stumble because he sees the light of this world. ¹⁰But if someone walks during the night, he stumbles because the light is not in him."

11:1 Ἦν δέ τις ἀσθενῶν, Λάζαρος ἀπὸ Βηθανίας, ἐκ τῆς κώμης Μαρίας καὶ Μάρθας τῆς ἀδελφῆς αὐτῆς.

Ἦν. Impf act ind 3rd sg εἰμί. The use of ἦν is a common way in the FG to introduce a new chacter in the main narrative (see 3:1; 4:46; 5:5; cf. LXX Exod 2:1; 1 Sam 1:1; Job 1:1; Luke 14:2; Acts 9:10, 36; 16:1). On the function of the imperfect in the FG, see 1:39 on ἦν.

δέ. Transitional particle that marks narrative development (Runge 2010, 28-36).

τις. Nominative subject of Ἦν.

ἀσθενῶν. Pres act ptc masc nom sg ἀσθενέω. The participle could be regarded either as a second element of the imperfect periphrastic construction ("a certain man was sick") or as an attributive participle modifying τις ("there was a certain man who was sick").

Λάζαρος. Nominative in apposition to τις. Λάζαρος presupposes the Hebrew name לעזר, a shortened form of אלעזר (Barrett, 389). The only other occurrence of this name in the NT is in the parable of Lazarus and the rich man (Luke 16:19-31).

ἀπὸ Βηθανίας. Source.

ἐκ τῆς κώμης. Source.

Μαρίας καὶ Μάρθας. Possessive genitives broadly defined qualifying τῆς κώμης ("the village of Mary and Martha" = "the village where Mary and Martha lived").

τῆς ἀδελφῆς. Genitive in apposition to Μάρθας.

αὐτῆς. Genitive of relationship qualifying ἀδελφῆς.

11:2 ἦν δὲ Μαριὰμ ἡ ἀλείψασα τὸν κύριον μύρῳ καὶ ἐκμάξασα τοὺς πόδας αὐτοῦ ταῖς θριξὶν αὐτῆς, ἧς ὁ ἀδελφὸς Λάζαρος ἠσθένει.

ἦν. Impf act ind 3rd sg εἰμί. On the function of the imperfect in the FG, see 1:39 on ἦν.

δὲ. Marker of narrative development.

Μαριὰμ. Nominative subject of ἦν.

ἡ ἀλείψασα . . . καὶ ἐκμάξασα. Predicate nominative. Two substantival participles governed by one article and joined by καί form a TSKS (article-substantive-καί-substantive) construction. In such formulations, according to the Granville Sharp rule, the single article indicates that both participles have the same referent; see 5:24 on ὁ . . . ἀκούων καὶ πιστεύων.

ἡ ἀλείψασα. Aor act ptc fem nom sg ἀλείφω (substantival). The aorist participle does not refer to an event antecedent to the narrative time but to an event subsequent to the time of the narration, i.e., to Mary's anointing of Jesus' feet described in 12:3. This, however, does not invalidate the general rule about the temporal reference of the aorist participle because, as Zerwick explains, "the participle has the article, and so is not subordinated to any verb, but simply used to describe Mary, and to identify her for the readers of the gospel, among the many Maries, as 'the one who anointed . . .', so that the time with respect to which the anointing is to be considered is the time when the gospel is composed, or read" (§266).

ἐκμάξασα. Aor act ptc fem nom sg ἐκμάσσω (substantival). The temporal reference of this participle is the same as that of ἀλείψασα (see above).

τὸν κύριον. Accusative direct object of ἀλείψασα.
μύρῳ. Dative of material (Wallace 1996, 170).
τοὺς πόδας. Accusative direct object of ἐκμάξασα.
αὐτοῦ. Possessive genitive qualifying πόδας.
ταῖς θριξὶν. Dative of means/instrument (Wallace 1996, 163).
αὐτῆς. Possessive genitive qualifying θριξὶν.
ἧς. Genitive of relationship qualifying ἀδελφὸς. It introduces the relative clause that provides further information about Mary's identity.
ὁ ἀδελφὸς. Nominative subject of ἠσθένει. Fronted for emphasis.
Λάζαρος. Nominative in apposition to ὁ ἀδελφὸς.
ἠσθένει. Impf act ind 3rd sg ἀσθενέω. On the function of the imperfect in the FG, see 1:39 on ἦν.

11:3 ἀπέστειλαν οὖν αἱ ἀδελφαὶ πρὸς αὐτὸν λέγουσαι· κύριε, ἴδε ὃν φιλεῖς ἀσθενεῖ.

ἀπέστειλαν. Aor act ind 3rd pl ἀποστέλλω.
οὖν. Postpositive inferential conjunction.
αἱ ἀδελφαὶ. Nominative subject of ἀπέστειλαν.
πρὸς αὐτὸν. Locative (motion toward).
λέγουσαι. Pres act ptc fem nom pl λέγω (manner). James suggests that the imperfective aspect of this participle "seems to function as a future ('with the intent of saying') and so to involve a temporal rather than an aspectual contrast" (207; cf. BDF §339.2). On participles that follow the main verb, see βαπτίζων in 1:31.
κύριε. Vocative of direct address.
ἴδε. An interjection (originally aor act impv 2nd sg ὁράω) that is used "when that which is to be observed is in the nom[inative]" (BDAG, 466).
ὃν. Introduces a headless relative clause that, in its entirety (ὃν φιλεῖς), serves as the nominative subject of ἀσθενεῖ. Within its clause, ὃν is the accusative direct object of φιλεῖς.
φιλεῖς. Pres act ind 2nd sg φιλέω.
ἀσθενεῖ. Pres act ind 3rd sg ἀσθενέω. The verb stands in final, emphatic position.

11:4 ἀκούσας δὲ ὁ Ἰησοῦς εἶπεν· αὕτη ἡ ἀσθένεια οὐκ ἔστιν πρὸς θάνατον ἀλλ' ὑπὲρ τῆς δόξης τοῦ θεοῦ, ἵνα δοξασθῇ ὁ υἱὸς τοῦ θεοῦ δι' αὐτῆς.

ἀκούσας. Aor act ptc masc nom sg ἀκούω (temporal). On participles that precede the main verb, see ἐμβλέψας in 1:36.
δὲ. Marker of narrative development.

ὁ Ἰησοῦς. Nominative subject of εἶπεν.

εἶπεν. Aor act ind 3rd sg λέγω.

αὕτη ἡ ἀσθένεια. Nominative subject of ἔστιν. Fronted as a topical frame.

οὐκ . . . ἀλλ'. A point/counterpoint set ("not this . . . but that") that negates the incorrect conclusion (Lazarus' illness will lead to death) and affirms the correct one (the purpose of his illness is to reveal God's glory). On the function of ἀλλά in a point/counterpoint set, see 1:8.

ἔστιν. Pres act ind 3rd sg εἰμί. The enclitic ἐστιν is accented ἔστιν when it comes at the beginning of a sentence, when it expresses existence, or when it follows ἀλλ', εἰ, καί, οὐκ, ὅτι, or τοῦτ'. The third condition is fulfilled here.

πρὸς θάνατον. Result ("the final outcome of this illness is not death" or "this illness will not end in death" [LN 89.44]; cf. Young, 101).

ὑπὲρ τῆς δόξης. Purpose ("for the sake of the glory of God" [Robertson, 632]; "in order to reveal the glory of God" [Barrett, 390]).

τοῦ θεοῦ. Possessive genitive qualifying δόξης.

ἵνα. Introduces a purpose clause.

δοξασθῇ. Aor pass subj 3rd sg δοξάζω. Subjunctive with ἵνα. The primary (personal) agency of the passive verb is not expressed, but the implied agent is most likely God. Such a formulation has been traditionally called "divine passive," but the usual explanation that the direct mention of God is avoided out of reverence or respect is in many cases inadequate because, as Porter explains, "the relatively frequent mention of God in the Gospels minimalizes this rationale" (Porter 1994, 65). In this verse, for example, God is mentioned twice, suggesting that the absence of expressed personal agency is stylistic and conventional rather than theological.

ὁ υἱὸς. Nominative subject of δοξασθῇ.

τοῦ θεοῦ. Genitive of relationship qualifying υἱός.

δι' αὐτῆς. Secondary (intermediate) agency.

11:5 ἠγάπα δὲ ὁ Ἰησοῦς τὴν Μάρθαν καὶ τὴν ἀδελφὴν αὐτῆς καὶ τὸν Λάζαρον.

ἠγάπα. Impf act ind 3rd sg ἀγαπάω. On the function of the imperfect in the FG, see 1:39 on ἦν.

δὲ. Marker of narrative development.

ὁ Ἰησοῦς. Nominative subject of ἠγάπα.

τὴν Μάρθαν. Accusative direct object of ἠγάπα.

καὶ . . . καὶ. Coordinating conjunctions, linking three direct objects of ἠγάπα.

τὴν ἀδελφὴν. Accusative direct object of ἠγάπα.
αὐτῆς. Genitive of relationship qualifying ἀδελφὴν.
τὸν Λάζαρον. Accusative direct object of ἠγάπα.

11:6 Ὡς οὖν ἤκουσεν ὅτι ἀσθενεῖ, τότε μὲν ἔμεινεν ἐν ᾧ ἦν τόπῳ δύο ἡμέρας,

Ὡς. Temporal conjunction (BDAG, 1105.8.a; BDF §455.2) that introduces a temporal clause in a left-dislocation, resumed by the temporal adverb τότε. The temporal clause is dislocated because it is too complex to be placed in a marked position (see Runge 2010, 297–312).

οὖν. The specific function of this conjunction is not easy to determine. (1) If οὖν functions as an inferential conjunction, Jesus' prolonged stay in the place where he was should be interpreted as an expression of his love for Martha, Mary, and Lazarus. (2) If οὖν functions as a mere transitional particle, then "[i]t just carries along the narrative with no necessary thought of cause or result" (Robertson, 1191). (3) If the combination Ὡς οὖν denotes contrast, as BDAG (737.2.d) suggests, the sense would be, "Although Jesus dearly loved this Bethany family (v. 5), he then (τότε) surprisingly still (μέν) remained where he was, rather than hurrying to their side" (Harris 2015, 208).

ἤκουσεν. Aor act ind 3rd sg ἀκούω.

ὅτι. Introduces the clausal complement (indirect discourse) of ἤκουσεν.

ἀσθενεῖ. Pres act ind 3rd sg ἀσθενέω. The present tense from the original utterance (see ἀσθενεῖ in 11:3) is retained in indirect discourse (see 1:39 on μένει).

τότε. Adverb of time, which resumes the temporal clause Ὡς οὖν ἤκουσεν ὅτι ἀσθενεῖ. Fronted for emphasis. On the function of the resumptive element, see 7:10 on τότε.

μὲν. Correlative particle that is usually combined with δέ, but in this instance δέ is omitted. BDF (§447.3) notes that the use of anacoluthic μέν (without correlative δέ) represents "a more or less serious breach of good sentence structure."

ἔμεινεν. Aor act ind 3rd sg μένω.

ἐν ᾧ ... τόπῳ. Locative. ἐν ᾧ ... τόπῳ stands for ἐν τῷ τόπῳ ᾧ. The clause in which this PP occurs (ἐν ᾧ ἦν τόπῳ δύο ἡμέρας) is an internally headed relative clause because the antecedent of ᾧ is incorporated into the relative clause (Culy, Parsons, and Stigall, 115; see also 6:14 on ὅ).

ἦν. Impf act ind 3rd sg εἰμί. On the function of the imperfect in the FG, see 1:39 on ἦν.

δύο ἡμέρας. Accusative indicating extent of time.

11:7 ἔπειτα μετὰ τοῦτο λέγει τοῖς μαθηταῖς· ἄγωμεν εἰς τὴν Ἰουδαίαν πάλιν.

ἔπειτα. Temporal adverb.

μετὰ τοῦτο. Temporal. The antecedent of the pronoun is Jesus' extended stay in the place where he was. ἔπειτα μετὰ τοῦτο ("then, after this") is a pleonasm that is perpetrated for emphasis (Barrett, 391).

λέγει. Pres act ind 3rd sg λέγω. The historical present gives prominence to Jesus' instruction to his disciples (see 1:15 on μαρτυρεῖ). The conversation between Jesus and his disciples, recounted in vv. 7-11, serves to tie the Lazarus story to the narrative in the preceding chapters (Brown, 1:432).

τοῖς μαθηταῖς. Dative indirect object of λέγει.

ἄγωμεν. Pres act subj 1st pl ἄγω (hortatory subjunctive).

εἰς τὴν Ἰουδαίαν. Locative.

πάλιν. Adverb "pert[aining] to return to a position or state" (BDAG, 752.1). For Jesus' previous visits to Judea, see 2:13; 5:1; 7:14.

11:8 λέγουσιν αὐτῷ οἱ μαθηταί· ῥαββί, νῦν ἐζήτουν σε λιθάσαι οἱ Ἰουδαῖοι, καὶ πάλιν ὑπάγεις ἐκεῖ;

λέγουσιν. Pres act ind 3rd pl λέγω. The historical present gives prominence to the objection of Jesus' disciples (see 1:15 on μαρτυρεῖ). This verse is connected to the previous one by asyndeton.

αὐτῷ. Dative indirect object of λέγουσιν.

οἱ μαθηταί. Nominative subject of λέγουσιν.

ῥαββί. Vocative of direct address.

νῦν. The literary context of this passage (see 10:31-39, which describes a double attempt of Jewish leaders to stone Jesus), indicates that this νῦν does not refer to the time coextensive with the events of the narrative, as elsewhere in the FG (4:23; 5:25; 11:22; 12:27, 31; 13:31, 36; 14:29; 15:22, 24; 16:5, 22, 29, 30; 17:5, 7, 13), but to the time shortly before the immediate present (BDAG, 681.1.b; Barrett, 391).

ἐζήτουν. Impf act ind 3rd pl ζητέω. ἐζήτουν refers to the unsuccessful attempts at stoning Jesus (see 10:31-39). The meaning of νῦν in this clause (see above) suggests that ἐζήτουν cannot be taken as an illustration of Porter's claim that "the time-based conception of the Imperfect is not only unnecessary but potentially misleading," which he applies to this verse by translating νῦν ἐζήτουν σε λιθάσαι οἱ Ἰουδαῖοι as "the Jews are now seeking to stone you" (1989, 209; 1994, 35; for a critique of Porter's view, see McKay 1992, 213; 1994, 40). Rather, the imperfect ἐζήτουν describes the events that occurred in a recent past, as illustrated in McKay's translation of the clause: "[Q]uite recently (just now) the Jews were trying to stone you" (1994, 40).

σε. Accusative direct object of λιθάσαι.

λιθάσαι. Aor act inf λιθάζω (complementary). The subject of the infinitive (οἱ Ἰουδαῖοι) is in the nominative case because it is the same as the subject of ἐζήτουν (Wallace 1996, 192). The perfective aspect of the infinitive λιθάσαι indicates the intent of the Jewish leaders to complete the task (see λιθάσωσιν in 10:31). James suggests that "[a]n imperfective infinitive, λιθάζειν 'to try to stone,' in 11:8 would imply that their stoning was less goal-oriented" (206).

οἱ Ἰουδαῖοι. Nominative subject of ἐζήτουν. Unlike other occurrences of this term in ch. 11 (see vv. 19, 31, 33, 36, and 45), the term οἱ Ἰουδαῖοι in this verse refers to Jewish religious authorities who are hostile to Jesus.

καὶ. Coordinating conjunction.

πάλιν. Adverb "pert[aining] to repetition in the same (or similar) manner" (BDAG, 752.2). Fronted for emphasis.

ὑπάγεις. Pres act ind 2nd sg ὑπάγω.

ἐκεῖ. Adverb of place.

11:9 ἀπεκρίθη Ἰησοῦς· οὐχὶ δώδεκα ὧραί εἰσιν τῆς ἡμέρας; ἐάν τις περιπατῇ ἐν τῇ ἡμέρᾳ, οὐ προσκόπτει, ὅτι τὸ φῶς τοῦ κόσμου τούτου βλέπει·

ἀπεκρίθη. Aor mid ind 3rd sg ἀποκρίνομαι. On the voice, see "Deponency" in the Series Introduction. This verse is connected to the previous one by asyndeton.

Ἰησοῦς. Nominative subject of ἀπεκρίθη.

οὐχὶ. The negative particle which, like the negative particle οὐ, indicates that Jesus expects an affirmative answer to his rhetorical question (BDF §440). οὐχί functions as a marker of "a somewhat more emphatic affirmative response" than a simple οὐ (LN 69.12)

δώδεκα ὧραί. Nominative subject of εἰσιν. Fronted for emphasis. ὧραί, which has a circumflex accent on the penult, acquired an additional accent, the acute, on the ultima from the enclitic εἰσιν (Smyth §183; Carson 1985, 48).

εἰσιν. Pres act ind 3rd pl εἰμί.

τῆς ἡμέρας. Genitive of time. δώδεκα ὧραί . . . τῆς ἡμέρας (lit. "twelve hours of the day") refers to the twelve hours of daylight.

ἐάν. Introduces the protasis of a third-class condition. This group of conditional clauses encompasses the present general condition, a mere hypothetical situation, and a more probable future. ἐάν τις περιπατῇ ἐν τῇ ἡμέρᾳ, οὐ προσκόπτει is an example of the present general condition because "[t]here is no hint of uncertainty about this even occurring" (Wallace 1996, 698).

τις. Nominative subject of περιπατῇ.

περιπατῇ. Pres act subj 3rd sg περιπατέω. Subjunctive with ἐάν. As Wallace (1996, 698) explains, "The subjunctive is used because the subject is undefined, not because the time is future."

ἐν τῇ ἡμέρᾳ. Temporal.

οὐ. Negative particle normally used with indicative verbs. It marks the beginning of the apodosis of a third-class condition.

προσκόπτει. Pres act ind 3rd sg προσκόπτω. The verb means "to strike one's foot against something as one walks and in this way to lose one's balance temporarily—'to stumble'" (LN 15.228).

ὅτι. Introduces a causal clause.

τὸ φῶς. Accusative direct object of βλέπει. Fronted for emphasis.

τοῦ κόσμου τούτου. Objective genitive ("the light that illuminates this world") or genitive of source if "this world" stands for "the sun" ("the light of the sun to see by" [Harris 2015, 209]). The term κόσμος here denotes the totality of creation.

βλέπει. Pres act ind 3rd sg βλέπω.

11:10 ἐὰν δέ τις περιπατῇ ἐν τῇ νυκτί, προσκόπτει, ὅτι τὸ φῶς οὐκ ἔστιν ἐν αὐτῷ.

ἐάν. Introduces the protasis of a third-class condition. Like the conditional clause in the previous verse, this is an example of the present general condition.

δέ. Marker of discursive development.

τις. Nominative subject of περιπατῇ.

περιπατῇ. Pres act subj 3rd sg περιπατέω. Subjunctive with ἐάν.

ἐν τῇ νυκτί. Temporal.

προσκόπτει. Pres act ind 3rd sg προσκόπτω. The verb marks the beginning of the apodosis of a third-class condition.

ὅτι. Introduces a causal clause.

τὸ φῶς. Nominative subject of ἔστιν. Fronted as a topical frame.

οὐκ. Negative particle normally used with indicative verbs.

ἔστιν. Pres act ind 3rd sg εἰμί. The enclitic ἐστιν is accented ἔστιν when it comes at the beginning of a sentence, when it expresses existence, or when it follows ἀλλ', εἰ, καί, οὐκ, ὅτι, or τοῦτ'. The last two conditions are fulfilled here.

ἐν αὐτῷ. Locative.

John 11:11-16

¹¹He said these things, and after this he said to them, "Lazarus, our friend, has fallen asleep, but I am going that I may wake him up." ¹²Then the disciples said to him, "Lord, if he has fallen asleep, he will get well." ¹³Jesus, however, had not spoken about his death, but they thought that he spoke about natural sleep. ¹⁴Thereupon Jesus told them plainly, "Lazarus has died. ¹⁵I am glad for your sake—so that you may believe—that I was not there. But let us go to him." ¹⁶Then Thomas called Didymus said to his fellow disciples, "Let us also go, so that we may die with him."

11:11 Ταῦτα εἶπεν, καὶ μετὰ τοῦτο λέγει αὐτοῖς· Λάζαρος ὁ φίλος ἡμῶν κεκοίμηται· ἀλλὰ πορεύομαι ἵνα ἐξυπνίσω αὐτόν.

Ταῦτα. Accusative direct object of εἶπεν. Fronted as a topical frame. This verse is connected to the previous one by asyndeton.

εἶπεν. Aor act ind 3rd sg λέγω. The aorist verb form is unmarked and "functions as a closing speech mark" (James, 214).

καὶ. Coordinating conjunction.

μετὰ τοῦτο. Temporal. Fronted as a temporal frame.

λέγει. Pres act ind 3rd sg λέγω. The historical present λέγει stands in contrast to the unmarked aorist εἶπεν, giving prominence to Jesus' explanation of Lazarus' situation (see 1:15 on μαρτυρεῖ).

αὐτοῖς. Dative indirect object of λέγει.

Λάζαρος. Nominative subject of κεκοίμηται.

ὁ φίλος. Nominative in apposition to Λάζαρος.

ἡμῶν. Genitive of relationship qualifying φίλος.

κεκοίμηται. Prf mid ind 3rd sg κοιμάομαι. Campbell, who holds that prominence—which he defines as "the degree to which an element stands out from others in its environment" (2007, 206)—is one of the pragmatic implicatures of the perfect tense, argues that the prominence of κεκοίμηται "highlights the point that Jesus is making: though Lazarus is dead, it is a though he sleeps. Jesus sets out to raise him from death, as though waking a sleeping man" (207). In this context, κεκοίμηται functions as a double entendre, which, by causing an evident misunderstanding (see vv. 12-13), provides occasion for further explanation and moves the conversation forward. For other examples of words with multiple meanings that are typically misunderstood by Jesus' audience, see 3:3-4; 4:14-15; 6:33-34; 8:21-22; 11:23-24; 14:7-8.

ἀλλὰ. Marker of contrast.

πορεύομαι. Pres mid ind 1st sg πορεύομαι.

ἵνα. Introduces a purpose clause.

ἐξυπνίσω. Aor act subj 1st sg ἐξυπνίζω. Subjunctive with ἵνα. ἐξυπνίζω means "to cause to wake up, to awaken someone, to wake up someone" (LN 23.77).

αὐτόν. Accusative direct object of ἐξυπνίσω.

11:12 εἶπαν οὖν οἱ μαθηταὶ αὐτῷ· κύριε, εἰ κεκοίμηται σωθήσεται.

εἶπαν. Aor act ind 3rd pl λέγω.

οὖν. Postpositive inferential conjunction and/or transitional particle (see 1:22 and 11:6).

οἱ μαθηταί. Nominative subject of εἶπαν.

αὐτῷ. Dative indirect object of εἶπαν.

κύριε. Vocative of direct address.

εἰ. Introduces the protasis of a first-class condition. Porter suggests that this conditional particle can be translated with "since" because Lazarus' "being asleep allows there to be the expectation of his being saved: since he is asleep, he can expect to be saved. If he is dead, this expectation is removed" (1994, 256–57).

κεκοίμηται. Prf mid ind 3rd sg κοιμάομαι.

σωθήσεται. Fut pass ind 3rd sg σῴζω. This verb is the only content of the apodosis. In this context, σωθήσεται refers to recovering from illness (Barrett, 393). Its primary (personal) agency is not expressed.

11:13 εἰρήκει δὲ ὁ Ἰησοῦς περὶ τοῦ θανάτου αὐτοῦ, ἐκεῖνοι δὲ ἔδοξαν ὅτι περὶ τῆς κοιμήσεως τοῦ ὕπνου λέγει.

εἰρήκει. Plprf act ind 3rd sg λέγω. This use of the pluperfect, according to Fanning, "highlights the antecedent past occurrence while still implying the past state consequent upon it" (307). James (208) regards it as "an example of an anterior past (that is, the past-in-the-past)."

δέ. Marker of narrative development.

ὁ Ἰησοῦς. Nominative subject of εἰρήκει.

περὶ τοῦ θανάτου. Reference.

αὐτοῦ. Subjective genitive qualifying θανάτου ("he died"). The antecedent of the pronoun is Lazarus.

ἐκεῖνοι. Nominative subject of ἔδοξαν. The demonstrative pronoun acts as a third-person personal pronoun with a simple anaphoric force (Wallace 1996, 328–29).

δέ. Marker of narrative development.

ἔδοξαν. Aor act ind 3rd pl δοκέω.

ὅτι. Introduces the clausal complement (indirect discourse) of ἔδοξαν.

περὶ τῆς κοιμήσεως. Reference. Fronted for emphasis. κοίμησις ("the state of being asleep" [LN 23.66]) is a NT *hapax legomenon*.

τοῦ ὕπνου. Epexegetical genitive, explaining κοιμήσεως and thus creating a somewhat redundant expression ("sleep which is slumber" or "sleep that is literal/actual sleep"; cf. Harris 2015, 209–10) to stress the fact that an ordinary sleep is in view (LN 23.66).

λέγει. Pres act ind 3rd sg λέγω. The present tense is retained from direct discourse (see 1:39 on μένει).

11:14 τότε οὖν εἶπεν αὐτοῖς ὁ Ἰησοῦς παρρησίᾳ· Λάζαρος ἀπέθανεν,

τότε οὖν. A combination of the temporal adverb and the postpositive inferential conjunction, in which τότε functions as a connective particle that introduces "a subsequent event, but not one taking place at a definite time ('thereupon,' not 'at that time')" (BDF §459.2). τότε οὖν = "now" (in contrast to the preceding time).

αὐτοῖς. Dative indirect object of εἶπεν.
ὁ Ἰησοῦς. Nominative subject of εἶπεν.
παρρησίᾳ. Dative of manner ("plainly," "without obscurity or ambiguity of speech" [Barrett, 393]).
Λάζαρος. Nominative subject of ἀπέθανεν.
ἀπέθανεν. Aor act ind 3rd sg ἀποθνῄσκω. The verb stands in final, emphatic position.

11:15 καὶ χαίρω δι' ὑμᾶς ἵνα πιστεύσητε, ὅτι οὐκ ἤμην ἐκεῖ· ἀλλ' ἄγωμεν πρὸς αὐτόν.

καὶ. Coordinating conjunction.
χαίρω. Pres act ind 1st sg χαίρω.
δι' ὑμᾶς. Causal.
ἵνα. Introduces a parenthetical purpose clause (ἵνα πιστεύσητε) that is added to clarify the prepositional phrase δι' ὑμᾶς. Its precise function, however, is uncertain because there is no clear indication in this chapter that Jesus' raising of Lazarus affected the faith of his disciples. The only result that is explicitly noted by the evangelist is the belief of the crowd that witnessed the miracle (11:42, 45).

πιστεύσητε. Aor act subj 2nd pl πιστεύω. Subjunctive with ἵνα.
ὅτι. Introduces the clausal complement of χαίρω.
οὐκ. Negative particle normally used with indicative verbs.
ἤμην. Impf mid ind 1st sg εἰμί.
ἐκεῖ. Adverb of place.
ἀλλ'. Marker of contrast.

ἄγωμεν. Pres act subj 1st pl ἄγω (hortatory subjunctive).
πρὸς αὐτόν. Locative (motion toward).

11:16 εἶπεν οὖν Θωμᾶς ὁ λεγόμενος Δίδυμος τοῖς συμμαθηταῖς· ἄγωμεν καὶ ἡμεῖς ἵνα ἀποθάνωμεν μετ' αὐτοῦ.

εἶπεν. Aor act ind 3rd sg λέγω.

οὖν. Postpositive inferential conjunction and/or transitional particle (see 1:22 and 11:6).

Θωμᾶς. Nominative subject of εἶπεν. The Hebrew/Aramaic equavalent of Θωμᾶς (תְּאוֹם) means "twin." In the Acts of Thomas 11–12, 31, 45, 39, 54–56, Thomas is identified with Judas (see Mark 6:3) and portrayed as the twin brother of Jesus. In the FG, in addition to this verse Thomas is mentioned in 14:5; 20:24-29; 21:2. Elsewhere in the NT, his name appears only on the lists of the Twelve (Matt 10:3; Mark 3:18; Luke 6:15; Acts 1:13).

ὁ λεγόμενος. Pres pass ptc masc nom sg λέγω (attributive). The participle modifies Θωμᾶς, standing in the third attributive position (see 1:18 on ὁ ὤν).

Δίδυμος. Nominative complement to Θωμᾶς in a double nominative subject-complement construction. The passive formulation Θωμᾶς ὁ λεγόμενος Δίδυμος ("Thomas called Didymus") is derived from the hypothetical active clause τις λέγει Θωμᾶν Δίδυμον ("someone calls Thomas Didymus") that employs a double accusative object-complement construction. When the active clause is transformed into a passive formulation, the accusative direct object (Θωμᾶν) becomes the nominative subject, and the accusative complement (Δίδυμον) becomes the nominative complement (Culy 2009). Δίδυμος, like the Hebrew version of Thomas' name (see Θωμᾶς above), means "twin" (BDAG, 242).

τοῖς συμμαθηταῖς. Dative indirect object of εἶπεν. συμμαθητής ("fellow disciple") is a NT *hapax legomenon*.

ἄγωμεν. Pres act subj 1st pl ἄγω (hortatory subjunctive).

καί. Adverbial use (adjunctive).

ἡμεῖς. Nominative subject of ἄγωμεν.

ἵνα. Introduces a purpose clause.

ἀποθάνωμεν. Aor act subj 1st pl ἀποθνῄσκω. Subjunctive with ἵνα.

μετ' αὐτοῦ. Association/accompaniment.

John 11:17-27

¹⁷Now when Jesus came, he found him having lain in the tomb four days already. ¹⁸Bethany was near Jerusalem, about fifteen stadia away, ¹⁹and many of the Jews had come out to Martha and Mary in order to console them concerning their brother. ²⁰When Martha heard that Jesus was coming, she went to meet him, while Mary remained in the house. ²¹Then Martha said to Jesus, "Lord, if you had been here, my brother would not have died. ²²But even now I know that whatever you ask God for, God will give you." ²³Jesus said to her, "Your brother will rise again." ²⁴Martha said to him, "I know that he will rise again in the resurrection on the last day." ²⁵Jesus said to her, "I am the resurrection and the life. The one who believes in me, even if he dies, will live, ²⁶and everyone who lives and believes in me will never die. Do you believe this?" ²⁷She said to him, "Yes, Lord, I believe that you are the Messiah, the Son of God, the one coming into the world."

11:17 Ἐλθὼν οὖν ὁ Ἰησοῦς εὗρεν αὐτὸν τέσσαρας ἤδη ἡμέρας ἔχοντα ἐν τῷ μνημείῳ.

Ἐλθών. Aor act ptc masc nom sg ἔρχομαι (temporal). On participles that precede the main verb, see ἐμβλέψας in 1:36.

οὖν. Postpositive inferential conjunction and/or transitional particle (see 1:22 and 11:6).

ὁ Ἰησοῦς. Nominative subject of εὗρεν.

εὗρεν. Aor act ind 3rd sg εὑρίσκω.

αὐτόν. Accusative direct object of εὗρεν.

τέσσαρας ἤδη ἡμέρας. There are four textual variants of this formulation:

(1) τέσσαρας ἤδη ἡμέρας (𝔓⁷⁵ B C* Θ ƒ¹³ vg^ms)
(2) τέσσαρας ἡμέρας ἤδη (ℵ A^c C² K L W Γ Δ Ψ ƒ¹ 33 565 579 700 𝔐 sy^h et al.)
(3) ἤδη τέσσαρας ἡμέρας (𝔓⁶⁶ [1 p vg^ms])
(4) τέσσαρας ἡμέρας (A*^vid D e)

Reading (1) has the strongest textual support, and the awkward placement of ἤδη separating the words τέσσαρας ἡμέρας best explains the emergence of other variants (Metzger, 198–99).

τέσσαρας ... ἡμέρας. Accusative indicating extent of time. Fronted for emphasis.

ἤδη. Adverb ("already").

ἔχοντα. Pres act ptc masc acc sg ἔχω (attributive). The participle modifies αὐτόν. When ἔχω is combined with temporal indications of time, as here, it refers to a certain state or condition ("having lain in the grave") (BDAG, 422.7.b).

ἐν τῷ μνημείῳ. Locative.

11:18 ἦν δὲ ἡ Βηθανία ἐγγὺς τῶν Ἱεροσολύμων ὡς ἀπὸ σταδίων δεκαπέντε.

ἦν. Impf act ind 3rd sg εἰμί. On the function of the imperfect in the FG, see 1:39 on ἦν.

δὲ. Marker of narrative development.

ἡ Βηθανία. Nominative subject of ἦν.

ἐγγὺς τῶν Ἱεροσολύμων. Locative. ἐγγὺς is an adverb that here functions as an improper preposition (see 1:3 on χωρὶς αὐτοῦ) indicating close spatial proximity (BDAG, 271.1.b).

ὡς. Particle used with numerals to denote an estimate ("about, approximately").

ἀπὸ σταδίων δεκαπέντε. Separation. Louw and Nida note that "ἀπό with a statement of measurement may be analyzed as marking the extent of the measurement from a particular point" (LN 84 n. 3).

11:19 πολλοὶ δὲ ἐκ τῶν Ἰουδαίων ἐληλύθεισαν πρὸς τὴν Μάρθαν καὶ Μαριὰμ ἵνα παραμυθήσωνται αὐτὰς περὶ τοῦ ἀδελφοῦ.

πολλοί. Nominative subject of ἐληλύθεισαν. Fronted as a topical frame.

δὲ. Marker of narrative development.

ἐκ τῶν Ἰουδαίων. Replaces the partitive genitive. The term "the Jews" here refers to Judeans and not to the Jewish authorities who are hostile to Jesus as elsewhere in the FG.

ἐληλύθεισαν. Plprf act ind 3rd pl ἔρχομαι. The function of this pluperfect is similar to the function of εἰρήκει in 11:13.

πρὸς τὴν Μάρθαν καὶ Μαριάμ. Locative (motion toward). The presence of a single article before the names of two distinct individuals occurs elsewhere in the NT (Matt 17:1; Mark 15:47; Acts 13:2) and indicates that the persons in question are conceptualized as a contextually defined coherent group (Wallace 1996, 277–78). In this case, Martha and Mary are united under one article because they are sisters who are grieving the death of their brother.

ἵνα. Introduces a purpose clause.

παραμυθήσωνται. Aor mid subj 3rd pl παραμυθέομαι. Subjunctive with ἵνα.

αὐτάς. Accusative direct object of παραμυθήσωνται.
περὶ τοῦ ἀδελφοῦ. Reference.

11:20 Ἡ οὖν Μάρθα ὡς ἤκουσεν ὅτι Ἰησοῦς ἔρχεται ὑπήντησεν αὐτῷ· Μαριὰμ δὲ ἐν τῷ οἴκῳ ἐκαθέζετο.

Ἡ ... Μάρθα. Nominative subject of ἤκουσεν. Fronted as a topical frame.
οὖν. Postpositive inferential conjunction and/or transitional particle (see 1:22 and 11:6).
ὡς. Temporal conjunction (BDAG, 1105.8.a; BDF §455.2) introducing a clause that is fronted as a temporal frame.
ἤκουσεν. Aor act ind 3rd sg ἀκούω.
ὅτι. Introduces the clausal complement (indirect discourse) of ἤκουσεν.
Ἰησοῦς. Nominative subject of ἔρχεται.
ἔρχεται. Pres mid ind 3rd sg ἔρχομαι. The present tense is retained from direct discourse (see 1:39 on μένει).
ὑπήντησεν. Aor act ind 3rd sg ὑπαντάω.
αὐτῷ. Dative complement of ὑπήντησεν.
Μαριάμ. Nominative subject of ἐκαθέζετο.
δὲ. Marker of narrative development.
ἐν τῷ οἴκῳ. Locative. Fronted for emphasis.
ἐκαθέζετο. Impf mid ind 3rd sg καθέζομαι. The imperfect ἐκαθέζετο, which refers to Mary's ongoing condition (imperfective aspect), stands in contrast with the aorist ὑπήντησεν, which refers to Martha's immediate action (perfective aspect). James argues that this contrast "creates a cliffhanger, as the audience is left wondering what role Mary will play in the narrative" (193). Since, however, the fulfillment of the audience's expectation is delayed until v. 29, which uses another imperfect (ἤρχετο) to describe Mary's reaction to Martha's report, we could probably conclude with du Toit that "the imperfect establishes cohesion in the text" (221).

11:21 εἶπεν οὖν ἡ Μάρθα πρὸς τὸν Ἰησοῦν· κύριε, εἰ ἦς ὧδε οὐκ ἂν ἀπέθανεν ὁ ἀδελφός μου·

εἶπεν. Aor act ind 3rd sg λέγω.
οὖν. Postpositive inferential conjunction and/or transitional particle (see 1:22 and 11:6).
ἡ Μάρθα. Nominative subject of εἶπεν.
πρὸς τὸν Ἰησοῦν. Locative (motion toward).

κύριε. Nominative of direct address.

εἰ. Introduces the protasis of a second-class (contrary-to-fact) condition. Typically, the present contrary-to-fact conditions have the imperfect in both the protasis and the apodosis, while the past contrary-to-fact conditions have the aorist in both the protasis and the apodosis. Most of the exceptions to this rule involve the imperfect of εἰμί in the protasis, as here (Wallace 1996, 695 n. 26). εἰ ἦς ὧδε οὐκ ἂν ἀπέθανεν ὁ ἀδελφός μου is therefore a past contrary-to-fact condition. Had Jesus been there (but he was not), Lazarus would not have died (but he did). The formal features of this construction, however, should be distinguished from its rhetorical function. Martha is using a conditional sentence to communicate indirectly that Jesus should have been there. Thus, though formally this is a second-class condition, rhetorically it functions as a rebuke (Wallace 1996, 703; Young, 230).

ἦς. Impf act ind 2nd sg εἰμί.

ὧδε. Adverb of place.

οὐκ. Negative particle normally used with indicative verbs. It marks the beginning of the apodosis of a second-class (contrary-to-fact) condition.

ἄν. Marker of contingency in the apodosis of the second-class condition.

ἀπέθανεν. Aor act ind 3rd sg ἀποθνῄσκω.

ὁ ἀδελφός. Nominative subject of ἀπέθανεν.

μου. Genitive of relationship qualifying ἀδελφός.

11:22 [ἀλλὰ] καὶ νῦν οἶδα ὅτι ὅσα ἂν αἰτήσῃ τὸν θεὸν δώσει σοι ὁ θεός.

[ἀλλὰ]. Marker of contrast. ἀλλὰ is printed within square brackets because the manuscript evidence for its inclusion ($\mathfrak{P}^{45.66}$ $\aleph^2$ A C³ D K L W Γ Δ Θ Ψ f^{13} 565 579 700 892ˢ 1424 $\mathfrak{M}$ lat sy co) and its exclusion ($\mathfrak{P}^{75}$ $\aleph$* B C* 1 33 1241 *l*844 *l*2211 bo^{mss}) is evenly balanced.

καὶ. Adverbial use (ascensive).

νῦν. Temporal adverb focusing on time coextensive with the event of the narrative (BDAG, 681.1.a). Fronted as a temporal frame.

οἶδα. Prf act ind 1st sg οἶδα (see 1:26 on οἴδατε).

ὅτι. Introduces the clausal complement (indirect discourse) of οἶδα.

ὅσα. The relative pronoun introduces a headless relative clause that, in its entirety (ὅσα ἂν αἰτήσῃ τὸν θεὸν), serves as the direct object of δώσει. Within its clause, which is fronted as a topical frame, ὅσα is the accusative direct object (thing) of αἰτήσῃ in a double accusative person-thing construction.

ἄν. Marker of contingency.

αἰτήσῃ. Aor mid subj 2nd sg αἰτέω. Subjunctive with ἄν. In a double accusative construction, αἰτέω means to "ask someone for something" (BDAG, 30).

τὸν θεόν. Accusative direct object (person) of αἰτήσῃ in a double accusative person-thing construction.

δώσει. Fut act ind 3rd sg δίδωμι.

σοι. Dative indirect object of δώσει.

ὁ θεός. Nominative subject of δώσει.

11:23 λέγει αὐτῇ ὁ Ἰησοῦς· ἀναστήσεται ὁ ἀδελφός σου.

λέγει. Pres act ind 3rd sg λέγω. The historical present gives prominence to Jesus' promise to Martha that her brother will rise again (see 1:15 on μαρτυρεῖ). This verse is connected to the previous one by asyndeton.

αὐτῇ. Dative indirect object of λέγει.

ὁ Ἰησοῦς. Nominative subject of λέγει.

ἀναστήσεται. Fut mid ind 3rd sg ἀνίστημι. ἀναστήσεται functions as a double entendre because the Johannine Jesus uses the future tense as a reference to the near future, while Martha understands it as a reference to the eschatological future. For other examples of words with multiple meanings that are typically misunderstood by Jesus' audience, see 3:3-4; 4:14-15; 6:33-34; 8:21-22; 11:11-12; 14:7-8.

ὁ ἀδελφός. Nominative subject of ἀναστήσεται.

σου. Genitive of relationship qualifying ἀδελφός.

11:24 λέγει αὐτῷ ἡ Μάρθα· οἶδα ὅτι ἀναστήσεται ἐν τῇ ἀναστάσει ἐν τῇ ἐσχάτῃ ἡμέρᾳ.

λέγει. Pres act ind 3rd sg λέγω. The historical present gives prominence to Martha's reply to Jesus (see 1:15 on μαρτυρεῖ). This verse is connected to the previous one by asyndeton.

αὐτῷ. Dative indirect object of λέγει.

ἡ Μάρθα. Nominative subject of λέγει.

οἶδα. Prf act ind 1st sg οἶδα (see 1:26 on οἴδατε).

ὅτι. Introduces the clausal complement (indirect discourse) of οἶδα.

ἀναστήσεται. Fut mid ind 3rd sg ἀνίστημι.

ἐν τῇ ἀναστάσει. Temporal ("at the time of the resurrection," "when all come back from the dead" [BBE]) or locative ("in the resurrected state"). The noun ἀνάστασις is used in the FG only here and in the next verse. Elsewhere in the New Testament, this term occurs in Matt 22:31; Luke 20:35; Acts 1:22; Rom 6:5; 1 Cor 15:12-13; Rev 20:5-6.

ἐν τῇ ἐσχάτῃ ἡμέρᾳ. Temporal. The PP "on the last day" occurs only in the FG (6:39, 40, 44; 11:24; 12:48; cf. τῇ ἐσχάτῃ ἡμέρᾳ in 6:54). Other NT formulations use the plural "the last days" (ἐν ταῖς ἐσχάταις ἡμέραις [Acts 2:17]; ἐν ἐσχάταις ἡμέραις [2 Tim 3:1; Jas 5:3]; ἐπ᾽ ἐσχάτου τῶν ἡμερῶν [Heb 1:2]; ἐπ᾽ ἐσχάτων τῶν ἡμερῶν [2 Pet 3:3]).

11:25 εἶπεν αὐτῇ ὁ Ἰησοῦς· ἐγώ εἰμι ἡ ἀνάστασις καὶ ἡ ζωή· ὁ πιστεύων εἰς ἐμὲ κἂν ἀποθάνῃ ζήσεται,

εἶπεν. Aor act ind 3rd sg λέγω. This verse is connected to the previous one by asyndeton.

αὐτῇ. Dative indirect object of εἶπεν.

ὁ Ἰησοῦς. Nominative subject of εἶπεν.

ἐγώ εἰμι ἡ ἀνάστασις καὶ ἡ ζωή. This is one of Jesus' "I am" pronouncements in the FG with an explicit predicate; for other statements of this type, see 6:35, 48, 51; 8:12; 10:7, 9, 11, 14; 14:6; 15:1, 5.

ἐγώ. Nominative subject of ἐγώ. Fronted for emphasis.

εἰμι. Pres act ind 1st sg εἰμί.

ἡ ἀνάστασις. Predicate nominative.

καί. Coordinating conjunction.

ἡ ζωή. Predicate nominative.

ὁ πιστεύων. Pres act ptc masc nom sg πιστεύω (substantival). Nominative subject of ζήσεται. Fronted as a topical frame. The imperfective aspect of the present-tense participle indicates that believing is seen as an action in progress without regard for its beginning or end. This clause is connected to the previous one by asyndeton.

εἰς ἐμέ. Goal of actions or feelings directed toward someone (BDAG, 290.4.c.β). For πιστεύειν εἰς + accusative ("trust or believe in someone"), see 1:12 on εἰς τὸ ὄνομα.

κἄν. Formed by crasis from καὶ ἐάν. καί is ascensive ("even"). Louw and Nida call κἄν "an emphatic marker of concession—'even if, even though'" (LN 89.73). ἐάν introduces the protasis of a third-class condition.

ἀποθάνῃ. Aor act subj 3rd sg ἀποθνῄσκω.

ζήσεται. Fut mid ind 3rd sg ζάω. This verb provides the only content of the apodosis.

11:26 καὶ πᾶς ὁ ζῶν καὶ πιστεύων εἰς ἐμὲ οὐ μὴ ἀποθάνῃ εἰς τὸν αἰῶνα. πιστεύεις τοῦτο;

καί. Coordinating conjunction.

πᾶς ὁ ζῶν καὶ πιστεύων. Nominative subject of ἀποθάνῃ. Fronted as a topical frame. On πᾶς + articular participle, see 3:8 on πᾶς ὁ γεγεννημένος. Two substantival participles governed by one article and joined by καί form a TSKS (article-substantive-καί-substantive) construction. In such formulations, according to the Granville Sharp rule, the single article indicates that both participles have the same referent; see 5:24 on ὁ ... ἀκούων καὶ πιστεύων.

ζῶν. Pres act ptc masc nom sg ζάω (substantival). On the function of this participle, see πᾶς ὁ ζῶν καὶ πιστεύων above.

πιστεύων. Pres act ptc masc nom sg πιστεύω (substantival). On the function of this participle, see πᾶς ὁ ζῶν καὶ πιστεύων above.

εἰς ἐμὲ. Goal of actions or feelings directed toward someone (BDAG, 290.4.c.β). For πιστεύειν εἰς + accusative ("trust or believe in someone"), see 1:12 on εἰς τὸ ὄνομα.

οὐ μὴ. Emphatic negation, which is usually followed by the aorist subjunctive.

ἀποθάνῃ. Aor act subj 3rd sg ἀποθνῄσκω. The subjunctive is used with οὐ μὴ to express emphatic negation.

εἰς τὸν αἰῶνα. Temporal.

πιστεύεις. Pres act ind 2nd sg πιστεύω.

τοῦτο. Accusative direct object of πιστεύεις.

11:27 λέγει αὐτῷ· ναὶ κύριε, ἐγὼ πεπίστευκα ὅτι σὺ εἶ ὁ χριστὸς ὁ υἱὸς τοῦ θεοῦ ὁ εἰς τὸν κόσμον ἐρχόμενος.

λέγει. Pres act ind 3rd sg λέγω. The historical present gives prominence to Martha's confession of Jesus' messiahship (see 1:15 on μαρτυρεῖ). This verse is connected to the previous one by asyndeton.

αὐτῷ. Dative indirect object of λέγει.

ναὶ. Affirmative particle.

κύριε. Vocative of direct address.

ἐγώ. Nominative subject of πεπίστευκα. Fronted as a topical frame.

πεπίστευκα. Prf act ind 1st sg πιστεύω. Stative aspect of the perfect tense points to a state of faith without any reference to its origin or progress. Porter mentions this verb as an example of inadequacy of the traditional explanation of the perfect tense that postulates the continuum between an event in the past and its present result: "[W]hen Jesus asks Martha if she believes (πιστεύεις [v 26]), she answers ἐγὼ πεπίστευκα (I indeed believe)" (1989, 255; *pace* Fanning, 113, 139, who argues that the present state of belief implies a previous act of believing).

ὅτι. Introduces the clausal complement (indirect discourse) of πεπίστευκα. Indirect discourse is placed within direct discourse (Porter 1994, 272).

σύ. Nominative subject of εἶ. Fronted as a topical frame.

εἶ. Pres act ind 2nd sg εἰμί.

ὁ χριστὸς. Predicate nominative (see 1:20).

ὁ υἱὸς. Nominative in apposition to ὁ χριστὸς.

τοῦ θεοῦ. Genitive of relationship qualifying υἱός.

ὁ . . . ἐρχόμενος. Pres mid ptc masc nom sg ἔρχομαι (substantival). This could be regarded either as a nominative in apposition to ὁ χριστὸς or as a nominative in apposition to ὁ υἱὸς.

εἰς τὸν κόσμον. Locative. The PP, placed between the article and the participle, functions as an attributive modifier of ἐρχόμενος (see 1:15 on ὀπίσω μου).

John 11:28-37

²⁸And when she said this, she went away and called Mary, her sister, saying in private, "The Teacher is here and is asking for you." ²⁹When she heard [this], she rose quickly and came to him. ³⁰Now Jesus had not yet come into the village but was still at the place where Martha had met him. ³¹The Jews, who were with her in the house and were consoling her, when they saw Mary, that she quickly rose and went out, followed her because they thought that she was going to the tomb to weep there. ³²When Mary came where Jesus was, as soon as she saw him, she fell at his feet, saying to him, "Lord, if you had been here, my brother would not have died." ³³Then when Jesus saw her weeping and the Jews who came with her weeping, he was deeply disturbed in the spirit and troubled. ³⁴And he said, "Where have you put him?" They said to him, "Lord, come and see." ³⁵Jesus wept. ³⁶Then the Jews said, "See how he loved him!" ³⁷But some of them said, "Could not this man who opened the eyes of the blind man do something so that also this one should not die?"

11:28 Καὶ τοῦτο εἰποῦσα ἀπῆλθεν καὶ ἐφώνησεν Μαριὰμ τὴν ἀδελφὴν αὐτῆς λάθρᾳ εἰποῦσα· ὁ διδάσκαλος πάρεστιν καὶ φωνεῖ σε.

Καὶ. Coordinating conjunction.

τοῦτο. Accusative direct object of εἰποῦσα. The anaphoric demonstrative refers to Mary's confession in the previous verse.

εἰποῦσα. Aor act ptc fem nom sg λέγω (temporal). On participles that precede the main verb, see ἐμβλέψας in 1:36.

ἀπῆλθεν. Aor act ind 3rd sg ἀπέρχομαι.

καὶ. Coordinating conjunction.

ἐφώνησεν. Aor act ind 3rd sg φωνέω.

Μαριὰμ. Accusative direct object of ἐφώνησεν.

τὴν ἀδελφὴν. Accusative in apposition to Μαριάμ.
αὐτῆς. Genitive of relationship qualifying ἀδελφὴν.
λάθρᾳ. Adverb of manner qualifying either ἐφώνησεν (KJV; GNT; LEB; NIV) or εἰποῦσα (NRSV; HCSB; ESV). The placement of the adverb in close proximity to the participle favors the latter.
εἰποῦσα. Aor act ptc fem nom sg λέγω (manner). On participles that follow the main verb, see βαπτίζων in 1:31.
ὁ διδάσκαλος. Nominative subject of πάρεστιν. Fronted for emphasis. Besides Martha, several other characters in the FG apply this title for Jesus: two of John's disciples (1:38), Nicodemus (3:2), Jesus' disciples (13:13-14), and Mary Magdalene (20:16). It is, however, somewhat surprising that Martha uses this title just after she confessed her faith in Jesus as the Messiah (cf Barrett, 397).
πάρεστιν. Pres act ind 3rd sg πάρειμι.
καὶ. Coordinating conjunction.
φωνεῖ. Pres act ind 3rd sg φωνέω.
σε. Accusative direct object of φωνεῖ.

11:29 ἐκείνη δὲ ὡς ἤκουσεν ἠγέρθη ταχὺ καὶ ἤρχετο πρὸς αὐτόν.

ἐκείνη. Nominative subject of ἤκουσεν. The demonstrative pronoun refers to Μαριάμ in the preceding verse, functioning as a third-person personal pronoun with a simple anaphoric force (Wallace 1996, 328–29).
δὲ. Marker of narrative development.
ὡς. Temporal conjunction (BDAG, 1105.8.a; BDF §455.2), introducing a clause that is fronted as a temporal frame.
ἤκουσεν. Aor act ind 3rd sg ἀκούω.
ἠγέρθη. Aor mid ind 3rd sg ἐγείρω. This is an intransitive θη–middle form. On the voice, see "Deponency" in the Series Introduction.
ταχὺ. Adverbial accusative ("quickly, without delay").
καὶ. Coordinating conjunction, connecting two finite verbs.
ἤρχετο. Impf mid ind 3rd sg ἔρχομαι.
πρὸς αὐτόν. Locative (motion toward).

11:30 οὔπω δὲ ἐληλύθει ὁ Ἰησοῦς εἰς τὴν κώμην, ἀλλ' ἦν ἔτι ἐν τῷ τόπῳ ὅπου ὑπήντησεν αὐτῷ ἡ Μάρθα.

οὔπω. Adverb of time.
δὲ. Marker of narrative development.
ἐληλύθει. Plprf act ind 3rd sg ἔρχομαι. The function of this pluperfect is similar to the function of εἰρήκει in 11:13.
ὁ Ἰησοῦς. Nominative subject of ἐληλύθει.

εἰς τὴν κώμην. Locative.
ἀλλ'. Marker of contrast.
ἦν. Impf act ind 3rd sg εἰμί. On the function of the imperfect in the FG, see 1:39 on ἦν.
ἔτι. Adverb ("still").
ἐν τῷ τόπῳ. Locative.
ὅπου. Marker of a position in space.
ὑπήντησεν. Aor act ind 3rd sg ὑπαντάω.
αὐτῷ. Dative complement of ὑπήντησεν.
ἡ Μάρθα. Nominative subject of ὑπήντησεν.

11:31 οἱ οὖν Ἰουδαῖοι οἱ ὄντες μετ' αὐτῆς ἐν τῇ οἰκίᾳ καὶ παραμυθούμενοι αὐτήν, ἰδόντες τὴν Μαριὰμ ὅτι ταχέως ἀνέστη καὶ ἐξῆλθεν, ἠκολούθησαν αὐτῇ δόξαντες ὅτι ὑπάγει εἰς τὸ μνημεῖον ἵνα κλαύσῃ ἐκεῖ.

οἱ ... Ἰουδαῖοι. Nominative subject of ἠκολούθησαν. In this context, οἱ ... Ἰουδαῖοι is a geographic designation for Judeans (see 11:19 on ἐκ τῶν Ἰουδαίων). Fronted as a topical frame.

οὖν. Postpositive inferential conjunction and/or transitional particle (see 1:22 and 11:6).

οἱ ὄντες. Pres act ptc masc nom pl εἰμί (attributive). The participle modifies οἱ ... Ἰουδαῖοι, standing in the second attributive position (see 1:29 on ὁ αἴρων).

μετ' αὐτῆς. Association/accompaniment.
ἐν τῇ οἰκίᾳ. Locative.
καί. Coordinating conjunction.

παραμυθούμενοι. Pres mid ptc masc nom pl παραμυθέομαι (attributive). This participle also modifies οἱ ... Ἰουδαῖοι (see οἱ ὄντες above), standing in the second attributive position (see 1:29 on ὁ αἴρων). παραμυθέομαι means "to console, to comfort, to encourage" (LN 25.153).

αὐτήν. Accusative direct object of παραμυθέομαι.

ἰδόντες. Aor act ptc masc nom pl ὁράω (temporal). On participles that precede the main verb, see ἐμβλέψας in 1:36.

τὴν Μαριάμ. Accusative direct object of ἰδόντες. Barrett says that "τὴν Μαριάμ is attracted out of the ὅτι clause into the principal sentence" (398), but it is more accurate to say that τὴν Μαριάμ anticipates the subject of the ὅτι clause (see ἀνέστη below).

ὅτι. Introduces the clausal complement (indirect discourse) of ἰδόντες.

ταχέως. Adverb of manner.

ἀνέστη. Aor act ind 3rd sg ἀνίστημι. The implied subject of ἀνέστη (Mary) "is anticipated in the main clause as its object" (Zerwick §207).

καί. Coordinating conjunction.

ἐξῆλθεν. Aor act ind 3rd sg ἐξέρχομαι.

ἠκολούθησαν. Aor act ind 3rd pl ἀκολουθέω.

αὐτῇ. Dative direct object of ἠκολούθησαν.

δόξαντες. Aor act ptc masc nom pl δοκέω (causal). The variant λέγοντες, attested in a number of manuscripts ($\mathfrak{P}^{66}$ A C² K Γ Δ Θ Ψ 892ˢ 1424 *l*844 *l*2211 𝔐 lat syʰ sa ly), "may have arisen when it was asked how the evangelist could have known the thoughts of the Jews" (Metzger, 199).

ὅτι. Introduces the clausal complement (indirect discourse) of δόξαντες.

ὑπάγει. Pres act ind 3rd sg ὑπάγω.

εἰς τὸ μνημεῖον. Locative (motion toward). Here is εἰς used for πρός (Zerwick §97). For other examples of this usage, see 11:38; 20:1, 3, 4, 8.

ἵνα. Introduces a purpose clause.

κλαύσῃ. Aor act subj 3rd sg κλαίω. Subjunctive with ἵνα.

ἐκεῖ. Adverb of place.

11:32 Ἡ οὖν Μαριὰμ ὡς ἦλθεν ὅπου ἦν Ἰησοῦς ἰδοῦσα αὐτὸν ἔπεσεν αὐτοῦ πρὸς τοὺς πόδας λέγουσα αὐτῷ· κύριε, εἰ ἧς ὧδε οὐκ ἄν μου ἀπέθανεν ὁ ἀδελφός.

Ἡ . . . Μαριάμ. Nominative subject of ἦλθεν. Fronted as a topical frame.

οὖν. Postpositive inferential conjunction and/or transitional particle (see 1:22 and 11:6).

ὡς. Temporal conjunction (BDAG, 1105.8.a; BDF §455.2), introducing a clause that is fronted as a temporal frame.

ἦλθεν. Aor act ind 3rd sg ἔρχομαι.

ὅπου. Marker of a position in space.

ἦν. Impf act ind 3rd sg εἰμί. On the function of the imperfect in the FG, see 1:39 on ἦν.

Ἰησοῦς. Nominative subject of ἦν.

ἰδοῦσα. Aor act ptc fem nom sg ὁράω (temporal). On participles that precede the main verb, see ἐμβλέψας in 1:36.

αὐτόν. Accusative direct object of ἰδοῦσα.

ἔπεσεν. Aor act ind 3rd sg πίπτω.

αὐτοῦ. Possessive genitive qualifying πόδας.

πρὸς τοὺς πόδας. Locative (motion toward). Though the variant εἰς τοὺς πόδας ($\mathfrak{P}^{66}$ A C³ K Γ Δ Θ *f*¹³ 700 892ˢ 1424 *l*2211 𝔐) represents the more difficult reading, πρὸς τοὺς πόδας is probably original because of its early and diversified external support (ℵ B C* D L W Ψ *f*¹ 33 579 1241 *l*844 sy^h) (Metzger, 200).

λέγουσα. Pres act ptc fem nom sg λέγω (manner). On participles that follow the main verb, see βαπτίζων in 1:31.

αὐτῷ. Dative indirect object of λέγουσα.

κύριε. Vocative of direct address.

εἰ. Introduces the protasis of a second-class (contrary-to-fact) condition. Mary's words are the verbatim repetition of Martha's words in 11:21, except for the fronting of the possessive genitive μου. Mary's contrary-to-fact conditional clause serves the same rhetorical purpose as Martha's—to provide an indirect rebuke of Jesus' delayed arrival.

ἦς. Impf act ind 2nd sg εἰμί.

ὧδε. Adverb of place.

οὐκ. Negative particle normally used with indicative verbs. It marks the beginning of the apodosis of a second-class (contrary-to-fact) condition.

ἄν. Marker of contingency in the apodosis of the second-class condition.

μου. Genitive of relationship qualifying ἀδελφός. The preposed pronoun is thematically salient (Levinsohn 2000, 64).

ἀπέθανεν. Aor act ind 3rd sg ἀποθνήσκω.

ὁ ἀδελφός. Nominative subject of ἀπέθανεν.

11:33 Ἰησοῦς οὖν ὡς εἶδεν αὐτὴν κλαίουσαν καὶ τοὺς συνελθόντας αὐτῇ Ἰουδαίους κλαίοντας, ἐνεβριμήσατο τῷ πνεύματι καὶ ἐτάραξεν ἑαυτὸν

Ἰησοῦς. Nominative subject of εἶδεν. Fronted as a topical frame.

οὖν. Postpositive inferential conjunction and/or transitional particle (see 1:22 and 11:6).

ὡς. Temporal conjunction (BDAG, 1105.8.a; BDF §455.2), introducing a clause that is fronted as a temporal frame.

εἶδεν. Aor act ind 3rd sg ὁράω.

αὐτὴν. The first accusative direct object of εἶδεν in a double accusative object-complement construction.

κλαίουσαν. Pres act ptc fem acc sg κλαίω (predicative). Accusative complement to αὐτὴν in a double accusative object-complement construction. In this context, κλαίω means "to weep or lament for the dead" (BDAG, 545.1).

καί. Coordinating conjunction.

τοὺς ... Ἰουδαίους. The second accusative direct object of εἶδεν in a double accusative object-complement construction. In this context, "the Jews" is a geographic designation for Judeans (see 11:19 on ἐκ τῶν Ἰουδαίων).

συνελθόντας. Aor act ptc masc acc pl συνέρχομαι (attributive). The participle modifies τοὺς ... Ἰουδαίους, standing in the first attributive position (see 5:37 on πέμψας).

αὐτῇ. Dative complement of συνελθόντας.

κλαίοντας. Pres act ptc masc acc pl κλαίω (predicative). Accusative complement to τοὺς ... Ἰουδαίους in a double accusative object-complement construction.

ἐνεβριμήσατο. Aor mid ind 3rd sg ἐμβριμάομαι. In this context, ἐμβριμάομαι means "to have an intense, strong feeling of concern, often with the implication of indignation" (LN 25.56). The usage of this verb and its cognates in biblical (LXX Dan 11:30; Lam 2:6) and non-biblical literature (Lucian, *Men.* 20) shows that ἐμβριμάομαι usually implies anger. In the FG, the verb is used only in the Lazarus narrative (here and in 11:38). Elsewhere in the NT, it occurs in Matt 9:30; Mark 1:43; 14:5.

τῷ πνεύματι. Locative dative ("in the spirit") or dative of respect ("with reference to the spirit"). A parallel construction in 11:38 (ἐν ἑαυτῷ) indicates that this is his—i.e., Jesus'—spirit.

καὶ. Coordinating conjunction.

ἐτάραξεν. Aor act ind 3rd sg ταράσσω. In this context, ταράσσω means "to cause acute emotional distress or turbulence" (LN 25.244). The verb is used in this sense also in 12:27; 13:21; 14:1, 27.

ἑαυτόν. Accusative direct object of ἐτάραξεν (lit. "he troubled himself").

11:34 καὶ εἶπεν· ποῦ τεθείκατε αὐτόν; λέγουσιν αὐτῷ· κύριε, ἔρχου καὶ ἴδε.

καὶ. Coordinating conjunction.

εἶπεν. Aor act ind 3rd sg λέγω.

ποῦ. Interrogative adverb of place. Fronted for emphasis.

τεθείκατε. Prf act ind 2nd pl τίθημι. In this context, τίθημι denotes the disposal of a dead body in a tomb (see Matt 27:60; Mark 6:29; 15:46-47; 16:6; Luke 23:53, 55; John 19:41-42; Rev 11:9). Porter notes that the perfect tense can be used, as here, "in a past context, often parallel with other past-referring verb forms" (1989, 260); in this case, "Jesus is not inquiring about any continuing effect on Mary and Martha about the place where they laid the body" (261).

αὐτόν. Accusative direct object of τεθείκατε.

λέγουσιν. Pres act ind 3rd pl λέγω. The historical present gives prominence to the response of the Jews (see 1:15 on μαρτυρεῖ). This clause is connected to the previous one by asyndeton.

αὐτῷ. Dative indirect object of λέγουσιν.

κύριε. Vocative of direct address.

ἔρχου καὶ ἴδε. Wallace (1996, 489, 491) regards ἔρχου as a type of conditional imperative ("if X, then Y will happen") because the trailing imperative (ἴδε) "function[s] semantically like a *future indicative*": "Come and see" = "If you come, you *will* see" (491). The identical clause is found in 1:46.

ἔρχου. Pres mid impv 2nd sg ἔρχομαι.

καὶ. Coordinating conjunction.

ἴδε. Aor act impv 2nd sg ὁράω.

11:35 ἐδάκρυσεν ὁ Ἰησοῦς.

ἐδάκρυσεν. Aor act ind 3rd sg δακρύω. This verse is connected to the previous one by asyndeton. δακρύω means "to weep, with the clear implication of shedding tears" (LN 25.137). Barrett (400) emphasizes that δακρύω is different from κλαίω that is used of Mary and the Jews who came with her (11:33).

ὁ Ἰησοῦς. Nominative subject of ἐδάκρυσεν.

11:36 ἔλεγον οὖν οἱ Ἰουδαῖοι· ἴδε πῶς ἐφίλει αὐτόν.

ἔλεγον. Impf act ind 3rd pl λέγω. The imperfect marks a transition from Jesus, who was the main actor in the preceding narrative, to the Judean mourners. It is probably used for a repeated action, denoting an ongoing conversation among the members of this group (James, 209).

οὖν. Postpositive inferential conjunction.

οἱ Ἰουδαῖοι. Nominative subject of ἔλεγον. In this context, "the Jews" is a geographic designation for Judeans (see 11:19 on ἐκ τῶν Ἰουδαίων).

ἴδε. An interjection (originally aor act impv 2nd sg ὁράω) that is "used when more than one pers[on] is addressed, and when that which is to be observed is in the nom[inative]" (BDAG, 466).

πῶς. Interrogative adverb used in exclamations (BDF §436).

ἐφίλει. Impf act ind 3rd sg φιλέω.

αὐτόν. Accusative direct object of ἐφίλει.

11:37 τινὲς δὲ ἐξ αὐτῶν εἶπαν· οὐκ ἐδύνατο οὗτος ὁ ἀνοίξας τοὺς ὀφθαλμοὺς τοῦ τυφλοῦ ποιῆσαι ἵνα καὶ οὗτος μὴ ἀποθάνῃ;

τινὲς. Nominative subject of εἶπαν. Fronted as a topical frame.

δὲ. Marker of narrative development.

ἐξ αὐτῶν. Replaces the partitive genitive.

εἶπαν. Aor act ind 3rd pl λέγω. This aorist stands in contrast to the imperfect ἔλεγον in v. 36 and receives more semantic weight because of its departure from the unmarked word order (James, 209).

οὐκ. The negative particle indicates that the rhetorical question expects an affirmative answer.

ἐδύνατο. Aor mid ind 3rd sg δύναμαι.

οὗτος ὁ ἀνοίξας. Nominative subject of ἐδύνατο. The use of the near-demonstrative indicates spatial proximity between the interlocutors and Jesus.

ὁ ἀνοίξας. Aor act ptc masc nom sg ἀνοίγω (substantival).

τοὺς ὀφθαλμοὺς. Accusative direct object of ἀνοίξας.

τοῦ τυφλοῦ. Possessive genitive qualifying ὀφθαλμοὺς.

ποιῆσαι. Aor act inf ποιέω (complementary).

ἵνα. Introduces a result clause (Zerwick §352).

καὶ. Adverbial use (adjunctive).

οὗτος. Nominative subject of ἀποθάνῃ.

μὴ. Negative particle normally used with non-indicative verbs.

ἀποθάνῃ. Aor act subj 3rd sg ἀποθνῄσκω. Subjunctive with ἵνα. The verb stands in final, emphatic position.

John 11:38-44

[38]Then Jesus, because he was again deeply moved within himself, came to the tomb. It was a cave, and a stone was lying against it. [39]Jesus said, "Take away the stone." The sister of the dead man, Martha, said to him, "Lord, he already stinks because he has been there four days." [40]Jesus said to her, "Did I not tell you that if you believed, you would see the glory of God?" [41]Then they took away the stone. Jesus lifted up his eyes and said, "Father, I thank you that you have heard me. [42]I knew that you always hear me, but I have spoken for the sake of the crowd standing around, so that they may believe that you sent me." [43]And when he said these things, he cried with a loud voice, "Lazarus, come out!" [44]The dead man came out, having been bound with linen strips with respect to his feet and hands, and his face was wrapped with a face-cloth. Jesus said to them, "Unbind him, and let him go away."

11:38 Ἰησοῦς οὖν πάλιν ἐμβριμώμενος ἐν ἑαυτῷ ἔρχεται εἰς τὸ μνημεῖον· ἦν δὲ σπήλαιον καὶ λίθος ἐπέκειτο ἐπ' αὐτῷ.

Ἰησοῦς. Nominative subject of ἔρχεται.

οὖν. Postpositive inferential conjunction and/or transitional particle (see 1:22 and 11:6).

πάλιν. Adverb "pert[aining] to repetition in the same (or similar) manner" (BDAG, 752.2).

ἐμβριμώμενος. Pres mid ptc masc nom sg ἐμβριμάομαι (causal; cf. Wallace 1996, 631).

ἐν ἑαυτῷ. Locative. This PP interprets the dative τῷ πνεύματι in 11:33.

ἔρχεται. Pres mid ind 3rd sg ἔρχομαι. The historical present marks the narrative transition to a new scene and calls attention to Jesus' arrival to the tomb in which Lazarus was buried (Battle, 128). This is the first of several historical presents in vv. 38-44 (see λέγει in vv. 39 [2x], 40, 44), which could be regarded as an example of "the overuse of a device in a series of clauses, like building to a crescendo" (Runge 2010, 133; cf. James, 216).

εἰς τὸ μνημεῖον. Locative (motion toward). Here εἰς is used for πρός (Zerwick §97). It is clear from the context that Jesus came to the tomb but did not enter it (see 11:31; 20:1, 3, 4, 8).

ἦν. Impf act ind 3rd sg εἰμί. The subject ("it") is embedded in the verb form. On the function of the imperfect in the FG, see 1:39 on ἦν.

δὲ. Marker of narrative development.

σπήλαιον. Predicate nominative.

καὶ. Coordinating conjunction.

λίθος. Nominative subject of ἐπέκειτο. Fronted for emphasis. λίθος denotes a stone that is used to seal the tomb (cf. 20:1).

ἐπέκειτο. Impf mid ind 3rd sg ἐπίκειμαι.

ἐπ' αὐτῷ. Locative. The antecedent of the pronoun is σπήλαιον.

11:39 λέγει ὁ Ἰησοῦς· ἄρατε τὸν λίθον. λέγει αὐτῷ ἡ ἀδελφὴ τοῦ τετελευτηκότος Μάρθα· κύριε, ἤδη ὄζει, τεταρταῖος γάρ ἐστιν.

λέγει. Pres act ind 3rd sg λέγω. The historical present gives prominence to Jesus' command (see 1:15 on μαρτυρεῖ). This verse is connected to the previous one by asyndeton.

ὁ Ἰησοῦς. Nominative subject of λέγει.

ἄρατε. Aor act impv 2nd pl αἴρω. The evangelist uses the participle of the same verb to describe the position of the sealing stone ("taken away from the tomb") when Mary Magdalene arrived at Jesus' burial place: βλέπει τὸν λίθον ἠρμένον ἐκ τοῦ μνημείου (20:1).

τὸν λίθον. Accusative direct object of ἄρατε.

λέγει. Pres act ind 3rd sg λέγω. The historical present gives prominence to Martha's objection (see 1:15 on μαρτυρεῖ). This clause is connected to the previous one by asyndeton.

αὐτῷ. Dative indirect object of λέγει.

ἡ ἀδελφὴ. Nominative subject of λέγει.

τοῦ τετελευτηκότος. Prf act ptc masc gen sg τελευτάω (substantival). Genitive of relationship qualifying ἀδελφὴ.

Μάρθα. Nominative in apposition to ἡ ἀδελφὴ.

κύριε. Vocative of direct address.

ἤδη. Adverb ("already").

ὄζει. Pres act ind 3rd sg ὄζω. ὄζω ("to stink, to have a bad smell" [LN 79.47]) is a NT *hapax legomenon*. The implied subject of the verb ("he") refers to "the dead man" (τοῦ τετελευτηκότος), i.e., his corpse: "(the body) already stinks" (LN 79.47). The verb stands in final, emphatic position.

τεταρταῖος. Predicate adjective. Another NT *hapax legomenon* that means "happening on the fourth day" (BDAG, 1000). Fronted for emphasis.

γάρ. Postpositive conjunction introducing a clause that explains the previous statement, i.e., why there will be an unpleasant odor.

ἐστιν. Pres act ind 3rd sg εἰμί. The implied subject of the verb ("he") refers to "the dead man" (τοῦ τετελευτηκότος), i.e., his corpse.

11:40 λέγει αὐτῇ ὁ Ἰησοῦς· οὐκ εἶπόν σοι ὅτι ἐὰν πιστεύσῃς ὄψῃ τὴν δόξαν τοῦ θεοῦ;

λέγει. Pres act ind 3rd sg λέγω. The historical present gives prominence to Jesus' words that follow (see 1:15 on μαρτυρεῖ). This verse is connected to the previous one by asyndeton.

αὐτῇ. Dative indirect object of λέγει.

ὁ Ἰησοῦς. Nominative subject of λέγει.

οὐκ. The negative particle indicates that Jesus' question expects an affirmative answer.

εἶπόν. Aor act ind 1st sg λέγω. εἶπόν, which has a circumflex accent on the penult, acquired an additional accent, the acute, on the ultima from the enclitic σοι (Smyth §183; Carson 1985, 48).

σοι. Dative indirect object of εἶπόν.

ὅτι. Introduces the clausal complement (indirect discourse) of εἶπόν. Indirect discourse is placed within direct discourse (see 11:27).

ἐάν. Introduces the protasis of a third-class condition.

πιστεύσῃς. Aor act subj 2nd sg πιστεύω. Subjunctive with ἐάν.

ὄψῃ. Fut mid ind 2nd sg ὁράω. The verb marks the beginning of the apodosis of a third-class condition.

τὴν δόξαν. Accusative direct object of τὴν δόξαν.

τοῦ θεοῦ. Objective genitive qualifying δόξαν ("glorification of God," "God glorified") or genitive of source/origin ("glory from God").

11:41 ἦραν οὖν τὸν λίθον. ὁ δὲ Ἰησοῦς ἦρεν τοὺς ὀφθαλμοὺς ἄνω καὶ εἶπεν· πάτερ, εὐχαριστῶ σοι ὅτι ἤκουσάς μου.

ἦραν. Aor act ind 3rd pl αἴρω. The embedded subject ("they") is not specified, but presumably it refers to the Jews who accompanied Jesus and the sisters to the tomb.

οὖν. Postpositive inferential conjunction and/or transitional particle (see 1:22 and 11:6).

τὸν λίθον. Accusative direct object of ἦραν.

ὁ ... Ἰησοῦς. Nominative subject of ἦρεν. Fronted as a topical frame.

δὲ. Marker of narrative development.

ἦρεν. Aor act ind 3rd sg αἴρω.

τοὺς ὀφθαλμοὺς. Accusative direct object of ἦρεν.

ἄνω. Adverb ("up, upwards, toward above" [LN 84.25]).

καὶ. Coordinating conjunction.

εἶπεν. Aor act ind 3rd sg λέγω.

πάτερ. Vocative of direct address. In his prayers in the FG, Jesus regularly addresses God as Father (11:41; 12:27, 28; 17:1, 5, 11, 21, 24, 25).

εὐχαριστῶ. Pres act ind 1st sg εὐχαριστέω.

σοι. Dative complement of εὐχαριστῶ.

ὅτι. Introduces the clausal complement (indirect discourse) of εὐχαριστῶ.

ἤκουσάς. Aor act ind 2nd sg ἀκούω. ἤκουσάς, which has an acute accent on the antepenult, acquired an additional accent, the acute, on the ultima from the enclitic μου (Smyth §183; Carson 1985, 48).

μου. Genitive complement of ἤκουσάς.

11:42 ἐγὼ δὲ ᾔδειν ὅτι πάντοτέ μου ἀκούεις, ἀλλὰ διὰ τὸν ὄχλον τὸν περιεστῶτα εἶπον, ἵνα πιστεύσωσιν ὅτι σύ με ἀπέστειλας.

ἐγώ. Nominative subject of ᾔδειν. Fronted as a topical frame.

δὲ. Marker of discursive development.

ᾔδειν. Plprf act ind 1st sg οἶδα. In the FG, every occurrence of the pluperfect within direct discourse is a pluperfect of οἶδα (1:31, 33; 4:10; 8:19 [2x]; 11:42). The pluperfect tense has the imperfect meaning, describing the state of knowing in the past without any reference to how this knowledge was gained (see 1:26 on οἴδατε).

ὅτι. Introduces the clausal complement (indirect discourse) of ᾔδειν.

πάντοτέ. Adverb. πάντοτέ, which has an acute accent on the antepenult, acquired an additional accent, the acute, on the ultima from the enclitic μου (Smyth §183; Carson 1985, 48).

μου. Genitive complement of ἀκούεις.

ἀκούεις. Pres act ind 2nd sg ἀκούω.

ἀλλὰ. Marker of contrast.

διὰ τὸν ὄχλον. Causal or purpose. Fronted for emphasis.

τὸν περιεστῶτα. Prf act ptc masc acc sg περιΐστημι (attributive). The participle modifies τὸν ὄχλον, standing in the second attributive position (see 1:29 on ὁ αἴρων). περιΐστημι means "to stand around someone or encircle" (LN 17.4).

εἶπον. Aor act ind 1st sg λέγω.

ἵνα. Introduces a purpose clause.

πιστεύσωσιν. Aor act subj 3rd pl πιστεύω. Subjunctive with ἵνα.

ὅτι σύ με ἀπέστειλας. This clause occurs five times in the FG: three times as the content of faith (11:42; 17:8, 21) and twice as the content of knowledge (17:23, 25).

ὅτι. Introduces the clausal complement (indirect discourse) of πιστεύσωσιν.

σύ. Nominative subject of ἀπέστειλας. Fronted for emphasis.

με. Accusative direct object of ἀπέστειλας.

ἀπέστειλας. Aor act ind 2nd sg ἀποστέλλω.

11:43 καὶ ταῦτα εἰπὼν φωνῇ μεγάλῃ ἐκραύγασεν· Λάζαρε, δεῦρο ἔξω.

καὶ. Coordinating conjunction.

ταῦτα. Accusative direct object of εἰπὼν.

εἰπών. Aor act ptc masc nom sg λέγω (temporal). On participles that precede the main verb, see ἐμβλέψας in 1:36.

φωνῇ μεγάλῃ. Dative of means/instrument. Fronted as a topical frame.

ἐκραύγασεν. Aor act ind 3rd sg κραυγάζω.

Λάζαρε. Vocative of direct address.

δεῦρο. Adverb of place functioning as an imperative ("here, hither, come here" [LN 84.24]).

ἔξω. Adverb ("outside").

11:44 ἐξῆλθεν ὁ τεθνηκὼς δεδεμένος τοὺς πόδας καὶ τὰς χεῖρας κειρίαις καὶ ἡ ὄψις αὐτοῦ σουδαρίῳ περιεδέδετο. λέγει αὐτοῖς ὁ Ἰησοῦς· λύσατε αὐτὸν καὶ ἄφετε αὐτὸν ὑπάγειν.

ἐξῆλθεν. Aor act ind 3rd sg ἐξέρχομαι. This verse is connected to the previous one by asyndeton.

ὁ τεθνηκὼς. Prf act ptc masc nom sg θνῄσκω (substantival). The context indicates that the participle refers to the state of the man prior to his exit from the tomb.

δεδεμένος. Prf pass ptc masc nom sg δέω (predicative). The participle modifies ὁ τεθνηκὼς, standing in the second predicate position (see 1:29 on ἐρχόμενον). Fanning emphasizes that the perfect passive participle "often emphasizes the *resulting state* and only implies the anterior occurrence" (416). The primary (personal) agency of the verb is not expressed.

τοὺς πόδας καὶ τὰς χεῖρας. Accusatives of respect or accusative of retained object with the passive (Robertson, 485–86). In this context, both articles function as possessive pronouns ("bound with respect to his feet and his hands").

κειρίαις. Dative of means/instrument. κειρία ("band of cloth, strip of cloth" [LN 6.156]) is a NT *hapax legomenon*.

καὶ. Coordinating conjunction.

ἡ ὄψις. Nominative subject of περιεδέδετο.

αὐτοῦ. Possessive genitive qualifying ὄψις.

σουδαρίῳ. Dative of means/instrument. σουδάριον is a Greek transliteration of the Latin *sudarium*, "a face-cloth for wiping perspiration" (BDAG, 934).

περιεδέδετο. Plprf pass ind 3rd sg περιδέω ("to tie or wrap an object around something" [LN 18.14]). The primary (personal) agency of the verb is not expressed. This pluperfect has a descriptive function (Campbell 2007, 219). Barrett notes that "[i]t is difficult to visualize the emergence of Lazarus thus bound" (403).

λέγει. Pres act ind 3rd sg λέγω. The historical present gives prominence to Jesus' command that follows (see 1:15 on μαρτυρεῖ). This clause is connected to the previous one by asyndeton.

αὐτοῖς. Dative indirect object of λέγει.

ὁ Ἰησοῦς. Nominative subject of λέγει.

λύσατε. Aor act impv 2nd pl λύω.

αὐτὸν. Accusative direct object of λύσατε.

καὶ. Coordinating conjunction.

ἄφετε. Aor act impv 2nd pl ἀφίημι. This combination of ἀφίημι and the complementary infinitive ὑπάγειν (see below) implies two verbal ideas—permitting and leaving (Caragounis 2004, 167).

αὐτόν. Accusative direct object of ἄφετε.
ὑπάγειν. Pres act inf ὑπάγω (complementary).

John 11:45-54

⁴⁵Therefore, many of the Jews, those who had come to Mary and had seen what Jesus did, believed in him. ⁴⁶But some of them went to the Pharisees, and they told them what Jesus had done. ⁴⁷Then the chief priests and the Pharisees called together the Sanhedrin and said, "What are we going to do, for this man is performing many signs. ⁴⁸If we let him go on like this, all will believe in him, and the Romans will come and destroy both our place and our nation." ⁴⁹But one of them, Caiaphas, who was high priest that year, said to them, "You do not know anything! ⁵⁰Nor do you consider that it is advantageous for you that one man should die for the people and not that the whole nation should perish." ⁵¹He did not say this on his own, but, because he was high priest that year, he prophesied that Jesus was about to die for the nation, ⁵²and not for the nation only, but that he may also gather into one the scattered children of God. ⁵³So from that day on they plotted that they might kill him. ⁵⁴Jesus therefore no longer walked about publicly among the Jews but went from there to the district near the desert, to a town called Ephraim, and he remained there with the disciples.

11:45 Πολλοὶ οὖν ἐκ τῶν Ἰουδαίων οἱ ἐλθόντες πρὸς τὴν Μαριὰμ καὶ θεασάμενοι ἃ ἐποίησεν ἐπίστευσαν εἰς αὐτόν·

Πολλοί. Nominative subject of ἐπίστευσαν. Fronted as a topical frame.

οὖν. Postpositive inferential conjunction. While in the FG the inferential force of οὖν is frequently either elusive or nonexistent (see 1:22 and 11:6), the participial descriptions of those who believed in Jesus indicate that this was the consequence of the miracle described in the previous verse.

ἐκ τῶν Ἰουδαίων. Replaces the partitive genitive. In this context, "the Jews" is a geographic designation for Judeans (see 11:19 on ἐκ τῶν Ἰουδαίων).

οἱ ἐλθόντες ... καὶ θεασάμενοι. Nominative in apposition to Πολλοί. The Granville Sharp rule is not applicable here because both substantival participles are in the plural. However, the contextual markers and the singular article that governs both participles indicate that the participles describe two identical groups: those who have come to visit Mary are also those who have seen what Jesus had done (Wallace 1996, 281–83). Many English translations (e.g., "Therefore many of the Jews who had come to visit Mary, and had seen what Jesus did" [NIV]; "Then many of the Jews who had come with Mary and saw the things which he did" [LEB]) wrongly suggest that Πολλοί constitute a subgroup of a larger group of Jews who witnessed the raising of Lazarus. The Greek syntax, however, indicates that Πολλοί are all those who visited Mary and saw the miracle described in the previous section, i.e., that all of them came to faith in Jesus.

ἐλθόντες. Aor act ptc masc nom pl ἔρχομαι (substantival).
πρὸς τὴν Μαριάμ. Locative (motion toward)
θεασάμενοι. Aor mid ptc masc nom pl θεάομαι (substantival).
ἅ. Introduces a headless relative clause that, in its entirety (ἃ ἐποίησεν), serves as the direct object of θεασάμενοι. Within its clause, ἅ is the accusative direct object of ἐποίησεν.
ἐποίησεν. Aor act ind 3rd sg ποιέω.
ἐπίστευσαν. Aor act ind 3rd pl πιστεύω.
εἰς αὐτόν. Goal of actions or feelings directed toward someone (BDAG, 290.4.c.β). For πιστεύειν εἰς + accusative ("trust or believe in someone"), see 1:12 on εἰς τὸ ὄνομα.

11:46 τινὲς δὲ ἐξ αὐτῶν ἀπῆλθον πρὸς τοὺς Φαρισαίους καὶ εἶπαν αὐτοῖς ἃ ἐποίησεν Ἰησοῦς.

τινές. Nominative subject of ἀπῆλθον. Fronted as a topical frame.
δέ. Marker of narrative development.
ἐξ αὐτῶν. Replaces the partitive genitive. The antecedent of the pronoun is Πολλοί from the previous verse, i.e., the Jews who believed in Jesus because they witnessed the raising of Lazarus. The expression τινὲς ... ἐξ αὐτῶν thus qualifies the sweeping statement in the previous verse, suggesting that the reaction to Jesus' miracle was not a unanimous belief in Jesus but a division among the witnesses.
ἀπῆλθον. Aor act ind 3rd pl ἀπέρχομαι.
πρὸς τοὺς Φαρισαίους. Locative (motion toward).
καί. Coordinating conjunction.
εἶπαν. Aor act ind 3rd pl λέγω.
αὐτοῖς. Dative indirect object of αὐτοῖς.
ἅ. Introduces a headless relative clause that, in its entirety (ἃ ἐποίησεν Ἰησοῦς), serves as the direct object of εἶπαν. Within its clause, ἅ is the accusative direct object of ἐποίησεν.
ἐποίησεν. Aor act ind 3rd sg ποιέω.
Ἰησοῦς. Nominative subject of ἐποίησεν.

11:47 Συνήγαγον οὖν οἱ ἀρχιερεῖς καὶ οἱ Φαρισαῖοι συνέδριον καὶ ἔλεγον· τί ποιοῦμεν ὅτι οὗτος ὁ ἄνθρωπος πολλὰ ποιεῖ σημεῖα;

Συνήγαγον. Aor act ind 3rd pl συνάγω.

οὖν. Postpositive inferential conjunction and/or transitional particle (see 1:22 and 11:6).

οἱ ἀρχιερεῖς καὶ οἱ Φαρισαῖοι. Nominative subjects of Συνήγαγον and ἔλεγον.

συνέδριον. Accusative direct object of Συνήγαγον. This is the only occurrence of the name of the highest indigenous judicial body in Judaea in the FG. The absence of the article suggests that this may have been "an ad hoc council" (Keener, 2:1074).

καὶ. Coordinating conjunction.

ἔλεγον. Impf act ind 3rd pl λέγω. This imperfect stands in contrast to the aorist Συνήγαγον, which has the same subject, and carries more semantic weight in this context because it introduces a key conversation among the chief priests and the Pharisees (James, 209).

τί. Interrogative pronoun, functioning as the accusative direct object of ποιοῦμεν. Fronted for emphasis.

ποιοῦμεν. Pres act ind 1st pl ποιέω. BDF (§366.4) suggests that the present indicative is used here in a deliberative sense in place of the future, i.e., as an equivalent to τί ποιῶμεν ("What should we do?") or τί ποιήσμεν ("What will we do?"). The next verse confirms that they are deliberating about the most appropriate course of action in the future in response to Jesus' activity.

ὅτι. Introduces a causal clause.

οὗτος ὁ ἄνθρωπος. Nominative subject of ποιεῖ.

πολλὰ ... σημεῖα. Accusative direct object of ποιεῖ. The use of the term σημεῖα for Jesus' miracles is one of the distinctive features of the FG (see 2:11, 23; 3:2; 4:48, 54; 6:2, 14, 26; 7:31; 9:16; 12:18, 37; 20:30; cf. Barrett, 75-78; Keener, 1:272-79; Thompson, 65-68).

ποιεῖ. Pres act ind 3rd sg ποιέω.

11:48 ἐὰν ἀφῶμεν αὐτὸν οὕτως, πάντες πιστεύσουσιν εἰς αὐτόν, καὶ ἐλεύσονται οἱ Ῥωμαῖοι καὶ ἀροῦσιν ἡμῶν καὶ τὸν τόπον καὶ τὸ ἔθνος.

ἐὰν. Introduces the protasis of a third-class condition. This verse is connected to the previous one by asyndeton.

ἀφῶμεν. Aor act subj 1st pl ἀφίημι. Subjunctive with ἐάν.

αὐτὸν. Accusative direct object of ἀφῶμεν.

οὕτως. Adverb of manner ("in this manner, thus, so").

πάντες. Nominative subject of πιστεύσουσιν.

πιστεύσουσιν. Fut act ind 3rd pl πιστεύω.

εἰς αὐτόν. Goal of actions or feelings directed toward someone (BDAG, 290.4.c.β). For πιστεύειν εἰς + accusative ("trust or believe in someone"), see 1:12 on εἰς τὸ ὄνομα.

καί. Coordinating conjunction. MHT (2:422) calls this καί "the consecutive use of καί in parataxis" because the second clause is the result of the first, but this is not a semantic quality of this conjunction but a conclusion based on its use in a specific context.

ἐλεύσονται. Fut mid ind 3rd pl ἔρχομαι.

οἱ Ῥωμαῖοι. Nominative subject of ἐλεύσονται.

καί. Coordinating conjunction.

ἀροῦσιν. Fut act ind 3rd pl αἴρω. In this context, αἴρω means "to destroy, with the implication of removal and doing away with" (LN 20.43).

ἡμῶν. Possessive genitive qualifying both τὸν τόπον and ἔθνος.

καὶ ... καί. "Both ... and."

τὸν τόπον. Accusative direct object of ἀροῦσιν. In this context, τόπον ("space, place, room") could refer to a privileged position of the Jewish leaders (Beasley-Murray, 196), the temple in Jerusalem (LN 80.1; Barrett, 405), the city of Jerusalem (Barrett, 405), or the land (Harris 2015, 220).

τὸ ἔθνος. Accusative direct object of ἀροῦσιν.

11:49 εἷς δέ τις ἐξ αὐτῶν Καϊάφας, ἀρχιερεὺς ὢν τοῦ ἐνιαυτοῦ ἐκείνου, εἶπεν αὐτοῖς· ὑμεῖς οὐκ οἴδατε οὐδέν,

εἷς ... τις. Nominative subject of εἶπεν. Fronted as a topical frame. Caragounis claims that "in the NT the cardinal numbers εἷς, μία, ἕν, are losing their numerical value and are being reduced to an indefinite pronoun" and adds that "[o]ccasionally the indefinite significance of εἷς is strengthened by the addition of τις" (2004, 113). This conclusion, however, is not applicable here because εἷς ... τις refers to a specific individual, Caiaphas, who is immediately identified in the text. The same combination of εἷς and τις also occurs in Mark 14:47 and Luke 22:50. For a similar critique of Caragounis' thesis regarding Luke 22:50, see Culy, Parsons, and Stigall (691).

δέ. Marker of narrative development.

ἐξ αὐτῶν. Replaces the partitive genitive.

Καϊάφας. Nominative in apposition to εἷς ... τις.

ἀρχιερεύς. Predicate nominative. Fronted for emphasis.

ὤν. Pres act ptc masc nom sg εἰμί (attributive). The participle modifies Καϊάφας.

τοῦ ἐνιαυτοῦ ἐκείνου. Genitive of time (BDF 186.2).

εἶπεν. Aor act ind 3rd sg λέγω.

αὐτοῖς. Dative indirect object of εἶπεν.

ὑμεῖς. Nominative subject of οἴδατε. The personal pronoun is contrastive, highlighting the differences of opinion of the members of the Sanhedrin ("you") and Caiaphas.

οὐκ. Negative particle normally used with indicative verbs.

οἴδατε. Prf act ind 2nd pl οἶδα (see 1:26 on οἴδατε).

οὐδέν. Accusative direct object of οἴδατε. The two negatives οὐκ ... οὐδέν reinforce each other: lit. "you do not know nothing" = "you do not know anything" (see 3:27 on οὐδὲ).

11:50 οὐδὲ λογίζεσθε ὅτι συμφέρει ὑμῖν ἵνα εἷς ἄνθρωπος ἀποθάνῃ ὑπὲρ τοῦ λαοῦ καὶ μὴ ὅλον τὸ ἔθνος ἀπόληται.

οὐδὲ. Negative coordinating conjunction (οὐ + δέ).

λογίζεσθε. Pres mid/pass ind 2nd pl λογίζομαι.

ὅτι. Introduces the clausal complement (indirect discourse) of λογίζομαι.

συμφέρει. Pres act ind 3rd sg συμφέρω. The verb means "to be advantageous, to be better off, to be to someone's advantage" (LN 65.44).

ὑμῖν. Dative of advantage. The omission of ὑμῖν from some witnesses (ℵ sa^ms pbo) or its replacement with ἡμῖν (A K W Δ Θ Ψ $f^{1.13}$ 33 565 579 700 892^s 𝔐 et al.) is most likely secondary in comparison with the strong external support for ὑμῖν ($\mathfrak{P}^{45.66}$ B D L Γ 1241 1424 it vg^d bo) and its concurrence with the contemptuous declaration ὑμεῖς οὐκ οἴδατε οὐδέν at the end of the previous verse (Metzger, 200).

ἵνα. Introduces two conjoined substantival clauses that function as the subject of συμφέρει. A similar construction (συμφέρει + dat + ἵνα ... καὶ μὴ) occurs in Matt 5:29.

εἷς ἄνθρωπος. Nominative subject of ἀποθάνῃ. Fronted for emphasis.

ἀποθάνῃ. Aor act subj 3rd sg ἀποθνῄσκω. Subjunctive with ἵνα.

ὑπὲρ τοῦ λαοῦ. Substitution ("in the place of the people"; cf. Robertson, 631; Zerwick §91; Wallace 1996, 387). This function of the PP is confirmed by the clause that follows (καὶ μὴ ὅλον τὸ ἔθνος ἀπόληται). For other prepositional phrases with ὑπέρ in the FG, see 6:51; 10:11, 15; 11:51, 52; 13:37, 38; 15:13; 17:19; 18:14.

καὶ. Coordinating conjunction.

μὴ. Negative particle normally used with non-indicative verbs.

ὅλον τὸ ἔθνος. Nominative subject of ἀπόληται. Fronted for emphasis.

ἀπόληται. Aor mid subj 3rd sg ἀπόλλυμι. Subjunctive with ἵνα.

11:51 τοῦτο δὲ ἀφ' ἑαυτοῦ οὐκ εἶπεν, ἀλλ' ἀρχιερεὺς ὢν τοῦ ἐνιαυτοῦ ἐκείνου ἐπροφήτευσεν ὅτι ἔμελλεν Ἰησοῦς ἀποθνῄσκειν ὑπὲρ τοῦ ἔθνους,

τοῦτο. The anaphoric demonstrative serves as the accusative direct object of εἶπεν.

δὲ. Marker of narrative development.

ἀφ' ἑαυτοῦ. Agency. The preposition ἀπό indicates an agent responsible for something (BDAG, 107.5.e.α).

οὐκ . . . ἀλλ'. A point/counterpoint set ("not this . . . but that") that negates the incorrect conclusion (Caiaphas spoke on his own) and affirms the correct one (Caiaphas prophesied). On the function of ἀλλά in a point/counterpoint set, see 1:8.

εἶπεν. Aor act ind 3rd sg λέγω. The verb stands in final, emphatic position.

ἀρχιερεὺς. Predicate nominative. Fronted for emphasis.

ὢν. Pres act ptc masc nom sg εἰμί (causal). On participles that precede the main verb, see ἐμβλέψας in 1:36. See 11:49, where the same participial clause (ἀρχιερεὺς ὢν τοῦ ἐνιαυτοῦ ἐκείνου) has attributive function.

τοῦ ἐνιαυτοῦ ἐκείνου. Genitive of time (BDF 186.2).

ἐπροφήτευσεν. Aor act ind 3rd sg προφητεύω. The verb stands in final, emphatic position.

ὅτι. Introduces the clausal complement (indirect discourse) of ἐπροφήτευσεν.

ἔμελλεν. Impf act ind 3rd sg μέλλω. On the augment, see ἤμελλεν in 4:47.

Ἰησοῦς. Nominative subject of ἔμελλεν.

ἀποθνῄσκειν. Pres act inf ἀποθνῄσκω (complementary).

ὑπὲρ τοῦ ἔθνους. Substitution ("in the place of the nation"); see ὑπὲρ τοῦ λαοῦ in the previous verse.

11:52 καὶ οὐχ ὑπὲρ τοῦ ἔθνους μόνον ἀλλ' ἵνα καὶ τὰ τέκνα τοῦ θεοῦ τὰ διεσκορπισμένα συναγάγῃ εἰς ἕν.

καὶ. Coordinating conjunction.

οὐχ . . . μόνον ἀλλ' . . . καὶ. A point/counterpoint set ("not only this . . . but also that") which supplements the initial explanation of the purpose of Jesus' death (to die for the nation) with another purpose (to gather into one the dispersed children of God).

ὑπὲρ τοῦ ἔθνους. Substitution ("in the place of the nation"). For other prepositional phrases with ὑπέρ in the FG, see 6:51; 10:11, 15; 11:50, 51; 13:37, 38; 15:13; 17:19; 18:14.

ἵνα. Introduces a purpose clause.
τὰ τέκνα. Accusative direct object of συναγάγῃ.
τοῦ θεοῦ. Genitive of relationship qualifying τέκνα.
τὰ διεσκορπισμένα. Prf pass ptc neut acc pl διασκορπίζω (attributive). The primary (personal) agency of the verb is not expressed. The participle modifies τὰ τέκνα, standing in the second attributive position (see 1:29 on ὁ αἴρων). In this formulation, the noun and its participial modifier are separated by a genitive phrase.
συναγάγῃ. Aor act subj 3rd sg συνάγω. Subjunctive with ἵνα.
εἰς ἕν. Purpose or spatial.

11:53 ἀπ' ἐκείνης οὖν τῆς ἡμέρας ἐβουλεύσαντο ἵνα ἀποκτείνωσιν αὐτόν.

ἀπ' ἐκείνης ... τῆς ἡμέρας. Temporal ("from that day on"). Fronted as a temporal frame.
οὖν. Postpositive inferential conjunction.
ἐβουλεύσαντο. Aor mid ind 3rd pl βουλεύω.
ἵνα. Introduces a purpose clause.
ἀποκτείνωσιν. Aor act subj 3rd pl ἀποκτείνω. Subjunctive with ἵνα.
αὐτόν. Accusative direct object of ἀποκτείνωσιν.

11:54 Ὁ οὖν Ἰησοῦς οὐκέτι παρρησίᾳ περιεπάτει ἐν τοῖς Ἰουδαίοις, ἀλλ' ἀπῆλθεν ἐκεῖθεν εἰς τὴν χώραν ἐγγὺς τῆς ἐρήμου, εἰς Ἐφραὶμ λεγομένην πόλιν, κἀκεῖ ἔμεινεν μετὰ τῶν μαθητῶν.

Ὁ ... Ἰησοῦς. Nominative subject of περιεπάτει.
οὖν. Postpositive inferential conjunction.
οὐκέτι ... ἀλλ'. A point/counterpoint set ("no longer this ... but that") that negates one type of behavior (walking openly among the Jews) and affirms another type of behavior (going to the district near the desert).
παρρησίᾳ. Dative of manner ("openly, publicly").
περιεπάτει. Impf act ind 3rd sg περιπατέω. On the function of the imperfect in the FG, see 1:39 on ἦν.
ἐν τοῖς Ἰουδαίοις. Locative. The term "the Jews" refers to the Jewish authorities hostile to Jesus.
ἀπῆλθεν. Aor act ind 3rd sg ἀπέρχομαι.
ἐκεῖθεν. Adverb of place.
εἰς τὴν χώραν. Locative.
ἐγγὺς τῆς ἐρήμου. Locative. ἐγγὺς is an adverb that here functions as an improper preposition (see 1:3 on χωρὶς αὐτοῦ) indicating close spatial proximity (BDAG, 271.1.b).

εἰς . . . πόλιν. Locative. The accusative object of the preposition is part of a double accusative object-complement construction.

Ἐφραίμ. Accusative complement to Ἐφραίμ in a double accusative object-complement construction. In this formulation, the complement is placed before the object of the preposition.

λεγομένην. Pres pass ptc fem acc sg λέγω (attributive). The participle modifies πόλιν.

κἀκεῖ. Formed by crasis from καὶ ἐκεῖ. καὶ is a coordinating conjunction, and ἐκεῖ is an adverb of place.

ἔμεινεν. Aor act ind 3rd sg μένω.

μετὰ τῶν μαθητῶν. Association/accompaniment.

John 11:55-57

⁵⁵Now the Passover of the Jews was near, and many went up to Jerusalem from the [surrounding] country before the Passover that they might purify themselves. ⁵⁶They were looking for Jesus and were asking one another as they stood in the temple, "What do you think? That he will not come to the festival at all?" ⁵⁷Now the chief priests and the Pharisees had given orders that if anyone knew where he was, he should report it, so that they could arrest him.

11:55 Ἦν δὲ ἐγγὺς τὸ πάσχα τῶν Ἰουδαίων, καὶ ἀνέβησαν πολλοὶ εἰς Ἱεροσόλυμα ἐκ τῆς χώρας πρὸ τοῦ πάσχα ἵνα ἁγνίσωσιν ἑαυτούς.

Ἦν. Impf act ind 3rd sg εἰμί. On the function of the imperfect in the FG, see 1:39 on ἦν.

δὲ. Marker of narrative development.

ἐγγὺς. Predicate adverb indicating close temporal proximity (see 2:1 on ἐκεῖ).

τὸ πάσχα. Nominative subject of Ἦν. This is the third Passover recorded in the FG (see 2:13 and 6:4).

τῶν Ἰουδαίων. Subjective genitive qualifying πάσχα ("the Passover that the Jews celebrate").

καὶ. Coordinating conjunction.

ἀνέβησαν. Aor act ind 3rd pl ἀναβαίνω. On the meaning of the verb, see 2:13 on ἀνέβη.

πολλοὶ. Nominative subject of ἀνέβησαν.

εἰς Ἱεροσόλυμα. Locative.

ἐκ τῆς χώρας. Source.

πρὸ τοῦ πάσχα. Temporal.

ἵνα. Introduces a purpose clause.

ἁγνίσωσιν. Aor act subj 3rd pl ἁγνίζω. Subjunctive with ἵνα. ἁγνίζω means "to purify and cleanse ritually and thus acquire a state of ritual acceptability" (LN 53.30).

ἑαυτούς. Accusative direct object of ἁγνίσωσιν.

11:56 ἐζήτουν οὖν τὸν Ἰησοῦν καὶ ἔλεγον μετ' ἀλλήλων ἐν τῷ ἱερῷ ἑστηκότες· τί δοκεῖ ὑμῖν; ὅτι οὐ μὴ ἔλθῃ εἰς τὴν ἑορτήν;

ἐζήτουν. Impf act ind 3rd pl ζητέω. On the function of the imperfect in the FG, see 1:39 on ἦν. Although in this context the verb ζητέω simply means "to look/search for," Dennis (164–65) argues that it carries malicious intent. He derives this conclusion from other uses of ζητέω in the FG, which typically describe the pursuit of Jesus for violent purposes, such as to kill him (5:18; 7:1, 19, 20, 25; 8:37), to arrest him (7:30), or to stone him (11:8).

οὖν. Postpositive inferential conjunction and/or transitional particle (see 1:22 and 11:6).

τὸν Ἰησοῦν. Accusative direct object of ἐζήτουν.

καί. Coordinating conjunction.

ἔλεγον. Impf act ind 3rd pl λέγω. The verb describes an ongoing conversation among the Jews who came to the temple (imperfective aspect).

μετ' ἀλλήλων. Association/accompaniment.

ἐν τῷ ἱερῷ. Locative. Elsewhere in the FG, this PP occurs in 2:14; 5:14; 7:28; 8:20; 10:23; 18:20.

ἑστηκότες. Prf act ptc masc nom pl ἵστημι (temporal). On participles that follow the main verb, see βαπτίζων in 1:31.

τί. Interrogative pronoun, functioning as the nominative subject of δοκεῖ.

δοκεῖ. Pres act ind 3rd sg δοκέω.

ὑμῖν. Dative complement of δοκεῖ (lit. "What does it seem to you?").

ὅτι. This could be either (1) a subordinating conjunction ("that") introducing the clausal complement (indirect discourse) of δοκεῖ ("What do you think? That he will not come to the festival at all?"), or (2) ὅτι-*recitativum* introducing a direct rhetorical question ("What do you think? He will surely not come to the festival, will he?"). The function of ὅτι determines the nature of the expected answer. (1) If ὅτι introduces the clausal complement of δοκεῖ, the expected answer is negative: "(Do you think) that he will not come to the festival at all?" = he certainly will not come to the festival. (2) If ὅτι introduces a direct rhetorical question, the expected answer is cautiously affirmative: "He will surely not come to the festival, will he?" = he will probably come to the festival (Haubeck and von Siebenthal, 573). Considering the command to report Jesus' whereabouts to the authorities and the threat to arrest him, described in the next verse, the first option is more likely.

οὐ μή. Emphatic negation, which is usually followed by the aorist subjunctive.

ἔλθῃ. Aor act subj 3rd sg ἔρχομαι. The subjunctive is used with οὐ μή to express emphatic negation.

εἰς τὴν ἑορτήν. Locative.

11:57 δεδώκεισαν δὲ οἱ ἀρχιερεῖς καὶ οἱ Φαρισαῖοι ἐντολὰς ἵνα ἐάν τις γνῷ ποῦ ἐστιν μηνύσῃ, ὅπως πιάσωσιν αὐτόν.

δεδώκεισαν. Plprf act ind 3rd pl δίδωμι. This pluperfect has a supplemental function (Campbell 2007, 219).

δέ. Marker of narrative development.

οἱ ἀρχιερεῖς καὶ οἱ Φαρισαῖοι. Nominative subjects of δεδώκεισαν (see 11:47).

ἐντολάς. Accusative direct object of δεδώκεισαν.

ἵνα. Introduces an epexegetical clause that explains the content of ἐντολάς.

ἐάν. Introduces the protasis of a third-class condition.

τις. Nominative subject of γνῷ.

γνῷ. Aor act subj 3rd sg γινώσκω. Subjunctive with ἵνα.

ποῦ. Interrogative adverb of place.

ἐστιν. Pres act ind 3rd sg εἰμί.

μηνύσῃ. Aor act subj 3rd sg μηνύω. Subjunctive with ἵνα. μηνύω means "to provide information concerning something, with emphasis upon the fact that such information is secret or known only to a select few" (LN 33.209).

ὅπως. Introduces a purpose clause. This is the only occurrence of this conjunction in the FG.

πιάσωσιν. Aor act subj 3rd pl πιάζω. Subjunctive with ὅπως. On the meaning and the use of this verb in the FG, see 7:30 on πιάσαι.

αὐτόν. Accusative direct object of πιάσωσιν.

John 12:1-8

¹Then, six days before the Passover, Jesus came to Bethany, where Lazarus was, whom Jesus raised from the dead. ²So they made a dinner for him, and Martha served, but Lazarus was one of the guests reclining with him. ³Then Mary took a pound of expensive ointment made from pure nard and anointed Jesus' feet and wiped his feet with her hair. The house was filled with fragrance of the ointment. ⁴But Judas Iscariot, one

of his disciples, the one who was about to betray him, said, ⁵"Why was this ointment not sold for three hundred denarii and the money given to the poor?" ⁶He said this not because he cared for the poor but because he was a thief and, since he was in charge of the money-bag, he used to steal what was put in [it]. ⁷Then Jesus said, "Leave her alone. [She bought it] in order that she might keep it for the day of my burial. ⁸For the poor you always have with you, but you do not always have me."

12:1 Ὁ οὖν Ἰησοῦς πρὸ ἓξ ἡμερῶν τοῦ πάσχα ἦλθεν εἰς Βηθανίαν, ὅπου ἦν Λάζαρος, ὃν ἤγειρεν ἐκ νεκρῶν Ἰησοῦς.

Ὁ ... Ἰησοῦς. Nominative subject of ἦλθεν.

οὖν. Postpositive transitional particle (see 1:22 and 11:6). An inferential οὖν would suggest that Jesus went to Bethany to avoid arrest.

πρὸ ἓξ ἡμερῶν τοῦ πάσχα. Temporal. In this "remarkable Hellenistic manner of indicating distance," the preposition πρό governs "not the point from which the distance is measured, but the distance itself" (Zerwick §71; cf. MHT 3:248; BDB §213.2). Thus, πρὸ ἓξ ἡμερῶν τοῦ πάσχα (lit. "before six days of the Passover") stands for ἓξ ἡμέρας πρὸ τοῦ πάσχα ("six days before the Passover"). Fronted as a temporal frame.

ἦλθεν. Aor act ind 3rd sg ἔρχομαι.

εἰς Βηθανίαν. Locative.

ὅπου. Marker of a position in space.

ἦν. Impf act ind 3rd sg εἰμί. On the function of the imperfect in the FG, see 1:39 on ἦν.

Λάζαρος. Nominative subject of ἦν. The longer reading, Λάζαρος ὁ τεθνηκώς, is attested in various manuscripts, some of which are quite early (𝔓⁶⁶ A D K Γ Δ Θ Ψ 0217ᵛⁱᵈ ƒ¹·¹³ 33 565 579 1241 1424 𝔐 lat syˢ·ʰ et al.), but strong external support for the shorter reading (ℵ B L W *l*844 *l*2211 syᵖ it sa pbo) suggests that it is more likely that the substantival participle ὁ τεθνηκώς represents an early scribal addition to rather than an early deletion from the original text (Metzger, 201).

ὅν. Accusative direct object of ἤγειρεν. The antecedent of the relative pronoun is Λάζαρος. According to Caragounis (2004, 175), the relative clause ὃν ἤγειρεν ἐκ νεκρῶν Ἰησοῦς functions as a substitute for the participle ἐγερθείς.

ἤγειρεν. Aor act ind 3rd sg ἐγείρω.

ἐκ νεκρῶν. Separation.

Ἰησοῦς. Nominative subject of ἤγειρεν.

12:2 ἐποίησαν οὖν αὐτῷ δεῖπνον ἐκεῖ, καὶ ἡ Μάρθα διηκόνει, ὁ δὲ Λάζαρος εἷς ἦν ἐκ τῶν ἀνακειμένων σὺν αὐτῷ.

ἐποίησαν. Aor act ind 3rd pl ποιέω. Since the subject ("they") is not identified, this is equivalent to a passive formulation "a dinner was given" (Brown, 1:448).

οὖν. Postpositive inferential conjunction and/or transitional particle (see 1:22 and 11:6).

αὐτῷ. Dative of advantage. The referent of the pronoun could be either Jesus or Lazarus (Harris 2015, 224; Keener, 2:862). The former is more likely because the narrator identifies Lazarus by name in the second half of the verse and refers to Jesus only with a pronoun (σὺν αὐτῷ), as here.

δεῖπνον. Accusative direct object of ἐποίησαν. δεῖπνον denotes the main meal of the day that is normally eaten toward evening. In the FG, the term occurs here and in 13:2, 4; 21:20.

ἐκεῖ. Adverb of place.

καὶ. Coordinating conjunction.

ἡ Μάρθα. Nominative subject of διηκόνει.

διηκόνει. Impf act ind 3rd sg διακονέω. The imperfective aspect of the verb portrays Martha's serving at dinner as an action in progress. For a similar description of Martha's responsibilities during Jesus' visit of her home, see Luke 10:40.

ὁ ... Λάζαρος. Nominative subject of ἦν.

δὲ. Marker of narrative development.

εἷς. Predicate nominative. Fronted for emphasis.

ἦν. Impf act ind 3rd sg εἰμί. On the function of the imperfect in the FG, see 1:39 on ἦν.

ἐκ τῶν ἀνακειμένων. Replaces the partitive genitive.

τῶν ἀνακειμένων. Pres mid ptc masc gen pl ἀνάκειμαι (substantival).

σὺν αὐτῷ. Accompaniment/association. The referent of the pronoun is Jesus.

12:3 Ἡ οὖν Μαριὰμ λαβοῦσα λίτραν μύρου νάρδου πιστικῆς πολυτίμου ἤλειψεν τοὺς πόδας τοῦ Ἰησοῦ καὶ ἐξέμαξεν ταῖς θριξὶν αὐτῆς τοὺς πόδας αὐτοῦ· ἡ δὲ οἰκία ἐπληρώθη ἐκ τῆς ὀσμῆς τοῦ μύρου.

Ἡ ... Μαριάμ. Nominative subject of ἤλειψεν. Fronted as a topical frame.

οὖν. Postpositive inferential conjunction and/or transitional particle (see 1:22 and 11:6).

λαβοῦσα. Aor act ptc fem nom sg λαμβάνω (attendant circumstance). On participles that precede the main verb, see ἐμβλέψας in 1:36.

λίτραν. Accusative direct object of λαβοῦσα. λίτρα is a loanword from Latin (*libra*) denoting a Roman pound (= 327.45 grams).

μύρου ... πολυτίμου. Partitive genitive qualifying λίτραν ("a pound of expensive ointment"). The adjective πολυτίμου ("very precious, valuable, expensive") stands in the fourth attributive position (see 3:15 on ζωὴν αἰώνιον).

νάρδου πιστικῆς. Genitive of material qualifying μύρου ("ointment made from pure nard"). The adjective πιστικῆς ("genuine, pure") also stands in the fourth attributive position. It is noteworthy that the only other occurrence of this adjective in the NT is in Mark 14:3. The anarthrous noun phrase νάρδου πιστικῆς is placed within the anarthrous noun phrase μύρου ... πολυτίμου, creating a composite structure in which two genitive nouns are followed by two genitive adjectives: noun [noun-adjective] adjective.

ἤλειψεν. Aor act ind 3rd sg ἀλείφω.

τοὺς πόδας. Accusative direct object of ἤλειψεν.

τοῦ Ἰησοῦ. Possessive genitive qualifying πόδας.

καὶ. Coordinating conjunction.

ἐξέμαξεν. Aor act ind 3rd sg ἐκμάσσω. The imperfect of ἐκμάσσω and the dative ταῖς θριξὶν (see below) are also used in Luke 7:38 (ταῖς θριξὶν τῆς κεφαλῆς αὐτῆς ἐξέμασσεν).

ταῖς θριξὶν. Dative of means/instrument.

αὐτῆς. Possessive genitive qualifying θριξὶν.

τοὺς πόδας. Accusative direct object of ἐξέμαξεν.

αὐτοῦ. Possessive genitive qualifying πόδας.

ἡ ... οἰκία. Nominative subject of ἐπληρώθη.

δὲ. Marker of narrative development.

ἐπληρώθη. Aor pass ind 3rd sg πληρόω.

ἐκ τῆς ὀσμῆς. Instrumental (impersonal) agency ("filled with the fragrance") or cause ("filled because of the fragrance"; cf. Robertson, 598).

τοῦ μύρου. Genitive of source qualifying ὀσμῆς ("fragrance coming out of the ointment")

12:4 Λέγει δὲ Ἰούδας ὁ Ἰσκαριώτης εἷς [ἐκ] τῶν μαθητῶν αὐτοῦ, ὁ μέλλων αὐτὸν παραδιδόναι·

Λέγει. Pres act ind 3rd sg λέγω. The historical present gives prominence to Judas' question (see 1:15 on μαρτυρεῖ).

δὲ. Marker of narrative development.

Ἰούδας ὁ Ἰσκαριώτης. Nominative subject of λέγει. On the meaning, see 6:71.

εἷς. Nominative in apposition to Ἰούδας.

[ἐκ] τῶν μαθητῶν. Replaces the partitive genitive. The preposition ἐκ is placed within square brackets because it is missing from some early witnesses ($\mathfrak{P}^{66.75vid}$ B L W 33 579), but its absence from the original text is in doubt considering other occurrences of the expression εἷς ἐκ in the FG (1:40; 6:8, 71; 13:23; 28:26; 20:24; cf. Metzger, 201).

αὐτοῦ. Genitive of relationship qualifying μαθητῶν.

ὁ μέλλων. Pres act ptc masc nom sg μέλλω (substantival [NRSV; CEB; ESV; LEB] or attributive [HCSB; NASB; NIV]). If the participle is substantival, it functions as the second nominative in apposition to Ἰούδας.

αὐτὸν. Accusative direct object of παραδιδόναι.

παραδιδόναι. Pres act inf παραδίδωμι (complementary).

12:5 διὰ τί τοῦτο τὸ μύρον οὐκ ἐπράθη τριακοσίων δηναρίων καὶ ἐδόθη πτωχοῖς;

διὰ τί. Causal. In direct questions, διὰ τί (lit. "because of what?") means "why?" (BDAG, 225.B.2.b).

τοῦτο τὸ μύρον. Nominative subject of ἐπράθη.

οὐκ. Negative particle normally used with indicative verbs.

ἐπράθη. Aor pass ind 3rd sg πιπράσκω. The primary (personal) agency of the passive verb is not expressed.

τριακοσίων δηναρίων. Genitive of price. Three hundred denarii are equivalent to a year's earnings for a laborer.

καὶ. Coordinating conjunction.

ἐδόθη. Aor pass ind 3rd sg δίδωμι. The context indicates that the subject of the verb is no longer τοῦτο τὸ μύρον; rather, the implied subject of ἐδόθη ("it") refers to three hundred denarii that could be received for the fragrant ointment. The primary (personal) agency of the passive verb is again not expressed.

πτωχοῖς. Dative indirect object of ἐδόθη.

12:6 εἶπεν δὲ τοῦτο οὐχ ὅτι περὶ τῶν πτωχῶν ἔμελεν αὐτῷ, ἀλλ' ὅτι κλέπτης ἦν καὶ τὸ γλωσσόκομον ἔχων τὰ βαλλόμενα ἐβάσταζεν.

εἶπεν. Aor act ind 3rd sg λέγω.

δὲ. Marker of narrative development.

τοῦτο. Accusative direct object of εἶπεν.

John 12:4-7

οὐχ ... ἀλλ'. A point/counterpoint set ("not this . . . but that") that negates the incorrect explanation of Judas' words (Judas cared for the poor) and replaces it with the correct explanation (Judas was a thief). On the function of ἀλλά in a point/counterpoint set, see 1:8.

ὅτι. Introduces a causal clause.

περὶ τῶν πτωχῶν. Reference.

ἔμελεν. Impf act ind 3rd sg μέλω. The verb is used mostly impersonally with dative of person ("it is a care/concern, is of interest to someone" [BDAG 626.1]).

αὐτῷ. Dative complement of ἔμελεν (lit. "it was a care to him" = "he cared").

ὅτι. Introduces a causal clause.

κλέπτης. Predicate nominative. Fronted for emphasis.

ἦν. Impf act ind 3rd sg εἰμί. On the function of the imperfect in the FG, see 1:39 on ἦν.

καὶ. Coordinating conjunction.

τὸ γλωσσόκομον. Accusative direct object of ἔχων. γλωσσόκομον denotes "a box in which money was kept" (LN 6.143).

ἔχων. Pres act ptc masc nom sg ἔχω (causal). On participles that precede the main verb, see ἐμβλέψας in 1:36.

τὰ βαλλόμενα. Pres pass ptc neut acc pl βάλλω (substantival). Accusative direct object of ἐβάσταζεν.

ἐβάσταζεν. Impf act ind 3rd sg βαστάζω. The verb stands in final, emphatic position. The expression τὰ βαλλόμενα ἐβάσταζεν (lit. "he used to lift what was put in [it]") is here used with moral implication, indicating that Judas used to steal the contributions to the money-bag (BDAG, 171.3.b). On the function of the imperfect in the FG, see 1:39 on ἦν.

12:7 εἶπεν οὖν ὁ Ἰησοῦς· ἄφες αὐτήν, ἵνα εἰς τὴν ἡμέραν τοῦ ἐνταφιασμοῦ μου τηρήσῃ αὐτό·

εἶπεν. Aor act ind 3rd sg λέγω.

οὖν. Postpositive inferential conjunction and/or transitional particle (see 1:22 and 11:6).

ὁ Ἰησοῦς. Nominative subject of εἶπεν.

ἄφες. Aor act impv 2nd sg ἀφίημι. Since this imperative is the only verb in the clause, it has its full verbal force of "allowing" or "letting" (Caragounis 2004, 164).

αὐτήν. Accusative direct object of ἄφες.

ἵνα. Introduces a purpose clause.

εἰς τὴν ἡμέραν. Temporal.

τοῦ ἐνταφιασμοῦ. Genitive of time qualifying ἡμέραν ("the day when I will be buried"). ἐνταφιασμός refers to "the performance of what is customary for burial" (BDAG, 339).

μου. Objective genitive qualifying ἐνταφιασμοῦ.

τηρήσῃ. Aor act subj 3rd sg τηρέω. Subjunctive with ἵνα.

αὐτό. Accusative direct object of τηρήσῃ. The referent of αὐτό is not clear. There are two main options, each resulting in a different meaning of Jesus' words. (1) If αὐτό refers to the rest of the ointment, the sense would be "Leave her alone, in order that she may keep it for the day of my burial" (cf. ESV). On this reading, the unused ointment was intended for the actual preparation of Jesus' body for burial. While this reading makes good sense of the Greek syntax, there are no contextual indications that there was a leftover portion intended for future use (Haubeck and von Siebenthal, 574). (2) If αὐτό refers to the entire amount of ointment that Mary poured over Jesus' feet, the ἵνα clause is elliptical, requiring some kind of introduction: "Leave her alone. [She bought it] in order that she might keep it for the day of my burial" (cf. NRSV). On this reading, Mary's anointing of Jesus' feet was an anticipation of the actual anointing of Jesus' body after his death. This interpretation is supported by the Johannine passion narrative, which mentions only Joseph of Arimathea and Nicodemus as being involved in the burial preparations after the crucifixion (19:38-42).

12:8 τοὺς πτωχοὺς γὰρ πάντοτε ἔχετε μεθ' ἑαυτῶν, ἐμὲ δὲ οὐ πάντοτε ἔχετε.

τοὺς πτωχοὺς. Accusative direct object of the first ἔχετε. Fronted as a topical frame.

γὰρ. Postpositive conjunction that introduces the explanation for the preceding command.

πάντοτε. Adverb of time.

ἔχετε. Pres act ind 2nd pl ἔχω.

μεθ' ἑαυτῶν. Association/accompaniment. In Koine Greek, the third-person form of the reflexive pronoun ἑαυτῶν is frequently used, as here, in place of ὑμῶν αὐτῶν (MHT 3:42; see Matt 26:11; Mark 14:7).

ἐμὲ. Accusative direct object of the second ἔχετε. Fronted as a topical frame.

δὲ. Marker of narrative development.

οὐ. Negative particle normally used with indicative verbs.

πάντοτε. Adverb of time.

ἔχετε. Pres act ind 2nd pl ἔχω.

John 12:9-11

⁹Then the great crowd of the Jews learned that he was there and came, not only because of Jesus but also to see Lazarus, whom he raised from the dead. ¹⁰So the chief priests plotted that they might kill Lazarus as well, ¹¹because on account of him many of the Jews were departing and believing in Jesus.

12:9 Ἔγνω οὖν [ὁ] ὄχλος πολὺς ἐκ τῶν Ἰουδαίων ὅτι ἐκεῖ ἐστιν καὶ ἦλθον οὐ διὰ τὸν Ἰησοῦν μόνον, ἀλλ᾽ ἵνα καὶ τὸν Λάζαρον ἴδωσιν ὃν ἤγειρεν ἐκ νεκρῶν.

Ἔγνω. Aor act ind 3rd sg γινώσκω.

οὖν. Postpositive inferential conjunction and/or transitional particle (see 1:22 and 11:6).

[ὁ] ὄχλος πολύς. Nominative subject of Ἔγνω. The adjective πολύς has attributive function although it stands in the second predicate position (see 5:36 on μείζω). The evidence for and against the presence of the definite article before ὄχλος is indeterminate. The variants ὄχλος πολύς ($\mathfrak{P}^{66*.75}$ ℵ² A B² K Q Γ Δ Θ Ψ f^1 33 565 1424 $\mathfrak{M}$) and ὁ ὄχλος ὁ πολύς ($\mathfrak{P}^{66c}$ W l2211) could represent scribal corrections of the difficult expression ὁ ὄχλος πολύς (ℵ* B* L 892ˢ 1241 l844 boᵐˢ), but, as Metzger explains, this formulation is "such unusual Greek . . . that serious doubts arise whether the evangelist could have written it thus" (202).

ἐκ τῶν Ἰουδαίων. Replaces the partitive genitive. The Jews mentioned here and in v. 11 are portrayed as a group that has a friendly disposition toward Jesus, in distinction from the Jewish authorities who plot to kill not only Jesus but also Lazarus.

ὅτι. Introduces the clausal complement (indirect discourse) of Ἔγνω.

ἐκεῖ. Adverb of place.

ἐστιν. Pres act ind 3rd sg εἰμί. The present tense is retained from direct discourse (see 1:39 on μένει).

καὶ. Coordinating conjunction.

ἦλθον. Aor act ind 3rd pl ἔρχομαι.

οὐ . . . μόνον, ἀλλ᾽ . . . καί. A point/counterpoint set ("not only this . . . but also that") that supplements the initial explanation of the crowd's arrival (because of Jesus) with another purpose (to see Lazarus).

διὰ τὸν Ἰησοῦν. Causal.

ἵνα. Introduces a purpose clause.

τὸν Λάζαρον. Accusative direct object of ἴδωσιν.

ἴδωσιν. Aor act subj 3rd pl ὁράω. Subjunctive with ἵνα.

ὅν. Accusative direct object of ἤγειρεν.

ἤγειρεν. Aor act ind 3rd sg ἐγείρω.
ἐκ νεκρῶν. Separation.

12:10 ἐβουλεύσαντο δὲ οἱ ἀρχιερεῖς ἵνα καὶ τὸν Λάζαρον ἀποκτείνωσιν,

ἐβουλεύσαντο. Aor mid ind 3rd pl βουλεύω (see 11:53).
δὲ. Marker of narrative development.
οἱ ἀρχιερεῖς. Nominative subject of ἐβουλεύσαντο.
ἵνα. Introduces a purpose clause.
καὶ. Adverbial use (adjunctive).
τὸν Λάζαρον. Accusative direct object of ἀποκτείνωσιν. Fronted for emphasis.
ἀποκτείνωσιν. Aor act subj 3rd pl ἀποκτείνω. Subjunctive with ἵνα.

12:11 ὅτι πολλοὶ δι᾽ αὐτὸν ὑπῆγον τῶν Ἰουδαίων καὶ ἐπίστευον εἰς τὸν Ἰησοῦν.

ὅτι. Introduces a causal clause.
πολλοὶ. Nominative subject of ὑπῆγον.
δι᾽ αὐτὸν. Causal.
ὑπῆγον. Impf act ind 3rd pl ὑπάγω. This and the next verb depict two unfolding actions (departing and believing in Jesus), which the narrator presents as an explanation of the murderous plot of the chief priests against Lazarus. On the function of the imperfect in the FG, see 1:39 on ἦν.
τῶν Ἰουδαίων. Partitive genitive qualifying πολλοὶ.
καὶ. Coordinating conjunction.
ἐπίστευον. Impf act ind 3rd pl πιστεύω. On the function of this verb, see ὑπῆγον above.
εἰς τὸν Ἰησοῦν. Goal of actions or feelings directed toward someone (BDAG, 290.4.c.β). For πιστεύειν εἰς + accusative ("trust or believe in someone"), see 1:12 on εἰς τὸ ὄνομα.

John 12:12-19

[12]On the next day, the large crowd that had come to the festival, upon hearing that Jesus was coming to Jerusalem, [13]took branches of palm trees and went out to meet him and kept shouting, "Hosanna! Blessed is the one who comes in the name of the Lord, that is, the King of Israel!" [14]Jesus found a young donkey and sat on it, as it is written, [15]"Do not be afraid, daughter of Zion. Look, your king is coming, sitting on the foal of a donkey." [16]His disciples did not understand these things at first, but when Jesus was glorified, then they remembered that these things had

been written about him and [that] they did these things to him. ¹⁷So the crowd that was with him when he called Lazarus out of the tomb and raised him from the dead kept testifying. ¹⁸Because of this too the crowd went to meet him because they heard that he had done this sign. ¹⁹Then the Pharisees said to one another, "You see that you are accomplishing nothing! Look, the world has gone after him!"

12:12 Τῇ ἐπαύριον ὁ ὄχλος πολὺς ὁ ἐλθὼν εἰς τὴν ἑορτήν, ἀκούσαντες ὅτι ἔρχεται ὁ Ἰησοῦς εἰς Ἱεροσόλυμα

Τῇ ἐπαύριον. The article functions as a nominalizer, changing the adverb ἐπαύριον ("tomorrow") into the dative of time (see 1:29). Fronted as a temporal frame. This verse is connected to the previous one by asyndeton.

ὁ ὄχλος πολύς. Nominative subject of ἔλαβον (v. 13). The adjective πολύς has attributive function although it stands in the second predicate position (see 5:36 on μείζω).

ὁ ἐλθών. Aor act ptc masc nom sg ἔρχομαι (attributive). The participle modifies ὁ ὄχλος, standing in the second attributive position (see 1:29 on ὁ αἴρων).

εἰς τὴν ἑορτήν. Locative.

ἀκούσαντες. Aor act ptc masc nom pl ἀκούω (temporal). The plural form of the participle is a *constructio ad sensum* because the subject is a collective noun (BDF §134.1). On participles that precede the main verb, see ἐμβλέψας in 1:36.

ὅτι. Introduces the clausal complement (indirect discourse) of ἀκούσαντες.

ἔρχεται. Pres mid ind 3rd sg ἔρχομαι. The present tense is retained from the corresponding direct discourse (see 1:39 on μένει).

ὁ Ἰησοῦς. Nominative subject of ἔρχεται.

εἰς Ἱεροσόλυμα. Locative.

12:13 ἔλαβον τὰ βαΐα τῶν φοινίκων καὶ ἐξῆλθον εἰς ὑπάντησιν αὐτῷ καὶ ἐκραύγαζον· ὡσαννά· εὐλογημένος ὁ ἐρχόμενος ἐν ὀνόματι κυρίου, [καὶ] ὁ βασιλεὺς τοῦ Ἰσραήλ.

ἔλαβον. Aor act ind 3rd pl λαμβάνω. The plural form of this and other verbs in this verse is again a *constructio ad sensum* because the subject (ὁ ὄχλος πολύς) is a collective noun (see 12:12 on ἀκούσαντες).

τὰ βαΐα. Accusative direct object of ἔλαβον. βάϊον ("palm branch"), a loanword from Coptic (BDF §6), is a NT *hapax legomenon*.

τῶν φοινίκων. Partitive genitive qualifying βαΐα. Louw and Nida suggest that the genitive τῶν φοινίκων ("of palm trees") "may have been added redundantly, since the term βάϊον may not have been regarded as sufficiently well known to readers" (LN 3.53).

καὶ. Coordinating conjunction.

ἐξῆλθον. Aor act ind 3rd pl ἐξέρχομαι. ἐξῆλθον ("they went out") suggests that the crowd mentioned in v. 12 (ὁ ὄχλος πολὺς ὁ ἐλθὼν εἰς τὴν ἑορτήν) consisted of the pilgrims to the festival who were already in Jerusalem when Jesus arrived; see vv. 17-18, which mention two crowds—one that came with Jesus and one that came out of the city to meet him.

εἰς ὑπάντησιν. Purpose (BDAG, 290.4.f).

αὐτῷ. Dative complement of ὑπάντησιν: εἰς ὑπάντησιν τινί = "to meet someone" (BDAG, 1029).

καὶ. Coordinating conjunction.

ἐκραύγαζον. Impf act ind 3rd pl κραυγάζω. The imperfective aspect of the verb portrays the shouting of the crowd as an action in progress.

ὡσαννά. The indeclinable ὡσαννά is a Greek transliteration of the Hebrew expression הוֹשִׁיעָה נָּא, which functions as "a shout of praise, *hosanna* (lit.='help' or 'save, I pray,' an appeal that became a liturgical formula; as a part of the Hallel (Ps 113–118 Hebr.) it was familiar to everyone in Israel)" (BDAG, 1106). In the FG, ὡσαννά is used either as a cry for salvation (Bultmann, 418 n. 1) or as a shout of praise (Schnackenburg, 2:375).

εὐλογημένος ὁ ἐρχόμενος ἐν ὀνόματι κυρίου. A verbatim quotation of LXX Ps 117:26 (εὐλογημένος ὁ ἐρχόμενος ἐν ὀνόματι κυρίου), which is quoted in the exactly same way in the Synoptic Gospels (Matt 21:9; 23:39; Mark 11:9; Luke 13:35).

εὐλογημένος. Prf pass ptc masc nom sg εὐλογέω (perfect periphrastic). A form of εἰμί, such as the optative εἴη or the imperative ἔστω, must be supplied.

ὁ ἐρχόμενος. Pres mid ptc masc nom sg ἔρχομαι (substantival). Nominative subject of a verbless equative clause.

ἐν ὀνόματι. Manner.

κυρίου. Possessive genitive qualifying ὀνόματι.

[καὶ]. Epexegetical conjunction ("that is, namely"). The manuscript evidence for (ℵ*.2b B L Q W Ψ 579 bo) and against (𝔓66 ℵ2a A D K Γ Δ Θ $f^{1.13}$ 565 sa ly pbo bo^mss 𝔐) the presence of this conjunction in the text is evenly balanced.

ὁ βασιλεὺς. Nominative in apposition to ὁ ἐρχόμενος.

τοῦ Ἰσραήλ. Genitive of subordination qualifying βασιλεὺς.

John 12:13-15

12:14 εὑρὼν δὲ ὁ Ἰησοῦς ὀνάριον ἐκάθισεν ἐπ' αὐτό, καθώς ἐστιν γεγραμμένον·

εὑρών. Aor act ptc masc nom sg εὑρίσκω (attendant circumstance or temporal). On participles that precede the main verb, see ἐμβλέψας in 1:36.
δέ. Marker of narrative development.
ὁ Ἰησοῦς. Nominative subject of ἐκάθισεν.
ὀνάριον. Accusative direct object of εὑρών. ὀνάριον, a diminutive of ὄνος (called πῶλος ὄνου in v. 15; cf. BDF §111.3), is a NT *hapax legomenon*.
ἐκάθισεν. Aor act ind 3rd sg καθίζω.
ἐπ' αὐτό. Locative.
καθώς ἐστιν γεγραμμένον. The OT introductory formula (cf. 2:17; 6:31. 45; 7:38; 10:34).
καθώς. Introduces a comparative clause.
ἐστιν. Pres act ind 3rd sg εἰμί.
γεγραμμένον. Prf pass ptc neut nom sg γράφω (perfect periphrastic).

12:15 μὴ φοβοῦ, θυγάτηρ Σιών· ἰδοὺ ὁ βασιλεύς σου ἔρχεται, καθήμενος ἐπὶ πῶλον ὄνου.

μὴ φοβοῦ, θυγάτηρ Σιών· ἰδοὺ ὁ βασιλεύς σου ἔρχεται, καθήμενος ἐπὶ πῶλον ὄνου. A composite OT quotation. The source of the first part is impossible to determine, but two possible candidates are LXX Zeph 3:16b (θάρσει Σιων μὴ παρείσθωσαν αἱ χεῖρές σου) and LXX Isa 40:9b (μὴ φοβεῖσθε εἰπὸν ταῖς πόλεσιν Ιουδα ἰδοὺ ὁ θεὸς ὑμῶν). The second part comes from LXX Zech 9:9 (χαῖρε σφόδρα θύγατερ Σιων κήρυσσε θύγατερ Ιερουσαλημ ἰδοὺ ὁ βασιλεύς σου ἔρχεταί σοι δίκαιος καὶ σώζων αὐτός πραΰς καὶ ἐπιβεβηκὼς ἐπὶ ὑποζύγιον καὶ πῶλον νέον), but except for the clause ἰδοὺ ὁ βασιλεύς σου ἔρχεταί, the Fourth Evangelist does not follow closely his scriptural source. Cf. Matt 21:5, which combines Isa 62:11 with Zech 9:9.
μή. Negative particle introducing prohibition.
φοβοῦ. Pres mid impv 2nd sg φοβέομαι (prohibition). Whether this prohibition refers to an action that has already begun cannot be concluded from the use of the present imperative (*pace* Harris 2015, 228) but only from the context, which in this case does not provide enough clues for such an inference.
θυγάτηρ. Nominative for vocative (Wallace 1996, 56–59).
Σιών. Genitive of relationship qualifying θυγάτηρ.

ἰδού. An interjection (originally ἰδοῦ [aor mid impv 2nd sg ὁράω] but accented with the acute rather than the circumflex) that "draws attention to what follows" (BDAG, 468).

ὁ βασιλεύς. Nominative subject of ἔρχεται. Fronted for emphasis.

σου. Genitive of subordination qualifying βασιλεύς.

ἔρχεται. Pres mid ind 3rd sg ἔρχομαι.

καθήμενος. Pres mid ptc masc nom sg κάθημαι (manner). On participles that follow the main verb, see βαπτίζων in 1:31.

ἐπὶ πῶλον. Locative. πῶλος denotes "the young of a donkey—'foal, colt'" (LN 4.33).

ὄνου. Genitive of relationship qualifying πῶλον. "In this context the reference is obviously to a female donkey" (LN 4.31).

12:16 ταῦτα οὐκ ἔγνωσαν αὐτοῦ οἱ μαθηταὶ τὸ πρῶτον, ἀλλ' ὅτε ἐδοξάσθη Ἰησοῦς τότε ἐμνήσθησαν ὅτι ταῦτα ἦν ἐπ' αὐτῷ γεγραμμένα καὶ ταῦτα ἐποίησαν αὐτῷ.

ταῦτα. Accusative direct object of ἔγνωσαν. This verse is connected to the previous one by asyndeton.

οὐκ ... ἀλλ'. A point/counterpoint set ("not this ... but that") that replaces the idea that the disciples understood "these things" at first with the assertion that they understood them when Jesus was glorified. On the function of ἀλλά in a point/counterpoint set, see 1:8.

ἔγνωσαν. Aor act ind 3rd pl γινώσκω.

αὐτοῦ. Genitive of relationship qualifying μαθηταὶ. The preposed pronoun is thematically salient (Levinsohn 2000, 64).

οἱ μαθηταί. Nominative subject of ἔγνωσαν.

τὸ πρῶτον. Adverbial accusative indicating time or sequence ("first, in the first place, before, earlier, to begin with"; BDAG, 893.1.a.β). When used with the article, as here, τὸ πρῶτον means "the first time" (BDAG, 893.1.a.β).

ὅτε. Introduces a temporal clause in a left-dislocation, resumed by the temporal adverb τότε. Runge explains that "[t]he dislocated temporal information provides the answer to the question of when they would understand. It is too complex to place in marked focus, as it could be mistaken to be a temporal frame of reference. The dislocation allows the information to be introduced and then reiterated in a form simple enough for emphasis" (2010, 311).

ἐδοξάσθη. Aor pass ind 3rd sg δοξάζω. The unexpressed primary agent of the action is most likely God. In this context, glorification refers to Jesus' death and resurrection (see 7:39; 12:23; 13:31, 32; 17:1). By using δοξάζω as a description of the cross-events, the evangelist indicates that the death of Jesus "marked the turning point . . . of the movement that led on to his resurrection and exaltation, i.e. his glorification" (Carson 1991, 434). On δοξάζω as a double entendre, see 7:39.

Ἰησοῦς. Nominative subject of ἐδοξάσθη.

τότε. Adverb of time, which resumes the temporal clause ὅτε ἐδοξάσθη Ἰησοῦς. Fronted for emphasis. On the function of the resumptive element, see 7:10 on τότε.

ἐμνήσθησαν. Aor mid ind 3rd pl μιμνῄσκομαι. On the voice, see "Deponency" in the Series Introduction; on the meaning, see 2:17. A similar comment, which places the disciples' recollection and understanding of the past events in the time after Easter, occurs in 2:22.

ὅτι. Introduces the clausal complement (indirect discourse) of ἐμνήσθησαν.

ταῦτα. Nominative subject of ἦν.

ἦν. Impf act ind 3rd sg εἰμί. Neuter plural subjects typically take singular verbs (see 1:28 on ἐγένετο).

ἐπ' αὐτῷ. Reference, "indicating the one to whom, for whom, or about whom someth[ing] is done" (BDAG, 366.14.a).

γεγραμμένα. Prf pass ptc neut nom pl γράφω (pluperfect periphrastic).

καὶ. Coordinating conjunction. Another ὅτι is implied after καὶ.

ταῦτα. Accusative direct object of ἐποίησαν.

ἐποίησαν. Aor act ind 3rd pl ποιέω. The unspecified subject of the verb could be either the crowd praising Jesus in 12:13 or, less likely, Jesus' disciples (Daise, 82).

αὐτῷ. Dative of advantage.

12:17 Ἐμαρτύρει οὖν ὁ ὄχλος ὁ ὢν μετ' αὐτοῦ ὅτε τὸν Λάζαρον ἐφώνησεν ἐκ τοῦ μνημείου καὶ ἤγειρεν αὐτὸν ἐκ νεκρῶν.

Ἐμαρτύρει. Impf act ind 3rd sg μαρτυρέω. On the function of the imperfect in the FG, see 1:39 on ἦν.

οὖν. Postpositive inferential conjunction and/or transitional particle (see 1:22 and 11:6).

ὁ ὄχλος. Nominative subject of Ἐμαρτύρει.

ὁ ὢν. Pres act ptc masc nom sg εἰμί (attributive). The participle modifies ὁ ὄχλος, standing in the second attributive position (see 1:29 on ὁ αἴρων).

μετ' αὐτοῦ. Association/accompaniment.

ὅτε. Introduces a temporal clause. The variant ὅτι ($\mathfrak{P}^{66}$ D K L 579 it vg^{mss} syp co) is probably a scribal amelioration seeking to avoid the impression that there were two crowds with Jesus (Metzger, 202).

τὸν Λάζαρον. Accusative direct object of ἐφώνησεν.

ἐφώνησεν. Aor act ind 3rd sg φωνέω.
ἐκ τοῦ μνημείου. Separation.
καί. Coordinating conjunction.
ἤγειρεν. Aor act ind 3rd sg ἐγείρω.
αὐτόν. Accusative direct object of ἤγειρεν.
ἐκ νεκρῶν. Separation.

12:18 διὰ τοῦτο [καὶ] ὑπήντησεν αὐτῷ ὁ ὄχλος, ὅτι ἤκουσαν τοῦτο αὐτὸν πεποιηκέναι τὸ σημεῖον.

διὰ τοῦτο. Causal. The demonstrative pronoun is cataphoric, referring to the ὅτι clause that follows. The pilgrims to the festival (v. 12) went to meet Jesus not because he raised Lazarus (anaphoric demonstrative) but because they heard from the eyewitnesses (the crowd mentioned in v. 17) that he raised Lazarus (cataphoric demonstrative).

[καί]. Adverbial use (adjunctive). The external support for the inclusion of καί is strong ($\mathfrak{P}^{66c}$ A [B²] K L Q Γ Θ Ψ $f^{1.13}$ 565 579 1241 1424 𝔐 et al.), but it is absent in some early manuscripts ($\mathfrak{P}^{66*.75c}$ Δ it pbo).

ὑπήντησεν. Aor act ind 3rd sg ὑπαντάω.
αὐτῷ. Dative complement of ὑπήντησεν.
ὁ ὄχλος. Nominative subject of ὑπήντησεν. This crowd (see v. 12) should be distinguished from the crowd that was with Jesus when he raised Lazarus (v. 17).
ὅτι. Introduces a causal clause.
ἤκουσαν. Aor act ind 3rd pl ἀκούω. The plural verb form is a *constructio ad sensum* because the implied subject (ὁ ὄχλος) is a collective noun (see 12:12-13). Wallace (1996, 401 n. 16) suggests that the change from the singular (ὑπήντησεν) to the plural (ἤκουσαν) may be the evangelist's subconscious shift "from one to the other due to natural number" rather than an indication that one verb views the group collectively and another individually.

τοῦτο ... τὸ σημεῖον. Accusative direct object of πεποιηκέναι. The demonstrative pronoun, which is separated from the noun it modifies by the accusative + infinitive construction for emphasis, is anaphoric, referring to the raising of Lazarus mentioned in v. 17. The use of the term σημεῖα for Jesus' miracles is one of the distinctive features of the FG (see 2:11, 23; 3:2; 4:48, 54; 6:2, 14, 26; 7:31; 9:16; 11:47; 12:37; 20:30; cf. Barrett, 75–78; Keener, 1:272–79; Thompson, 65–68).

αὐτόν. Accusative subject of the infinitive πεποιηκέναι.
πεποιηκέναι. Prf act inf ποιέω (indirect discourse). John uses the infinitive instead of an ὅτι clause to avoid repetition after the preceding ὅτι ἤκουσαν (BDF §388).

12:19 οἱ οὖν Φαρισαῖοι εἶπαν πρὸς ἑαυτούς· θεωρεῖτε ὅτι οὐκ ὠφελεῖτε οὐδέν· ἴδε ὁ κόσμος ὀπίσω αὐτοῦ ἀπῆλθεν.

οἱ ... Φαρισαῖοι. Nominative subject of εἶπαν.
οὖν. Postpositive inferential conjunction.
εἶπαν. Aor act ind 3rd pl λέγω.
πρὸς ἑαυτούς. Locative (motion toward). The PP functions like an indirect object of εἶπαν.
θεωρεῖτε. Pres act ind or impv 2nd pl θεωρέω. θεωρέω here refers to mental perception, not to physical sight (Zerwick and Grosvenor, 325).
ὅτι. Introduces the clausal complement (indirect discourse) of θεωρεῖτε.
οὐκ. Negative particle normally used with indicative verbs.
ὠφελεῖτε. Pres act ind 2nd pl ὠφελέω.
οὐδέν. Accusative direct object of ὠφελεῖτε. The two negatives οὐκ ... οὐδέν reinforce each other: lit. "you are not accomplishing nothing" = "you are accomplishing nothing" (see 3:27 on οὐδὲ).
ἴδε. An interjection (originally aor act impv 2nd sg ὁράω) that is "used when more than one pers[on] is addressed, and when that which is to be observed is in the nom[inative]" (BDAG, 466). This clause is connected to the preceding one by asyndeton.
ὁ κόσμος. Nominative subject of ἀπῆλθεν. The expression ὁ κόσμος ("the world" = "everyone") is ironic (Thompson, 266) and cynical (Smith, 237). Fronted for emphasis.
ὀπίσω αὐτοῦ. Locative. ὀπίσω is an improper preposition (see 1:3 on χωρὶς αὐτοῦ), functioning here as "a marker of position behind an entity that precedes" (BDAG, 716.2.a). In this context, it functions as a "marker of one who is followed as a leader" (LN 36.35).
ἀπῆλθεν. Aor act ind 3rd sg ἀπέρχομαι.

John 12:20-26

²⁰Now some Greeks were among those who went up in order to worship at the festival. ²¹So they came to Philip, who was from Bethsaida in Galilee, and were asking him, saying, "Sir, we wish to see Jesus." ²²Philip went and told Andrew; Andrew and Philip went and told Jesus. ²³Jesus answered them, saying, "The hour is come for the Son of Man to be glorified. ²⁴Truly, truly I say to you, unless a seed of wheat falls into the ground and dies, it remains by itself alone; but if it dies, it bears much fruit. ²⁵The one who loves his life loses it, and the one who hates his life in this world will keep it for eternal life. ²⁶If someone serves me, he must

follow me, and where I am, there will my servant also be. If someone serves me, the Father will honor him."

12:20 Ἦσαν δὲ Ἕλληνές τινες ἐκ τῶν ἀναβαινόντων ἵνα προσκυνήσωσιν ἐν τῇ ἑορτῇ·

Ἦσαν. Impf act ind 3rd pl εἰμί. On the function of the imperfect in the FG, see 1:39 on ἦν.

δὲ. Marker of narrative development.

Ἕλληνές τινες. Nominative subject of Ἦσαν. Ἕλληνές denotes either persons of non-Jewish birth (Barrett, 421) or Greek-speaking Jews (Robinson, 120). Either way, the designation "Greeks" clearly marks them as "the other" (Michaels, 686). Ἕλληνές, which has an acute accent on the antepenult, acquired an additional accent, the acute, on the ultima from the enclitic τινες (Smyth §183; Carson 1985, 48).

ἐκ τῶν ἀναβαινόντων. Replaces the partitive genitive.

ἀναβαινόντων. Pres act ptc masc gen pl ἀναβαίνω (substantival). On the function of the participle, see ἐκ τῶν ἀναβαινόντων above. On the meaning of ἀναβαίνω, see 2:13 on ἀνέβη.

ἵνα. Introduces a purpose clause.

προσκυνήσωσιν. Aor act subj 3rd pl προσκυνέω. Subjunctive with ἵνα.

ἐν τῇ ἑορτῇ. Locative ("at the festival [in Jerusalem]") or temporal ("during the festival").

12:21 οὗτοι οὖν προσῆλθον Φιλίππῳ τῷ ἀπὸ Βηθσαϊδὰ τῆς Γαλιλαίας καὶ ἠρώτων αὐτὸν λέγοντες· κύριε, θέλομεν τὸν Ἰησοῦν ἰδεῖν.

οὗτοι. Nominative subject of προσῆλθον. The demonstrative pronoun refers to Ἕλληνές τινες from the previous verse, acting as a third-person personal pronoun with a simple anaphoric force (Wallace 1996, 328–29).

οὖν. Postpositive inferential conjunction and/or transitional particle (see 1:22 and 11:6).

προσῆλθον. Aor act ind 3rd pl προσέρχομαι.

Φιλίππῳ. Dative of destination (Wallace 1996, 147–48).

τῷ ἀπὸ Βηθσαϊδὰ. The article functions as an adjectivizer, changing the PP ἀπὸ Βηθσαϊδὰ into an attributive modifier of Φιλίππῳ.

ἀπὸ Βηθσαϊδὰ. Locative (cf. 1:44).

τῆς Γαλιλαίας. Partitive genitive qualifying Βηθσαϊδὰ. Galilee denotes the territory within which Bethsaida lies (MHT 3:210).

καὶ. Coordinating conjunction.

ἠρώτων. Impf act ind 3rd pl ἐρωτάω.
αὐτὸν. Accusative direct object of ἠρώτων.
λέγοντες. Pres act ptc masc nom pl λέγω (pleonastic).
κύριε. Vocative of direct address.
θέλομεν. Pres act ind 1st pl θέλω.
τὸν Ἰησοῦν. Accusative direct object of ἰδεῖν. Fronted for emphasis.
ἰδεῖν. Aor act inf ὁράω (complementary). ἰδεῖν ("to see") here means "to have an interview with" (Barrett, 422).

12:22 ἔρχεται ὁ Φίλιππος καὶ λέγει τῷ Ἀνδρέᾳ, ἔρχεται Ἀνδρέας καὶ Φίλιππος καὶ λέγουσιν τῷ Ἰησοῦ.

ἔρχεται. Pres mid ind 3rd sg ἔρχομαι. All verbs in this verse, including ἀποκρίνεται in v. 23, are historical presents, marking a narrative transition from the Greek pilgrims, via Philip and Andrew, to Jesus and giving thematic prominence to his reply to their request (see 1:15 on μαρτυρεῖ). This verse is connected to the previous one by asyndeton.
ὁ Φίλιππος. Nominative subject of ἔρχεται.
καὶ. Coordinating conjunction.
λέγει. Pres act ind 3rd sg λέγω. Historical present (see ἔρχεται above).
τῷ Ἀνδρέᾳ. Dative indirect object of λέγει.
ἔρχεται. Pres mid ind 3rd sg ἔρχομαι. Historical present (see ἔρχεται above).
Ἀνδρέας καὶ Φίλιππος. Compound nominative subject of ἔρχεται. When the verb precedes its two (or more) subjects, as here, it is in the singular, agreeing with the first (BDF §135).
καὶ. Coordinating conjunction.
λέγουσιν. Pres act ind 3rd pl λέγω. Historical present (see ἔρχεται above). This verb is in the plural because it follows its two subjects, Ἀνδρέας καὶ Φίλιππος.
τῷ Ἰησοῦ. Dative indirect object of λέγουσιν.

12:23 Ὁ δὲ Ἰησοῦς ἀποκρίνεται αὐτοῖς λέγων· ἐλήλυθεν ἡ ὥρα ἵνα δοξασθῇ ὁ υἱὸς τοῦ ἀνθρώπου.

Ὁ ... Ἰησοῦς. Nominative subject of ἀποκρίνεται.
δὲ. Marker of narrative development.
ἀποκρίνεται. Pres mid ind 3rd sg ἀποκρίνομαι. Historical present (see ἔρχεται in 12:22).
αὐτοῖς. Dative indirect object of ἀποκρίνεται.
λέγων. Pres act ptc masc nom sg λέγω (pleonastic).

ἐλήλυθεν. Prf act ind 3rd sg ἔρχομαι. Fronted for emphasis. The perfect tense (stative aspect), which here has the force of the present, is marked for prominence (Porter 1994, 41). Caragounis (2004, 275), conversely, thinks that this aorist is future-referring because it points to the cross, which is viewed as an imminently approaching event. He argues that using "the aorist indicative in place of the future indicative underscores two points which the future indicative does not: the *certainty* and *immediacy* (or *imminence*) of action contemplated" (268).

ἡ ὥρα. Nominative subject of ἐλήλυθεν. This verse marks the shift from the time when Jesus' hour has not yet come (2:4; 7:30; 8:20) to the time when his hour has arrived (12:27; 13:1; 16:32; 17:1). Jesus' description of the arrival of the hour circumvents the request of the Greeks or answers it only indirectly.

ἵνα. Introduces an epexegetical clause that clarifies ἡ ὥρα. In classical Greek, an epexegetical ἵνα clause is equivalent to an epexegetical infinitive (Wallace 1996, 476; BDF §379; cf. Zerwick §411). Since this ἵνα clause explains "the hour," it could also be regarded as equivalent to a temporal clause (Barrett, 423; Caragounis 2004, 220 n. 292); see 4:21, 23; 5:25; 16:25, in which the formulation ἔρχεται ὥρα is followed by ὅτε (Zerwick §428; Young, 187).

δοξασθῇ. Aor pass subj 3rd sg δοξάζω. Subjunctive with ἵνα. The unexpressed primary agent of the action is most likely God. In this context, glorification refers to Jesus' death and resurrection (see 7:39; 12:16; 13:31, 32; 17:1). On δοξάζω as a double entendre, see 7:39 on ἐδοξάσθη.

ὁ υἱὸς. Nominative subject of δοξασθῇ.

τοῦ ἀνθρώπου. Genitive of relationship qualifying υἱὸς.

12:24 ἀμὴν ἀμὴν λέγω ὑμῖν, ἐὰν μὴ ὁ κόκκος τοῦ σίτου πεσὼν εἰς τὴν γῆν ἀποθάνῃ, αὐτὸς μόνος μένει· ἐὰν δὲ ἀποθάνῃ, πολὺν καρπὸν φέρει.

ἀμὴν ἀμὴν λέγω ὑμῖν. Metacomment (see 1:51).

ἀμὴν ἀμὴν. Asseverative particles that mark the beginning of Jesus' solemn declaration (see 1:51). This verse is connected to the previous one by asyndeton.

λέγω. Pres act ind 1st sg λέγω.

ὑμῖν. Dative indirect object of λέγω.

ἐὰν. Introduces the protasis of a third-class condition.

μὴ. Negative particle normally used with non-indicative verbs. ἐὰν μή can be translated "unless."

ὁ κόκκος. Nominative subject of ἀποθάνῃ. The article is generic ("a representative grain" [Barrett, 423]).

τοῦ σίτου. Attributive genitive qualifying κόκκος ("wheat seed"), genitive of source ("seed out of wheat"), or epexegetical genitive ("seed which is wheat"; cf. LN 3.31).

πεσών. Aor act ptc masc nom sg πίπτω (attendant circumstance or temporal). On participles that precede the main verb, see ἐμβλέψας in 1:36.

εἰς τὴν γῆν. Locative.

ἀποθάνῃ. Aor act subj 3rd sg ἀποθνῄσκω. Subjunctive with ἐάν.

αὐτὸς μόνος. Predicate nominative. Fronted for emphasis. αὐτὸς functions as an intensive pronoun, which is modified by the adjective μόνος ("by itself alone").

μένει. Pres act ind 3rd sg μένω. This present tense is traditionally called a "timeless present" because, as McKay explains, it refers to an activity that "tends to, or does, happen in present circumstances, but is not necessarily happening now" (1994, 40–41).

ἐάν. Introduces the protasis of a third-class condition.

δέ. Marker of narrative development.

ἀποθάνῃ. Aor act subj 3rd sg ἀποθνῄσκω. Subjunctive with ἐάν.

πολὺν καρπόν. Accusative direct object of φέρει. The adjective πολὺν stands in the first (anarthrous) attributive position (see 2:6 on λίθιναι ὑδρίαι). Fronted for emphasis.

φέρει. Pres act ind 3rd sg φέρω. This is another example of the so-called timeless present (see μένει above).

12:25 ὁ φιλῶν τὴν ψυχὴν αὐτοῦ ἀπολλύει αὐτήν, καὶ ὁ μισῶν τὴν ψυχὴν αὐτοῦ ἐν τῷ κόσμῳ τούτῳ εἰς ζωὴν αἰώνιον φυλάξει αὐτήν.

ὁ φιλῶν. Pres act ptc masc nom sg φιλέω (substantival). Nominative subject of ἀπολλύει. Fronted as a topical frame. This verse is connected to the previous one by asyndeton.

τὴν ψυχήν. Accusative direct object of φιλῶν. The term ψυχή does not mean "soul" in contrast to "body" (anthropological dualism) but denotes physical life or one's self (Brown, 1:467).

αὐτοῦ. Possessive genitive qualifying ψυχήν.

ἀπολλύει. Pres act ind 3rd sg ἀπόλλυμι. Here ἀπόλλυμι means "to lose someth[ing] that one already has" (BDAG, 116.3). The synoptic parallel in Mark 8:35 has the future tense: ὃς γὰρ ἐὰν θέλῃ τὴν ψυχὴν αὐτοῦ σῶσαι ἀπολέσει αὐτήν.

αὐτήν. Accusative direct object of ἀπολλύει.

καί. Coordinating conjunction.

ὁ μισῶν. Pres act ptc masc nom sg μισέω (substantival). Nominative subject of φυλάξει. Fronted as a topical frame.

τὴν ψυχὴν. Accusative direct object of μισῶν.

αὐτοῦ. Possessive genitive qualifying ψυχὴν.

ἐν τῷ κόσμῳ τούτῳ. Locative, with temporal implications ("the present age"; cf. Barrett, 424).

εἰς ζωὴν αἰώνιον. Purpose or result (Harris 2015, 232). On the use of this phrase in the FG, see 3:15 on ζωὴν αἰώνιον.

φυλάξει. Fut act ind 3rd sg φυλάσσω.

αὐτήν. Accusative direct object of φυλάξει.

12:26 ἐάν ἐμοί τις διακονῇ, ἐμοὶ ἀκολουθείτω, καὶ ὅπου εἰμὶ ἐγὼ ἐκεῖ καὶ ὁ διάκονος ὁ ἐμὸς ἔσται· ἐάν τις ἐμοὶ διακονῇ τιμήσει αὐτὸν ὁ πατήρ.

ἐάν. Introduces the protasis of a third-class condition. This verse is connected to the previous one by asyndeton.

ἐμοί. Dative direct object of διακονῇ. Fronted for emphasis.

τις. Nominative subject of διακονῇ.

διακονῇ. Pres act subj 3rd sg διακονέω. Subjunctive with ἐάν.

ἐμοί. Dative direct object of ἀκολουθείτω. Fronted as a topical frame.

ἀκολουθείτω. Pres act impv 3rd sg ἀκολουθέω. The verb stands in final, emphatic position.

καὶ. Coordinating conjunction.

ὅπου. Marker of a position in space.

εἰμί. Pres act ind 1st sg εἰμί. Frey calls attention to a contrast between the present tense (εἰμί), which is used in reference to Jesus, and the future tense (ἔσται), which is used in reference to Jesus' followers, and concludes that "Jesus, who alone uses the 'revelation formula' ἐγώ εἰμι of himself, is time-overarching. He is already present before the becoming of Abraham, and the future of the disciples is also already present for him" (2018, 82–83).

ἐγώ. Nominative subject of εἰμί.

ἐκεῖ. Adverb of place.

καὶ. Adverbial use (adjunctive).

ὁ διάκονος ὁ ἐμός. Nominative subject of ἔσται. The possessive adjective ἐμός stands in the second attributive position (see 1:9 on τὸ φῶς τὸ ἀληθινόν). Fronted for emphasis.

ἔσται. Fut mid ind 3rd sg εἰμί.

ἐάν. Introduces the protasis of a third-class condition. This clause is connected to the previous one by asyndeton.

τις. Nominative subject of διακονῇ.

ἐμοί. Dative direct object of διακονῇ.

διακονῇ. Pres act subj 3rd sg διακονέω.

τιμήσει. Fut act ind 3rd sg τιμάω.
αὐτόν. Accusative direct object of τιμήσει.
ὁ πατήρ. Nominative subject of τιμήσει.

John 12:27-33

²⁷"Now my soul is troubled. And what shall I say? 'Father, deliver me from this hour'? No, but for this reason I have come to this hour. ²⁸Father, glorify your name!" Then a voice came from heaven, "I both have glorified [it] and will glorify [it] again." ²⁹Then the crowd that stood by and heard it was saying that it was thunder; others were saying, "An angel has spoken to him." ³⁰Jesus answered and said, "This voice has happened not for my sake but for your sake. ³¹Now is the judgment of this world; now the ruler of this world will be thrown out. ³²And I, when I am lifted up from the earth, will draw all people to myself." ³³He was saying this to indicate by what sort of death he was about to die.

12:27 Νῦν ἡ ψυχή μου τετάρακται, καὶ τί εἴπω; πάτερ, σῶσόν με ἐκ τῆς ὥρας ταύτης; ἀλλὰ διὰ τοῦτο ἦλθον εἰς τὴν ὥραν ταύτην.

Νῦν. Temporal adverb focusing on time coextensive with the event of the narrative (BDAG, 681.1.a). Fronted as a temporal frame. This verse is connected to the previous one by asyndeton.

ἡ ψυχή. Nominative subject of τετάρακται.

μου. Possessive genitive qualifying ψυχή. Fronted as a topical frame.

τετάρακται. Prf pass ind 3rd sg ταράσσω. The perfect tense (stative aspect) expresses Jesus' present state of anguish (see Νῦν above). On the meaning of the verb, see 11:33 on ἐτάραξεν.

καὶ. Coordinating conjunction.

τί. Accusative direct object of εἴπω.

εἴπω. Aor act subj 1st sg λέγω (deliberative subjunctive).

πάτερ, σῶσόν με ἐκ τῆς ὥρας ταύτης. The punctuation adopted by NA²⁸/UBS⁵ marks this clause as a question (cf. NRSV; NASB; NAB; JB; NIV; REB; HCSB; ESV; NET; Barrett, 425; Brown, 1:465; BDF §448.4), while the punctuation adopted by SBLGNT marks it as a petition (cf. KJV; ASV; TCNT; NEB; Harris 2015, 233), which is parallel to Jesus' prayer in Gethsemane in the Synoptics (Mark 14:36; Matt 26:39; Luke 22:42). The first question ("What shall I say?") probably indicates that what follows is another question that clarifies the first ("[Shall I say,] 'Father, save me from this hour'?"). If so, Jesus does not offer a real prayer for deliverance but merely considers it and then dismisses it (see ἀλλὰ below).

πάτερ. Vocative of direct address. In his prayers in the FG, Jesus regularly addresses God as Father (11:41; 12:27, 28; 17:1, 5, 11, 21, 24, 25).

σῶσόν. Aor act impv 2nd sg σῴζω. σῶσόν, which has a circumflex accent on the penult, acquired an additional accent, the acute, on the ultima from the enclitic με (Smyth §183; Carson 1985, 48).

με. Accusative direct object of σῶσόν.

ἐκ τῆς ὥρας ταύτης. Separation. Harris remarks that "ἐκ here is indistinguishable from ἀπό; that is, it is not the case that ἐκ means 'bring me safely *out of*,' while ἀπό would mean, 'save me *from*'" (2015, 233).

ἀλλά. If the clause πάτερ, σῶσόν με ἐκ τῆς ὥρας ταύτης functions as a question, ἀλλά means "no" (BDF §448.4); if it functions as a petition, ἀλλά serves as a marker of contrast.

διὰ τοῦτο. Causal. The demonstrative pronoun is anaphoric, referring to Jesus' suffering that is anticipated by the prayer for deliverance that Jesus considers.

ἦλθον. Aor act ind 1st sg ἔρχομαι.

εἰς τὴν ὥραν ταύτην. Goal. On the arrival of Jesus' hour, see ἡ ὥρα in 12:23.

12:28 πάτερ, δόξασόν σου τὸ ὄνομα. ἦλθεν οὖν φωνὴ ἐκ τοῦ οὐρανοῦ· καὶ ἐδόξασα καὶ πάλιν δοξάσω.

πάτερ. Vocative of direct address. In his prayers in the FG, Jesus regularly addresses God as Father (11:41; 12:27, 28; 17:1, 5, 11, 21, 24, 25). This verse is connected to the previous one by asyndeton.

δόξασόν. Aor act impv 2nd sg δοξάζω. δόξασόν, which has an acute accent on the antepenult, acquired an additional accent, the acute, on the ultima from the enclitic με (Smyth §183; Carson 1985, 48).

σου. Possessive genitive qualifying ὄνομα. The preposed pronoun is thematically salient (Levinsohn 2000, 64).

τὸ ὄνομα. Accusative direct object of δόξασόν.

ἦλθεν. Aor act ind 3rd sg ἔρχομαι.

οὖν. Postpositive inferential conjunction and/or transitional particle (see 1:22 and 11:6).

φωνή. Nominative subject of ἦλθεν.

ἐκ τοῦ οὐρανοῦ. Source.

καὶ . . . καί. "Both . . . and" in the sense "on the one hand . . . on the other" (BDF §444.3).

ἐδόξασα. Aor act ind 1st sg δοξάζω.

πάλιν. Adverb "pert[aining] to repetition in the same (or similar) manner" (BDAG, 752.2). Fronted for emphasis.

δοξάσω. Fut act ind 1st sg δοξάζω.

12:29 ὁ οὖν ὄχλος ὁ ἑστὼς καὶ ἀκούσας ἔλεγεν βροντὴν γεγονέναι, ἄλλοι ἔλεγον· ἄγγελος αὐτῷ λελάληκεν.

ὁ . . . ὄχλος. Nominative subject of ἔλεγεν. Fronted as a topical frame.

οὖν. Postpositive inferential conjunction and/or transitional particle (see 1:22 and 11:6).

ὁ ἑστώς. Prf act ptc masc nom sg ἵστημι (attributive). The participle modifies ὁ . . . ὄχλος, standing in the second attributive position (see 1:29 on ὁ αἴρων).

καὶ. Coordinating conjunction, linking two attributive participles with the same function.

ἀκούσας. Aor act ptc masc nom sg ἀκούω (attributive). This participle also modifies ὁ . . . ὄχλος, standing in the second attributive position (see ὁ ἑστώς above). The implied direct object of ἀκούσας is τοῦτο/ταῦτα (Haubeck and von Siebenthal, 577). "In keeping with its economic nature, Greek regularly implies an object that was already mentioned in the preceding context, rather than restating it" (Wallace 1996, 409 n. 5).

ἔλεγεν. Impf act ind 3rd sg λέγω. The verb presents the discussion about the meaning of the voice from heaven as an ongoing conversation (imperfective aspect). On the function of the imperfect in the FG, see 1:39 on ἦν.

βροντὴν. Accusative subject of the infinitive γεγονέναι. Fronted for emphasis. βροντή denotes "the loud sound that accompanies a flash of lightning—'thunder'" (LN 14.15).

γεγονέναι. Prf act inf γίνομαι (indirect discourse).

ἄλλοι. Nominative subject of ἔλεγον.

ἔλεγον. Impf act ind 3rd pl λέγω (see ἔλεγεν above).

ἄγγελος. Nominative subject of λελάληκεν. Fronted for emphasis.

αὐτῷ. Dative indirect object of λελάληκεν.

λελάληκεν. Prf act ind 3rd sg λαλέω. In this account that has past implicature, the perfect tense refers to a past event (Porter 1989, 261–62).

12:30 ἀπεκρίθη Ἰησοῦς καὶ εἶπεν· οὐ δι' ἐμὲ ἡ φωνὴ αὕτη γέγονεν ἀλλὰ δι' ὑμᾶς.

ἀπεκρίθη. Aor mid ind 3rd sg ἀποκρίνομαι. On the voice, see "Deponency" in the Series Introduction. This verse is connected to the previous one by asyndeton.

Ἰησοῦς. Nominative subject of ἀπεκρίθη.

καὶ εἶπεν. Pleonastic clause under Semitic influence, which functions as a redundant quotative frame (see 1:25 on καὶ εἶπαν αὐτῷ).

καί. Coordinating conjunction.

εἶπεν. Aor act ind 3rd sg λέγω.

οὐ . . . ἀλλά. A point/counterpoint set ("not this . . . but that") that replaces the incorrect explanation of the purpose of the divine voice ("for my sake") with the correct explanation of its purpose ("for your sake"). On the function of ἀλλά in a point/counterpoint set, see 1:8.

δι' ἐμὲ. Purpose.

ἡ φωνὴ αὕτη. Nominative subject of γέγονεν.

γέγονεν. Prf act ind 3rd sg γίνομαι. Like λελάληκεν in v. 30, this perfect tense is also past-referring.

δι' ὑμᾶς. Purpose.

12:31 νῦν κρίσις ἐστὶν τοῦ κόσμου τούτου, νῦν ὁ ἄρχων τοῦ κόσμου τούτου ἐκβληθήσεται ἔξω·

νῦν. Temporal adverb focusing on time coextensive with the event of the narrative (BDAG, 681.1.a). Fronted as a temporal frame. This verse is connected to the previous one by asyndeton.

κρίσις. Nominative subject of ἐστίν. Fronted for emphasis. Elsewhere in the FG, κρίσις is mentioned in 3:19; 5:22, 24, 27, 29, 30; 7:24; 8:16; 16:8, 11.

ἐστὶν. Pres act ind 3rd sg εἰμί.

τοῦ κόσμου τούτου. Objective genitive qualifying κρίσις.

νῦν. See above.

ὁ ἄρχων. Nominative subject of ἐκβληθήσεται. Fronted as a topical frame.

τοῦ κόσμου τούτου. Genitive of subordination qualifying ἄρχων ("the ruler over this world"; cf. Wallace 1996, 103). The expression ὁ ἄρχων τοῦ κόσμου τούτου refers to the devil. The same designation for the devil is used in 16:11; in 14:30 the devil is called ὁ τοῦ κόσμου ἄρχων.

ἐκβληθήσεται. Fut pass ind 3rd sg ἐκβάλλω. The primary agent of the verb is not expressed.

ἔξω. Adverb ("outside").

12:32 κἀγὼ ἐὰν ὑψωθῶ ἐκ τῆς γῆς, πάντας ἑλκύσω πρὸς ἐμαυτόν.

κἀγώ. Formed by crasis from καὶ ἐγώ. καί is a coordinating conjunction; ἐγώ is the nominative subject of ὑψωθῶ. Fronted for emphasis.

ἐάν. Introduces the protasis of a third-class condition. In this clause, ἐάν refers to "a point of time which is somewhat conditional and simultaneous with another point of time" (LN 67.32), so that it almost means ὅταν (Haubeck and von Siebenthal, 577).

ὑψωθῶ. Aor pass subj 1st sg ὑψόω. Subjunctive with ἐάν. On the meaning of the verb ὑψόω in reference to Jesus' crucifixion, see ὑψωθῆναι in 3:14.

ἐκ τῆς γῆς. Separation. This PP refers to both exaltation "from the earth (on to a cross)" and "from the earth (up into heaven)" (Harris 2015, 234).

πάντας. Accusative direct object of ἑλκύσω. Fronted for emphasis. Since the variant πάντα ("all things"), despite its early attestation ($\mathfrak{P}^{66}$ ℵ* [D] latt Ir^{lat}), may reflect the concept of cosmic redemption that appears foreign to the Johannine theology, the UBS committee favored the reading πάντας (Metzger, 202; cf. SBLGNT, which also has πάντας).

ἑλκύσω. Fut act ind 1st sg ἕλκω.

πρὸς ἐμαυτόν. Spatial (motion toward).

12:33 τοῦτο δὲ ἔλεγεν σημαίνων ποίῳ θανάτῳ ἤμελλεν ἀποθνῄσκειν.

τοῦτο. Accusative direct object of ἔλεγεν.

δὲ. Marker of narrative development.

ἔλεγεν. Impf act ind 3rd sg λέγω. On the function of the imperfect in the FG, see 1:39 on ἦν.

σημαίνων. Pres act ptc masc nom sg σημαίνω (purpose) (Wallace 1996, 637; Young, 157). On participles that follow the main verb, see βαπτίζων in 1:31.

ποίῳ θανάτῳ. Dative of manner. ποίῳ is a qualitative interrogative pronoun, asking "What sort of?" (LN 58.30; Wallace 1996, 346).

ἤμελλεν. Impf act ind 3rd sg μέλλω. On the augment, see ἤμελλεν in 4:47.

ἀποθνῄσκειν. Pres act inf ἀποθνῄσκω (complementary).

John 12:34-36

³⁴So the crowd answered him, "We have heard from the law that the Messiah remains forever. And how do you say that the Son of Man must be lifted up? Who is this Son of Man?" ³⁵So Jesus said to them, "The light is still among you for a little while. Walk while you have the light, so that darkness may not overtake you. And the one who walks in the darkness does not know where he is going. ³⁶While you have the light, believe in the light, so that you may become sons of light." Jesus said these things, and after he departed, he hid from them.

12:34 Ἀπεκρίθη οὖν αὐτῷ ὁ ὄχλος· ἡμεῖς ἠκούσαμεν ἐκ τοῦ νόμου ὅτι ὁ χριστὸς μένει εἰς τὸν αἰῶνα, καὶ πῶς λέγεις σὺ ὅτι δεῖ ὑψωθῆναι τὸν υἱὸν τοῦ ἀνθρώπου; τίς ἐστιν οὗτος ὁ υἱὸς τοῦ ἀνθρώπου;

Ἀπεκρίθη. Aor mid ind 3rd sg ἀποκρίνομαι. On the voice, see "Deponency" in the Series Introduction.

οὖν. Postpositive inferential conjunction and/or transitional particle (see 1:22 and 11:6).

αὐτῷ. Dative indirect object of Ἀπεκρίθη.

ὁ ὄχλος. Nominative subject of Ἀπεκρίθη.

ἡμεῖς. Nominative subject of ἠκούσαμεν. The personal pronoun is emphatic and contrastive, differentiating the crowd ("we") from Jesus ("you").

ἠκούσαμεν. Aor act ind 1st pl ἀκούω.

ἐκ τοῦ νόμου. Source.

ὅτι. Introduces the clausal complement (indirect discourse) of ἠκούσαμεν.

ὁ χριστὸς. Nominative subject of μένει. Fronted as a topical frame.

μένει. Pres act ind 3rd sg μένω. The present tense is retained from the corresponding direct discourse (see 1:39 on μένει).

εἰς τὸν αἰῶνα. Temporal.

καὶ. Coordinating conjunction.

πῶς. Interrogative particle.

λέγεις. Pres act ind 2nd sing λέγω.

σὺ. Nominative subject of λέγεις. The personal pronoun is emphatic and contrastive, differentiating Jesus ("you") from the crowd ("we").

ὅτι. Introduces the clausal complement (indirect discourse) of λέγεις.

δεῖ. Pres act ind 3rd sg δεῖ.

ὑψωθῆναι. Aor pass inf ὑψόω (complementary). On the function of the infinitive with δεῖ, see 3:7 on γεννηθῆναι. The primary agent of the action is not expressed.

τὸν υἱὸν. Accusative subject of the infinitive ὑψωθῆναι.

τοῦ ἀνθρώπου. Genitive of relationship qualifying υἱόν.

τίς. Predicate nominative. "Interrogatives, by their nature, indicate the unknown component and hence cannot be the subject" (Wallace 1996, 40 n. 12).

ἐστιν. Pres act ind 3rd sg εἰμί.

οὗτος ὁ υἱὸς. Nominative subject of ἐστιν. Robertson (697) thinks that this οὗτος is contemptuous. Runge, conversely, argues that this usage is "better explained as marking the participant as being thematically salient, as being in the spotlight" (2010, 373 n. 22).

τοῦ ἀνθρώπου. Genitive of relationship qualifying υἱός.

John 12:34-35

12:35 εἶπεν οὖν αὐτοῖς ὁ Ἰησοῦς· ἔτι μικρὸν χρόνον τὸ φῶς ἐν ὑμῖν ἐστιν. περιπατεῖτε ὡς τὸ φῶς ἔχετε, ἵνα μὴ σκοτία ὑμᾶς καταλάβῃ· καὶ ὁ περιπατῶν ἐν τῇ σκοτίᾳ οὐκ οἶδεν ποῦ ὑπάγει.

εἶπεν. Aor act ind 3rd sg λέγω.

οὖν. Postpositive inferential conjunction and/or transitional particle (see 1:22 and 11:6).

αὐτοῖς. Dative indirect object of εἶπεν.

ὁ Ἰησοῦς. Nominative subject of εἶπεν.

ἔτι. Adverb ("still").

μικρὸν χρόνον. Accusative indicating extent of time.

τὸ φῶς. Nominative subject of ἐστιν. Fronted for emphasis.

ἐν ὑμῖν. Locative ("among you") or association ("with you").

ἐστιν. Pres act ind 3rd sg εἰμί.

περιπατεῖτε. Pres act impv 2nd pl περιπατέω. This clause is connected to the previous one by asyndeton.

ὡς. Temporal conjunction (BDAG, 1105.8.b; BDF §455.2).

τὸ φῶς. Accusative direct object of ἔχετε.

ἔχετε. Pres act ind 2nd pl ἔχω. The verb stands in final, emphatic position.

καὶ. Coordinating conjunction.

ἵνα. Introduces a purpose clause.

μὴ. Negative particle normally used with non-indicative verbs.

σκοτία. Nominative subject of καταλάβῃ. Fronted for emphasis.

ὑμᾶς. Accusative direct object of καταλάβῃ.

καταλάβῃ. Aor act subj 3rd sg καταλαμβάνω. Subjunctive with ἵνα.

καὶ. Coordinating conjunction, which indicates a close, though not specified, association between the clauses περιπατεῖτε ὡς τὸ φῶς ἔχετε, ἵνα μὴ σκοτία ὑμᾶς καταλάβῃ and ὁ περιπατῶν ἐν τῇ σκοτίᾳ οὐκ οἶδεν ποῦ ὑπάγει (Runge 2010, 25). Many English versions do not translate this καί (NRSV; CEB; HCSB; ESV; NET; NIV) or ascribe it a causative function (e.g., "for the one who walks in the dark does not know where he is going" [GNT]).

ὁ περιπατῶν. Pres act ptc masc nom sg περιπατέω (substantival). Nominative subject of οἶδεν. Fronted as a topical frame.

ἐν τῇ σκοτίᾳ. Locative.

οὐκ. Negative particle normally used with indicative verbs.

οἶδεν. Prf act ind 3rd sg οἶδα (see 1:26 on οἴδατε).

ποῦ. Interrogative adverb of place.

ὑπάγει. Pres act ind 3rd sg ὑπάγω.

12:36 ὡς τὸ φῶς ἔχετε, πιστεύετε εἰς τὸ φῶς, ἵνα υἱοὶ φωτὸς γένησθε. ταῦτα ἐλάλησεν Ἰησοῦς, καὶ ἀπελθὼν ἐκρύβη ἀπ' αὐτῶν.

ὡς. Temporal conjunction (BDAG, 1105.8.b; BDF §455.2), introducing a clause that is fronted as a temporal frame.

τὸ φῶς. Accusative direct object of ἔχετε.

ἔχετε. Pres act ind 2nd pl ἔχω.

πιστεύετε. Pres act impv 2nd pl πιστεύω.

εἰς τὸ φῶς. Goal of actions or feelings directed toward someone (BDAG, 290.4.c.β). For πιστεύειν εἰς + accusative ("trust or believe in someone"), see 1:12 on εἰς τὸ ὄνομα.

ἵνα. Introduces a purpose clause.

υἱοί. Predicate nominative. Fronted for emphasis. This preverbal predicate nominative is most likely qualitative because the idea is that "[t]hose who believe in Jesus themselves take on the quality of light" (Barrett, 429).

φωτός. Descriptive genitive qualifying υἱοί ("people characterized by light" or "people worthy of light"). The expression "son(s) of . . ." is a Semitic idiom for ascribing certain characteristic to a person or a group (Moule, 174–75). The phrase "sons of light" (בני אור) is a technical term for the members of the Qumran community (1QS 1.9; 2.16; 3.13, 14, 25; 1QM 1.1, 3, 9, 11, 13). The NT examples include Mark 3:17 ("sons of thunder"); Luke 16:8 ("sons of light"); John 17:12 ("son of perdition"); Eph 2:2 ("sons of disobedience"); 5:8 ("children of light"); 1 Thess 5:5 ("sons of light and sons of the day").

γένησθε. Aor mid subj 2nd pl γίνομαι. Subjunctive with ἵνα.

ταῦτα. Accusative direct object of ἐλάλησεν. This clause is connected to the previous one by asyndeton.

ἐλάλησεν. Prf act ind 3rd sg λαλέω.

Ἰησοῦς. Nominative subject of ἐλάλησεν.

καί. Coordinating conjunction.

ἀπελθών. Aor act ptc masc nom sg ἀπέρχομαι (temporal). On participles that precede the main verb, see ἐμβλέψας in 1:36.

ἐκρύβη. Aor mid ind 3rd sg κρύπτω. On the voice, see "Deponency" in the Series Introduction.

ἀπ' αὐτῶν. Separation.

John 12:37-43

[37]Although he has done so many signs in their presence, they were not believing in him, [38]so that the word of Isaiah, the prophet, might be fulfilled, which he spoke, "Lord, who has believed our message, and to

whom has the arm of the Lord been revealed?" ³⁹For this reason they could not believe because Isaiah said elsewhere, ⁴⁰"He has blinded their eyes and hardened their heart, so that they might not see with their eyes and understand with their heart and turn, and I will heal them." ⁴¹Isaiah said these things because he saw his glory, and he spoke about him. ⁴²Yet despite that, even many of the rulers believed in him, but because of the Pharisees they were not confessing [it], so that they would not be expelled from the synagogue. ⁴³For they loved the glory that comes from human beings more than the glory that comes from God.

12:37 Τοσαῦτα δὲ αὐτοῦ σημεῖα πεποιηκότος ἔμπροσθεν αὐτῶν οὐκ ἐπίστευον εἰς αὐτόν,

Τοσαῦτα . . . σημεῖα. Accusative direct object of πεποιηκότος. The demonstrative adjective Τοσαῦτα ("so great, so many") is separated from the noun it modifies (σημεῖα) and fronted for emphasis. The use of the term σημεῖα for Jesus' miracles is one of the distinctive features of the FG (see 2:11, 23; 3:2; 4:48, 54; 6:2, 14, 26; 7:31; 9:16; 11:47; 12:18; 20:30; cf. Barrett, 75–78; Keener, 1:272–79; Thompson, 65–68).

δὲ. Marker of narrative development.

αὐτοῦ. Genitive subject of πεποιηκότος.

πεποιηκότος. Prf act ptc masc gen sg ποιέω (genitive absolute, concessive). Although the perfect participle "often emphasizes the *resulting state* and only implies the anterior occurrence" (Fanning, 416), in some cases, as here, it "emphasizes the actual *completion* of the action and only implies the result" (418).

ἔμπροσθεν αὐτῶν. Locative. ἔμπροσθέν is an adverb of place that here functions as an improper preposition (see 1:3 on χωρὶς αὐτοῦ); lit. "before them" = "in their presence."

οὐκ. Negative particle normally used with indicative verbs.

ἐπίστευον. Impf act ind 3rd pl πιστεύω. The imperfective aspect portrays the unbelief of the people as an ongoing process. On the function of the imperfect in the FG, see 1:39 on ἦν.

εἰς αὐτόν. Goal of actions or feelings directed toward someone (BDAG, 290.4.c.β). For πιστεύειν εἰς + accusative ("trust or believe in someone"), see 1:12 on εἰς τὸ ὄνομα.

12:38 ἵνα ὁ λόγος Ἡσαΐου τοῦ προφήτου πληρωθῇ ὃν εἶπεν· κύριε, τίς ἐπίστευσεν τῇ ἀκοῇ ἡμῶν; καὶ ὁ βραχίων κυρίου τίνι ἀπεκαλύφθη;

ἵνα ὁ λόγος Ἡσαΐου τοῦ προφήτου πληρωθῇ. This OT introductory formula and its variations—ἵνα ἡ γραφὴ πληρωθῇ (13:18; 17:12; 19:24,

36) and ἵνα πληρωθῇ ὁ λόγος (15:25)—occur only in the FG. Matthew uses a similar formula to introduce the so-called fulfillment citations, but his version includes the substantival participle of λέγω: ἵνα πληρωθῇ τὸ ῥηθὲν (Matt 1:22; 2:15; 4:14; 12:17; 21:4).

ἵνα. Introduces a purpose clause.

ὁ λόγος. Nominative subject of πληρωθῇ.

Ἡσαΐου. Subjective genitive qualifying λόγος ("the word that Isaiah spoke").

τοῦ προφήτου. Genitive in apposition to Ἡσαΐου.

πληρωθῇ. Aor pass subj 3rd sg πληρόω. Subjunctive with ἵνα.

ὅν. Accusative direct object of εἶπεν. The antecedent of the relative pronoun is ὁ λόγος.

εἶπεν. Aor act ind 3rd sg λέγω.

κύριε τίς ἐπίστευσεν τῇ ἀκοῇ ἡμῶν καὶ ὁ βραχίων κυρίου τίνι ἀπεκαλύφθη. A verbatim quotation of LXX Isa 53:1 (κύριε τίς ἐπίστευσεν τῇ ἀκοῇ ἡμῶν καὶ ὁ βραχίων κυρίου τίνι ἀπεκαλύφθη). See Rom 10:16, where Paul quotes the first half of LXX Isa 53:1.

κύριε. Vocative of direct address.

τίς. Nominative subject of ἐπίστευσεν.

ἐπίστευσεν. Aor act ind 3rd sg πιστεύω.

τῇ ἀκοῇ. Dative direct object of ἐπίστευσεν. The dative conveys the thing to which someone gives credence (BDAG, 816.1.a.δ). ἀκοή here denotes "that which is heard," i.e., "account, report, message" (BDAG, 36.4.b).

ἡμῶν. Subjective genitive qualifying ἀκοῇ ("the message that we spoke").

καὶ. Coordinating conjunction.

ὁ βραχίων. Nominative subject of ἀπεκαλύφθη.

κυρίου. Possessive genitive qualifying βραχίων.

τίνι. Dative indirect object of ἀπεκαλύφθη.

ἀπεκαλύφθη. Aor pass ind 3rd sg ἀποκαλύπτω.

12:39 διὰ τοῦτο οὐκ ἠδύναντο πιστεύειν, ὅτι πάλιν εἶπεν Ἡσαΐας·

διὰ τοῦτο. Causal. The demonstrative pronoun is cataphoric, referring to the ὅτι clause that follows.

οὐκ. Negative particle normally used with indicative verbs.

ἠδύναντο. Impf mid ind 3rd pl δύναμαι. On the augment, see ἠδύνατο in 9:33.

πιστεύειν. Pres act inf πιστεύω (complementary).

ὅτι. Introduces a causal clause.

πάλιν. Adverb marking "a discourse or narrative item added to items of a related nature" (BDAG, 752.3).

εἶπεν. Aor act ind 3rd sg λέγω.
Ἡσαΐας. Nominative subject of εἶπεν.

12:40 τετύφλωκεν αὐτῶν τοὺς ὀφθαλμοὺς καὶ ἐπώρωσεν αὐτῶν τὴν καρδίαν, ἵνα μὴ ἴδωσιν τοῖς ὀφθαλμοῖς καὶ νοήσωσιν τῇ καρδίᾳ καὶ στραφῶσιν, καὶ ἰάσομαι αὐτούς.

τετύφλωκεν αὐτῶν τοὺς ὀφθαλμοὺς καὶ ἐπώρωσεν αὐτῶν τὴν καρδίαν. A loose quotation of LXX Isa 6:10a (ἐπαχύνθη γὰρ ἡ καρδία τοῦ λαοῦ τούτου καὶ τοῖς ὡσὶν αὐτῶν βαρέως ἤκουσαν καὶ τοὺς ὀφθαλμοὺς αὐτῶν ἐκάμμυσαν). The quotations of LXX Isa 6:10a in Matt 13:15a and Acts 28:27a follow closely their scriptural base text.

τετύφλωκεν. Prf act ind 3rd sg τυφλόω. The implied subject of the verb is probably God.

αὐτῶν. Possessive genitive qualifying ὀφθαλμοὺς. The preposed pronoun is thematically salient (Levinsohn 2000, 64).

τοὺς ὀφθαλμοὺς. Accusative direct object of τετύφλωκεν. τυφλόω τοὺς ὀφθαλμοὺς (lit. "to blind the eyes") is an idiom for "caus[ing] someone to no longer have the capacity for understanding" (LN 32.25).

καὶ. Coordinating conjunction.

ἐπώρωσεν. Aor act ind 3rd sg πωρόω. πωρόω ("to harden") is here used figuratively, meaning "to cause to be completely unwilling to learn, to cause the mind to be closed" (LN 27.51).

αὐτῶν. Possessive genitive qualifying καρδίαν. The preposed pronoun is thematically salient (Levinsohn 2000, 64).

τὴν καρδίαν. Accusative direct object of ἐπώρωσεν. τὴν καρδίαν is a distributive singular (MHT 3:23). πωρόω τὴν καρδίαν (lit. "to maim the heart") is an idiom that means "to close someone's mind, to make someone unable to learn" (LN 27.53).

ἵνα μὴ ἴδωσιν τοῖς ὀφθαλμοῖς καὶ νοήσωσιν τῇ καρδίᾳ καὶ στραφῶσιν καὶ ἰάσομαι αὐτούς. A loose quotation of LXX Isa 6:10b (μήποτε ἴδωσιν τοῖς ὀφθαλμοῖς καὶ τοῖς ὡσὶν ἀκούσωσιν καὶ τῇ καρδίᾳ συνῶσιν καὶ ἐπιστρέψωσιν καὶ ἰάσομαι αὐτούς). Matt 13:15b and Acts 28:27b quote LXX Isa 6:10b verbatim.

ἵνα. Introduces a purpose-result clause, which "indicates both the intention and its sure accomplishment" (Wallace 1996, 473).

μὴ. Negative particle normally used with non-indicative verbs.

ἴδωσιν. Aor act subj 3rd pl ὁράω. Subjunctive with ἵνα.

τοῖς ὀφθαλμοῖς. Dative of means/instrument. Since human anatomy is involved, the article functions like a possessive pronoun (Wallace 1996, 215).

καὶ. Coordinating conjunction.

νοήσωσιν. Aor act subj 3rd pl νοέω. Subjunctive with ἵνα.

τῇ καρδίᾳ. Dative of means/instrument. τῇ καρδίᾳ is a distributive singular. Since human anatomy is involved, the article functions like a possessive pronoun (Wallace 1996, 215).

καὶ. Coordinating conjunction.

στραφῶσιν. Aor pass subj 3rd pl στρέφω. Subjunctive with ἵνα.

καὶ. Coordinating conjunction.

ἰάσομαι. Fut mid ind 1st sg ἰάομαι. καί + future indicative after ἵνα with the subjunctive is used to indicate some further consequence (MHT 3:100; BDF §369.3).

αὐτούς. Accusative direct object of ἰάσομαι.

12:41 ταῦτα εἶπεν Ἡσαΐας ὅτι εἶδεν τὴν δόξαν αὐτοῦ, καὶ ἐλάλησεν περὶ αὐτοῦ.

ταῦτα. Accusative direct object of εἶπεν. The demonstrative pronoun refers to the scriptural quotations in 12:38-40. This verse is connected to the previous one by asyndeton.

εἶπεν. Aor act ind 3rd sg λέγω.

Ἡσαΐας. Nominative subject of εἶπεν.

ὅτι. Introduces a causal clause. The reading ὅτι ($\mathfrak{P}^{66.75}$ ℵ A B L Θ Ψ f^1 33 et al.) is preferable to the variant ὅτε (D K Γ Δ f^{13} 565 700 892 1241 1424 𝔐 sy Eus) because it has stronger external support and because it "appears, on the surface, to be somewhat less appropriate in the context," which could have caused scribal amelioration (Metzger, 203).

εἶδεν. Aor act ind 3rd sg ὁράω.

τὴν δόξαν. Accusative direct object of εἶδεν.

αὐτοῦ. Possessive genitive qualifying δόξαν. The personal pronoun refers to Jesus.

καὶ. Coordinating conjunction.

ἐλάλησεν. Prf act ind 3rd sg λαλέω.

περὶ αὐτοῦ. Reference. αὐτοῦ refers to Jesus.

12:42 ὅμως μέντοι καὶ ἐκ τῶν ἀρχόντων πολλοὶ ἐπίστευσαν εἰς αὐτόν, ἀλλὰ διὰ τοὺς Φαρισαίους οὐχ ὡμολόγουν ἵνα μὴ ἀποσυνάγωγοι γένωνται·

ὅμως. Adversative particle ("all the same, nevertheless, yet") (BDAG, 710).

μέντοι. Adverbial particle with adversative sense ("though, to be sure, indeed") (BDAG, 630.2). The combination ὅμως μέντοι is "a marker of an implied clause of concession" (LN 89.75) that can be translated "yet, despite that" (BDAG, 630.2). The contrast is between the general rejection of Jesus by his contemporaries (12:37), which was predicted by the prophet Isaiah (12:38-41), and the fact that many of the authorities secretly believed in Jesus.

καί. Adjunctive ("also") or ascensive ("even").

ἐκ τῶν ἀρχόντων. Replaces the partitive genitive.

πολλοί. Nominative subject of ἐπίστευσαν.

ἐπίστευσαν. Aor act ind 3rd pl πιστεύω.

εἰς αὐτόν. Goal of actions or feelings directed toward someone (BDAG, 290.4.c.β). For πιστεύειν εἰς + accusative ("trust or believe in someone"), see 1:12 on εἰς τὸ ὄνομα.

ἀλλά. Marker of contrast.

διὰ τοὺς Φαρισαίους. Causal.

οὐχ. Negative particle normally used with indicative verbs.

ὡμολόγουν. Impf act ind 3rd pl ὁμολογέω. The imperfective aspect of the verb portrays the reluctance to confess Jesus as an ongoing process. On the function of the imperfect in the FG, see 1:39 on ἦν.

ἵνα. Introduces a purpose clause.

μή. Negative particle normally used with non-indicative verbs.

ἀποσυνάγωγοι. Predicate nominative. Fronted for emphasis. This is the second of the three occurrences of this adjective in the FG (9:22; 12:42; 16:2). For a reconstruction of the historical background of this expression, see Martyn (35–66, 148–67; cf. Barrett, 137–44).

γένωνται. Aor mid subj 3rd pl γίνομαι. Subjunctive with ἵνα.

12:43 ἠγάπησαν γὰρ τὴν δόξαν τῶν ἀνθρώπων μᾶλλον ἤπερ τὴν δόξαν τοῦ θεοῦ.

ἠγάπησαν. Aor act ind 3rd pl ἀγαπάω.

γάρ. Postpositive conjunction that introduces the explanation for the authorities' refrain from publicly acknowledging their faith in Jesus.

τὴν δόξαν. Accusative direct object of ἠγάπησαν.

τῶν ἀνθρώπων. Genitive of source qualifying δόξαν ("the glory/fame/praise that comes from human beings") or subjective genitive ("the glory/fame/praise that human beings give").

μᾶλλον. Comparative of the adverb μάλα, functioning as a "marker of an alternative to someth[ing], *rather*" (BDAG, 614.3).

ἤπερ. Strengthened form of the comparative particle ἤ. A NT *hapax legomenon*.

τὴν δόξαν. Accusative direct object of an implied ἠγάπησαν ("more than [they loved] the glory of God").

τοῦ θεοῦ. Genitive of source qualifying δόξαν ("the glory/fame/praise that comes from God") or subjective genitive ("the glory/fame/praise that God gives").

John 12:44-50

⁴⁴Jesus cried out and said, "The one who believes in me does not believe in me but in the one who sent me, ⁴⁵and the one who sees me sees the one who sent me. ⁴⁶I have come as light into the world, so that everyone who believes in me should not remain in darkness. ⁴⁷And if anyone hears my words and does not keep [them], I do not judge him. For I did not come to judge the world but to save the world. ⁴⁸The one who rejects me and does not accept my words has one who judges him; the word that I have spoken—that will judge him on the last day. ⁴⁹For I have not spoken on my own, but the Father himself who sent me has given me a commandment what I should say and what I should speak. ⁵⁰And I know that his commandment is eternal life. So, the things that I speak, just as the Father has told me, so I speak."

12:44 Ἰησοῦς δὲ ἔκραξεν καὶ εἶπεν· ὁ πιστεύων εἰς ἐμὲ οὐ πιστεύει εἰς ἐμὲ ἀλλ' εἰς τὸν πέμψαντά με,

Ἰησοῦς. Nominative subject of ἔκραξεν.

δὲ. Marker of narrative development.

ἔκραξεν. Aor act ind 3rd sg κράζω.

καὶ εἶπεν. Pleonastic clause under Semitic influence, which functions as a redundant quotative frame (see 1:25 on καὶ εἶπαν αὐτῷ).

καὶ. Coordinating conjunction.

εἶπεν. Aor act ind 3rd sg λέγω.

ὁ πιστεύων. Pres act ptc masc nom sg πιστεύω (substantival). Nominative subject of πιστεύει. Fronted as a topical frame.

εἰς ἐμὲ. Goal of actions or feelings directed toward someone (BDAG, 290.4.c.β). For πιστεύειν εἰς + accusative ("trust or believe in someone"), see 1:12 on εἰς τὸ ὄνομα.

οὐ . . . ἀλλ'. A point/counterpoint set whose sense here is "not so much A as B" or "B rather than A" (Zerwick §445). Thus, believing in Jesus means not only believing in him but also (or rather) believing in the one who sent him.

πιστεύει. Pres act ind 3rd sg πιστεύω.

εἰς ἐμὲ. See εἰς ἐμὲ above.

εἰς τὸν πέμψαντά. See εἰς ἐμὲ above.

τὸν πέμψαντά. Aor act ptc masc acc sg πέμπω (substantival). πέμψαντά, which has an acute accent on the antepenult, acquired an additional accent, the acute, on the ultima from the enclitic με (Smyth §183; Carson 1985, 48). On the use of the participial forms of πέμπω to either identify or describe God in the FG, see τοῦ πέμψαντός in 4:34.

με. Accusative direct object of πέμψαντά.

12:45 καὶ ὁ θεωρῶν ἐμὲ θεωρεῖ τὸν πέμψαντά με.

καὶ. Coordinating conjunction.

ὁ θεωρῶν. Pres act ptc masc nom sg θεωρέω (substantival). Nominative subject of θεωρεῖ. Fronted as a topical frame.

ἐμὲ. Accusative direct object of θεωρῶν.

θεωρεῖ. Pres act ind 3rd sg θεωρέω.

τὸν πέμψαντά. Aor act ptc masc acc sg πέμπω (substantival). Accusative direct object of θεωρεῖ. πέμψαντά, which has an acute accent on the antepenult, acquired an additional accent, the acute, on the ultima from the enclitic με (Smyth §183; Carson 1985, 48). On the use of the participial forms of πέμπω to either identify or describe God in the FG, see τοῦ πέμψαντός in 4:34.

με. Accusative direct object of πέμψαντά.

12:46 ἐγὼ φῶς εἰς τὸν κόσμον ἐλήλυθα, ἵνα πᾶς ὁ πιστεύων εἰς ἐμὲ ἐν τῇ σκοτίᾳ μὴ μείνῃ.

ἐγὼ. Nominative subject of ἐλήλυθα. Fronted as a topical frame. This verse is connected to the previous one by asyndeton.

φῶς. Nominative complement to ἐγὼ ("as light").

εἰς τὸν κόσμον. Locative. On the portrayal of the world in the FG, see 1:10 on ἐν τῷ κόσμῳ.

ἐλήλυθα. Prf act ind 1st sg ἔρχομαι.

ἵνα. Introduces a purpose clause.

πᾶς ὁ πιστεύων. Nominative subject of μείνῃ. On πᾶς + articular participle, see 3:8 on πᾶς ὁ γεγεννημένος. Fronted as a topical frame.

ὁ πιστεύων. Pres act ptc masc nom sg πιστεύω (substantival). On the function of this participle, see πᾶς ὁ πιστεύων above.

εἰς ἐμὲ. Goal of actions or feelings directed toward someone (BDAG, 290.4.c.β). For πιστεύειν εἰς + accusative ("trust or believe in someone"), see 1:12 on εἰς τὸ ὄνομα.

ἐν τῇ σκοτίᾳ. Locative.

μὴ. Negative particle normally used with non-indicative verbs.

μείνῃ. Aor act subj 3rd sg μένω. Subjunctive with ἵνα. The verb stands in final, emphatic position.

12:47 καὶ ἐάν τίς μου ἀκούσῃ τῶν ῥημάτων καὶ μὴ φυλάξῃ, ἐγὼ οὐ κρίνω αὐτόν· οὐ γὰρ ἦλθον ἵνα κρίνω τὸν κόσμον, ἀλλ' ἵνα σώσω τὸν κόσμον.

καί. Coordinating conjunction.
ἐάν. Introduces the protasis of a third-class condition.
τίς. Nominative subject of ἀκούσῃ.
μου. Subjective genitive qualifying τῶν ῥημάτων ("the words that I speak"; cf. 3:34). The preposed pronoun is thematically salient (Levinsohn 2000, 64).
ἀκούσῃ. Aor act subj 3rd sg ἀκούω. Subjunctive with ἐάν.
τῶν ῥημάτων. Genitive direct object of ἀκούσῃ.
καί. Coordinating conjunction.
μή. Negative particle normally used with non-indicative verbs.
φυλάξῃ. Aor act subj 3rd sg φυλάσσω.
ἐγώ. Nominative subject of κρίνω. Fronted as a topical frame.
οὐ. Negative particle normally used with indicative verbs.
κρίνω. Pres act ind 1st sg κρίνω.
αὐτόν. Accusative direct object of κρίνω.
οὐ . . . ἀλλ'. A point/counterpoint set ("not this . . . but that") that replaces the incorrect explanation of the purpose of Jesus' coming (to judge the world) with the correct explanation of his purpose (to save the world). On the function of ἀλλά in a point/counterpoint set, see 1:8.
γάρ. Postpositive conjunction that introduces the explanation of Jesus' assertion that he does not judge anyone who does not keep his words.
ἦλθον. Aor act ind 1st sg ἔρχομαι.
ἵνα. Introduces a purpose clause.
κρίνω. Aor act subj 1st sg κρίνω. Subjunctive with ἵνα.
τὸν κόσμον. Accusative direct object of κρίνω. On the portrayal of the world in the FG, see 1:10 on ἐν τῷ κόσμῳ.
ἵνα. Introduces a purpose clause.
σώσω. Aor act subj 1st sg σῴζω. Subjunctive with ἵνα.
τὸν κόσμον. Accusative direct object of σώσω.

12:48 ὁ ἀθετῶν ἐμὲ καὶ μὴ λαμβάνων τὰ ῥήματά μου ἔχει τὸν κρίνοντα αὐτόν· ὁ λόγος ὃν ἐλάλησα ἐκεῖνος κρινεῖ αὐτὸν ἐν τῇ ἐσχάτῃ ἡμέρᾳ.

ὁ ἀθετῶν . . . καὶ . . . λαμβάνων. Nominative subject of ἔχει. Two substantival participles governed by one article and joined by καί form a TSKS (article-substantive-καί-substantive) construction. In such formulations, according to the Granville Sharp rule, the single article indicates that both participles have the same referent; see 5:24 on ὁ . . . ἀκούων καὶ πιστεύων. Fronted as a topical frame. This verse is connected to the previous one by asyndeton.

ἀθετῶν. Pres act ptc masc nom sg ἀθετέω (substantival). In this context, ἀθετέω means "to reject by not recognizing someth[ing] or someone" (BDAG, 24.2).

ἐμὲ. Accusative direct object of ἀθετῶν.

μὴ. Negative particle normally used with non-indicative verbs.

λαμβάνων. Pres act ptc masc nom sg λαμβάνω (substantival). λαμβάνω here means "to accept as true" (LN 31.50).

τὰ ῥήματά. Accusative direct object of λαμβάνων. ῥήματά, which has an acute accent on the antepenult, acquired an additional accent, the acute, on the ultima from the enclitic μου (Smyth §183; Carson 1985, 48).

μου. Subjective genitive qualifying ῥήματά (see 12:47).

ἔχει. Pres act ind 3rd sg ἔχω.

τὸν κρίνοντα. Pres act ptc masc acc sg κρίνω (substantival). Accusative direct object of ἔχει.

αὐτόν. Accusative direct object of κρίνοντα.

ὁ λόγος. Nominative subject of κρινεῖ in a left-dislocation, resumed by ἐκεῖνος (see Runge 2010, 287–313). The left-dislocation shifts focus on the word that Jesus spoke.

ὃν. Accusative direct object of ἐλάλησα. The antecedent of the relative pronoun is ὁ λόγος.

ἐλάλησα. Aor act ind 1st sg λαλέω.

ἐκεῖνος. Nominative subject of κρινεῖ, resuming ὁ λόγος. The anaphoric demonstrative reinforces what is already made prominent through the left-dislocation of ὁ λόγος.

κρινεῖ. Fut act ind 3rd sg κρίνω.

αὐτὸν. Accusative direct object of κρινεῖ.

ἐν τῇ ἐσχάτῃ ἡμέρᾳ. Temporal. The PP "on the last day" occurs only in the FG (6:39, 40, 44; 11:24; 12:48; cf. τῇ ἐσχάτῃ ἡμέρᾳ in 6:54). Other NT formulations use the plural "the last days" (ἐν ταῖς ἐσχάταις ἡμέραις [Acts 2:17]; ἐν ἐσχάταις ἡμέραις [2 Tim 3:1; Jas 5:3]; ἐπ' ἐσχάτου τῶν ἡμερῶν [Heb 1:2]; ἐπ' ἐσχάτων τῶν ἡμερῶν [2 Pet 3:3]).

12:49 ὅτι ἐγὼ ἐξ ἐμαυτοῦ οὐκ ἐλάλησα, ἀλλ' ὁ πέμψας με πατὴρ αὐτός μοι ἐντολὴν δέδωκεν τί εἴπω καὶ τί λαλήσω.

ὅτι. Introduces a causal clause.
ἐγώ. Nominative subject of ἐλάλησα. Fronted for emphasis.
ἐξ ἐμαυτοῦ. Source/origin (lit. "from myself").
οὐκ . . . ἀλλ'. A point/counterpoint set ("not this . . . but that") that replaces the erroneous explanation of the origin of Jesus' message (he spoke on his own) with the accurate explanation (the Father himself told him what to say). On the function of ἀλλά in a point/counterpoint set, see 1:8.
ἐλάλησα. Aor act ind 1st sg λαλέω.
ὁ . . . πατὴρ αὐτός. Nominative subject of δέδωκεν. αὐτός functions as an intensive pronoun ("the Father himself"), "setting an item off fr[om] everything else through emphasis and contrast" (BDAG, 152.1).
πέμψας. Aor act ptc masc nom sg πέμπω (attributive). The participle modifies πατὴρ, standing in the first attributive position (article-attributive participle-noun) (Wallace 1996, 306, 618). On the use of the participial forms of πέμπω to either identify or describe God in the FG, see τοῦ πέμψαντός in 4:34. ὁ πέμψας με πατήρ is a common Johannine expression (5:37; 8:16, 18; 12:49; 14:24).
με. Accusative direct object of πέμψας.
μοι. Dative indirect object of δέδωκεν.
ἐντολήν. Accusative direct object of δέδωκεν. Fronted for emphasis.
δέδωκεν. Prf act ind 3rd sg δίδωμι. The perfect tense verb form is marked for prominence, expressing that "what the Father 'has given' to the Son . . . is definitely in his hand" (Frey 2018, 81).
τί. Accusative direct object of εἴπω.
εἴπω. Aor act subj 1st sg λέγω (deliberative subjunctive).
καί. Coordinating conjunction.
τί. Accusative direct object of λαλήσω.
λαλήσω. Aor act subj 1st sg λαλέω (deliberative subjunctive). There is no distinction in meaning between τί εἴπω and τί λαλήσω (Barrett, 435).

12:50 καὶ οἶδα ὅτι ἡ ἐντολὴ αὐτοῦ ζωὴ αἰώνιός ἐστιν. ἃ οὖν ἐγὼ λαλῶ, καθὼς εἴρηκέν μοι ὁ πατήρ, οὕτως λαλῶ.

καί. Coordinating conjunction.
οἶδα. Prf act ind 1st sg οἶδα (see 1:26 on οἴδατε).
ὅτι. Introduces the clausal complement (indirect discourse) of οἶδα.
ἡ ἐντολή. Nominative subject of ἐστιν.

αὐτοῦ. Subjective genitive qualifying ἐντολή.

ζωὴ αἰώνιος. Predicate nominative. Fronted for emphasis. On the use of this phrase in the FG, see 3:15 on ζωὴν αἰώνιον. αἰώνιός, which has an acute accent on the antepenult, acquired an additional accent, the acute, on the ultima from the enclitic ἐστιν (Smyth §183; Carson 1985, 48).

ἐστιν. Pres act ind 3rd sg εἰμί.

ἅ. The relative pronoun introduces the headless relative clause that, in its entirety (ἃ οὖν ἐγὼ λαλῶ), serves as the direct object of the second λαλῶ. Within its clause, ἅ is the accusative direct object of the first λαλῶ.

οὖν. Postpositive inferential conjunction and/or transitional particle (see 1:22 and 11:6).

ἐγώ. Nominative subject of the first λαλῶ. Fronted for emphasis.

λαλῶ. Pres act ind 1st sg λαλέω.

καθώς. Introduces a comparative clause.

εἴρηκέν. Prf act ind 3rd sg λέγω. εἴρηκέν, which has an acute accent on the antepenult, acquired an additional accent, the acute, on the ultima from the enclitic μοι (Smyth §183; Carson 1985, 48).

μοι. Indirect object of εἴρηκέν.

ὁ πατήρ. Nominative subject of εἴρηκέν.

οὕτως. Adverb of manner ("in this manner, thus, so") that functions as a correlative to καθώς (BDAG, 741.1.a).

λαλῶ. Pres act ind 1st sg λαλέω.

John 13:1-11

[1]Now before the festival of the Passover, when Jesus knew that his hour had come to depart from this world to the Father, having loved his own who were in the world, he loved them to the end. [2]And while a supper was taking place, when the devil had already put into the heart of Judas son of Simon Iscariot that he should betray him, [3]because he knew that the Father had given him all things into his hands and that he had come from God and was going to God, [4]he got up from the supper and took off his outer garment and, after he took a towel, he tied it around himself. [5]Then he poured water into the basin and began washing the feet of the disciples and to wipe them with the towel which he had tied around him. [6]So he came to Simon Peter. He said to him, "Lord, are you going to wash my feet?" [7]Jesus answered and said to him, "What I am doing you do not know now, but you will understand after these things." [8]Peter said to him, "You shall never wash my feet." Jesus answered him, "Unless I wash you, you have no share with me." [9]Simon Peter said to him, "Lord, not only my feet but also my hands and my head!" [10]Jesus said to him,

"The one who has had a bath does not need to wash except for the feet but is entirely clean. And you are clean, but not all." ¹¹For he knew the one who was going to betray him. Because of this he said, "Not all of you are clean."

13:1 Πρὸ δὲ τῆς ἑορτῆς τοῦ πάσχα εἰδὼς ὁ Ἰησοῦς ὅτι ἦλθεν αὐτοῦ ἡ ὥρα ἵνα μεταβῇ ἐκ τοῦ κόσμου τούτου πρὸς τὸν πατέρα, ἀγαπήσας τοὺς ἰδίους τοὺς ἐν τῷ κόσμῳ εἰς τέλος ἠγάπησεν αὐτούς.

Πρὸ . . . τῆς ἑορτῆς. Temporal. Fronted as a temporal frame. Temporal references in 18:28, 19:14, 31, 42 indicate that the PP Πρὸ . . . τῆς ἑορτῆς in this verse means one day before the Passover.

δὲ. Marker of narrative development.

τοῦ πάσχα. Epexegetical genitive, explaining τῆς ἑορτῆς ("the festival, which is the Passover"; cf. Wallace 1996, 99). For other references to the Passover in the FG, see 2:13, 6:4, and 11:55.

εἰδὼς. Prf act ptc masc nom sg οἶδα (temporal or causal); see 1:26 on οἴδατε. On participles that precede the main verb, see ἐμβλέψας in 1:36.

ὁ Ἰησοῦς. Nominative subject of ἠγάπησεν.

ὅτι. Introduces the clausal complement (indirect discourse) of εἰδὼς.

ἦλθεν. Aor act ind 3rd sg ἔρχομαι.

αὐτοῦ. Genitive of purpose qualifying ὥρα ("the hour destined for him"). The preposed pronoun is thematically salient (Levinsohn 2000, 64).

ἡ ὥρα. Nominative subject of ἦλθεν. On the arrival of Jesus' hour, see ἡ ὥρα in 12:23.

ἵνα. Introduces an epexegetical clause that explains ἡ ὥρα or, alternatively, a temporal clause if this ἵνα is regarded as equivalent to ὅτε. On ἡ ὥρα followed by the ἵνα clause, see 12:23.

μεταβῇ. Aor act subj 3rd sg μεταβαίνω. Subjunctive with ἵνα. μεταβαίνω ("go/pass over") indicates transfer from one place to another.

ἐκ τοῦ κόσμου τούτου. Separation.

πρὸς τὸν πατέρα. Locative (motion toward).

ἀγαπήσας. Aor act ptc masc nom sg ἀγαπάω (causal). On participles that precede the main verb, see ἐμβλέψας in 1:36.

τοὺς ἰδίους. Accusative direct object of ἀγαπήσας. The masculine substantival adjective refers to "persons who in some sense belong to a so-called 'reference person'—'his own people'" (LN 10.12). This expression here refers to Jesus' followers (cf. 1:11, where it referred to the Jews).

τοὺς ἐν τῷ κόσμῳ. The article functions as an adjectivizer, changing the prepositional phrase ἐν τῷ κόσμῳ into an attributive modifier of τοὺς ἰδίους.

ἐν τῷ κόσμῳ. Locative, with temporal implications ("this age"; cf. Barrett, 438).

εἰς τέλος. An idiom (lit. "into end") that indicates "a degree of completeness, with the possible implication of purpose or result—'completely, totally, entirely, wholly'" and/or functions as a temporal expression— "he loved them to the end" (LN 78.47; cf. BDAG, 289.2.a.α; 289.3), i.e., "to the last moment of his life" (Barrett, 438). Fronted for emphasis.

ἠγάπησεν. Aor act ind 3rd sg ἀγαπάω.

αὐτούς. Accusative direct object of ἠγάπησεν.

13:2 Καὶ δείπνου γινομένου, τοῦ διαβόλου ἤδη βεβληκότος εἰς τὴν καρδίαν ἵνα παραδοῖ αὐτὸν Ἰούδας Σίμωνος Ἰσκαριώτου,

Καὶ. Coordinating conjunction.

δείπνου. Genitive subject of γινομένου.

γινομένου. Pres mid ptc neut gen sg γίνομαι (genitive absolute, temporal). The present-tense participle γινομένου, which has strong manuscript support (ℵ* B L W Ψ 070 579 1241 d r¹), indicates that the supper was in progress when the narrated events took place (Porter 1994, 188). The aorist-tense participle γενομένου, which also has considerable textual support (𝔓⁶⁶ ℵ² A D K Γ Δ Θ f¹·¹³ 33 565 700 892 1424 l844 𝔐 lat), is without doubt the more difficult reading of the two because it presumes that the supper had ended when the events described in ch. 13 occurred, which is contradicted by the account itself that indicates that the supper was still in progress when Jesus washed his disciples' feet and identified his betrayer. The reading γινομένου therefore seems more suitable to the context, especially given its strong textual support (Metzger, 203).

τοῦ διαβόλου. Genitive subject of βεβληκότος.

ἤδη. Adverb ("already").

βεβληκότος. Prf act ptc masc gen sg βάλλω (genitive absolute, temporal). The perfect tense of the participle refers to an action that took place in the past, but the emphasis falls on the consequence of that action, i.e., on the state Judas was in at the supper (Fanning, 162).

εἰς τὴν καρδίαν. Locative. βάλλω εἰς τὴν καρδίαν is an idiom (lit. "to throw into the heart") for "caus[ing] someone to think in a particular manner, often as a means of inducing some behavior—'to make think, to fill the heart, to cause to decide'" (LN 30.29). The PP most likely refers to Judas' heart because in Greek the definite article typically functions as a possessive pronoun when one's body part is specified (but see Barrett, 439, who thinks that this is a reference to the devil's heart). To indicate this, I have followed many English versions that add the genitive "of Judas son of Simon Iscariot" after "the heart" and, to avoid repetition, I have replaced the name "Judas son of Simon Iscariot," which in Greek serves as the subject of the ἵνα clause, with the personal pronoun "he."

ἵνα. Introduces a direct object clause (also known as a "content ἵνα clause") of βεβληκότος (Wallace 1996, 475; Zerwick §§406–7).

παραδοῖ. Aor act subj 3rd sg παραδίδωμι. Subjunctive with ἵνα.

αὐτὸν. Accusative direct object of παραδοῖ. The personal pronoun refers to Jesus.

Ἰούδας. Nominative subject of παραδοῖ. Harris suggests that "an explicit ref. to Judas was perhaps delayed for dramatic effect" (243). In some manuscripts, the genitive case Ἰούδα is placed after the PP εἰς τὴν καρδίαν (A K Γ Δ Θ f¹ 33 700 892 1424 𝔐 [a f q] sy). However, if this smooth formulation, which makes perfectly clear that it was Judas' heart into which the devil put the idea of betraying Jesus, were the original reading, it is difficult to explain why it would have been changed to a more difficult construction in which the nominative case Ἰούδας comes after παραδοῖ αὐτὸν (Metzger, 204).

Σίμωνος Ἰσκαριώτου. Genitive of relationship in an elliptical construction ("[the son] of Simon Iscariot"); see 6:71; 13:26; 21:15.

13:3 εἰδὼς ὅτι πάντα ἔδωκεν αὐτῷ ὁ πατὴρ εἰς τὰς χεῖρας καὶ ὅτι ἀπὸ θεοῦ ἐξῆλθεν καὶ πρὸς τὸν θεὸν ὑπάγει,

εἰδώς. Prf act ptc masc nom sg οἶδα (causal). On participles that precede the main verb, see ἐμβλέψας in 1:36.

ὅτι. Introduces the first clausal complement (indirect discourse) of εἰδώς.

πάντα. Accusative direct object of ἔδωκεν.

ἔδωκεν. Aor act ind 3rd sg δίδωμι.

αὐτῷ. Dative indirect object of ἔδωκεν.

ὁ πατὴρ. Nominative subject of ἔδωκεν.

εἰς τὰς χεῖρας. Locative. The article functions as a possessive pronoun ("into his hands"). The combination αὐτῷ . . . εἰς τὰς χεῖρας is awkward ("to him . . . into his hands").

καὶ. Coordinating conjunction.

ὅτι. Introduces the second clausal complement (indirect discourse) of εἰδώς.

ἀπὸ θεοῦ. Source.

ἐξῆλθεν. Aor act ind 3rd sg ἐξέρχομαι.

καὶ. Coordinating conjunction.

πρὸς τὸν θεὸν. Locative (motion toward).

ὑπάγει. Pres act ind 3rd sg ὑπάγω. The present tense is retained from the corresponding direct discourse (see 1:39 on μένει). The verb ὑπάγω ("go away") is frequently used in chs. 13–16 (13:3, 33, 36; 14:4, 5, 28; 16:5, 10, 17), where it refers to Jesus' departure in death and his return to the Father.

13:4 ἐγείρεται ἐκ τοῦ δείπνου καὶ τίθησιν τὰ ἱμάτια καὶ λαβὼν λέντιον διέζωσεν ἑαυτόν·

ἐγείρεται. Pres mid ind 3rd sg ἐγείρω. On the voice, see "Deponency" in the Series Introduction. Here ἐγείρω means "to get up, normally from a lying or reclining position but possibly from a seated position" (LN 17.9). ἐγείρεται is the first verb in a string of historical presents in this chapter. It marks the transition from the background information to the account of Jesus' washing of the disciples' feet and gives prominence to Jesus' preparation to perform this surprising act (see 1:15 on μαρτυρεῖ). The reason for the use of some of the historical presents in this account, however, is not always clear. Fanning suggests that "the choice of tenses in some of these cases is due to a combination of a kind of 'linguistic momentum' (use of one historical present prompts several in series) and an idiomatic predilection to use the historical present more commonly with some verbs" (235).

ἐκ τοῦ δείπνου. Separation.

καὶ. Coordinating conjunction.

τίθησιν. Pres act ind 3rd sg τίθημι. This is another historical present that continues to give prominence to Jesus' preparation to wash his disciples' feet (see ἐγείρεται above). Here τίθημι means "to remove or take off clothing" (LN 49.21). This use of τίθημι + τὰ ἱμάτια ("to take off the outer garment") is parallel to λαμβάνω + τὰ ἱμάτια ("to put on the outer garment") in 13:12.

τὰ ἱμάτια. Accusative direct object of τίθησιν. ἱμάτιον means "outer clothing, cloak, robe" (BDAG, 475.2). The plural is here used for the singular (BDF §141.8; MHT 3:27).

καὶ. Coordinating conjunction.

λαβών. Aor act ptc masc nom sg λαμβάνω (temporal). On participles that precede the main verb, see ἐμβλέψας in 1:36.

λέντιον. Accusative direct object of λαβών. λέντιον, a Greek transliteration of the Latin *linteum*, denotes "a piece of cloth (probably made of linen) used primarily for drying" (LN 6.161). It occurs only twice in the NT—here and in v. 5.

διέζωσεν. Aor act ind 3rd sg διαζώννυμι. The verb means "to tuck up or hold a garment firmly in place by wrapping a belt, girdle, or piece of cloth around it" (LN 49.14).

ἑαυτόν. Accusative direct object of διέζωσεν. The reflexive pronoun indicates that "[t]he subject acts upon himself" (Wallace 1996, 413).

13:5 εἶτα βάλλει ὕδωρ εἰς τὸν νιπτῆρα καὶ ἤρξατο νίπτειν τοὺς πόδας τῶν μαθητῶν καὶ ἐκμάσσειν τῷ λεντίῳ ᾧ ἦν διεζωσμένος.

εἶτα. Adverb ("then, next").

βάλλει. Pres act ind 3rd sg βάλλω. The historical present marks another preparatory act for Jesus' washing of the disciples' feet (see ἐγείρεται above).

ὕδωρ. Accusative direct object of βάλλει.

εἰς τὸν νιπτῆρα. Locative. The noun νιπτήρ ("wash basin") is a NT *hapax legomenon*. Since the basin was not mentioned before, τὸν functions as the article of simple identification, specifying a piece of standard equipment in the room (Wallace 1996, 217).

καὶ. Coordinating conjunction.

ἤρξατο. Aor mid ind 3rd sg ἄρχω.

νίπτειν. Pres act inf νίπτω (complementary). νίπτω means "to cleanse with use of water, *wash*" (BDAG, 674.1). The imperfective aspect of the verb portrays the washing of the disciples' feet as an action in progress.

τοὺς πόδας. Accusative direct object of νίπτειν.

τῶν μαθητῶν. Possessive genitive qualifying πόδας.

καὶ. Coordinating conjunction.

ἐκμάσσειν. Pres act inf ἐκμάσσω (complementary). ἐκμάσσω means "to wipe dry" (LN 79.83). The imperfective aspect of the verb portrays the wiping of the disciples' feet as an action in progress.

τῷ λεντίῳ. Dative of means/instrument.

ᾧ. The relative pronoun ᾧ stands for ὅ, serving as the direct object of διεζωσμένος. It is in the dative because it is attracted to its antecedent τῷ λεντίῳ.

ἦν. Impf act ind 3rd sg εἰμί.

διεζωσμένος. Prf mid ptc masc nom sg διαζώννυμι (pluperfect periphrastic).

13:6 Ἔρχεται οὖν πρὸς Σίμωνα Πέτρον· λέγει αὐτῷ· κύριε, σύ μου νίπτεις τοὺς πόδας;

Ἔρχεται. Pres mid ind 3rd sg ἔρχομαι. The historical present calls attention to Jesus' approach to Peter and the conversation between them.

οὖν. Postpositive inferential conjunction and/or transitional particle (see 1:22 and 11:6).
πρὸς Σίμωνα Πέτρον. Locative (motion toward).
λέγει. Pres act ind 3rd sg λέγω. The historical present gives prominence to Peter's question (see 1:15 on μαρτυρεῖ).
αὐτῷ. Dative indirect object of λέγει.
κύριε. Vocative of direct address.
σύ. Nominative subject of νίπτεις. The personal pronoun is emphatic and contrastive.
μου. Possessive genitive qualifying πόδας. The preposed pronoun is thematically salient (Levinsohn 2000, 64) and contrasted with σύ.
νίπτεις. Pres act ind 2nd sg νίπτω. This has been traditionally labeled a "conative present" because it refers to an action that has not yet occurred but is only intended (Fanning, 220–21). Fanning (220) notes that in cases such as this, "the intention or desire to do an act is, by easy association, seen as part of the process of doing the act itself," which in many instances remains incomplete; v. 12, however, indicates that the act of washing Peter's feet was not merely contemplated but also performed.
τοὺς πόδας. Accusative direct object of νίπτεις.

13:7 ἀπεκρίθη Ἰησοῦς καὶ εἶπεν αὐτῷ· ὃ ἐγὼ ποιῶ σὺ οὐκ οἶδας ἄρτι, γνώσῃ δὲ μετὰ ταῦτα.

ἀπεκρίθη. Aor mid ind 3rd sg ἀποκρίνομαι. On the voice, see "Deponency" in the Series Introduction. This verse is connected to the previous one by asyndeton.
Ἰησοῦς. Nominative subject of ἀπεκρίθη.
καὶ εἶπεν αὐτῷ. Pleonastic clause under Semitic influence, which functions as a redundant quotative frame (see 1:25 on καὶ εἶπαν αὐτῷ).
καὶ. Coordinating conjunction.
εἶπεν. Aor act ind 3rd sg λέγω.
αὐτῷ. Dative indirect object of εἶπεν.
ὅ. Introduces a headless relative clause that, in its entirety (ὃ ἐγὼ ποιῶ), serves as the direct object of οἶδας. Within its clause, ὅ is the accusative direct object of ποιῶ.
ἐγώ. Nominative subject of ποιῶ. Fronted for emphasis.
ποιῶ. Pres act ind 1st sg ποιέω.
σύ. Nominative subject of οἶδας. The personal pronoun is emphatic and contrastive, juxtaposing the act of Jesus and Peter's failure to understand its significance.
οὐκ. Negative particle normally used with indicative verbs.
οἶδας. Prf act ind 2nd sg οἶδα; see 1:26 on οἴδατε.

ἄρτι. Adverb of time.

γνώσῃ. Fut mid ind 2nd sg γινώσκω.

δὲ. Marker of narrative development.

μετὰ ταῦτα. Temporal. It is not clear to which events the demonstrative ταῦτα points, but if 2:22 and 12:16 are taken as an interpretive key, this PP refers not to the conversation following Jesus' washing of the disciples' feet but to the time after Jesus' death and resurrection (Brown, 2:552; Schnackenburg, 3:19; Barrett, 440).

13:8 λέγει αὐτῷ Πέτρος· οὐ μὴ νίψῃς μου τοὺς πόδας εἰς τὸν αἰῶνα. ἀπεκρίθη Ἰησοῦς αὐτῷ· ἐὰν μὴ νίψω σε, οὐκ ἔχεις μέρος μετ' ἐμοῦ.

λέγει. Pres act ind 3rd sg λέγω. Historical present (see 13:4 on ἐγείρεται). This verse is connected to the previous one by asyndeton.

αὐτῷ. Dative indirect object of λέγει.

Πέτρος. Nominative subject of λέγει.

οὐ μὴ. Emphatic negation, which is usually followed by the aorist subjunctive.

νίψῃς. Aor act subj 2nd sg νίπτω. Used with οὐ μὴ to express emphatic negation.

μου. Possessive genitive qualifying πόδας. The preposed pronoun is thematically salient (Levinsohn 2000, 64).

τοὺς πόδας. Accusative direct object of νίψῃς.

εἰς τὸν αἰῶνα. Temporal. εἰς τὸν αἰῶνα with a negative means "never" (Harris 2015, 243).

ἀπεκρίθη. Aor mid ind 3rd sg ἀποκρίνομαι. On the voice, see "Deponency" in the Series Introduction. This clause is connected to the previous one by asyndeton.

Ἰησοῦς. Nominative subject of ἀπεκρίθη.

αὐτῷ. Dative indirect object of ἀπεκρίθη.

ἐὰν. Introduces the protasis of a third-class condition.

μὴ. Negative particle normally used with non-indicative verbs. ἐὰν μή can be translated "unless."

νίψω. Aor act subj 1st sg νίπτω. Subjunctive with ἐάν.

σε. Accusative direct object of νίψω.

οὐκ. Negative particle normally used with indicative verbs.

ἔχεις. Pres act ind 2nd sg ἔχω.

μέρος. Accusative direct object of ἔχεις.

μετ' ἐμοῦ. Association/accompaniment.

13:9 λέγει αὐτῷ Σίμων Πέτρος· κύριε, μὴ τοὺς πόδας μου μόνον ἀλλὰ καὶ τὰς χεῖρας καὶ τὴν κεφαλήν.

λέγει. Pres act ind 3rd sg λέγω. Historical present (see 13:4 on ἐγείρεται). This verse is connected to the previous one by asyndeton.

αὐτῷ. Dative indirect object of λέγει.

Σίμων Πέτρος. Nominative subject of λέγει.

κύριε. Vocative of direct address.

μὴ ... μόνον ἀλλὰ καὶ. A point/counterpoint set ("not only ... but also") that corrects the first direct object of Jesus' washing (Peter's feet) by supplementing it by two additional direct objects (Peter's hands and head). On the function of ἀλλά in a point/counterpoint set, see 1:8. The negative particle μὴ is used rather than οὐ because the elliptical construction presumes the addition of the prohibitive subjunctive νίψῃς.

τοὺς πόδας. Accusative direct object of an implied νίψαι.

μου. Possessive genitive qualifying πόδας.

τὰς χεῖρας. Accusative direct object of an implied νίψαι. In this context, the article functions as a first-person possessive pronoun ("my hands").

καὶ. Coordinating conjunction.

τὴν κεφαλήν. Accusative direct object of an implied νίψαι. In this context, the article functions as a first-person possessive pronoun ("my head").

13:10 λέγει αὐτῷ ὁ Ἰησοῦς· ὁ λελουμένος οὐκ ἔχει χρείαν εἰ μὴ τοὺς πόδας νίψασθαι, ἀλλ' ἔστιν καθαρὸς ὅλος· καὶ ὑμεῖς καθαροί ἐστε, ἀλλ' οὐχὶ πάντες.

λέγει. Pres act ind 3rd sg λέγω. Historical present (see 13:4 on ἐγείρεται). This verse is connected to the previous one by asyndeton.

αὐτῷ. Dative indirect object of λέγει.

ὁ Ἰησοῦς. Nominative subject of λέγει.

ὁ λελουμένος. Prf pass ptc masc nom sg λούω (substantival). Nominative subject of ἔχει. λούω means "to use water to cleanse a body of physical impurity, *wash*, as a rule of the whole body, *bathe*" (BDAG, 603.1). The perfect participle refers to a past action, but the context clearly indicates that the emphasis is on the state of cleanliness attained though bathing.

οὐκ ... εἰ μή. A point/counterpoint set that corrects the negated clause ("the one who has been bathed does not need to wash") by introducing an exception ("except for his feet"); on the function of the excepted element, see 3:13 on οὐδεὶς ... εἰ μή. Because of the strong external attestation of the excepted clause, εἰ μὴ τοὺς πόδας (B C* [K] L W Ψ f^{13} 892 it vg^d sy^h Or^{txt}), its omission in some manuscripts (ℵ aur c vgst Or^{com}) is, according to the UBS committee, either accidental or deliberate, seeking to reconcile Jesus' assertion with the generalizing statement ἀλλ' ἔστιν καθαρὸς ὅλος that follows (Metzger, 204). This view is not shared by many modern scholars, who argue that the excepted clause represents an addition to an originally shorter text (ὁ λελουμένος οὐκ ἔχει χρείαν νίψασθαι) that arose because of the copyists' failure to understand that Jesus' act of washing represents a bath that completely cleanses a person (Bultmann, 469–70 n. 2; Brown, 2:566–68; Barrett, 441–42; Schnackenburg, 3:20–22; Beasley-Murray, 229 n. f). The longer reading, then, presumes two washings: one complete and primary, in which the whole body is immersed in water, and one partial and secondary, which involves only the foot washing. The most problematic aspect of this interpretation is that it ostensibly downplays the significance of Jesus' act of washing the disciples' feet, which creates a tension with v. 8 that depicts the foot washing as absolutely necessary. Since, however, good sense can be made of two washings (see Talbert, 200–201), especially considering a distinction in meaning between λούω ("washing of the whole body") and νίπτω ("washing of a part of the body"), the argument for a shorter or longer text cannot be based on the question of which reading "is more intelligible in the context" (*pace* Barrett, 441) but must include the weight of the external evidence, which here favors the longer text.

ἔχει. Pres act ind 3rd sg ἔχω.

χρείαν. Accusative direct object of ἔχει. χρείαν ἔχω (lit. "to have need of") is an idiom for "to need."

τοὺς πόδας. Accusative direct object of νίψασθαι. Fronted for emphasis.

νίψασθαι. Aor mid inf νίπτω (epexegetical to χρείαν).

ἀλλ'. Marker of contrast.

ἔστιν. Pres act ind 3rd sg εἰμί. The enclitic ἐστιν is accented ἔστιν when it comes at the beginning of a sentence, when it expresses existence, or when it follows ἀλλ', εἰ, καί, οὐκ, ὅτι, or τοῦτ'. The third condition is fulfilled here.

καθαρὸς. Predicate adjective. In the FG, καθαρὸς is used only here, in the next verse, and in 15:3.

ὅλος. The adjective ὅλος is here equivalent to the adverb ὅλως, indicating "a degree of totality or completeness" (LN 78.44).

καί. Coordinating conjunction.

ὑμεῖς. Nominative subject of ἐστε. Fronted as a topical frame. Note a shift to the second-person plural address.
καθαροί. Predicate nominative. Fronted for emphasis.
ἐστε. Pres act ind 2nd pl εἰμί.
ἀλλ'. Marker of contrast.
οὐχὶ. A strengthened form of the negative particle οὐ.
πάντες. Nominative subject of an implied ἐστέ (see 13:11, which reproduces the complete sentence).

13:11 ᾔδει γὰρ τὸν παραδιδόντα αὐτόν· διὰ τοῦτο εἶπεν ὅτι οὐχὶ πάντες καθαροί ἐστε.

ᾔδει. Plprf act ind 3rd sg οἶδα. The pluperfect of οἶδα is rendered by the imperfect. This pluperfect has an explicatory function (Campbell 2007, 220).
γὰρ. Postpositive conjunction that introduces the narrator's explanation of Jesus' declaration in the previous verse that not all of his disciples are clean.
τὸν παραδιδόντα. Pres act ptc masc acc sg παραδίδωμι (substantival). Accusative direct object of ᾔδει. The present-tense participle refers to an action that has not yet occurred.
αὐτόν. Accusative direct object of παραδιδόντα. The personal pronoun refers to Jesus.
διὰ τοῦτο. Causal. The demonstrative pronoun is anaphoric, referring to the previous explanatory clause. In this context, the PP διὰ τοῦτο functions as a connective; on this function of διὰ τοῦτο, see 1:31.
εἶπεν. Aor act ind 3rd sg λέγω.
ὅτι. ὅτι-*recitativum* that introduces the clausal complement (direct discourse) of εἶπεν.
οὐχὶ. A strengthened form of the negative particle οὐ.
πάντες. Nominative subject of ἐστε. Fronted for emphasis.
καθαροί. Predicate nominative.
ἐστε. Pres act ind 2nd pl εἰμί.

John 13:12-17

[12]So when he had washed their feet and put on his outer garment and reclined at table again, he said to them, "Do you understand what I have done for you? [13]You call me 'Teacher' and 'Lord,' and you speak rightly, for I am that. [14]If then I, the Lord and the Teacher, have washed your feet, you also ought to wash one another's feet. [15]For I have given you an example so that just as I have done for you, you also should do. [16]Truly,

truly I say to you, a slave is not greater than his master nor a messenger greater than the one who sent him. ¹⁷If you know these things, you are blessed if you do them."

13:12 Ὅτε οὖν ἔνιψεν τοὺς πόδας αὐτῶν [καὶ] ἔλαβεν τὰ ἱμάτια αὐτοῦ καὶ ἀνέπεσεν πάλιν εἶπεν αὐτοῖς· γινώσκετε τί πεποίηκα ὑμῖν;

Ὅτε. Introduces a temporal clause.

οὖν. Postpositive inferential conjunction and/or transitional particle (see 1:22 and 11:6).

ἔνιψεν. Aor act ind 3rd sg νίπτω.

τοὺς πόδας. Accusative direct object of ἔνιψεν.

αὐτῶν. Possessive genitive qualifying πόδας. The personal pronoun refers to the disciples.

[καὶ]. Coordinating conjunction. It is printed within square brackets because the external evidence for its inclusion (B C*,³ D K W Γ Δ Θ $f^{1.13}$ 579 700 892 1424 𝔐 lat sy^h) and exclusion ($\mathfrak{P}^{66}$ ℵ A C² L Ψ 33 1241 *l*844 it vg^s sy^{s,p}) is evenly balanced.

ἔλαβεν. Aor act ind 3rd sg λαμβάνω. In this context, λαμβάνω means not merely "to take along" but also "to put on" an outer garment (LN 49.10, 49 n. 5); see 13:4 on τίθησιν.

τὰ ἱμάτια. Accusative direct object of ἔλαβεν (see 13:4).

αὐτοῦ. Possessive genitive qualifying ἱμάτια. The personal pronoun refers to Jesus.

καὶ. Coordinating conjunction.

ἀνέπεσεν. Aor act ind 3rd sg ἀναπίπτω. The verb means "to recline on a couch to eat" (BDAG, 70.1).

πάλιν. Adverb "pert[aining] to repetition in the same (or similar) manner" (BDAG, 752.2).

εἶπεν. Aor act ind 3rd sg λέγω.

αὐτοῖς. Dative indirect object of εἶπεν.

γινώσκετε. Pres act ind 2nd pl γινώσκω.

τί. Accusative direct object of πεποίηκα.

πεποίηκα. Prf act ind 1st sg ποιέω.

ὑμῖν. Dative of advantage.

13:13 ὑμεῖς φωνεῖτέ με· ὁ διδάσκαλος, καί· ὁ κύριος, καὶ καλῶς λέγετε· εἰμὶ γάρ.

ὑμεῖς. Nominative subject of φωνεῖτέ. Fronted as a topical frame. This verse is connected to the previous one by asyndeton.

φωνεῖτε. Pres act ind 2nd pl φωνέω. φωνεῖτέ, which has a circumflex accent on the penult, acquired an additional accent, the acute, on the ultima from the enclitic με (Smyth §183; Carson 1985, 48).

με. Accusative direct object of φωνεῖτέ.

ὁ διδάσκαλος. Articular nominative used for vocative (BDF §147.3; MHT 1:70; Wallace 1996, 61).

καί. Coordinating conjunction.

ὁ κύριος. Articular nominative used for vocative (BDF §147.3; MHT 1:70; Wallace 1996, 61).

καὶ. Coordinating conjunction.

καλῶς. Adverb of manner. Fronted for emphasis.

λέγετε. Pres act ind 2nd pl λέγω.

εἰμί. Pres act ind 1st sg εἰμί.

γάρ. Postpositive conjunction that introduces Jesus' explanation of why it is right to call him Teacher and Lord.

13:14 εἰ οὖν ἐγὼ ἔνιψα ὑμῶν τοὺς πόδας ὁ κύριος καὶ ὁ διδάσκαλος, καὶ ὑμεῖς ὀφείλετε ἀλλήλων νίπτειν τοὺς πόδας·

εἰ. Introduces the protasis of a first-class condition, which functions as the premise of the *a minore ad maius* rhetorical argument, known as *qal wahomer* (קל וחומר) in the rabbinic literature.

οὖν. Postpositive inferential conjunction and/or transitional particle (see 1:22 and 11:6).

ἐγώ. Nominative subject of ἔνιψα. Fronted as a topical frame.

ἔνιψα. Aor act ind 1st sg νίπτω.

ὑμῶν. Possessive genitive qualifying πόδας. The preposed pronoun is thematically salient (Levinsohn 2000, 64).

τοὺς πόδας. Accusative direct object of ἔνιψα.

ὁ κύριος. Nominative in apposition to ἐγώ.

καί. Coordinating conjunction.

ὁ διδάσκαλος. Nominative in apposition to ἐγώ.

καί. Adverbial use (adjunctive). It marks the beginning of the apodosis of a first-class condition, which functions as the inference of the *a minore ad maius* rhetorical argument (see εἰ above).

ὑμεῖς. Nominative subject of ὀφείλετε. Fronted for emphasis.

ὀφείλετε. Pres act ind 2nd pl ὀφείλω.

ἀλλήλων. Possessive genitive qualifying πόδας. The preposed reciprocal pronoun is thematically salient (Levinsohn 2000, 64).

νίπτειν. Pres act inf νίπτω (complementary).

τοὺς πόδας. Accusative direct object of νίπτειν.

John 13:12-17

13:15 ὑπόδειγμα γὰρ ἔδωκα ὑμῖν ἵνα καθὼς ἐγὼ ἐποίησα ὑμῖν καὶ ὑμεῖς ποιῆτε.

ὑπόδειγμα. Accusative direct object of ἔδωκα. Fronted for emphasis. ὑπόδειγμα here denotes "a model of behavior as an example to be imitated" (LN 58.59). Elsewhere in the NT, the noun is used in this sense in Heb 4:11; Jas 5:10; 2 Pet 2:6.

γὰρ. Postpositive conjunction that introduces the explanation for the previous instruction to wash one another's feet.

ἔδωκα. Aor act ind 1st sg δίδωμι.

ὑμῖν. Dative indirect object of ἔδωκα.

ἵνα. Introduces a purpose clause.

καθὼς . . . καὶ. A point/counterpoint set ("just as . . . also") in which the comparative clause provides a paradigm that should be imitated.

ἐγώ. Nominative subject of ἐποίησα. Fronted as a topical frame.

ἐποίησα. Aor act ind 1st sg ποιέω.

ὑμῖν. Dative of advantage.

ὑμεῖς. Nominative subject of ποιῆτε. Fronted for emphasis.

ποιῆτε. Pres act subj 2nd pl ποιέω. Subjunctive with ἵνα.

13:16 ἀμὴν ἀμὴν λέγω ὑμῖν, οὐκ ἔστιν δοῦλος μείζων τοῦ κυρίου αὐτοῦ οὐδὲ ἀπόστολος μείζων τοῦ πέμψαντος αὐτόν.

ἀμὴν ἀμὴν λέγω ὑμῖν. Metacomment (see 1:51).

ἀμὴν ἀμήν. Asseverative particles that mark the beginning of Jesus' solemn declaration (see 1:51). This verse is connected to the previous one by asyndeton.

λέγω. Pres act ind 1st sg λέγω.

ὑμῖν. Dative indirect object of λέγω.

οὐκ . . . οὐδέ. "Neither . . . nor." οὐδέ is a combination of the negative particle οὐ and the marker of narrative development δέ.

ἔστιν. Pres act ind 3rd sg εἰμί. The enclitic ἐστιν is accented ἔστιν when it comes at the beginning of a sentence, when it expresses existence, or when it follows ἀλλ', εἰ, καί, οὐκ, ὅτι, or τοῦτ'. The third condition is fulfilled here.

δοῦλος. Nominative subject of ἔστιν.

μείζων. Predicate adjective. μείζων is a comparative from μέγας.

τοῦ κυρίου. Genitive of comparison.

αὐτοῦ. Genitive of subordination qualifying κυρίου.

ἀπόστολος. Nominative subject of an implied ἐστίν. This is the only occurrence of this noun in the FG. It is not used here as a technical term for an apostle but as a designation for a messenger without extraordinary status (BDAG, 122.1)

μείζων. Predicate adjective (see above).

τοῦ πέμψαντος. Aor act ptc masc gen sg πέμπω (substantival). Genitive of comparison.

αὐτόν. Accusative direct object of πέμψαντος.

13:17 εἰ ταῦτα οἴδατε, μακάριοί ἐστε ἐὰν ποιῆτε αὐτά.

εἰ. Introduces the protasis of a first-class condition. This verse is connected to the previous one by asyndeton. It combines two types of conditional clauses: (1) a first-class condition, which includes only the protasis (εἰ ταῦτα οἴδατε); and (2) a third-class condition, which begins with the apodosis (μακάριοί ἐστε) followed by the protasis (ἐὰν ποιῆτε αὐτά). In this combination, "the knowledge is assumed as true, the future performance is assumed as possible" (Harris 2015, 245).

ταῦτα. Accusative direct object of οἴδατε. The demonstrative pronoun most likely refers to Jesus' statement in v. 16 that a slave is not greater than his master nor a messenger greater than the one who sent him (Barrett, 444).

οἴδατε. Prf act ind 2nd pl οἶδα (see 1:26 on οἴδατε).

μακάριοί. Predicate adjective, which marks the beginning of the apodosis of a third-class condition. Fronted for emphasis. μακάριοί, which has an acute accent on the antepenult, acquired an additional accent, the acute, on the ultima from the enclitic ἐστε (Smyth §183; Carson 1985, 48).

ἐστε. Pres act ind 2nd pl εἰμί.

ἐάν. Introduces the protasis of a third-class condition.

ποιῆτε. Pres act subj 2nd pl ποιέω. Subjunctive with ἐάν.

αὐτά. Accusative direct object of ποιῆτε. Grammatically, αὐτά refers to ταῦτα in the protasis of a first-class condition. If, however, ταῦτα denotes the knowledge of a hierarchical relationship between slaves and masters as well as messengers and senders, as suggested above, it is not clear how the disciples can *do* these things. Barrett helpfully suggests that this is an *ad sensum* construction, in which v. 16 has a parenthetical function: "If you know that, in view of these considerations and of what you have seen, it is a good thing to wash one another's feet, happy are you if you do it" (444).

John 13:18-20

[18]"I am not speaking about all of you. I know whom I have chosen. But [this has happened] in order that the Scripture may be fulfilled, 'The one who ate my bread has lifted his heel against me.' [19]From now on I am telling you before it happens, so that when it happens you may believe that I am. [20]Truly, truly I say to you, the one who receives anyone I send receives me, and the one who receives me receives the one who sent me."

13:18 Οὐ περὶ πάντων ὑμῶν λέγω· ἐγὼ οἶδα τίνας ἐξελεξάμην· ἀλλ' ἵνα ἡ γραφὴ πληρωθῇ· ὁ τρώγων μου τὸν ἄρτον ἐπῆρεν ἐπ' ἐμὲ τὴν πτέρναν αὐτοῦ.

Οὐ. Negative particle normally used with indicative verbs. This verse is connected to the previous one by asyndeton.

περὶ πάντων ὑμῶν. Reference.

λέγω. Pres act ind 1st sg λέγω.

ἐγὼ. Nominative subject of οἶδα. This clause is connected to the previous one by asyndeton.

οἶδα. Prf act ind 1st sg οἶδα (see 1:26 on οἴδατε).

τίνας. Accusative direct object of ἐξελεξάμην. In indirect discourse, the interrogative pronoun functions like a relative pronoun.

ἐξελεξάμην. Aor mid ind 1st sg ἐκλέγω.

ἀλλ'. Marker of contrast.

ἵνα ἡ γραφὴ πληρωθῇ. This OT introductory formula is used nowhere else in the NT except in the FG, where it occurs four times (13:18; 17:12; 19:24, 36). Three times (here and in 19:24, 36) it precedes the scriptural quotation, and only once (17:12) it follows the scriptural reference. On the variations of this formula in the FG, see 12:38.

ἵνα. Introduces a purpose clause. The ἵνα clause is elliptical, requiring an introduction, such as τοῦτο γέγονεν. Alternatively, but less likely, the ἵνα clause functions as a substitute for the imperative: "But let the Scripture be fulfilled" (Turner 1965, 147–48).

ἡ γραφὴ. Nominative subject of πληρωθῇ.

πληρωθῇ. Aor pass subj 3rd sg πληρόω. Subjunctive with ἵνα.

ὁ τρώγων μου τὸν ἄρτον ἐπῆρεν ἐπ' ἐμὲ τὴν πτέρναν αὐτοῦ. A quotation of Ps 41:10b (LXX Ps 40:10b). John's citation is closer to the Hebrew text (אוֹכֵל לַחְמִי הִגְדִּיל עָלַי עָקֵב ["the one who ate my bread has lifted the heel against me"]) than to the Greek text (ὁ ἐσθίων ἄρτους μου ἐμεγάλυνεν ἐπ' ἐμὲ πτερνισμόν ["the one who ate my breads magnified deception against me"]), but it agrees with neither one exactly.

ὁ τρώγων. Pres act ptc masc nom sg τρώγω (substantival). Nominative subject of ἐπῆρεν. Fronted as a topical frame.

μου. Possessive genitive qualifying τρώγων. The variant reading μετ' ἐμοῦ, though widely attested ($\mathfrak{P}^{66}$ ℵ A D K W Γ Δ Θ Ψ $f^{1.13}$ 33 579 700 1241 1424 𝔐 lat sy et al.), is probably a scribal assimilation to Mark 14:18 (Metzger, 205).

τὸν ἄρτον. Accusative direct object of τρώγων.

ἐπῆρεν. Aor act ind 3rd sg ἐπαίρω.

ἐπ' ἐμὲ. Hostile opposition (BDAG, 366.12.b).

τὴν πτέρναν. Accusative direct object of ἐπῆρεν. πτέρνα ("heel") is a NT *hapax legomenon*, which is here used in an idiomatic expression ἐπαίρω τὴν πτέρναν (lit. "to lift one's heel") to denote antagonism and opposition (LN 8.52; 39.3).

αὐτοῦ. Possessive genitive qualifying πτέρναν.

13:19 ἀπ' ἄρτι λέγω ὑμῖν πρὸ τοῦ γενέσθαι, ἵνα πιστεύσητε ὅταν γένηται ὅτι ἐγώ εἰμι.

ἀπ' ἄρτι. Temporal ("from now on"). Fronted as a temporal frame. This combination of letters (απαρτι) could also be written ἀπαρτί ("exactly, certainly, expressly"; BDAG, 97) or ἀπάρτι ("just now, even now"; BDAG, 97). The parallel in 14:29 (νῦν εἴρηκα ὑμῖν πρὶν γενέσθαι) indicates that ἀπ' ἄρτι here means "now" (Barrett, 445). Elsewhere in the FG, ἀπ' ἄρτι occurs only in 14:7. This verse is connected to the previous one by asyndeton.

λέγω. Pres act ind 1st sg λέγω.

ὑμῖν. Dative indirect object of λέγω.

πρὸ τοῦ. Used with the infinitive to denote time (see γενέσθαι below).

γενέσθαι. Aor mid inf γίνομαι. Used with πρὸ τοῦ to indicate subsequent time. The implied subject of the infinitive is Judas' betrayal.

ἵνα. Introduces a purpose clause.

πιστεύσητε. Aor act subj 2nd pl πιστεύω. Subjunctive with ἵνα.

ὅταν. Introduces an indefinite temporal clause.

γένηται. Aor mid subj 3rd sg γίνομαι. Subjunctive with ὅταν. The implied subject of the verb is Judas' betrayal.

ὅτι. Introduces the clausal complement (indirect discourse) of πιστεύσητε.

ἐγώ. Nominative subject of εἰμι. Fronted for emphasis.

εἰμι. Pres act ind 1st sg εἰμί. In the OT, ἐγώ εἰμι functions as divine self-designation (see LXX Exod 3:14; Isa 41:4; 43:10; 46:4; 48:12).

13:20 ἀμὴν ἀμὴν λέγω ὑμῖν, ὁ λαμβάνων ἄν τινα πέμψω ἐμὲ λαμβάνει, ὁ δὲ ἐμὲ λαμβάνων λαμβάνει τὸν πέμψαντά με.

ἀμὴν ἀμὴν λέγω ὑμῖν. Metacomment (see 1:51).

ἀμὴν ἀμὴν. Asseverative particles that mark the beginning of Jesus' solemn declaration (see 1:51). This verse is connected to the previous one by asyndeton.

λέγω. Pres act ind 1st sg λέγω.

ὑμῖν. Dative indirect object of λέγω.

ὁ λαμβάνων. Pres act ptc masc nom sg λαμβάνω (substantival). Nominative subject of the first λαμβάνει. Fronted as a topical frame.

ἄν. ἄν stands for ἐάν (BDF §107) and introduces the protasis of a third-class condition, whose direct object (τινα) functions as the antecedent of the implied direct object of λαμβάνων. Lit. "if I send anyone, the one who receives him receives me" = "the one who receives anyone I send receives me."

τινα. Accusative direct object of πέμψω.

πέμψω. Aor act subj 1st sg πέμπω.

ἐμὲ. Accusative direct object of the first λαμβάνει. Fronted for emphasis.

λαμβάνει. Pres act ind 3rd sg λαμβάνω.

ὁ . . . λαμβάνων. Pres act ptc masc nom sg λαμβάνω (substantival). Nominative subject of the second λαμβάνει. Fronted as a topical frame.

δὲ. Marker of narrative development.

ἐμὲ. Accusative direct object of λαμβάνων. Fronted for emphasis.

λαμβάνει. Pres act ind 3rd sg λαμβάνω.

τὸν πέμψαντά. Aor act ptc masc acc sg πέμπω (substantival). Accusative direct object of the second λαμβάνει. πέμψαντά, which has an acute accent on the antepenult, acquired an additional accent, the acute, on the ultima from the enclitic με (Smyth §183; Carson 1985, 48). On the use of the participial forms of πέμπω to either identify or describe God in the FG, see τοῦ πέμψαντός in 4:34.

με. Accusative direct object of πέμψαντά.

John 13:21-30

[21]After he had said these things, Jesus was troubled in spirit and testified and said, "Truly, truly I say to you, one of you will betray me." [22]The disciples began looking at one another, being uncertain about whom he was speaking. [23]One of his disciples, whom Jesus loved, was reclining close beside Jesus. [24]Simon Peter therefore nodded to him to ask Jesus who it was about whom he was speaking. [25]So he leaned back accordingly

closer to Jesus' chest and said to him, "Lord, who is it?" [26]Jesus answered, "That is the one for whom I will dip a piece of bread, and I will give it to him." So when he had dipped the piece of bread, he took and gave it to Judas son of Simon Iscariot. [27]And after [Judas received] the piece of bread, then Satan entered into him. Then Jesus said to him, "What you are about to do, do quickly!" [28]Now no one of those reclining at table knew for what purpose he said this to him. [29]For some were thinking that, since Judas had the money-bag, Jesus told him, "Buy what we need for the festival," or that he should give something to the poor. [30]So after he had received the piece of bread, he immediately went out. And it was night.

13:21 Ταῦτα εἰπὼν [ὁ] Ἰησοῦς ἐταράχθη τῷ πνεύματι καὶ ἐμαρτύρησεν καὶ εἶπεν· ἀμὴν ἀμὴν λέγω ὑμῖν ὅτι εἷς ἐξ ὑμῶν παραδώσει με.

Ταῦτα. Accusative direct object of εἰπών. The demonstrative refers to Jesus' speech in vv. 18-20. This verse is connected to the previous one by asyndeton.

εἰπών. Aor act ptc masc nom sg λέγω (temporal). On participles that precede the main verb, see ἐμβλέψας in 1:36.

[ὁ] Ἰησοῦς. Nominative subject of ἐταράχθη, ἐμαρτύρησεν, and εἶπεν. The external evidence for the presence of the article is strong ($\mathfrak{P}^{66c}$ A C D K W Γ Δ Θ Ψ $f^{1.13}$ 33 579 700 892 1241 1424 𝔐 Or), but it is absent in some early manuscripts ($\mathfrak{P}^{66*}$ ℵ B L).

ἐταράχθη. Aor pass ind 3rd sg ταράσσω. On the meaning of the verb, see 11:33 on ἐτάραξεν.

τῷ πνεύματι. Dative of sphere ("in spirit") or dative of respect ("with respect to spirit"). The reference is to Jesus' spirit (see 11:33).

καί. Coordinating conjunction.

ἐμαρτύρησεν. Aor act ind 3rd sg μαρτυρέω.

καὶ εἶπεν. Pleonastic clause under Semitic influence, which functions as a redundant quotative frame (see 1:25 on καὶ εἶπαν αὐτῷ).

καί. Coordinating conjunction.

εἶπεν. Aor act ind 3rd sg λέγω.

ἀμὴν ἀμὴν λέγω ὑμῖν. Metacomment (see 1:51).

ἀμὴν ἀμήν. Asseverative particles that mark the beginning of Jesus' solemn declaration (see 1:51).

λέγω ὑμῖν ὅτι εἷς ἐξ ὑμῶν παραδώσει με. The same formulation of Jesus' prediction of his betrayal is found in Mark 14:18 and Matt 16:21.

λέγω. Pres act ind 1st sg λέγω.

ὑμῖν. Dative indirect object of λέγω.

ὅτι. Introduces the clausal complement (direct discourse [CEB; HCSB; ESV; NIV; NRSV] or indirect discourse [ASV; KJV; LEB; NASB]) of εἶπεν.
εἷς. Nominative subject of παραδώσει.
ἐξ ὑμῶν. Replaces the partitive genitive.
παραδώσει. Fut act ind 3rd sg παραδίδωμι.
με. Accusative direct object of παραδώσει.

13:22 ἔβλεπον εἰς ἀλλήλους οἱ μαθηταὶ ἀπορούμενοι περὶ τίνος λέγει.

ἔβλεπον. Impf act ind 3rd pl βλέπω. On the function of the imperfect in the FG, see 1:39 on ἦν. This verse is connected to the previous one by asyndeton.
εἰς ἀλλήλους. Locative.
οἱ μαθηταί. Nominative subject of ἔβλεπον.
ἀπορούμενοι. Pres mid ptc masc nom pl ἀπορέω (manner). On participles that follow the main verb, see βαπτίζων in 1:31. ἀπορέω means "to be in perplexity, with the implication of serious anxiety—'to be at a loss, to be uncertain, to be anxious, to be in doubt, consternation'" (LN 32.9).
περὶ τίνος. Reference. The PP with the interrogative τίνος introduces the indirect question.
λέγει. Pres act ind 3rd sg λέγω. The present tense is retained from the corresponding direct speech (see 1:39 on μένει).

13:23 ἦν ἀνακείμενος εἷς ἐκ τῶν μαθητῶν αὐτοῦ ἐν τῷ κόλπῳ τοῦ Ἰησοῦ, ὃν ἠγάπα ὁ Ἰησοῦς.

ἦν. Impf act ind 3rd sg εἰμί. This verse is connected to the previous one by asyndeton.
ἀνακείμενος. Pres mid ptc masc nom sg ἀνάκειμαι (imperfect periphrastic). The formulation ἀνάκειμαι ἐν τῷ κόλπῳ is an idiom (lit. "to recline on the bosom") for taking the place of honor at a meal (LN 17.25). This expression means that the Beloved Disciple was at the right of Jesus, since guests would be reclining on their left elbow to have the right hand free for dining.
εἷς. Nominative subject of ἦν.
ἐκ τῶν μαθητῶν. Replaces the partitive genitive.
αὐτοῦ. Genitive of relationship qualifying μαθητῶν.
ἐν τῷ κόλπῳ. Locative (see ἀνακείμενος above). κόλπος denotes "the region of the body extending from the breast to the legs, especially when a person is in a seated position" (LN 8.39).

τοῦ Ἰησοῦ. Possessive genitive qualifying κόλπῳ.

ὅν. Accusative direct object of ἠγάπα. The relative pronoun refers to εἷς ἐκ τῶν μαθητῶν αὐτοῦ.

ἠγάπα. Impf act ind 3rd sg ἀγαπάω. This is the first appearance of the Beloved Disciple in the FG (see 19:26; 20:2; 21:7, 20). The Fourth Evangelist regularly identifies him with the relative clause ὃν ἠγάπα ὁ Ἰησοῦς (13:23; 19:26 [ὃν ἠγάπα]; 21: 7, 20) or ὃν ἐφίλει ὁ Ἰησοῦς (20:2). In all instances the verbs are in the imperfect, which portrays Jesus' love for this disciple as an ongoing process.

ὁ Ἰησοῦς. Nominative subject of ἠγάπα.

13:24 νεύει οὖν τούτῳ Σίμων Πέτρος πυθέσθαι τίς ἂν εἴη περὶ οὗ λέγει.

νεύει. Pres act ind 3rd sg νεύω. The verb means to "nod to someone as a signal" (BDAG, 670). The historical present gives prominence to Peter's signal.

οὖν. Postpositive inferential conjunction. Peter's gesture is presented as consequence of the Beloved Disciple's place at table close to Jesus.

τούτῳ. Dative indirect object of νεύει. The demonstrative pronoun refers to the Beloved Disciple introduced in the previous verse.

Σίμων Πέτρος. Nominative subject of νεύει.

πυθέσθαι. Aor mid inf πυνθάνομαι (purpose).

τίς. Nominative subject of εἴη.

ἄν. Marker of contingency.

εἴη. Pres act opt 3rd sg εἰμί. This is the only optative in the FG.

περὶ οὗ. Reference.

λέγει. Pres act ind 3rd sg λέγω. The present tense is retained from the corresponding direct speech (see 1:39 on μένει).

13:25 ἀναπεσὼν οὖν ἐκεῖνος οὕτως ἐπὶ τὸ στῆθος τοῦ Ἰησοῦ λέγει αὐτῷ· κύριε, τίς ἐστιν;

ἀναπεσών. Aor act ptc masc nom sg ἀναπίπτω (attendant circumstance or temporal). On participles that precede the main verb, see ἐμβλέψας in 1:36. The expression ἀναπίπτω ἐπὶ τὸ στῆθος (lit. "to lie down on the chest") is a synonym for ἀνάκειμαι ἐν τῷ κόλπῳ in v. 23, functioning as another idiom for taking the place of honor at a meal, which the Fourth Evangelist uses for the sake of variety (LN 17.25). Since, however, v. 23 uses the present participle of ἀνάκειμαι, while this verse uses the aorist participle of ἀναπίπτω, it is possible to understand the entire expression here more literally: "He moved closer to the side (of Jesus)" (LN 17.25) or "He leaned back from where he lay" (BDAG, 70.2).

οὖν. Postpositive inferential conjunction and/or transitional particle (see 1:22 and 11:6).

ἐκεῖνος. Nominative subject of λέγει. The demonstrative pronoun refers to the Beloved Disciple introduced in v. 23, acting as a third-person personal pronoun with a simple anaphoric force (Wallace 1996, 328–29).

οὕτως. Adverb of manner, which refers to what precedes ("accordingly") or indicates an action "to the exclusion of other considerations, *without further ado*" (BDAG, 742.4).

ἐπὶ τὸ στῆθος. Locative.

τοῦ Ἰησοῦ. Possessive genitive qualifying στῆθος.

λέγει. Pres act ind 3rd sg λέγω. Historical present (see 13:4 on ἐγείρεται).

αὐτῷ. Dative indirect object of λέγει.

κύριε. Vocative of direct address.

τίς. Predicate nominative. "Interrogatives, by their nature, indicate the unknown component and hence cannot be the subject" (Wallace 1996, 40 n. 12).

ἐστιν. Pres act ind 3rd sg εἰμί.

13:26 ἀποκρίνεται [ὁ] Ἰησοῦς· ἐκεῖνός ἐστιν ᾧ ἐγὼ βάψω τὸ ψωμίον καὶ δώσω αὐτῷ. βάψας οὖν τὸ ψωμίον [λαμβάνει καὶ] δίδωσιν Ἰούδᾳ Σίμωνος Ἰσκαριώτου.

ἀποκρίνεται. Pres mid ind 3rd sg ἀποκρίνομαι. Historical present (see 13:4 on ἐγείρεται). This verse is connected to the previous one by asyndeton.

[ὁ] Ἰησοῦς. Nominative subject of ἀποκρίνεται. The article is attested in some manuscripts (ℵ* A C³ K Γ Δ Θ Ψ *f*¹ 33 565 700 1241 𝔐) but absent from others (𝔓⁶⁶ B W 579ᵛⁱᵈ).

ἐκεῖνός. Nominative subject of ἐστιν. The anaphoric demonstrative refers to a disciple who will betray Jesus (see v. 21), whose identity will be revealed. ἐκεῖνός, which has a circumflex accent on the penult, acquired an additional accent, the acute, on the ultima from the enclitic ἐστιν (Smyth §183; Carson 1985, 48).

ἐστιν. Pres act ind 3rd sg εἰμί.

ᾧ. Introduces a headless relative clause that, in its entirety (ᾧ ἐγὼ βάψω τὸ ψωμίον καὶ δώσω αὐτῷ), serves as the predicate nominative. Within its clause, ᾧ is the dative of advantage vis-à-vis βάψω ("for whom I will dip a piece of bread").

ἐγώ. Nominative subject of βάψω. Fronted as a topical frame.

βάψω. Fut act ind 1st sg βάπτω.

τὸ ψωμίον. Accusative direct object of βάψω and δώσω. ψωμίον denotes "a small piece or bit of bread" (LN 5.4).

καὶ. Coordinating conjunction.

δώσω. Fut act ind 1st sg δίδωμι.

αὐτῷ. Dative indirect object of δώσω. If the function of this dative is regarded to be identical to the function of the relative pronoun ᾧ, αὐτῷ could be seen as a pleonastic personal pronoun under Semitic influence (BDF §297; Harris 2015, 249; Barrett, 447). If, however, these two datives have different functions, as I am suggesting (see ᾧ above), αὐτῷ is not redundant with ᾧ.

βάψας. Aor act ptc masc nom sg βάπτω (temporal). On participles that precede the main verb, see ἐμβλέψας in 1:36.

οὖν. Postpositive inferential conjunction and/or transitional particle (see 1:22 and 11:6).

τὸ ψωμίον. Accusative direct object of βάψας.

[λαμβάνει καὶ]. These two words are placed within square brackets because it is not easy to decide whether they are included in some manuscripts (ℵ²ᵃ B C L 33 892 1241 syʰᵐᵍ Or) because the copyists wanted to allude to Jesus' taking of bread at the Last Supper (Matt 26:26; Mark 14:22; Luke 22:19; 1 Cor 11:23) or whether they are excluded from others (𝔓⁶⁶⁽*⁾·ᶜ ℵ*·²ᵇ A D K W Γ Δ Θ Ψ f¹·¹³ 565 579 700 1424 𝔐 lat syʰ) because the copyists considered them unnecessary (Metzger, 205).

λαμβάνει. Pres act ind 3rd sg λαμβάνω. The historical present calls attention to Jesus' act that identifies his betrayer.

καὶ. Coordinating conjunction.

δίδωσιν. Pres act ind 3rd sg δίδωμι. The historical present calls attention to Jesus' act that identifies his betrayer.

Ἰούδᾳ. Dative indirect object of δίδωσιν.

Σίμωνος Ἰσκαριώτου. Genitive of relationship in an elliptical construction ("[the son] of Simon Iscariot"); see 6:71; 13:2; 21:15.

13:27 καὶ μετὰ τὸ ψωμίον τότε εἰσῆλθεν εἰς ἐκεῖνον ὁ σατανᾶς. λέγει οὖν αὐτῷ ὁ Ἰησοῦς· ὃ ποιεῖς ποίησον τάχιον.

καὶ. Coordinating conjunction.

μετὰ τὸ ψωμίον. Temporal ("after the piece of bread" = "after Judas received the piece of bread"). The PP stands in a left-dislocation and is resumed by the temporal adverb τότε (Runge 2010, 300).

τότε. Adverb of time, which resumes the PP μετὰ τὸ ψωμίον. Fronted for emphasis. On the function of the resumptive element, see 7:10 on τότε.

εἰσῆλθεν. Aor act ind 3rd sg εἰσέρχομαι.

εἰς ἐκεῖνον. Locative. The demonstrative pronoun refers to Judas.

ὁ σατανᾶς. Nominative subject of εἰσῆλθεν. This is the only occurrence of this noun in the FG. John typically uses the term διάβολός (6:70; 8:44; 13:2).

λέγει. Pres act ind 3rd sg λέγω. Historical present (see 13:4 on ἐγείρεται).

οὖν. Postpositive inferential conjunction and/or transitional particle (see 1:22 and 11:6).

αὐτῷ. Dative indirect object of λέγει.

ὁ Ἰησοῦς. Nominative subject of λέγει.

ὅ. Introduces a headless relative clause that, in its entirety (ὃ ποιεῖς), serves as the direct object of ποίησον. Within its clause, ὅ is the direct object of ποιεῖς.

ποιεῖς. Pres act ind 2nd sg ποιέω. The context indicates that the present tense refers to an action that is intended but not yet performed.

ποίησον. Aor act impv 2nd sg ποιέω.

τάχιον. Temporal adverb "with focus on speed of action" (BDAG, 992.1). τάχιον is a comparative of ταχέως, whose sense here is probably positive ("quickly, soon, without delay"; cf. BDAG, 992.1.b.β; MHT 3:30), but it could also be a true comparative, with the object of comparison deduced from the context ("more quickly than Judas would have done but for the exposure" [Robertson, 664]), or elative ("as quickly as possible"; cf. BDF §244.1; Zerwick §150).

13:28 τοῦτο [δὲ] οὐδεὶς ἔγνω τῶν ἀνακειμένων πρὸς τί εἶπεν αὐτῷ·

τοῦτο. Accusative direct object of εἶπεν. The demonstrative pronoun is anaphoric, referring to Jesus' words to Judas in v. 27.

[δὲ]. Marker of narrative development. It is within square brackets because some early manuscripts do not include it (B W Ψ 579 sa[ms] bo[ms]).

οὐδεὶς. Nominative subject of ἔγνω. Fronted for emphasis.

ἔγνω. Aor act ind 3rd sg γινώσκω.

τῶν ἀνακειμένων. Pres mid/pass ptc masc gen pl ἀνάκειμαι (substantival). Partitive genitive qualifying οὐδείς.

πρὸς τί. Purpose (BDF §239.7).

εἶπεν. Aor act ind 3rd sg λέγω.

αὐτῷ. Dative indirect object of εἶπεν.

13:29 τινὲς γὰρ ἐδόκουν, ἐπεὶ τὸ γλωσσόκομον εἶχεν Ἰούδας, ὅτι λέγει αὐτῷ [ὁ] Ἰησοῦς· ἀγόρασον ὧν χρείαν ἔχομεν εἰς τὴν ἑορτήν, ἢ τοῖς πτωχοῖς ἵνα τι δῷ.

τινὲς. Nominative subject of ἐδόκουν.

γὰρ. Postpositive conjunction that introduces the rationale for the previous comment, which demonstrates that the disciples were in the dark regarding the meaning and purpose of Jesus' instruction to Judas.

ἐδόκουν. Impf act ind 3rd pl δοκέω. On the function of the imperfect in the FG, see 1:39 on ἦν.

ἐπεὶ. Causal conjunction.

τὸ γλωσσόκομον. Accusative direct object of εἶχεν (see 12:6). Fronted for emphasis.

εἶχεν. Impf act ind 3rd sg ἔχω.

Ἰούδας. Nominative subject of εἶχεν.

ὅτι. Introduces the clausal complement (indirect discourse) of ἐδόκουν.

λέγει. Pres act ind 3rd sg λέγω. The present tense is retained from the corresponding direct discourse (see 1:39 on μένει).

αὐτῷ. Dative indirect object of λέγει.

[ὁ] Ἰησοῦς. Nominative subject of λέγει. The article is missing in Sinaiticus and Vaticanus.

ἀγόρασον. Aor act impv 2nd sg ἀγοράζω.

ὧν. Introduces a headless relative clause that, in its entirety (ὧν χρείαν ἔχομεν), serves as the direct object of ἀγόρασον. Within its clause, ὧν is the objective genitive qualifying χρείαν ("what we need").

χρείαν. Accusative direct object of ἔχομεν. Fronted for emphasis.

ἔχομεν. Pres act ind 1st pl ἔχω.

εἰς τὴν ἑορτήν. Purpose.

ἢ. Marker of an alternative/disjunctive particle (BDAG, 432.1).

τοῖς πτωχοῖς. Dative indirect object of δῷ. τοῖς πτωχοῖς is placed before ἵνα for emphasis because the elements that belong to a dependent clause normally come after the subordinating conjunction (BDF §475.1).

ἵνα. Introduces an imperatival clause (Wallace 1996, 476–77).

τι. Accusative direct object of δῷ.

δῷ. Aor act subj 3rd sg δίδωμι. Subjunctive with ἵνα.

13:30 λαβὼν οὖν τὸ ψωμίον ἐκεῖνος ἐξῆλθεν εὐθύς. ἦν δὲ νύξ.

λαβών. Aor act ptc masc nom sg λαμβάνω (temporal). On participles that precede the main verb, see ἐμβλέψας in 1:36.

οὖν. Postpositive inferential conjunction and/or transitional particle (see 1:22 and 11:6).

τὸ ψωμίον. Accusative direct object of λαβών.

ἐκεῖνος. Nominative subject of ἐξῆλθεν. The demonstrative pronoun refers to Ἰούδας from the previous verse, acting as a third-person personal pronoun with a simple anaphoric force (Wallace 1996, 328–29).

ἐξῆλθεν. Aor act ind 3rd sg ἐξέρχομαι.

εὐθύς. Temporal adverb.

ἦν. Impf act ind 3rd sg εἰμί. On the function of the imperfect in the FG, see 1:39 on ἦν.

δέ. Marker of narrative development.

νύξ. Nominative subject of ἦν.

John 13:31-35

[31]So when he went out, Jesus said, "Now the Son of Man is glorified, and God is glorified in him. [32]If God is glorified in him, God will also glorify him in himself and will glorify him immediately. [33]Little children, yet a little while I am with you. You will seek me, and just as I said to the Jews, 'Where I am going you cannot come,' now I say also to you. [34]I give you a new commandment that you love one another. Just as I have loved you, you also should love one another. [35]By this all people will know that you are my disciples, if you have love among yourselves."

13:31 Ὅτε οὖν ἐξῆλθεν, λέγει Ἰησοῦς· νῦν ἐδοξάσθη ὁ υἱὸς τοῦ ἀνθρώπου καὶ ὁ θεὸς ἐδοξάσθη ἐν αὐτῷ·

Ὅτε. Introduces a temporal clause, which is fronted as a temporal frame.

οὖν. Postpositive inferential conjunction and/or transitional particle (see 1:22 and 11:6).

ἐξῆλθεν. Aor act ind 3rd sg ἐξέρχομαι.

λέγει. Pres act ind 3rd sg λέγω. Historical present (see 13:4 on ἐγείρεται).

Ἰησοῦς. Nominative subject of λέγει.

νῦν. Temporal adverb focusing on time coextensive with the event of the narrative (BDAG, 681.1.a). Fronted for emphasis.

ἐδοξάσθη. Aor pass ind 3rd sg δοξάζω. The primary agent of the verb is not expressed. In this context, glorification refers to Jesus' death and resurrection (see 7:39; 12:16, 23; 13:32; 17:1; on δοξάζω as a double entendre, see 7:39). Because of the temporal marker νῦν ("now"), Porter (1994, 36) regards ἐδοξάσθη as an "aorist for present action." Fanning (269–73) and Wallace (1996, 563–64), however, call it a "proleptic or futuristic aorist" because it describes a future event as if it has already occurred. Fanning (274) adds that this aorist portrays Jesus' glorification as an action that has already started but is not yet completed, though its completion is viewed as certain (see 7:39, which asserts that Jesus was not yet glorified). According to Caragounis, the use of the aorist ἐδοξάσθη to indicate that Jesus' glorification through the cross has already begun "finds its explanation in the fact that the aorist indicative can be used to underscore the *certainty* and *imminence* of an action which will take place sometime in the future" (2004, 275). The key to understanding this and other similar declarations that present salvation and its consequences as though they have already been completed (e.g., ἐγὼ νενίκηκα τὸν κόσμον [16:33]; ὁ ἄρχων τοῦ κόσμου τούτου κέκριται [16:11]) is provided, as Frey explains, "by statements for which the only possible explanation is that a post-Easter perspective has penetrated into the words of the pre-Easter Jesus" (2018, 83).

ὁ υἱὸς. Nominative subject of the first ἐδοξάσθη.
τοῦ ἀνθρώπου. Genitive of relationship qualifying υἱὸς.
καὶ. Coordinating conjunction.
ὁ θεὸς. Nominative subject of the second ἐδοξάσθη.
ἐδοξάσθη. Aor pass ind 3rd sg δοξάζω. The primary agent of the verb is again not expressed. For the temporal reference of the verb, see ἐδοξάσθη above.
ἐν αὐτῷ. Locative. The personal pronoun refers to the Son of Man.

13:32 [εἰ ὁ θεὸς ἐδοξάσθη ἐν αὐτῷ], καὶ ὁ θεὸς δοξάσει αὐτὸν ἐν αὐτῷ, καὶ εὐθὺς δοξάσει αὐτόν.

[εἰ ὁ θεὸς ἐδοξάσθη ἐν αὐτῷ]. This clause is absent from several early, and quite diversified, manuscripts ($\mathfrak{P}^{66}$ ℵ* B C* D L W 1 579 it vg^{mss} sy$^{s.h}$ ly cw bo^{pt}), but the priority of the shorter text is not thereby established because this could have been an inadvertent omission caused by homoeoteleuton in vv. 31b-32a (καὶ ὁ θεὸς ἐδοξάσθη ἐν αὐτῷ εἰ ὁ θεὸς ἐδοξάσθη ἐν αὐτῷ) or a deliberate erasure because of a presumed redundancy of these two clauses (Metzger, 206). Because of these uncertainties, the UBS committee decided to print this clause within square brackets.

εἰ. Introduces the protasis of a first-class condition.

ὁ θεὸς. Nominative subject of ἐδοξάσθη.

ἐδοξάσθη. Aor pass ind 3rd sg δοξάζω. On the meaning of the verb, see 13:31.

ἐν αὐτῷ. Locative. Like in v. 31, the personal pronoun refers to the Son of Man.

καί. Adverbial use (adjunctive). It marks the beginning of the apodosis of a first-class condition.

ὁ θεὸς. Nominative subject of δοξάσει.

δοξάσει. Fut act ind 3rd sg δοξάζω. Barrett relates the clause καὶ ὁ θεὸς δοξάσει αὐτὸν ἐν αὐτῷ in this verse to Jesus' prayer in 17:5: "The glory achieved by Jesus in his death on the cross is sealed by his exaltation to the glory which he had with the Father before the world was" (450). On δοξάζω as a double entendre, see 7:39 on ἐδοξάσθη.

αὐτόν. Accusative direct object of δοξάσει.

ἐν αὐτῷ. Locative. This reading is attested in the earliest manuscript tradition ($\mathfrak{P}^{66}$ ℵ*·2b B), although it is not clear whether the breathing should be smooth (αὐτῷ) or rough (αὑτῷ). The variant ἐν ἑαυτῷ (ℵ²ᵃ A D K L W Γ Δ Θ Ψ $f^{1.13}$ 33 565 700 892 1241 1424 *l*844 𝔐) is probably a scribal modification to clarify that the pronoun refers to God.

καί. Coordinating conjunction.

εὐθὺς. Temporal adverb. Fronted for emphasis.

δοξάσει. Fut act ind 3rd sg δοξάζω.

αὐτόν. Accusative direct object of δοξάσει.

13:33 τεκνία, ἔτι μικρὸν μεθ' ὑμῶν εἰμι· ζητήσετέ με, καὶ καθὼς εἶπον τοῖς Ἰουδαίοις ὅτι ὅπου ἐγὼ ὑπάγω ὑμεῖς οὐ δύνασθε ἐλθεῖν, καὶ ὑμῖν λέγω ἄρτι.

τεκνία. Vocative of direct address. τεκνίον is a diminutive of τέκνον. This is the only occurrence of this form of address in the FG, but it is frequent in 1 John (2:1, 12, 28; 3:7, 18; 4:4; 5:21). This verse is connected to the previous one by asyndeton.

ἔτι. Adverb ("still").

μικρὸν. Adverbial accusative ("a short time, a little while" [BDAG, 651.1.d.β]).

μεθ' ὑμῶν. Association/accompaniment.

εἰμι. Pres act ind 1st sg εἰμί.

ζητήσετέ. Fut act ind 2nd pl ζητέω. ζητήσετέ, which has an acute accent on the antepenult, acquired an additional accent, the acute, on the ultima from the enclitic με (Smyth §183; Carson 1985, 48). This clause is connected to the previous one by asyndeton.

John 13:32-34

με. Accusative direct object of ζητήσετέ.
καί. Coordinating conjunction.
καθὼς ... καί. A point/counterpoint set ("just as ... also") that compares Jesus' declaration to the Jews with his declaration to his disciples.
εἶπον. Aor act ind 1st sg λέγω.
τοῖς Ἰουδαίοις. Dative indirect object of εἶπον.
ὅτι. ὅτι-*recitativum* that introduces the clausal complement (direct discourse) of εἶπον.
ὅπου. Marker of a position in space.
ἐγώ. Nominative subject of ὑπάγω.
ὑπάγω. Pres act ind 1st sg ὑπάγω. On the use of ὑπάγω in chs. 13–16, see 13:3 on ὑπάγει.
ὑμεῖς. Nominative subject of δύνασθε.
οὐ. Negative particle normally used with indicative verbs.
δύνασθε. Pres mid ind 2nd pl δύναμαι.
ἐλθεῖν. Aor act inf ἔρχομαι (complementary).
ὑμῖν. Dative indirect object of λέγω.
λέγω. Pres act ind 1st sg λέγω.
ἄρτι. Adverb of time.

13:34 Ἐντολὴν καινὴν δίδωμι ὑμῖν, ἵνα ἀγαπᾶτε ἀλλήλους, καθὼς ἠγάπησα ὑμᾶς ἵνα καὶ ὑμεῖς ἀγαπᾶτε ἀλλήλους.

Ἐντολὴν καινήν. Accusative direct object of δίδωμι. The adjective καινήν stands in the fourth attributive position (see 3:15 on ζωὴν αἰώνιον). Ἐντολὴν καινήν functions as a forward-pointing reference to the ἵνα clause that follows (see 8:41 on ἕνα πατέρα). This verse is connected to the previous one by asyndeton.
δίδωμι. Pres act ind 1st sg δίδωμι.
ὑμῖν. Dative indirect object of δίδωμι.
ἵνα. Introduces an epexegetical clause that explains Ἐντολὴν καινήν. In classical Greek, an epexegetical ἵνα clause is equivalent to an epexegetical infinitive (Wallace 1996, 476; BDF §379; Brown, 2:607; Barrett, 452). Even though this ἵνα clause could also be understood as imperatival in force (Zerwick §415; Beasley-Murray, 242 n. b; Caragounis 2004, 220), it is probably better to classify it as epexegetical because it does not function independently (cf. the second ἵνα clause in this verse) but provides the content of the nominal phrase in the main clause.
ἀγαπᾶτε. Pres act subj 2nd pl ἀγαπάω. Subjunctive with ἵνα.
ἀλλήλους. Accusative direct object of ἀγαπᾶτε. ἀλλήλων is a reciprocal pronoun that "is used to indicate an interchange between two or

more groups. It is thus always *plural* and . . . occurs only in the oblique cases" (Wallace 1996, 351), as here.

καθὼς . . . καί. A point/counterpoint set ("just as . . . also") in which the comparative clause provides a paradigm that should be imitated.

ἠγάπησα. Aor act ind 1st sg ἀγαπάω. This aorist verb form does not refer to Jesus' present love for his disciples, as Porter claims (1989, 227), but "must refer complexively to the example Jesus set in his three-year association with the disciples, as he seeks to prepare them for his departure" (McKay 1992, 219).

ὑμᾶς. Accusative direct object of ἠγάπησα.

ἵνα. Introduces an imperatival clause that conveys Jesus' instruction. While some scholars suggest that this is a purpose (final) clause ("I have loved you in order that you also love one another"; cf. Brown, 2:607; Harris 2015, 252), the καθὼς . . . καί construction indicates that the ἵνα clause functions as an imperatival counterpoint of the comparative clause.

ὑμεῖς. Nominative subject of ἀγαπᾶτε. Fronted for emphasis.

ἀγαπᾶτε. Pres act subj 2nd pl ἀγαπάω. Subjunctive with ἵνα.

ἀλλήλους. Accusative direct object of ἀγαπᾶτε.

13:35 ἐν τούτῳ γνώσονται πάντες ὅτι ἐμοὶ μαθηταί ἐστε, ἐὰν ἀγάπην ἔχητε ἐν ἀλλήλοις.

ἐν τούτῳ. Instrumental. The PP marks the beginning of the apodosis of a third-class condition, which here precedes the protasis. This verse is connected to the previous one by asyndeton.

γνώσονται. Fut mid ind 3rd pl γινώσκω.

πάντες. Nominative subject of γνώσονται.

ὅτι. Introduces the clausal complement (indirect discourse) of γνώσονται.

ἐμοί. Dative of possession ("disciples belonging to me") or dative of advantage ("disciples for me"). Fronted for emphasis.

μαθηταί. Predicate nominative. Fronted for emphasis. This preverbal predicate nominative is most likely qualitative because mutual love is the identifying mark of discipleship rather than of the particular disciples.

ἐστε. Pres act ind 2nd pl εἰμί.

ἐάν. Introduces the protasis of a third-class condition.

ἀγάπην. Accusative direct object of ἔχητε. Fronted for emphasis.

ἔχητε. Pres act subj 2nd pl ἔχω. Subjunctive with ἐάν.

ἐν ἀλλήλοις. Locative, i.e., "the sphere in which love is exercised" (Harris 2015, 252; Turner 1965, 121) or, if ἐν stands for εἰς, advantage ("for one another").

John 13:36-38

³⁶Simon Peter said to him, "Lord, where are you going?" Jesus answered him, "Where I am going you cannot follow me now, but you will follow later." ³⁷Peter said to him, "Lord, why can I not follow you now? I will lay down my life for you." ³⁸Jesus answered, "Will you lay down your life for me? Truly, truly I say to you, the rooster will not crow until you have denied me three times."

13:36 Λέγει αὐτῷ Σίμων Πέτρος· κύριε, ποῦ ὑπάγεις; ἀπεκρίθη [αὐτῷ] Ἰησοῦς· ὅπου ὑπάγω οὐ δύνασαί μοι νῦν ἀκολουθῆσαι, ἀκολουθήσεις δὲ ὕστερον.

Λέγει. Pres act ind 3rd sg λέγω. The historical present marks the narrative transition to a new scene (Battle, 128). This verse is connected to the previous one by asyndeton.

αὐτῷ. Dative indirect object of Λέγει.

Σίμων Πέτρος. Nominative subject of Λέγει.

κύριε. Vocative of direct address.

ποῦ. Interrogative adverb of place.

ὑπάγεις. Pres act ind 2nd sg ὑπάγω. On the use of ὑπάγω in chs. 13–16, see 13:3 on ὑπάγει.

ἀπεκρίθη. Aor mid ind 3rd sg ἀποκρίνομαι. On the voice, see "Deponency" in the Series Introduction. This clause is connected to the previous one by asyndeton.

[αὐτῷ]. Dative indirect object of ἀπεκρίθη. The personal pronoun is placed within square brackets despite the strong external support for its inclusion ($\mathfrak{P}^{66}$ ℵ A C³ D K W Γ Δ Θ Ψ $f^{1.13}$ 33 565 1241 1424 𝔐 et al.) because it is omitted in some early, and quite diverse, manuscripts (B C* L lat sa^ms pbo bo).

Ἰησοῦς. Nominative subject of ἀπεκρίθη.

ὅπου. Marker of a position in space.

ὑπάγω. Pres act ind 1st sg ὑπάγω.

οὐ. Negative particle normally used with indicative verbs.

δύνασαί. Pres mid ind 2nd sg δύναμαι. δύνασαί, which has an acute accent on the antepenult, acquired an additional accent, the acute, on the ultima from the enclitic μοι (Smyth §183; Carson 1985, 48).

μοι. Dative direct object of ἀκολουθῆσαι.

νῦν. Temporal adverb focusing on time coextensive with the event of the narrative (BDAG, 681.1.a). Fronted for emphasis.

ἀκολουθῆσαι. Aor act inf ἀκολουθέω (complementary).

ἀκολουθήσεις. Fut act ind 2nd sg ἀκολουθέω.

δέ. Marker of narrative development.

ὕστερον. Adverbial accusative, which indicates "a point of time that is subsequent to another point of time" (BDAG, 1044.2).

13:37 λέγει αὐτῷ ὁ Πέτρος· κύριε, διὰ τί οὐ δύναμαί σοι ἀκολουθῆσαι ἄρτι; τὴν ψυχήν μου ὑπὲρ σοῦ θήσω.

λέγει. Pres act ind 3rd sg λέγω. Historical present (see 13:4 on ἐγείρεται). This verse is connected to the previous one by asyndeton.

αὐτῷ. Dative indirect object of λέγει.

ὁ Πέτρος. Nominative subject of λέγει.

κύριε. Vocative of direct address.

διὰ τί. Causal.

οὐ. Negative particle normally used with indicative verbs.

δύναμαί. Pres mid ind 1st sg δύναμαι. δύναμαί, which has an acute accent on the antepenult, acquired an additional accent, the acute, on the ultima from the enclitic σοι (Smyth §183; Carson 1985, 48).

σοι. Dative direct object of ἀκολουθῆσαι.

ἀκολουθῆσαι. Aor act inf ἀκολουθέω (complementary).

ἄρτι. Adverb of time that refers to the immediate present ("at once, immediately, now" [BDAG, 136.1]).

τὴν ψυχήν. Accusative direct object of θήσω. Fronted for emphasis. This clause is connected to the previous one by asyndeton.

μου. Possessive genitive qualifying ψυχήν.

ὑπὲρ σοῦ. Substitution ("instead of you"). For other prepositional phrases with ὑπέρ in the FG, see 6:51; 10:11, 15; 11:50, 51, 52; 13:38; 15:13; 17:19; 18:14.

θήσω. Fut act ind 1st sg τίθημι. The expression τὴν ψυχήν τίθημι (lit. "to lay down one's life") is an idiom for "to die, with the implication of voluntary or willing action" (LN 23.113).

13:38 ἀποκρίνεται Ἰησοῦς· τὴν ψυχήν σου ὑπὲρ ἐμοῦ θήσεις; ἀμὴν ἀμὴν λέγω σοι, οὐ μὴ ἀλέκτωρ φωνήσῃ ἕως οὗ ἀρνήσῃ με τρίς.

ἀποκρίνεται. Pres mid ind 3rd sg ἀποκρίνομαι. Historical present (see 13:4 on ἐγείρεται). This verse is connected to the previous one by asyndeton.

Ἰησοῦς. Nominative subject of ἀποκρίνεται.

τὴν ψυχήν. Accusative direct object of θήσεις. Fronted as a topical frame.

σου. Possessive genitive qualifying ψυχήν.

ὑπὲρ ἐμοῦ. Substitution ("instead of me"). For other prepositional phrases with ὑπέρ in the FG, see 6:51; 10:11, 15; 11:50, 51, 52; 13:37; 15:13; 17:19; 18:14.

θήσεις. Fut act ind 2nd sg τίθημι. On the meaning of the expression τὴν ψυχήν τίθημι, see the previous verse. The verb stands in final, emphatic position.

ἀμὴν ἀμὴν λέγω σοι. Metacomment (see 1:51).

ἀμὴν ἀμὴν. Asseverative particles that mark the beginning of Jesus' solemn declaration (see 1:51). This clause is connected to the previous one by asyndeton.

λέγω. Pres act ind 1st sg λέγω.

σοι. Dative indirect object of λέγω.

οὐ μὴ. Emphatic negation, which is usually followed by the aorist subjunctive.

ἀλέκτωρ. Nominative subject of φωνήσῃ.

φωνήσῃ. Aor act subj 3rd sg φωνέω. Used with οὐ μὴ to express emphatic negation.

ἕως οὗ. Temporal (BDAG, 423.1.b.β.ℵ). In this idiomatic PP, ἕως serves as an improper preposition (see 1:3 on χωρὶς αὐτοῦ). ἕως οὗ is an abbreviated version for ἕως τοῦ χρόνου ᾧ ("until the time at which"), in which the relative pronoun is attracted to the case of its omitted antecedent (Harris 2015, 254).

ἀρνήσῃ. Aor mid subj 2nd sg ἀρνέομαι. Subjunctive in indefinite temporal clause (Wallace 1996, 479).

με. Accusative direct object of ἀρνήσῃ.

τρίς. Adverb of measure ("three times").

John 14:1-7

¹"Let not your hearts be troubled. Believe in God; believe also in me. ²In my Father's house are many dwelling places. If it were not so, would I have told you that I go to prepare a place for you? ³And if I go and prepare a place for you, I will come again and will take you to myself, so that where I am you may be also. ⁴And you know the way to where I am going." ⁵Thomas said to him, "Lord, we do not know where you are going. How can we know the way?" ⁶Jesus said to him, "I am the way, and the truth, and the life. No one comes to the Father except through me. ⁷If you have known me, you will know my Father also. And from now on you do know him, and you have seen him."

John 14:1-7

14:1 Μὴ ταρασσέσθω ὑμῶν ἡ καρδία· πιστεύετε εἰς τὸν θεὸν καὶ εἰς ἐμὲ πιστεύετε.

Μὴ. Negative particle normally used with non-indicative verbs. This verse is connected to the previous one by asyndeton.

ταρασσέσθω. Pres pass impv 3rd sg ταράσσω. On the meaning of the verb, see 11:33 on ἐτάραξεν.

ὑμῶν. Possessive genitive qualifying καρδία. The preposed pronoun is thematically salient (Levinsohn 2000, 64).

ἡ καρδία. Nominative subject of ταρασσέσθω. ἡ καρδία is a distributive singular.

πιστεύετε. Pres act impv (or ind) 2nd pl πιστεύω. This clause is connected to the previous one by asyndeton. Since both cases of πιστεύετε in this verse could be either imperatives or indicatives, the sentence πιστεύετε εἰς τὸν θεὸν καὶ εἰς ἐμὲ πιστεύετε can be translated in several ways: (1) "Believe in God; believe also in me" (if both verbs are imperatives; cf. NRSV; ASV; HCSB; REB; Schnackenburg, 3:57); (2) "You believe in God and you believe in me" (if both verbs are indicatives); (3) "(If) you believe in God, you (will) also believe in me" (if the first clause is construed as an imperatival condition and the second as an apodosis introduced by καί; cf. Barrett, 456); (4) "You believe in God; believe also in me" (if the first verb is indicative and the second verb is imperative; cf. LEB; NET; Brown, 2:617); (5) "Do you believe in God? Then believe also in me" (if the first verb is indicative and the clause is construed as a question; cf. Bultmann, 600). My translation reflects option (1).

εἰς τὸν θεὸν. Goal of actions or feelings directed toward someone (BDAG, 290.4.c.β). For πιστεύειν εἰς + accusative ("trust or believe in someone"), see 1:12 on εἰς τὸ ὄνομα.

καὶ. Adverbial use (adjunctive) (ASV; CEB; ESV; KJV; LEB; NASB; NIV; NRSV), but some translations regard it is as a coordinating conjunction (GNT; NCV).

εἰς ἐμὲ. See εἰς τὸν θεὸν above. Fronted for emphasis.

πιστεύετε. Pres act impv (or ind) 2nd pl πιστεύω.

14:2 ἐν τῇ οἰκίᾳ τοῦ πατρός μου μοναὶ πολλαί εἰσιν· εἰ δὲ μή, εἶπον ἂν ὑμῖν ὅτι πορεύομαι ἑτοιμάσαι τόπον ὑμῖν;

ἐν τῇ οἰκίᾳ. Locative. Fronted as a spatial frame. This verse is connected to the previous one by asyndeton.

τοῦ πατρός. Possessive genitive qualifying οἰκίᾳ.

μου. Genitive of relationship qualifying πατρός.

μοναὶ πολλαί. Nominative subject of εἰσιν. μονή refers to "a place where one may remain or dwell" (LN 85.76). Fronted for emphasis.

εἰσιν. Pres act ind 3rd pl εἰμί.

εἰ δὲ μή. A formulaic expression for "if not" or "otherwise" (BDAG, 278.6.d; BDF §376; §480; Zerwick and Grosvenor, 330), which can be used, as here, after an affirmative clause as an ellipsis for the protasis of the second-class (contrary-to-fact) condition.

εἶπον. Aor act ind 1st sg λέγω. It marks the beginning of the apodosis of a second-class condition.

ἄν. Marker of contingency in the apodosis of the second-class condition.

ὑμῖν. Dative indirect object of εἶπον.

ὅτι. This could be (1) ὅτι-*recitativum* introducing direct discourse, (2) the subordinating conjunction "that" introducing indirect discourse, or (3) the subordinating conjunction "because" introducing a causal clause. If ὅτι introduces direct or indirect discourse, the conditional clause εἰ δὲ μή, εἶπον ἄν ὑμῖν ὅτι πορεύομαι ἑτοιμάσαι τόπον ὑμῖν is best construed as a question (as indicated by the punctuation in NA[28]/UBS[5]): "If it were not so, would I have told you that I go to prepare a place for you?" (NRSV; ESV; cf. CEB; NIV; NLT). It could also be construed as a statement: "If it were not so, I would have told you that I go to prepare a place for you" (Brown, 2:619). If ὅτι introduces a causal clause, the conditional clause εἰ δὲ μή, εἶπον ἄν ὑμῖν ὅτι πορεύομαι ἑτοιμάσαι τόπον ὑμῖν is best construed as a statement (as indicated by the punctuation in SBLGNT): "If it were not so, I would have told you; for I go to prepare a place for you" (ASV; NASB; cf. LEB; NET; REB). The absence of ὅτι from some manuscripts ($\mathfrak{P}^{66*}$ C² N Γ Δ Θ 700 1241 1424 𝔐 a e f q) could be explained "as a simplification introduced by copyists who took it as ὅτι *recitativum*, which is often omitted as superfluous," as Metzger (206) suggests, but ὅτι may also have been omitted to indicate that πορεύομαι ἑτοιμάσαι τόπον ὑμῖν is a new statement unrelated to the previous condition: "If it were not so, I would have told you. I go to prepare a place for you" (KJV; cf. Brown, 2:617, 620).

πορεύομαι. Pres mid ind 1st sg πορεύομαι.

ἑτοιμάσαι. Aor act inf ἑτοιμάζω (purpose).

τόπον. Accusative direct object of ἑτοιμάσαι.

ὑμῖν. Dative of advantage.

14:3 καὶ ἐὰν πορευθῶ καὶ ἑτοιμάσω τόπον ὑμῖν, πάλιν ἔρχομαι καὶ παραλήμψομαι ὑμᾶς πρὸς ἐμαυτόν, ἵνα ὅπου εἰμὶ ἐγὼ καὶ ὑμεῖς ἦτε.

καί. Coordinating conjunction.

ἐάν. Introduces the protasis of a third-class condition. In this formulation, however, the meaning of "ἐάν approaches closely that of ὅταν" (BDAG, 268.2; cf. Haubeck and von Siebenthal, 584).

πορευθῶ. Aor mid subj 1st sg πορεύομαι. Subjunctive with ἐάν. On the voice, see "Deponency" in the Series Introduction.

καί. Coordinating conjunction.

ἑτοιμάσω. Aor act subj 1st sg ἑτοιμάζω. Subjunctive with ἐάν.

τόπον. Accusative direct object of ἑτοιμάσω.

ὑμῖν. Dative of advantage.

πάλιν. Adverb "pert[aining] to repetition in the same (or similar) manner" (BDAG, 752.2). Fronted for emphasis.

ἔρχομαι. Pres mid ind 1st sg ἔρχομαι. The context (see the adverb πάλιν and the subsequent verb παραλήμψομαι) indicates that ἔρχομαι refers to the future (Caragounis 2004, 160; Young, 111).

καί. Coordinating conjunction.

παραλήμψομαι. Fut mid ind 1st sg παραλαμβάνω.

ὑμᾶς. Accusative direct object of παραλήμψομαι.

πρὸς ἐμαυτόν. Locative (motion toward).

ἵνα. Introduces a purpose clause.

ὅπου. Marker of a position in space.

εἰμί. Pres act ind 1st sg εἰμί.

ἐγώ. Nominative subject of εἰμί.

καί. Adverbial use (adjunctive).

ὑμεῖς. Nominative subject of ἦτε. Fronted for emphasis.

ἦτε. Pres act subj 2nd pl εἰμί. Subjunctive with ἵνα.

14:4 καὶ ὅπου [ἐγὼ] ὑπάγω οἴδατε τὴν ὁδόν.

καί. Coordinating conjunction.

ὅπου. Marker of a position in space.

[ἐγώ]. Nominative subject of ὑπάγω. This personal pronoun (attested in ℵ A B C K N Q Γ Δ Ψ 33 579 700 892 1241 *l*844 𝔐 et al.) is placed within square brackets because it is absent from some early manuscripts (𝔓⁶⁶ D L W Θ *f*¹³ 1 565 1424 it pbo bo^ms).

ὑπάγω. Pres act ind 1st sg ὑπάγω. On the use of ὑπάγω in chs. 13–16, see 13:3 on ὑπάγει.

οἴδατε. Prf act ind 2nd pl οἶδα (see 1:26 on οἴδατε).

τὴν ὁδόν. Accusative direct object of οἴδατε. Many copyists have tried to smooth out the syntactical roughness of the short reading by adding the conjunction καί before and the verb οἴδατε after τὴν ὁδόν (𝔓⁶⁶* A C³ D K N Γ Δ Θ Ψ *f*¹·¹³ 565 700 892 1241 1424 *l*844 𝔐 lat sy sa ly), turning a single sentence into two parallel clauses, καὶ ὅπου ἐγὼ ὑπάγω οἴδατε καὶ τὴν ὁδὸν οἴδατε, which reflect a distinction between "where" and "the way" that Thomas makes in the next verse (Metzger, 207).

14:5 Λέγει αὐτῷ Θωμᾶς· κύριε, οὐκ οἴδαμεν ποῦ ὑπάγεις· πῶς δυνάμεθα τὴν ὁδὸν εἰδέναι;

Λέγει. Pres act ind 3rd sg λέγω. The historical present gives prominence to Thomas' reply to Jesus (see 1:15 on μαρτυρεῖ). This verse is connected to the previous one by asyndeton.

αὐτῷ. Dative indirect object of Λέγει.
Θωμᾶς. Nominative subject of Λέγει (see 11:16).
κύριε. Vocative of direct address.
οὐκ. Negative particle normally used with indicative verbs.
οἴδαμεν. Prf act ind 1st pl οἶδα (see 1:26 on οἴδατε).
ποῦ. Indirect interrogative adverb of place.
ὑπάγεις. Pres act ind 2nd sg ὑπάγω. On the use of ὑπάγω in chs. 13–16, see 13:3 on ὑπάγει.
πῶς. Interrogative particle.
δυνάμεθα. Pres mid ind 1st pl δύναμαι.
τὴν ὁδὸν. Accusative direct object of εἰδέναι. Fronted for emphasis.
εἰδέναι. Prf act inf οἶδα (complementary).

14:6 λέγει αὐτῷ [ὁ] Ἰησοῦς· ἐγώ εἰμι ἡ ὁδὸς καὶ ἡ ἀλήθεια καὶ ἡ ζωή· οὐδεὶς ἔρχεται πρὸς τὸν πατέρα εἰ μὴ δι' ἐμοῦ.

λέγει. Pres act ind 3rd sg λέγω. The historical present gives prominence to Jesus' answer to Thomas' question (see 1:15 on μαρτυρεῖ) and marks a shift in the direction of the conversation between Thomas and Jesus (Runge 2010, 138). This verse is connected to the previous one by asyndeton.

αὐτῷ. Dative indirect object of λέγει.
[ὁ] Ἰησοῦς. Nominative subject of λέγει. Although the definite article is well attested (A B C³ D K N Q W Γ Δ Θ Ψ $f^{1.13}$ 33 565 𝔐 et al.), it is absent in 𝔓⁶⁶ ℵ C* L.
ἐγώ εἰμι ἡ ὁδὸς καὶ ἡ ἀλήθεια καὶ ἡ ζωή. This is one of Jesus' "I am" pronouncements in the FG with an explicit predicate; for other statements of this type, see 6:35, 48, 51; 8:12; 10:7, 9, 11, 14; 11:25; 15:1, 5.
ἐγώ. Nominative subject of εἰμι. Fronted for emphasis.
εἰμι. Pres act ind 1st sg εἰμί.
ἡ ὁδὸς. Predicate nominative. The definite article is anaphoric, referring to τὴν ὁδὸν in the previous verse (Harris 2015, 256).

καί. Coordinating conjunction. Brown (2:621) proposes that this and the next καί are epexegetical or explanatory, but this conclusion cannot be derived from a semantic quality of καί, whose primary function is to connect items of equal status (Runge 2010, 24), but from the perceived relationship between the three predicate nominatives—ἡ ὁδὸς, ἡ ἀλήθεια, and ἡ ζωή. Since Jesus responds to Thomas' question about "the way" and, after making the "I am" pronouncement, points out that the only access to the Father is through him, it is conceivable, as Brown suggests, that ἡ ὁδὸς represents the dominant notion and that the other two predicates "are just explanations of the way" (621).

ἡ ἀλήθεια. Predicate nominative.
καί. Coordinating conjunction.
ἡ ζωή. Predicate nominative.
οὐδεὶς ... εἰ μή. A point/counterpoint set that corrects the negated clause ("no one comes to the Father") by introducing an exception ("except through me"); on the function of the excepted element, see 3:13 on οὐδεὶς ... εἰ μή. This sentence is connected to the previous one by asyndeton.
οὐδεὶς. Nominative subject of ἔρχεται. This clause is connected to the previous one by asyndeton.
ἔρχεται. Pres mid ind 3rd sg ἔρχομαι.
πρὸς τὸν πατέρα. Locative (motion toward).
δι᾽ ἐμοῦ. Agency.

14:7 εἰ ἐγνώκατέ με, καὶ τὸν πατέρα μου γνώσεσθε. καὶ ἀπ᾽ ἄρτι γινώσκετε αὐτὸν καὶ ἑωράκατε αὐτόν.

εἰ. Introduces the protasis of a first-class condition. This verse is connected to the previous one by asyndeton.
ἐγνώκατέ. Perf act ind 2nd pl γινώσκω. ἐγνώκατέ, which has an acute accent on the antepenult, acquired an additional accent, the acute, on the ultima from the enclitic με (Smyth §183; Carson 1985, 48). The second-person plural indicates that Jesus no longer addresses only Thomas but speaks to all his disciples. The perfect-tense verb form is marked for prominence, highlighting the disciples' knowledge of Jesus as a condition of knowing the Father. Although, in principle, the first-class conditional clause presumes the reality of the condition for the sake of the argument, the text that follows indicates that in this case the apodosis describes the current state of affairs at the moment of speaking, turning the conditional clause into a promise: "If you have come to know me [as in fact you do], you shall know my Father also" (Metzger, 207). Some copyists, however, interpreted Jesus' words as a reproach by

changing the perfect-tense ἐγνώκατέ into the pluperfect ἐγνώκειτε in the protasis (A B C D¹ K L N Q Γ Δ Θ Ψ $f^{1.13}$ 33 565 700 892 1241 1424 *l*844 𝔐 et al.) and by replacing the future-tense γνώσεσθε with either ἂν ᾔδειτε (B C* [L] Q Ψ 1 33 565 et al.) or ἐγνώκειτε ἂν (A C³ K N Γ Δ Θ f^{13} 700 892 1241 1424 𝔐 et al.) in the apodosis, thus effectively turning a first-class condition into a second-class (contrary-to-fact) condition: "If you had come to know me [which, alas, you do not], you would have knowledge of my Father also" (Metzger, 207). Metzger suggests that the latter reading probably developed under the influence of 8:19 or 14:8-9.

με. Accusative direct object of ἐγνώκατέ.

καί. Adverbial use (adjunctive). καί marks the beginning of the apodosis of a first-class condition.

τὸν πατέρα. Accusative direct object of γνώσεσθε.

μου. Genitive of relationship qualifying πατέρα.

γνώσεσθε. Fut mid ind 2nd pl γινώσκω. For the text-critical comments, see ἐγνώκατέ above.

καί. Coordinating conjunction.

ἀπ' ἄρτι. Temporal. In this context, ἀπ' ἄρτι does not mean "henceforth," referring to the future knowledge of God, but describes the disciples' present knowledge of the Father acquired through Jesus (Schnackenburg, 3:68). Elsewhere in the FG, ἀπ' ἄρτι occurs only in 13:19.

γινώσκετε. Pres act ind 2nd pl γινώσκω.

αὐτόν. Accusative direct object of γινώσκετε. The personal pronoun refers to τὸν πατέρα from the previous clause.

καί. Coordinating conjunction.

ἑωράκατε. Perf act ind 2nd pl ὁράω. The perfect-tense verb form attributes the greatest semantic weight to the act of seeing God, which becomes the main topic of conversation in the following dialogue between Philip and Jesus.

αὐτόν. Accusative direct object of ἑωράκατε.

John 14:8-14

⁸Philip said to him, "Lord, show us the Father, and it is enough for us." ⁹Jesus said to him, "Have I been with you such a long time, and you still do not know me, Philip? The one who has seen me has seen the Father. How can you say, 'Show us the Father'? ¹⁰Do you not believe that I am in the Father and the Father is in me? The words that I say to you I do not speak on my own, but the Father, because he dwells in me, does his works. ¹¹Believe me that I am in the Father and the Father is in me. But if not, believe because of the works themselves. ¹²Truly, truly I say to

you, the one who believes in me, the works that I am doing he will also do; even greater [works] than these will he do because I am going to the Father. ¹³And whatever you ask in my name, this I will do, in order that the Father may be glorified in the Son. ¹⁴If you ask me anything in my name, I will do it."

14:8 Λέγει αὐτῷ Φίλιππος· κύριε, δεῖξον ἡμῖν τὸν πατέρα, καὶ ἀρκεῖ ἡμῖν.

Λέγει. Pres act ind 3rd sg λέγω. The historical present gives prominence to Philip's request (see 1:15 on μαρτυρεῖ). This verse is connected to the previous one by asyndeton.
αὐτῷ. Dative indirect object of Λέγει.
Φίλιππος. Nominative subject of Λέγει.
κύριε. Vocative of direct address.
δεῖξον. Aor act impv 2nd sg δείκνυμι.
ἡμῖν. Dative indirect object of δεῖξον.
τὸν πατέρα. Accusative direct object of δεῖξον. Philip's uncomprehending request shows that he completely misunderstood Jesus' statement that knowing Jesus means knowing the Father also.
καὶ. Coordinating conjunction.
ἀρκεῖ. Pres act ind 3rd sg ἀρκέω. ἀρκέω is an impersonal verb (BDF §129) that here means to "be enough, sufficient, adequate" (BDAG, 131.1).
ἡμῖν. Dative of advantage.

14:9 λέγει αὐτῷ ὁ Ἰησοῦς· τοσούτῳ χρόνῳ μεθ' ὑμῶν εἰμι καὶ οὐκ ἔγνωκάς με, Φίλιππε; ὁ ἑωρακὼς ἐμὲ ἑώρακεν τὸν πατέρα· πῶς σὺ λέγεις· δεῖξον ἡμῖν τὸν πατέρα;

λέγει. Pres act ind 3rd sg λέγω. The historical present gives prominence to Jesus' response to Philip's request (see 1:15 on μαρτυρεῖ) and marks a shift in the direction of the conversation between Philip and Jesus (Runge 2010, 138). This verse is connected to the previous one by asyndeton.
αὐτῷ. Dative indirect object of λέγει.
ὁ Ἰησοῦς. Nominative subject of λέγει.
τοσούτῳ χρόνῳ. An irregular dative indicating extent of time. Fronted for emphasis. Wallace notes that "[a]lthough the dative largely has the force of *point*, it occasionally overlaps with the accusative of time" (1996, 156; cf. Zerwick §54). The variant reading τοσοῦτον χρόνον (𝔓⁶⁶·⁷⁵ ℵ²ᵃ A B K N Γ Δ Θ Ψ 𝔐 et al.) is probably a scribal correction,

adjusting the case of this nominal phrase to its more common usage (accusative) for a duration of time.

μεθ' ὑμῶν. Association/accompaniment.

εἰμι. Pres act ind 1st sg εἰμί. τοσούτῳ χρόνῳ indicates that this present tense describes "a situation which began in the past and continues in the present" (Fanning, 217). McKay (1994, 41) calls this usage "extension from past."

καὶ. Coordinating conjunction.

οὐκ. Negative particle normally used with indicative verbs.

ἔγνωκάς. Prf act ind 2nd sg γινώσκω. Like εἰμι above, ἔγνωκάς describes a situation that started in the past, but the emphasis falls on the present state of affairs, i.e., Philip's current failure to understand Jesus. ἔγνωκάς, which has an acute accent on the antepenult, acquired an additional accent, the acute, on the ultima from the enclitic με (Smyth §183; Carson 1985, 48).

με. Accusative direct object of ἔγνωκάς.

Φίλιππε. Vocative of direct address.

ὁ ἑωρακὼς. Prf act ptc masc nom sg ὁράω (substantival). Fronted as a topical frame. Both verb forms of ὁράω in this verse are in the perfect tense, which functions as a semantic marker for prominence. This clause is connected to the preceding one by asyndeton.

ἐμὲ. Accusative direct object of ἑωρακὼς.

ἑώρακεν. Prf act ind 3rd sg ὁράω.

τὸν πατέρα. Accusative direct object of ἑώρακεν.

πῶς. Interrogative particle. This clause is connected to the previous one by asyndeton.

σὺ. Nominative subject of λέγεις.

λέγεις. Pres act ind 2nd sing λέγω.

δεῖξον. Aor act impv 2nd sg δείκνυμι.

ἡμῖν. Dative indirect object of δεῖξον.

τὸν πατέρα. Accusative direct object of δεῖξον.

14:10 οὐ πιστεύεις ὅτι ἐγὼ ἐν τῷ πατρὶ καὶ ὁ πατὴρ ἐν ἐμοί ἐστιν; τὰ ῥήματα ἃ ἐγὼ λέγω ὑμῖν ἀπ' ἐμαυτοῦ οὐ λαλῶ, ὁ δὲ πατὴρ ἐν ἐμοὶ μένων ποιεῖ τὰ ἔργα αὐτοῦ.

οὐ. Negative particle that introduces a question that expects an affirmative answer. This verse is connected to the previous one by asyndeton.

πιστεύεις. Pres act ind 2nd sg πιστεύω.

ὅτι. Introduces the clausal complement (indirect discourse) of πιστεύεις.

ἐγὼ ἐν τῷ πατρὶ καὶ ὁ πατὴρ ἐν ἐμοί. The reciprocal formula of immanence that describes the unity between the Father and the Son.

This formula is repeated in 14:11. For other versions of this formula, see 10:38 (ἐν ἐμοὶ ὁ πατὴρ κἀγὼ ἐν τῷ πατρί) and 17:21 (σύ, πάτερ, ἐν ἐμοὶ κἀγὼ ἐν σοί).

ἐγώ. Nominative subject of an implied εἰμί. Fronted as a topical frame.

ἐν τῷ πατρί. State of being, describing a close personal relationship between the Son and the Father.

καί. Coordinating conjunction.

ὁ πατήρ. Nominative subject of ἐστιν. Fronted as a topical frame.

ἐν ἐμοί. State of being, describing a close personal relationship between the Father and the Son.

ἐστιν. Pres act ind 3rd sg εἰμί.

τὰ ῥήματα. Accusative direct object of λαλῶ. Fronted as a topical frame. This clause is connected to the preceding one by asyndeton.

ἅ. Accusative direct object of λέγω. The antecedent of the relative pronoun is τὰ ῥήματα.

ἐγώ. Nominative subject of λέγω.

λέγω. Pres act ind 1st sg λέγω.

ὑμῖν. Dative indirect object of λέγω.

ἀπ' ἐμαυτοῦ. Agency (see 5:19 on ἀφ' ἑαυτοῦ). Fronted for emphasis.

οὐ. Negative particle normally used with indicative verbs.

λαλῶ. Pres act ind 1st sg λαλέω.

ὁ ... πατήρ. Nominative subject of ποιεῖ.

δέ. Marker of narrative development.

ἐν ἐμοί. State of being, describing a close personal relationship between the Father and the Son.

μένων. Pres act ptc masc nom sg μένω. Since the participle is not preceded by an article, it cannot be attributive, as some English translations imply (e.g., "the Father who dwells in me does his works" [NRSV; CEB; ESV]; "it is the Father who dwells in me doing his own work" [REB]; "the Father who resides in me crafts each word into a divine act" [MSG]). Even many copyists understood the participle to be attributive and added ὁ before ἐν ἐμοὶ μένων (ℵ A D K N Q W Γ Δ Θ $f^{1.13}$ 33 565 1241 1424 𝔐 et al.). The more difficult reading ($\mathfrak{P}^{66.75}$ B L Ψ) presumes that the participle is adverbial, although its specific function is not completely clear. It could be causal ("the Father does his works because he dwells in me") or instrumental ("the Father does his works by dwelling in me").

ποιεῖ. Pres act ind 3rd sg ποιέω.

τὰ ἔργα. Accusative direct object of ποιεῖ.

αὐτοῦ. Subjective genitive qualifying ἔργα.

14:11 πιστεύετέ μοι ὅτι ἐγὼ ἐν τῷ πατρὶ καὶ ὁ πατὴρ ἐν ἐμοί· εἰ δὲ μή, διὰ τὰ ἔργα αὐτὰ πιστεύετε.

πιστεύετέ. Pres act impv 2nd pl πιστεύω. πιστεύετέ, which has an acute accent on the antepenult, acquired an additional accent, the acute, on the ultima from the enclitic μοι (Smyth §183; Carson 1985, 48). This verse is connected to the previous one by asyndeton.

μοι. Dative complement of πιστεύετέ. The dative denotes "the pers[on] to whom one gives credence or whom one believes" (BDAG, 816.1.b). The meaning of πιστεύετέ μοι is therefore not "believe in me" but "accept the following statement as true" (Barrett, 460).

ὅτι. Introduces the clausal complement (indirect discourse) of πιστεύετέ.

ἐγὼ ἐν τῷ πατρὶ καὶ ὁ πατὴρ ἐν ἐμοί. The reciprocal formula of immanence that describes the unity between the Father and the Son. This is a verbatim repetition of the formulation in 14:10. For other versions of this formula, see 10:38 (ἐν ἐμοὶ ὁ πατὴρ κἀγὼ ἐν τῷ πατρί) and 17:21 (σύ, πάτερ, ἐν ἐμοὶ κἀγὼ ἐν σοί).

ἐγώ. Nominative subject of an implied εἰμί.

ἐν τῷ πατρί. State of being, describing a close personal relationship between the Son and the Father.

καί. Coordinating conjunction.

ὁ πατήρ. Nominative subject of an implied ἐστίν.

ἐν ἐμοί. State of being, describing a close personal relationship the Father and the Son.

εἰ δὲ μή. A formulaic expression for "if not" or "otherwise" (BDAG, 278.6.d; BDF §376; §480; Zerwick and Grosvenor, 330), which can be used, as here, after an affirmative clause as an ellipsis for the protasis of a first-class condition.

διὰ τὰ ἔργα αὐτά. Causal. αὐτά functions as an intensive pronoun. The PP marks the beginning of the apodosis of a first-class condition.

πιστεύετε. Pres act impv 2nd pl πιστεύω.

14:12 Ἀμὴν ἀμὴν λέγω ὑμῖν, ὁ πιστεύων εἰς ἐμὲ τὰ ἔργα ἃ ἐγὼ ποιῶ κἀκεῖνος ποιήσει καὶ μείζονα τούτων ποιήσει, ὅτι ἐγὼ πρὸς τὸν πατέρα πορεύομαι·

Ἀμὴν ἀμὴν λέγω ὑμῖν. Metacomment (see 1:51).

Ἀμὴν ἀμήν. Asseverative particles that mark the beginning of Jesus' solemn declaration (see 1:51). This verse is connected to the previous one by asyndeton.

λέγω. Pres act ind 1st sg λέγω.

ὑμῖν. Dative indirect object of λέγω.

ὁ πιστεύων. Pres act ptc masc nom sg πιστεύω (substantival). Nominative subject of ποιήσει in a left-dislocation, resumed by κἀκεῖνος (see Runge 2010, 287–313). The left-dislocation shifts focus on a believer in Jesus.

εἰς ἐμὲ. Goal of actions or feelings directed toward someone (BDAG, 290.4.c.β). For πιστεύειν εἰς + accusative ("trust or believe in someone"), see 1:12 on εἰς τὸ ὄνομα.

τὰ ἔργα. Accusative direct object of ποιήσει. Fronted for emphasis.

ἅ. Accusative direct object of ποιῶ. The antecedent of the relative pronoun is τὰ ἔργα.

ἐγὼ. Nominative subject of ποιῶ. The personal pronoun is emphatic and distinctive.

ποιῶ. Pres act ind 1st sg ποιέω.

κἀκεῖνος. Formed by crasis from καὶ ἐκεῖνος. καὶ is adverbial (adjunctive); ἐκεῖνος is the nominative subject of ποιήσει, resuming ὁ πιστεύων. The anaphoric demonstrative reinforces what is already made prominent through the left-dislocation of ὁ πιστεύων.

ποιήσει. Fut act ind 3rd sg ποιέω.

καὶ. Adverbial (ascensive).

μείζονα. Accusative direct object of ποιήσει. μείζονα is the comparative adjective from μέγας.

τούτων. Genitive of comparison.

ποιήσει. Fut act ind 3rd sg ποιέω.

ὅτι. Introduces a causal clause.

ἐγὼ. Nominative subject of πορεύομαι. Fronted as a topical frame.

πρὸς τὸν πατέρα. Locative (motion toward). Fronted for emphasis.

πορεύομαι. Pres mid ind 1st sg πορεύομαι. The context indicates that this present tense refers to "an activity whose completion is still in the future" (McKay 1994, 41).

14:13 καὶ ὅ τι ἂν αἰτήσητε ἐν τῷ ὀνόματί μου τοῦτο ποιήσω, ἵνα δοξασθῇ ὁ πατὴρ ἐν τῷ υἱῷ.

καὶ. Coordinating conjunction.

ὅ τι ἂν. Accusative direct object of αἰτήσητε in a left-dislocation, resumed by τοῦτο (see Runge 2010, 287–313). ὅ τι is the neuter singular form of the indefinite relative pronoun ὅστις (printed as two words to distinguish it from ὅτι; cf. MHT 2:179), whose indefiniteness is heightened with the marker of contingency ἄν.

αἰτήσητε. Aor act subj 2nd pl αἰτέω. Subjunctive with ἄν.

ἐν τῷ ὀνόματί. Instrumental. With the exception of Mark 16:17, the phrase ἐν τῷ ὀνόματί μου occurs only in the FG in Jesus' farewell discourse: here, 14:14, 26; 15:16; 16:23, 24, 26. ὀνόματί, which has an acute accent on the antepenult, acquired an additional accent, the acute, on the ultima from the enclitic μου (Smyth §183; Carson 1985, 48).

μου. Possessive genitive qualifying ὀνόματί.

τοῦτο. Accusative direct object of αἰτήσητε, resuming ὅ τι ἄν.

ποιήσω. Fut act ind 1st sg ποιέω.

ἵνα. Introduces a purpose clause.

δοξασθῇ. Aor pass subj 3rd sg δοξάζω. Subjunctive with ἵνα.

ὁ πατὴρ. Nominative subject of δοξασθῇ.

ἐν τῷ υἱῷ. Locative.

14:14 ἐάν τι αἰτήσητέ με ἐν τῷ ὀνόματί μου ἐγὼ ποιήσω.

ἐάν τι αἰτήσητέ με ἐν τῷ ὀνόματί μου ἐγὼ ποιήσω. The omission of entire v. 14 in a few manuscripts (X f^1 565 b vg^{ms} sy^s) could have happened accidentally during transcription because of parablepsis—an eye skip from v. 14 to v. 15 due to their similar beginnings (εαν)—or deliberately to avoid a repetition of the first half of 14:13 or possible contradiction with 16:23 (Metzger, 208).

ἐάν. Introduces the protasis of a third-class condition. This verse is connected to the previous one by asyndeton.

τι. Accusative direct object (thing) of αἰτήσητέ in a double accusative person-thing construction.

αἰτήσητέ. Aor act subj 2nd pl αἰτέω. Subjunctive with ἐάν. On the meaning of αἰτέω in a double accusative construction, see 11:22. αἰτήσητέ, which has an acute accent on the antepenult, acquired an additional accent, the acute, on the ultima from the enclitic με (Smyth §183; Carson 1985, 48).

με. Accusative direct object (person) of αἰτήσητέ in a double accusative person-thing construction. The omission of this personal pronoun in some copies (A D K L Q Ψ 1241 1424 *l*844 *pm* it vg^{mss} co) may have been motivated by a desire to adjust the wording of the clause to v. 13a, which does not have με after αἰτήσητε, or to avoid contradiction with 16:23, where Jesus declares that his disciples will ask nothing of him and advises them to ask anything of the Father in Jesus' name.

ἐν τῷ ὀνόματί. Instrumental (see 14:13, 26; 15:16; 16:23, 24, 26). ὀνόματί, which has an acute accent on the antepenult, acquired an additional accent, the acute, on the ultima from the enclitic μου (Smyth §183; Carson 1985, 48).

μου. Possessive genitive qualifying ὀνόματί.

ἐγώ. Nominative subject of ποιήσω. The personal pronoun marks the beginning of the apodosis of a third-class condition. Fronted for emphasis.

ποιήσω. Fut act ind 1st sg ποιέω.

John 14:15-21

[15]"If you love me, you will keep my commandments. [16]And I will ask the Father, and he will give you another Paraclete, in order that he may be with you forever, [17]the Spirit of truth, whom the world cannot receive because it neither sees him nor knows him. You know him because he remains with you and will be in you. [18]I will not leave you orphaned; I am coming to you. [19]Yet a little while and the world will no longer see me, but you will see me. Because I live, you also will live. [20]On that day you will know that I am in my Father, and you are in me, and I am in you. [21]The one who has my commandments and keeps them—that one is the one who loves me; and the one who loves me will be loved by my Father, and I will love him and will reveal myself to him."

14:15 Ἐὰν ἀγαπᾶτέ με, τὰς ἐντολὰς τὰς ἐμὰς τηρήσετε·

Ἐάν. Introduces the protasis of a third-class condition. This verse is connected to the previous one by asyndeton.

ἀγαπᾶτε. Pres act subj 2nd pl ἀγαπάω. Subjunctive with ἐάν. ἀγαπᾶτέ, which has a circumflex accent on the penult, acquired an additional accent, the acute, on the ultima from the enclitic με (Smyth §183; Carson 1985, 48).

με. Accusative direct object of ἀγαπᾶτέ.

τὰς ἐντολὰς τὰς ἐμάς. Accusative direct object of τηρήσετε. Fronted for emphasis. It marks the beginning of the apodosis of a third-class condition. The possessive adjective ἐμάς stands in the second attributive position (see 1:9 on τὸ φῶς τὸ ἀληθινόν).

τηρήσετε. Fut act ind 2nd pl τηρέω. Although the aorist imperative τηρήσατε has strong manuscript support (A D K Q W Γ Δ Θ $f^{1.13}$ 565 700 892 1241 1424 *l*844 𝔐), the future-tense τηρήσετε (B L Ψ co Epiph) is probably preferable because it is more coherent with Jesus' words in the next verse than the imperative (Metzger, 208). The idea that keeping Jesus' commandments depends on one's love for Jesus is repeated in 14:21 (ὁ ἔχων τὰς ἐντολάς μου καὶ τηρῶν αὐτὰς ἐκεῖνός ἐστιν ὁ ἀγαπῶν με) and 14:23 (ἐάν τις ἀγαπᾷ με τὸν λόγον μου τηρήσει).

14:16 κἀγὼ ἐρωτήσω τὸν πατέρα καὶ ἄλλον παράκλητον δώσει ὑμῖν, ἵνα μεθ' ὑμῶν εἰς τὸν αἰῶνα ᾖ,

κἀγώ. Formed by crasis from καὶ ἐγώ. καὶ is a coordinating conjunction; ἐγώ is the nominative subject of ἐρωτήσω. Fronted as a topical frame.
ἐρωτήσω. Fut act ind 1st sg ἐρωτάω.
τὸν πατέρα. Accusative direct object of ἐρωτήσω.
καί. Coordinating conjunction.
ἄλλον παράκλητον. Accusative direct object of δώσει. This is the first of the four occurrences of the verbal adjective παράκλητος in the FG (14:16, 26; 15:26; 16:7), which the evangelist uses as an exclusive designation for the Holy Spirit. In the formulation ἄλλον παράκλητον, the adjective ἄλλον modifies the substantival adjective παράκλητον ("another Paraclete"), standing in the first (anarthrous) attributive position (see 2:6 on λίθιναι ὑδρίαι). The implication of the idea that the Holy Spirit is "another Paraclete" is that Jesus himself is a Paraclete, although this is not explicitly stated in the FG. In 1 John 2:1, however, παράκλητος is applied to Jesus Christ: παράκλητον ἔχομεν πρὸς τὸν πατέρα Ἰησοῦν Χριστὸν δίκαιον. According to Louw and Nida, "The principal difficulty encountered in rendering παράκλητος is the fact that this term covers potentially such a wide area of meaning. The traditional rendering of 'Comforter' is especially misleading because it suggests only one very limited aspect of what the Holy Spirit does. A term such as 'Helper' is highly generic and can be particularly useful in some languages. . . . A rendering based upon the concept of legal advocate seems in most instances to be too restrictive" (LN 12.19). For a thorough analysis of this Johannine term, see Brown (2:1135–43). Since no translation could capture the complexity of the functions of παράκλητος, I have decided to use an anglicized transliteration ("Paraclete") of the Greek word.
δώσει. Fut act ind 3rd sg δίδωμι.
ὑμῖν. Dative indirect object of δώσει.
ἵνα. Introduces a purpose clause.
μεθ' ὑμῶν. Association/accompaniment.
εἰς τὸν αἰῶνα. Temporal.
ᾖ. Pres act subj 3rd sg εἰμί. Subjunctive with ἵνα.

14:17 τὸ πνεῦμα τῆς ἀληθείας, ὃ ὁ κόσμος οὐ δύναται λαβεῖν, ὅτι οὐ θεωρεῖ αὐτὸ οὐδὲ γινώσκει· ὑμεῖς γινώσκετε αὐτό, ὅτι παρ' ὑμῖν μένει καὶ ἐν ὑμῖν ἔσται.

τὸ πνεῦμα. Accusative in apposition to παράκλητον from the previous verse.

τῆς ἀληθείας. Objective genitive expressing the activity of πνεῦμα ("the Spirit who communicates the truth"; cf. Barrett, 463), attributive genitive qualifying πνεῦμα ("the true/truth-giving Spirit"; cf. Harris 2015, 260), or epexegetical genitive explaining πνεῦμα ("the Spirit, which is the truth"; cf. 1 John 5:6: τὸ πνεῦμά ἐστιν ἡ ἀλήθεια). The expression τὸ πνεῦμα τῆς ἀληθείας occurs three times in the FG (14:17; 15:26; 16:13) and once in 1 John (4:6). Similar expressions are found in T. Jud. 20.1, 5 ("the spirit of truth and the spirit of error"), 1QS 3.18-19 (רוחות האמת והעול = "the spirits of truth and of deceit") and 1QS 4.23 (רוחי אמת ועול = "the spirits of truth and deceit").

ὅ. Accusative direct object of δύναται. The antecedent of the relative pronoun is τὸ πνεῦμα.

ὁ κόσμος. Nominative subject of δύναται. On the portrayal of the world in the FG, see 1:10 on ἐν τῷ κόσμῳ.

οὐ. Negative particle normally used with indicative verbs.

δύναται. Pres mid ind 3rd sg δύναμαι.

λαβεῖν. Aor act inf λαμβάνω (complementary).

ὅτι. Introduces a causal clause.

οὐ ... οὐδὲ. "Neither ... nor." οὐδὲ is a combination of the negative particle οὐ and the marker of narrative development δέ.

θεωρεῖ. Pres act ind 3rd sg θεωρέω.

αὐτὸ. Accusative direct object of θεωρεῖ. The personal pronoun refers to τὸ πνεῦμα.

γινώσκει. Pres act ind 3rd sg γινώσκω.

ὑμεῖς. Nominative subject of γινώσκετε. Fronted for emphasis. This clause is connected to the previous one by asyndeton.

γινώσκετε. Pres act ind 2nd pl γινώσκω. This present tense reflects a post-resurrection (i.e., the audience's) perspective. From the narrative perspective, it anticipates the future gift of the Spirit described in 20:22 (Barrett, 463).

αὐτό. Accusative direct object of γινώσκετε. The personal pronoun refers to τὸ πνεῦμα.

ὅτι. Introduces a causal clause.

παρ' ὑμῖν. Association. Fronted for emphasis.

μένει. Pres act ind 3rd sg μένω.

καὶ. Coordinating conjunction.

ἐν ὑμῖν. State of being, describing a close personal relationship between the Holy Spirit and Jesus' disciples. Fronted for emphasis.

ἔσται. Fut mid ind 3rd sg εἰμί. Some manuscripts have the present-tense ἐστιν ($\mathfrak{P}^{66*}$ B D* W 1 565 *l*844 it), but the future-tense ἔσται not only has good external support ($\mathfrak{P}^{66c.75vid}$ ℵ A Θ Ψ f^{13} 28 33^{vid} 700 syr$^{s.h}$

et al.) but also seems to be a better reading on internal grounds because the present-tense verbs γινώσκετε and μένει "anticipate the future gift" (Barrett, 463; cf. Metzger, 208).

14:18 Οὐκ ἀφήσω ὑμᾶς ὀρφανούς, ἔρχομαι πρὸς ὑμᾶς.

Οὐκ. Negative particle normally used with indicative verbs. This verse is connected to the previous one by asyndeton.

ἀφήσω. Fut act ind 1st sg ἀφίημι.

ὑμᾶς. Accusative direct object of ἀφήσω in a double accusative object-complement construction.

ὀρφανούς. Accusative complement to ὑμᾶς in a double accusative object-complement construction. If ὀρφανούς is regarded as an adjective, it functions as a predicate adjective vis-à-vis ὑμᾶς: "I will not leave you orphaned/bereft/desolate" (NRSV; REB; ASV) (Wallace 1996, 184, 187). If ὀρφανούς is regarded as an anarthrous noun, it functions as a nominal complement to the pronoun ὑμᾶς: "I will not leave you as orphans" (ESV; LEB; NASB; NIV).

ἔρχομαι. Pres mid ind 1st sg ἔρχομαι. The context indicates that this present tense is here used to express future time.

πρὸς ὑμᾶς. Locative (motion toward).

14:19 ἔτι μικρὸν καὶ ὁ κόσμος με οὐκέτι θεωρεῖ, ὑμεῖς δὲ θεωρεῖτέ με, ὅτι ἐγὼ ζῶ καὶ ὑμεῖς ζήσετε.

ἔτι. Adverb ("still"). This verse is connected to the previous one by asyndeton.

μικρὸν. Adverbial accusative ("a short time, a little while" [BDAG, 651.1.d.β]).

καὶ. Coordinating conjunction.

ὁ κόσμος. Nominative subject of θεωρεῖ.

με. Accusative direct object of θεωρεῖ.

οὐκέτι. Negative adverb of time ("no longer, no further").

θεωρεῖ. Pres act ind 3rd sg θεωρέω. The context indicates that this is a futuristic present.

ὑμεῖς. Nominative subject of θεωρεῖτέ. The second-person plural personal pronoun is emphatic and contrastive, distinguishing the addressees (the disciples) from the world.

δὲ. Marker of narrative development.

θεωρεῖτέ. Pres act ind 2nd pl θεωρέω. This present tense also refers to the future (see θεωρεῖ above). θεωρεῖτέ, which has a circumflex accent on the penult, acquired an additional accent, the acute, on the ultima from the enclitic με (Smyth §183; Carson 1985, 48).

με. Accusative direct object of θεωρεῖτέ.
ὅτι. Introduces a causal clause.
ἐγώ. Nominative subject of ζῶ. Fronted for emphasis.
ζῶ. Pres act ind 1st sg ζάω.
καί. Adverbial use (adjunctive).
ὑμεῖς. Nominative subject of ζήσετε. Fronted for emphasis.
ζήσετε. Fut act ind 2nd pl ζάω.

14:20 ἐν ἐκείνῃ τῇ ἡμέρᾳ γνώσεσθε ὑμεῖς ὅτι ἐγὼ ἐν τῷ πατρί μου καὶ ὑμεῖς ἐν ἐμοὶ κἀγὼ ἐν ὑμῖν.

ἐν ἐκείνῃ τῇ ἡμέρᾳ. Temporal. This verse is connected to the previous one by asyndeton. Elsewhere in the FG, this PP occurs in 5:9; 16:23, 26.
γνώσεσθε. Fut mid ind 2nd pl γινώσκω.
ὑμεῖς. Nominative subject of γνώσεσθε.
ὅτι. Introduces the clausal complement (indirect discourse) of γνώσεσθε.
ἐγώ. Nominative subject of an implied εἰμί. Fronted as a topical frame.
ἐν τῷ πατρί. State of being, describing a close personal relationship between the Son and the Father.
μου. Genitive of relationship qualifying πατρί.
καί. Coordinating conjunction.
ὑμεῖς. Nominative subject of an implied ἐστέ. Fronted as a topical frame.
ἐν ἐμοί. State of being, describing a close personal relationship the disciples and Jesus.
κἀγώ. Formed by crasis from καὶ ἐγώ. καί is a coordinating conjunction; ἐγώ is the nominative subject of an implied εἰμί.
ἐν ὑμῖν. State of being, describing a close personal relationship between Jesus and his disciples.

14:21 ὁ ἔχων τὰς ἐντολάς μου καὶ τηρῶν αὐτὰς ἐκεῖνός ἐστιν ὁ ἀγαπῶν με· ὁ δὲ ἀγαπῶν με ἀγαπηθήσεται ὑπὸ τοῦ πατρός μου, κἀγὼ ἀγαπήσω αὐτὸν καὶ ἐμφανίσω αὐτῷ ἐμαυτόν.

ὁ ἔχων... καὶ τηρῶν. Nominative subject of ἐστιν in a left-dislocation, resumed by ἐκεῖνός (see Runge 2010, 287–313). The left-dislocation shifts focus to the person who has Jesus' commandments and keeps them. Two substantival participles governed by one article and joined by καί form a TSKS (article-substantive-καί-substantive) construction. In such formulations, according to the Granville Sharp rule, the single article indicates that both participles have the same referent; see 5:24 on ὁ ... ἀκούων καὶ πιστεύων. This verse is connected to the previous one by asyndeton.

ἔχων. Pres act ptc masc nom sg ἔχω (substantival). In this formulation, ἔχω means "to grasp firmly with the mind" (Barrett, 465).

τὰς ἐντολάς. Accusative direct object of ἔχων.

μου. Subjective genitive qualifying ἐντολάς.

καὶ. Coordinating conjunction.

τηρῶν. Pres act ptc masc nom sg τηρέω (substantival).

αὐτάς. Accusative direct object of τηρῶν.

ἐκεῖνός. Nominative subject of ἐστιν, resuming ὁ ἔχων ... καὶ τηρῶν. The anaphoric demonstrative reinforces what is already made prominent through the left-dislocation of ὁ ἔχων ... καὶ τηρῶν. ἐκεῖνός, which has a circumflex accent on the penult, acquired an additional accent, the acute, on the ultima from the enclitic ἐστιν (Smyth §183; Carson 1985, 48).

ἐστιν. Pres act ind 3rd sg εἰμί.

ὁ ἀγαπῶν. Pres act ptc masc nom sg ἀγαπάω (substantival). Predicate nominative. On the connection between the love for Jesus and the obedience to his commandments, see 14:15 on τηρήσετε.

με. Accusative direct object of ἀγαπῶν.

ὁ ... ἀγαπῶν. Pres act ptc masc nom sg ἀγαπάω (substantival). Nominative subject of ἀγαπηθήσεται. Fronted as a topical frame.

δὲ. Marker of narrative development.

με. Accusative direct object of ἀγαπῶν.

ἀγαπηθήσεται. Fut pass ind 3rd sg ἀγαπάω. For other references to God's love for the disciples in the FG, see 14:23; 16:27; 17:23, 26.

ὑπὸ τοῦ πατρός. Primary (ultimate) agency.

μου. Genitive of relationship qualifying πατρός.

κἀγὼ. Formed by crasis from καὶ ἐγώ. καὶ is a coordinating conjunction; ἐγώ is the nominative subject of ἀγαπήσω.

ἀγαπήσω. Fut act ind 1st sg ἀγαπάω.

αὐτὸν. Accusative direct object of ἀγαπήσω.

καὶ. Coordinating conjunction.

ἐμφανίσω. Fut act ind 1st sg ἐμφανίζω.

αὐτῷ. Dative indirect object of ἐμφανίσω. The verb means "to make known, to make plain, to reveal, to bring to the light, to disclose" (LN 28.36).

ἐμαυτόν. Accusative direct object of ἐμφανίσω.

John 14:22-26

²²Judas (not Iscariot) said to him, "Lord, what has happened that you are about to reveal yourself to us and not to the world?" ²³Jesus answered and said to him, "If anyone loves me, he will keep my word, and my Father will love him, and we will come to him, and we will make our dwelling with him. ²⁴The one who does not love me does not keep my word. And the word that you hear is not my own but comes from the Father who sent me. ²⁵I have told you these things while I am residing with you. ²⁶But the Paraclete, the Holy Spirit, whom the Father will send in my name—that one will teach you everything and remind you of everything that I have said to you."

14:22 Λέγει αὐτῷ Ἰούδας, οὐχ ὁ Ἰσκαριώτης· κύριε, [καὶ] τί γέγονεν ὅτι ἡμῖν μέλλεις ἐμφανίζειν σεαυτὸν καὶ οὐχὶ τῷ κόσμῳ;

Λέγει. Pres act ind 3rd sg λέγω. The historical present introduces and gives prominence to Judas' question (see 1:15 on μαρτυρεῖ). This verse is connected to the previous one by asyndeton.

αὐτῷ. Dative indirect object of Λέγει.

Ἰούδας. Nominative subject of Λέγει. Elsewhere in the NT, the apostle named Judas is mentioned only in Luke 6:16 (Ἰούδαν Ἰακώβου) and Acts 1:13 (Ἰούδας Ἰακώβου).

οὐχ. Negative particle normally used with indicative verbs.

ὁ Ἰσκαριώτης. Nominative in apposition to Ἰούδας. The negative appositional remark distinguishes this Judas from Judas Iscariot mentioned in 6:71; 12:4; 13:2, 26-30.

κύριε. Vocative of direct address.

[καὶ]. Coordinating conjunction. If καὶ is original (it is attested in $\mathfrak{P}^{66c}$ ℵ K Q W Γ Δ Ψ $f^{1.13}$ 𝔐 et al. but missing in $\mathfrak{P}^{66*.75}$ A B D L Θ et al.), it introduces a question (Zerwick §459).

τί. Interrogative pronoun, functioning as the nominative subject of γέγονεν (lit. "What has happened . . . ?").

γέγονεν. Prf act ind 3rd sg γίνομαι.

ὅτι. This subordinate conjunction could be (1) causal, introducing the reason for Judas' question: "What has happened (to account for the fact) that . . . ?" or "Why is it that . . . ?" (Zerwick and Grosvenor, 331; Zerwick §420); (2) consecutive, introducing the consequences of the incident about which Judas inquires: "What has happened (with the result) that . . . ?" (Robertson, 1001; Harris 2015, 262); or (3) epexegetical, explaining the preceding interrogative pronoun τί: "What has happened (to the effect) that . . . ?" or: "How is it that . . . ?" (Wallace 1996, 459–60).

ἡμῖν. Dative indirect object of ἐμφανίζειν. It is fronted for emphasis and contrasted with τῷ κόσμῳ at the end of the clause.
μέλλεις. Pres act ind 2nd sg μέλλω.
ἐμφανίζειν. Pres act inf ἐμφανίζω (complementary).
σεαυτὸν. Accusative direct object of ἐμφανίζειν.
καὶ. Coordinating conjunction.
οὐχὶ. A strengthened form of the negative particle οὐ.
τῷ κόσμῳ. Dative indirect object of ἐμφανίζειν.

14:23 ἀπεκρίθη Ἰησοῦς καὶ εἶπεν αὐτῷ· ἐάν τις ἀγαπᾷ με τὸν λόγον μου τηρήσει, καὶ ὁ πατήρ μου ἀγαπήσει αὐτὸν καὶ πρὸς αὐτὸν ἐλευσόμεθα καὶ μονὴν παρ' αὐτῷ ποιησόμεθα.

ἀπεκρίθη. Aor mid ind 3rd sg ἀποκρίνομαι. On the voice, see "Deponency" in the Series Introduction. This verse is connected to the previous one by asyndeton.
Ἰησοῦς. Nominative subject of ἀπεκρίθη.
καὶ εἶπεν αὐτῷ. Pleonastic clause under Semitic influence, which functions as a redundant quotative frame (see 1:25 on καὶ εἶπαν αὐτῷ).
καὶ. Coordinating conjunction.
εἶπεν. Aor act ind 3rd sg λέγω.
αὐτῷ. Dative indirect object of εἶπεν.
ἐάν. Introduces the protasis of a third-class condition.
τις. Nominative subject of ἀγαπᾷ.
ἀγαπᾷ. Pres act subj 3rd sg ἀγαπάω.
με. Accusative direct object of ἀγαπᾷ.
τὸν λόγον. Accusative direct object of τηρήσει. It marks the beginning of the apodosis of a third-class condition.
μου. Subjective genitive qualifying λόγον.
τηρήσει. Fut act ind 3rd sg τηρέω. On the connection between the love for Jesus and the obedience to his commandments, see 14:15 on τηρήσετε.
καὶ. Coordinating conjunction.
ὁ πατήρ. Nominative subject of ἀγαπήσει.
μου. Genitive of relationship qualifying πατήρ.
ἀγαπήσει. Fut act ind 3rd sg ἀγαπάω.
αὐτὸν. Accusative direct object of ἀγαπήσει.
καὶ. Coordinating conjunction.
πρὸς αὐτὸν. Locative (motion toward).

ἐλευσόμεθα. Fut mid ind 1st pl ἔρχομαι. Barrett (466) argues that the plural verb form indicates that neither ἐλευσόμεθα nor ποιησόμεθα refers to the resurrection appearances or the parousia on the last day.

καί. Coordinating conjunction.

μονήν. Accusative direct object of ποιησόμεθα. On the meaning of μονή, see 14:2.

παρ' αὐτῷ. Association.

ποιησόμεθα. Fut mid ind 1st pl ποιέω. On the plural verb form, see ἐλευσόμεθα above. The middle voice emphasizes the Father and the Son's participation in making their dwelling with the person who keeps Jesus' word.

14:24 ὁ μὴ ἀγαπῶν με τοὺς λόγους μου οὐ τηρεῖ· καὶ ὁ λόγος ὃν ἀκούετε οὐκ ἔστιν ἐμὸς ἀλλὰ τοῦ πέμψαντός με πατρός.

ὁ . . . ἀγαπῶν. Pres act ptc masc nom sg ἀγαπάω (substantival). Nominative subject of τηρεῖ. Fronted as a topical frame.

μή. Negative particle normally used with non-indicative verbs. This verse is connected to the previous one by asyndeton.

με. Accusative direct object of ἀγαπῶν.

τοὺς λόγους. Accusative direct object of τηρεῖ.

μου. Subjective genitive qualifying λόγους.

οὐ. Negative particle normally used with indicative verbs.

τηρεῖ. Pres act ind 3rd sg τηρέω.

καί. Coordinating conjunction.

ὁ λόγος. Nominative subject of ἔστιν.

ὅν. Accusative direct object of ἀκούετε. The antecedent of the relative pronoun is ὁ λόγος.

ἀκούετε. Pres act ind 2nd pl ἀκούω.

οὐκ . . . ἀλλά. A point/counterpoint set ("not this . . . but that") that replaces the erroneous explanation of the origin of the word that the disciples hear (it is Jesus' own word) with the accurate explanation (it is the word of the Father who sent him). On the function of ἀλλά in a point/counterpoint set, see 1:8.

ἔστιν. Pres act ind 3rd sg εἰμί. The enclitic ἐστιν is accented ἔστιν when it comes at the beginning of a sentence, when it expresses existence, or when it follows ἀλλ', εἰ, καί, οὐκ, ὅτι, or τοῦτ'. The third condition is fulfilled here.

ἐμός. Predicate adjective.

τοῦ . . . πατρός. Subjective genitive ("the word comes from the Father") or possessive genitive ("the word belongs to the Father"), with the implied head noun ὁ λόγος functioning as an understood predicate nominative.

πέμψαντός. Aor act ptc masc gen sg πέμπω (attributive). The participle modifies τοῦ . . . πατρός, standing in the first attributive position (see 5:37 on πέμψας). According to Caragounis (2004, 175), the participial expression πέμψαντός με could have been replaced by the relative clause ὃς ἔπεμψεν με. πέμψαντός, which has an acute accent on the antepenult, acquired an additional accent, the acute, on the ultima from the enclitic με (Smyth §183; Carson 1985, 48). On the use of the participial forms of πέμπω to either identify or describe God in the FG, see τοῦ πέμψαντός in 4:34. ὁ πέμψας με πατὴρ is a common Johannine expression (5:37; 8:16, 18; 12:49; 14:24).

με. Accusative direct object of πέμψαντός.

14:25 Ταῦτα λελάληκα ὑμῖν παρ' ὑμῖν μένων·

Ταῦτα. Accusative direct object of λελάληκα. The demonstrative pronoun is anaphoric, referring to Jesus' speech in the previous verses. Fronted for prominence. This verse is connected to the previous one by asyndeton.

λελάληκα. Prf act ind 1st sg λαλέω. The perfect tense refers to both the past (cf. the anaphoric Ταῦτα) and the present (cf. the present participle μένων indicating a concurrent action). Frey argues that the resultative aspect of the perfect tense conveys that what Jesus "'has spoken' (λελάληκα: 6.63; 8.40; 14.25; 15.3, 11; 16.1, 4, 6, 25, 33; 18.20) is enduringly valid revelation. The use of the perfect here results from an authorial choice of the linguistic expression. It characterizes the Johannine style and expresses, beyond this, the constitutive relatedness of the post-Easter community to the enduringly valid word and work of Christ and his connection back to the initiative of the Father, who sent and authorized him" (2018, 81). The clause ταῦτα λελάληκα ὑμῖν is repeated in 15:11; 16:1, 4, 6, 33.

ὑμῖν. Dative indirect object of λελάληκα.

παρ' ὑμῖν. Association.

μένων. Pres act ptc masc nom sg μένω (temporal). On participles that follow the main verb, see βαπτίζων in 1:31.

14:26 ὁ δὲ παράκλητος, τὸ πνεῦμα τὸ ἅγιον, ὃ πέμψει ὁ πατὴρ ἐν τῷ ὀνόματί μου, ἐκεῖνος ὑμᾶς διδάξει πάντα καὶ ὑπομνήσει ὑμᾶς πάντα ἃ εἶπον ὑμῖν [ἐγώ].

ὁ . . . παράκλητος. Nominative subject of διδάξει in a left-dislocation, resumed by ἐκεῖνος (see Runge 2010, 287–313). The left-dislocation shifts focus on the Paraclete and his role after Jesus' departure. On the meaning of παράκλητος, see 14:16.

δὲ. Marker of narrative development.

τὸ πνεῦμα τὸ ἅγιον. Nominative in apposition to ὁ . . . παράκλητος. The adjective ἅγιον stands in the second attributive position (see 1:9 on τὸ φῶς τὸ ἀληθινόν).

ὅ. Accusative direct object of πέμψει. The antecedent of the relative pronoun is τὸ πνεῦμα.

πέμψει. Fut act ind 3rd sg πέμπω.

ὁ πατήρ. Nominative subject of πέμψει.

ἐν τῷ ὀνόματί. Instrumental (see 14:13, 14; 15:16; 16:23, 24, 26). ὀνόματί, which has an acute accent on the antepenult, acquired an additional accent, the acute, on the ultima from the enclitic μου (Smyth §183; Carson 1985, 48).

μου. Possessive genitive qualifying ὀνόματί.

ἐκεῖνος. Nominative subject of διδάξει, resuming ὁ . . . παράκλητος. The anaphoric demonstrative reinforces what is already made prominent through the left-dislocation of ὁ . . . παράκλητος. Wallace (1996, 331–32) rightly emphasizes that the masculine gender of ἐκεῖνος cannot be taken as an affirmation of the personality of the Holy Spirit because it is required by the masculine gender of ὁ . . . παράκλητος to which ἐκεῖνος refers.

ὑμᾶς. Accusative direct object (person) of διδάξει in a double accusative person-thing construction.

διδάξει. Fut act ind 3rd sg διδάσκω.

πάντα. Accusative direct object (thing) of διδάξει in a double accusative person-thing construction.

καὶ. Coordinating conjunction.

ὑπομνήσει. Fut act ind 3rd sg ὑπομιμνῄσκω.

ὑμᾶς. Accusative direct object (person) of ὑπομνήσει in a double accusative person-thing construction.

πάντα. Accusative direct object (thing) of ὑπομνήσει in a double accusative person-thing construction.

ἅ. Accusative direct object of εἶπον.

εἶπον. Aor act ind 1st sg λέγω.

ὑμῖν. Dative indirect object of εἶπον.

[ἐγώ]. Nominative subject of εἶπον. This emphatic pronoun (attested in B L 060 [33]) is omitted in a number of manuscripts ($\mathfrak{P}^{75}$ ℵ A D K Γ Δ Θ Ψ $f^{1.13}$ 565 579 700 892^s 1241 1424 *l*844 $\mathfrak{M}$ co), but since there are no compelling internal reasons for its inclusion or omission, it is printed within square brackets (Metzger, 209).

John 14:27-31

[27]"Peace I leave with you, my peace I give to you. Not as the world gives do I give to you. Do not let your hearts be troubled, and do not let them be fearful. [28]You have heard that I said to you, 'I am going away, and I am coming to you.' If you loved me, you would rejoice that I am going to the Father because the Father is greater than I. [29]And now I tell you before it happens, so that when it does happen you may believe. [30]I will no longer talk much with you, for the ruler of the world is coming. And he has no hold over me, [31]but [this has happened] so that the world may know that I love the Father; and as the Father has commanded me, so I am doing. Get up, let us go from here!"

14:27 Εἰρήνην ἀφίημι ὑμῖν, εἰρήνην τὴν ἐμὴν δίδωμι ὑμῖν· οὐ καθὼς ὁ κόσμος δίδωσιν ἐγὼ δίδωμι ὑμῖν. μὴ ταρασσέσθω ὑμῶν ἡ καρδία μηδὲ δειλιάτω.

Εἰρήνην. Accusative direct object of ἀφίημι. Fronted for emphasis. Here and in 16:33, εἰρήνη is used as a word of farewell. In 20:19, 21, 26, εἰρήνη is used as a greeting. This verse is connected to the previous one by asyndeton.

ἀφίημι. Pres act ind 1st sg ἀφίημι. In this context, ἀφίημι means "to have someth[ing] continue or remain in a place" (BDAG, 156.4) or "to bequeath" (Barrett, 468).

ὑμῖν. Dative indirect object of ἀφίημι.

εἰρήνην τὴν ἐμὴν. Accusative direct object of δίδωμι. Fronted as a topical frame. The article before ἐμὴν indicates that it stands in an attributive position vis-à-vis εἰρήνην, although the noun itself is anarthrous. Such constructions are common in the NT (e.g., Luke 7:32; 15:22; Acts 7:35; 11:21; 25:23). According to BDF (§270.3), when "an attributive adjective used in postposition with an anarthrous substantive" takes the article, the latter functions as the means by which "the definiteness of the substantive is supplied only as an afterthought through the additional phrase" (Zerwick §192).

δίδωμι. Pres act ind 1st sg δίδωμι.

ὑμῖν. Dative indirect object of δίδωμι.

οὐ. Negative particle normally used with indicative verbs.

καθώς. Introduces a comparative clause, which is negated by the negative particle: "not in the same way as . . ." Another possibility is to understand καθὼς in the sense of ποῖος: "not of the kind as . . ." (BDAG, 493.1). This clause is connected to the previous one by asyndeton.

ὁ κόσμος. Nominative subject of δίδωσιν.

δίδωσιν. Pres act ind 3rd sg δίδωμι.

ἐγώ. Nominative subject of δίδωμι.

δίδωμι. Pres act ind 1st sg δίδωμι.

ὑμῖν. Dative indirect object of δίδωμι.

μὴ . . . μηδέ. Negative particles that are used with non-indicative verbs; μηδὲ also indicates development ("neither . . . nor").

ταρασσέσθω. Pres pass impv 3rd sg ταράσσω. On the meaning of the verb, see 11:33 on ἐτάραξεν.

ὑμῶν. Possessive genitive qualifying καρδία. The preposed pronoun is thematically salient (Levinsohn 2000, 64).

ἡ καρδία. Nominative subject of ταρασσέσθω. ἡ καρδία is a distributive singular.

δειλιάτω. Pres act impv 3rd sg δειλιάω. The verb means "to be cowardly, to lack courage" (LN 25.267).

14:28 ἠκούσατε ὅτι ἐγὼ εἶπον ὑμῖν· ὑπάγω καὶ ἔρχομαι πρὸς ὑμᾶς. εἰ ἠγαπᾶτέ με ἐχάρητε ἂν ὅτι πορεύομαι πρὸς τὸν πατέρα, ὅτι ὁ πατὴρ μείζων μού ἐστιν.

ἠκούσατε. Aor act ind 2nd pl ἀκούω. This verse is connected to the previous one by asyndeton.

ὅτι. Introduces the clausal complement (indirect discourse) of ἠκούσατε.

ἐγώ. Nominative subject of εἶπον. Fronted as a topical frame.

εἶπον. Aor act ind 1st sg λέγω.

ὑμῖν. Dative indirect object of εἶπον.

ὑπάγω. Pres act ind 1st sg ὑπάγω. On the use of ὑπάγω in chs. 13–16, see 13:3 on ὑπάγει.

καί. Coordinating conjunction.

ἔρχομαι. Pres mid ind 1st sg ἔρχομαι; cf. 14: 3, 18.

πρὸς ὑμᾶς. Locative (motion toward).

εἰ. Introduces the protasis of a second-class (contrary-to-fact) condition, which is connected to the previous clause by asyndeton. Typically, the present contrary-to-fact conditions have the imperfect in both the protasis and the apodosis, while the past contrary-to-fact conditions have the aorist in both the protasis and the apodosis. This conditional clause represents a mixed form because the protasis has the imperfect and the apodosis has the aorist, but the meaning could hardly be "if you loved me now you would have rejoiced in the past"; rather, as Zerwick (§317) suggests, "it seems clear enough that the reference is to a present situation but without the present expression of joy as 'you would be glad.'"

ἠγαπᾶτε. Impf act ind 2nd pl ἀγαπάω. ἠγαπᾶτε, which has a circumflex accent on the penult, acquired an additional accent, the acute, on the ultima from the enclitic με (Smyth §183; Carson 1985, 48).

με. Accusative direct object of ἠγαπᾶτε.

ἐχάρητε. Aor mid ind 2nd pl χαίρω. On the voice, see 8:56 on ἐχάρη; see also "Deponency" in the Series Introduction. The verb marks the beginning of the apodosis of a second-class (contrary-to-fact) condition.

ἄν. Marker of contingency in the apodosis of the second-class condition.

ὅτι. Introduces either the clausal complement of ἐχάρητε ("that I am going") or a causal clause ("because I am going").

πορεύομαι. Pres mid ind 1st sg πορεύομαι. This present tense refers to the future, which is accentuated by the next verse (Caragounis 2004, 160).

πρὸς τὸν πατέρα. Locative (motion toward).

ὅτι. Introduces a causal clause.

ὁ πατὴρ. Nominative subject of ἐστιν.

μείζων. Predicate adjective. μείζων is a comparative from μέγας.

μού. Genitive of comparison. The enclitic μού is accented because it is followed by the enclitic ἐστιν. "When several enclitics occur in succession, each receives an accent from the following, only the last having no accent" (Smyth §185).

ἐστιν. Pres act ind 3rd sg εἰμί.

14:29 καὶ νῦν εἴρηκα ὑμῖν πρὶν γενέσθαι, ἵνα ὅταν γένηται πιστεύσητε.

καὶ. Coordinating conjunction.

νῦν. Temporal adverb focusing on time coextensive with the event of the narrative (BDAG, 681.1.a). Fronted as a temporal frame.

εἴρηκα. Prf act ind 1st sg λέγω. While here the perfect tense may refer to a recent past ("now I have told you"), the temporal adverb νῦν indicates that the emphasis falls on the act of speaking in the present ("now I tell you"; cf. Porter 1989, 255).

ὑμῖν. Dative indirect object of εἴρηκα.

πρὶν. Subordinating conjunction ("before").

γενέσθαι. Aor mid inf γίνομαι. Used with πρὶν to denote subsequent time. The infinitive is here used without its accusative subject, which is understood from the context (BDAG, 863.a.β).

ἵνα. Introduces a purpose clause.

ὅταν. Introduces an indefinite temporal clause.

γένηται. Aor mid subj 3rd sg γίνομαι. Subjunctive with ὅταν.

πιστεύσητε. Aor act subj 2nd pl πιστεύω. Subjunctive with ἵνα.

14:30 Οὐκέτι πολλὰ λαλήσω μεθ' ὑμῶν, ἔρχεται γὰρ ὁ τοῦ κόσμου ἄρχων· καὶ ἐν ἐμοὶ οὐκ ἔχει οὐδέν,

Οὐκέτι. Negative adverb of time ("no longer, no further"). This verse is connected to the previous one by asyndeton.

πολλὰ. Accusative direct object of λαλήσω.

λαλήσω. Fut act ind 1st sg λαλέω.

μεθ' ὑμῶν. Association/accompaniment.

ἔρχεται. Pres mid ind 3rd sg ἔρχομαι.

γὰρ. Postpositive conjunction that introduces the explanation of Jesus' declaration that he will no longer talk much with his disciples.

ὁ ... ἄρχων. Nominative subject of ἔρχεται.

τοῦ κόσμου. Genitive of subordination qualifying ἄρχων. The expression ὁ τοῦ κόσμου ἄρχων refers to the devil; see 12:31 and 16:11, which use the designation ὁ ἄρχων τοῦ κόσμου τούτου.

καὶ. Coordinating conjunction.

ἐν ἐμοὶ. Locative, "denoting the object to which someth[ing] happens" (BDAG, 329.8). Combined with ἔχει, the PP means: "he has no hold on me" (BDAG, 422.9.a).

οὐκ. Negative particle normally used with indicative verbs.

ἔχει. Pres act ind 3rd sg ἔχω.

οὐδέν. Accusative direct object of ἔχει. Lit. "he has nothing on me" (CEB) = "he has no power over me" (NRSV; HCSB; LEB).

14:31 ἀλλ' ἵνα γνῷ ὁ κόσμος ὅτι ἀγαπῶ τὸν πατέρα, καὶ καθὼς ἐνετείλατό μοι ὁ πατήρ, οὕτως ποιῶ. ἐγείρεσθε, ἄγωμεν ἐντεῦθεν.

ἀλλ'. Marker of contrast.

ἵνα. Introduces a purpose clause. The ἵνα clause is elliptical, requiring an introduction, such as τοῦτο γέγονεν: "But [this has happened] so that the world may know ..." (BDF §448.7; Haubeck and von Siebenthal, 586–87). Alternatively, the ἵνα clause could be viewed as a substitute for the imperative: "But the world must know ..." (Wallace 1996, 477; Zerwick and Grosvenor, 332; Moule, 144).

γνῷ. Aor act subj 3rd sg γινώσκω. Subjunctive with ἵνα.
ὁ κόσμος. Nominative subject of γνῷ.
ὅτι. Introduces the clausal complement (indirect discourse) of γνῷ.
ἀγαπῶ. Pres act ind 1st sg ἀγαπάω.
τὸν πατέρα. Accusative direct object of ἀγαπῶ.
καὶ. Coordinating conjunction.
καθὼς . . . οὕτως. A point/counterpoint set ("just as . . . so") that compares the Father's giving of instructions to Jesus' activity.
ἐνετείλατο. Aor mid ind 3rd sg ἐντέλλω. ἐνετείλατο, which has an acute accent on the antepenult, acquired an additional accent, the acute, on the ultima from the enclitic μοι (Smyth §183; Carson 1985, 48).
μοι. Dative indirect object of ἐνετείλατο.
ὁ πατήρ. Nominative subject of ἐνετείλατο.
ποιῶ. Pres act ind 1st sg ποιέω.
ἐγείρεσθε. Pres mid impv 2nd pl ἐγείρω. This clause is connected to the previous one by asyndeton.
ἄγωμεν. Pres act subj 1st pl ἄγω (hortatory subjunctive).
ἐντεῦθεν. Adverb of place.

John 15:1-8

¹"I am the true vineyard, and my Father is the vinedresser. ²Every vine in me that does not bear fruit—he takes it away; and every [vine] that bears fruit—he prunes it in order that it may bear more fruit. ³You are already clean because of the word that I have spoken to you. ⁴Abide in me, and I [will abide] in you. Just as the vine cannot bear fruit by itself unless it abides in the vineyard, so neither [can] you unless you abide in me. ⁵I am the vineyard; you are the vines. The one who abides in me and I in him—this one bears much fruit, because apart from me you are not able to do anything. ⁶If anyone does not abide in me, he is thrown away like a vine and withers. And they gather them up and throw [them] into the fire; and they are burned. ⁷If you abide in me, and my words abide in you, ask whatever you wish, and it will happen for you. ⁸My Father is glorified by this: that you bear much fruit and become my disciples."

15:1 Ἐγώ εἰμι ἡ ἄμπελος ἡ ἀληθινὴ καὶ ὁ πατήρ μου ὁ γεωργός ἐστιν.

Ἐγώ εἰμι ἡ ἄμπελος ἡ ἀληθινή. This is one of Jesus' "I am" pronouncements in the FG with an explicit predicate; for other statements of this type, see 6:35, 48, 51; 8:12; 10:7, 9, 11, 14; 11:25; 14:6; 15:5.

Ἐγώ. Nominative subject of εἰμι. Fronted for emphasis. This verse is connected to the previous one by asyndeton.

εἰμι. Pres act ind 1st sg εἰμί.

ἡ ἄμπελος ἡ ἀληθινή. Predicate nominative. The adjective ἀληθινή stands in the second attributive position (see 1:9 on τὸ φῶς τὸ ἀληθινόν). Most English versions and commentaries translate ἄμπελος as "vine," i.e., the plant *Vitis vinifera*. An alternative rendering is proposed by Caragounis (2004, 247–61), who argues that the meaning of ἄμπελος changed over time, from "vine" in classical Greek to "vineyard" in proto-Neo-Hellenic or proto–Modern Greek. Since this rendering makes better sense of the imagery employed in this passage (see Caragounis 2012, 254–55), I have adopted it in the translation above.

καὶ. Coordinating conjunction.

ὁ πατήρ. Nominative subject of ἐστιν.

μου. Genitive of relationship qualifying πατήρ.

ὁ γεωργός. Predicate nominative. Fronted for emphasis.

ἐστιν. Pres act ind 3rd sg εἰμί.

15:2 πᾶν κλῆμα ἐν ἐμοὶ μὴ φέρον καρπὸν αἴρει αὐτό, καὶ πᾶν τὸ καρπὸν φέρον καθαίρει αὐτὸ ἵνα καρπὸν πλείονα φέρῃ.

πᾶν κλῆμα. Traditional grammarians regard this nominal phrase either as a pendent accusative (Wallace 1996, 198) or as a pendent nominative (Zerwick and Grosvenor, 333; Zerwick §25; Harris 2015, 266), both of which presume that the sentence is characterized by an awkward syntax. A more satisfying explanation is offered by discourse analysis, which pays attention to the cognitive function of a dislocated element. In that regard, πᾶν κλῆμα functions as the accusative direct object of αἴρει in a left-dislocation, resumed by αὐτό. κλῆμα is usually understood as a branch of the plant *Vitis vinifera*, but Caragounis has shown that the meaning of this noun changed in proto-Neo-Hellenic Greek, denoting "no longer merely the branch or twig but the whole plant, the vine itself" (2012, 251). Since this rendering makes more sense with both verbs αἴρει (a vine is taken up from a vineyard) and καθαίρει (pruning is done not to a branch but to the plant itself by removing superfluous or sickly branches), I have adopted it in my translation above. This verse is connected to the previous one by asyndeton.

ἐν ἐμοί. State of being, describing a close personal relationship. The PP modifies κλῆμα ("every vine in me").

μή. Negative particle normally used with non-indicative verbs.

φέρον. Pres act ptc neut acc sg φέρω (attributive or conditional). If the participle is viewed as attributive, it modifies κλῆμα, standing in the fourth attributive position (noun-attributive participle): "every vine that does not bear fruit . . ." If the participle is regarded as conditional, it conveys a condition on which the fulfillment of the verb depends: "every vine, if it does not bear fruit, . . ." (Moule, 104).

καρπὸν. Accusative direct object of φέρον.

αἴρει. Pres act ind 3rd sg αἴρω. The implied subject of the verb is the Father from the preceding verse.

αὐτό. Accusative direct object of αἴρει, resuming πᾶν κλῆμα (see above). αὐτό is placed in an unmarked position (following the verb), which occurs relatively infrequently in the FG (1:12; 7:38; 15:2; 17:2; cf. Runge 2010, 297). Much more common are left-dislocations that have the resumptive pronoun in a marked position (at the beginning of the clause).

καὶ. Coordinating conjunction.

πᾶν τὸ . . . φέρον. Accusative direct object of καθαίρει in a left-dislocation, resumed by αὐτὸ (see Runge 2010, 287–313). Like πᾶν κλῆμα above, πᾶν τὸ . . . φέρον introduces a new entity in the discourse ("every [vine] that bears fruit"), which is resumed by a pronoun in an unmarked position.

τὸ . . . φέρον. Pres act ptc neut acc sg φέρω (substantival).

καρπὸν. Accusative direct object of φέρον.

καθαίρει. Pres act ind 3rd sg καθαίρω. The implied subject of the verb is again the Father from the previous verse. καθαίρω is a NT *hapax legomenon*, which here "involves a play on two different meanings. The one meaning involves pruning of a plant, while the other meaning involves a cleansing process" (LN 43.12). Another wordplay (paronomasia) is created through the similar-sounding verbs αἴρει . . . καθαίρει, which share the same stem.

αὐτὸ. Accusative direct object of καθαίρει, resuming πᾶν τὸ . . . φέρον.

ἵνα. Introduces a purpose clause.

καρπὸν πλείονα. Accusative direct object of φέρῃ. πλείονα is masc acc sg of πλείων, a comparative of πολύς. Fronted for emphasis.

φέρῃ. Pres act subj 3rd sg φέρω. Subjunctive with ἵνα.

15:3 ἤδη ὑμεῖς καθαροί ἐστε διὰ τὸν λόγον ὃν λελάληκα ὑμῖν·

ἤδη. Adverb ("already"). This verse is connected to the previous one by asyndeton.

ὑμεῖς. Nominative subject of ἐστε.

καθαροί. Predicate adjective. Fronted for emphasis.

ἐστε. Pres act ind 2nd pl εἰμί.

διὰ τὸν λόγον. Causal ("because of the word") or instrumental ("by the word").

ὅν. Accusative direct object of λελάληκα. The antecedent of the relative pronoun is τὸν λόγον.

λελάληκα. Prf act ind 1st sg λαλέω. On the significance of the verbal aspect of λελάληκα, see 14:25.

ὑμῖν. Dative indirect object of λελάληκα.

15:4 μείνατε ἐν ἐμοί, κἀγὼ ἐν ὑμῖν. καθὼς τὸ κλῆμα οὐ δύναται καρπὸν φέρειν ἀφ' ἑαυτοῦ ἐὰν μὴ μένῃ ἐν τῇ ἀμπέλῳ, οὕτως οὐδὲ ὑμεῖς ἐὰν μὴ ἐν ἐμοὶ μένητε.

μείνατε. Aor act impv 2nd pl μένω. In this context, μένω ("remain, continue, abide") describes "someone who does not leave a certain realm or sphere" (BDAG, 631.1.a.β). The perfective aspect of the aorist imperative indicates that the command to abide in Jesus is viewed as a summary occurrence without regard to its progress. Fanning (370) suggests that the use of the aorist for this purpose underlines the urgency of the command "even though the desired action is a thing to be done not only (or perhaps not at all) in the immediate circumstance but as a customary practice." This verse is connected to the previous one by asyndeton.

ἐν ἐμοί. State of being, describing a close personal relationship between the disciples and Jesus (LN 89.119).

κἀγώ. Formed by crasis from καὶ ἐγώ. καὶ is a coordinating conjunction that may express a comparison ("Abide in me as I abide in you" [NRSV]) or a consequence ("Abide in me and then I will abide in you"). If the latter, the imperative μείνατε functions as a "conditional imperative" because it conveys the idea that "if X, then Y will happen" (Wallace 1996, 489). ἐγώ is the nominative subject of an implied μένω or μενῶ.

ἐν ὑμῖν. State of being, describing a close personal relationship between Jesus and the disciples.

καθὼς ... οὕτως. A point/counterpoint set ("just as ... so") that compares the vine's abiding in the vineyard to the disciples' abiding in Jesus. This clause is connected to the previous one by asyndeton.

τὸ κλῆμα. Nominative subject of δύναται.

οὐ ... οὐδέ. "Neither ... nor." οὐδέ is a combination of the negative particle οὐ and the marker of narrative development δέ.

δύναται. Pres mid ind 3rd sg δύναμαι.

καρπόν. Accusative direct object of φέρειν.

φέρειν. Pres act inf φέρω (complementary).

ἀφ' ἑαυτοῦ. Agency (see 5:19 on ἀφ' ἑαυτοῦ).

ἐάν. Introduces the protasis of a third-class condition.

μή. Negative particle normally used with non-indicative verbs. ἐὰν μή can be translated "unless."

μένῃ. Pres act subj 3rd sg μένω. Subjunctive with ἐάν.
ἐν τῇ ἀμπέλῳ. Locative.
ὑμεῖς. Nominative subject of an implied δύνασθε. The personal pronoun is emphatic.
ἐάν. Introduces the protasis of a third-class condition.
μή. Negative particle normally used with non-indicative verbs. ἐὰν μή = "unless."
ἐν ἐμοί. State of being, describing a close personal relationship between the disciples and Jesus. Fronted for emphasis.
μένητε. Pres act subj 2nd pl μένω. Subjunctive with ἐάν.

15:5 ἐγώ εἰμι ἡ ἄμπελος, ὑμεῖς τὰ κλήματα. ὁ μένων ἐν ἐμοὶ κἀγὼ ἐν αὐτῷ οὗτος φέρει καρπὸν πολύν, ὅτι χωρὶς ἐμοῦ οὐ δύνασθε ποιεῖν οὐδέν.

ἐγώ εἰμι ἡ ἄμπελος. This is the last of Jesus' "I am" pronouncements with an explicit predicate in the FG; for other statements of this type, see 6:35, 48, 51; 8:12; 10:7, 9, 11, 14; 11:25; 14:6; 15:1.
ἐγώ. Nominative subject of εἰμί. The personal pronoun is emphatic and contrastive, distinguishing the speaker from the addressees. This verse is connected to the previous one by asyndeton.
εἰμι. Pres act ind 1st sg εἰμί.
ἡ ἄμπελος. Predicate nominative. On the meaning, see 15:1.
ὑμεῖς. Nominative subject of an implied ἐστέ. The personal pronoun is emphatic and contrastive, distinguishing the addressees from the speaker.
τὰ κλήματα. Predicate nominative.
ὁ μένων. Pres act ptc masc nom sg μένω (substantival). Nominative subject of φέρει in a left-dislocation, resumed by οὗτος (see Runge 2010, 287–313). The participial construction is continued by an implied finite verb (see κἀγώ below) "because ὁ μένων was felt to be the equivalent of ἐάν τις μένῃ" (BDF §468.3). This clause is connected to the previous one by asyndeton.
ἐν ἐμοί. State of being, describing a close personal relationship between a believer and Jesus.
κἀγώ. Formed by crasis from καὶ ἐγώ. καί is a coordinating conjunction; ἐγώ is the nominative subject of an implied μένω.
ἐν αὐτῷ. State of being, describing a close personal relationship between Jesus and a believer.
οὗτος. Nominative subject of φέρει, resuming ὁ μένων.
φέρει. Pres act ind 3rd sg φέρω.

καρπὸν πολύν. Accusative direct object of φέρει. The adjective πολὺν stands in the fourth attributive position (see 3:15 on ζωὴν αἰώνιον). For a reversed order, see πολὺν καρπὸν in 12:24.

ὅτι. Introduces a causal clause.

χωρὶς ἐμοῦ. Separation. χωρίς ("without, apart from") is an improper preposition. On a distinction between improper and proper prepositions, see 1:3 on χωρὶς αὐτοῦ.

οὐ. Negative particle normally used with indicative verbs.

δύνασθε. Pres mid ind 2nd pl δύναμαι.

ποιεῖν. Pres act inf ποιέω (complementary).

οὐδέν. Accusative direct object of ποιεῖν. The two negatives οὐ ... οὐδέν reinforce each other: lit. "you are not able to do nothing" = "you are not able to do anything" or "you are able to do nothing at all" (see 3:27 on οὐδὲ).

15:6 ἐὰν μή τις μένῃ ἐν ἐμοί, ἐβλήθη ἔξω ὡς τὸ κλῆμα καὶ ἐξηράνθη καὶ συνάγουσιν αὐτὰ καὶ εἰς τὸ πῦρ βάλλουσιν καὶ καίεται.

ἐάν. Introduces the protasis of a third-class condition. This verse is connected to the previous one by asyndeton.

μή. Negative particle normally used with non-indicative verbs. ἐὰν μή = "unless."

τις. Nominative subject of μένῃ.

μένῃ. Pres act subj 3rd sg μένω. Subjunctive with ἐάν.

ἐν ἐμοί. State of being, describing a close personal relationship between a believer and Jesus.

ἐβλήθη. Aor pass ind 3rd sg βάλλω. The verb marks the beginning of the apodosis of a third-class condition. The implied subject is τις from the protasis. In this conditional structure, the aorist verb form does not describe an action that is antecedent to action in the protasis (for a critique of this view, see Porter 1994, 266). Rather, since it depicts a consequence of the condition in the protasis, ἐβλήθη may refer to an immediate sequence (the so-called dramatic aorist; Moule, 12–13), to an act that is valid for all time (the so-called gnomic aorist; cf. BDF §333.1), or to the future (the so-called proleptic aorist; cf. Zerwick §257; Fanning, 269–70; Caragounis 2004, 276).

ἔξω. Adverb ("outside").

ὡς. Comparative particle, introducing an elliptical clause that presumes the repetition of the main verb (see τὸ κλῆμα below).

τὸ κλῆμα. Nominative subject of an implied ἐβλήθη: "like a vine is thrown away."

καί. Coordinating conjunction.

ἐξηράνθη. Aor mid ind 3rd sg ξηραίνω. Like ἐβλήθη above, the implied subject of ἐξηράνθη is τις from the protasis. Brown (2:661) notes that "[w]hen a man is made the immediate subject of these verbs, it is very awkward." ξηραίνω is a derivative of ξηρός ("dry") and means "to become dry, dry up, wither" (BDAG, 684.1.b). If the sense of the verb is transitive, ἐξηράνθη is the true passive. If the sense is intransitive, it is better to classify ἐξηράνθη as the middle voice (see "Deponency" in the Series Introduction) rather than the passive in the active sense (see BDAG, 684.1.b).

καί. Coordinating conjunction.

συνάγουσιν. Pres act ind 3rd pl συνάγω. This is an example of indefinite plural, i.e., "the use of the third-person plural to indicate no one in particular, but rather 'someone'" (Wallace 1996, 402). Wallace suggests that in many cases "it is better to convert an indefinite plural into a passive in which the object becomes the subject" (Wallace 1996, 402). Such use of third-person plural active in place of passive is typical in Hebrew and Aramaic (MHT 2:447–48).

αὐτά. Accusative direct object of συνάγουσιν. The personal pronoun refers to the vines that are thrown away, but the plural form is awkward because the previous clause uses the singular τὸ κλῆμα. This is why some copyists (ℵ D L Δ Ψ $f^{1.13}$ 33 565 *l*844 et al.) changed the plural αὐτά to the singular αὐτό (Metzger, 209).

καί. Coordinating conjunction.

εἰς τὸ πῦρ. Spatial.

βάλλουσιν. Pres act ind 3rd pl βάλλω. Indefinite plural (see συνάγουσιν above).

καί. Coordinating conjunction.

καίεται. Pres pass ind 3rd sg καίω. The implied subject of the verb is αὐτά.

15:7 ἐὰν μείνητε ἐν ἐμοὶ καὶ τὰ ῥήματά μου ἐν ὑμῖν μείνῃ, ὃ ἐὰν θέλητε αἰτήσασθε, καὶ γενήσεται ὑμῖν.

ἐάν. Introduces the protasis of a third-class condition. This verse is connected to the previous one by asyndeton.

μείνητε. Aor act subj 2nd pl μένω. Subjunctive with ἐάν.

ἐν ἐμοί. State of being, describing a close personal relationship between the disciples and Jesus.

καί. Coordinating conjunction.

τὰ ῥήματά. Nominative subject of μείνῃ. ῥήματά, which has an acute accent on the antepenult, acquired an additional accent, the acute, on the ultima from the enclitic μου (Smyth §183; Carson 1985, 48).

μου. Subjective genitive qualifying ῥήματά.

ἐν ὑμῖν. Locative.

μείνῃ. Aor act subj 3rd sg μένω. Subjunctive with ἐάν. Neuter plural subjects typically take singular verbs (see 1:28 on ἐγένετο).

ὃ ἐάν. The relative pronoun ὃ and the particle ἐάν (= ἄν) form an indefinite relative pronoun (see Culy 2004, 27–28), which introduces a headless relative clause that, in its entirety (ὃ ἐὰν θέλητε), serves as the direct object of αἰτήσασθε. Within its clause, ὃ ἐάν is the accusative direct object of θέλητε.

θέλητε. Pres act subj 2nd pl θέλω. Subjunctive with ἐάν.

αἰτήσασθε. Aor mid impv 2nd pl αἰτέω.

καί. Coordinating conjunction.

γενήσεται. Fut mid ind 3rd sg γίνομαι.

ὑμῖν. Dative of advantage.

15:8 ἐν τούτῳ ἐδοξάσθη ὁ πατήρ μου, ἵνα καρπὸν πολὺν φέρητε καὶ γένησθε ἐμοὶ μαθηταί.

ἐν τούτῳ. Instrumental. The demonstrative pronoun could be anaphoric, referring to God's response to prayer in 15:7, but it is more likely that it is cataphoric, referring to the ἵνα clause that follows. This verse is connected to the previous one by asyndeton.

ἐδοξάσθη. Aor pass ind 3rd sg δοξάζω. The aorist tense may refer to the future (the so-called proleptic aorist; BDF §333.2; Fanning, 270; Caragounis 2004, 276) or describe a timeless action (the so-called gnomic aorist; Harris 2015, 268; McKay 1994, 48; Caragounis 2004, 276).

ὁ πατήρ. Nominative subject of ἐδοξάσθη.

μου. Genitive of relationship qualifying πατήρ.

ἵνα. Introduces an epexegetical clause that explains τούτῳ (Haubeck and von Siebenthal, 588; Harris 2015, 268). An epexegetical ἵνα clause is equivalent to an epexegetical infinitive: ἐν τούτῳ ἐδοξάσθη ὁ πατήρ μου, ἵνα καρπὸν πολὺν φέρητε = ἐν τῷ φέρειν ὑμᾶς (BDF §394). This could also be regarded as a ἵνα clause that is appositional to τούτῳ: "My Father is glorified by this, [*namely, that* you bear much fruit . . .]" (Wallace 1996, 475–76).

καρπὸν πολύν. Accusative direct object of φέρητε. The adjective πολύν stands in the fourth attributive position (see 3:15 on ζωὴν αἰώνιον). The same expression occurs in 15:5. For a reversed order, see πολὺν καρπόν in 12:24.

φέρητε. Pres act subj 2nd pl φέρω. Subjunctive with ἵνα.

καί. Coordinating conjunction.

γένησθε. Aor mid subj 2nd pl γίνομαι. Subjunctive with ἵνα. If the original reading is γένησθε (𝔓⁶⁶ᵛⁱᵈ B D L Θ 1 565 [579] *l*844), it is coordinate with φέρητε as part of the ἵνα clause, suggesting that bearing much fruit and becoming Jesus' disciples are two related ways of glorifying the Father rather than one action being the consequence of the other. As Brown explains, "[T]he sense is not that when the hearers bear fruit, they will become his disciples, but that in bearing fruit they show how they are disciples" (2:662–63). The variant reading that has the future-tense γενήσεσθε (attested in ℵ A K Γ Δ Ψ *f*¹³ 33 700 892ˢ 1241 1424 𝔐) probably indicates that καὶ γενήσεσθε ἐμοὶ μαθηταί should be construed as an independent clause, in which case becoming Jesus' disciples represents a consequence of fruit bearing (BDF §369.3). A decision between these two readings is difficult. Some scholars (Brown, 2:662; Barrett, 475) prefer γενήσεσθε over γένησθε (printed in NA²⁸/UBS⁵ and SBLGNT because of its diverse external support; cf. Metzger, 209), but they still regard fruit bearing and becoming a disciple as two inseparable expressions of discipleship rather than as two subsequent activities.

ἐμοὶ. Dative of possession ("disciples belonging to me") or dative of advantage ("disciples for me").

μαθηταί. Predicate nominative.

John 15:9-17

⁹"Just as the Father has loved me, I also have loved you. Abide in my love. ¹⁰If you keep my commandments, you will abide in my love, just as I have kept the commandments of my Father and abide in his love. ¹¹I have spoken these things to you in order that my joy may be in you, and that your joy may be complete. ¹²My commandment is this: that you love one another as I have loved you. ¹³No one has greater love than this: that someone lay down his life for his friends. ¹⁴You are my friends if you do what I command you. ¹⁵No longer do I call you servants because a servant does not know what his master is doing. But I have called you friends because everything that I have heard from my Father I have made known to you. ¹⁶You did not choose me, but I chose you and appointed you, so that you should go and bear fruit and that your fruit should remain, so that whatever you ask the Father in my name he may give to you. ¹⁷These things I command you that you love one another."

15:9 Καθὼς ἠγάπησέν με ὁ πατήρ, κἀγὼ ὑμᾶς ἠγάπησα· μείνατε ἐν τῇ ἀγάπῃ τῇ ἐμῇ.

Καθὼς . . . κἀγώ. A point/counterpoint set ("just as . . . also") that compares the Father's love for Jesus with Jesus' love for his disciples. κἀγώ is formed by crasis from καὶ ἐγώ. καί is adverbial (adjunctive). ἐγώ is the nominative subject of ἠγάπησα. This verse is connected to the previous one by asyndeton.

ἠγάπησέν. Aor act ind 3rd sg ἀγαπάω. ἠγάπησέν, which has an acute accent on the antepenult, acquired an additional accent, the acute, on the ultima from the enclitic με (Smyth §183; Carson 1985, 48).

με. Accusative direct object of ἠγάπησέν.

ὁ πατήρ. Nominative subject of ἠγάπησέν.

ὑμᾶς. Accusative direct object of ἠγάπησα.

ἠγάπησα. Aor act ind 1st sg ἀγαπάω.

μείνατε. Aor act impv 2nd pl μένω (see 15:4). This clause is connected to the preceding one by asyndeton.

ἐν τῇ ἀγάπῃ τῇ ἐμῇ. State or condition. The possessive adjective ἐμῇ stands in the second attributive position (see 1:9 on τὸ φῶς τὸ ἀληθινόν). The meaning of the PP is subjective: "my love" = "my love for you" (Zerwick and Grosvenor, 332).

15:10 ἐὰν τὰς ἐντολάς μου τηρήσητε, μενεῖτε ἐν τῇ ἀγάπῃ μου, καθὼς ἐγὼ τὰς ἐντολὰς τοῦ πατρός μου τετήρηκα καὶ μένω αὐτοῦ ἐν τῇ ἀγάπῃ.

ἐάν. Introduces the protasis of a third-class condition. This verse is connected to the previous one by asyndeton.

τὰς ἐντολάς. Accusative direct object of τηρήσητε.

μου. Subjective genitive qualifying ἐντολάς.

τηρήσητε. Aor act subj 2nd pl τηρέω. Subjunctive with ἐάν.

μενεῖτε. Fut act ind 2nd pl μένω.

ἐν τῇ ἀγάπῃ. State or condition (see 15:9).

μου. Subjective genitive qualifying ἀγάπη.

καθώς. Introduces a clause that compares, on the one hand, the disciples' obedience to Jesus' commandments to Jesus' obedience to the commandments of the Father, and, on the other hand, the disciples' abiding in Jesus' love to Jesus' abiding in the Father's love.

ἐγώ. Nominative subject of τετήρηκα and μένω.

τὰς ἐντολάς. Accusative direct object of τετήρηκα.

τοῦ πατρός. Subjective genitive qualifying ἐντολάς.

μου. Genitive of relationship qualifying πατρός.

τετήρηκα. Prf act ind 1st sg τηρέω.
καί. Coordinating conjunction.
μένω. Pres act ind 1st sg μένω.
αὐτοῦ. Both subjective and objective genitive qualifying ἀγάπη (Haubeck and von Siebenthal, 588). Fronted for emphasis.
ἐν τῇ ἀγάπῃ. State or condition.

15:11 Ταῦτα λελάληκα ὑμῖν ἵνα ἡ χαρὰ ἡ ἐμὴ ἐν ὑμῖν ᾖ καὶ ἡ χαρὰ ὑμῶν πληρωθῇ.

Ταῦτα. Accusative direct object of λελάληκα. Fronted for emphasis. This verse is connected to the previous one by asyndeton.
λελάληκα. Prf act ind 1st sg λαλέω (see 6:63). On the significance of the verbal aspect of λελάληκα, see 14:25.
ὑμῖν. Dative indirect object of λελάληκα.
ἵνα. Introduces a purpose clause.
ἡ χαρὰ ἡ ἐμή. Nominative subject of ᾖ. The possessive adjective ἐμὴ stands in the second attributive position (see 1:9 on τὸ φῶς τὸ ἀληθινόν).
ἐν ὑμῖν. Locative.
ᾖ. Pres act subj 3rd sg εἰμί. Subjunctive with ἵνα.
καί. Coordinating conjunction.
ἡ χαρά. Nominative subject of πληρωθῇ.
ὑμῶν. Subjective genitive qualifying χαρά.
πληρωθῇ. Aor pass subj 3rd sg πληρόω.

15:12 Αὕτη ἐστὶν ἡ ἐντολὴ ἡ ἐμή, ἵνα ἀγαπᾶτε ἀλλήλους καθὼς ἠγάπησα ὑμᾶς.

Αὕτη. Predicate nominative. Fronted for emphasis. Culy (2004, 11) explains that in equative clauses, demonstratives "will tend to function as the predicate when they are cataphoric and as the subject when they are anaphoric." In this construction, the demonstrative Αὕτη is cataphoric, i.e., it points forward to the ἵνα clause. This verse is connected to the previous one by asyndeton.
ἐστίν. Pres act ind 3rd sg εἰμί.
ἡ ἐντολὴ ἡ ἐμή. Nominative subject of ἐστίν. The possessive adjective ἐμή stands in the second attributive position (see 1:9 on τὸ φῶς τὸ ἀληθινόν). The singular ("my commandment") replaces the plural from v. 10 ("my commandments").
ἵνα. Introduces an epexegetical clause that explains Αὕτη (Harris 2015, 269; Zerwick and Grosvenor, 332) or, alternatively, a clause that is appositional to Αὕτη (Wallace 1996, 475–76).

ἀγαπᾶτε. Pres act subj 2nd pl ἀγαπάω. Subjunctive with ἵνα.
ἀλλήλους. Accusative direct object of ἀγαπᾶτε.
καθώς. Introduces a comparative clause.
ἠγάπησα. Aor act ind 1st sg ἀγαπάω.
ὑμᾶς. Accusative direct object of ἠγάπησα.

15:13 μείζονα ταύτης ἀγάπην οὐδεὶς ἔχει, ἵνα τις τὴν ψυχὴν αὐτοῦ θῇ ὑπὲρ τῶν φίλων αὐτοῦ.

μείζονα . . . ἀγάπην. Accusative direct object of ἔχει. μείζονα is the comparative adjective from μέγας, which stands in the first (anarthrous) attributive position (see 2:6 on λίθιναι ὑδρίαι). In this formulation, the noun and its adjectival modifier are separated by a genitive of comparison, ταύτης. This verse is connected to the previous one by asyndeton.
ταύτης. Genitive of comparison. This elliptical formulation implies the addition of τῆς ἀγάπης ("than this [love]").
οὐδεὶς. Nominative subject of ἔχει.
ἔχει. Pres act ind 3rd sg ἔχω.
ἵνα. Introduces an epexegetical clause that explains ταύτης. An epexegetical ἵνα clause is equivalent to an epexegetical infinitive (BDF §394).
τις. Nominative subject of θῇ.
τὴν ψυχὴν. Accusative direct object of θῇ.
αὐτοῦ. Possessive genitive qualifying ψυχὴν.
θῇ. Aor act subj 3rd sg τίθημι. Subjunctive with ἵνα.
ὑπὲρ τῶν φίλων. Representation ("on behalf of his friends") and substitution ("in the place of his friends"; cf. Harris 2015, 269). For other prepositional phrases with ὑπέρ in the FG, see 6:51; 10:11, 15; 11:50, 51, 52; 13:37, 38; 17:19; 18:14.
αὐτοῦ. Genitive of relationship qualifying φίλων.

15:14 ὑμεῖς φίλοι μού ἐστε ἐὰν ποιῆτε ἃ ἐγὼ ἐντέλλομαι ὑμῖν.

ὑμεῖς. Nominative subject of ἐστε. The personal pronoun introduces the apodosis of a third-class condition, which here precedes the protasis. ὑμεῖς is emphatic and contrastive, distinguishing the disciples who should obey the commandments from Jesus, who gives the commandments. This verse is connected to the previous one by asyndeton.
φίλοι. Predicate nominative. Fronted for emphasis.
μού. Genitive of relationship qualifying φίλοι. The enclitic μού is accented because it is followed by the enclitic ἐστε. "When several enclitics occur in succession, each receives an accent from the following, only the last having no accent" (Smyth §185).

ἐστε. Pres act ind 2nd pl εἰμί.
ἐάν. Introduces the protasis of a third-class condition.
ποιῆτε. Pres act subj 2nd pl ποιέω. Subjunctive with ἐάν.
ἅ. Introduces a headless relative clause that, in its entirety (ἃ ἐγὼ ἐντέλλομαι ὑμῖν), serves as the direct object of ποιῆτε. Within its clause, ἃ is the accusative direct object of ἐντέλλομαι.
ἐγώ. Nominative subject of ἐντέλλομαι. The personal pronoun is emphatic and contrastive (see ὑμεῖς above).
ἐντέλλομαι. Pres mid ind 1st sg ἐντέλλομαι.
ὑμῖν. Dative indirect object of ἐντέλλομαι.

15:15 οὐκέτι λέγω ὑμᾶς δούλους, ὅτι ὁ δοῦλος οὐκ οἶδεν τί ποιεῖ αὐτοῦ ὁ κύριος· ὑμᾶς δὲ εἴρηκα φίλους, ὅτι πάντα ἃ ἤκουσα παρὰ τοῦ πατρός μου ἐγνώρισα ὑμῖν.

οὐκέτι. Negative adverb of time ("no longer, no further"). This verse is connected to the previous one by asyndeton.
λέγω. Pres act ind 1st sg λέγω.
ὑμᾶς. Accusative direct object of λέγω in a double accusative object-complement construction.
δούλους. Accusative complement to ὑμᾶς in a double accusative object-complement construction. δοῦλος could mean "slave" or "servant." The latter seems more appropriate in this context because "the implication that hitherto Jesus had treated his disciples as slaves seems too harsh" (Brown, 2:664).
ὅτι. Introduces a causal clause.
ὁ δοῦλος. Nominative subject of οἶδεν. The article is generic ("a servant").
οὐκ. Negative particle normally used with indicative verbs.
οἶδεν. Prf act ind 3rd sg οἶδα (see 1:26 on οἴδατε).
τί. Indirect interrogative ("what") that functions as a substitute for the relative pronoun, introducing a headless relative clause that, in its entirety (τί ποιεῖ αὐτοῦ ὁ κύριος), serves as the direct object of οἶδεν. Within its clause, τί is accusative direct object of ποιεῖ.
ποιεῖ. Pres act ind 3rd sg ποιέω.
αὐτοῦ. Genitive of subordination qualifying κύριος. The preposed pronoun is thematically salient (Levinsohn 2000, 64).
ὁ κύριος. Nominative subject of ποιεῖ.
ὑμᾶς. Accusative direct object of εἴρηκα in a double accusative object-complement construction.
δέ. Marker of narrative development.
εἴρηκα. Prf act ind 1st sg λέγω.

φίλους. Accusative complement to ὑμᾶς in a double accusative object-complement construction.

ὅτι. Introduces a causal clause.

πάντα. Accusative direct object of ἐγνώρισα.

ἅ. Accusative direct object of ἤκουσα. The antecedent of the relative pronoun is πάντα.

ἤκουσα. Aor act ind 1st sg ἀκούω.

παρὰ τοῦ πατρός. Source.

μου. Genitive of relationship qualifying πατρός.

ἐγνώρισα. Aor act ind 1st sg γνωρίζω. The verb means "to cause information to be known by someone—'to make known'" (LN 28.26). Louw and Nida add that, in this context, "the focal component of meaning in γνωρίζω . . . would seem to be upon the resulting knowledge, not upon the communicative process" (28 n. 7).

ὑμῖν. Dative indirect object of ἐγνώρισα.

15:16 οὐχ ὑμεῖς με ἐξελέξασθε, ἀλλ' ἐγὼ ἐξελεξάμην ὑμᾶς καὶ ἔθηκα ὑμᾶς ἵνα ὑμεῖς ὑπάγητε καὶ καρπὸν φέρητε καὶ ὁ καρπὸς ὑμῶν μένῃ, ἵνα ὅ τι ἂν αἰτήσητε τὸν πατέρα ἐν τῷ ὀνόματί μου δῷ ὑμῖν.

οὐχ . . . ἀλλ'. A point/counterpoint set ("not this . . . but that") that negates the incorrect explanation of election (you chose me) and replaces it with the correct one (I chose you). On the function of ἀλλά in a point/counterpoint set, see 1:8. This verse is connected to the previous one by asyndeton.

ὑμεῖς. Nominative subject of ἐξελέξασθε. The personal pronoun is emphatic and contrastive, juxtaposing the disciples to Jesus with regard to election (Wallace 1996, 322).

με. Accusative direct object of ἐξελέξασθε.

ἐξελέξασθε. Aor mid ind 2nd pl ἐκλέγω. The middle voice emphasizes the subject's interest in the action ("you did not choose me for yourself").

ἐγώ. Nominative subject of ἐξελεξάμην and ἔθηκα. The personal pronoun is emphatic and contrastive (see ὑμεῖς above).

ἐξελεξάμην. Aor mid ind 1st sg ἐκλέγω. The middle voice again emphasizes the subject's interest in the action ("I chose you for myself").

ὑμᾶς. Accusative direct object of ἐξελεξάμην.

καί. Coordinating conjunction.

ἔθηκα. Aor act ind 1st sg τίθημι. The same verb is used in 15:13 to express the idea of laying down one's life. In this verse, however, τίθημι means "to assign someone to a particular task, function, or role" (LN 37.96).

ὑμᾶς. Accusative direct object of ἔθηκα.
ἵνα. Introduces a purpose clause.
ὑμεῖς. Nominative subject of ὑπάγητε.
ὑπάγητε. Pres act subj 2nd pl ὑπάγω. Subjunctive with ἵνα.
καὶ. Coordinating conjunction.
καρπὸν. Accusative direct object of φέρητε.
φέρητε. Pres act subj 2nd pl φέρω. Subjunctive with ἵνα.
καὶ. Coordinating conjunction.
ὁ καρπὸς. Nominative subject of μένῃ.
ὑμῶν. Subjective genitive qualifying καρπὸς.
μένῃ. Pres act subj 3rd sg μένω. Subjunctive with ἵνα.
ἵνα. Introduces a purpose clause. This second ἵνα clause could be regarded as coordinate with the first ἵνα clause, indicating two distinct purposes of Jesus' election and appointment of the disciples (Barrett, 478) or subordinate to the first ἵνα clause, indicating that granting the disciples' requests by the Father is dependent on the disciples' bearing fruit that will last (Schnackenburg, 3:112).

ὅ τι ἄν. Introduces a headless relative clause that, in its entirety (ὅ τι ἄν αἰτήσητε τὸν πατέρα ἐν τῷ ὀνόματί μου), serves as the direct object of δῷ. On the meaning of ὅ τι ἄν, see 14:13. Within its clause, ὅ τι ἄν functions as an accusative direct object (thing) of αἰτήσητε in a double accusative person-thing construction.

αἰτήσητε. Aor act subj 2nd pl αἰτέω. On the meaning of αἰτέω in a double accusative construction, see 11:22.

τὸν πατέρα. Accusative direct object (person) of αἰτήσητε in a double accusative person-thing construction.

ἐν τῷ ὀνόματί. Instrumental (see 14:13, 14, 26; 16:23, 24, 26). ὀνόματί, which has an acute accent on the antepenult, acquired an additional accent, the acute, on the ultima from the enclitic μου (Smyth §183; Carson 1985, 48).

μου. Possessive genitive qualifying ὀνόματί.
δῷ. Aor act subj 3rd sg δίδωμι. Subjunctive with ἵνα.
ὑμῖν. Dative indirect object of δῷ.

15:17 Ταῦτα ἐντέλλομαι ὑμῖν, ἵνα ἀγαπᾶτε ἀλλήλους.

Ταῦτα. Accusative direct object of ἐντέλλομαι. The demonstrative pronoun could be anaphoric, referring to Jesus' previous message, but it is more likely that it is cataphoric, pointing forward to the ἵνα clause that follows. This verse is connected to the previous one by asyndeton.

ἐντέλλομαι. Pres mid ind 1st sg ἐντέλλομαι.
ὑμῖν. Dative indirect object of ἐντέλλομαι.

ἵνα. Introduces either an epexegetical clause that explains Ταῦτα (see 13:34 and 15:12) or, less likely, a purpose clause (if Ταῦτα is regarded as anaphoric).

ἀγαπᾶτε. Pres act subj 2nd pl ἀγαπάω. Subjunctive with ἵνα.

ἀλλήλους. Accusative direct object of ἀγαπᾶτε.

John 15:18-27

¹⁸"If the world hates you, know that it has hated me before [it hated] you. ¹⁹If you were of the world, the world would love its own. Yet because you are not of the world, but I chose you out of the world—because of this the world hates you. ²⁰Remember the word that I said to you, 'A slave is not greater than his master.' If they persecuted me, they will persecute you too; if they kept my word, they will keep yours too. ²¹But they will do all these things to you on account of my name because they do not know the one who sent me. ²²If I had not come and spoken to them, they would not have sin. But now they have no excuse for their sin. ²³The one who hates me hates my Father also. ²⁴If I had not done among you the works that no one else did, they would not have sin. But now they have both seen and hated both me and my Father. ²⁵But [this has happened] in order that the word that is written in their law might be fulfilled, 'They hated me without a cause.' ²⁶When the Paraclete comes, whom I will send to you from the Father—the Spirit of truth who comes from the Father—that one will testify about me. ²⁷You also will testify because you have been with me from the beginning."

15:18 Εἰ ὁ κόσμος ὑμᾶς μισεῖ, γινώσκετε ὅτι ἐμὲ πρῶτον ὑμῶν μεμίσηκεν.

Εἰ. Introduces the protasis of a first-class condition. This verse is connected to the previous one by asyndeton.

ὁ κόσμος. Nominative subject of μισεῖ. On the portrayal of the world in the FG, see 1:10 on ἐν τῷ κόσμῳ.

ὑμᾶς. Accusative direct object of μισεῖ.

μισεῖ. Pres act ind 3rd sg μισέω.

γινώσκετε. Pres act impv 2nd pl γινώσκω.

ὅτι. Introduces the clausal complement (indirect discourse) of γινώσκετε.

ἐμὲ. Accusative direct object of μεμίσηκεν.

πρῶτον. The superlative used for the comparative πρότερον, functioning as a comparative adjective modifying ἐμὲ ("earlier than [it hated] you"; cf. Harris 2015, 272; BDAG, 893.1.a.α) or an adverbial neuter accusative indicating time or sequence ("before [it hated] you"; cf. Harris 2015, 272; BDAG, 893.1.a.β).

ὑμῶν. Genitive of comparison (if πρῶτον is a comparative adjective) or genitive of reference (if πρῶτον is an adverbial accusative).

μεμίσηκεν. Prf act ind 3rd sg μισέω. The perfect-tense verb form is marked for prominence, while the context (see πρῶτον above) indicates that μεμίσηκεν describes an attitude—a state of hatred—that has begun in the past and continues in the present.

15:19 εἰ ἐκ τοῦ κόσμου ἦτε, ὁ κόσμος ἂν τὸ ἴδιον ἐφίλει· ὅτι δὲ ἐκ τοῦ κόσμου οὐκ ἐστέ, ἀλλ' ἐγὼ ἐξελεξάμην ὑμᾶς ἐκ τοῦ κόσμου, διὰ τοῦτο μισεῖ ὑμᾶς ὁ κόσμος.

εἰ. Introduces the protasis of a second-class (contrary-to-fact) condition. This is the present contrary-to-fact condition because the verbs in both the protasis and the apodosis are in the imperfect. This verse is connected to the previous one by asyndeton.

ἐκ τοῦ κόσμου. Source/origin that determines the character of a person (Zerwick §§134–35). On the portrayal of the world in the FG, see 1:10 on ἐν τῷ κόσμῳ.

ἦτε. Impf act ind 2nd pl εἰμί.

ὁ κόσμος. Nominative subject of ἐφίλει.

ἄν. Marker of contingency in the apodosis of the second-class condition.

τὸ ἴδιον. Accusative direct object of ἐφίλει. The adjective ἴδιος ("one's own") is here used as a substantive ("what it owns, one's property").

ἐφίλει. Impf act ind 3rd sg φιλέω.

ὅτι. Introduces a causal clause. In this verse, the ὅτι clause precedes the explanatory clause introduced by διὰ τοῦτο. For a typical Johannine order (διὰ τοῦτο . . . ὅτι), see 5:16, 18; 8:47; 10:17; 12:18, 39.

δὲ. Marker of narrative development.

ἐκ τοῦ κόσμου. Source/origin that determines the character of a person (see above).

οὐκ . . . ἀλλ'. A point/counterpoint set ("not this . . . but that") that negates the claim that Jesus' disciples belong to the world and replaces it with the claim that Jesus has chosen them out of the world. On the function of ἀλλά in a point/counterpoint set, see 1:8.

ἐστέ. Pres act ind 2nd pl εἰμί.

ἐγώ. Nominative subject of ἐξελεξάμην. Fronted for emphasis.

ἐξελεξάμην. Aor mid ind 1st sg ἐκλέγω.

ὑμᾶς. Accusative direct object of ἐξελεξάμην.

ἐκ τοῦ κόσμου. Separation.

διὰ τοῦτο. Causal. The demonstrative pronoun is anaphoric, referring to the previous ὅτι clause. In this context, the PP διὰ τοῦτο functions as a connective; on this function of διὰ τοῦτο, see 1:31.
μισεῖ. Pres act ind 3rd sg μισέω.
ὑμᾶς. Accusative direct object of μισεῖ.
ὁ κόσμος. Nominative subject of μισεῖ.

15:20 μνημονεύετε τοῦ λόγου οὗ ἐγὼ εἶπον ὑμῖν· οὐκ ἔστιν δοῦλος μείζων τοῦ κυρίου αὐτοῦ. εἰ ἐμὲ ἐδίωξαν, καὶ ὑμᾶς διώξουσιν· εἰ τὸν λόγον μου ἐτήρησαν, καὶ τὸν ὑμέτερον τηρήσουσιν.

μνημονεύετε. Pres act impv 2nd pl μνημονεύω. This verse is connected to the previous one by asyndeton.
τοῦ λόγου. Genitive direct object of μνημονεύετε.
οὗ. The relative pronoun οὗ stands for ὅν, serving as the direct object of εἶπον. It is in the genitive because it is attracted to the case of its antecedent τοῦ λόγου.
ἐγώ. Nominative subject of εἶπον. Fronted as a topical frame.
εἶπον. Aor act ind 1st sg λέγω.
ὑμῖν. Dative indirect object of εἶπον.
οὐκ ἔστιν δοῦλος μείζων τοῦ κυρίου αὐτοῦ. A verbatim repetition of 13:16. This clause is connected to the previous one by asyndeton.
οὐκ. Negative particle normally used with indicative verbs.
ἔστιν. Pres act ind 3rd sg εἰμί. The enclitic ἐστιν is accented ἔστιν when it comes at the beginning of a sentence, when it expresses existence, or when it follows ἀλλ', εἰ, καί, οὐκ, ὅτι, or τοῦτ'. The third condition is fulfilled here.
δοῦλος. Nominative subject of ἔστιν.
μείζων. Predicate adjective. μείζων is a comparative from μέγας.
τοῦ κυρίου. Genitive of comparison.
αὐτοῦ. Genitive of relationship qualifying κυρίου. This clause is connected to the previous one by asyndeton.
εἰ. Introduces the protasis of a first-class condition. This verse is connected to the previous one by asyndeton.
ἐμέ. Accusative direct object of ἐδίωξαν.
ἐδίωξαν. Aor act ind 3rd pl διώκω.
καί. Adverbial use (adjunctive). καί marks the beginning of the apodosis of a first-class condition.
ὑμᾶς. Accusative direct object of διώξουσιν.
διώξουσιν. Fut act ind 3rd pl διώκω.
εἰ. Introduces the protasis of a first-class condition, which is connected to the previous clause by asyndeton. This conditional clause (εἰ

τὸν λόγον μου ἐτήρησαν, καὶ τὸν ὑμέτερον τηρήσουσιν) is parallel to the previous one (εἰ ἐμὲ ἐδίωξαν, καὶ ὑμᾶς διώξουσιν), but since these clauses build a couplet of opposites, it is not possible to claim that both times the first-class condition means "since" (Wallace 1996, 708; Brown, 2:687; contra Harris 2015, 272). Rather, each condition envisions one hypothetical response to Jesus (persecution or acceptance) and, regardless of its likelihood in real life, presents it as a reality for the sake of the argument that whatever happened to Jesus will also happen to his followers.

τὸν λόγον. Accusative direct object of ἐτήρησαν.
μου. Subjective genitive qualifying λόγον.
ἐτήρησαν. Aor act ind 3rd pl τηρέω.
καί. Adverbial use (adjunctive). καί marks the beginning of the apodosis of a first-class condition.
τὸν ὑμέτερον. Accusative direct object of τηρήσουσιν. The expression is elliptical, presuming the repetition of τὸν λόγον from the protasis: [τὸν λόγον] τὸν ὑμέτερον.
τηρήσουσιν. Fut act ind 3rd pl τηρέω.

15:21 ἀλλὰ ταῦτα πάντα ποιήσουσιν εἰς ὑμᾶς διὰ τὸ ὄνομά μου, ὅτι οὐκ οἴδασιν τὸν πέμψαντά με.

ἀλλά. Marker of contrast.
ταῦτα πάντα. Accusative direct object of ποιήσουσιν.
ποιήσουσιν. Fut act ind 3rd pl ποιέω.
εἰς ὑμᾶς. Spatial, with hostile connotation (Zerwick and Grosvenor, 333), serving as an equivalent to a dative of indirect object ὑμῖν (Moule, 69).
διὰ τὸ ὄνομά. Causal. ὄνομα is a synecdoche for the whole person. ὄνομά, which has an acute accent on the antepenult, acquired an additional accent, the acute, on the ultima from the enclitic μου (Smyth §183; Carson 1985, 48).
μου. Possessive genitive qualifying ὄνομά.
ὅτι. Introduces a causal clause.
οὐκ. Negative particle normally used with indicative verbs.
οἴδασιν. Prf act ind 3rd pl οἶδα (see 1:26 on οἴδατε).
τὸν πέμψαντά. Aor act ptc masc acc sg πέμπω (substantival). Accusative direct object of οἴδασιν. πέμψαντά, which has an acute accent on the antepenult, acquired an additional accent, the acute, on the ultima from the enclitic με (Smyth §183; Carson 1985, 48). On the use of the participial forms of πέμπω to either identify or describe God in the FG, see τοῦ πέμψαντός in 4:34.
με. Accusative direct object of πέμψαντά.

15:22 Εἰ μὴ ἦλθον καὶ ἐλάλησα αὐτοῖς, ἁμαρτίαν οὐκ εἴχοσαν· νῦν δὲ πρόφασιν οὐκ ἔχουσιν περὶ τῆς ἁμαρτίας αὐτῶν.

Εἰ. Introduces the protasis of a second-class (contrary-to-fact) condition. The apodosis does not have the marker of contingency because in Hellenistic Greek "the addition of ἄν is no longer obligatory" (BDF §360.1). Typically, the present contrary-to-fact conditions have the imperfect in both the protasis and the apodosis, while the past contrary-to-fact conditions have the aorist in both the protasis and the apodosis. This conditional clause represents a mixed form because the protasis has the verbs in the aorist (ἦλθον and ἐλάλησα), while the apodosis has the imperfect (εἴχοσαν). It is connected to the previous verse by asyndeton.

μὴ. This negative particle is regularly used in contrary-to-fact protases because they employ the so-called unreal indicative (BDF §428.2).

ἦλθον. Aor act ind 1st sg ἔρχομαι.

καὶ. Coordinating conjunction.

ἐλάλησα. Aor act ind 1st sg λαλέω.

αὐτοῖς. Dative indirect object of ἐλάλησα.

ἁμαρτίαν. Accusative direct object of εἴχοσαν. It marks the beginning of the apodosis of a second-class (contrary-to-fact) condition. The phrase ἁμαρτίαν ἔχειν is found only in the Johannine literature (John 9:41; 15:22, 24; 19:11; 1 John 1:8).

οὐκ. Negative particle normally used with indicative verbs.

εἴχοσαν. Impf act ind 3rd pl ἔχω. εἴχοσαν, a form probably imported from -μι verbs, is here used instead of a more common εἶχον (MHT 2:194; Robertson, 335–36; Zerwick and Grosvenor, 333).

νῦν. Temporal adverb focusing on time coextensive with the event of the narrative (BDAG, 681.1.a). The temporal clause introduced by νῦν, which highlights the contrast between the hypothetical situation envisioned in the conditional clause and the actual situation, confirms the contrary-to-fact character of the protasis (Robertson, 1013).

δὲ. Marker of narrative development with a contrastive nuance.

πρόφασιν. Accusative direct object of ἔχουσιν. Fronted for emphasis. This is the only occurrence of πρόφασις in the FG, which in this context denotes "what is said in defense of a particular action, but without real justification—'excuse'" (LN 33.437).

οὐκ. Negative particle normally used with indicative verbs.

ἔχουσιν. Pres act ind 3rd pl ἔχω.

περὶ τῆς ἁμαρτίας. Reference.

αὐτῶν. Subjective genitive qualifying ἁμαρτίας.

15:23 ὁ ἐμὲ μισῶν καὶ τὸν πατέρα μου μισεῖ.

ὁ ... μισῶν. Pres act ptc masc nom sg μισέω (substantival). Nominative subject of μισεῖ. Fronted as a topical frame. This verse is connected to the previous one by asyndeton.
ἐμὲ. Accusative direct object of μισῶν.
καὶ. Adverbial use (adjunctive).
τὸν πατέρα. Accusative direct object of μισεῖ.
μου. Genitive of relationship qualifying πατέρα.
μισεῖ. Pres act ind 3rd sg μισέω.

15:24 εἰ τὰ ἔργα μὴ ἐποίησα ἐν αὐτοῖς ἃ οὐδεὶς ἄλλος ἐποίησεν, ἁμαρτίαν οὐκ εἴχοσαν· νῦν δὲ καὶ ἑωράκασιν καὶ μεμισήκασιν καὶ ἐμὲ καὶ τὸν πατέρα μου.

εἰ. Introduces the protasis of a second-class (contrary-to-fact) condition, which is connected to the previous verse by asyndeton. Like in 15:22, the apodosis does not include the marker of contingency ἄν. Another similarity with 15:22 is a mixed form of the conditional clause: the protasis refers to the past, having the aorist verb forms (ἐποίησα and ἐποίησεν), while the apodosis refers to the present, having the imperfect (εἴχοσαν).
τὰ ἔργα. Accusative direct object of ἐποίησα.
μὴ. This negative particle, which is normally used with non-indicative verbs, negates ἐποίησα because this verb here functions as an "unreal" indicative (see 15:22).
ἐποίησα. Aor act ind 1st sg ποιέω.
ἐν αὐτοῖς. Locative ("among them").
ἅ. Accusative direct object of ἐποίησεν. The antecedent of the relative pronoun is τὰ ἔργα.
οὐδεὶς ἄλλος. Nominative subject of ἐποίησεν ("no one else").
ἐποίησεν. Aor act ind 3rd sg ποιέω.
ἁμαρτίαν. Accusative direct object of εἴχοσαν. It marks the beginning of the apodosis of a second-class (contrary-to-fact) condition. The phrase ἁμαρτίαν ἔχειν is found only in the Johannine literature (John 9:41; 15:22, 24; 19:11; 1 John 1:8).
οὐκ. Negative particle normally used with indicative verbs.
εἴχοσαν. Impf act ind 3rd pl ἔχω. On the verbal form, see 15:22.
νῦν. Temporal adverb focusing on time coextensive with the event of the narrative (BDAG, 681.1.a). Like in 15:22, the temporal clause highlights the contrast between the hypothetical situation envisioned in

the conditional clause and the actual situation, which substantiates the contrary-to-fact character of the protasis (Robertson, 1013).

δὲ. Marker of narrative development.

καὶ ... καὶ. "Both ... and."

ἑωράκασιν. Prf act ind 3rd pl ὁράω. The perfect-tense verb form functions as a semantic marker, highlighting the importance of seeing Jesus' mighty works. The temporal adverb νῦν indicates that the emphasis falls on the "the *state* or condition existing at the time of speaking," although "there is also a clear implication of the *anterior occurrence* which produced it" (Fanning, 291). The implied direct object of ἑωράκασιν is τὰ ἔργα μου (Barrett, 481). "In keeping with its economic nature, Greek regularly implies an object that was already mentioned in the preceding context, rather than restating it" (Wallace 1996, 409 n. 5).

μεμισήκασιν. Prf act ind 3rd pl μισέω. On the function of the perfect-tense verb form, see ἑωράκασιν above.

καὶ ... καὶ. "Both ... and."

ἐμὲ. Accusative direct object of μεμισήκασιν.

τὸν πατέρα. Accusative direct object of μεμισήκασιν.

μου. Genitive of relationship qualifying πατέρα.

15:25 ἀλλ' ἵνα πληρωθῇ ὁ λόγος ὁ ἐν τῷ νόμῳ αὐτῶν γεγραμμένος ὅτι ἐμίσησάν με δωρεάν.

ἀλλ'. Marker of contrast.

ἵνα πληρωθῇ ὁ λόγος ὁ ἐν τῷ νόμῳ ... γεγραμμένος. This OT introductory formula occurs nowhere else in the NT. On its variations in the FG, see 12:38.

ἵνα. Introduces a purpose clause. The ἵνα clause is elliptical, requiring an introduction, such as τοῦτο γέγονεν (BDF §448.7). It is also possible to regard the ἵνα clause as a substitute for the imperative: "But the word that is written in their Law must be fulfilled" (ESV; cf. REB; Wallace 1996, 477).

πληρωθῇ. Aor pass subj 3rd sg πληρόω. Subjunctive with ἵνα.

ὁ λόγος. Nominative subject of πληρωθῇ.

ὁ ... γεγραμμένος. Prf pass ptc masc nom sg γράφω (attributive). The participle modifies ὁ λόγος, standing in the second attributive position (see 1:29 on ὁ αἴρων).

ἐν τῷ νόμῳ. Locative.

αὐτῶν. Possessive genitive qualifying νόμῳ. By speaking about "their law," Jesus distinguishes himself and his disciples from the Jews, whose hatred is described as without cause in their own sacred text.

ὅτι. ὅτι-*recitativum* that introduces the clausal complement (direct discourse) of γεγραμμένος.

ἐμίσησάν με δωρεάν. A quotation of either Ps 35:19 (LXX Ps 34:19) or Ps 69:5 (LXX Ps 68:5). John's citation agrees neither with the Hebrew (שֹׂנְאַי חִנָּם) nor the Greek version (οἱ μισοῦντές με δωρεάν) of these passages.

ἐμίσησάν. Aor act ind 3rd pl μισέω. ἐμίσησάν, which has an acute accent on the antepenult, acquired an additional accent, the acute, on the ultima from the enclitic με (Smyth §183; Carson 1985, 48).

με. Accusative direct object of ἐμίσησάν.

δωρεάν. Adverbial accusative ("without cause, without reason, for no reason" [LN 89.20]; cf. Wallace 1996, 200).

15:26 Ὅταν ἔλθῃ ὁ παράκλητος ὃν ἐγὼ πέμψω ὑμῖν παρὰ τοῦ πατρός, τὸ πνεῦμα τῆς ἀληθείας ὃ παρὰ τοῦ πατρὸς ἐκπορεύεται, ἐκεῖνος μαρτυρήσει περὶ ἐμοῦ·

Ὅταν. Introduces an indefinite temporal clause. This verse is connected to the previous one by asyndeton.

ἔλθῃ. Aor act subj 3rd sg ἔρχομαι. Subjunctive with ὅταν.

ὁ παράκλητος. Nominative subject of ἔλθῃ. On the meaning of παράκλητος, see 14:16.

ὅν. Accusative direct object of πέμψω. The antecedent of the relative pronoun is ὁ παράκλητος.

ἐγώ. Nominative subject of πέμψω. Fronted for emphasis. In this verse, Jesus is presented as a sender of the Spirit from the Father (ὃν ἐγὼ πέμψω ὑμῖν παρὰ τοῦ πατρός); see 14:26, which presents God as a sender of the Spirit in Jesus' name (ὃ πέμψει ὁ πατὴρ ἐν τῷ ὀνόματί μου).

πέμψω. Fut act ind 1st sg πέμπω.

ὑμῖν. Dative indirect object of πέμψω.

παρὰ τοῦ πατρός. Source.

τὸ πνεῦμα. Nominative in apposition to ὁ παράκλητος.

τῆς ἀληθείας. Objective genitive or attributive genitive qualifying πνεῦμα (see 14:17).

ὅ. Nominative subject of ἐκπορεύεται. The antecedent of the relative pronoun is τὸ πνεῦμα.

παρὰ τοῦ πατρός. Source.

ἐκπορεύεται. Pres mid ind 3rd sg ἐκπορεύομαι.

ἐκεῖνος. Nominative subject of μαρτυρήσει. The demonstrative pronoun is anaphoric, referring to ὁ παράκλητος. The masculine gender of ἐκεῖνος, as Wallace (1996, 331–32) emphasizes, "has nothing to do with the natural gender of πνεῦμα" because πνεῦμα is not its antecedent. Thus, the gender of ἐκεῖνος cannot be taken as an affirmation of the personality of the Spirit (*pace* Young, 78; Barrett, 482).

μαρτυρήσει. Fut act ind 3rd sg μαρτυρέω.
περὶ ἐμοῦ. Reference.

15:27 καὶ ὑμεῖς δὲ μαρτυρεῖτε, ὅτι ἀπ' ἀρχῆς μετ' ἐμοῦ ἐστε.

καὶ. Adverbial use (adjunctive).
ὑμεῖς. Nominative subject of μαρτυρεῖτε.
δὲ. Marker of narrative development.
μαρτυρεῖτε. Pres act ind or impv 2nd pl μαρτυρέω. Some English translations understand μαρτυρεῖτε as a descriptive present (REB: "you ... are my witnesses"; cf. ASV), others as a futuristic present (NASB: "you will testify"; cf. CEB; HCSB; ESV; LEB; NET), and still others as an imperative (NRSV: "you ... are to testify"; NIV: "you ... must testify").
ὅτι. Introduces a causal clause.
ἀπ' ἀρχῆς. Temporal. ἀρχή refers to the beginning of Jesus' ministry.
μετ' ἐμοῦ. Association/accompaniment.
ἐστε. Pres act ind 2nd pl εἰμί. The PP ἀπ' ἀρχῆς indicates that ἐστε denotes "a situation which began in the past and continues in the present" (Fanning, 217).

John 16:1-15

¹"I have said these things to you so that you may not fall away. ²They will put you out of the synagogues. Indeed, an hour is coming that everyone who kills you will think that he is offering service to God. ³And they will do these things because they did not know either the Father or me. ⁴But I have said these things to you so that when their hour comes you may remember them [and] that I told [them] to you. I did not say these things to you from the beginning because I was with you. ⁵But now I am going to the one who sent me, yet none of you asks me, 'Where are you going?' ⁶But because I have said these things to you, sorrow has filled your hearts. ⁷Nevertheless, I tell you the truth: it is advantageous for you that I go away. For if I do not go away, the Paraclete will not come to you; but if I go, I will send him to you. ⁸And when he comes, he will convict the world concerning sin and justice and judgment: ⁹concerning sin, because they do not believe in me; ¹⁰and concerning justice, because I am going to the Father and you will see me no longer; ¹¹and concerning judgment, because the ruler of this world has been condemned. ¹²I still have many things to say to you, but you are not able to bear [them] now.

¹³But when he—the Spirit of truth—comes, he will guide you into all the truth. For he will not speak on his own, but whatever he hears he will speak, and he will proclaim to you the things that are to come. ¹⁴He will glorify me because he will take from what is mine and will proclaim [it] to you. ¹⁵All that the Father has is mine. Because of this I said that he will take from what is mine and will proclaim [it] to you."

16:1 Ταῦτα λελάληκα ὑμῖν ἵνα μὴ σκανδαλισθῆτε.

Ταῦτα. Accusative direct object of λελάληκα. The demonstrative pronoun is anaphoric, referring to 15:18-27. This verse is connected to the previous one by asyndeton.

λελάληκα. Prf act ind 1st sg λαλέω. On the significance of the verbal aspect of λελάληκα, see 14:25.

ὑμῖν. Dative indirect object of λελάληκα.

ἵνα. Introduces a purpose clause.

μὴ. Negative particle normally used with non-indicative verbs.

σκανδαλισθῆτε. Aor pass subj 2nd pl σκανδαλίζω. Subjunctive with ἵνα. The meaning of the passive voice of σκανδαλίζω ("cause to sin") is to "let oneself be led into sin" or "fall away" (BDAG, 926.1.a). The only other occurrence of σκανδαλίζω in the FG is in 6:61.

16:2 ἀποσυναγώγους ποιήσουσιν ὑμᾶς· ἀλλ' ἔρχεται ὥρα ἵνα πᾶς ὁ ἀποκτείνας ὑμᾶς δόξῃ λατρείαν προσφέρειν τῷ θεῷ.

ἀποσυναγώγους. Accusative complement to ὑμᾶς in a double accusative object-complement construction. This is the last of the three occurrences of this adjective in the FG (9:22; 12:42; 16:2). For a reconstruction of the historical background of this expression, see Martyn (35-66, 148-67; cf. Barrett, 137-44). This verse is connected to the previous one by asyndeton.

ποιήσουσιν. Fut act ind 3rd pl ποιέω. ἀποσυναγώγους indicates that the implied subject of ποιήσουσιν is the synagogue leaders.

ὑμᾶς. Accusative direct object of ποιήσουσιν in a double accusative object-complement construction.

ἀλλ'. This conjunction here does not indicate contrast but introduces "an additional point in an emphatic way" (BDF §448.6).

ἔρχεται. Pres mid ind 3rd sg ἔρχομαι. This is a futuristic present because, from the narrative perspective, the persecution of Jesus' disciples has not happened yet.

ὥρα. Nominative subject of ἔρχεται.

ἵνα. Introduces an epexegetical clause that clarifies ἡ ὥρα or, alternatively, a temporal clause in which ἵνα stands for ὅτε (BDF §382.1; Caragounis 2004, 220). In the FG, ἔρχεται ὥρα is typically followed by ὅτε (4:21, 23; 5:25; 16:25). In addition to this verse, the combination ἔρχεται ὥρα + ἵνα occurs in 12:23 and 16:32.

πᾶς ὁ ἀποκτείνας. Nominative subject of δόξῃ. On πᾶς + articular participle, see 3:8 on πᾶς ὁ γεγεννημένος.

ὁ ἀποκτείνας. Aor act ptc masc nom sg ἀποκτείνω (substantival). On the function of this participle, see πᾶς ὁ ἀποκτείνας above.

ὑμᾶς. Accusative direct object of ἀποκτείνας.

δόξῃ. Aor act subj 3rd sg δοκέω. Subjunctive with ἵνα.

λατρείαν. Accusative direct object of προσφέρειν.

προσφέρειν. Pres act inf προσφέρω (indirect discourse).

τῷ θεῷ. Dative indirect object of προσφέρειν.

16:3 καὶ ταῦτα ποιήσουσιν ὅτι οὐκ ἔγνωσαν τὸν πατέρα οὐδὲ ἐμέ.

καὶ. Coordinating conjunction.

ταῦτα. Accusative direct object of ποιήσουσιν. The demonstrative pronoun is anaphoric, referring to the persecution described in v. 2.

ποιήσουσιν. Fut act ind 3rd pl ποιέω.

ὅτι. Introduces a causal clause.

οὐκ ... οὐδὲ. "Neither ... nor." οὐδὲ is a combination of the negative particle οὐ and the marker of narrative development δέ.

ἔγνωσαν. Aor act ind 3rd pl γινώσκω.

τὸν πατέρα. Accusative direct object of ἔγνωσαν.

ἐμέ. Accusative direct object of ἔγνωσαν.

16:4 ἀλλὰ ταῦτα λελάληκα ὑμῖν ἵνα ὅταν ἔλθῃ ἡ ὥρα αὐτῶν μνημονεύητε αὐτῶν ὅτι ἐγὼ εἶπον ὑμῖν. Ταῦτα δὲ ὑμῖν ἐξ ἀρχῆς οὐκ εἶπον, ὅτι μεθ' ὑμῶν ἤμην.

ἀλλὰ. Marker of contrast.

ταῦτα. Accusative direct object of λελάληκα. The demonstrative is anaphoric, referring to Jesus' prediction in vv. 2-3.

λελάληκα. Prf act ind 1st sg λαλέω. On the significance of the verbal aspect of λελάληκα, see 14:25.

ὑμῖν. Dative indirect object of λελάληκα.

ἵνα. Introduces a purpose clause.

ὅταν. Introduces an indefinite temporal clause.

ἔλθῃ. Aor act subj 3rd sg ἔρχομαι. Subjunctive with ὅταν.

ἡ ὥρα. Nominative subject of ἔλθῃ.

αὐτῶν. Genitive of purpose qualifying ὥρα. The personal pronoun probably refers to the persecution described in v. 2 ("the hour destined for these things"), but it could also refer to the agents of persecution ("their [= the persecutors'] time"; cf. Harris 2015, 274). αὐτῶν is omitted in some manuscripts (א* D K Γ Δ Ψ 1 565 700 892ˢ 1241 1424 *l*844 𝔐 et al.), but its external attestation is quite strong (𝔓⁶⁶ᵛⁱᵈ א² A B L Θ *f*¹³ 33 118 *l*2211 et al.). Internal considerations also support its presence in the text because, as Metzger observes, "αὐτῶν after ὥρα was more likely to be removed as superfluous than added by copyists" (210).

μνημονεύητε. Pres act subj 2nd pl μνημονεύω. Subjunctive with ἵνα.

αὐτῶν. Genitive direct object of μνημονεύητε (BDAG, 655.1.a). The personal pronoun refers to ταῦτα above, which, in turn, refers to Jesus' predictions of excommunication and martyrdom.

ὅτι. Introduces the clausal complement (indirect discourse) of μνημονεύητε. Since the ὅτι clause is placed after the direct object of μνημονεύητε, it provides a different content of what is remembered: the disciples will remember not only Jesus' predictions of the coming persecution (αὐτῶν) but also the fact that Jesus told these things to them in advance (ὅτι ἐγὼ εἶπον ὑμῖν). To differentiate these two objects of remembering and to smooth the English translation, I have added a conjunction "and" between them, which does not occur in the Greek text.

ἐγώ. Nominative subject of εἶπον. Fronted as a topical frame.

εἶπον. Aor act ind 1st sg λέγω. The unexpressed direct object of εἶπον is the same as the expressed direct object of μνημονεύητε.

ὑμῖν. Dative indirect object of εἶπον.

Ταῦτα. Accusative direct object of εἶπον. Ταῦτα is again anaphoric, referring to Jesus' prediction of the persecution of his followers in vv. 2-3.

δέ. Marker of narrative development.

ὑμῖν. Dative indirect object of εἶπον.

ἐξ ἀρχῆς. Temporal. ἀρχή refers either to the beginning of the disciples' association with Jesus or to the beginning of Jesus' ministry (Harris 2015, 276).

οὐκ. Negative particle normally used with indicative verbs.

εἶπον. Aor act ind 1st sg λέγω.

ὅτι. Introduces a causal clause.

μεθ' ὑμῶν. Association/accompaniment.

ἤμην. Impf mid ind 1st sg εἰμί. By using the imperfect tense, the Johannine Jesus portrays his time with the disciples as though it is already a past event. Frey argues that here Jesus "speaks to the disciples in a retrospective review of his ministry. The standpoint of the narrated scene in which he speaks to the disciples prior to his death and a standpoint in which he looks back at the passion and Easter are juxtaposed in a way that is unmistakable" (2018, 83).

16:5 νῦν δὲ ὑπάγω πρὸς τὸν πέμψαντά με, καὶ οὐδεὶς ἐξ ὑμῶν ἐρωτᾷ με· ποῦ ὑπάγεις;

νῦν. Temporal adverb focusing on time coextensive with the event of the narrative (BDAG, 681.1.a). Fronted as a temporal frame.

δὲ. Marker of narrative development.

ὑπάγω. Pres act ind 1st sg ὑπάγω. On the use of ὑπάγω in chs. 13–16, see 13:3 on ὑπάγει.

πρὸς τὸν πέμψαντά. Locative (motion toward).

τὸν πέμψαντά. Aor act ptc masc acc sg πέμπω (substantival). πέμψαντά, which has an acute accent on the antepenult, acquired an additional accent, the acute, on the ultima from the enclitic με (Smyth §183; Carson 1985, 48). On the use of the participial forms of πέμπω to either identify or describe God in the FG, see τοῦ πέμψαντός in 4:34.

με. Accusative direct object of πέμψαντά.

καὶ. Coordinating conjunction linking two clauses that stand in adversative relationship (see 1:5).

οὐδεὶς. Nominative subject of ἐρωτᾷ.

ἐξ ὑμῶν. Replaces the partitive genitive.

ἐρωτᾷ. Pres act ind 3rd sg ἐρωτάω.

με. Accusative direct object of ἐρωτᾷ.

ποῦ. Indirect interrogative adverb of place.

ὑπάγεις. Pres act ind 2nd sg ὑπάγω.

16:6 ἀλλ' ὅτι ταῦτα λελάληκα ὑμῖν ἡ λύπη πεπλήρωκεν ὑμῶν τὴν καρδίαν.

ἀλλ'. Marker of contrast.

ὅτι. Introduces a causal clause that is placed before the main clause for emphasis.

ταῦτα. Accusative direct object of λελάληκα. ταῦτα refers to Jesus' announcement of his departure in v. 5.

λελάληκα. Prf act ind 1st sg λαλέω. On the significance of the verbal aspect of λελάληκα, see 14:25.

ὑμῖν. Dative indirect object of λελάληκα.

ἡ λύπη. Nominative subject of πεπλήρωκεν.

πεπλήρωκεν. Prf act ind 3rd sg πληρόω.

ὑμῶν. Possessive genitive qualifying καρδίαν. The preposed pronoun is thematically salient (Levinsohn 2000, 64).

τὴν καρδίαν. Accusative direct object of πεπλήρωκεν. τὴν καρδίαν is a distributive singular (MHT 3:23).

16:7 ἀλλ' ἐγὼ τὴν ἀλήθειαν λέγω ὑμῖν, συμφέρει ὑμῖν ἵνα ἐγὼ ἀπέλθω. ἐὰν γὰρ μὴ ἀπέλθω, ὁ παράκλητος οὐκ ἐλεύσεται πρὸς ὑμᾶς· ἐὰν δὲ πορευθῶ, πέμψω αὐτὸν πρὸς ὑμᾶς.

ἀλλ'. Marker of contrast.

ἐγώ. Nominative subject of λέγω. Fronted as a topical frame.

τὴν ἀλήθειαν. Accusative direct object of λέγω. Fronted for emphasis.

λέγω. Pres act ind 1st sg λέγω.

ὑμῖν. Dative indirect object of λέγω.

συμφέρει. Pres act ind 3rd sg συμφέρω. This verb occurs twice more in the FG (11:50; 18:14). In each case, συμφέρω ("to be advantageous") refers to the benefits of Jesus' death.

ὑμῖν. Dative of advantage.

ἵνα. Introduces a substantival clause that serves as the subject of συμφέρει (Wallace 1996, 475).

ἐγώ. Nominative subject of ἀπέλθω.

ἀπέλθω. Aor act subj 1st sg ἀπέρχομαι. Subjunctive with ἵνα.

ἐάν. Introduces the protasis of a third-class condition.

γάρ. Postpositive conjunction that introduces the explanation of Jesus' assertion that it is advantageous for his disciples that he goes away.

μή. Negative particle normally used with non-indicative verbs.

ἀπέλθω. Aor act subj 1st sg ἀπέρχομαι. Subjunctive with ἐάν.

ὁ παράκλητος. Nominative subject of ἐλεύσεται. It marks the beginning of the apodosis of a third-class condition. On the meaning of παράκλητος, see 14:16.

οὐκ. Negative particle normally used with indicative verbs.

ἐλεύσεται. Fut mid ind 3rd sg ἔρχομαι.

πρὸς ὑμᾶς. Locative (motion toward).

ἐάν. Introduces the protasis of a third-class condition.

δέ. Marker of narrative development.

πορευθῶ. Aor mid subj 1st sg πορεύομαι. Subjunctive with ἐάν. On the voice, see "Deponency" in the Series Introduction.

πέμψω. Fut act ind 1st sg πέμπω. It marks the beginning of the apodosis of a third-class condition.

αὐτόν. Accusative direct object of πέμψω. The personal pronoun is masculine because its antecedent is ὁ παράκλητος.

πρὸς ὑμᾶς. Locative (motion toward).

John 16:1-15

16:8 Καὶ ἐλθὼν ἐκεῖνος ἐλέγξει τὸν κόσμον περὶ ἁμαρτίας καὶ περὶ δικαιοσύνης καὶ περὶ κρίσεως·

Καί. Coordinating conjunction.

ἐλθών. Aor act ptc masc nom sg ἔρχομαι (temporal; cf. Caragounis 2004, 175). On participles that precede the main verb, see ἐμβλέψας in 1:36.

ἐκεῖνος. Nominative subject of ἐλέγξει. The demonstrative pronoun refers to ὁ παράκλητος from the previous verse, acting as a third-person personal pronoun with a simple anaphoric force (Wallace 1996, 328–29).

ἐλέγξει. Fut act ind 3rd sg ἐλέγχω. In this context, ἐλέγχω could mean "to bring to light, expose, set forth" (BDAG, 315.1) or "to convict, convince someone of someth[ing], point someth[ing] out to someone" (BDAG, 315.2). The two meanings are closely related because the purpose of exposing the actions of the world regarding sin, justice, and judgment is to prove that it is guilty (Schnackenburg, 3:128–29).

τὸν κόσμον. Accusative direct object of ἐλέγξει.

περὶ ἁμαρτίας. Reference. ἁμαρτίας and the next two genitives after περί (δικαιοσύνης and κρίσεως) are anarthrous because "the author is dealing with basic ideas rather than with individual instances" (Brown, 2:705).

καί. Coordinating conjunction.

περὶ δικαιοσύνης. Reference. The term δικαιοσύνη occurs only here and in v. 10 in the FG.

καί. Coordinating conjunction.

περὶ κρίσεως. Reference. Elsewhere in the FG, κρίσις is mentioned in 3:19; 5:22, 24, 27, 29, 30; 7:24; 8:16; 12:31; 16:11.

16:9 περὶ ἁμαρτίας μέν, ὅτι οὐ πιστεύουσιν εἰς ἐμέ·

περὶ ἁμαρτίας. Reference.

μέν . . . δέ . . . δέ. A point/counterpoint set that correlates the clause introduced by μέν in this verse with the clauses introduced by δέ in vv. 9 and 10. Runge argues that "μέν simply creates anticipation of a related clause . . . introduced by δέ" (2010, 75 n. 7) and adds that μέν is "always prospective, even in instances where δέ does not follow" (76).

ὅτι. Introduces a causal clause that explains why the world will be condemned with regard to sin: "concerning sin, because they do not believe in me" (cf. ASV; HCSB; ESV; LEB; NRSV; NIV). Alternatively, ὅτι introduces an epexegetical clause that expounds the meaning of ἁμαρτία: "concerning sin—in that they do not believe in me" (cf. CJB; NCV; Bultmann, 563; Brown, 2:703, 706).

οὐ. Negative particle normally used with indicative verbs.
πιστεύουσιν. Pres act ind 3rd pl πιστεύω.
εἰς ἐμέ. Goal of actions or feelings directed toward someone (BDAG, 290.4.c.β). For πιστεύειν εἰς + accusative ("trust or believe in someone"), see 1:12 on εἰς τὸ ὄνομα.

16:10 περὶ δικαιοσύνης δέ, ὅτι πρὸς τὸν πατέρα ὑπάγω καὶ οὐκέτι θεωρεῖτέ με·

περὶ δικαιοσύνης. Reference.
δέ. Marker of narrative development, which is part of the μέν . . . δέ . . . δὲ point/counterpoint set (see. v. 9).
ὅτι. Introduces a causal clause that explains why the world will be condemned with regard to justice: "concerning justice, because I am going to the Father and you will see me no longer" (cf. ASV; HCSB; ESV; LEB; NRSV; NIV). Alternatively, ὅτι introduces an epexegetical clause that expounds the meaning of δικαιοσύνη: "concerning justice—in that I am going to the Father and you will see me no longer" (cf. CJB; NCV; Bultmann, 563–65; Brown, 2:703). The connection between δικαιοσύνη and Jesus' going to the Father is not so apparent, but the sense becomes clearer if we recall that Jesus' speech in vv. 8–11 presumes a forensic setting, i.e., a lawsuit between God and the world. In this context, δικαιοσύνη points to Jesus' innocence declared by God (Bultmann, 564). As Brown explains, "Jesus is just in the sense of one who has been vindicated in court. . . . He stands in the Father's presence and so partakes of the justice of God, before whom there can be nothing unjust" (2:706).
πρὸς τὸν πατέρα. Locative (motion toward).
ὑπάγω. Pres act ind 1st sg ὑπάγω. On the use of ὑπάγω in chs. 13–16, see 13:3 on ὑπάγει.
καί. Coordinating conjunction.
οὐκέτι. Negative adverb of time ("no longer, no further").
θεωρεῖτέ. Pres act ind 2nd pl θεωρέω. οὐκέτι indicates that this is a futuristic present. θεωρεῖτέ, which has a circumflex accent on the penult, acquired an additional accent, the acute, on the ultima from the enclitic με (Smyth §183; Carson 1985, 48).
με. Accusative direct object of θεωρεῖτέ.

16:11 περὶ δὲ κρίσεως, ὅτι ὁ ἄρχων τοῦ κόσμου τούτου κέκριται.

περὶ . . . κρίσεως. Reference.
δέ. Marker of narrative development, which is part of the μέν . . . δέ . . . δὲ point/counterpoint set (see v. 9).

ὅτι. Introduces a causal clause that explains why the world will be condemned with regard to judgment: "concerning judgment, because the ruler of this world has been condemned" (cf. ASV; HCSB; ESV; LEB; NRSV; NIV). Alternatively, ὅτι introduces an epexegetical clause that expounds the meaning of κρίσις: "concerning judgment—in that the ruler of this world has been condemned" (cf. CJB; NCV; Bultmann, 565; Brown, 2:703).

ὁ ἄρχων. Nominative subject of κέκριται.

τοῦ κόσμου τούτου. Genitive of subordination qualifying ἄρχων. The same designation for the devil (ὁ ἄρχων τοῦ κόσμου τούτου) is used in 12:31; in 14:30 the devil is called ὁ τοῦ κόσμου ἄρχων.

κέκριται. Prf pass ind 3rd sg κρίνω. The verb stands in final, emphatic position. Jesus presents the final condemnation of "the ruler of this world" as though it has already occurred because "a post-Easter perspective has penetrated into the words of the pre-Easter Jesus" (Frey 2018, 83).

16:12 Ἔτι πολλὰ ἔχω ὑμῖν λέγειν, ἀλλ' οὐ δύνασθε βαστάζειν ἄρτι·

Ἔτι. Adverb ("still"). This verse is connected to the previous one by asyndeton.

πολλὰ. Accusative direct object of ἔχω.

ἔχω. Pres act ind 1st sg ἔχω.

ὑμῖν. Dative indirect object of ἔχω.

λέγειν. Pres act inf λέγω (complementary).

ἀλλ'. Marker of contrast.

οὐ. Negative particle normally used with indicative verbs.

δύνασθε. Pres mid ind 2nd pl δύναμαι.

βαστάζειν. Pres act inf βαστάζω (complementary).

ἄρτι. Adverb of time ("now, at the present time" [BDAG, 136.3]).

16:13 ὅταν δὲ ἔλθῃ ἐκεῖνος, τὸ πνεῦμα τῆς ἀληθείας, ὁδηγήσει ὑμᾶς ἐν τῇ ἀληθείᾳ πάσῃ· οὐ γὰρ λαλήσει ἀφ' ἑαυτοῦ, ἀλλ' ὅσα ἀκούσει λαλήσει καὶ τὰ ἐρχόμενα ἀναγγελεῖ ὑμῖν.

ὅταν. Introduces an indefinite temporal clause, which is fronted as a temporal frame.

δὲ. Marker of narrative development.

ἔλθῃ. Aor act subj 3rd sg ἔρχομαι.

ἐκεῖνος. Nominative subject of ἔλθῃ. The demonstrative pronoun refers to ὁ παράκλητος from v. 7, acting as a third-person personal pronoun with a simple anaphoric force (Wallace 1996, 328–29).

τὸ πνεῦμα. Nominative in apposition to ἐκεῖνος.

τῆς ἀληθείας. Objective genitive or attributive genitive qualifying πνεῦμα (see 14:17).

ὁδηγήσει. Fut act ind 3rd sg ὁδηγέω.

ὑμᾶς. Accusative direct object of ὁδηγήσει.

ἐν τῇ ἀληθείᾳ πάσῃ. This PP (attested in ℵ² D L W et al.) suggests that truth is the sphere of the Spirit's action (Brown, 2:707; Barrett, 489), while the variants εἰς τὴν ἀλήθειαν πᾶσαν (A B vgst Or) and εἰς πᾶσαν τὴν ἀλήθειαν (Κ Γ Δ Ψ 068 f^{13} 700 892^s 1241 1424 l844 l2211 𝔐) suggest that truth is the goal of the Spirit's action (Brown, 2:707; Barrett, 489). The difference in meaning, however, should not be pressed too much because in the NT ἐν and εἰς are sometimes used interchangeably (BDF §218; Brown, 2:707). It is, in fact, quite likely that copyists substituted ἐν + dative with εἰς + accusative because they regarded the latter as more idiomatic after ὁδηγήσει (Metzger, 210).

οὐ ... ἀλλ'. A point/counterpoint set ("not this ... but that") that replaces the inaccurate explanation of the source of the Spirit's message (he will speak on his own) with the accurate one (he will speak whatever he hears). On the function of ἀλλά in a point/counterpoint set, see 1:8.

γάρ. Postpositive conjunction that introduces the clause that explains the claim that the Spirit will guide the believers into all truth.

λαλήσει. Fut act ind 3rd sg λαλέω.

ἀφ' ἑαυτοῦ. Agency (see 5:19 on ἀφ' ἑαυτοῦ).

ὅσα. The relative pronoun introduces a headless relative clause that, in its entirety (ὅσα ἀκούσει), serves as the direct object of λαλήσει. Within its clause, ὅσα is the accusative direct object of ἀκούσει.

ἀκούσει. Fut act ind 3rd sg ἀκούω. In addition to the future-tense ἀκούσει (B D W Θ Ψ 1 579 l844 l2211 et al.), some manuscripts have the present-tense ἀκούει (ℵ L 33 b e), and others the subjunctive ἀκούσῃ with ἄν (Α Κ Γ Δ f^{13} 565 700 1241 1424 𝔐). Metzger (210) argues for the priority of the future tense because the present tense appears to be a dogmatic improvement whose purpose is to convey the eternal relationship between the Holy Spirit and the Father, while the subjunctive represents a grammatical improvement (Barrett, 489–90). Brown (2:707), however, thinks that the present tense is the *lectio difficilior* because all other verbs in the immediate context are in the future, tempting a copyist to conform ἀκούει to ἀκούσει. The decision is difficult, but the weight of external evidence tips the balance in favor of ἀκούσει.

λαλήσει. Fut act ind 3rd sg λαλέω.

καί. Coordinating conjunction.

τὰ ἐρχόμενα. Pres mid ptc neut acc pl ἔρχομαι (substantival). Accusative direct object of ἀναγγελεῖ. The neuter plural form of the participle refers to the events that are to happen (lit. "the things that are to come"; on the meaning and the function of this participial expression in the FG, see Frey 1997–2000, 3:179–222).

ἀναγγελεῖ. Fut act ind 3rd sg ἀναγγέλλω.

ὑμῖν. Dative indirect object of ἀναγγελεῖ.

16:14 ἐκεῖνος ἐμὲ δοξάσει, ὅτι ἐκ τοῦ ἐμοῦ λήμψεται καὶ ἀναγγελεῖ ὑμῖν.

ἐκεῖνος. Nominative subject of δοξάσει. The demonstrative pronoun refers to ὁ παράκλητος from v. 7, acting as a third-person personal pronoun with a simple anaphoric force (Wallace 1996, 328–29). This verse is connected to the previous one by asyndeton.

ἐμὲ. Accusative direct object of δοξάσει.

δοξάσει. Fut act ind 3rd sg δοξάζω.

ὅτι. Introduces a causal clause.

ἐκ τοῦ ἐμοῦ. Separation. The article τοῦ nominalizes the possessive adjective ἐμοῦ ("that which is mine").

λήμψεται. Fut mid ind 3rd sg λαμβάνω.

καὶ. Coordinating conjunction.

ἀναγγελεῖ. Fut act ind 3rd sg ἀναγγέλλω.

ὑμῖν. Dative indirect object of ἀναγγελεῖ.

16:15 πάντα ὅσα ἔχει ὁ πατὴρ ἐμά ἐστιν· διὰ τοῦτο εἶπον ὅτι ἐκ τοῦ ἐμοῦ λαμβάνει καὶ ἀναγγελεῖ ὑμῖν.

πάντα. Nominative subject of ἐστιν. This verse is connected to the previous one by asyndeton.

ὅσα. Accusative direct object of ἔχει. The antecedent of the relative pronoun is πάντα. πάντα ὅσα = "all things that" (see 4:29).

ἔχει. Pres act ind 3rd sg ἔχω.

ὁ πατὴρ. Nominative subject of ἔχει.

ἐμά. Predicate adjective. Fronted for emphasis.

ἐστιν. Pres act ind 3rd sg εἰμί. Neuter plural subjects typically take singular verbs (see 1:28 on ἐγένετο).

διὰ τοῦτο. Causal. The demonstrative pronoun is anaphoric, referring to Jesus' previous assertion that all things that the Father has are his. In this context, the PP διὰ τοῦτο functions as a connective; on this function of διὰ τοῦτο, see 1:31.

εἶπον. Aor act ind 1st sg λέγω.

ὅτι. Introduces the clausal complement (direct [NRSV] or indirect [REB] discourse) of εἶπον.

ἐκ τοῦ ἐμοῦ. Separation (see 16:14).

λαμβάνει. Pres act ind 3rd sg λαμβάνω. This is a futuristic present (cf. λήμψεται in 16:14).

καί. Coordinating conjunction.

ἀναγγελεῖ. Fut act ind 3rd sg ἀναγγέλλω.

ὑμῖν. Dative indirect object of ἀναγγελεῖ.

John 16:16-24

[16]"A little while and you will see me no longer, and again a little while and you will see me." [17]Then some of his disciples said to one another, "What is this that he is saying to us, 'A little while and you will not see me, and again a little while and you will see me,' and 'Because I am going to the Father'?" [18]So they kept on saying, "What is this that he is saying, 'A little while'? We do not know what he is talking about." [19]Jesus knew that they wanted to ask him, and he said to them, "Are you deliberating with one another about this, namely, that I said, 'A little while and you will not see me, and again a little while and you will see me'? [20]Truly, truly I say to you, you will weep and mourn, but the world will rejoice; you will become sorrowful, but your sorrow will turn into joy. [21]A woman, when she gives birth, has pain because her hour has come. But when she has delivered the child, she no longer remembers the anguish because of the joy that a human being has been born into the world. [22]So you also have sorrow now, but I will see you again, and your hearts will rejoice, and no one will take away your joy from you. [23]And on that day you will ask me nothing. Truly, truly I say to you, if you ask the Father for anything in my name, he will give [it] to you. [24]Until now you have not asked for anything in my name. Ask and you will receive, so that your joy may be complete."

16:16 Μικρὸν καὶ οὐκέτι θεωρεῖτέ με, καὶ πάλιν μικρὸν καὶ ὄψεσθέ με.

Μικρόν. Adverbial accusative ("a short time, a little while" [BDAG, 651.1.d.β]). This verse is connected to the previous one by asyndeton.

καί. Coordinating conjunction.

οὐκέτι. Negative adverb of time ("no longer, no further").

θεωρεῖτε. Pres act ind 2nd pl θεωρέω. Μικρόν indicates that the verb refers to the not-so-distant future. θεωρεῖτε, which has a circumflex accent on the penult, acquired an additional accent, the acute, on the ultima from the enclitic με (Smyth §183; Carson 1985, 48).

με. Accusative direct object of θεωρεῖτέ.

καί. Coordinating conjunction.

πάλιν. Adverb "pert[aining] to repetition in the same (or similar) manner" (BDAG, 752.2).

μικρὸν. Adverbial accusative (see above).

καί. Coordinating conjunction.

ὄψεσθέ. Fut mid ind 2nd pl ὁράω. ὄψεσθέ, which has an acute accent on the antepenult, acquired an additional accent, the acute, on the ultima from the enclitic με (Smyth §183; Carson 1985, 48).

με. Accusative direct object of ὄψεσθέ.

16:17 εἶπαν οὖν ἐκ τῶν μαθητῶν αὐτοῦ πρὸς ἀλλήλους· τί ἐστιν τοῦτο ὃ λέγει ἡμῖν· μικρὸν καὶ οὐ θεωρεῖτέ με, καὶ πάλιν μικρὸν καὶ ὄψεσθέ με; καί· ὅτι ὑπάγω πρὸς τὸν πατέρα;

εἶπαν. Aor act ind 3rd pl λέγω.

οὖν. Postpositive inferential conjunction and/or transitional particle (see 1:22 and 11:6).

ἐκ τῶν μαθητῶν. Replaces the partitive genitive. The PP presumes addition of τινές, which functions as the implied subject of εἶπαν (BDF §164.2).

αὐτοῦ. Genitive of relationship qualifying μαθητῶν.

πρὸς ἀλλήλους. Locative (motion toward). The PP functions like an indirect object of εἶπαν.

τί. Predicate nominative (see τοῦτο below).

ἐστιν. Pres act ind 3rd sg εἰμί.

τοῦτο. Nominative subject of ἐστιν. In a question in which a linking verb joins an interrogative pronoun and a demonstrative pronoun, as here, the demonstrative functions as a subject because it is "a substitute for something already revealed in the context (a known quantity)," while the interrogative is "anticipatory of a substantive not yet revealed (an unknown quantity)" (Wallace 1996, 44 n. 24).

ὅ. Accusative direct object of λέγει. The antecedent of the relative pronoun is τοῦτο.

λέγει. Pres act ind 3rd sg λέγω.

ἡμῖν. Dative indirect object of λέγει.

μικρὸν καὶ οὐ θεωρεῖτέ με, καὶ πάλιν μικρὸν καὶ ὄψεσθέ με. A quotation of Jesus' words from 16:16. The only difference is the replacement of the negative adverb οὐκέτι with the negative particle οὐ.

μικρὸν. Adverbial accusative (see 16:16).

καί. Coordinating conjunction.

οὐ. Negative particle normally used with indicative verbs.

θεωρεῖτε. Pres act ind 2nd pl θεωρέω (see 16:16). θεωρεῖτε, which has a circumflex accent on the penult, acquired an additional accent, the acute, on the ultima from the enclitic με (Smyth §183; Carson 1985, 48).

με. Accusative direct object of θεωρεῖτε.

καὶ. Coordinating conjunction.

πάλιν. Adverb "pert[aining] to repetition in the same (or similar) manner" (BDAG, 752.2).

μικρὸν. Adverbial accusative (see 16:16).

καὶ. Coordinating conjunction.

ὄψεσθέ. Fut mid ind 2nd pl ὁράω (see 16:16).

με. Accusative direct object of ὄψεσθέ.

καί. Coordinating conjunction.

ὅτι ὑπάγω πρὸς τὸν πατέρα. A quotation of Jesus' words from 16:10b. The only difference is the placement of the PP after the verb.

ὅτι. Introduces a causal clause. In Jesus' original speech, the ὅτι clause explained why the world would be condemned regarding justice. In the question of the disciples, the function of the quoted ὅτι clause is obfuscated.

ὑπάγω. Pres act ind 1st sg ὑπάγω. On the use of ὑπάγω in chs. 13–16, see 13:3 on ὑπάγει.

πρὸς τὸν πατέρα. Locative (motion toward).

16:18 ἔλεγον οὖν· τί ἐστιν τοῦτο [ὃ λέγει] τὸ μικρόν; οὐκ οἴδαμεν τί λαλεῖ.

ἔλεγον. Impf act ind 3rd pl λέγω. On the function of the imperfect in the FG, see 1:39 on ἦν.

οὖν. Postpositive inferential conjunction and/or transitional particle (see 1:22 and 11:6).

τί. Predicate nominative (see 16:17).

ἐστιν. Pres act ind 3rd sg εἰμί.

τοῦτο. Nominative subject of ἐστιν (see 16:17).

[ὃ λέγει]. This relative clause is placed within square brackets because the external evidence in favor of its presence (ℵ² A B D² K L N Γ Δ Θ Ψ 068 33 700 892ˢ 1241 1424 [*l*844] 𝔐 lat sy ly bo) and its absence (𝔓⁵·⁶⁶ ℵ* D* W *f*¹³ 1 565 579 it sa pbo) is evenly balanced.

ὅ. Accusative direct object of λέγει. The antecedent of the relative pronoun is τοῦτο.

λέγει. Pres act ind 3rd sg λέγω.

τὸ μικρόν. The article τό is used to introduce a quotation, here μικρόν (BDF §267.1).

οὐκ. Negative particle normally used with indicative verbs.

οἴδαμεν. Prf act ind 1st pl οἶδα (see 1:26 on οἴδατε).
τί. Accusative direct object of λαλεῖ.
λαλεῖ. Pres act ind 3rd sg λαλέω.

16:19 Ἔγνω [ὁ] Ἰησοῦς ὅτι ἤθελον αὐτὸν ἐρωτᾶν, καὶ εἶπεν αὐτοῖς· περὶ τούτου ζητεῖτε μετ' ἀλλήλων ὅτι εἶπον· μικρὸν καὶ οὐ θεωρεῖτέ με, καὶ πάλιν μικρὸν καὶ ὄψεσθέ με;

Ἔγνω. Aor act ind 3rd sg γινώσκω. This verse is connected to the previous one by asyndeton.

[ὁ] Ἰησοῦς. Nominative subject of Ἔγνω. Although the external attestation for the definite article is strong, it is absent in some early manuscripts ($\mathfrak{P}^{5*}$ B L W).

ὅτι. Introduces the clausal complement (indirect discourse) of Ἔγνω.

ἤθελον. Impf act ind 3rd pl θέλω. For the augment, see 1:43 on ἠθέλησεν.

αὐτὸν. Accusative direct object of ἐρωτᾶν.

ἐρωτᾶν. Pres act inf ἐρωτάω (complementary).

καὶ. Coordinating conjunction.

εἶπεν. Aor act ind 3rd sg λέγω.

αὐτοῖς. Dative indirect object of εἶπεν.

περὶ τούτου. Reference.

ζητεῖτε. Pres act ind 2nd pl ζητέω. In this context, ζητέω means "to seek information, investigate, examine, consider, deliberate" (BDAG, 428.2).

μετ' ἀλλήλων. Association/accompaniment.

ὅτι. Introduces a clause that stands in apposition to τούτου: "Are you deliberating with one another about this, namely, that I said . . . ?" (Wallace 1996, 458–59).

εἶπον. Aor act ind 1st sg λέγω.

μικρὸν καὶ οὐ θεωρεῖτέ με, καὶ πάλιν μικρὸν καὶ ὄψεσθέ με. A quotation of Jesus' words from 16:16. Like the previous quotation in 16:17, this citation replaces the negative adverb οὐκέτι with the negative particle οὐ.

μικρὸν. Adverbial accusative (see 16:16).

καὶ. Coordinating conjunction.

οὐ. Negative particle normally used with indicative verbs.

θεωρεῖτέ. Pres act ind 2nd pl θεωρέω (see 16:16). θεωρεῖτέ, which has a circumflex accent on the penult, acquired an additional accent, the acute, on the ultima from the enclitic με (Smyth §183; Carson 1985, 48).

με. Accusative direct object of θεωρεῖτέ.

καὶ. Coordinating conjunction.

πάλιν. Adverb "pert[aining] to repetition in the same (or similar) manner" (BDAG, 752.2).

μικρὸν. Adverbial accusative (see 16:16).

καὶ. Coordinating conjunction.

ὄψεσθέ. Fut mid ind 2nd pl ὁράω (see 16:16).

με. Accusative direct object of ὄψεσθέ.

16:20 ἀμὴν ἀμὴν λέγω ὑμῖν ὅτι κλαύσετε καὶ θρηνήσετε ὑμεῖς, ὁ δὲ κόσμος χαρήσεται· ὑμεῖς λυπηθήσεσθε, ἀλλ' ἡ λύπη ὑμῶν εἰς χαρὰν γενήσεται.

ἀμὴν ἀμὴν λέγω ὑμῖν. Metacomment (see 1:51).

ἀμὴν ἀμὴν. Asseverative particles that mark the beginning of Jesus' solemn declaration (see 1:51). This verse is connected to the previous one by asyndeton.

λέγω. Pres act ind 1st sg λέγω.

ὑμῖν. Dative indirect object of λέγω.

ὅτι. Introduces the clausal complement (direct [NRSV; REB; NET; ESV; NIV] or indirect [ASV; CEB; NASB; LEB] discourse) of λέγω.

κλαύσετε. Fut act ind 2nd pl κλαίω. In the FG, κλαίω is used only in the settings related to death (11:31, 33; 20:11, 13, 15).

καὶ. Coordinating conjunction.

θρηνήσετε. Fut act ind 2nd pl θρηνέω. This is the only occurrence of θρηνέω ("mourn for, lament") in the FG. κλαίω and θρηνέω are used together in Luke 7:32.

ὑμεῖς. Nominative subject of κλαύσετε. The personal pronoun is emphatic and contrastive, distinguishing the disciples from the world.

ὁ ... κόσμος. Nominative subject of χαρήσεται. Fronted as a topical frame.

δὲ. Marker of narrative development with a contrastive nuance.

χαρήσεται. Fut mid ind 3rd sg χαίρω. On the voice, see 8:56 on ἐχάρη; see also "Deponency" in the Series Introduction.

ὑμεῖς. Nominative subject of λυπηθήσεσθε. Fronted for emphasis. This clause is connected to the previous one by asyndeton.

λυπηθήσεσθε. Fut pass ind 2nd pl λυπέω.

ἀλλ'. Marker of contrast.

ἡ λύπη. Nominative subject of γενήσεται. λύπη here denotes "pain of mind or spirit, grief, sorrow, affliction" (BDAG, 604).

ὑμῶν. Subjective genitive qualifying λύπη.

εἰς χαρὰν. Occasionally, as here, εἰς + accusative replaces the predicate nominative (BDF §145.1; Wallace 1996, 47). Fronted for emphasis.

γενήσεται. Fut mid ind 3rd sg γίνομαι.

16:21 ἡ γυνὴ ὅταν τίκτῃ λύπην ἔχει, ὅτι ἦλθεν ἡ ὥρα αὐτῆς· ὅταν δὲ γεννήσῃ τὸ παιδίον, οὐκέτι μνημονεύει τῆς θλίψεως διὰ τὴν χαρὰν ὅτι ἐγεννήθη ἄνθρωπος εἰς τὸν κόσμον.

ἡ γυνὴ. Nominative subject of ἔχει. The article is generic ("a woman"). Fronted as a topical frame. This verse is connected to the previous one by asyndeton.

ὅταν. Introduces an indefinite temporal clause.

τίκτῃ. Pres act subj 3rd sg τίκτω. Subjunctive with ὅταν.

λύπην. Accusative direct object of ἔχει. In this context, λύπη denotes physical pain. Fronted for emphasis.

ἔχει. Pres act ind 3rd sg ἔχω.

ὅτι. Introduces a causal clause.

ἦλθεν. Aor act ind 3rd sg ἔρχομαι. The perfective aspect of the aorist tense portrays the arrival of the time to deliver a baby as a complete action (McKay 1994, 48).

ἡ ὥρα. Nominative subject of ἦλθεν.

αὐτῆς. Genitive of purpose qualifying ὥρα.

ὅταν. Introduces an indefinite temporal clause.

δὲ. Marker of narrative development with a contrastive nuance.

γεννήσῃ. Aor act subj 3rd sg γεννάω. Subjunctive with ὅταν.

τὸ παιδίον. Accusative direct object of γεννήσῃ.

οὐκέτι. Negative adverb of time ("no longer, no further"). Fronted for emphasis.

μνημονεύει. Pres act ind 3rd sg μνημονεύω.

τῆς θλίψεως. Genitive direct object of μνημονεύει.

διὰ τὴν χαρὰν. Causal.

ὅτι. Introduces an epexegetical clause that explains χαρὰν.

ἐγεννήθη. Aor pass ind 3rd sg γεννάω.

ἄνθρωπος. Nominative subject of ἐγεννήθη.

εἰς τὸν κόσμον. Locative.

16:22 καὶ ὑμεῖς οὖν νῦν μὲν λύπην ἔχετε· πάλιν δὲ ὄψομαι ὑμᾶς, καὶ χαρήσεται ὑμῶν ἡ καρδία, καὶ τὴν χαρὰν ὑμῶν οὐδεὶς αἴρει ἀφ' ὑμῶν.

καὶ. Adverbial use (adjunctive).

ὑμεῖς. Nominative subject of ἔχετε. Fronted for emphasis.

οὖν. Postpositive inferential conjunction and/or transitional particle (see 1:22 and 11:6).

νῦν. Temporal adverb focusing on time coextensive with the event of the narrative (BDAG, 681.1.a).

μὲν ... δὲ. A point/counterpoint set that correlates the clause introduced by μέν with the clause introduced by δέ. On the function of these particles, see 16:9.

λύπην. Accusative direct object of ἔχετε. Fronted for emphasis.

ἔχετε. Pres act ind 2nd pl ἔχω. The variant ἕξετε ($\mathfrak{P}^{66}$ ℵ^2 A D L N W^{txt} Θ Ψ 33 *l*844 it vg^{mss}) is probably a scribal modification to adjust the statement about having sorrow in this verse to λυπηθήσεσθε in v. 20 (Metzger, 211). The external evidence for ἔχετε is notable ($\mathfrak{P}^{22}$ ℵ* B C K W$^{v.1}$ Γ Δ *f*$^{1.13}$ 565 579 1241 1424 𝔐 et al.), and the present tense better fits the current context (see νῦν above).

πάλιν. Adverb "pert[aining] to repetition in the same (or similar) manner" (BDAG, 752.2). Fronted for emphasis.

δὲ. Marker of narrative development.

ὄψομαι. Fut mid ind 1st sg ὁράω.

ὑμᾶς. Accusative direct object of ὄψομαι.

καὶ. Coordinating conjunction.

χαρήσεται. Fut mid ind 3rd sg χαίρω. On the voice, see "Deponency" in the Series Introduction.

ὑμῶν. Possessive genitive qualifying καρδία. The preposed pronoun is thematically salient (Levinsohn 2000, 64).

ἡ καρδία. Nominative subject of χαρήσεται. ἡ καρδία is a distributive singular.

καὶ. Coordinating conjunction.

τὴν χαρὰν. Accusative direct object of αἴρει.

ὑμῶν. Subjective genitive qualifying χαρὰν.

οὐδεὶς. Nominative subject of αἴρει. Fronted for emphasis.

αἴρει. Pres act ind 3rd sg αἴρω. Two previous clauses (πάλιν δὲ ὄψομαι ὑμᾶς, καὶ χαρήσεται ὑμῶν ἡ καρδία) indicate that αἴρει is a futuristic present. The future-tense ἀρεῖ in some manuscripts ($\mathfrak{P}^5$ B D* Γ it et al.) is most likely a scribal adjustment of the present-tense αἴρει to other future-tense verbs in this verse (Metzger, 211).

ἀφ' ὑμῶν. Separation.

16:23 Καὶ ἐν ἐκείνῃ τῇ ἡμέρᾳ ἐμὲ οὐκ ἐρωτήσετε οὐδέν. ἀμὴν ἀμὴν λέγω ὑμῖν, ἄν τι αἰτήσητε τὸν πατέρα ἐν τῷ ὀνόματί μου δώσει ὑμῖν.

Καὶ. Coordinating conjunction.

ἐν ἐκείνῃ τῇ ἡμέρᾳ. Temporal. Elsewhere in the FG, this PP occurs in 5:9; 14:20; 16:26.

ἐμὲ. Accusative direct object (person) of ἐρωτήσετε in a double accusative person-thing construction.

οὐκ. Negative particle normally used with indicative verbs.

ἐρωτήσετε. Fut act ind 2nd pl ἐρωτάω. Although in Hellenistic Greek the meaning of ἐρωτάω could overlap with the meaning of αἰτέω ("to ask for something"; BDAG, 395.2), it seems that in this verse ἐρωτάω means "to put a query to someone, to ask a question" (BDAG, 395.1; cf. Brown, 2:718; Barrett, 494; see also John 16:19, 30).

οὐδέν. Accusative direct object (thing) of ἐρωτήσετε in a double accusative person-thing construction. The two negatives οὐκ ... οὐδέν reinforce each other (see 3:27 on οὐδέ).

ἀμὴν ἀμὴν λέγω ὑμῖν. Metacomment (see 1:51).

ἀμὴν ἀμὴν. Asseverative particles that mark the beginning of Jesus' solemn declaration (see 1:51). This clause is connected to the previous one by asyndeton.

λέγω. Pres act ind 1st sg λέγω.

ὑμῖν. Dative indirect object of λέγω.

ἄν. ἄν stands for ἐάν (BDF §107; Caragounis 2004, 228) and introduces the protasis of a third-class condition (see 13:20).

τι. Accusative direct object (thing) of αἰτήσητε in a double accusative person-thing construction.

αἰτήσητε. Aor act subj 2nd pl αἰτέω. Subjunctive with ἐάν. On the meaning of αἰτέω in a double accusative construction, see 11:22.

τὸν πατέρα. Accusative direct object (person) of αἰτήσητε in a double accusative person-thing construction.

ἐν τῷ ὀνόματί. Instrumental (see 14:13, 14, 26; 15:16; 16:24, 26). ὀνόματί, which has an acute accent on the antepenult, acquired an additional accent, the acute, on the ultima from the enclitic μου (Smyth §183; Carson 1985, 48). The PP ἐν τῷ ὀνόματί μου occurs in two different locations: before ($\mathfrak{P}^{22vid}$ A C³ D K N W Γ Θ Ψ f^{13} 1 565 579 700 892ˢ 1241 1424 𝔐 et al.) and after ($\mathfrak{P}^{5vid}$ ℵ B C* L Δ *l*844 et al.) δώσει ὑμῖν. The first option presumes that the disciples make their requests to the Father in Jesus' name. The second option presumes that the Father will give them things in Jesus' name. The former is probably to be preferred because it has a more diversified textual support and agrees with 15:16 (ὅ τι ἂν αἰτήσητε τὸν πατέρα ἐν τῷ ὀνόματί μου δῷ ὑμῖν), 16:24 (ἕως ἄρτι οὐκ ᾐτήσατε οὐδὲν ἐν τῷ ὀνόματί μου), and 16:26 (ἐν ἐκείνῃ τῇ ἡμέρᾳ ἐν τῷ ὀνόματί μου αἰτήσεσθε) (Metzger, 211). Some scholars (Brown, 2:723; Schnackenburg, 3:160), however, prefer the latter because this rendering is more difficult, so that the scribes would be more likely to conform the unusual reading to the more usual pattern than the other way around.

μου. Possessive genitive qualifying ὀνόματί.

δώσει. Fut act ind 3rd sg δίδωμι. It marks the beginning of the apodosis of a third-class condition.

ὑμῖν. Dative indirect object of δώσει.

16:24 ἕως ἄρτι οὐκ ᾐτήσατε οὐδὲν ἐν τῷ ὀνόματί μου· αἰτεῖτε καὶ λήμψεσθε, ἵνα ἡ χαρὰ ὑμῶν ᾖ πεπληρωμένη.

ἕως ἄρτι. Temporal. ἕως functions here as a preposition of time ("until") and the adverb ἄρτι as a substantive. ἕως ἄρτι = "until now" (BDAG, 423.1.b.γ). This verse is connected to the previous one by asyndeton.

οὐκ. Negative particle normally used with indicative verbs.

ᾐτήσατε. Aor act ind 2nd pl αἰτέω.

οὐδὲν. Accusative direct object of ᾐτήσατε. The two negatives οὐκ . . . οὐδὲν reinforce each other (see 3:27 on οὐδὲ).

ἐν τῷ ὀνόματί. Instrumental (see 14:13, 14, 26; 15:16; 16:23, 26). ὀνόματί, which has an acute accent on the antepenult, acquired an additional accent, the acute, on the ultima from the enclitic μου (Smyth §183; Carson 1985, 48).

μου. Possessive genitive qualifying ὀνόματί.

αἰτεῖτε. Pres act impv 2nd pl αἰτέω. This clause is connected to the previous one by asyndeton.

καὶ. Coordinating conjunction.

λήμψεσθε. Fut mid ind 2nd pl λαμβάνω.

ἵνα. Introduces a purpose clause.

ἡ χαρὰ. Nominative subject of ᾖ.

ὑμῶν. Subjective genitive qualifying χαρὰ.

ᾖ. Pres act subj 3rd sg εἰμί. Subjunctive with ἵνα.

πεπληρωμένη. Prf pass ptc fem nom sg πληρόω (perfect periphrastic).

John 16:25-33

[25]"I have said these things to you in figurative speech. An hour is coming when I will no longer speak to you in figurative speech, but I will tell you about the Father in plain words. [26]On that day you will ask in my name, and I do not say to you that I will ask the Father on your behalf. [27]For the Father himself loves you because you love me and believe that I came from God. [28]I came from the Father and have come into the world; again, I am leaving the world and going to the Father." [29]His disciples said, "Look, now you are speaking in plain words and are using no figurative saying. [30]Now we know that you know all things and have no need that anyone should question you. By this we believe that you came from

God." ³¹Jesus answered them, "Do you now believe? ³²Look! An hour is coming—and has come—that you will be scattered, each one to his own home, and you will leave me alone. Yet I am not alone because the Father is with me. ³³I have said these things to you so that in me you may have peace. In the world you have affliction. But take courage! I have conquered the world."

16:25 Ταῦτα ἐν παροιμίαις λελάληκα ὑμῖν· ἔρχεται ὥρα ὅτε οὐκέτι ἐν παροιμίαις λαλήσω ὑμῖν, ἀλλὰ παρρησίᾳ περὶ τοῦ πατρὸς ἀπαγγελῶ ὑμῖν.

Ταῦτα. Accusative direct object of λελάληκα. The demonstrative pronoun is anaphoric, referring to the preceding section in 16:16-24 or, more broadly, to the entirety of Jesus' speech in 15:1–16:24. This verse is connected to the previous one by asyndeton.

ἐν παροιμίαις. Manner. Fronted for emphasis. This is the second occurrence of the term παροιμία ("veiled saying, figure of speech, in which esp. lofty ideas are concealed" [BDAG, 780.2]) in the FG (10:6; 16:25, 29). In addition to the Johannine usage, this term occurs in the NT only in 2 Pet 2:22. The fourth evangelist never uses the synoptic term παραβολή (cf. Matt 13:3, 10, 13, 34, 34, 53; 21:45; 22:1; Mark 3:23; 4:2, 10, 11, 13, 30, 33; 12:1; Luke 8:9, 10, 11).

λελάληκα. Prf act ind 1st sg λαλέω. On the significance of the verbal aspect of λελάληκα, see 14:25.

ὑμῖν. Dative indirect object of λελάληκα.

ἔρχεται. Pres mid ind 3rd sg ἔρχομαι. This clause is connected to the previous one by asyndeton.

ὥρα. Nominative subject of ἔρχεται.

ὅτε. Introduces a temporal clause.

οὐκέτι. Negative adverb of time ("no longer, no further").

ἐν παροιμίαις. Manner.

λαλήσω. Fut act ind 1st sg λαλέω.

ὑμῖν. Dative indirect object of λαλήσω.

ἀλλά. Marker of contrast.

παρρησίᾳ. Dative of manner. παρρησίᾳ ("in plain words") is here contrasted to ἐν παροιμίαις ("in figures of speech").

περὶ τοῦ πατρός. Reference.

ἀπαγγελῶ. Fut act ind 1st sg ἀπαγγέλλω.

ὑμῖν. Dative indirect object of ἀπαγγελῶ.

John 16:25-27

16:26 ἐν ἐκείνῃ τῇ ἡμέρᾳ ἐν τῷ ὀνόματί μου αἰτήσεσθε, καὶ οὐ λέγω ὑμῖν ὅτι ἐγὼ ἐρωτήσω τὸν πατέρα περὶ ὑμῶν·

ἐν ἐκείνῃ τῇ ἡμέρᾳ. Temporal. This verse is connected to the previous one by asyndeton. Elsewhere in the FG, this PP occurs in 5:9; 14:20; 16:23.

ἐν τῷ ὀνόματί. Instrumental (see 14:13, 14, 26; 15:16; 16:23, 24). Fronted for emphasis. ὀνόματί, which has an acute accent on the antepenult, acquired an additional accent, the acute, on the ultima from the enclitic μου (Smyth §183; Carson 1985, 48).

μου. Possessive genitive qualifying ὀνόματί.

αἰτήσεσθε. Fut mid ind 2nd pl αἰτέω.

καὶ. Coordinating conjunction.

οὐ. Negative particle normally used with indicative verbs.

λέγω. Pres act ind 1st sg λέγω.

ὑμῖν. Dative indirect object of λέγω.

ὅτι. Introduces the clausal complement (indirect discourse) of λέγω.

ἐγὼ. Nominative subject of ἐρωτήσω. Fronted for emphasis.

ἐρωτήσω. Fut act ind 1st sg ἐρωτάω.

τὸν πατέρα. Accusative direct object of ἐρωτήσω.

περὶ ὑμῶν. Advantage/representation. περί is here used instead of ὑπέρ (Zerwick §96; Wallace 1996, 379).

16:27 αὐτὸς γὰρ ὁ πατὴρ φιλεῖ ὑμᾶς, ὅτι ὑμεῖς ἐμὲ πεφιλήκατε καὶ πεπιστεύκατε ὅτι ἐγὼ παρὰ [τοῦ] θεοῦ ἐξῆλθον.

αὐτὸς . . . ὁ πατὴρ. Nominative subject of φιλεῖ. αὐτὸς functions as an intensive pronoun ("the Father himself"), which expresses the idea that the Father himself, without prompting, loves Jesus' disciples (BDAG, 152.1.d). Fronted for emphasis.

γὰρ. Postpositive conjunction that introduces the explanation of Jesus' statement in v. 26 that he will not ask the Father on behalf of his disciples.

φιλεῖ. Pres act ind 3rd sg φιλέω.

ὑμᾶς. Accusative direct object of φιλεῖ.

ὅτι. Introduces a causal clause.

ὑμεῖς. Nominative subject of πεφιλήκατε.

ἐμὲ. Accusative direct object of πεφιλήκατε and πεπιστεύκατε. Fronted for emphasis.

πεφιλήκατε. Prf act ind 2nd pl φιλέω. By describing the disciples' attitude toward Jesus with the perfect-tense verbs πεφιλήκατε and πεπιστεύκατε, the evangelist uses semantic markers to underscore the disciples' love for and belief in Jesus (Porter 1989, 280).

καί. Coordinating conjunction.

πεπιστεύκατε. Prf act ind 2nd pl πιστεύω.

ὅτι. Introduces the clausal complement (indirect discourse) of πεπιστεύκατε.

ἐγώ. Nominative subject of ἐξῆλθον.

παρὰ [τοῦ] θεοῦ. Source. Fronted for emphasis. παρὰ τοῦ θεοῦ has the same meaning as ἀπὸ θεοῦ (see 13:3; cf. Harris 2015, 282). The definite article is printed within square brackets because the evidence in favor of its presence (C³ K W Γ Δ Ψ f¹·¹³ 565 700 892ˢ 1241 1424 𝔐) or absence (𝔓⁵ ℵ*·²ᵇ A N Θ 33 579) is evenly balanced.

ἐξῆλθον. Aor act ind 1st sg ἐξέρχομαι.

16:28 ἐξῆλθον παρὰ τοῦ πατρὸς καὶ ἐλήλυθα εἰς τὸν κόσμον· πάλιν ἀφίημι τὸν κόσμον καὶ πορεύομαι πρὸς τὸν πατέρα.

ἐξῆλθον. Aor act ind 1st sg ἐξέρχομαι. This verse is connected to the previous one by asyndeton.

παρὰ τοῦ πατρός. Source (see παρὰ [τοῦ] θεοῦ in the previous verse). The variant reading ἐκ τοῦ πατρός (B C* L Ψ 33) most likely arose through assimilation to the prefix of the compound verb ἐξῆλθον, which occurs twice (at the end of v. 27 and at the beginning of v. 28) before this PP (Metzger, 212).

καί. Coordinating conjunction.

ἐλήλυθα. Prf act ind 1st sg ἔρχομαι. While the perfect ἐλήλυθα, like the aorist ἐξῆλθον, has past implicature, Porter emphasizes that in this verse "a profitable contrast is made between Jesus' coming from the Father (ἐξῆλθον) with his entrance into the world (ἐλήλυθα εἰς τὸν κόσμον), with the marked Perfect used of his entrance" (1989, 262).

εἰς τὸν κόσμον. Locative. On the portrayal of the world in the FG, see 1:10 on ἐν τῷ κόσμῳ.

πάλιν. Adverb "pert[aining] to repetition in the same (or similar) manner" (BDAG, 752.2). This clause is connected to the previous one by asyndeton.

ἀφίημι. Pres act ind 1st sg ἀφίημι. Both present-tense verbs (ἀφίημι and πορεύομαι) refer to the future.

τὸν κόσμον. Accusative direct object of ἀφίημι.

καί. Coordinating conjunction.

πορεύομαι. Pres mid ind 1st sg πορεύομαι.

πρὸς τὸν πατέρα. Locative (motion toward).

16:29 Λέγουσιν οἱ μαθηταὶ αὐτοῦ· ἴδε νῦν ἐν παρρησίᾳ λαλεῖς καὶ παροιμίαν οὐδεμίαν λέγεις.

Λέγουσιν. Pres act ind 3rd pl λέγω. The historical present gives prominence to the disciples' words (see 1:15 on μαρτυρεῖ). This verse is connected to the previous one by asyndeton.
οἱ μαθηταὶ. Nominative subject of Λέγουσιν.
αὐτοῦ. Genitive of relationship qualifying μαθηταὶ.
ἴδε. An interjection that here stands for ἰδού (Zerwick and Grosvenor, 335).
νῦν. Temporal adverb focusing on time coextensive with the event of the narrative (BDAG, 681.1.a).
ἐν παρρησίᾳ. Manner ("in plainness of speech" = "plainly"). Fronted for emphasis.
λαλεῖς. Pres act ind 2nd sg λαλέω.
καὶ. Coordinating conjunction.
παροιμίαν οὐδεμίαν. Accusative direct object of λέγεις. This is the last occurrence of the term παροιμία in the FG (10:6; 16:25, 29). The adjective οὐδεμίαν is emphatic, standing in the fourth attributive position (see 3:15 on ζωὴν αἰώνιον).
λέγεις. Pres act ind 2nd sg λέγω.

16:30 νῦν οἴδαμεν ὅτι οἶδας πάντα καὶ οὐ χρείαν ἔχεις ἵνα τίς σε ἐρωτᾷ· ἐν τούτῳ πιστεύομεν ὅτι ἀπὸ θεοῦ ἐξῆλθες.

νῦν. Temporal adverb focusing on time coextensive with the event of the narrative (BDAG, 681.1.a). Fronted for emphasis. This verse is connected to the previous one by asyndeton.
οἴδαμεν. Prf act ind 1st pl οἶδα (see 1:26 on οἴδατε).
ὅτι. Introduces the clausal complement (indirect discourse) of οἴδαμεν.
οἶδας. Prf act ind 2nd sg οἶδα (see 1:26 on οἴδατε).
πάντα. Accusative direct object of οἶδας.
καὶ. Coordinating conjunction.
οὐ. Negative particle normally used with indicative verbs.
χρείαν. Accusative direct object of ἔχεις.
ἔχεις. Pres act ind 2nd sg ἔχω.
ἵνα. Introduces an epexegetical clause that explains χρείαν. An epexegetical ἵνα clause is equivalent to an epexegetical infinitive (BDF §394).
τίς. Nominative subject of ἐρωτᾷ.
σε. Accusative direct object of ἐρωτᾷ.
ἐρωτᾷ. Pres act subj 3rd sg ἐρωτάω. Subjunctive with ἵνα.

ἐν τούτῳ. Instrumental (BDF §219.2). The demonstrative pronoun is anaphoric, referring to the disciples' confession of Jesus' omniscience. This clause is connected to the previous one by asyndeton.

πιστεύομεν. Pres act ind 1st pl πιστεύω.

ὅτι. Introduces the clausal complement (indirect discourse) of πιστεύομεν.

ἀπὸ θεοῦ. Source.

ἐξῆλθες. Aor act ind 2nd sg ἐξέρχομαι.

16:31 ἀπεκρίθη αὐτοῖς Ἰησοῦς· ἄρτι πιστεύετε;

ἀπεκρίθη. Aor mid ind 3rd sg ἀποκρίνομαι. On the voice, see "Deponency" in the Series Introduction. This verse is connected to the previous one by asyndeton.

αὐτοῖς. Dative indirect object of ἀπεκρίθη.

Ἰησοῦς. Nominative subject of ἀπεκρίθη.

ἄρτι. Adverb of time ("now, at the present time" [BDAG, 136.3]). Fronted for emphasis.

πιστεύετε. Pres act ind 2nd pl πιστεύω.

16:32 ἰδοὺ ἔρχεται ὥρα καὶ ἐλήλυθεν ἵνα σκορπισθῆτε ἕκαστος εἰς τὰ ἴδια κἀμὲ μόνον ἀφῆτε· καὶ οὐκ εἰμὶ μόνος, ὅτι ὁ πατὴρ μετ' ἐμοῦ ἐστιν.

ἰδού. An interjection (originally ἰδοῦ [aor mid impv 2nd sg ὁράω] but accented with the acute rather than the circumflex) that "draws attention to what follows" (BDAG, 468). This verse is connected to the previous one by asyndeton.

ἔρχεται. Pres mid ind 3rd sg ἔρχομαι. The context indicates that this is a futuristic present.

ὥρα. Nominative subject of ἔρχεται. On the arrival of Jesus' hour, see ἡ ὥρα in 12:23.

καί. Coordinating conjunction.

ἐλήλυθεν. Prf act ind 3rd sg ἔρχομαι. In contrast to the present tense of ἔρχομαι (see ἔρχεται above), which refers to the future, the perfect tense of the same verb conveys that the anticipated hour has already arrived.

ἵνα. Introduces an epexegetical clause that clarifies ὥρα or, alternatively, a temporal clause in which ἵνα stands for ὅτε (BDF §382.1). For other instances of ἔρχεται ὥρα + ἵνα, see 12:23 and 16:2.

σκορπισθῆτε. Aor pass subj 2nd pl σκορπίζω. Subjunctive with ἵνα. σκορπίζω means "to cause a group or a gathering to disperse or scatter" (LN 15.135).

ἕκαστος. Nominative in apposition to the embedded second-person subject of σκορπισθῆτε.

εἰς τὰ ἴδια. Locative, if τὰ ἴδια means "one's own home" (BDAG, 467.4.b), or goal of an action, if τὰ ἴδια means "one's own occupation" (Brown, 2:727).

κἀμὲ. Formed by crasis from καὶ ἐμέ. καὶ is a coordinating conjunction. ἐμέ is the accusative direct object of ἀφῆτε in a double accusative object-complement construction.

μόνον. Accusative complement to ἐμέ (see κἀμὲ above) in a double accusative object-complement construction.

ἀφῆτε. Aor act subj 2nd pl ἀφίημι. Subjunctive with ἵνα.

καὶ. Coordinating conjunction linking two clauses that stand in adversative relationship (see 1:5).

οὐκ. Negative particle normally used with indicative verbs.

εἰμὶ. Pres act ind 1st sg εἰμί.

μόνος. Predicate adjective.

ὅτι. Introduces a causal clause.

ὁ πατὴρ. Nominative subject of ἐστιν. Fronted for emphasis.

μετ' ἐμοῦ. Association/accompaniment.

ἐστιν. Pres act ind 3rd sg εἰμί.

16:33 Ταῦτα λελάληκα ὑμῖν ἵνα ἐν ἐμοὶ εἰρήνην ἔχητε. ἐν τῷ κόσμῳ θλῖψιν ἔχετε· ἀλλὰ θαρσεῖτε, ἐγὼ νενίκηκα τὸν κόσμον.

Ταῦτα. Accusative direct object of λελάληκα. The demonstrative pronoun is anaphoric, but it is not clear whether it refers to the preceding verse or the entire preceding discourse. This verse is connected to the previous one by asyndeton.

λελάληκα. Prf act ind 1st sg λαλέω. On the significance of the verbal aspect of λελάληκα, see 14:25.

ὑμῖν. Dative indirect object of λελάληκα.

ἵνα. Introduces a purpose clause.

ἐν ἐμοὶ. State of being.

εἰρήνην. Accusative direct object of ἔχητε. Fronted for emphasis. Here and in 14:27, εἰρήνη is used as a word of farewell. In 20:19, 21, 26, εἰρήνη is used as a greeting.

ἔχητε. Pres act subj 2nd pl ἔχω. Subjunctive with ἵνα.

ἐν τῷ κόσμῳ. Locative. This clause is connected to the previous one by asyndeton. On the portrayal of the world in the FG, see 1:10 on ἐν τῷ κόσμῳ.

θλῖψιν. Accusative direct object of ἔχετε. Fronted for emphasis.

ἔχετε. Pres act ind 2nd pl ἔχω.

ἀλλά. Marker of contrast.
θαρσεῖτε. Pres act impv 2nd pl θαρσέω.
ἐγώ. Nominative subject of νενίκηκα. The personal pronoun is emphatic.
νενίκηκα. Prf act ind 1st sg νικάω. This is the only occurrence of this verb in the FG. The perfect-tense verb form calls attention to the completion of Jesus' victory over the world (Fanning, 298). Since, however, this victory is accomplished in Jesus' death, νενίκηκα conveys "a post-Easter perspective" that "has penetrated into the words of the pre-Easter Jesus" (Frey 2018, 83).
τὸν κόσμον. Accusative direct object of νενίκηκα.

John 17:1-5

¹Jesus said these things and, after he lifted his eyes to heaven, he said, "Father, the hour has come. Glorify your Son, so that the Son may glorify you, ²since you have given him authority over all flesh, so that everyone whom you have given him—he might give eternal life to them. ³And the eternal life is this: that they may know you, the only true God, and whom you have sent, Jesus Christ. ⁴I glorified you on earth by completing the work that you have given me to do. ⁵And now, Father, glorify me in your own presence with the glory that I had in your presence before the world existed."

17:1 Ταῦτα ἐλάλησεν Ἰησοῦς καὶ ἐπάρας τοὺς ὀφθαλμοὺς αὐτοῦ εἰς τὸν οὐρανὸν εἶπεν· πάτερ, ἐλήλυθεν ἡ ὥρα· δόξασόν σου τὸν υἱόν, ἵνα ὁ υἱὸς δοξάσῃ σέ,

Ταῦτα. Accusative direct object of ἐλάλησεν. The demonstrative pronoun is anaphoric, referring to the entire farewell discourse. This verse is connected to the previous one by asyndeton.
ἐλάλησεν. Aor act ind 3rd sg λαλέω.
Ἰησοῦς. Nominative subject of ἐλάλησεν.
καί. Coordinating conjunction.
ἐπάρας. Aor act ptc masc nom sg ἐπαίρω (temporal or manner). On participles that precede the main verb, see ἐμβλέψας in 1:36.
τοὺς ὀφθαλμούς. Accusative direct object of ἐπάρας.
αὐτοῦ. Possessive genitive qualifying ὀφθαλμούς.
εἰς τὸν οὐρανόν. Locative.
εἶπεν. Aor act ind 3rd sg λέγω.
πάτερ. Vocative of direct address. In his prayers in the FG, Jesus regularly addresses God as Father (11:41; 12:27, 28; 17:1, 5, 11, 21, 24, 25).

ἐλήλυθεν. Prf act ind 3rd sg ἔρχομαι.
ἡ ὥρα. Nominative subject of ἐλήλυθεν. Beginning with 12:23, Jesus makes several statements that his hour has arrived (12:23, 27; 13:1; 16:32; 17:1). This is the last mention of the arrival of Jesus' hour in the FG. Brown remarks that "obviously 'the hour' is a long period of time, beginning with the first indication that the process which would lead to Jesus' death had been set in motion, and terminating with his return to his Father" (2:740).
δόξασόν. Aor act impv 2nd sg δοξάζω. In this context, glorification refers to Jesus' death and resurrection (see 7:39; 12:16, 23; 13:31, 32). On δοξάζω as a double entendre, see 7:39 on ἐδοξάσθη. δόξασόν, which has an acute accent on the antepenult, acquired an additional accent, the acute, on the ultima from the enclitic με (Smyth §183; Carson 1985, 48). This clause is connected to the previous one by asyndeton.
σου. Genitive of relationship qualifying υἱόν. The preposed pronoun is thematically salient (Levinsohn 2000, 64).
τὸν υἱόν. Accusative direct object of δόξασόν.
ἵνα. Introduces a purpose clause.
ὁ υἱὸς. Nominative subject of δοξάσῃ. Many copies include the personal pronoun σου after ὁ υἱὸς (A C². ³ D K L N Γ Δ Θ Ψ *f*¹³ 33 565ˢ 579 700 892ˢ 1241 1424 *l*844 𝔐 et al.). It is difficult to decide between the shorter and the longer reading on internal grounds because copyists could have omitted the pronoun as superfluous, or they could have added it to "enhance the solemnity of the style" (Metzger, 212). The weight of external attestation for ὁ υἱὸς without σου (ℵ B C* W 0109 0301 d e ff² pbo Orᵖᵗ et al.), however, tips the balance in favor of the shorter reading.
δοξάσῃ. Aor act subj 3rd sg δοξάζω. Subjunctive with ἵνα.
σέ. Accusative direct object of δοξάσῃ.

17:2 καθὼς ἔδωκας αὐτῷ ἐξουσίαν πάσης σαρκός, ἵνα πᾶν ὃ δέδωκας αὐτῷ δώσῃ αὐτοῖς ζωὴν αἰώνιον.

καθὼς. Introduces a causal clause (BDAG, 494.3; BDF §453.2). This verse is connected to the previous one by asyndeton.
ἔδωκας. Aor act ind 2nd sg δίδωμι.
αὐτῷ. Dative indirect object of ἔδωκας.
ἐξουσίαν. Accusative direct object of ἔδωκας.
πάσης σαρκός. Genitive of subordination or objective genitive qualifying ἐξουσίαν. The expression πᾶσα σάρξ is a Semitism (כל בשר) for "all people," which occurs only here in the FG.

ἵνα. Introduces either a purpose clause or an epexegetical clause that explains ἐξουσίαν.

πᾶν. Pendent nominative in a left-dislocation, resumed by αὐτοῖς. πᾶν serves to introduce a new entity into the discourse. The neuter singular is sometimes used with reference to persons, as here, "if it is not the individuals but a general quality that is to be emphasized" (BDF §138.1). Caragounis adds that the neuter singular "expresses an inclusiveness that is absent from the masculine (and even more so from the feminine) . . . , especially when strengthened by πᾶν" (2004, 237). For other examples of this usage in the FG, see 3:6; 6:37; 17:2, 24.

ὅ. Accusative direct object of δέδωκας. The neuter agrees with its antecedent πᾶν, although it refers to a person (see above). The entire relative clause ὅ δέδωκας αὐτῷ is, like πᾶν to which it refers, in a left-dislocation.

δέδωκας. Prf act ind 2nd sg δίδωμι.

αὐτῷ. Dative indirect object of δέδωκας.

δώσῃ. Aor act subj 3rd sg δίδωμι. Subjunctive with ἵνα.

αὐτοῖς. Dative indirect object of δώσῃ, resuming πᾶν ὅ δέδωκας αὐτῷ. The plural form of the personal pronoun is a *constructio ad sensum* because its antecedent πᾶν ὅ designates the sum of all individuals who are given to Jesus by the Father. αὐτοῖς is placed in an unmarked position (following the verb), which occurs relatively infrequently in the FG (here and in 1:12; 7:38; 15:2; cf. Runge 2010, 297). Much more common are left-dislocations that have the resumptive pronoun in a marked position (at the beginning of the clause).

ζωὴν αἰώνιον. Accusative direct object of δώσῃ. On the use of this phrase in the FG, see 3:15 on ζωὴν αἰώνιον.

17:3 αὕτη δέ ἐστιν ἡ αἰώνιος ζωὴ ἵνα γινώσκωσιν σὲ τὸν μόνον ἀληθινὸν θεὸν καὶ ὃν ἀπέστειλας Ἰησοῦν Χριστόν.

αὕτη. Predicate nominative. Fronted for emphasis. Culy (2004, 11) explains that in equative clauses, demonstratives "will tend to function as the predicate when they are cataphoric and as the subject when they are anaphoric." In this construction, αὕτη is cataphoric, pointing forward to the ἵνα clause.

δέ. Marker of narrative development.

ἐστιν. Pres act ind 3rd sg εἰμί.

ἡ αἰώνιος ζωή. Nominative subject of ἐστιν. On the use of this phrase in the FG, see 3:15 on ζωὴν αἰώνιον. This is the only occurrence of the articular formulation of this expression in John.

ἵνα. Introduces an epexegetical clause that explains αὕτη (Harris 2015, 286; Zerwick §410) or, alternatively, a clause that is appositional to αὕτη (Wallace 1996, 475; Haubeck and von Siebenthal, 593).

γινώσκωσιν. Pres act subj 3rd pl γινώσκω. Subjunctive with ἵνα. The implied subject of γινώσκωσιν ("they") should be supplied from αὐτοῖς in v. 2.

σὲ. The first accusative direct object of γινώσκωσιν.

τὸν μόνον ἀληθινὸν θεὸν. Accusative in apposition to σὲ. Two adjectives—μόνον and ἀληθινὸν—stand in the first attributive position (see 2:10 on τὸν καλὸν οἶνον).

καὶ. Coordinating conjunction.

ὃν. The parallelism between two coordinated formulations after γινώσκωσιν—σὲ τὸν μόνον ἀληθινὸν θεὸν and ὃν ἀπέστειλας Ἰησοῦν Χριστόν—indicates that the headless relative clause (ὃν ἀπέστειλας) functions as the second direct object of γινώσκωσιν (Barrett, 504). Within its clause, ὃν is the accusative direct object of ἀπέστειλας.

ἀπέστειλας. Aor act ind 2nd sg ἀποστέλλω.

Ἰησοῦν Χριστόν. Accusative in apposition to the headless relative clause ὃν ἀπέστειλας (see above).

17:4 ἐγώ σε ἐδόξασα ἐπὶ τῆς γῆς τὸ ἔργον τελειώσας ὃ δέδωκάς μοι ἵνα ποιήσω·

ἐγώ. Nominative subject of ἐδόξασα. Fronted as a topical frame. This verse is connected to the previous one by asyndeton.

σε. Accusative direct object of ἐδόξασα. Fronted for emphasis.

ἐδόξασα. Aor act ind 1st sg δοξάζω. In this verse, the aorist tense is used as a reference to the glorification of the Father through the entirety of Jesus' ministry, compared to the purpose clause ἵνα ὁ υἱὸς δοξάσῃ σέ in v. 1, which refers to the glorification of the Father through Jesus' impending death (Barrett, 504).

ἐπὶ τῆς γῆς. Locative.

τὸ ἔργον. Accusative direct object of τελειώσας.

τελειώσας. Aor act ptc masc nom sg τελειόω (means or causal). On participles that follow the main verb, see βαπτίζων in 1:31.

ὃ. Accusative direct object of δέδωκάς. The antecedent of the relative pronoun is τὸ ἔργον.

δέδωκάς. Prf act ind 2nd sg δίδωμι. δέδωκάς, which has an acute accent on the antepenult, acquired an additional accent, the acute, on the ultima from the enclitic μοι (Smyth §183; Carson 1985, 48).

μοι. Dative indirect object of δέδωκάς.

ἵνα. Introduces either a purpose clause ("the work that you have given me that I should do") or a complementary clause that replaces an infinitive ("the work that you have given me to do"; cf. Zerwick §§406–7; Wallace 1996, 476).

ποιήσω. Aor act subj 1st sg ποιέω. Subjunctive with ἵνα.

17:5 καὶ νῦν δόξασόν με σύ, πάτερ, παρὰ σεαυτῷ τῇ δόξῃ ᾗ εἶχον πρὸ τοῦ τὸν κόσμον εἶναι παρὰ σοί.

καὶ. Coordinating conjunction.

νῦν. Temporal adverb focusing on time coextensive with the event of the narrative (BDAG, 681.1.a). Fronted as a temporal frame.

δόξασόν. Aor act impv 2nd sg δοξάζω. δόξασόν, which has an acute accent on the antepenult, acquired an additional accent, the acute, on the ultima from the enclitic με (Smyth §183; Carson 1985, 48).

με. Accusative direct object of δόξασόν.

σύ. Nominative subject of δόξασόν.

πάτερ. Vocative of direct address. In his prayers in the FG, Jesus regularly addresses God as Father (11:41; 12:27, 28; 17:1, 5, 11, 21, 24, 25).

παρὰ σεαυτῷ. Association. σεαυτῷ is a reflexive pronoun (lit. "at your own side" = "in your own presence").

τῇ δόξῃ. Dative of means/instrument.

ᾗ. The relative pronoun ᾗ stands for ἥν, serving as the direct object of εἶχον. It is in the dative because it is attracted to its antecedent τῇ δόξῃ.

εἶχον. Impf act ind 1st sg ἔχω.

πρὸ τοῦ. Used with the infinitive to denote time (see εἶναι below).

εἶναι. Pres act inf εἰμί. Used with πρὸ τοῦ to indicate subsequent time.

τὸν κόσμον. Accusative subject of the infinitive εἶναι. The term κόσμος here denotes the totality of creation.

παρὰ σοί. Association (lit. "by your side" = "in your presence").

John 17:6-8

⁶"I have made your name known to the people whom you gave me out of the world. They were yours, and you gave them to me, and they have kept your word. ⁷Now they know that all things that you have given me are from you, ⁸because the words that you gave to me I have given to them, and they received [them] and know truly that I came from you, and they believed that you sent me."

17:6 Ἐφανέρωσά σου τὸ ὄνομα τοῖς ἀνθρώποις οὓς ἔδωκάς μοι ἐκ τοῦ κόσμου. σοὶ ἦσαν κἀμοὶ αὐτοὺς ἔδωκας καὶ τὸν λόγον σου τετήρηκαν.

Ἐφανέρωσά. Aor act ind 1st sg φανερόω. The notion of revealing the name of God is found only in this verse. Elsewhere in the FG, φανερόω occurs in 1:31 (revealing the one coming after John); 2:11 (revealing Jesus' glory through his signs); 3:21 (revealing Jesus' deeds); 7:4 (Jesus revealing himself to the world); 9:3 (revealing God's works); and 21:1, 14 (revealing/making visible the risen Jesus). Ἐφανέρωσά, which has an acute accent on the antepenult, acquired an additional accent, the acute, on the ultima from the enclitic με (Smyth §183; Carson 1985, 48). This verse is connected to the previous one by asyndeton.

σου. Possessive genitive qualifying ὄνομα. The preposed pronoun is thematically salient (Levinsohn 2000, 64).

τὸ ὄνομα. Accusative direct object of Ἐφανέρωσά.

τοῖς ἀνθρώποις. Dative indirect object of Ἐφανέρωσά.

οὕς. Accusative direct object of ἔδωκάς. The antecedent of the relative pronoun is τοῖς ἀνθρώποις.

ἔδωκάς. Aor act ind 2nd sg δίδωμι. ἔδωκάς, which has an acute accent on the antepenult, acquired an additional accent, the acute, on the ultima from the enclitic μοι (Smyth §183; Carson 1985, 48).

μοι. Dative indirect object of ἔδωκάς.

ἐκ τοῦ κόσμου. Separation. On the portrayal of the world in the FG, see 1:10 on ἐν τῷ κόσμῳ.

σοί. If σοί is masc nom pl of the possessive adjective σός, it functions as a predicate nominative. If σοί is dat sg of the personal pronoun σύ, it functions as a dative of possession. Either way, the meaning is similar: "they were yours." This clause is connected to the previous one by asyndeton.

ἦσαν. Impf act ind 3rd pl εἰμί.

κἀμοί. Formed by crasis from καὶ ἐμοί. καί is a coordinating conjunction. ἐμοί is the dative indirect object of ἔδωκας.

αὐτούς. Accusative direct object of ἔδωκας.

ἔδωκας. Aor act ind 2nd sg δίδωμι.

καί. Coordinating conjunction.

τὸν λόγον. Accusative direct object of τετήρηκαν.

σου. Subjective genitive qualifying λόγον.

τετήρηκαν. Prf act ind 3rd pl τηρέω. The third-person plural ending -αν for -ασι is attested in Greek literature since the second century BCE (BDF §83.1).

17:7 νῦν ἔγνωκαν ὅτι πάντα ὅσα δέδωκάς μοι παρὰ σοῦ εἰσιν·

νῦν. Temporal adverb focusing on time coextensive with the event of the narrative (BDAG, 681.1.a). Fronted as a temporal frame. This verse is connected to the previous one by asyndeton.

ἔγνωκαν. Prf act ind 3rd pl γινώσκω. ἔγνωκαν stands for ἐγνώκασιν (BDF §83.1). νῦν indicates that this perfect tense describes a state of knowledge in the present (Porter 1989, 265). The first-person singular variants ἔγνων (ℵ) and ἔγνωκα (W 579 sy^hmg) are probably scribal corrections under the influence of the first-person singular verb Ἐφανέρωσά in v. 6. The variant ἔγνωσαν (C Ψ f^13 33 700 1241) is most likely a scribal assimilation to ἔγνωσαν in v. 8 (Metzger, 213).

ὅτι. Introduces the clausal complement (indirect discourse) of ἔγνωκαν.

πάντα. Nominative subject of εἰσιν.

ὅσα. Accusative direct object of δέδωκάς. The antecedent of the relative pronoun is πάντα. πάντα ὅσα = "all things that" (see 4:29).

δέδωκάς. Prf act ind 2nd sg δίδωμι. δέδωκάς, which has an acute accent on the antepenult, acquired an additional accent, the acute, on the ultima from the enclitic μοι (Smyth §183; Carson 1985, 48).

μοι. Dative indirect object of δέδωκάς.

παρὰ σοῦ. Source.

εἰσιν. Pres act ind 3rd pl εἰμί.

17:8 ὅτι τὰ ῥήματα ἃ ἔδωκάς μοι δέδωκα αὐτοῖς, καὶ αὐτοὶ ἔλαβον καὶ ἔγνωσαν ἀληθῶς ὅτι παρὰ σοῦ ἐξῆλθον, καὶ ἐπίστευσαν ὅτι σύ με ἀπέστειλας.

ὅτι. Introduces a causal clause.

τὰ ῥήματα. Accusative direct object of δέδωκα.

ἅ. Accusative direct object of ἔδωκάς. The antecedent of the relative pronoun is τὰ ῥήματα.

ἔδωκάς. Aor act ind 2nd sg δίδωμι. ἔδωκάς, which has an acute accent on the antepenult, acquired an additional accent, the acute, on the ultima from the enclitic μοι (Smyth §183; Carson 1985, 48).

μοι. Dative indirect object of ἔδωκάς.

δέδωκα. Prf act ind 1st sg δίδωμι.

αὐτοῖς. Dative indirect object of δέδωκα.

καί. Coordinating conjunction.

αὐτοί. Nominative subject of ἔλαβον.

ἔλαβον. Aor act ind 3rd pl λαμβάνω.

καί. Coordinating conjunction.

ἔγνωσαν. Aor act ind 3rd pl γινώσκω.

ἀληθῶς. Adverb ("truly, really").

ὅτι. Introduces the clausal complement (indirect discourse) of ἔγνωσαν.

παρὰ σοῦ. Source (see 17:7). Fronted for emphasis.

ἐξῆλθον. Aor act ind 1st sg ἐξέρχομαι.

καὶ. Coordinating conjunction.

ἐπίστευσαν. Aor act ind 3rd pl πιστεύω.

ὅτι σύ με ἀπέστειλας. This clause occurs five times in the FG: three times as the content of faith (11:42; 17:8, 21) and twice as the content of knowledge (17:23, 25).

ὅτι. Introduces the clausal complement (indirect discourse) of ἐπίστευσαν.

σύ. Nominative subject of ἀπέστειλας. Fronted for emphasis.

με. Accusative direct object of ἀπέστειλας.

ἀπέστειλας. Aor act ind 2nd sg ἀποστέλλω.

John 17:9-19

⁹"I am asking on their behalf. I am not asking on behalf of the world but on behalf of those whom you have given me because they are yours. ¹⁰And all mine are yours and yours [are] mine, and I have been glorified in them. ¹¹And I am no longer in the world, yet they are in the world, and I am coming to you. Holy Father, keep them in your name, which you have given me, so that they may be one, just as we [are]. ¹²While I was with them, I was keeping them in your name, which you have given me, and I guarded [them], and none of them has perished except the son of destruction, in order that the Scripture may be fulfilled. ¹³And now I am coming to you, and I am saying these things in the world so that they may have my joy completed in themselves. ¹⁴I have given them your word, and the world hates them because they are not of the world, just as I am not of the world. ¹⁵I do not ask that you take them out of the world, but that you keep them from the evil one. ¹⁶They are not of the world, just as I am not of the world. ¹⁷Consecrate them in the truth; your word is truth. ¹⁸Just as you have sent me into the world, I also am going to send them into the world. ¹⁹And I consecrate myself for them, so that they also may be consecrated in the truth."

John 17:9-19

17:9 Ἐγὼ περὶ αὐτῶν ἐρωτῶ, οὐ περὶ τοῦ κόσμου ἐρωτῶ ἀλλὰ περὶ ὧν δέδωκάς μοι, ὅτι σοί εἰσιν,

Ἐγώ. Nominative subject of ἐρωτῶ. Fronted as a topical frame. This verse is connected to the previous one by asyndeton.

περὶ αὐτῶν. Advantage/representation. περί is here used instead of ὑπέρ (Zerwick §96; BDF §229.1; Wallace 1996, 363). Fronted for emphasis.

ἐρωτῶ. Pres act ind 1st sg ἐρωτάω.

οὐ ... ἀλλά. A point/counterpoint set ("not this ... but that") that replaces the incorrect explanation of the purpose of Jesus' intercessory prayer (he prays on behalf of the world) with the correct one (he prays on behalf of those whom the Father gave him). On the function of ἀλλά in a point/counterpoint set, see 1:8.

περὶ τοῦ κόσμου. Advantage/representation (see περὶ αὐτῶν above).

ἐρωτῶ. Pres act ind 1st sg ἐρωτάω.

περὶ ὧν. Advantage/representation (see περὶ αὐτῶν above). περὶ ὧν is an abbreviated version of περὶ τούτων οὕς ("on behalf of those whom"), in which the relative pronoun is attracted to the case of its omitted antecedent.

δέδωκάς. Prf act ind 2nd sg δίδωμι. δέδωκάς, which has an acute accent on the antepenult, acquired an additional accent, the acute, on the ultima from the enclitic μοι (Smyth §183; Carson 1985, 48).

μοι. Dative indirect object of δέδωκάς.

ὅτι. Introduces a causal clause.

σοί. Predicate nominative (if σοί is masc nom pl of the possessive adjective σός) or dative of possession (if σοί is dat sg of the personal pronoun σύ); for a similar usage, see 17:6. Fronted for emphasis.

εἰσιν. Pres act ind 3rd pl εἰμί.

17:10 καὶ τὰ ἐμὰ πάντα σά ἐστιν καὶ τὰ σὰ ἐμά, καὶ δεδόξασμαι ἐν αὐτοῖς.

καί. Coordinating conjunction.

τὰ ἐμὰ πάντα. Nominative subject of ἐστιν. Although the indefinite adjective πάντα stands in the second predicate position (article-noun-adjective), it has attributive function vis-à-vis the nominalized adjective τὰ ἐμά ("my things") because the pronominal adjectives such as πᾶς are exceptions to the rules about the relation of the adjective to the noun when the article is present (Wallace 1996, 308).

σά. Predicate adjective. Fronted for emphasis.

ἐστιν. Pres act ind 3rd sg εἰμί.

καί. Coordinating conjunction.
τὰ σά. Nominative subject of an implied ἐστίν.
ἐμά. Predicate nominative.
καί. Coordinating conjunction.
δεδόξασμαι. Prf pass ind 1st sg δοξάζω.
ἐν αὐτοῖς. Locative ("in them") or instrumental ("through them"). The personal pronoun is either neuter plural, referring to τὰ ἐμὰ πάντα in the first half of this verse, or masculine plural, referring to ὧν, i.e., the disciples, in v. 9. The former is the most natural reading of the syntax. The latter presumes that the first two paratactic clauses in v. 10, καὶ τὰ ἐμὰ πάντα σά ἐστιν καὶ τὰ σὰ ἐμά, function as a parenthesis, so that the third clause, καὶ δεδόξασμαι ἐν αὐτοῖς, resumes the thought of v. 10 (Barrett, 507).

17:11 καὶ οὐκέτι εἰμὶ ἐν τῷ κόσμῳ, καὶ αὐτοὶ ἐν τῷ κόσμῳ εἰσίν, κἀγὼ πρὸς σὲ ἔρχομαι. πάτερ ἅγιε, τήρησον αὐτοὺς ἐν τῷ ὀνόματί σου ᾧ δέδωκάς μοι, ἵνα ὦσιν ἓν καθὼς ἡμεῖς.

καί. Coordinating conjunction.
οὐκέτι. Negative adverb of time ("no longer, no further"). Fronted for emphasis.
εἰμί. Pres act ind 1st sg εἰμί. οὐκέτι indicates that this is a futuristic present.
ἐν τῷ κόσμῳ. Locative.
καί. Coordinating conjunction linking two clauses that stand in adversative relationship (see 1:5).
αὐτοί. Nominative subject of εἰσίν.
ἐν τῷ κόσμῳ. Locative. Fronted for emphasis.
εἰσίν. Pres act ind 3rd pl εἰμί. Since Jesus continues describing the impending events, this is also a futuristic present.
κἀγώ. Formed by crasis from καὶ ἐγώ. καί is a coordinating conjunction; ἐγώ is the nominative subject of ἔρχομαι.
πρὸς σέ. Locative (motion toward). Fronted for emphasis.
ἔρχομαι. Pres mid ind 1st sg ἔρχομαι. Futuristic present (see above).
πάτερ ἅγιε. Vocative of direct address. In his prayers in the FG, Jesus regularly addresses God as Father (11:41; 12:27, 28; 17:1, 5, 11, 21, 24, 25), but only here he uses the expression "Holy Father."
τήρησον. Aor act impv 2nd sg τηρέω. The combination τηρεῖν τινα ἔν τινι means "to keep someone (unharmed) by or through something" (BDAG, 1002.2.b).
αὐτούς. Accusative direct object of τήρησον.

ἐν τῷ ὀνόματί. State of being ("in your name") or instrumental ("by your name"). ὀνόματί, which has an acute accent on the antepenult, acquired an additional accent, the acute, on the ultima from the enclitic σου (Smyth §183; Carson 1985, 48).

σου. Possessive genitive qualifying ὀνόματί.

ᾧ. The relative pronoun ᾧ stands for ὅ, serving as the direct object of δέδωκάς. It is in the dative because it is attracted to its antecedent τῷ ὀνόματί. The dative singular ᾧ has the strongest external support ($\mathfrak{P}^{60.66vid}$ ℵ A B C K L W Γ Δ Θ Ψ f^{13} 1 565 579 700 1241 *l*844 𝔐) and may account for the emergence of two major variants: the accusative singular ὅ (D* 1424), which changes the attracted relative to its proper case, and the accusative plural οὕς (D¹ N 209 892ˢ aur f q vg saᵐˢˢ), which takes αὐτούς as the antecedent of the relative pronoun, possibly under the influence of οὕς ἔδωκάς μοι in v. 6 (Metzger, 213).

δέδωκάς. Prf act ind 2nd sg δίδωμι. δέδωκάς, which has an acute accent on the antepenult, acquired an additional accent, the acute, on the ultima from the enclitic μοι (Smyth §183; Carson 1985, 48).

μοι. Dative indirect object of δέδωκάς.

ἵνα. Introduces a purpose clause.

ὦσιν. Pres act subj 3rd pl εἰμί. Subjunctive with ἵνα.

ἕν. Predicate nominative. The neuter form of the numerical term εἷς, μία, ἕν shows that "[t]he disciples are to be kept by God not as units but as a unity" (Barrett, 508).

καθώς. Introduces a comparative clause.

ἡμεῖς. Nominative subject of an implied ὦμεν.

17:12 ὅτε ἤμην μετ' αὐτῶν ἐγὼ ἐτήρουν αὐτοὺς ἐν τῷ ὀνόματί σου ᾧ δέδωκάς μοι, καὶ ἐφύλαξα, καὶ οὐδεὶς ἐξ αὐτῶν ἀπώλετο εἰ μὴ ὁ υἱὸς τῆς ἀπωλείας, ἵνα ἡ γραφὴ πληρωθῇ.

ὅτε. Introduces a temporal clause, which is fronted as a temporal frame.

ἤμην. Impf mid ind 1st sg εἰμί. Frey (2018, 83) argues that the Johannine Jesus uses the imperfect tense to describe his time with his disciples because he already views it from the post-Easter perspective.

μετ' αὐτῶν. Association/accompaniment.

ἐγώ. Nominative subject of ἤμην.

ἐτήρουν. Impf act ind 1st sg τηρέω. On the meaning of τηρέω, see 17:11. The imperfective aspect of the verb portrays Jesus' protection of his disciples as an ongoing process.

αὐτούς. Accusative direct object of ἐτήρουν.

ἐν τῷ ὀνόματί σου ᾧ δέδωκάς μοι. A verbatim repetition of a portion of 17:11.

ἐν τῷ ὀνόματί. State of being ("in your name") or instrumental ("by your name"). On the second accent, see 17:11.

σου. Possessive genitive qualifying ὀνόματί.

ᾧ. The relative pronoun ᾧ stands for ὅ, serving as the direct object of δέδωκάς. It is in the dative because it is attracted to its antecedent τῷ ὀνόματί.

δέδωκάς. Prf act ind 2nd sg δίδωμι (see 17:11).

μοι. Dative indirect object of δέδωκάς.

καί. Coordinating conjunction.

ἐφύλαξα. Aor act ind 1st sg φυλάσσω. The aorist ἐφύλαξα (perfective aspect) "sums up the process represented by the imperfect ἐτήρουν" (Barrett, 508). Elsewhere in the FG, φυλάσσω is used only in 12:25, 47.

καί. Coordinating conjunction.

οὐδεὶς . . . εἰ μή. A point/counterpoint set that corrects the negated clause ("no one of them was lost") by introducing an exception ("except the son of destruction"); on the function of the excepted element, see 3:13 on οὐδεὶς . . . εἰ μή.

οὐδεὶς. Nominative subject of ἀπώλετο.

ἐξ αὐτῶν. Replaces the partitive genitive.

ἀπώλετο. Aor mid ind 3rd sg ἀπόλλυμι. In this context, ἀπόλλυμι means "to destroy or to cause the destruction of persons, objects, or institutions" (LN 20.31). The middle voice means "to perish" (BDAG, 116.1.b.α).

ὁ υἱός. The excepted nominative subject of ἀπώλετο.

τῆς ἀπωλείας. Descriptive genitive qualifying υἱός ("a person destined for destruction" or "a person doomed to be lost"). The expression "son of . . ." is a Semitic idiom for ascribing certain characteristic to a person or a group (Moule, 174–75). For other NT examples of this idiom, see 12:36 on φωτός. Two similar expressions occur in the DSS: בני השחת = "the sons of pit" (CD 6.15) and אנשי (ה)שחת = "the men of pit" (1QS 9.16, 22; cf. 1QS 10.19-20).

ἵνα ἡ γραφὴ πληρωθῇ. This OT introductory formula is used nowhere else in the NT except in the FG, where it occurs four times (13:18; 17:12; 19:24, 36). This is the only instance when it follows the scriptural reference. On the variations of this formula in the FG, see 12:38. The evangelist probably alludes to Ps 41:10b (LXX Ps 40:10b) quoted in John 13:18. Another possibility is LXX Prov 24:22a. John does not quote any of these texts directly but uses them creatively to explain the theme of Judas the betrayer.

ἵνα. Introduces a purpose clause.

ἡ γραφὴ. Nominative subject of πληρωθῇ.

πληρωθῇ. Aor pass subj 3rd sg πληρόω. Subjunctive with ἵνα. The verb stands in final, emphatic position.

17:13 νῦν δὲ πρὸς σὲ ἔρχομαι καὶ ταῦτα λαλῶ ἐν τῷ κόσμῳ ἵνα ἔχωσιν τὴν χαρὰν τὴν ἐμὴν πεπληρωμένην ἐν ἑαυτοῖς.

νῦν. Temporal adverb focusing on time coextensive with the event of the narrative (BDAG, 681.1.a). Fronted as a temporal frame.

δὲ. Marker of narrative development.

πρὸς σὲ. Locative (motion toward). Fronted for emphasis.

ἔρχομαι. Pres mid ind 1st sg ἔρχομαι. νῦν indicates that Jesus' return to the Father has already started, although its completion lies in the future.

καὶ. Coordinating conjunction.

ταῦτα. Accusative direct object of λαλῶ. ταῦτα could refer to the entire farewell discourse or to Jesus' intercessory prayer (Barrett, 509).

λαλῶ. Pres act ind 1st sg λαλέω.

ἐν τῷ κόσμῳ. Locative. On the portrayal of the world in the FG, see 1:10 on ἐν τῷ κόσμῳ.

ἵνα. Introduces a purpose clause.

ἔχωσιν. Pres act subj 3rd pl ἔχω. Subjunctive with ἵνα.

τὴν χαρὰν τὴν ἐμὴν. Accusative direct object of ἔχωσιν in a double accusative object-complement construction. The possessive adjective ἐμὴν stands in the second attributive position (see 1:9 on τὸ φῶς τὸ ἀληθινόν).

πεπληρωμένην. Prf pass ptc fem acc sg πληρόω (predicative). Accusative complement to τὴν χαρὰν τὴν ἐμὴν in a double accusative object-complement construction. Fanning emphasizes that the perfect passive participle "often emphasizes the *resulting state* and only implies the anterior occurrence" (416).

ἐν ἑαυτοῖς. Locative.

17:14 ἐγὼ δέδωκα αὐτοῖς τὸν λόγον σου καὶ ὁ κόσμος ἐμίσησεν αὐτούς, ὅτι οὐκ εἰσὶν ἐκ τοῦ κόσμου καθὼς ἐγὼ οὐκ εἰμὶ ἐκ τοῦ κόσμου.

ἐγὼ. Nominative subject of δέδωκα. Fronted as a topical frame. This verse is connected to the previous one by asyndeton.

δέδωκα. Prf act ind 1st sg δίδωμι.

αὐτοῖς. Dative indirect object of δέδωκα.

τὸν λόγον. Accusative direct object of δέδωκα.

σου. Objective genitive qualifying λόγον.

καί. Coordinating conjunction.

ὁ κόσμος. Nominative subject of ἐμίσησεν. On the portrayal of the world in the FG, see 1:10 on ἐν τῷ κόσμῳ.

ἐμίσησεν. Aor act ind 3rd sg μισέω. The context indicates that this aorist tense describes the current and future attitude of the unbelieving world toward Jesus' followers (Porter 1989, 78; Campbell 2007, 121). Caragounis, alternatively, argues that ἐμίσησεν presents the world's hatred as a fact that has already occurred (cf. 15:18-19), though he concedes that "this process, which has already begun, will continue and be accentuated in the future" (2004, 329). A third possibility is to say that ἐμίσησεν "is written from the evangelist's standpoint" (Barrett, 509), i.e., that it describes the hatred of the world from the post-resurrection perspective.

αὐτούς. Accusative direct object of ἐμίσησεν.

ὅτι. Introduces a causal clause.

οὐκ. Negative particle normally used with indicative verbs.

εἰσίν. Pres act ind 3rd pl εἰμί.

ἐκ τοῦ κόσμου. Source/origin that determines the character of a person (Zerwick §§134–35). Although the comparative clause that follows compares the origin of the disciples to the origin of Jesus, "they do not share Jesus' ontic 'of-ness' but its consequences: The world hates both the inherently alien Jesus, whose 'of-ness' was maintained, and those made aliens by acknowledging the 'of-ness' of Jesus" (Keck, 284). On the portrayal of the world in the FG, see 1:10 on ἐν τῷ κόσμῳ.

καθώς. Introduces a comparative clause.

ἐγώ. Nominative subject of εἰμί. Fronted for emphasis.

οὐκ. Negative particle normally used with indicative verbs.

εἰμί. Pres act ind 1st sg εἰμί.

ἐκ τοῦ κόσμου. See above.

17:15 οὐκ ἐρωτῶ ἵνα ἄρῃς αὐτοὺς ἐκ τοῦ κόσμου, ἀλλ' ἵνα τηρήσῃς αὐτοὺς ἐκ τοῦ πονηροῦ.

οὐκ . . . ἀλλ'. A point/counterpoint set ("not this . . . but that") that replaces the inaccurate petition for the disciples regarding their relationship to the world (that God may take them out of the world) with the accurate one (that God may protect them from the evil one). On the function of ἀλλά in a point/counterpoint set, see 1:8. This verse is connected to the previous one by asyndeton.

ἐρωτῶ. Pres act ind 1st sg ἐρωτάω.

ἵνα. Introduces a complementary clause that replaces an infinitive (Zerwick §§406–7; Wallace 1996, 476; BDAG, 476.2.a.γ). Zerwick (§406) explains that in Hellenistic Greek, a ἵνα clause "began to be more and more used for the infinitive expressing the object (which in a certain sense is an 'end in view') with verbs of asking, commanding or the like," as here. For other NT examples of ἐρωτάω with a ἵνα clause, see Mark 7:26; Luke 7:36; 16:27; John 4:47.

ἄρῃς. Aor act subj 2nd sg αἴρω. Subjunctive with ἵνα.

αὐτοὺς. Accusative direct object of ἄρῃς.

ἐκ τοῦ κόσμου. Separation. On the portrayal of the world in the FG, see 1:10 on ἐν τῷ κόσμῳ.

ἵνα. Introduces a complementary clause that replaces an infinitive (see above).

τηρήσῃς. Aor act subj 2nd sg τηρέω. Subjunctive with ἵνα. The combination τηρεῖν τινα ἔκ τινος means "to keep someone from someone or someth[ing]" (BDAG, 1002.2.d).

αὐτοὺς. Accusative direct object of τηρήσῃς.

ἐκ τοῦ πονηροῦ. Separation. ἐκ is here used for ἀπό (Zerwick §87); see Matt 6:13 (ῥῦσαι ἡμᾶς ἀπὸ τοῦ πονηροῦ). If the nominalized adjective τοῦ πονηροῦ is masculine, it denotes "the evil one" = "the devil" (BDAG, 851.1.b.β; cf. ASV; ESV; LEB; NRSV; NET; NIV; REB); if it is neuter, it denotes "that which is evil" (BDAG, 852.1.b.γ; cf. KJV; RHE; WBT). The use of this substantive in 1 John 2:13-14; 3:12; 5:18-19 favors the former.

17:16 ἐκ τοῦ κόσμου οὐκ εἰσὶν καθὼς ἐγὼ οὐκ εἰμὶ ἐκ τοῦ κόσμου.

ἐκ τοῦ κόσμου οὐκ εἰσὶν καθὼς ἐγὼ οὐκ εἰμὶ ἐκ τοῦ κόσμου. A verbatim repetition of 17:14b (οὐκ εἰσὶν ἐκ τοῦ κόσμου καθὼς ἐγὼ οὐκ εἰμὶ ἐκ τοῦ κόσμου). The only difference is the placement of the PP ἐκ τοῦ κόσμου before οὐκ εἰσὶν.

ἐκ τοῦ κόσμου. Source/origin that determines the character of a person (Zerwick §§134–35). The PP is fronted for emphasis. This verse is connected to the previous one by asyndeton.

οὐκ. Negative particle normally used with indicative verbs.

εἰσὶν. Pres act ind 3rd pl εἰμί.

καθὼς. Introduces a comparative clause.

ἐγὼ. Nominative subject of εἰμί. Emphatic use.

οὐκ. Negative particle normally used with indicative verbs.

εἰμὶ. Pres act ind 1st sg εἰμί.

ἐκ τοῦ κόσμου. See above.

17:17 ἁγίασον αὐτοὺς ἐν τῇ ἀληθείᾳ· ὁ λόγος ὁ σὸς ἀλήθειά ἐστιν.

ἁγίασον. Aor act impv 2nd sg ἁγιάζω. This verse is connected to the previous one by asyndeton.

αὐτοὺς. Accusative direct object of ἁγίασον.

ἐν τῇ ἀληθείᾳ. Locative ("in the sphere of truth"; Schnackenburg, 3:185; cf. NRSV; ASV; ESV; LEB; NET), instrumental ("by the truth"; cf. HCSB; NIV; REB), or both: "Here 'truth' is both the agency of the consecration and the realm into which they are consecrated" (Brown, 2:761).

ὁ λόγος ὁ σὸς. Nominative subject of ἐστιν. Fronted for emphasis. The possessive adjective σὸς stands in the second attributive position (see 1:9 on τὸ φῶς τὸ ἀληθινόν). This verse is connected to the previous one by asyndeton.

ἀλήθειά. Predicate nominative. ἀλήθειά, which has an acute accent on the antepenult, acquired an additional accent, the acute, on the ultima from the enclitic ἐστιν (Smyth §183; Carson 1985, 48).

ἐστιν. Pres act ind 3rd sg εἰμί.

17:18 καθὼς ἐμὲ ἀπέστειλας εἰς τὸν κόσμον, κἀγὼ ἀπέστειλα αὐτοὺς εἰς τὸν κόσμον·

καθὼς . . . κἀγὼ. A point/counterpoint set ("just as . . . also") that compares God's sending of Jesus into the world with Jesus' sending of his disciples. κἀγώ is formed by crasis from καὶ ἐγώ. καί is adverbial (adjunctive). ἐγώ is the nominative subject of ἀπέστειλα. This verse is connected to the previous one by asyndeton.

ἐμὲ. Accusative direct object of ἀπέστειλας. Fronted for emphasis.

ἀπέστειλας. Aor act ind 2nd sg ἀποστέλλω.

εἰς τὸν κόσμον. Locative. See 3:17 and 10:36 for other examples of the combination ἀποστέλλω + εἰς τὸν κόσμον in the FG. On the portrayal of the world in the FG, see 1:10 on ἐν τῷ κόσμῳ.

ἀπέστειλα. Aor act ind 1st sg ἀποστέλλω. This aorist is usually construed as past-referring, although commentators regularly note that the disciples are not officially sent into the world until after the resurrection, when Jesus tells them in 20:21: καθὼς ἀπέσταλκέν με ὁ πατήρ, κἀγὼ πέμπω ὑμᾶς ("As the Father sent me, I also send you"). One possibility is to take Jesus' declaration in 4:38 (ἐγὼ ἀπέστειλα ὑμᾶς θερίζειν ὃ οὐχ ὑμεῖς κεκοπιάκατε ["I sent you to reap what you have not labored for"]) as a type of sending to which Jesus refers here. Another possibility is to interpret Jesus' statement as a past event not from the narrative perspective but from the post-resurrection (i.e., the audience's) perspective

(Brown, 2:762; Michaels, 872–73). A third possibility, which is reflected in my translation, is to regard ἀπέστειλα as an example of the "futuristic or proleptic aorist" (Porter 1994, 37; cf. Campbell 2007, 121).

αὐτούς. Accusative direct object of ἀπέστειλα.

εἰς τὸν κόσμον. See above.

17:19 καὶ ὑπὲρ αὐτῶν ἐγὼ ἁγιάζω ἐμαυτόν, ἵνα ὦσιν καὶ αὐτοὶ ἡγιασμένοι ἐν ἀληθείᾳ.

καί. Coordinating conjunction.

ὑπὲρ αὐτῶν. Representation or substitution. For other prepositional phrases with ὑπέρ in the FG, see 6:51; 10:11, 15; 11:50, 51, 52; 13:37, 38; 15:13; 18:14.

ἐγώ. Nominative subject of ἁγιάζω. Fronted for emphasis.

ἁγιάζω. Pres act ind 1st sg ἁγιάζω. Barrett notes that "[t]here is nothing in the word ἁγιάζειν itself to make a reference to the death of Jesus necessary: this reference lies rather in the context, especially in the use of ὑπέρ" (511).

ἐμαυτόν. Accusative direct object of ἁγιάζω.

ἵνα. Introduces a purpose clause.

ὦσιν. Pres act subj 3rd pl εἰμί. Subjunctive with ἵνα.

καί. Adverbial use (adjunctive).

αὐτοί. Nominative subject of ὦσιν.

ἡγιασμένοι. Prf pass ptc masc nom pl ἁγιάζω (perfect periphrastic).

ἐν ἀληθείᾳ. Although this PP could be adverbial (ἐν ἀληθείᾳ = ἀληθῶς; cf. LN 70.4), it probably has the same sense as the PP with the article (ἐν τῇ ἀληθείᾳ) in 17:17. In this verse, however, "'truth' is more the realm of the disciples' consecration than the agency of that consecration" (Brown, 2:762).

John 17:20-26

[20]"I am asking not only on behalf of these but also on behalf of those who will believe in me through their word, [21]that they all may be one, just as you, Father, [are] in me and I [am] in you, that they also may be in us, so that the world may believe that you sent me. [22]And the glory that you have given to me I have given to them, so that they may be one, just as we [are] one— [23]I in them and you in me—so that they may be perfected into one, so that the world may know that you sent me and loved them just as you loved me. [24]Father, those whom you have given to me—I desire that they also may be with me where I am, so that they may see my glory that you have given me because you loved me before

the foundation of the world. ²⁵Righteous Father, the world did not know you (though I knew you), and these came to know that you sent me. ²⁶And I made known to them your name, and I will make [it] known, so that the love with which you have loved me may be in them, and I [may be] in them."

17:20 Οὐ περὶ τούτων δὲ ἐρωτῶ μόνον, ἀλλὰ καὶ περὶ τῶν πιστευόντων διὰ τοῦ λόγου αὐτῶν εἰς ἐμέ,

Οὐ ... μόνον ἀλλὰ καί. A point/counterpoint set ("not only this ... but also that") which supplements the initial group for whom Jesus prays (his disciples) with another group of (those who will come to faith through them).

περὶ τούτων. Advantage/representation. περί is here used instead of ὑπέρ (see 17:9). The demonstrative pronoun is anaphoric, referring to Jesus' disciples on whose behalf Jesus prayed until now.

δέ. Marker of narrative development.

ἐρωτῶ. Pres act ind 1st sg ἐρωτάω.

περὶ τῶν πιστευόντων. Advantage/representation (see περὶ τούτων above).

τῶν πιστευόντων. Pres act ptc masc gen pl πιστεύω (substantival). This present participle denotes "a relatively future action" vis-à-vis the finite verb of the clause ("those who will believe") (BDF §339.2a; Zerwick §283).

διὰ τοῦ λόγου. Means.

αὐτῶν. Subjective genitive qualifying λόγου. The antecedent of the personal pronoun is Jesus' disciples.

εἰς ἐμέ. Goal of actions or feelings directed toward someone (BDAG, 290.4.c.β). Even though εἰς ἐμέ is separated by διὰ τοῦ λόγου αὐτῶν from πιστευόντων, it most likely belongs with this verb. For πιστεύειν εἰς + accusative ("trust or believe in someone"), see 1:12 on εἰς τὸ ὄνομα. Barrett's (511–12) proposal to take εἰς ἐμέ with λόγου ("their word of testimony to me") is problematic because the formulation διὰ τοῦ λόγου αὐτῶν εἰς ἐμέ is not really analogous to ὁ λόγος ἡμῶν ὁ πρὸς ὑμᾶς in 2 Cor 1:18 as he suggests. In such a case, we would expect an adjectivizing article that could turn the PP εἰς ἐμέ into an attributive modifier of λόγου, i.e., διὰ τοῦ λόγου αὐτῶν τοῦ εἰς ἐμέ.

17:21 ἵνα πάντες ἓν ὦσιν, καθὼς σύ, πάτερ, ἐν ἐμοὶ κἀγὼ ἐν σοί, ἵνα καὶ αὐτοὶ ἐν ἡμῖν ὦσιν, ἵνα ὁ κόσμος πιστεύῃ ὅτι σύ με ἀπέστειλας.

ἵνα. Introduces a complementary clause that conveys the content of Jesus' prayer (Wallace 1996, 476; BDAG, 476.2.a.γ).

πάντες. Nominative subject of ὦσιν.

ἕν. Predicate nominative that conveys the notion of unity (see 17:11). Fronted for emphasis.

ὦσιν. Pres act subj 3rd pl εἰμί. Subjunctive with ἵνα.

καθώς. Introduces a comparative clause that portrays the unity between Jesus and the Father as the model for the unity among believers.

σύ, πάτερ, ἐν ἐμοὶ κἀγὼ ἐν σοί. The reciprocal formula of immanence that describes the unity between the Father and the Son. For other versions of this formula, see 10:38 (ἐν ἐμοὶ ὁ πατὴρ κἀγὼ ἐν τῷ πατρί), 14:10, 11 (ἐγὼ ἐν τῷ πατρὶ καὶ ὁ πατὴρ ἐν ἐμοί).

σύ. Nominative subject of an implied εἶ.

πάτερ. Vocative of direct address. In his prayers in the FG, Jesus regularly addresses God as Father (11:41; 12:27, 28; 17:1, 5, 11, 21, 24, 25).

ἐν ἐμοί. State of being, describing a close personal relationship between the Father and the Son.

κἀγώ. Formed by crasis from καὶ ἐγώ. καί is a coordinating conjunction; ἐγώ is the nominative subject of an implied εἰμί.

ἐν σοί. State of being, describing a close personal relationship between the Son and the Father.

ἵνα. Introduces a complementary clause that conveys additional content of Jesus' prayer (see above).

καί. Adverbial use (adjunctive).

αὐτοί. Nominative subject of ὦσιν.

ἐν ἡμῖν. State of being, describing a close personal relationship between the believers, the Father, and the Son.

ὦσιν. Pres act subj 3rd pl εἰμί. Subjunctive with ἵνα. Many copyists have added ἓν before ὦσιν (ℵ A C³ K L N Γ Δ Θ Ψ $f^{1.13}$ 33 565 579 700 1241 1424 *l*844 𝔐 et al.), most likely under the influence of ἓν ὦσιν at the beginning of this verse. The reading without ἕν, however, is preferable because of its better attestation ($\mathfrak{P}^{66vid}$ B C* D W it sa ly pbo bo^ms). Metzger adds that the longer reading "clouds the thought more than illumines it" (Metzger, 214).

ἵνα. Introduces a purpose or, perhaps, result clause. Unlike the first two ἵνα clauses in this verse, this third ἵνα clause does not depend on ἐρωτῶ from v. 20. Rather, it conveys the goal of the believers' unity through their indwelling in Jesus and the Father (Bultmann, 514 n. 4).

ὁ κόσμος. Nominative subject of πιστεύῃ. On the portrayal of the world in the FG, see 1:10 on ἐν τῷ κόσμῳ.

πιστεύῃ. Pres act subj 3rd sg πιστεύω. Subjunctive with ἵνα.

ὅτι σύ με ἀπέστειλας. This clause occurs five times in the FG: three times as the content of faith (11:42; 17:8, 21) and twice as the content of knowledge (17:23, 25).

    ὅτι. Introduces the clausal complement (indirect discourse) of πιστεύῃ.

    σύ. Nominative subject of ἀπέστειλας. Fronted for emphasis.

    με. Accusative direct object of ἀπέστειλας.

    ἀπέστειλας. Aor act ind 2nd sg ἀποστέλλω.

17:22 κἀγὼ τὴν δόξαν ἣν δέδωκάς μοι δέδωκα αὐτοῖς, ἵνα ὦσιν ἓν καθὼς ἡμεῖς ἕν·

κἀγώ. Formed by crasis from καὶ ἐγώ. καί is a coordinating conjunction; ἐγώ is the nominative subject of δέδωκα.

τὴν δόξαν. Accusative direct object of δέδωκα.

ἥν. Accusative direct object of δέδωκάς. The antecedent of the relative pronoun is τὴν δόξαν.

δέδωκάς. Prf act ind 2nd sg δίδωμι. δέδωκάς, which has an acute accent on the antepenult, acquired an additional accent, the acute, on the ultima from the enclitic μοι (Smyth §183; Carson 1985, 48).

    μοι. Dative indirect object of δέδωκάς.

    δέδωκα. Prf act ind 1st sg δίδωμι.

    αὐτοῖς. Dative indirect object of δέδωκα.

    ἵνα. Introduces a purpose clause.

    ὦσιν. Pres act subj 3rd pl εἰμί. Subjunctive with ἵνα.

    ἕν. Predicate nominative that conveys the notion of unity (see 17:11).

καθώς. Introduces a comparative clause that presents the unity between the Father and the Son as the model for the unity of the believers (see 17:21).

    ἡμεῖς. Nominative subject of an implied ἐσμέν. Fronted for emphasis.

    ἕν. Predicate nominative (see above).

17:23 ἐγὼ ἐν αὐτοῖς καὶ σὺ ἐν ἐμοί, ἵνα ὦσιν τετελειωμένοι εἰς ἕν, ἵνα γινώσκῃ ὁ κόσμος ὅτι σύ με ἀπέστειλας καὶ ἠγάπησας αὐτοὺς καθὼς ἐμὲ ἠγάπησας.

ἐγώ. Nominative subject of an implied εἰμί. The personal pronoun is contrasted to σύ. Robertson remarks that in cases of contrastive pronouns, as here, "[t]he amount of emphasis will vary very greatly according to circumstances and may sometimes vanish entirely so far as we can determine" (677). This verse is connected to the previous one by asyndeton.

ἐν αὐτοῖς. State of being, describing a close personal relationship between Jesus and the believers.

καὶ. Coordinating conjunction.

σὺ. Nominative subject of an implied εἶ. The personal pronoun is contrasted to ἐγὼ (see above).

ἐν ἐμοί. State of being, describing a close personal relationship between the Father and the Son.

ἵνα. Introduces a purpose clause.

ὦσιν. Pres act subj 3rd pl εἰμί. Subjunctive with ἵνα.

τετελειωμένοι. Prf pass ptc masc nom pl τελειόω (perfect periphrastic).

εἰς ἕν. This PP could be understood in three different ways: (1) as conveying the goal and result, "that they may be perfected into one" (ASV; cf. Harris 2015, 293); (2) as a substitution for ἐν ἑνί, "in order that they may be completed in one" (LEB; cf. Harris 2015, 293); or (3) as a replacement for the predicate nominative, "that they may become completely one" (NRSV; cf. Wallace 1996, 47). The neuter form of the numerical term εἷς, μία, ἕν is again used to convey the idea of unity (see 17:11). The third option, which is favored by many English translations (CEB; HCSB; ESV; GNT; NET; NRSV; REB), assigns adverbial function to the passive participle τετελειωμένοι and construes the ἵνα clause as copulative. But the subject of the clause ("they") and εἰς ἕν are not connected to each other by the present subjunctive of εἰμί, as Wallace (1996, 47 n. 38) claims; rather, the subjunctive of εἰμί connects the subject of the clause and the perfect participle into a periphrastic construction ("that they may be perfected"). Regarding the first two alternatives, option (1) is preferable because it offers a better explanation of the syntax of the clause.

ἵνα. Introduces a purpose clause.

γινώσκῃ. Pres act subj 3rd sg γινώσκω. Subjunctive with ἵνα.

ὁ κόσμος. Nominative subject of γινώσκῃ.

ὅτι σύ με ἀπέστειλας. This clause occurs five times in the FG: three times as the content of faith (11:42; 17:8, 21) and twice as the content of knowledge (17:23, 25).

ὅτι. Introduces the clausal complement (indirect discourse) of γινώσκῃ.

σύ. Nominative subject of ἀπέστειλας. Fronted for emphasis.

με. Accusative direct object of ἀπέστειλας.

ἀπέστειλας. Aor act ind 2nd sg ἀποστέλλω.

καὶ. Coordinating conjunction.

ἠγάπησας. Aor act ind 2nd sg ἀγαπάω.

αὐτούς. Accusative direct object of the first ἠγάπησας.

καθώς. Introduces a comparative clause that presents the Father's love for the Son as the paradigm of the Father's love for the believers (see 17:21).

ἐμέ. Accusative direct object of the second ἠγάπησας. Fronted for emphasis.

ἠγάπησας. Aor act ind 2nd sg ἀγαπάω.

17:24 Πάτερ, ὃ δέδωκάς μοι, θέλω ἵνα ὅπου εἰμὶ ἐγὼ κἀκεῖνοι ὦσιν μετ' ἐμοῦ, ἵνα θεωρῶσιν τὴν δόξαν τὴν ἐμήν, ἣν δέδωκάς μοι ὅτι ἠγάπησάς με πρὸ καταβολῆς κόσμου.

Πάτερ. Vocative of direct address. In his prayers in the FG, Jesus regularly addresses God as Father (11:41; 12:27, 28; 17:1, 5, 11, 21, 24, 25). This verse is connected to the previous one by asyndeton.

ὅ. Introduces a headless relative clause that, in its entirety (ὃ δέδωκάς μοι), serves as the subject of the ἵνα clause in a left-dislocation, resumed by κἀκεῖνοι. (Runge 2010, 287–313). The left-dislocation calls attention to the portrayal of the believers as those who are given to the Son by the Father. Within its clause, ὅ is the accusative direct object of δέδωκάς. The neuter singular is sometimes used with reference to persons, as here, "if it is not the individuals but a general quality that is to be emphasized" (BDF §138.1; cf. Caragounis 2004, 236–37). For other examples of this usage in the FG, see 3:6; 6:37; 17:2. Some copyists replaced ὅ with οὕς (A C K L N Γ Δ Ψ $f^{1.13}$ 33 565 700 892^s 1241 1424 *l*844 𝔐 lat sy$^{p.h}$ et al.), which better anticipates κἀκεῖνοι. The neuter singular, however, is to be preferred because it is the *lectio difficilior* and is attested by several text types (𝔓^{60} ℵ B D W 579 sy^s bo) (Metzger, 214).

δέδωκάς. Prf act ind 2nd sg δίδωμι. δέδωκάς, which has an acute accent on the antepenult, acquired an additional accent, the acute, on the ultima from the enclitic μοι (Smyth §183; Carson 1985, 48).

μοι. Dative indirect object of δέδωκάς.

θέλω. Pres act ind 1st sg θέλω.

ἵνα. Introduces a complementary clause that completes the meaning of the helping verb θέλω. In classical Greek, a complementary ἵνα clause is equivalent to a complementary infinitive (Wallace 1996, 476; BDF §392.1a).

ὅπου. Marker of a position in space.

εἰμί. Pres act ind 1st sg εἰμί.

ἐγώ. Nominative subject of εἰμί.

κἀκεῖνοι. Formed by crasis from καὶ ἐκεῖνοι. καὶ is adverbial (adjunctive); ἐκεῖνοι is the nominative subject of ὦσιν, resuming ὃ δέδωκάς μοι. The anaphoric demonstrative reinforces what is already made prominent through the left-dislocation of the relative clause.

ὦσιν. Pres act subj 3rd pl εἰμί. Subjunctive with ἵνα.

μετ' ἐμοῦ. Association/accompaniment.

ἵνα. Introduces a purpose clause.

θεωρῶσιν. Pres act subj 3rd pl θεωρέω. Subjunctive with ἵνα.

τὴν δόξαν τὴν ἐμήν. Accusative direct object of θεωρῶσιν. The possessive adjective ἐμήν stands in the second attributive position (see 1:9 on τὸ φῶς τὸ ἀληθινόν).

ἣν. Accusative direct object of δέδωκάς. The antecedent of the relative pronoun is τὴν δόξαν.

δέδωκάς. Prf act ind 2nd sg δίδωμι. δέδωκάς, which has an acute accent on the antepenult, acquired an additional accent, the acute, on the ultima from the enclitic μοι (Smyth §183; Carson 1985, 48).

μοι. Dative indirect object of δέδωκάς.

ὅτι. Introduces a causal clause.

ἠγάπησάς. Aor act ind 2nd sg ἀγαπάω. ἠγάπησάς, which has an acute accent on the antepenult, acquired an additional accent, the acute, on the ultima from the enclitic με (Smyth §183; Carson 1985, 48).

με. Accusative direct object of ἠγάπησάς.

πρὸ καταβολῆς. Temporal. The noun καταβολῆς (lit. "foundation") is definite although it does not have the article because it denotes the creation of the world. This is the only occurrence of this term in the FG.

κόσμου. Objective genitive qualifying καταβολῆς. The term κόσμος here denotes the totality of creation.

17:25 πάτερ δίκαιε, καὶ ὁ κόσμος σε οὐκ ἔγνω, ἐγὼ δέ σε ἔγνων, καὶ οὗτοι ἔγνωσαν ὅτι σύ με ἀπέστειλας·

πάτερ δίκαιε. Vocative of direct address. In his prayers in the FG, Jesus regularly addresses God as Father (11:41; 12:27, 28; 17:1, 5, 11, 21, 24, 25), but only here he uses the expression "righteous Father."

καὶ ... δέ ... καὶ. "Both ... (but ...) and." The two clauses introduced with καί make two juxtaposed statements: "*both* the world did not know you ... *and* these came to know that you sent me," although, as Moule rightly notes, "the first καί does not seem so easily explicable" (167). Since the middle clause with δέ ("I knew you") stands in tension with the first statement, it is probably best to take it as a parenthesis (Barrett, 515; Brown, 2:773). To avoid the awkwardness of the "both ... and" construction, I have not translated the first καί.

ὁ κόσμος. Nominative subject of ἔγνω. On the portrayal of the world in the FG, see 1:10 on ἐν τῷ κόσμῳ.

σε. Accusative direct object of ἔγνω.

οὐκ. Negative particle normally used with indicative verbs.

ἔγνω. Aor act ind 3rd sg γινώσκω.

ἐγώ. Nominative subject of ἔγνων. The personal pronoun is emphatic and contrastive, distinguishing Jesus from the world.

σε. Accusative direct object of ἔγνων.

ἔγνων. Aor act ind 1st sg γινώσκω.

οὗτοι. Nominative subject of ἔγνωσαν.

ἔγνωσαν. Aor act ind 3rd pl γινώσκω.

ὅτι σύ με ἀπέστειλας. This clause occurs five times in the FG: three times as the content of faith (11:42; 17:8, 21) and twice as the content of knowledge (17:23, 25).

ὅτι. Introduces the clausal complement (indirect discourse) of ἔγνωσαν.

σύ. Nominative subject of ἀπέστειλας. The personal pronoun is emphatic.

με. Accusative direct object of ἀπέστειλας.

ἀπέστειλας. Aor act ind 2nd sg ἀποστέλλω.

17:26 καὶ ἐγνώρισα αὐτοῖς τὸ ὄνομά σου καὶ γνωρίσω, ἵνα ἡ ἀγάπη ἣν ἠγάπησάς με ἐν αὐτοῖς ᾖ κἀγὼ ἐν αὐτοῖς.

καί. Coordinating conjunction.

ἐγνώρισα. Aor act ind 1st sg γνωρίζω.

αὐτοῖς. Dative indirect object of ἐγνώρισα.

τὸ ὄνομά. Accusative direct object of ἐγνώρισα. ὄνομά, which has an acute accent on the antepenult, acquired an additional accent, the acute, on the ultima from the enclitic σου (Smyth §183; Carson 1985, 48).

σου. Possessive genitive qualifying ὄνομά.

καί. Coordinating conjunction.

γνωρίσω. Fut act ind 1st sg γνωρίζω.

ἵνα. Introduces a purpose clause.

ἡ ἀγάπη. Nominative subject of ᾖ. The article is cataphoric, anticipating the relative clause that defines the love mentioned here (Wallace 1996, 220–21).

ἥν. The relative pronoun presupposes a cognate accusative (accusative of the inner object): ἀγάπην ἠγάπησας (lit. "you loved a love" = "the love with which you loved"; cf. Zerwick and Grosvenor, 337).

ἠγάπησάς. Aor act ind 2nd sg ἀγαπάω. ἠγάπησάς, which has an acute accent on the antepenult, acquired an additional accent, the acute, on the ultima from the enclitic με (Smyth §183; Carson 1985, 48).

με. Accusative direct object of ἠγάπησάς.

ἐν αὐτοῖς. Locative ("within them" or "among them").

ᾖ. Pres act subj 3rd sg εἰμί. Subjunctive with ἵνα.

κἀγώ. Formed by crasis from καὶ ἐγώ. καί is a coordinating conjunction; ἐγώ is the nominative subject of an implied ὦ.

ἐν αὐτοῖς. State of being, describing a close personal relationship between Jesus and the believers.

John 18:1-11

¹After Jesus had said these things, he went out with his disciples across the Kedron ravine, where there was a garden, into which he and his disciples entered. ²Now Judas, the one who betrayed him, also knew the place because Jesus often met there with his disciples. ³So Judas brought a cohort and officers from the chief priests and the Pharisees and came there with lanterns and torches and weapons. ⁴Then Jesus, because he knew all the things that were coming upon him, went out and said to them, "Whom are you looking for?" ⁵They answered him, "Jesus the Nazarene." He said to them, "I am [he]." Now Judas, the one who betrayed him, was also standing with them. ⁶So when he said to them, "I am [he]," they drew back and fell to the ground. ⁷Then he asked them again, "Whom are you looking for?" And they said, "Jesus the Nazarene." ⁸Jesus answered, "I told you that I am [he]. So if you are looking for me, let these [men] go." ⁹[This has happened] in order that the word that he had said might be fulfilled, "Those whom you have given me—I have not lost any one of them." ¹⁰Then Simon Peter, because he had a sword, drew it and struck the slave of the high priests and cut off his right ear. The slave's name was Malchus. ¹¹So Jesus said to Peter, "Put your sword into its sheath. The cup that the Father has given me—shall I not drink it?"

18:1 Ταῦτα εἰπὼν Ἰησοῦς ἐξῆλθεν σὺν τοῖς μαθηταῖς αὐτοῦ πέραν τοῦ χειμάρρου τοῦ Κεδρὼν ὅπου ἦν κῆπος, εἰς ὃν εἰσῆλθεν αὐτὸς καὶ οἱ μαθηταὶ αὐτοῦ.

Ταῦτα. Accusative direct object of εἰπών. Ταῦτα is anaphoric, referring to Jesus' prayer in ch. 17. This verse is connected to the previous one by asyndeton.

εἰπών. Aor act ptc masc nom sg λέγω (temporal). On participles that precede the main verb, see ἐμβλέψας in 1:36.

Ἰησοῦς. Nominative subject of ἐξῆλθεν.

ἐξῆλθεν. Aor act ind 3rd sg ἐξέρχομαι.

σὺν τοῖς μαθηταῖς. Association/accompaniment.

αὐτοῦ. Genitive of relationship qualifying μαθηταῖς.

πέραν τοῦ χειμάρρου. Locative (see 1:28). πέραν is an improper preposition (see 1:3 on χωρὶς αὐτοῦ) that specifies the location where Jesus went out with his disciples (BDAG, 796.b.β). χείμαρρος ("winter torrent, ravine") is a NT *hapax legomenon*.

τοῦ Κεδρών. Epexegetical genitive, explaining χειμάρρου ("ravine which is called Kidron"). Even though this reading has weaker external support (A Δ vg) than the two variants, τῶν κέδρων ("of the cedars"; ℵ² B C K L N Γ Θ Ψ *f*¹·¹³ 33 565 579 700 892ˢ 1241 1424 *l*844 𝔐 Or) and τοῦ κέδρου ("of the cedar"; ℵ* D W a b r¹), it is preferable on internal grounds because both variants appear to be scribal corrections of a lack of concord between the article τοῦ and the indeclinable proper noun Κεδρών (from the Hebrew קִדְרוֹן) (Metzger, 214).

ὅπου. Marker of a position in space.

ἦν. 3rd sg εἰμί.

κῆπος. Nominative subject of ἦν.

εἰς ὅν. Locative. The antecedent of the relative pronoun is κῆπος.

εἰσῆλθεν. Aor act ind 3rd sg εἰσέρχομαι.

αὐτὸς καὶ οἱ μαθηταὶ. Compound nominative subject of εἰσῆλθεν. When the verb precedes its two (or more) subjects, as here, it is in the singular, agreeing with the first (BDF §135).

αὐτοῦ. Genitive of relationship qualifying μαθηταί.

18:2 ᾜδει δὲ καὶ Ἰούδας ὁ παραδιδοὺς αὐτὸν τὸν τόπον, ὅτι πολλάκις συνήχθη Ἰησοῦς ἐκεῖ μετὰ τῶν μαθητῶν αὐτοῦ.

ᾜδει. Plprf act ind 3rd sg οἶδα. The pluperfect tense of οἶδα has the imperfect meaning.

δὲ. Marker of narrative development.

καὶ. Adverbial use (adjunctive).

Ἰούδας. Nominative subject of ᾜδει.

ὁ παραδιδοὺς. Pres act ptc masc nom sg παραδίδωμι (substantival). Nominative in apposition to Ἰούδας.

αὐτὸν. Accusative direct object of παραδιδοὺς.

τὸν τόπον. Accusative direct object of ᾜδει.

ὅτι. Introduces a causal clause.

πολλάκις. Adverb ("pert[aining] to a number of related points of time, many times, often, frequently" [BDAG, 846]).

συνήχθη. Aor pass ind 3rd sg συνάγω.

Ἰησοῦς. Nominative subject of συνήχθη.

ἐκεῖ. Adverb of place.

μετὰ τῶν μαθητῶν. Association/accompaniment.
αὐτοῦ. Genitive of relationship qualifying μαθητῶν.

18:3 ὁ οὖν Ἰούδας λαβὼν τὴν σπεῖραν καὶ ἐκ τῶν ἀρχιερέων καὶ ἐκ τῶν Φαρισαίων ὑπηρέτας ἔρχεται ἐκεῖ μετὰ φανῶν καὶ λαμπάδων καὶ ὅπλων.

ὁ . . . Ἰούδας. Nominative subject of ἔρχεται.

οὖν. Postpositive inferential conjunction and/or transitional particle (see 1:22 and 11:6).

λαβών. Aor act ptc masc nom sg λαμβάνω (attendant circumstance or temporal). On participles that precede the main verb, see ἐμβλέψας in 1:36. Brown suggests that λαμβάνω "implies little more than accompaniment as a guide" and that "no particular authority is necessarily attributed to Judas" (2:807; cf. Barrett, 518; BDF §418.5).

τὴν σπεῖραν. Accusative direct object of λαβών. σπεῖρα refers to "a Roman military unit of about six hundred soldiers, though only a part of such a cohort was often referred to as a cohort" (LN 55.9).

καί. Coordinating conjunction.

ἐκ τῶν ἀρχιερέων. In this PP, ἐκ stands for ἀπό (Zerwick §87), denoting agency ("sent by the chief priests").

καί. Coordinating conjunction.

ἐκ τῶν Φαρισαίων. ἐκ stands for ἀπό, denoting agency ("sent by the Pharisees").

ὑπηρέτας. Accusative direct object of λαβών.

ἔρχεται. Pres mid ind 3rd sg ἔρχομαι. The historical present grants prominence to Judas' arrival with the arresting party.

ἐκεῖ. Adverb of place.

μετὰ φανῶν καὶ λαμπάδων καὶ ὅπλων. Manner (attendant circumstance). φανός is a NT *hapax legomenon* that denotes "a small fire which was carried about for the sake of its light and which had some type of protection from wind and weather—'lantern'" (LN 6.103). λαμπάς denotes "a stick or bundle of sticks carried about as a light—'torch'" (6.102). ὅπλον denotes "an instrument used in fighting, whether offensive or defensive—'weapon'" (6.29).

18:4 Ἰησοῦς οὖν εἰδὼς πάντα τὰ ἐρχόμενα ἐπ' αὐτὸν ἐξῆλθεν καὶ λέγει αὐτοῖς· τίνα ζητεῖτε;

Ἰησοῦς. Nominative subject of ἐξῆλθεν.

οὖν. Postpositive inferential conjunction and/or transitional particle (see 1:22 and 11:6).

εἰδώς. Prf act ptc masc nom sg οἶδα (causal). On participles that precede the main verb, see ἐμβλέψας in 1:36.
πάντα τὰ ἐρχόμενα. Accusative direct object of εἰδώς (see 3:8 on πᾶς ὁ γεγεννημένος).
τὰ ἐρχόμενα. Pres mid ptc neut acc pl ἔρχομαι (substantival). On the meaning of this participle, see τὰ ἐρχόμενα in 16:13. On the function of this participle, see πάντα τὰ ἐρχόμενα above.
ἐπ' αὐτὸν. Locative.
ἐξῆλθεν. Aor act ind 3rd sg ἐξέρχομαι.
καὶ. Coordinating conjunction.
λέγει. Pres act ind 3rd sg λέγω. The historical present gives prominence to Jesus' question to the arresting party (see 1:15 on μαρτυρεῖ).
αὐτοῖς. Dative indirect object of λέγει.
τίνα. Accusative direct object of ζητεῖτε.
ζητεῖτε. Pres act ind 2nd pl ζητέω. In this context, ζητέω carries malicious intent (Dennis, 165).

18:5 ἀπεκρίθησαν αὐτῷ· Ἰησοῦν τὸν Ναζωραῖον. λέγει αὐτοῖς· ἐγώ εἰμι. εἱστήκει δὲ καὶ Ἰούδας ὁ παραδιδοὺς αὐτὸν μετ' αὐτῶν.

ἀπεκρίθησαν. Aor mid ind 3rd pl ἀποκρίνομαι. On the voice, see "Deponency" in the Series Introduction. This verse is connected to the previous one by asyndeton.
αὐτῷ. Dative indirect object of ἀπεκρίθησαν.
Ἰησοῦν. Accusative direct object of an implied ζητοῦμεν.
τὸν Ναζωραῖον. Accusative in apposition to Ἰησοῦν. ὁ Ναζωραῖος = ὁ ἀπὸ Ναζαρέτ (see 1:45).
λέγει. Pres act ind 3rd sg λέγω. The historical present gives prominence to Jesus' declaration of his identity (see 1:15 on μαρτυρεῖ). This clause is connected to the previous one by asyndeton.
αὐτοῖς. Dative indirect object of λέγει.
ἐγώ. Nominative subject of εἰμι. The personal pronoun has an identifying function, confirming that Jesus is the one whom they seek. Fronted for emphasis.
εἰμι. Pres act ind 1st sg εἰμί.
εἱστήκει. Plprf act ind 3rd sg ἵστημι. The pluperfect tense of ἵστημι has the imperfect meaning. This pluperfect has a descriptive function (Campbell 2007, 219).
δὲ. Marker of narrative development.
καὶ. Adverbial use (adjunctive).
Ἰούδας. Nominative subject of εἱστήκει.

ὁ παραδιδούς. Pres act ptc masc nom sg παραδίδωμι. Nominative in apposition to Ἰούδας (see 18:2).
αὐτόν. Accusative direct object of παραδιδούς.
μετ' αὐτῶν. Association/accompaniment.

18:6 ὡς οὖν εἶπεν αὐτοῖς· ἐγώ εἰμι, ἀπῆλθον εἰς τὰ ὀπίσω καὶ ἔπεσαν χαμαί.

ὡς. Temporal conjunction (BDAG, 1105.8.a; BDF §455.2).
οὖν. Postpositive inferential conjunction and/or transitional particle (see 1:22 and 11:6).
εἶπεν. Aor act ind 3rd sg λέγω.
αὐτοῖς. Dative indirect object of εἶπεν.
ἐγώ. Nominative subject of εἰμι (see 18:5).
εἰμι. Pres act ind 1st sg εἰμί.
ἀπῆλθον. Aor act ind 3rd pl ἀπέρχομαι.
εἰς τὰ ὀπίσω. Locative (lit. "to the things behind" = "backward"). The article functions as a nominalizer, changing the adverb ὀπίσω ("behind") into the object of the preposition εἰς.
καί. Coordinating conjunction.
ἔπεσαν. Aor act ind 3rd pl πίπτω.
χαμαί. Adverb ("to/on the ground" [BDAG, 1076.2]).

18:7 Πάλιν οὖν ἐπηρώτησεν αὐτούς· τίνα ζητεῖτε; οἱ δὲ εἶπαν· Ἰησοῦν τὸν Ναζωραῖον.

Πάλιν. Adverb "pert[aining] to repetition in the same (or similar) manner" (BDAG, 752.2). Fronted for emphasis.
οὖν. Postpositive inferential conjunction and/or transitional particle (see 1:22 and 11:6).
ἐπηρώτησεν. Aor act ind 3rd sg ἐπερωτάω.
αὐτούς. Accusative direct object of ἐπηρώτησεν.
τίνα. Accusative direct object of ζητεῖτε.
ζητεῖτε. Pres act ind 2nd pl ζητέω (see 18:4).
οἱ δέ. A construction that is frequently used in narrative literature to indicate the change of the speaker in a dialogue. The nominative article stands in place of a third-person personal pronoun and functions as the subject of εἶπαν.
εἶπαν. Aor act ind 3rd pl λέγω.
Ἰησοῦν. Accusative direct object of an implied ζητοῦμεν.
τὸν Ναζωραῖον. Accusative in apposition to Ἰησοῦν. On the meaning of ὁ Ναζωραῖος, see 18:5.

τοῦ ἀρχιερέως. Possessive genitive qualifying δοῦλον ("the servant that belongs to the high priest") or objective genitive ("the one who serves the high priest").

καὶ. Coordinating conjunction.

ἀπέκοψεν. Aor act ind 3rd sg ἀποκόπτω.

αὐτοῦ. Possessive genitive qualifying ὠτάριον. Fronted for emphasis.

τὸ ὠτάριον τὸ δεξιόν. Accusative direct object of ἀπέκοψεν. ὠτάριον (used here and in Mark 14:47) is a diminutive of οὖς (used in Luke 22:50), but the two versions are probably equivalent (Barrett, 521). The adjective δεξιόν stands in the second attributive position (see 1:9 on τὸ φῶς τὸ ἀληθινόν).

ἦν. Impf act ind 3rd sg εἰμί. This imperfect, which interrupts the main storyline, is used in a clause that provides background information about the servant's name (du Toit, 224).

δὲ. Marker of narrative development.

ὄνομα. Nominative subject of ἦν. The principle that in equative clauses with proper names the subject will be a proper name is not applicable when the other noun is ὄνομα. Wallace explains that "[t]he reason that ὄνομα is an exception is due to its lexical force: The very nature of the word connotes a known quantity" (1996, 43 n. 21).

τῷ δούλῳ. Dative of possession.

Μάλχος. Predicate nominative.

18:11 εἶπεν οὖν ὁ Ἰησοῦς τῷ Πέτρῳ· βάλε τὴν μάχαιραν εἰς τὴν θήκην· τὸ ποτήριον ὃ δέδωκέν μοι ὁ πατὴρ οὐ μὴ πίω αὐτό;

εἶπεν. Aor act ind 3rd sg λέγω.

οὖν. Postpositive inferential conjunction and/or transitional particle (see 1:22 and 11:6).

ὁ Ἰησοῦς. Nominative subject of εἶπεν.

τῷ Πέτρῳ. Dative indirect object of εἶπεν.

βάλε. Aor act impv 2nd sg βάλλω.

τὴν μάχαιραν. Accusative direct object of βάλε. The article is here used as a possessive pronoun ("your sword"; cf. Harris 2015, 297).

εἰς τὴν θήκην. Locative. The article is also used as a possessive pronoun ("its sheath"; cf. Harris 2015, 297).

τὸ ποτήριον. This could be viewed as a pendent nominative (Wallace 1996, 53; Barrett, 522; Harris 2015, 297), but it is better to take it as the accusative direct object of πίω in a left-dislocation that serves to introduce a new entity into the discourse, placing "the pronominal trace in an unmarked position following the verb" (Runge 2010, 297).

For a similar construction, see πᾶν κλῆμα in 15:2. This clause is connected to the previous one by asyndeton.

ὅ. Accusative direct object of δέδωκέν. The antecedent of the relative pronoun is τὸ ποτήριον.

δέδωκέν. Prf act ind 3rd sg δίδωμι. δέδωκέν, which has an acute accent on the antepenult, acquired an additional accent, the acute, on the ultima from the enclitic μοι (Smyth §183; Carson 1985, 48). The perfect tense "expresses that what the Father 'has given' to the Son . . . is definitely in his hand" (Frey 2018, 81).

μοι. Dative indirect object of δέδωκέν.

ὁ πατὴρ. Nominative subject of δέδωκέν.

οὐ μὴ. A combination of negative particles that serves as a "marker of a strongly emphatic affirmative response to a question" (LN 69.13). Elsewhere in the NT, οὐ μὴ is used in a question only in Luke 18:7.

πίω. Aor act subj 1st sg πίνω (deliberative subjunctive).

αὐτό. Accusative direct object of πίω, resuming τὸ ποτήριον (see above).

John 18:12-14

[12]Then the cohort and the commander and the officers of the Jews arrested Jesus and bound him [13]and brought [him] to Annas first, for he was the father-in-law of Caiaphas, who was high priest that year. [14]Now Caiaphas was the one who had advised the Jews that it was advantageous that one man die for the people.

18:12 Ἡ οὖν σπεῖρα καὶ ὁ χιλίαρχος καὶ οἱ ὑπηρέται τῶν Ἰουδαίων συνέλαβον τὸν Ἰησοῦν καὶ ἔδησαν αὐτὸν

Ἡ . . . σπεῖρα καὶ ὁ χιλίαρχος καὶ οἱ ὑπηρέται. Compound nominative subject of συνέλαβον. On the meaning of σπεῖρα, see 18:3. χιλίαρχος (lit. "leader of a thousand soldiers") denotes "military tribune, a commander of a cohort" (BDAG, 1084).

οὖν. Postpositive inferential conjunction and/or transitional particle (see 1:22 and 11:6).

τῶν Ἰουδαίων. Objective genitive qualifying ὑπηρέται ("those who serve the Jews"). According to 18:3, these were the officers sent by the chief priests and the Pharisees.

συνέλαβον. Aor act ind 3rd pl συλλαμβάνω.

τὸν Ἰησοῦν. Accusative direct object of συνέλαβον.

καὶ. Coordinating conjunction.

ἔδησαν. Aor act ind 3rd pl δέω.

αὐτὸν. Accusative direct object of ἔδησαν.

John 18:11-14

18:13 καὶ ἤγαγον πρὸς Ἅνναν πρῶτον· ἦν γὰρ πενθερὸς τοῦ Καϊάφα, ὃς ἦν ἀρχιερεὺς τοῦ ἐνιαυτοῦ ἐκείνου·

καὶ. Coordinating conjunction.

ἤγαγον. Aor act ind 3rd pl ἄγω.

πρὸς Ἅνναν. Locative (motion toward). Annas served as high priest from 6 to 15 CE.

πρῶτον. Adverbial accusative indicating time or sequence ("first, in the first place, before, earlier, to begin with"; BDAG, 893.1.a.β).

ἦν. Impf act ind 3rd sg εἰμί. On the function of the imperfect in the FG, see 1:39 on ἦν.

γὰρ. Postpositive conjunction introducing the clause that explains why Jesus was brought first to Annas.

πενθερὸς. Predicate nominative. πενθερὸς ("father-in-law") is a NT *hapax legomenon*.

τοῦ Καϊάφα. Genitive of relationship qualifying πενθερὸς.

ὅς. Nominative subject of ἦν. The antecedent of the relative pronoun is Καϊάφα.

ἦν. Impf act ind 3rd sg εἰμί. On the function of the imperfect in the FG, see 1:39 on ἦν.

ἀρχιερεὺς. Predicate nominative.

τοῦ ἐνιαυτοῦ ἐκείνου. Genitive of time.

18:14 ἦν δὲ Καϊάφας ὁ συμβουλεύσας τοῖς Ἰουδαίοις ὅτι συμφέρει ἕνα ἄνθρωπον ἀποθανεῖν ὑπὲρ τοῦ λαοῦ.

ἦν. Impf act ind 3rd sg εἰμί. On the function of the imperfect in the FG, see 1:39 on ἦν.

δὲ. Marker of narrative development.

Καϊάφας. Nominative subject of ἦν.

ὁ συμβουλεύσας. Aor act ptc masc nom sg συμβουλεύω (substantival). Predicate nominative.

τοῖς Ἰουδαίοις. Dative complement of συμβουλεύσας.

ὅτι. Introduces the clausal complement (indirect discourse) of συμβουλεύσας.

συμφέρει ἕνα ἄνθρωπον ἀποθανεῖν ὑπὲρ τοῦ λαοῦ. A slightly modified quotation of 11:50a (συμφέρει ὑμῖν ἵνα εἷς ἄνθρωπος ἀποθάνῃ ὑπὲρ τοῦ λαοῦ).

συμφέρει. Pres act ind 3rd sg συμφέρω. The present tense is retained from direct discourse (see 1:39 on μένει).

ἕνα ἄνθρωπον. Accusative subject of the infinitive ἀποθανεῖν. Fronted for emphasis.

ἀποθανεῖν. Aor act inf ἀποθνῄσκω. The infinitival clause ἕνα ἄνθρωπον ἀποθανεῖν ὑπὲρ τοῦ λαοῦ functions as the subject of συμφέρει.

ὑπὲρ τοῦ λαοῦ. Substitution (see 11:50).

John 18:15-18

¹⁵Simon Peter and another disciple followed Jesus. Now that disciple was known to the high priest and entered with Jesus into the courtyard of the high priest, ¹⁶but Peter was standing by the door outside. So the other disciple who was known by the high priest went out and spoke to the doorkeeper and brought Peter in. ¹⁷Then the maidservant, [who was] the doorkeeper, said to Peter, "You are not also [one] of the disciples of this man, are you?" He said, "I am not!" ¹⁸Now the servants and the officers were standing there, having made a charcoal fire because it was cold, and warming themselves; and Peter also was standing with them and warming himself.

18:15 Ἠκολούθει δὲ τῷ Ἰησοῦ Σίμων Πέτρος καὶ ἄλλος μαθητής. ὁ δὲ μαθητὴς ἐκεῖνος ἦν γνωστὸς τῷ ἀρχιερεῖ καὶ συνεισῆλθεν τῷ Ἰησοῦ εἰς τὴν αὐλὴν τοῦ ἀρχιερέως,

Ἠκολούθει. Impf act ind 3rd sg ἀκολουθέω. The verb supplies the background information about the events that transpired in the courtyard of the high priest while Jesus was examined by the religious authorities. On the function of the imperfect in the FG, see 1:39 on ἦν.

δὲ. Marker of narrative development.

τῷ Ἰησοῦ. Dative direct object of Ἠκολούθει.

Σίμων Πέτρος καὶ ἄλλος μαθητής. Compound nominative subject of Ἠκολούθει. When the verb precedes its two (or more) subjects, as here, it is in the singular, agreeing with the first (BDF §135).

ὁ ... μαθητὴς ἐκεῖνος. Nominative subject of ἦν. Runge argues that referring to the other disciple with the far-demonstrative "marks him as athematic, thus avoiding sending mixed signals about the center of attention. The spotlight remains on Peter" (2010, 377) even when the evangelist provides additional information about Peter's companion.

δὲ. Marker of narrative development.

ἦν. Impf act ind 3rd sg εἰμί. On the function of the imperfect in the FG, see 1:39 on ἦν.

γνωστὸς. Predicate adjective ("known") or predicate nominative, if γνωστὸς functions as a substantive ("acquaintance"; cf. REB; HCSB).

τῷ ἀρχιερεῖ. Dative of agency (Wallace 1996, 165) or dative complement of γνωστὸς (175). Dative of agency occurs regularly with

verbal adjectives ending in -τος, as here. Smyth (§1488) clarifies that "[t]he notion of agency does not belong to the dative, but it is a natural inference that the person interested is the agent."
καί. Coordinating conjunction.
συνεισῆλθεν. Aor act ind 3rd sg συνεισέρχομαι.
τῷ Ἰησοῦ. Dative complement of συνεισῆλθεν.
εἰς τὴν αὐλὴν. Locative.
τοῦ ἀρχιερέως. Possessive genitive qualifying αὐλήν.

18:16 ὁ δὲ Πέτρος εἱστήκει πρὸς τῇ θύρᾳ ἔξω. ἐξῆλθεν οὖν ὁ μαθητὴς ὁ ἄλλος ὁ γνωστὸς τοῦ ἀρχιερέως καὶ εἶπεν τῇ θυρωρῷ καὶ εἰσήγαγεν τὸν Πέτρον.

ὁ ... Πέτρος. Nominative subject of εἱστήκει.
δὲ. Marker of narrative development.
εἱστήκει. Plprf act ind 3rd sg ἵστημι. The pluperfect tense of ἵστημι has the imperfect meaning.
πρὸς τῇ θύρᾳ. Locative, indicating spatial proximity (BDAG, 874.2.a).
ἔξω. Adverb ("outside").
ἐξῆλθεν. Aor act ind 3rd sg ἐξέρχομαι.
οὖν. Postpositive inferential conjunction and/or transitional particle (see 1:22 and 11:6).
ὁ μαθητὴς ὁ ἄλλος. Nominative subject of ἐξῆλθεν. The article is anaphoric, pointing back to ἄλλος μαθητής, who was introduced in v. 15. The adjective ἄλλος stands in the second attributive position (see 1:9 on τὸ φῶς τὸ ἀληθινόν).
ὁ γνωστός. If the article is an adjectivizer, γνωστός stands in the second attributive position vis-à-vis the nominal phrase ὁ μαθητὴς ὁ ἄλλος ("the other disciple who was known"). If the article functions as a nominalizer, ὁ γνωστός is the nominative in apposition to ὁ μαθητὴς ὁ ἄλλος ("the other disciple, the acquaintance").
τοῦ ἀρχιερέως. Genitive of agency, if γνωστός is an adjective ("who was known by the high priest"; cf. Wallace 1996, 126), or genitive of relationship, if γνωστός is a substantive ("the acquaintance of the high priest").
καί. Coordinating conjunction.
εἶπεν. Aor act ind 3rd sg λέγω.
τῇ θυρωρῷ. Dative indirect object of εἶπεν. The noun θυρωρός ("one who guards the door giving access to a house or building—'doorkeeper'" [LN 46.8]) could be either masculine or feminine. The article τῇ indicates that the doorkeeper was a woman.
καί. Coordinating conjunction.

εἰσήγαγεν. Aor act ind 3rd sg εἰσάγω.
τὸν Πέτρον. Accusative direct object of εἰσήγαγεν.

18:17 λέγει οὖν τῷ Πέτρῳ ἡ παιδίσκη ἡ θυρωρός· μὴ καὶ σὺ ἐκ τῶν μαθητῶν εἶ τοῦ ἀνθρώπου τούτου; λέγει ἐκεῖνος· οὐκ εἰμί.

λέγει. Pres act ind 3rd sg λέγω. The historical present gives prominence to the question of the maidservant (see 1:15 on μαρτυρεῖ).

οὖν. Postpositive inferential conjunction and/or transitional particle (see 1:22 and 11:6).

τῷ Πέτρῳ. Dative indirect object of λέγει.

ἡ παιδίσκη. Nominative subject of λέγει.

ἡ θυρωρός. Nominative in apposition to ἡ παιδίσκη.

μή. Negative particle that introduces a question that expects a negative answer. Moulton regards the questions introduced by μή as cautious assertions, in which "μή is often equivalent to our 'perhaps'" (MHT 1:192).

καί. Adverbial use (adjunctive).

σύ. Nominative subject of εἶ. σύ is emphatic.

ἐκ τῶν μαθητῶν. Replaces the partitive genitive. The PP presumes addition of εἷς, which functions as predicate nominative.

εἶ. Pres act ind 2nd sg εἰμί.

τοῦ ἀνθρώπου τούτου. Genitive of relationship qualifying μαθητῶν.

λέγει. Pres act ind 3rd sg λέγω. The historical present gives prominence to Peter's reply (see 1:15 on μαρτυρεῖ). This clause is connected to the previous one by asyndeton.

ἐκεῖνος. Nominative subject of λέγει. The demonstrative pronoun refers to Peter, acting as a third-person personal pronoun with a simple anaphoric force (Wallace 1996, 328–29).

οὐκ. Negative particle normally used with indicative verbs.

εἰμί. Pres act ind 1st sg εἰμί.

18:18 εἱστήκεισαν δὲ οἱ δοῦλοι καὶ οἱ ὑπηρέται ἀνθρακιὰν πεποιηκότες, ὅτι ψῦχος ἦν, καὶ ἐθερμαίνοντο· ἦν δὲ καὶ ὁ Πέτρος μετ' αὐτῶν ἑστὼς καὶ θερμαινόμενος.

εἱστήκεισαν. Plprf act ind 3rd pl ἵστημι. The pluperfect tense of ἵστημι has the imperfect meaning.

δέ. Marker of narrative development.

οἱ δοῦλοι καὶ οἱ ὑπηρέται. Compound nominative subject of εἱστήκεισαν.

ἀνθρακιάν. Accusative direct object of πεποιηκότες.

πεποιηκότες. Prf act ptc masc nom pl ποιέω (temporal). On participles that follow the main verb, see βαπτίζων in 1:31.

ὅτι. Introduces a causal clause.

ψῦχος. Predicate adjective. Fronted for emphasis.

ἦν. Impf act ind 3rd sg εἰμί. On the function of the imperfect in the FG, see 1:39 on ἦν.

καί. Coordinating conjunction.

ἐθερμαίνοντο. Impf mid ind 3rd pl θερμαίνω. This is the direct middle, which is "semantically equivalent to an active voice with a reflexive pronoun as object; simply add *himself, herself*, etc. as direct object to the verb" (Wallace 1996, 417).

ἦν. Impf act ind 3rd sg εἰμί.

δέ. Marker of narrative development.

καί. Adverbial use (adjunctive).

ὁ Πέτρος. Nominative subject of ἦν.

μετ' αὐτῶν. Association/accompaniment.

ἑστώς. Prf act ptc masc nom sg ἵστημι (pluperfect periphrastic). The pluperfect periphrastic of ἵστημι is equivalent to the imperfect periphrastic: "Peter was also standing with them." Another possibility is to treat ἑστώς as an adverbial participle conveying manner: "Peter also was with them, standing and warming himself" (ESV; ASV).

καί. Coordinating conjunction.

θερμαινόμενος. Pres mid ptc masc nom sg θερμαίνω (imperfect periphrastic). This is again the direct middle (see ἐθερμαίνοντο above). Alternatively, θερμαινόμενος could be regarded as an adverbial participle conveying manner: "Peter also was with them, standing and warming himself" (ESV; ASV).

John 18:19-24

[19]Then the high priest questioned Jesus about his disciples and about his teaching. [20]Jesus answered him, "I have spoken openly to the world. I have always taught in the synagogue and in the temple, where all the Jews come together, and I have said nothing in secret. [21]Why are you asking me? Ask those who have heard what I said to them. Look, they know what I said." [22]When he had said these things, one of the officers, who was standing by, gave a slap in the face to Jesus, saying, "Do you answer the high priest in this way?" [23]Jesus answered him, "If I have spoken wrongly, testify about what is wrong. But if [I have spoken] rightly, why do you strike me?" [24]Then Annas sent him, tied up, to Caiaphas, the high priest.

John 18:19-24

18:19 Ὁ οὖν ἀρχιερεὺς ἠρώτησεν τὸν Ἰησοῦν περὶ τῶν μαθητῶν αὐτοῦ καὶ περὶ τῆς διδαχῆς αὐτοῦ.

Ὁ ... ἀρχιερεὺς. Nominative subject of ἠρώτησεν.

οὖν. Postpositive inferential conjunction and/or transitional particle (see 1:22 and 11:6).

ἠρώτησεν. Aor act ind 3rd sg ἐρωτάω.

τὸν Ἰησοῦν. Accusative direct object of ἠρώτησεν.

περὶ τῶν μαθητῶν. Reference.

αὐτοῦ. Genitive of relationship qualifying μαθητῶν.

καὶ. Coordinating conjunction.

περὶ τῆς διδαχῆς. Reference.

αὐτοῦ. Subjective genitive qualifying διδαχῆς.

18:20 ἀπεκρίθη αὐτῷ Ἰησοῦς· ἐγὼ παρρησίᾳ λελάληκα τῷ κόσμῳ, ἐγὼ πάντοτε ἐδίδαξα ἐν συναγωγῇ καὶ ἐν τῷ ἱερῷ, ὅπου πάντες οἱ Ἰουδαῖοι συνέρχονται, καὶ ἐν κρυπτῷ ἐλάλησα οὐδέν.

ἀπεκρίθη. Aor mid ind 3rd sg ἀποκρίνομαι. On the voice, see "Deponency" in the Series Introduction. This verse is connected to the previous one by asyndeton.

αὐτῷ. Dative indirect object of ἀπεκρίθη.

Ἰησοῦς. Nominative subject of ἀπεκρίθη.

ἐγώ. Nominative subject of λελάληκα. Fronted as a topical frame.

παρρησίᾳ. Dative of manner ("openly, publicly"); cf. 7:26; 11:54. It is contrasted to the PP ἐν κρυπτῷ. Fronted for emphasis.

λελάληκα. Prf act ind 1st sg λαλέω. The perfect-tense form serves as a semantic marker, giving prominence to Jesus' public speaking. On the significance of the verbal aspect of λελάληκα, see 14:25.

τῷ κόσμῳ. Dative indirect object of λελάληκα. On the portrayal of the world in the FG, see 1:10 on ἐν τῷ κόσμῳ.

ἐγώ. Nominative subject of ἐδίδαξα. Fronted as a topical frame.

πάντοτε. Adverb of time. Fronted for emphasis.

ἐδίδαξα. Aor act ind 1st sg διδάσκω.

ἐν συναγωγῇ. Locative. The FG contains only one instance of Jesus' teaching in the synagogue (6:59). In this context, the anarthrous συναγωγῇ may be stereotyped ("in the synagogue"; cf. HCSB; LEB) or generic ("in synagogues"; cf. ASV; ESV; NIV; NRSV; REB). The PP ἐν συναγωγῇ is equivalent to our phrase "in church" (MHT 1:236).

καί. Coordinating conjunction.

ἐν τῷ ἱερῷ. Locative. Elsewhere in the FG, this PP occurs in 2:14; 5:14; 7:28; 8:20; 10:23; 11:56.

ὅπου. Marker of a position in space.
πάντες οἱ Ἰουδαῖοι. Nominative subject of συνέρχονται. Fronted for emphasis.
συνέρχονται. Pres mid ind 3rd pl συνέρχομαι.
καί. Coordinating conjunction.
ἐν κρυπτῷ. Manner (lit. "in the hidden" = "secretly"). The adjective κρυπτός is here used as a substantive.
ἐλάλησα. Aor act ind 1st sg λαλέω.
οὐδέν. Accusative direct object of ἐλάλησα.

18:21 τί με ἐρωτᾷς; ἐρώτησον τοὺς ἀκηκοότας τί ἐλάλησα αὐτοῖς· ἴδε οὗτοι οἴδασιν ἃ εἶπον ἐγώ.

τί. Adverbial use of the interrogative pronoun ("why?"). This verse is connected to the previous one by asyndeton.
με. Accusative direct object of ἐρωτᾷς.
ἐρωτᾷς. Pres act ind 2nd sg ἐρωτάω.
ἐρώτησον. Aor act impv 2nd sg ἐρωτάω. This clause is connected to the previous one by asyndeton.
τοὺς ἀκηκοότας. Prf act ptc masc acc pl ἀκούω (substantival). Accusative direct object of ἐρώτησον.
τί. Indirect interrogative ("what?") that functions as a substitute for the relative pronoun, introducing a headless relative clause that, in its entirety (τί ἐλάλησα αὐτοῖς), serves as the direct object of ἀκηκοότας. Within its clause, τί is accusative direct object of ἐλάλησα.
ἐλάλησα. Aor act ind 1st sg λαλέω.
αὐτοῖς. Dative indirect object of ἐλάλησα.
ἴδε. An interjection (originally aor act impv 2nd sg ὁράω) that is used "when that which is to be observed is in the nom[inative]" (BDAG, 466). This clause is connected to the previous one by asyndeton.
οὗτοι. Nominative subject of οἴδασιν. The demonstrative pronoun refers to τοὺς ἀκηκοότας from the previous clause, acting as a third-person personal pronoun with a simple anaphoric force (Wallace 1996, 328–29).
οἴδασιν. Prf act ind 3rd pl οἶδα (see 1:26 on οἴδατε).
ἅ. Introduces a headless relative clause that, in its entirety (ἃ εἶπον ἐγώ), serves as the direct object of οἴδασιν. Within its clause, ἅ is accusative direct object of εἶπον.
εἶπον. Aor act ind 1st sg λέγω.
ἐγώ. Nominative subject of εἶπον.

18:22 ταῦτα δὲ αὐτοῦ εἰπόντος εἷς παρεστηκὼς τῶν ὑπηρετῶν ἔδωκεν ῥάπισμα τῷ Ἰησοῦ εἰπών· οὕτως ἀποκρίνῃ τῷ ἀρχιερεῖ;

ταῦτα. Accusative direct object of εἰπόντος.
δὲ. Marker of narrative development.
αὐτοῦ. Genitive subject of εἰπόντος.
εἰπόντος. Aor act ptc masc gen sg λέγω (genitive absolute, temporal).
εἷς. Nominative subject of ἔδωκεν. εἷς stands for τις (Zerwick §155).
παρεστηκὼς. Prf act ptc masc nom sg παρίστημι (attributive). The participle modifies εἷς and not the genitive τῶν ὑπηρετῶν, as many English translations seem to suggest (e.g., "one of the police standing nearby" [NRSV]; "one of the officers standing by" [ESV]).
τῶν ὑπηρετῶν. Partitive genitive qualifying εἷς.
ἔδωκεν. Aor act ind 3rd sg δίδωμι.
ῥάπισμα. Accusative direct object of ἔδωκεν. Here ῥάπισμα means "a blow on the face with someone's hand, a slap in the face" (BDAG, 904.2).
τῷ Ἰησοῦ. Dative indirect object of ἔδωκεν.
εἰπών. Aor act ptc masc nom sg λέγω (manner). On participles that follow the main verb, see βαπτίζων in 1:31.
οὕτως. Adverb of manner ("in this manner, thus, so").
ἀποκρίνῃ. Pres mid ind 2nd sg ἀποκρίνομαι.
τῷ ἀρχιερεῖ. Dative indirect object of ἀποκρίνῃ.

18:23 ἀπεκρίθη αὐτῷ Ἰησοῦς· εἰ κακῶς ἐλάλησα, μαρτύρησον περὶ τοῦ κακοῦ· εἰ δὲ καλῶς, τί με δέρεις;

ἀπεκρίθη. Aor mid ind 3rd sg ἀποκρίνομαι. On the voice, see "Deponency" in the Series Introduction. This verse is connected to the previous one by asyndeton.
αὐτῷ. Dative indirect object of ἀπεκρίθη.
Ἰησοῦς. Nominative subject of ἀπεκρίθη.
εἰ. Introduces the protasis of a first-class condition. Two opposing conditions in this verse—εἰ κακῶς ἐλάλησα and εἰ δὲ καλῶς—demonstrate that first-class conditional clauses assume the truthfulness of the condition for the sake of the argument and that, therefore, the particle εἰ should not be translated "since" (Wallace 1996, 690–94, 708).
κακῶς. Adverb of manner.
ἐλάλησα. Aor act ind 1st sg λαλέω.
μαρτύρησον. Aor act impv 2nd sg μαρτυρέω. It marks the beginning of the apodosis of a first-class condition.
περὶ τοῦ κακοῦ. Reference.
εἰ. Introduces the protasis of a first-class condition.

δέ. Marker of narrative development.

καλῶς. Adverb of manner. It modifies the implied verb ἐλάλησα.

τί. Adverbial use of the interrogative pronoun ("why?"). It marks the beginning of the apodosis of a first-class condition.

με. Accusative direct object of δέρεις.

δέρεις. Pres act ind 2nd sg δέρω.

18:24 ἀπέστειλεν οὖν αὐτὸν ὁ Ἅννας δεδεμένον πρὸς Καϊάφαν τὸν ἀρχιερέα.

ἀπέστειλεν οὖν αὐτὸν ὁ Ἅννας δεδεμένον πρὸς Καϊάφαν τὸν ἀρχιερέα. In an effort to harmonize the Johannine account of Jesus' trial before the Jewish authorities with the Synoptics, some copyists interpolated this verse after πρῶτον in v. 13 (225) or at the end of v. 13 (sy^s sy^{hmg} Cyr^{com}) (Metzger, 215).

ἀπέστειλεν. Aor act ind 3rd sg ἀποστέλλω.

οὖν. Postpositive inferential conjunction and/or transitional particle (see 1:22 and 11:6).

αὐτὸν. Accusative direct object of ἀπέστειλεν.

ὁ Ἅννας. Nominative subject of ἀπέστειλεν.

δεδεμένον. Prf pass ptc masc acc sg δέω (manner). On participles that follow the main verb, see βαπτίζων in 1:31.

πρὸς Καϊάφαν. Locative (motion toward).

τὸν ἀρχιερέα. Accusative in apposition to Καϊάφαν.

John 18:25-27

²⁵Now Simon Peter was standing and warming himself. So they said to him, "You are not also [one] of his disciples, are you?" He denied [it] and said, "I am not!" ²⁶One of the servants of the high priest, who was a relative of the one whose ear Peter had cut off, said, "Did I not see you in the garden with him?" ²⁷So again Peter denied [it], and at once a rooster crowed.

18:25 Ἦν δὲ Σίμων Πέτρος ἑστὼς καὶ θερμαινόμενος. εἶπον οὖν αὐτῷ· μὴ καὶ σὺ ἐκ τῶν μαθητῶν αὐτοῦ εἶ; ἠρνήσατο ἐκεῖνος καὶ εἶπεν· οὐκ εἰμί.

Ἦν δὲ Σίμων Πέτρος ἑστὼς καὶ θερμαινόμενος. A repetition of 18:18b: ἦν δὲ . . . ὁ Πέτρος . . . ἑστὼς καὶ θερμαινόμενος.

Ἦν. Impf act ind 3rd sg εἰμί.

δέ. Marker of narrative development.

Σίμων Πέτρος. Nominative subject of Ἦν.

ἑστώς. Prf act ptc masc nom sg ἵστημι (pluperfect periphrastic). The pluperfect periphrastic of ἵστημι is equivalent to the imperfect periphrastic.
καί. Coordinating conjunction.
θερμαινόμενος. Pres mid ptc masc nom sg θερμαίνω (imperfect periphrastic). This is the direct middle (see 18:18 on ἐθερμαίνοντο).
εἶπον. Aor act ind 3rd pl λέγω. The subject of the verb is not expressed.
οὖν. Postpositive inferential conjunction and/or transitional particle (see 1:22 and 11:6).
αὐτῷ. Dative indirect object of εἶπον.
μὴ καὶ σὺ ἐκ τῶν μαθητῶν αὐτοῦ εἶ. A repetition of 18:17b: μὴ καὶ σὺ ἐκ τῶν μαθητῶν εἶ τοῦ ἀνθρώπου τούτου.
μή. Negative particle that introduces either a question that expects a negative answer or a cautious assertion (see 18:17).
καί. Adverbial use (adjunctive).
σύ. Nominative subject of εἶ. σύ is emphatic.
ἐκ τῶν μαθητῶν. Replaces the partitive genitive. The PP presumes addition of εἷς, which functions as predicate nominative.
αὐτοῦ. Genitive of relationship qualifying μαθητῶν.
εἶ. Pres act ind 2nd sg εἰμί.
ἠρνήσατο. Aor mid ind 3rd sg ἀρνέομαι. This clause is connected to the previous one by asyndeton.
ἐκεῖνος. Nominative subject of ἠρνήσατο. The demonstrative pronoun refers to Σίμων Πέτρος, acting as a third-person personal pronoun with a simple anaphoric force (Wallace 1996, 328–29).
καὶ εἶπεν. Pleonastic clause under Semitic influence, which functions as a redundant quotative frame (see 1:25 on καὶ εἶπαν αὐτῷ).
καί. Coordinating conjunction.
εἶπεν. Aor act ind 3rd sg λέγω.
οὐκ. Negative particle normally used with indicative verbs.
εἰμί. Pres act ind 1st sg εἰμί.

18:26 λέγει εἷς ἐκ τῶν δούλων τοῦ ἀρχιερέως, συγγενὴς ὢν οὗ ἀπέκοψεν Πέτρος τὸ ὠτίον· οὐκ ἐγώ σε εἶδον ἐν τῷ κήπῳ μετ' αὐτοῦ;

λέγει. Pres act ind 3rd sg λέγω. The historical present gives prominence to the third question directed at Peter regarding his association with Jesus (see 1:15 on μαρτυρεῖ). This verse is connected to the previous one by asyndeton.
εἷς. Nominative subject of λέγει. εἷς is here used not as a cardinal number but as an indefinite pronoun (Caragounis 2004, 113).
ἐκ τῶν δούλων. Replaces the partitive genitive.

τοῦ ἀρχιερέως. Possessive genitive qualifying δούλων ("the servants that belong to the high priest") or objective genitive ("those who serve the high priest").

συγγενὴς. Predicate adjective ("related to"; cf. LEB) or predicate nominative, if συγγενὴς functions as a substantive ("a relative"; cf. ESV; NIV; NRSV; REB). Fronted for emphasis.

ὤν. Pres act ptc masc nom sg εἰμί (attributive). The participle modifies εἷς.

οὗ. Introduces a headless relative clause that, in its entirety (οὗ ἀπέκοψεν Πέτρος τὸ ὠτίον), functions as the genitive of relationship qualifying συγγενὴς. Within its clause, οὗ is the possessive genitive qualifying τὸ ὠτίον ("whose ear").

ἀπέκοψεν. Aor act ind 3rd sg ἀποκόπτω.

Πέτρος. Nominative subject of ἀπέκοψεν.

τὸ ὠτίον. Accusative direct object of ἀπέκοψεν.

οὐκ. Negative particle that introduces a question that expects an affirmative answer.

ἐγώ. Nominative subject of εἶδον.

σε. Accusative direct object of εἶδον. Fronted for emphasis.

εἶδον. Aor act ind 1st sg ὁράω.

ἐν τῷ κήπῳ. Locative.

μετ' αὐτοῦ. Association/accompaniment.

18:27 πάλιν οὖν ἠρνήσατο Πέτρος, καὶ εὐθέως ἀλέκτωρ ἐφώνησεν.

πάλιν. Adverb "pert[aining] to repetition in the same (or similar) manner" (BDAG, 752.2). Fronted for emphasis.

οὖν. Postpositive inferential conjunction and/or transitional particle (see 1:22 and 11:6).

ἠρνήσατο. Aor mid ind 3rd sg ἀρνέομαι.

Πέτρος. Nominative subject of ἠρνήσατο.

καί. Coordinating conjunction.

εὐθέως. Adverb ("at once").

ἀλέκτωρ. Nominative subject of ἐφώνησεν.

ἐφώνησεν. Aor act ind 3rd sg φωνέω.

John 18:28-40

[28]Then they led Jesus from Caiaphas to the governor's residence. Now it was early in the morning. And they themselves did not enter into the governor's residence so that they would not be defiled but could eat the Passover. [29]So Pilate went outside to them and said, "What accusation

do you bring against this man?" ³⁰They answered and said to him, "If this man had not been doing evil, we would not have handed him over to you." ³¹So Pilate said to them, "Take him yourselves and judge him according to your law!" The Jews said to him, "It is not permitted for us to kill anyone." ³²[This has happened] in order that the word of Jesus might be fulfilled, which he had said when he indicated by what sort of death he was about to die.

³³Then Pilate entered again into the governor's residence and summoned Jesus and said to him, "Are you the King of the Jews?" ³⁴Jesus answered, "Do you say this on your own, or did others say [this] to you about me?" ³⁵Pilate answered, "I am not a Jew, am I? Your own nation and the chief priests handed you over to me. What have you done?" ³⁶Jesus answered, "My kingdom is not from this world. If my kingdom were from this world, my subjects would be fighting so that I would not be handed over to the Jews. But, as a matter of fact, my kingdom is not from here." ³⁷Then Pilate said to him, "So then you are a king?" Jesus answered, "You say that I am a king. For this I have been born and for this I have come into the world: that I should testify to the truth. Everyone who is of the truth hears my voice." ³⁸Pilate said to him, "What is truth?" And after he had said this, he went out again to the Jews and said to them, "I find no basis for a charge in his case. ³⁹But it is your custom that I release for you one man at the Passover. So do you want that I release for you the King of the Jews?" ⁴⁰Then they shouted again, saying, "Not this man, but Barabbas!" Now Barabbas was an insurrectionist.

18:28 Ἄγουσιν οὖν τὸν Ἰησοῦν ἀπὸ τοῦ Καϊάφα εἰς τὸ πραιτώριον· ἦν δὲ πρωΐ· καὶ αὐτοὶ οὐκ εἰσῆλθον εἰς τὸ πραιτώριον, ἵνα μὴ μιανθῶσιν ἀλλὰ φάγωσιν τὸ πάσχα.

Ἄγουσιν. Pres act ind 3rd pl ἄγω. The subject of the verb is not expressed. The historical present marks the narrative transition from the Jewish to the Roman trial (Battle, 128).

οὖν. Postpositive inferential conjunction and/or transitional particle (see 1:22 and 11:6).

τὸν Ἰησοῦν. Accusative direct object of Ἄγουσιν.

ἀπὸ τοῦ Καϊάφα. Separation.

εἰς τὸ πραιτώριον. Locative. Here πραιτώριον (Lat. *praetorium*) designates "the governor's official residence" (BDAG, 859).

ἦν. Impf act ind 3rd sg εἰμί. On the function of the imperfect in the FG, see 1:39 on ἦν.

δέ. Marker of narrative development.

πρωΐ. Predicate adverb of time; see 2:1 on ἐκεῖ.

καί. Coordinating conjunction.

αὐτοί. Intensive pronoun that reinforces the implied subject of εἰσῆλθον ("they themselves").

οὐκ. Negative particle normally used with indicative verbs.

εἰσῆλθον. Aor act ind 3rd pl εἰσέρχομαι.

εἰς τὸ πραιτώριον. Locative.

ἵνα. Introduces a purpose clause.

μή. Negative particle normally used with non-indicative verbs.

μιανθῶσιν. Aor pass subj 3rd pl μιαίνω. Subjunctive with ἵνα. μιαίνω means "to cause something to be ceremonially impure, with the implication of serious defilement" (LN 53.34).

ἀλλά. Marker of contrast.

φάγωσιν. Aor act subj 3rd pl ἐσθίω. Subjunctive with ἵνα.

τὸ πάσχα. Accusative direct object of φάγωσιν.

18:29 Ἐξῆλθεν οὖν ὁ Πιλᾶτος ἔξω πρὸς αὐτοὺς καὶ φησίν· τίνα κατηγορίαν φέρετε [κατὰ] τοῦ ἀνθρώπου τούτου;

Ἐξῆλθεν. Aor act ind 3rd sg ἐξέρχομαι.

οὖν. Postpositive inferential conjunction and/or transitional particle (see 1:22 and 11:6).

ὁ Πιλᾶτος. Nominative subject of Ἐξῆλθεν.

ἔξω. Adverb ("outside").

πρὸς αὐτούς. Locative (motion toward).

καί. Coordinating conjunction.

φησίν. Pres act ind 3rd sg φημί. The historical present gives prominence to Pilate's question (see 1:15 on μαρτυρεῖ).

τίνα κατηγορίαν. Accusative direct object of φέρετε. Fronted for emphasis.

φέρετε. Pres act ind 2nd pl φέρω.

[κατὰ] τοῦ ἀνθρώπου τούτου. Opposition. The preposition has strong external support ($\mathfrak{P}^{66}$ ℵ^1 A C D^s K L N W Γ Δ Θ Ψ $f^{1.13}$ 33 565 700 𝔐 lat et al.), but it is absent in some early witnesses (ℵ* B 087^{vid} 579 e).

18:30 ἀπεκρίθησαν καὶ εἶπαν αὐτῷ· εἰ μὴ ἦν οὗτος κακὸν ποιῶν, οὐκ ἄν σοι παρεδώκαμεν αὐτόν.

ἀπεκρίθησαν. Aor mid ind 3rd pl ἀποκρίνομαι. On the voice, see "Deponency" in the Series Introduction. This verse is connected to the previous one by asyndeton.

καὶ εἶπαν αὐτῷ. Pleonastic clause under Semitic influence, which functions as a redundant quotative frame (see 1:25 on καὶ εἶπαν αὐτῷ).

καί. Coordinating conjunction.

εἶπαν. Aor act ind 3rd pl λέγω.

αὐτῷ. Dative indirect object of εἶπαν.

εἰ. Introduces the protasis of a second-class (contrary-to-fact) condition. Typically, the present contrary-to-fact conditions have the imperfect in both the protasis and the apodosis, while the past contrary-to-fact conditions have the aorist in both the protasis and the apodosis. Most of the exceptions to this rule involve the imperfect of εἰμί in the protasis, as here (Wallace 1996, 695 n. 26). If the participle ποιῶν is imperfect periphrastic, the entire conditional clause could be regarded as referring to the past: "If this man had not been doing evil, we would not have handed him over to you." If, however, the participle ποιῶν functions as a substantive, it is better to classify this conditional clause as a mixed form, i.e., the protasis referring to the present and the apodosis referring to the past: "If this man were not an evildoer, we would not have handed him over to you."

μή. Negative particle normally used with non-indicative verbs. εἰ μή can be translated "unless."

ἦν. Impf act ind 3rd sg εἰμί.

οὗτος. Nominative subject of ἦν.

κακόν. Accusative direct object of ποιῶν. The neuter adjective here functions as a substantive (BDAG, 501.1.c).

ποιῶν. Pres act ptc masc nom sg ποιέω. This participle could be either imperfect periphrastic ("if this man had not been doing evil") or an anarthrous substantive serving as the predicate nominative ("if this man were not a doer of evil"). It seems that the latter was favored by those copyists who replaced κακὸν ποιῶν (ℵ² B L W) with the substantive κακοποιός (A C³ Dˢ K N Γ Δ Θ f.¹³ 565 579 700 892ˢ 1241 1424 *l*844 𝔐 lat).

οὐκ. Negative particle normally used with indicative verbs. It marks the beginning of the apodosis of a second-class (contrary-to-fact) condition.

ἄν. Marker of contingency in the apodosis of the second-class condition.

σοι. Dative indirect object of παρεδώκαμεν.

παρεδώκαμεν. Aor act ind 1st pl παραδίδωμι.

αὐτόν. Accusative direct object of παρεδώκαμεν.

18:31 εἶπεν οὖν αὐτοῖς ὁ Πιλᾶτος· λάβετε αὐτὸν ὑμεῖς καὶ κατὰ τὸν νόμον ὑμῶν κρίνατε αὐτόν. εἶπον αὐτῷ οἱ Ἰουδαῖοι· ἡμῖν οὐκ ἔξεστιν ἀποκτεῖναι οὐδένα·

εἶπεν. Aor act ind 3rd sg λέγω.

οὖν. Postpositive inferential conjunction and/or transitional particle (see 1:22 and 11:6).

αὐτοῖς. Dative indirect object of εἶπεν.
ὁ Πιλᾶτος. Nominative subject of εἶπεν.
λάβετε. Aor act impv 2nd pl λαμβάνω.
αὐτὸν. Accusative direct object of λάβετε.
ὑμεῖς. Nominative subject of λάβετε. The personal pronoun is emphatic.
καὶ. Coordinating conjunction.
κατὰ τὸν νόμον. Standard. Fronted for emphasis.
ὑμῶν. Possessive genitive qualifying νόμον (see 8:17 and 10:34).
κρίνατε. Aor act impv 2nd pl κρίνω.
αὐτόν. Accusative direct object of κρίνατε.
εἶπον. Aor act ind 3rd pl λέγω. This clause is connected to the previous one by asyndeton.
αὐτῷ. Dative indirect object of εἶπον.
οἱ Ἰουδαῖοι. Nominative subject of εἶπον.
ἡμῖν. Dative complement of ἔξεστιν.
οὐκ. Negative particle normally used with indicative verbs.
ἔξεστιν. Pres act ind 3rd sg ἔξεστιν (impersonal). ἔξεστιν means "it is right, is authorized, is permitted, is proper" and can be followed by a dative of person and an infinitive, as here (BDAG, 348.1.b).
ἀποκτεῖναι. Aor act inf ἀποκτείνω (complementary). ἀποκτεῖναι could also be understood as the subject of ἔξεστιν, but since ἔξεστιν is an impersonal verb, it is better to regard it as complementary (see 3:7 on γεννηθῆναι).
οὐδένα. Accusative direct object of ἀποκτεῖναι. The two negatives οὐκ . . . οὐδένα reinforce each other (see 3:27 on οὐδὲ).

18:32 ἵνα ὁ λόγος τοῦ Ἰησοῦ πληρωθῇ ὃν εἶπεν σημαίνων ποίῳ θανάτῳ ἤμελλεν ἀποθνῄσκειν.

ἵνα ὁ λόγος τοῦ Ἰησοῦ πληρωθῇ ὃν εἶπεν. Only here and in 18:9 (ἵνα πληρωθῇ ὁ λόγος ὃν εἶπεν) is this introductory formula applied to the words of Jesus. In all other instances in the FG (12:38; 13:18; 15:25; 17:12; 19:24, 36), this formula and its variations are used to introduce scriptural quotations.
ἵνα. While this could be an imperatival ἵνα ("what Jesus said must be fulfilled"), it is more likely that it introduces a purpose clause. The ἵνα clause is elliptical, requiring an introduction, such as τοῦτο γέγονεν (BDF §448.7).
ὁ λόγος. Nominative subject of πληρωθῇ.
τοῦ Ἰησοῦ. Subjective genitive qualifying λόγος.
πληρωθῇ. Aor pass subj 3rd sg πληρόω. Subjunctive with ἵνα.

ὄν. Accusative direct object of εἶπεν. The antecedent of the relative pronoun is ὁ λόγος.

εἶπεν. Aor act ind 3rd sg λέγω.

σημαίνων ποίῳ θανάτῳ ἤμελλεν ἀποθνῄσκειν. A repetition of 12:33 (σημαίνων ποίῳ θανάτῳ ἤμελλεν ἀποθνῄσκειν). This summary statement refers to Jesus' prediction of his impending crucifixion in 12:32.

σημαίνων. Pres act ptc masc nom sg σημαίνω (temporal or purpose).

ποίῳ θανάτῳ. Dative of manner.

ἤμελλεν. Impf act ind 3rd sg μέλλω. On the augment, see ἤμελλεν in 4:47.

ἀποθνῄσκειν. Pres act inf ἀποθνῄσκω (complementary).

18:33 Εἰσῆλθεν οὖν πάλιν εἰς τὸ πραιτώριον ὁ Πιλᾶτος καὶ ἐφώνησεν τὸν Ἰησοῦν καὶ εἶπεν αὐτῷ· σὺ εἶ ὁ βασιλεὺς τῶν Ἰουδαίων;

Εἰσῆλθεν. Aor act ind 3rd sg εἰσέρχομαι.

οὖν. Postpositive inferential conjunction and/or transitional particle (see 1:22 and 11:6).

πάλιν. Adverb "pert[aining] to repetition in the same (or similar) manner" (BDAG, 752.2).

εἰς τὸ πραιτώριον. Locative.

ὁ Πιλᾶτος. Nominative subject of Εἰσῆλθεν.

καὶ. Coordinating conjunction.

ἐφώνησεν. Aor act ind 3rd sg φωνέω.

τὸν Ἰησοῦν. Accusative direct object of ἐφώνησεν.

καὶ. Coordinating conjunction.

εἶπεν. Aor act ind 3rd sg λέγω.

αὐτῷ. Dative indirect object of εἶπεν.

σὺ εἶ ὁ βασιλεὺς τῶν Ἰουδαίων. In all four Gospels, this is the first question that Pilate asks Jesus (Matt 27:11; Mark 15:2; Luke 23:3; John 18:33).

σὺ. Nominative subject of εἶ. Turner thinks that this personal pronoun is "without much emphasis" (MHT 3:37), but Brown (2:851) notes that σὺ could be emphatic if it expresses incredulity.

εἶ. Pres act ind 2nd sg εἰμί.

ὁ βασιλεὺς. Predicate nominative.

τῶν Ἰουδαίων. Genitive of subordination qualifying βασιλεὺς. On the lips of Pilate, "the Jews" refers to the whole Jewish nation and not to the hostile Jewish authorities, as elsewhere in the FG.

18:34 ἀπεκρίθη Ἰησοῦς· ἀπὸ σεαυτοῦ σὺ τοῦτο λέγεις ἢ ἄλλοι εἶπόν σοι περὶ ἐμοῦ;

ἀπεκρίθη. Aor mid ind 3rd sg ἀποκρίνομαι. On the voice, see "Deponency" in the Series Introduction. This verse is connected to the previous one by asyndeton.

Ἰησοῦς. Nominative subject of ἀπεκρίθη.

ἀπὸ σεαυτοῦ. Agency (BDAG, 107.5.e.α). Fronted for emphasis.

σύ. Nominative subject of λέγεις. σύ is contrastive, distinguishing Pilate from others (ἄλλοι).

τοῦτο. Accusative direct object of λέγεις.

λέγεις. Pres act ind 2nd sg λέγω.

ἤ. Marker of an alternative/disjunctive particle (BDAG, 432.1).

ἄλλοι. Nominative subject of εἶπόν. Fronted for emphasis.

εἶπόν. Aor act ind 3rd pl λέγω. The implied direct object of the verb is τοῦτο from the previous clause. "In keeping with its economic nature, Greek regularly implies an object that was already mentioned in the preceding context, rather than restating it" (Wallace 1996, 409 n. 5). εἶπόν, which has a circumflex accent on the penult, acquired an additional accent, the acute, on the ultima from the enclitic σοι (Smyth §183; Carson 1985, 48).

σοι. Dative indirect object of εἶπόν.

περὶ ἐμοῦ. Reference.

18:35 ἀπεκρίθη ὁ Πιλᾶτος· μήτι ἐγὼ Ἰουδαῖός εἰμι; τὸ ἔθνος τὸ σὸν καὶ οἱ ἀρχιερεῖς παρέδωκάν σε ἐμοί· τί ἐποίησας;

ἀπεκρίθη. Aor mid ind 3rd sg ἀποκρίνομαι. On the voice, see "Deponency" in the Series Introduction. This verse is connected to the previous one by asyndeton.

ὁ Πιλᾶτος. Nominative subject of ἀπεκρίθη.

μήτι. Negative particle that introduces a question that expects a negative answer. Although μήτι could be used in "questions in which the questioner is in doubt concerning the answer" (BDAG, 649), in this verse the expected answer is certainly "no."

ἐγώ. Nominative subject of εἰμι. Fronted as a topical frame.

Ἰουδαῖός. Predicate nominative. Fronted for emphasis.

εἰμι. Pres act ind 1st sg εἰμί.

τὸ ἔθνος τὸ σὸν καὶ οἱ ἀρχιερεῖς. Compound nominative subject of παρέδωκάν. Fronted for emphasis. The possessive adjective σόν stands in the second attributive position (see 1:9 on τὸ φῶς τὸ ἀληθινόν). This clause is connected to the previous one by asyndeton.

παρέδωκάν. Aor act ind 3rd pl παραδίδωμι. παρέδωκάν, which has an acute accent on the antepenult, acquired an additional accent, the acute, on the ultima from the enclitic σε (Smyth §183; Carson 1985, 48).

σε. Accusative direct object of παρέδωκάν.

ἐμοί. Dative indirect object of παρέδωκάν.

τί. Accusative direct object of ἐποίησας. This clause is connected to the previous one by asyndeton.

ἐποίησας. Aor act ind 2nd sg ποιέω.

18:36 ἀπεκρίθη Ἰησοῦς· ἡ βασιλεία ἡ ἐμὴ οὐκ ἔστιν ἐκ τοῦ κόσμου τούτου· εἰ ἐκ τοῦ κόσμου τούτου ἦν ἡ βασιλεία ἡ ἐμή, οἱ ὑπηρέται οἱ ἐμοὶ ἠγωνίζοντο [ἂν] ἵνα μὴ παραδοθῶ τοῖς Ἰουδαίοις· νῦν δὲ ἡ βασιλεία ἡ ἐμὴ οὐκ ἔστιν ἐντεῦθεν.

ἀπεκρίθη. Aor mid ind 3rd sg ἀποκρίνομαι. On the voice, see "Deponency" in the Series Introduction. This verse is connected to the previous one by asyndeton.

Ἰησοῦς. Nominative subject of ἀπεκρίθη.

ἡ βασιλεία ἡ ἐμή. Nominative subject of ἔστιν. Fronted as a topical frame. The possessive adjective ἐμή stands in the second attributive position (see 1:9 on τὸ φῶς τὸ ἀληθινόν). This nominal phrase is repeated twice more in this verse. Apart from these three references, the term βασιλεία occurs only twice more in the FG (3:3, 5), but in ch. 3 Jesus speaks about the kingdom of God, whereas here he speaks of his kingdom.

οὐκ. Negative particle normally used with indicative verbs.

ἔστιν. Pres act ind 3rd sg εἰμί. The enclitic ἐστιν is accented ἔστιν when it comes at the beginning of a sentence, when it expresses existence, or when it follows ἀλλ᾽, εἰ, καί, οὐκ, ὅτι, or τοῦτ᾽. The third condition is fulfilled here.

ἐκ τοῦ κόσμου τούτου. Source/origin or partaking/belonging. On the portrayal of the world in the FG, see 1:10 on ἐν τῷ κόσμῳ.

εἰ. Introduces the protasis of a second-class (contrary-to-fact) condition. This is the present contrary-to-fact condition because the verbs in both the protasis and the apodosis are in the imperfect. This clause is connected to the previous one by asyndeton.

ἐκ τοῦ κόσμου τούτου. Source/origin or partaking/belonging.

ἦν. Impf act ind 3rd sg εἰμί.

ἡ βασιλεία ἡ ἐμή. Nominative subject of ἦν (see above).

οἱ ὑπηρέται οἱ ἐμοί. Nominative subject of ἠγωνίζοντο. It marks the beginning of the apodosis of a second-class (contrary-to-fact) condition. The possessive adjective ἐμοί stands in the second attributive position. In 18:3, 12, 18 the term ὑπηρέται denotes the officers sent by the chief priests and the Pharisees, i.e., temple police. Here the evangelist applies it to Jesus' subjects, perhaps to create a deliberate contrast with the arresting party (Brown, 2:852).

ἠγωνίζοντο. Impf mid ind 3rd pl ἀγωνίζομαι. The verb means "to engage in intense struggle, involving physical or nonphysical force against strong opposition" (LN 39.29).

[ἄν]. Marker of contingency in the apodosis of the second-class condition. It is well attested, although many copyists placed it between οἱ ὑπηρέται and οἱ ἐμοί (A Dˢ K N Γ Δ Θ 565 700 892ˢ 1241 1424 𝔐 q).

ἵνα. Introduces a purpose clause.

μή. Negative particle normally used with non-indicative verbs.

παραδοθῶ. Aor pass subj 1st sg παραδίδωμι. Subjunctive with ἵνα.

τοῖς Ἰουδαίοις. Dative indirect object of παραδοθῶ.

νῦν. Here νῦν functions as a "temporal marker with focus not so much on the present time as the situation pert[aining] at a given moment," which, along with the following δέ, could be translated "but, as it is," "but, as things now stand," or, to mark a transition from the contrary-to-fact conditional clause to the real state of affairs, "but, as a matter of fact" (BDAG, 681.2.a).

δέ. Marker of narrative development.

ἡ βασιλεία ἡ ἐμή. Nominative subject of ἔστιν (see above).

οὐκ. Negative particle normally used with indicative verbs.

ἔστιν. Pres act ind 3rd sg εἰμί. The enclitic ἐστιν is accented ἔστιν when it comes at the beginning of a sentence, when it expresses existence, or when it follows ἀλλ', εἰ, καί, οὐκ, ὅτι, or τοῦτ'. The third condition is fulfilled here.

ἐντεῦθεν. Adverb of place.

18:37 εἶπεν οὖν αὐτῷ ὁ Πιλᾶτος· οὐκοῦν βασιλεὺς εἶ σύ; ἀπεκρίθη ὁ Ἰησοῦς· σὺ λέγεις ὅτι βασιλεύς εἰμι. ἐγὼ εἰς τοῦτο γεγέννημαι καὶ εἰς τοῦτο ἐλήλυθα εἰς τὸν κόσμον, ἵνα μαρτυρήσω τῇ ἀληθείᾳ· πᾶς ὁ ὢν ἐκ τῆς ἀληθείας ἀκούει μου τῆς φωνῆς.

εἶπεν. Aor act ind 3rd sg λέγω.

οὖν. Postpositive inferential conjunction and/or transitional particle (see 1:22 and 11:6).

αὐτῷ. Dative indirect object of εἶπεν.

ὁ Πιλᾶτος. Nominative subject of εἶπεν.

οὐκοῦν. An interrogative introducing a question that has inferential force ("so then"; BDAG, 736.2). A NT *hapax legomenon*.

βασιλεύς. Predicate nominative. Fronted for emphasis.

εἶ. Pres act ind 2nd sg εἰμί.

σύ. Nominative subject of εἶ.

ἀπεκρίθη. Aor mid ind 3rd sg ἀποκρίνομαι. On the voice, see "Deponency" in the Series Introduction. This clause is connected to the previous one by asyndeton.

ὁ Ἰησοῦς. Nominative subject of ἀπεκρίθη.

σὺ λέγεις. Asseverative clause ("you say it yourself, not I"), "in which there is always something of an implication that the statement would not have been made had the question not been asked" (BDF §441.3).

σύ. Nominative subject of λέγεις. σύ is emphatic and contrastive: "*you*, not I" (BDF §277.2).

λέγεις. Pres act ind 2nd sg λέγω.

ὅτι. Introduces the clausal complement (indirect discourse) of λέγεις.

βασιλεύς. Predicate nominative. Fronted for emphasis.

εἰμι. Pres act ind 1st sg εἰμί.

ἐγώ. Nominative subject of εἰμι. Fronted as a topical frame. This clause is connected to the previous one by asyndeton.

εἰς τοῦτο. Purpose. τοῦτο is cataphoric, referring to the ἵνα clause that follows.

γεγέννημαι. Prf pass ind 1st sg γεννάω. The perfect tense serves as a semantic marker, alerting the audience to the significance of Jesus' incarnation. The parallel structure of the two paratactic clauses ἐγὼ εἰς τοῦτο γεγέννημαι καὶ εἰς τοῦτο ἐλήλυθα εἰς τὸν κόσμον indicates that γεγέννημαι is synonymous with ἐλήλυθα εἰς τὸν κόσμον (Barrett, 537).

καί. Coordinating conjunction.

εἰς τοῦτο. Purpose.

ἐλήλυθα. Prf act ind 1st sg ἔρχομαι. The perfect tense is marked for prominence, calling attention to Jesus' coming into the world.

εἰς τὸν κόσμον. Locative. On the portrayal of the world in the FG, see 1:10 on ἐν τῷ κόσμῳ.

ἵνα. Introduces either a purpose clause or an epexegetical clause that explains τοῦτο.

μαρτυρήσω. Aor act subj 1st sg μαρτυρέω. Subjunctive with ἵνα.

τῇ ἀληθείᾳ. Dative complement of μεμαρτύρηκεν or dative of interest (see 5:33).

πᾶς ὁ ὤν. Nominative subject of ἀκούει. On πᾶς + articular participle, see 3:8 on πᾶς ὁ γεγεννημένος. Fronted as a topical frame. This clause is connected to the previous one by asyndeton.

ὁ ὤν. Pres act ptc masc nom sg εἰμί (substantival). On the function of this participle, see πᾶς ὁ ὤν above.

ἐκ τῆς ἀληθείας. Source/origin that determines the character of a person (Zerwick §§134–35).

ἀκούει. Pres act ind 3rd sg ἀκούω.

μου. Possessive genitive qualifying φωνῆς. The preposed pronoun is thematically salient (Levinsohn 2000, 64).

τῆς φωνῆς. Genitive direct object of ἀκούει.

18:38 λέγει αὐτῷ ὁ Πιλᾶτος· τί ἐστιν ἀλήθεια; Καὶ τοῦτο εἰπὼν πάλιν ἐξῆλθεν πρὸς τοὺς Ἰουδαίους καὶ λέγει αὐτοῖς· ἐγὼ οὐδεμίαν εὑρίσκω ἐν αὐτῷ αἰτίαν.

λέγει. Pres act ind 3rd sg λέγω. The historical present gives prominence to Pilate's question (see 1:15 on μαρτυρεῖ). This verse is connected to the previous one by asyndeton.

αὐτῷ. Dative indirect object of λέγει.

ὁ Πιλᾶτος. Nominative subject of λέγει.

τί. Predicate nominative. Fronted for emphasis.

ἐστιν. Pres act ind 3rd sg εἰμί.

ἀλήθεια. Nominative subject of ἐστιν.

Καὶ. Coordinating conjunction.

τοῦτο. Accusative direct object of εἰπὼν. The demonstrative pronoun is anaphoric, referring to Pilate's question about truth.

εἰπών. Aor act ptc masc nom sg λέγω (temporal). On participles that precede the main verb, see ἐμβλέψας in 1:36.

πάλιν. Adverb "pert[aining] to repetition in the same (or similar) manner" (BDAG, 752.2).

ἐξῆλθεν. Aor act ind 3rd sg ἐξέρχομαι.

πρὸς τοὺς Ἰουδαίους. Locative (motion toward).

καὶ. Coordinating conjunction.

λέγει. Pres act ind 3rd sg λέγω. The historical present gives prominence to Pilate's declaration of Jesus' innocence (see 1:15 on μαρτυρεῖ).

αὐτοῖς. Dative indirect object of λέγει.

ἐγώ. Nominative subject of εὑρίσκω. Fronted as a topical frame.

οὐδεμίαν ... αἰτίαν. Accusative direct object of εὑρίσκω. αἰτία is a technical term for "the basis of or grounds for an accusation in court" (LN 56.4). The adjective οὐδεμίαν is fronted for emphasis, standing in the first (anarthrous) attributive position (see 2:6 on λίθιναι ὑδρίαι).

εὑρίσκω. Pres act ind 1st sg εὑρίσκω. αἰτίαν εὑρίσκειν (ἔν τινι) = "find a basis for a charge (in his case)" (BDAG, 31.3.a).

ἐν αὐτῷ. Locative (see εὑρίσκω above).

18:39 ἔστιν δὲ συνήθεια ὑμῖν ἵνα ἕνα ἀπολύσω ὑμῖν ἐν τῷ πάσχα· βούλεσθε οὖν ἀπολύσω ὑμῖν τὸν βασιλέα τῶν Ἰουδαίων;

ἔστιν. Pres act ind 3rd sg εἰμί. The enclitic ἐστιν is accented ἔστιν when it comes at the beginning of a sentence, when it expresses existence, or when it follows ἀλλ', εἰ, καί, οὐκ, ὅτι, or τοῦτ'. The first two conditions are fulfilled here.

δὲ. Marker of narrative development.

συνήθεια. Nominative subject of ἔστιν.

ὑμῖν. Dative of possession. According to BDF (§189.1), "The classical distinction, whereby the genitive is used when the acquisition is recent or the emphasis is on the possessor . . . and the dative when the object possessed is to be stressed, is customarily preserved."

ἵνα. Introduces an epexegetical clause that explains συνήθεια.

ἕνα. Accusative direct object of ἀπολύσω. Fronted for emphasis.

ἀπολύσω. Aor act subj 1st sg ἀπολύω. Subjunctive with ἵνα.

ὑμῖν. Dative of advantage.

ἐν τῷ πάσχα. Temporal (see 2:23).

βούλεσθε. Pres mid ind 2nd pl βούλομαι. In classical Greek, "βούλεσθε (or βουλῇ) often introduces a doubtful question expressed (in 1st per[son]) directly by the subj[ect]" (Zerwick and Grosvenor, 340; cf. BDF §366.3).

οὖν. Postpositive inferential conjunction and/or transitional particle (see 1:22 and 11:6).

ἀπολύσω. Aor act subj 1st sg ἀπολύω (deliberative subjunctive).

ὑμῖν. Dative of advantage.

τὸν βασιλέα. Accusative direct object of ἀπολύσω.

τῶν Ἰουδαίων. Genitive of subordination qualifying βασιλέα (see 18:33).

18:40 ἐκραύγασαν οὖν πάλιν λέγοντες· μὴ τοῦτον ἀλλὰ τὸν Βαραββᾶν. ἦν δὲ ὁ Βαραββᾶς λῃστής.

ἐκραύγασαν. Aor act ind 3rd pl κραυγάζω.

οὖν. Postpositive inferential conjunction and/or transitional particle (see 1:22 and 11:6).

πάλιν. Adverb "pert[aining] to repetition in the same (or similar) manner" (BDAG, 752.2).

λέγοντες. Pres act ptc masc nom pl λέγω (pleonastic).

μὴ . . . ἀλλὰ. A point/counterpoint set ("not this one . . . but that one"). On the function of ἀλλά in a point/counterpoint set, see 1:8.

τοῦτον. Accusative direct object of an implied prohibition (μὴ ἀπολύσῃς).

τὸν Βαραββᾶν. Accusative direct object of an implied imperative (ἀπόλυσον).

ἦν. Impf act ind 3rd sg εἰμί. On the function of the imperfect in the FG, see 1:39 on ἦν.

δὲ. Marker of narrative development.

ὁ Βαραββᾶς. Nominative subject of ἦν.

λῃστής. Predicate nominative. λῃστής denotes "a person who engages in insurrection—'insurrectionist, rebel'" (LN 39.37).

John 19:1-16a

¹Thereupon Pilate ordered Jesus to be taken and had [him] scourged. ²And the soldiers wove a crown of thorns and placed [it] on his head and put a purple robe on him ³and kept coming up to him and saying, "Hail, king of the Jews!" And they kept giving him slaps in the face. ⁴And Pilate went out again and said to them, "Look, I am bringing him out to you so that you may know that I find no basis for a charge in his case." ⁵Then Jesus came out, wearing the crown made of thorns and the purple robe. And he said to them, "Behold the man!" ⁶So when they saw him, the chief priests and the officers shouted, saying, "Crucify! Crucify!" Pilate said to them, "Take him yourselves and crucify [him]. For I do not find a basis for a charge in his case." ⁷The Jews answered him, "We have a law, and according to that law he ought to die because he made himself the Son of God." ⁸So when Pilate heard this speech, he was even more afraid, ⁹and he entered the governor's residence again and said to Jesus, "Where are you from?" But Jesus did not give him an answer. ¹⁰Then Pilate said to him, "Are you not speaking to me? Do you not know that I have authority to release you, and I have authority to crucify you?" ¹¹Jesus answered him, "You would not have any authority over me unless it had been given to you from above. For this reason the one who handed me over to you has greater sin." ¹²From this time on Pilate was seeking to release him. But the Jews shouted, saying, "If you release this man, you are not a friend of the emperor! Everyone who makes himself a king is opposing the emperor." ¹³Then Pilate, when he heard these words, brought Jesus outside and sat down on the judgment seat at a place called the Stone Pavement, but Gabbatha in Aramaic. ¹⁴It was the day of preparation of the Passover. It was about the sixth hour. And he said to the Jews, "Here is your King!" ¹⁵Then they shouted, "Take him away! Take him away! Crucify him!" Pilate said to them, "Shall I crucify your King?" The chief priests answered, "We do not have a king

except the emperor." ¹⁶ᵃThereupon he handed him over to them in order that he might be crucified.

19:1 Τότε οὖν ἔλαβεν ὁ Πιλᾶτος τὸν Ἰησοῦν καὶ ἐμαστίγωσεν.

Τότε οὖν. A combination of the temporal adverb and the postpositive inferential conjunction, in which Τότε functions as a connective particle that introduces "a subsequent event, but not one taking place at a definite time ('thereupon,' not 'at that time')" (BDF §459.2). Τότε οὖν = "now" (in contrast to the preceding time). Fronted as a temporal frame.

ἔλαβεν. Aor act ind 3rd sg λαμβάνω. Both verbs in this verse—λαμβάνω and μαστιγόω—are causative because Pilate did not take and scourge Jesus himself (Wallace 1996, 411–12; Haubeck and von Siebenthal, 600).

ὁ Πιλᾶτος. Nominative subject of ἔλαβεν.
τὸν Ἰησοῦν. Accusative direct object of ἔλαβεν.
καὶ. Coordinating conjunction.
ἐμαστίγωσεν. Aor act ind 3rd sg μαστιγόω. The verb is causative (see ἔλαβεν above). Its implied direct object is τὸν Ἰησοῦν. "In keeping with its economic nature, Greek regularly implies an object that was already mentioned in the preceding context, rather than restating it" (Wallace 1996, 409 n. 5).

19:2 καὶ οἱ στρατιῶται πλέξαντες στέφανον ἐξ ἀκανθῶν ἐπέθηκαν αὐτοῦ τῇ κεφαλῇ καὶ ἱμάτιον πορφυροῦν περιέβαλον αὐτὸν

καὶ. Coordinating conjunction.
οἱ στρατιῶται. Nominative subject of ἐπέθηκαν.
πλέξαντες. Aor act ptc masc nom pl πλέκω (attendant circumstance or temporal). On participles that precede the main verb, see ἐμβλέψας in 1:36.
στέφανον. Accusative direct object of πλέξαντες.
ἐξ ἀκανθῶν. Source or, more specifically, material (BDAG, 297.3.h).
ἐπέθηκαν. Aor act ind 3rd pl ἐπιτίθημι. The implied direct object is στέφανον (see ἐμαστίγωσεν in v. 1).
αὐτοῦ. Possessive genitive qualifying κεφαλῇ. The preposed pronoun is thematically salient (Levinsohn 2000, 64).
τῇ κεφαλῇ. Dative complement of ἐπέθηκαν.
καὶ. Coordinating conjunction.
ἱμάτιον πορφυροῦν. Accusative direct object (thing) of περιέβαλον in a double accusative person-thing construction. Fronted for emphasis. The adjective πορφυροῦν ("purple") stands in the fourth attributive

position (see 3:15 on ζωὴν αἰώνιον). The purple color of the robe symbolizes royal status.

περιέβαλον. Aor act ind 3rd pl περιβάλλω.

αὐτόν. Accusative direct object (person) of περιέβαλον in a double accusative person-thing construction.

19:3 καὶ ἤρχοντο πρὸς αὐτὸν καὶ ἔλεγον· χαῖρε ὁ βασιλεὺς τῶν Ἰουδαίων· καὶ ἐδίδοσαν αὐτῷ ῥαπίσματα.

καί. Coordinating conjunction.

ἤρχοντο. Impf mid ind 3rd pl ἔρχομαι. The subject of the verb is οἱ στρατιῶται from the previous verse. The imperfective aspect of this and the other two indicative verbs in this verse (ἔλεγον and ἐδίδοσαν) portrays the mocking and abusive behavior of the soldiers as an unfolding process.

πρὸς αὐτόν. Locative (motion toward).

καί. Coordinating conjunction.

ἔλεγον. Impf act ind 3rd pl λέγω.

χαῖρε. Pres act impv 2nd sg χαίρω. The imperative functions as a stereotyped greeting (Wallace 1996, 493).

ὁ βασιλεύς. Nominative for vocative. Mark 15:18 and Matt 27:29 have the vocative (βασιλεῦ τῶν Ἰουδαίων). According to BDF (§147.3), "Attic used the nominative (with article) with simple substantives only in addressing inferiors, who were, so to speak, thereby addressed in the 3rd person." If the Johannine usage reflects the classical convention, the form of the soldiers' address to Jesus renounces the content of the address (Wallace 1996, 58). If, however, the articular nominative reflects Semitic usage, which does not conform to classical limitations, the subversive effect of the form may be absent (BDF §147.3). Moulton (70) disputes Semitic influence, arguing that the classical idiom was well established. In his view, the variant βασιλεῦ, attested in 𝔓⁶⁶ and ℵ, is inappropriate because it would admit the royal right to Jesus. Moulton extends this critique to the synoptic usage, maintaining that the appearance of βασιλεῦ in Mark 15:18 "is merely a note of the writer's imperfect sensibility to the more delicate shades of Greek idiom" (71).

τῶν Ἰουδαίων. Genitive of subordination qualifying βασιλεύς (see 18:33).

καί. Coordinating conjunction.

ἐδίδοσαν. Impf act ind 3rd pl δίδωμι.

αὐτῷ. Dative indirect object of ἐδίδοσαν.

ῥαπίσματα. Accusative direct object of ἐδίδοσαν.

19:4 Καὶ ἐξῆλθεν πάλιν ἔξω ὁ Πιλᾶτος καὶ λέγει αὐτοῖς· ἴδε ἄγω ὑμῖν αὐτὸν ἔξω, ἵνα γνῶτε ὅτι οὐδεμίαν αἰτίαν εὑρίσκω ἐν αὐτῷ.

Καὶ. Coordinating conjunction.
ἐξῆλθεν. Aor act ind 3rd sg ἐξέρχομαι.
πάλιν. Adverb "pert[aining] to repetition in the same (or similar) manner" (BDAG, 752.2).
ἔξω. Adverb ("outside").
ὁ Πιλᾶτος. Nominative subject of ἐξῆλθεν.
καὶ. Coordinating conjunction.
λέγει. Pres act ind 3rd sg λέγω. The historical present gives prominence to Pilate's repeated declaration of Jesus' innocence (see 18:38).
αὐτοῖς. Dative indirect object of λέγει. The personal pronoun refers to the Jews who were waiting outside of Pilate's residence (18:38).
ἴδε. An interjection (originally aor act impv 2nd sg ὁράω) that is "used when more than one pers[on] is addressed, and when that which is to be observed is in the nom[inative]" (BDAG, 466).
ἄγω. Pres act ind 1st sg ἄγω.
ὑμῖν. Dative indirect object of ἄγω.
αὐτὸν. Accusative direct object of ἄγω.
ἔξω. Adverb ("outside").
ἵνα. Introduces a purpose clause.
γνῶτε. Aor act subj 2nd pl γινώσκω. Subjunctive with ἵνα.
ὅτι. Introduces the clausal complement (indirect discourse) of γνῶτε.
οὐδεμίαν αἰτίαν. Accusative direct object of εὑρίσκω. Fronted for emphasis. The adjective οὐδεμίαν stands in the first (anarthrous) attributive position (see 2:6 on λίθιναι ὑδρίαι). On the meaning of αἰτία, see 18:38.
εὑρίσκω. Pres act ind 1st sg εὑρίσκω. On αἰτίαν εὑρίσκειν ἔν τινι, see 18:38.
ἐν αὐτῷ. Locative.

19:5 ἐξῆλθεν οὖν ὁ Ἰησοῦς ἔξω, φορῶν τὸν ἀκάνθινον στέφανον καὶ τὸ πορφυροῦν ἱμάτιον. καὶ λέγει αὐτοῖς· ἰδοὺ ὁ ἄνθρωπος.

ἐξῆλθεν. Aor act ind 3rd sg ἐξέρχομαι.
οὖν. Postpositive inferential conjunction and/or transitional particle (see 1:22 and 11:6).
ὁ Ἰησοῦς. Nominative subject of ἐξῆλθεν.
ἔξω. Adverb ("outside").
φορῶν. Pres act ptc masc nom sg φορέω (manner). On participles that follow the main verb, see βαπτίζων in 1:31.

τὸν ἀκάνθινον στέφανον. Accusative direct object of φορῶν. The adjective ἀκάνθινον stands in the first attributive position (see 2:10 on τὸν καλὸν οἶνον).

καί. Coordinating conjunction.

τὸ πορφυροῦν ἱμάτιον. Accusative direct object of φορῶν. The adjective πορφυροῦν stands in the first attributive position (see 2:10 on τὸν καλὸν οἶνον).

καί. Coordinating conjunction.

λέγει. Pres act ind 3rd sg λέγω. The implied subject of the verb is Pilate. The historical present gives prominence to Pilate's dramatic presentation of Jesus wearing the crown of thorns and the purple robe (see 1:15 on μαρτυρεῖ).

αὐτοῖς. Dative indirect object of λέγει.

ἰδού. An interjection (originally ἰδοῦ [aor mid impv 2nd sg ὁράω] but accented with the acute rather than the circumflex) that "draws attention to what follows" (BDAG, 468). Here it serves as a marker of strong emphasis that can be rendered "here" ("Here is the man!") (BDAG, 468.2).

ὁ ἄνθρωπος. Nominative subject of a verbless clause. ὁ is a deictic article, pointing out the person—Jesus—who is present at the moment of speaking (Wallace 1996, 221).

19:6 Ὅτε οὖν εἶδον αὐτὸν οἱ ἀρχιερεῖς καὶ οἱ ὑπηρέται ἐκραύγασαν λέγοντες· σταύρωσον σταύρωσον. λέγει αὐτοῖς ὁ Πιλᾶτος· λάβετε αὐτὸν ὑμεῖς καὶ σταυρώσατε· ἐγὼ γὰρ οὐχ εὑρίσκω ἐν αὐτῷ αἰτίαν.

Ὅτε. Introduces a temporal clause.

οὖν. Postpositive inferential conjunction and/or transitional particle (see 1:22 and 11:6).

εἶδον. Aor act ind 3rd pl ὁράω.

αὐτόν. Accusative direct object of εἶδον.

οἱ ἀρχιερεῖς καὶ οἱ ὑπηρέται. Compound nominative subject ἐκραύγασαν. The repetition of the article before ὑπηρέται indicates that the evangelists portrays the chief priests and the temple police as two distinct groups (MHT 3:182).

ἐκραύγασαν. Aor act ind 3rd pl κραυγάζω.

λέγοντες. Pres act ptc masc nom pl λέγω (pleonastic).

σταύρωσον. Aor act impv 2nd sg σταυρόω. In contrast to 19:15, the accusative direct object of the verb is not expressed.

σταύρωσον. Aor act impv 2nd sg σταυρόω. The repetition of the imperative conveys strong emotion (Robertson, 1200) and intensity (Brown, 2:876).

λέγει. Pres act ind 3rd sg λέγω. The historical present gives prominence to Pilate's third declaration of Jesus' innocence (see 18:38 and 19:4). This clause is connected to the previous one by asyndeton.

αὐτοῖς. Dative indirect object of λέγει.

ὁ Πιλᾶτος. Nominative subject of λέγει.

λάβετε. Aor act impv 2nd pl λαμβάνω.

αὐτὸν. Accusative direct object of λάβετε.

ὑμεῖς. Nominative subject of λάβετε. The personal pronoun is emphatic.

καὶ. Coordinating conjunction.

σταυρώσατε. Aor act impv 2nd pl σταυρόω.

ἐγὼ. Nominative subject of εὑρίσκω. The personal pronoun is emphatic and contrastive, differentiating Pilate's assessment of Jesus from that of the Jews.

γὰρ. Postpositive conjunction introducing the clause that explains why Pilate suggested that the Jews should crucify Jesus themselves.

οὐχ. Negative particle normally used with indicative verbs.

εὑρίσκω. Pres act ind 1st sg εὑρίσκω. On αἰτίαν εὑρίσκειν ἔν τινι, see 18:38.

ἐν αὐτῷ. Locative.

αἰτίαν. Accusative direct object of εὑρίσκω.

19:7 ἀπεκρίθησαν αὐτῷ οἱ Ἰουδαῖοι· ἡμεῖς νόμον ἔχομεν καὶ κατὰ τὸν νόμον ὀφείλει ἀποθανεῖν, ὅτι υἱὸν θεοῦ ἑαυτὸν ἐποίησεν.

ἀπεκρίθησαν. Aor mid ind 3rd pl ἀποκρίνομαι. On the voice, see "Deponency" in the Series Introduction. This verse is connected to the previous one by asyndeton.

αὐτῷ. Dative indirect object of ἀπεκρίθησαν.

οἱ Ἰουδαῖοι. Nominative subject of ἀπεκρίθησαν. In light of v. 6, this group consists of two subgroups—the chief priests and the temple police.

ἡμεῖς. Nominative subject of ἔχομεν. Fronted as a topical frame.

νόμον. Accusative direct object of ἔχομεν. Fronted for emphasis. The anarthrous νόμον probably denotes a particular statute of the Torah, such as the law of blasphemy in Lev 24:16 (Barrett, 541; Schnackenburg, 3:258), which is now introduced into the conversation between the Jewish leaders and Pilate (Wallace 1996, 217–18).

ἔχομεν. Pres act ind 1st pl ἔχω.

καὶ. Coordinating conjunction.

κατὰ τὸν νόμον. Standard. The article is anaphoric, denoting the previous reference to the law.

ὀφείλει. Pres act ind 3rd sg ὀφείλω.

ἀποθανεῖν. Aor act inf ἀποθνῄσκω (complementary).

ὅτι. Introduces a causal clause.

υἱόν. Accusative complement to ἑαυτὸν in a double accusative object-complement construction. Fronted for emphasis. The expression υἱὸν θεοῦ is monadic and does not require the article to be definite (Wallace 1996, 248–49). This conclusion is based on the rule known as Apollonius' canon, which states that both the head noun and the genitive noun either have the article or lack the article. A corollary to this rule is that "when both nouns are anarthrous, both will usually have the same semantic force" (250). In this case, since θεοῦ is a monadic noun and therefore definite, so is υἱόν.

θεοῦ. Genitive of relationship qualifying υἱόν.

ἑαυτὸν. Accusative direct object of ἐποίησεν in a double accusative object-complement construction.

ἐποίησεν. Aor act ind 3rd sg ποιέω.

19:8 Ὅτε οὖν ἤκουσεν ὁ Πιλᾶτος τοῦτον τὸν λόγον, μᾶλλον ἐφοβήθη,

Ὅτε. Introduces a temporal clause, which is fronted as a temporal frame.

οὖν. Postpositive inferential conjunction and/or transitional particle (see 1:22 and 11:6).

ἤκουσεν. Aor act ind 3rd sg ἀκούω.

ὁ Πιλᾶτος. Nominative subject of ἤκουσεν.

τοῦτον τὸν λόγον. Accusative direct object of ἤκουσεν.

μᾶλλον. Comparative of the adverb μάλα ("to a greater or higher degree, more" [BDAG, 613.1]).

ἐφοβήθη. Aor mid ind 3rd sg φοβέομαι. On the voice, see "Deponency" in the Series Introduction.

19:9 καὶ εἰσῆλθεν εἰς τὸ πραιτώριον πάλιν καὶ λέγει τῷ Ἰησοῦ· πόθεν εἶ σύ; ὁ δὲ Ἰησοῦς ἀπόκρισιν οὐκ ἔδωκεν αὐτῷ.

καὶ. Coordinating conjunction.

εἰσῆλθεν. Aor act ind 3rd sg εἰσέρχομαι.

εἰς τὸ πραιτώριον. Locative.

πάλιν. Adverb "pert[aining] to repetition in the same (or similar) manner" (BDAG, 752.2).

καὶ. Coordinating conjunction.

λέγει. Pres act ind 3rd sg λέγω. The historical present gives prominence to Pilate's question (see 1:15 on μαρτυρεῖ).
τῷ Ἰησοῦ. Dative indirect object of λέγει.
πόθεν. Interrogative adverb of place.
εἶ. Pres act ind 2nd sg εἰμί.
σύ. Nominative subject of εἶ.
ὁ ... Ἰησοῦς. Nominative subject of ἔδωκεν.
δὲ. Marker of narrative development.
ἀπόκρισιν. Accusative direct object of ἔδωκεν.
οὐκ. Negative particle normally used with indicative verbs.
ἔδωκεν. Aor act ind 3rd sg δίδωμι.
αὐτῷ. Dative indirect object of ἔδωκεν.

19:10 λέγει οὖν αὐτῷ ὁ Πιλᾶτος· ἐμοὶ οὐ λαλεῖς; οὐκ οἶδας ὅτι ἐξουσίαν ἔχω ἀπολῦσαί σε καὶ ἐξουσίαν ἔχω σταυρῶσαί σε;

λέγει. Pres act ind 3rd sg λέγω. The historical present gives prominence to Pilate's question (see 1:15 on μαρτυρεῖ).
οὖν. Postpositive inferential conjunction and/or transitional particle (see 1:22 and 11:6).
αὐτῷ. Dative indirect object of λέγει.
ὁ Πιλᾶτος. Nominative subject of λέγει.
ἐμοί. Dative indirect object of λαλεῖς. Fronted for emphasis.
οὐ. Negative particle normally used with indicative verbs.
λαλεῖς. Pres act ind 2nd sg λαλέω. The verb stands in final, emphatic position.
οὐκ. Negative particle normally used with indicative verbs. This question is connected to the previous one by asyndeton.
οἶδας. Prf act ind 2nd sg οἶδα (see 1:26 on οἴδατε).
ὅτι. Introduces the clausal complement (indirect discourse) of οἶδας.
ἐξουσίαν. Accusative direct object of ἔχω. Fronted for emphasis.
ἔχω. Pres act ind 1st sg ἔχω.
ἀπολῦσαί. Aor act inf ἀπολύω (epexegetical to ἐξουσίαν). ἀπολῦσαί, which has a circumflex accent on the penult, acquired an additional accent, the acute, on the ultima from the enclitic σε (Smyth §183; Carson 1985, 48).
σε. Accusative direct object of ἀπολῦσαί.
καὶ. Coordinating conjunction.
ἐξουσίαν. Accusative direct object of ἔχω. Fronted for emphasis.
ἔχω. Pres act ind 1st sg ἔχω.
σταυρῶσαί. Aor act inf σταυρόω (epexegetical to ἐξουσίαν). σταυρῶσαί, which has a circumflex accent on the penult, acquired an

σε. Accusative direct object of σταυρῶσαί.

19:11 ἀπεκρίθη [αὐτῷ] Ἰησοῦς· οὐκ εἶχες ἐξουσίαν κατ' ἐμοῦ οὐδεμίαν εἰ μὴ ἦν δεδομένον σοι ἄνωθεν· διὰ τοῦτο ὁ παραδούς μέ σοι μείζονα ἁμαρτίαν ἔχει.

ἀπεκρίθη. Aor mid ind 3rd sg ἀποκρίνομαι. On the voice, see "Deponency" in the Series Introduction. This verse is connected to the previous one by asyndeton.

[αὐτῷ]. Dative indirect object of ἀπεκρίθη. The pronoun is printed within square brackets because the external evidence for its inclusion ($\mathfrak{P}^{60vid}$ ℵ B D^s L W Ψ $f^{1.(13)}$ 33 565 579 c j sa^{mss}) and its exclusion ($\mathfrak{P}^{66c}$ A K N Γ Δ 700 892^s 1241 1424 *l*844 𝔐 lat sy^h sa^{ms} ly pbo bo) is evenly balanced.

Ἰησοῦς. Nominative subject of ἀπεκρίθη.

οὐκ. Negative particle normally used with indicative verbs. οὐκ marks the beginning of the apodosis of a second-class condition, which comes before the protasis and does not have the marker of contingency because in Hellenistic Greek "the addition of ἄν is no longer obligatory" (BDF §360.1).

εἶχες. Impf act ind 2nd sg ἔχω.

ἐξουσίαν ... οὐδεμίαν. Accusative direct object of εἶχες. The adjective οὐδεμίαν is emphatic, standing in the fourth attributive position (see 3:15 on ζωὴν αἰώνιον). The two negatives οὐκ ... οὐδεμίαν reinforce each other.

κατ' ἐμοῦ. Opposition.

εἰ. Introduces the protasis of a second-class (contrary-to-fact) condition. This conditional clause represents a mixed form because the protasis refers to the past and the apodosis refers to the present.

μή. This negative particle is regularly used in contrary-to-fact protases because they employ the so-called unreal indicative (BDF §428.2). εἰ μή can be translated "unless."

ἦν. Impf act ind 3rd sg εἰμί.

δεδομένον. Prf pass ptc neut nom sg δίδωμι (pluperfect periphrastic).

σοι. Dative indirect object of δεδομένον.

ἄνωθεν. Adverb of place that here designates "a source that is above, *from above*" (BDAG, 92.1).

διὰ τοῦτο. Causal. The demonstrative pronoun is anaphoric, referring to Jesus' assertion that Pilate would have no power over him unless it had been given to him from above. In this context, the PP διὰ τοῦτο functions as a connective; on this function of διὰ τοῦτο, see 1:31.

ὁ παραδούς. Aor act ptc masc nom sg παραδίδωμι (substantival). Nominative subject of ἔχει.

μέ. Accusative direct object of παραδούς. The enclitic μέ is accented because it is followed by the enclitic σοι. "When several enclitics occur in succession, each receives an accent from the following, only the last having no accent" (Smyth §185).

σοι. Dative indirect object of παραδούς.

μείζονα ἁμαρτίαν. Accusative direct object of ἔχει. Fronted for emphasis. μείζονα is the comparative adjective from μέγας, which stands in the first (anarthrous) attributive position (see 2:6 on λίθιναι ὑδρίαι). The phrase ἁμαρτίαν ἔχειν is found only in the Johannine literature (John 9:41; 15:22, 24; 19:11; 1 John 1:8).

ἔχει. Pres act ind 3rd sg ἔχω.

19:12 Ἐκ τούτου ὁ Πιλᾶτος ἐζήτει ἀπολῦσαι αὐτόν· οἱ δὲ Ἰουδαῖοι ἐκραύγασαν λέγοντες· ἐὰν τοῦτον ἀπολύσῃς, οὐκ εἶ φίλος τοῦ Καίσαρος· πᾶς ὁ βασιλέα ἑαυτὸν ποιῶν ἀντιλέγει τῷ Καίσαρι.

Ἐκ τούτου. Temporal ("from this time on") or causal ("because of this").

ὁ Πιλᾶτος. Nominative subject of ἐζήτει.

ἐζήτει. Impf act ind 3rd sg ζητέω. Contextual markers (see Ἐκ τούτου above) indicate that this imperfect conveys the beginning of Pilate's continuous but ultimately unsuccessful effort to release Jesus.

ἀπολῦσαι. Aor act inf ἀπολύω (complementary).

αὐτόν. Accusative direct object of ἀπολῦσαι.

οἱ . . . Ἰουδαῖοι. Nominative subject of ἐκραύγασαν.

δὲ. Marker of narrative development with a contrastive nuance.

ἐκραύγασαν. Aor act ind 3rd pl κραυγάζω.

λέγοντες. Pres act ptc masc nom pl λέγω (pleonastic).

ἐὰν. Introduces the protasis of a third-class condition.

τοῦτον. Accusative direct object of ἀπολύσῃς.

ἀπολύσῃς. Aor act subj 2nd sg ἀπολύω. Subjunctive with ἐάν.

οὐκ. Negative particle normally used with indicative verbs. οὐκ marks the beginning of the apodosis of a third-class condition.

εἶ. Pres act ind 2nd sg εἰμί.

φίλος. Predicate nominative.

τοῦ Καίσαρος. Genitive of relationship qualifying φίλος.

πᾶς ὁ ... ποιῶν. Nominative subject of ἀντιλέγει. On πᾶς + articular participle, see 3:8 on πᾶς ὁ γεγεννημένος. This clause is connected to the previous one by asyndeton.

ὁ ... ποιῶν. Pres act ptc masc nom sg ποιέω (substantival). On the function of this participle, see πᾶς ὁ ... ποιῶν above.

βασιλέα. Accusative complement to ἑαυτὸν in a double accusative object-complement construction.

ἑαυτόν. Accusative direct object of ποιῶν in a double accusative object-complement construction.

ἀντιλέγει. Pres act ind 3rd sg ἀντιλέγω.

τῷ Καίσαρι. Dative complement of ἀντιλέγει.

19:13 ὁ οὖν Πιλᾶτος ἀκούσας τῶν λόγων τούτων ἤγαγεν ἔξω τὸν Ἰησοῦν καὶ ἐκάθισεν ἐπὶ βήματος εἰς τόπον λεγόμενον Λιθόστρωτον, Ἑβραϊστὶ δὲ Γαββαθα.

ὁ ... Πιλᾶτος. Nominative subject of ἤγαγεν.

οὖν. Postpositive inferential conjunction and/or transitional particle (see 1:22 and 11:6).

ἀκούσας. Aor act ptc masc nom sg ἀκούω (temporal). On participles that precede the main verb, see ἐμβλέψας in 1:36.

τῶν λόγων τούτων. Genitive direct object of ἀκούσας. In 19:8 (Ὅτε οὖν ἤκουσεν ὁ Πιλᾶτος τοῦτον τὸν λόγον), the object of ἀκούειν is in the accusative, whereas here it is in the genitive. This distinction may reflect classical usage in which "the accusative represents what is directly grasped by the hearing (sound, news, what is said), and the genitive the source of what is heard, whether the person speaking or a voice conceived not as sound but as speaking" (Zerwick §69). If this distinction is applicable here, in 19:8 Pilate merely hears the argument of the Jewish leaders that Jesus broke a precept in the law by making himself the Son of God, while in 19:13 he understands and accepts their argument that if he releases Jesus, he would not be a friend of the emperor (Brown, 2:880).

ἤγαγεν. Aor act ind 3rd sg ἄγω.

ἔξω. Adverb ("outside").

τὸν Ἰησοῦν. Accusative direct object of ἤγαγεν.

καί. Coordinating conjunction.

ἐκάθισεν. Aor act ind 3rd sg καθίζω. The verb καθίζω could be either transitive ("to cause to sit down, *seat, set*" [BDAG, 491.1]) or intransitive ("to take a seated position, *sit down*" [BDAG, 492.3]). If the former, the missing direct object could be supplied from the context (see Wallace 1996, 409 n. 5), suggesting that Pilate caused Jesus to sit on the judicial bench. If the latter, Pilate himself sat on the judgment seat. This issue cannot be decided on the basis of the Greek grammar alone because both options are valid alternatives. What must also be considered are the narrative clues from the FG and the parallels in other ancient writings. The following three arguments support the first option: (1) seating Jesus on the judicial bench is consistent with other acts of mockery described in 19:2, 3, 5; (2) placing Jesus on the judgment seat is consistent with the Johannine theology, which portrays Jesus as the real judge of humanity; and (3) Justin, *1 Apol.* 35 and *Gos. Pet.* 7 show familiarity with a tradition about the Jews who put Jesus on the judicial bench. In favor of the second option speak the following considerations: (1) in the only other occurrence of καθίζω in the FG (12:14; cf. 8:2) the verb is intransitive; (2) in John Pilate seems to be more eager to release Jesus than to mock him; (3) Josephus, *J.W.* 2.172 contains a description of Pilate, who "took his seat on his tribunal in the great stadium" (ὁ Πιλᾶτος καθίσας ἐπὶ βήματος ἐν τῷ μεγάλῳ σταδίῳ; cf. Josephus, *J.W.* 2.301). On balance, the arguments in favor of the intransitive meaning of ἐκάθισεν appear more convincing (Brown, 2:880–81; Beasley-Murray, 342. Barrett, 544, thinks that both meanings are intended). This is also the sense of the verb in Matt 27:19 (Καθημένου δὲ αὐτοῦ ἐπὶ τοῦ βήματος).

ἐπὶ βήματος. Locative. βῆμα denotes "a raised platform mounted by steps and usually furnished with a seat, used by officials in addressing an assembly, often on judicial matters—'judgment seat, judgment place'" (LN 7.63). Elsewhere in the NT, βῆμα with this sense occurs in Matt 27:19; Acts 18:12, 16-17; 25:6, 10, 17; Rom 14:10; and 2 Cor 5:10.

εἰς τόπον. Locative. In this PP, εἰς stands for ἐν (Harris 2012, 84, 87).

λεγόμενον. Pres pass ptc masc acc sg λέγω (attributive). The participle modifies τόπον, standing in the fourth attributive position (see 1:6 on ἀπεσταλμένος).

Λιθόστρωτον. Accusative complement to τόπον in a double accusative subject-complement construction (see 1:41 on χριστός). Although the nominalized adjective Λιθόστρωτον does not have the article, it is definite because it is monadic (Wallace 1996, 248–49), denoting "an area in Jerusalem, paved with flat blocks of stone and forming a kind of courtyard" (LN 7.71). In the passive construction τόπον λεγόμενον Λιθόστρωτον, τόπον is the conceptual subject of the passive participle λεγόμενον. This formulation is derived from the (real or hypothetical) active clause τις λέγει τόπον Λιθόστρωτον. When the active clause is transformed into a passive clause, the direct object becomes the subject and the accusative complement becomes a nominative complement:

τόπος λέγεται Λιθόστρωτος (see 1:41 on χριστός). Here an additional step is required: τόπον is in the accusative as the object of the preposition εἰς and requires a complement in the same case.

Ἑβραϊστί. Adverb ("in Hebrew/Aramaic" [BDAG, 270]).

δὲ. Marker of narrative development.

Γαββαθα. This indeclinable noun is a NT *hapax legomenon*. In this clause, it functions as the accusative in apposition to Λιθόστρωτον.

19:14 ἦν δὲ παρασκευὴ τοῦ πάσχα, ὥρα ἦν ὡς ἕκτη. καὶ λέγει τοῖς Ἰουδαίοις· ἴδε ὁ βασιλεὺς ὑμῶν.

ἦν. Impf act ind 3rd sg εἰμί. On the function of the imperfect in the FG, see 1:39 on ἦν.

δὲ. Marker of narrative development.

παρασκευὴ. Nominative subject of ἦν. παρασκευὴ denotes the day of preparation for a festival.

τοῦ πάσχα. Objective genitive qualifying παρασκευὴ.

ὥρα. Nominative subject of ἦν.

ἦν. Impf act ind 3rd sg εἰμί. On the function of the imperfect in the FG, see 1:39 on ἦν.

ὡς. Particle used with numerals to denote an estimate ("about, approximately").

ἕκτη. Predicate adjective. ἕκτη (from ἕκτος) is an ordinal number meaning "sixth"; "the sixth hour of a day" = 12 p.m. based on a customary reckoning of the twelve-hour day from sunrise (6 a.m.) to sunset (6 p.m.). The variant τρίτη attested in some manuscripts (ℵ² Dˢ L Δ Ψ *l*844) is a scribal attempt to adjust the Johannine chronology to that of Mark 15:25 (ἦν δὲ ὥρα τρίτη καὶ ἐσταύρωσαν αὐτόν) (Metzger, 216).

καὶ. Coordinating conjunction.

λέγει. Pres act ind 3rd sg λέγω. The historical present gives prominence to Pilate's exclamation that follows (see 1:15 on μαρτυρεῖ).

τοῖς Ἰουδαίοις. Dative indirect object of λέγει.

ἴδε. An interjection (originally aor act impv 2nd sg ὁράω) that is "used when more than one pers[on] is addressed, and when that which is to be observed is in the nom[inative]" (BDAG, 466). This interjection is here used "to indicate a place or individual" and can be translated "here is" (BDAG, 466.3).

ὁ βασιλεὺς. Nominative of exclamation (see 1:29 on ὁ ἀμνὸς).

ὑμῶν. Genitive of subordination qualifying βασιλεὺς.

19:15 ἐκραύγασαν οὖν ἐκεῖνοι· ἆρον ἆρον, σταύρωσον αὐτόν. λέγει αὐτοῖς ὁ Πιλᾶτος· τὸν βασιλέα ὑμῶν σταυρώσω; ἀπεκρίθησαν οἱ ἀρχιερεῖς· οὐκ ἔχομεν βασιλέα εἰ μὴ Καίσαρα.

ἐκραύγασαν. Aor act ind 3rd pl κραυγάζω.

οὖν. Postpositive inferential conjunction and/or transitional particle (see 1:22 and 11:6).

ἐκεῖνοι. Nominative subject of ἐκραύγασαν. The demonstrative pronoun refers to the Jews mentioned in the previous verse, acting as a third-person personal pronoun with a simple anaphoric force (Wallace 1996, 328–29).

ἆρον. Aor act impv 2nd sg αἴρω. The direct object is not expressed, but it is clear from the context that it is Jesus.

ἆρον. Aor act impv 2nd sg αἴρω. The repetition of the imperative gives intensity to the request.

σταύρωσον. Aor act impv 2nd sg σταυρόω.

αὐτόν. Accusative direct object of σταύρωσον.

λέγει. Pres act ind 3rd sg λέγω. The historical present gives prominence to Pilate's question (see 1:15 on μαρτυρεῖ). This clause is connected to the previous one by asyndeton.

αὐτοῖς. Dative indirect object of λέγει.

ὁ Πιλᾶτος. Nominative subject of λέγει.

τὸν βασιλέα. Accusative direct object of σταυρώσω. Fronted for emphasis.

ὑμῶν. Genitive of subordination qualifying βασιλέα.

σταυρώσω. Aor act subj 1st sg σταυρόω (deliberative subjunctive). σταυρώσω is causative (see 19:1 on ἔλαβεν).

ἀπεκρίθησαν. Aor mid ind 3rd pl ἀποκρίνομαι. On the voice, see "Deponency" in the Series Introduction. This clause is connected to the previous one by asyndeton.

οἱ ἀρχιερεῖς. Nominative subject of ἀπεκρίθησαν.

οὐκ . . . εἰ μὴ. A point/counterpoint set that corrects the negated clause ("we do not have a king") by introducing an exception ("except the emperor"); on the function of the excepted element, see 3:13 on οὐδεὶς . . . εἰ μὴ.

ἔχομεν. Pres act ind 1st pl ἔχω.

βασιλέα. Accusative direct object of ἔχομεν.

Καίσαρα. Accusative direct object of ἔχομεν.

19:16a Τότε οὖν παρέδωκεν αὐτὸν αὐτοῖς ἵνα σταυρωθῇ.

Τότε οὖν. A combination of the temporal adverb and the postpositive inferential conjunction, in which Τότε functions as a connective particle that introduces "a subsequent event, but not one taking place at a definite time ('thereupon,' not 'at that time')" (BDF §459.2). Τότε οὖν = "now" (in contrast to the preceding time).

παρέδωκεν. Aor act ind 3rd sg παραδίδωμι.

αὐτὸν. Accusative direct object of παρέδωκεν.

αὐτοῖς. Dative indirect object of παρέδωκεν. Since the closest antecedent of the personal pronoun is οἱ ἀρχιερεῖς in v. 15, the impression is that Jesus was given over to the Jewish authorities to be crucified. Since 19:23 clearly states that the Roman soldiers were the ones who crucified Jesus, this impression may be the result of careless writing. It is, however, more likely, as Brown suggests, that "it reflects the later tendency to exculpate the Romans and inculpate the Jews" (2:884). The theme of Jewish culpability for Jesus' crucifixion is also found in Matt 27:22-25; Luke 23:25; Acts 2:36; 3:15; 10:39; Barn. 7:9; Justin, *1 Apol.* 35; Tertullian, *Apol.* 21.18.

ἵνα. Introduces a purpose clause.

σταυρωθῇ. Aor pass subj 3rd sg σταυρόω. Subjunctive with ἵνα.

John 19:16b-30

[16b]So they took Jesus, [17]and while he was carrying the cross by himself, he went out to [a place] called the Place of the Skull (which is called Golgotha in Aramaic), [18]where they crucified him, and with him two others, one on each side, and Jesus in the middle. [19]Pilate also had an inscription written and placed on the cross, and it was written: "Jesus the Nazarene, the King of the Jews." [20]Thus many of the Jews read this inscription because the place where Jesus was crucified was near the city; and it was written in Aramaic, in Latin, [and] in Greek. [21]Then the chief priests of the Jews said to Pilate, "Do not write, 'The King of the Jews,' but, 'That man said, "I am the King of the Jews."'" [22]Pilate answered, "What I have written I have written." [23]Then the soldiers, when they crucified Jesus, took his clothes and made four shares, for each soldier a share; also the tunic. Now the tunic was seamless, woven throughout from the top. [24]So they said to one another, "Let us not tear it, but let us cast lots for it, whose it will be." [This has happened] in order that the Scripture may be fulfilled that says, "They divided my clothes among themselves, and for my clothing they cast lots." So then the soldiers did these things. [25]Now his mother, and the sister of his mother, Mary

the [wife] of Clopas, and Mary Magdalene were standing near the cross of Jesus. ²⁶Then Jesus, when he saw his mother and the disciple whom he loved standing by, said to his mother, "Woman, here is your son!" ²⁷Then he said to the disciple, "Here is your mother!" And from that hour the disciple took her into his own home. ²⁸After this Jesus, when he knew that all things had already been completed, in order that the Scripture may be fulfilled, said, "I am thirsty." ²⁹A jar full of sour wine was standing there. Then they put a sponge full of the sour wine on a branch of hyssop and brought [it] to his mouth. ³⁰So when Jesus received the sour wine, he said, "It is completed." And he bowed his head and gave up his spirit.

19:16b-17 Παρέλαβον οὖν τὸν Ἰησοῦν, καὶ βαστάζων ἑαυτῷ τὸν σταυρὸν ἐξῆλθεν εἰς τὸν λεγόμενον Κρανίου Τόπον, ὃ λέγεται Ἑβραϊστὶ Γολγοθα,

Παρέλαβον. Aor act ind 3rd pl παραλαμβάνω. The implied subject seems to be οἱ ἀρχιερεῖς as the last-mentioned group of characters (see 19:16a on αὐτοῖς). Later in the chapter (v. 23) the evangelist clarifies that the soldiers, i.e., the Romans, crucified Jesus. Some scribes tried to reduce this ambiguity by various supplementations after Ἰησοῦν: καὶ ἤγαγον (Dˢ K Δ Θ 892ˢ 1241 1424 𝔐 lat syᵖ), καὶ ἀπήγαγον (A), ἀπήγαγον (𝔓⁶⁶ᵛⁱᵈ ℵ N W f¹ 565 579 syʰ), ἀπήγαγον εἰς τὸ πραιτώριον (Γ 700), ἤγαγον καὶ ἐπέθηκαν αὐτῷ τὸν σταυρὸν (f¹³ Orˡᵃᵗ).

οὖν. Postpositive inferential conjunction and/or transitional particle (see 1:22 and 11:6).

τὸν Ἰησοῦν. Accusative direct object of Παρέλαβον.

καὶ. Coordinating conjunction.

βαστάζων. Pres act ptc masc nom sg βαστάζω (manner). On participles that precede the main verb, see ἐμβλέψας in 1:36.

ἑαυτῷ. Dative of advantage ("for himself"; BDF §188.2) or dative of agency ("by himself").

τὸν σταυρὸν. Accusative direct object of βαστάζων. σταυρός here most likely denotes the horizontal beam (Lat. *patibulum*), not the entire cross.

ἐξῆλθεν. Aor act ind 3rd sg ἐξέρχομαι.

εἰς τὸν λεγόμενον Κρανίου Τόπον. Locative. The grammar of this PP is very awkward because it is not clear what the object of the preposition is. The expression probably presumes that τὸν stands for τόπον, and some copyists corrected the text to make this clear: εἰς τόπον λεγόμενον Κρανίου (𝔓⁶⁶ᵛⁱᵈ Γ aur c ff² saᵐˢˢ bo) or εἰς τόπον λεγόμενον Κρανίου Τόπον (f¹³ 700 892ˢ 1424 *pm* it saᵐˢˢ). The parallel formulations in Mark

15:22 and Matt 27:33 use the relative clauses introduced with the formulaic phrase ὅ ἐστιν.

λεγόμενον. Pres pass ptc masc acc sg λέγω (attributive). The participle modifies the implied τόπον (see above).

Κρανίου. Epexegetical genitive, explaining Τόπον (BDF §167; BDAG, 564). Fronted for emphasis. Κρανίου ("Skull") is a Greek translation of Γολγοθα.

Τόπον. Accusative complement to the implied τόπον in a double accusative subject-complement construction (see 1:41 on χριστός). Although Τόπον does not have the article, it is definite because its qualifying genitive Κρανίου is definite (a corollary of Apollonius' canon; cf. Wallace 1996, 248–49). Κρανίου Τόπος ("Skull Place") denotes "an eminence near Jerusalem, used as a place of execution" (BDAG, 204).

ὃ λέγεται Ἑβραϊστὶ Γολγοθα. Parenthetical clause that interrupts the plot of the narrative. The purpose of this editorial gloss is to provide the Aramaic translation of the Greek name Κρανίου Τόπον. For similar parenthetical comments, see 1:38, 41, 42; 20:16.

ὅ. Nominative subject of λέγεται. The antecedent of the relative pronoun is Τόπον. ὅ is neuter rather than masculine because in explanatory phrases the neuter is used without much regard to the gender of the word that the phrase explains (Robertson, 411; BDF §132.2).

λέγεται. Pres pass ind 3rd sg λέγω.

Ἑβραϊστὶ. Adverb ("in Hebrew/Aramaic" [BDAG, 270]).

Γολγοθα. Nominative complement to ὅ in a double nominative subject-complement construction (see 1:41 on χριστός). Γολγοθα is a Greek transliteration of the Aramaic term גֻּלְגַּלְתָּא (Hebrew גֻּלְגֹּלֶת).

19:18 ὅπου αὐτὸν ἐσταύρωσαν, καὶ μετ' αὐτοῦ ἄλλους δύο ἐντεῦθεν καὶ ἐντεῦθεν, μέσον δὲ τὸν Ἰησοῦν.

ὅπου. Marker of a position in space.

αὐτὸν. Accusative direct object of ἐσταύρωσαν.

ἐσταύρωσαν. Aor act ind 3rd pl σταυρόω. On the textual level, the implied subject continues to be οἱ ἀρχιερεῖς as the last-mentioned group of characters (see 19:16a on αὐτοῖς).

καὶ. Coordinating conjunction.

μετ' αὐτοῦ. Association/accompaniment.

ἄλλους δύο. Accusative direct object of ἐσταύρωσαν.

ἐντεῦθεν καὶ ἐντεῦθεν. Adverbial phrase denoting "extension from a source near the speaker" (BDAG, 339.1): lit. "from here and from there" = "on each side."

μέσον. Accusative neuter from the adjective μέσος, which is here used as an adverb ("in the middle"; Zerwick and Grosvenor, 342). It is also possible to view μέσον as the adjective modifying Ἰησοῦν (BDAG, 634.1.a), but in that case μέσον stands in the first predicate position (adjective-article-noun), functioning as the accusative complement to τὸν Ἰησοῦν in a double accusative object-complement construction: lit. "they crucified Jesus as middle" (Wallace 1996, 307–8).

δέ. Marker of narrative development.

τὸν Ἰησοῦν. Accusative direct object of ἐσταύρωσαν.

19:19 ἔγραψεν δὲ καὶ τίτλον ὁ Πιλᾶτος καὶ ἔθηκεν ἐπὶ τοῦ σταυροῦ· ἦν δὲ γεγραμμένον· Ἰησοῦς ὁ Ναζωραῖος ὁ βασιλεὺς τῶν Ἰουδαίων.

ἔγραψεν. Aor act ind 3rd sg γράφω. ἔγραψεν is causative because Pilate did not write the inscription himself.

δέ. Marker of narrative development.

καί. Adverbial use (adjunctive).

τίτλον. Accusative direct object of ἔγραψεν. τίτλος ("inscription") is a transliteration of the Latin term *titulus*. A NT *hapax legomenon*. Mark 15:26 and Luke 23:38 use the term ἐπιγραφή, while Matt 27:37 has αἰτία.

ὁ Πιλᾶτος. Nominative subject of ἔγραψεν.

καί. Coordinating conjunction.

ἔθηκεν. Aor act ind 3rd sg τίθημι. This verb is also causative (see ἔγραψεν above).

ἐπὶ τοῦ σταυροῦ. Locative.

ἦν. Impf act ind 3rd sg εἰμί (impersonal).

δέ. Marker of narrative development.

γεγραμμένον. Prf pass ptc neut nom sg γράφω (pluperfect periphrastic). "The normal use is to denote a state which existed in the past, with implication of a prior occurrence which produced it," as here (Fanning, 320).

Ἰησοῦς ὁ Ναζωραῖος ὁ βασιλεὺς τῶν Ἰουδαίων. All versions of the inscription on the cross in the canonical Gospels (ὁ βασιλεὺς τῶν Ἰουδαίων [Mark 15:26]; οὗτός ἐστιν Ἰησοῦς ὁ βασιλεὺς τῶν Ἰουδαίων [Matt 27:37]; ὁ βασιλεὺς τῶν Ἰουδαίων οὗτος [Luke 23:38]) agree that the official accusation against Jesus for which he was crucified was the claim that he was ὁ βασιλεὺς τῶν Ἰουδαίων ("the King of the Jews").

Ἰησοῦς. Nominative absolute.

ὁ Ναζωραῖος. Nominative in apposition to Ἰησοῦς. On the meaning of ὁ Ναζωραῖος, see 18:5.

ὁ βασιλεύς. Nominative in apposition to Ἰησοῦς.

τῶν Ἰουδαίων. Genitive of subordination qualifying βασιλεύς.

19:20 τοῦτον οὖν τὸν τίτλον πολλοὶ ἀνέγνωσαν τῶν Ἰουδαίων, ὅτι ἐγγὺς ἦν ὁ τόπος τῆς πόλεως ὅπου ἐσταυρώθη ὁ Ἰησοῦς· καὶ ἦν γεγραμμένον Ἑβραϊστί, Ῥωμαϊστί, Ἑλληνιστί.

τοῦτον ... τὸν τίτλον. Accusative direct object of ἀνέγνωσαν. Fronted as a topical frame.

οὖν. Postpositive inferential conjunction and/or transitional particle (see 1:22 and 11:6).

πολλοί. Nominative subject of ἀνέγνωσαν.

ἀνέγνωσαν. Aor act ind 3rd pl ἀναγινώσκω.

τῶν Ἰουδαίων. Partitive genitive qualifying πολλοί.

ὅτι. Introduces a causal clause.

ἐγγὺς ... τῆς πόλεως. Locative. ἐγγύς is an adverb that here functions as an improper preposition (see 1:3 on χωρὶς αὐτοῦ) indicating close spatial proximity (BDAG, 271.1.b).

ἦν. Impf act ind 3rd sg εἰμί. On the function of the imperfect in the FG, see 1:39 on ἦν.

ὁ τόπος. Nominative subject of ἦν.

ὅπου. Marker of a position in space.

ἐσταυρώθη. Aor pass ind 3rd sg σταυρόω.

ὁ Ἰησοῦς. Nominative subject of ἐσταυρώθη.

καί. Coordinating conjunction.

ἦν. Impf act ind 3rd sg εἰμί (impersonal).

γεγραμμένον. Prf pass ptc neut nom sg γράφω (pluperfect periphrastic); see the previous verse.

Ἑβραϊστί, Ῥωμαϊστί, Ἑλληνιστί. The arrangement of these three adverbs ("in Hebrew/Aramaic" [BDAG, 270], "in Latin" [908], "in Greek" [319]) represents the sequence "the national language, the official language, the common language." Some copyists, however, altered it into the sequence "in Hebrew, in Greek, in Latin" (A D^s K Γ Θ f^1 565 700 892^s 1241 1424 𝔐 lat sy) to reflect the geographical order from East to West (Metzger, 217).

19:21 ἔλεγον οὖν τῷ Πιλάτῳ οἱ ἀρχιερεῖς τῶν Ἰουδαίων· μὴ γράφε· ὁ βασιλεὺς τῶν Ἰουδαίων, ἀλλ' ὅτι ἐκεῖνος εἶπεν· βασιλεύς εἰμι τῶν Ἰουδαίων.

ἔλεγον. Impf act ind 3rd pl λέγω. On the function of the imperfect in the FG, see 1:39 on ἦν.

οὖν. Postpositive inferential conjunction and/or transitional particle (see 1:22 and 11:6).

τῷ Πιλάτῳ. Dative indirect object of ἔλεγον.

οἱ ἀρχιερεῖς. Nominative subject of ἔλεγον.

τῶν Ἰουδαίων. Genitive of subordination or partitive genitive qualifying ἀρχιερεῖς.

μὴ ... ἀλλ'. A point/counterpoint set ("not this ... but that") that seeks to replace Pilate's inscription asserting that Jesus is the King of the Jews with the inscription asserting that Jesus merely claims to be the King of the Jews. On the function of ἀλλά in a point/counterpoint set, see 1:8.

γράφε. Pres act impv 2nd sg γράφω. The present prohibition μὴ γράφε does not mean to stop writing the inscription because v. 19 indicates that this act has already been completed (see Wallace 1996, 717 n. 15, for a critique of the traditional view). It means, rather, to remove the original inscription: "Do not leave it written" (Brown, 2:897) or "Alter what you have written" (MHT, 3:76).

ὁ βασιλεὺς. Nominative absolute.

τῶν Ἰουδαίων. Genitive of subordination qualifying βασιλεὺς.

ὅτι. Introduces the clausal complement (direct discourse) of γράφε.

ἐκεῖνος. Nominative subject of εἶπεν. The far-demonstrative pronoun is here used as a contemptuous reference to Jesus. Contemptuous sense, however, is not a semantic value of ἐκεῖνος but a pragmatic effect that results from the use of the athematic demonstrative for a thematic participant (Runge 2010, 373).

εἶπεν. Aor act ind 3rd sg λέγω.

βασιλεύς. Predicate nominative. Fronted for emphasis. Although βασιλεύς is anarthrous, it is most likely definite like ὁ βασιλεὺς in the original inscription because, according to Colwell's rule, the definiteness of a preverbal anarthrous predicate nominative cannot be excluded (see 1:1 on θεὸς).

εἰμι. Pres act ind 1st sg εἰμί.

τῶν Ἰουδαίων. Genitive of subordination qualifying βασιλεύς.

19:22 ἀπεκρίθη ὁ Πιλᾶτος· ὃ γέγραφα, γέγραφα.

ἀπεκρίθη. Aor mid ind 3rd sg ἀποκρίνομαι. On the voice, see "Deponency" in the Series Introduction. This verse is connected to the previous one by asyndeton.

ὁ Πιλᾶτος. Nominative subject of ἀπεκρίθη.

ὅ. Introduces a headless relative clause that, in its entirety (ὃ γέγραφα), serves as the direct object of the second γέγραφα. Within its clause, ὅ is the accusative direct object of the first γέγραφα.

γέγραφα. Prf act ind 1st sg γράφω. The emphasis of this perfect tense falls on the past act of writing (BDF §342.4).

γέγραφα. Prf act ind 1st sg γράφω. The verb stands in final, emphatic position. The emphasis of this perfect tense falls on the current state of affairs created by the past act of writing (e.g., "What I have written stays written" [GNT]).

19:23 Οἱ οὖν στρατιῶται, ὅτε ἐσταύρωσαν τὸν Ἰησοῦν, ἔλαβον τὰ ἱμάτια αὐτοῦ καὶ ἐποίησαν τέσσαρα μέρη, ἑκάστῳ στρατιώτῃ μέρος, καὶ τὸν χιτῶνα. ἦν δὲ ὁ χιτὼν ἄραφος, ἐκ τῶν ἄνωθεν ὑφαντὸς δι' ὅλου.

Οἱ ... στρατιῶται. Nominative subject of ἔλαβον.

οὖν. Postpositive inferential conjunction and/or transitional particle (see 1:22 and 11:6).

ὅτε. Introduces a temporal clause.

ἐσταύρωσαν. Aor act ind 3rd pl σταυρόω.

τὸν Ἰησοῦν. Accusative direct object of ἐσταύρωσαν.

ἔλαβον. Aor act ind 3rd pl λαμβάνω.

τὰ ἱμάτια. Accusative direct object of ἔλαβον. The singular ἱμάτιον always denotes the outer garment, while the plural ἱμάτια could be used for clothing in general, as here.

αὐτοῦ. Possessive genitive qualifying ἱμάτια.

καί. Coordinating conjunction.

ἐποίησαν. Aor act ind 3rd pl ποιέω.

τέσσαρα μέρη. Accusative direct object of ἐποίησαν.

ἑκάστῳ στρατιώτῃ. Dative of advantage.

μέρος. Accusative in apposition to μέρη.

καί. Adverbial (adjunctive).

τὸν χιτῶνα. Accusative direct object of an implied ἔλαβον. χιτών ("tunic, shirt") denotes "a garment worn next to the skin" (BDAG, 1085).

ἦν. Impf act ind 3rd sg εἰμί. On the function of the imperfect in the FG, see 1:39 on ἦν.

δέ. Marker of narrative development.

ὁ χιτών. Nominative subject of ἦν.

ἄραφος. Predicate adjective ("seamless"). A NT *hapax legomenon*.

ἐκ τῶν ἄνωθεν. Source, indicating the beginning of weaving ("from the top"). The article functions as a nominalizer, changing the adverb ἄνωθεν ("from above") into the object of the preposition ἐκ.

ὑφαντός. Predicate adjective ("woven"). A NT *hapax legomenon*.

δι' ὅλου. Spatial. ὅλου functions as a substantive: "through the whole" = "throughout."

19:24 εἶπαν οὖν πρὸς ἀλλήλους· μὴ σχίσωμεν αὐτόν, ἀλλὰ λάχωμεν περὶ αὐτοῦ τίνος ἔσται· ἵνα ἡ γραφὴ πληρωθῇ [ἡ λέγουσα]· διεμερίσαντο τὰ ἱμάτιά μου ἑαυτοῖς καὶ ἐπὶ τὸν ἱματισμόν μου ἔβαλον κλῆρον. Οἱ μὲν οὖν στρατιῶται ταῦτα ἐποίησαν.

εἶπαν. Aor act ind 3rd pl λέγω.

οὖν. Postpositive inferential conjunction and/or transitional particle (see 1:22 and 11:6).

πρὸς ἀλλήλους. Locative (motion toward). The PP functions like an indirect object of εἶπαν.

μὴ ... ἀλλὰ. A point/counterpoint set ("not this ... but that") that replaces the idea to tear Jesus' tunic with the suggestion to cast lots for it. On the function of ἀλλά in a point/counterpoint set, see 1:8.

σχίσωμεν. Aor act subj 1st pl σχίζω (hortatory subjunctive).

αὐτόν. Accusative direct object of σχίσωμεν.

λάχωμεν. Aor act subj 1st pl λαγχάνω (hortatory subjunctive).

περὶ αὐτοῦ. Reference. αὐτοῦ refers to ὁ χιτὼν in v. 23.

τίνος. Possessive genitive qualifying the implied χιτών.

ἔσται. Fut mid ind 3rd sg εἰμί.

ἵνα ἡ γραφὴ πληρωθῇ [ἡ λέγουσα]. This OT introductory formula and its variations—ἵνα ἡ γραφὴ πληρωθῇ (13:18; 17:12; 19:36), ἵνα ὁ λόγος Ἡσαΐου τοῦ προφήτου πληρωθῇ (12:38), and ἵνα πληρωθῇ ὁ λόγος (15:25)—occur only in the FG. The formula typically precedes the scriptural quotation, as here.

ἵνα. Introduces a purpose clause. The ἵνα clause is elliptical, requiring an introduction, such as τοῦτο γέγονεν. Alternatively, but less likely, the ἵνα clause functions as a substitute for the imperative: "But let the Scripture be fulfilled" (Turner 1965, 147–48).

ἡ γραφὴ. Nominative subject of πληρωθῇ.

πληρωθῇ. Aor pass subj 3rd sg πληρόω. Subjunctive with ἵνα.

[ἡ λέγουσα]. Pres act ptc fem nom sg λέγω (attributive). The participle modifies ἡ γραφὴ, standing in the second attributive position (see 1:29 on ὁ αἴρων). It is placed within square brackets because it is not easy to decide whether this is an explanatory addition (A D^s K L N W Γ Θ Ψ $f^{1.13}$ 33 565 579 700 892^s 1241 1424 𝔐 lat sy^h sa^{mss} bo) or an intentional omission (ℵ B *l*844 it sa^{mss} ly pbo) to adjust the OT introductory formula to the wording in 13:18, 17:12, and 19:36 (Metzger, 217).

διεμερίσαντο τὰ ἱμάτιά μου ἑαυτοῖς καὶ ἐπὶ τὸν ἱματισμόν μου ἔβαλον κλῆρον. A verbatim quotation of LXX Ps 21:19 (διεμερίσαντο τὰ ἱμάτιά μου ἑαυτοῖς καὶ ἐπὶ τὸν ἱματισμόν μου ἔβαλον κλῆρον), which is a literal translation of the MT (Ps 22:19).

διεμερίσαντο. Aor mid ind 3rd pl διαμερίζω. The middle voice conveys a reflexive relationship: "divide among themselves" (BDAG, 233.2).

τὰ ἱμάτια. Accusative direct object of διεμερίσαντο. ἱμάτια, which has an acute accent on the antepenult, acquired an additional accent, the acute, on the ultima from the enclitic μου (Smyth §183; Carson 1985, 48).

μου. Possessive genitive qualifying ἱμάτια.

ἑαυτοῖς. Dative complement of διεμερίσαντο. The reflexive pronoun reinforces the reflexive relationship already expressed through διεμερίσαντο; BDF (§310.2) calls it "doubly reflexive."

καὶ. Coordinating conjunction.

ἐπὶ τὸν ἱματισμόν. Reference, indicating for what something is done (BDAG, 366.14.b.α).

μου. Possessive genitive qualifying ἱματισμόν.

ἔβαλον. Aor act ind 3rd pl βάλλω.

κλῆρον. Accusative direct object of ἔβαλον.

Οἱ... στρατιῶται. Nominative subject of ἐποίησαν.

μὲν οὖν. While in classical Greek this combination of particles is affirmative ("indeed"), in the NT it is usually resumptive ("so then"), as here (MHT 3:337).

ταῦτα. Accusative direct object of ἐποίησαν.

ἐποίησαν. Aor act ind 3rd pl ποιέω.

19:25 Εἱστήκεισαν δὲ παρὰ τῷ σταυρῷ τοῦ Ἰησοῦ ἡ μήτηρ αὐτοῦ καὶ ἡ ἀδελφὴ τῆς μητρὸς αὐτοῦ, Μαρία ἡ τοῦ Κλωπᾶ καὶ Μαρία ἡ Μαγδαληνή.

Εἱστήκεισαν. Plprf act ind 3rd pl ἵστημι. The pluperfect tense of ἵστημι has the imperfect meaning.

δὲ. Marker of narrative development.

παρὰ τῷ σταυρῷ. Locative. With dative, the preposition παρά indicates nearness in space: "at/by (the side of), beside, near, with" (BDAG, 757.B.1).

τοῦ Ἰησοῦ. Possessive genitive broadly defined qualifying σταυρῷ ("Jesus' cross" = "the cross on which Jesus was crucified").

ἡ μήτηρ... καὶ ἡ ἀδελφὴ... Μαρία... καὶ Μαρία. Compound nominative subject of Εἱστήκεισαν, consisting of four women. The absence of καί between the second and the third woman divides the group into two pairs. The women in the first pair are not named but are identified only through their relationships to Jesus and to each other. Since both women in the second pair have the same name, the first Mary is identified through her marriage and the second Mary through her place of origin. The absence of καί between the second and the third woman raises the possibility that Μαρία ἡ τοῦ Κλωπᾶ could be the apposition to ἡ ἀδελφὴ τῆς μητρὸς αὐτοῦ, but this is unlikely because this would mean that both Jesus' mother and her sister are named Mary. It is even less likely that only two women are meant—the first pair describing their relationship and the second pair providing their names—because Mary Magdalene would then be the sister of Jesus' mother, i.e., Jesus' aunt (Brown, 2:904–5; Schnackenburg 3:276–77).

αὐτοῦ. Genitive of relationship qualifying ἡ μήτηρ ("his mother").

τῆς μητρὸς. Genitive of relationship qualifying ἡ ἀδελφὴ ("the sister of the mother").

αὐτοῦ. Genitive of relationship qualifying τῆς μητρὸς ("of his mother"). ἡ ἀδελφὴ τῆς μητρὸς αὐτοῦ = "the sister of his mother."

ἡ. The article functions as a nominalizer, changing the genitive noun τοῦ Κλωπᾶ into the nominative in apposition to the first Μαρία (lit. "the one of Clopas"). Since the genitive noun most likely conveys marital relationship, the nominalized expression assumes the word γυνή after the article ("the wife of Clopas"). In the NT, the article followed by the genitive is frequently used to express personal relationships, such as son(s) (Mark 1:19; 2:14; 3:17, 18; 10:2; John 21:2), wife (John 19:25), mother (Matt 1:6), or disciples (Luke 5:33).

τοῦ Κλωπᾶ. Genitive of relationship qualifying the implied γυνή.

ἡ Μαγδαληνή. Nominative in apposition to the second Μαρία. Μαγδαληνή means "woman from Magdala" (BDAG, 608). It functions as a surname of this Mary, distinguishing her from other Marys in the NT. This is the first mention of Mary Magdalene in the FG.

19:26 Ἰησοῦς οὖν ἰδὼν τὴν μητέρα καὶ τὸν μαθητὴν παρεστῶτα ὃν ἠγάπα, λέγει τῇ μητρί· γύναι, ἴδε ὁ υἱός σου.

Ἰησοῦς. Nominative subject of λέγει.

οὖν. Postpositive inferential conjunction and/or transitional particle (see 1:22 and 11:6).

ἰδὼν. Aor act ptc masc nom sg ὁράω (temporal). On participles that precede the main verb, see ἐμβλέψας in 1:36.

τὴν μητέρα. The first accusative direct object of ἰδὼν. The article is here used as a possessive pronoun ("his mother"; cf. Harris 2015, 316).

καὶ. Coordinating conjunction.

τὸν μαθητὴν. The second accusative direct object of ἰδὼν in a double accusative object-complement construction (see παρεστῶτα below).

παρεστῶτα. Prf act ptc masc acc sg παρίστημι (predicative). Accusative complement to τὸν μαθητὴν in a double accusative object-complement construction.

ὅν. Accusative direct object of ἠγάπα. The antecedent of the relative pronoun is τὸν μαθητήν.

ἠγάπα. Impf act ind 3rd sg ἀγαπάω. On the use of ἀγαπάω to identify the Beloved Disciple in the FG, see 13:23.

λέγει. Pres act ind 3rd sg λέγω. The historical present gives prominence to Jesus' instruction to his mother (see 1:15 on μαρτυρεῖ).

τῇ μητρί. Dative indirect object of λέγει. The article is again used as a possessive pronoun.

γύναι. Vocative of direct address. On Jesus' use of this term to address his mother in the FG, see 2:4.

ἴδε. An interjection (originally aor act impv 2nd sg ὁράω) that is used "when that which is to be observed is in the nom[inative]" (BDAG, 466). This interjection here serves "to indicate a place or individual" and can be translated "here is" (BDAG, 466.3).

ὁ υἱός. Nominative of exclamation (see 1:29 on ὁ ἀμνὸς).

σου. Genitive of relationship qualifying υἱός.

19:27 εἶτα λέγει τῷ μαθητῇ· ἴδε ἡ μήτηρ σου. καὶ ἀπ' ἐκείνης τῆς ὥρας ἔλαβεν ὁ μαθητὴς αὐτὴν εἰς τὰ ἴδια.

εἶτα. Adverb ("then, next").

λέγει. Pres act ind 3rd sg λέγω. The historical present gives prominence to Jesus' instruction to the Beloved Disciple (see 1:15 on μαρτυρεῖ).

τῷ μαθητῇ. Dative indirect object of λέγει.

ἴδε. See 19:26.

ἡ μήτηρ. Nominative of exclamation (see 1:29 on ὁ ἀμνὸς).

σου. Genitive of relationship qualifying μήτηρ.

καί. Coordinating conjunction.

ἀπ' ἐκείνης τῆς ὥρας. Temporal ("from that hour").

ἔλαβεν. Aor act ind 3rd sg λαμβάνω.

ὁ μαθητής. Nominative subject of ἔλαβεν.

αὐτήν. Accusative direct object of ἔλαβεν. The personal pronoun refers to Jesus' mother.

εἰς τὰ ἴδια. Locative. In this context, τὰ ἴδια means "one's own home" (BDAG, 467.4.b).

19:28 Μετὰ τοῦτο εἰδὼς ὁ Ἰησοῦς ὅτι ἤδη πάντα τετέλεσται, ἵνα τελειωθῇ ἡ γραφή, λέγει· διψῶ.

Μετὰ τοῦτο. Temporal. The demonstrative pronoun refers to Jesus' instructions to his mother and the Beloved Disciple. This verse is connected to the previous one by asyndeton.

εἰδώς. Prf act ptc masc nom sg οἶδα (temporal or causal). On participles that precede the main verb, see ἐμβλέψας in 1:36.

ὁ Ἰησοῦς. Nominative subject of λέγει.

ὅτι. Introduces the clausal complement (indirect discourse) of εἰδώς.

ἤδη. Adverb ("already").

πάντα. Nominative subject of τετέλεσται.

τετέλεσται. Prf pass ind 3rd sg τελέω. Neuter plural subjects typically take singular verbs (see 1:28 on ἐγένετο).

ἵνα τελειωθῇ ἡ γραφή. This OT introductory formula is found nowhere else in the NT. The formula precedes the scriptural reference, but since no actual text is quoted, the scriptural source is unknown. Possible candidates are LXX Pss 68:22; 62:2; or 41:3.

ἵνα. Introduces a purpose clause.

τελειωθῇ. Aor pass subj 3rd sg τελειόω. Subjunctive with ἵνα.

ἡ γραφή. Nominative subject of τελειωθῇ.

λέγει. Pres act ind 3rd sg λέγω. The historical present marks the narrative transition to a new scene and gives prominence to Jesus' expression of thirst (see 1:15 on μαρτυρεῖ).

διψῶ. Pres act ind 1st sg διψάω.

19:29 σκεῦος ἔκειτο ὄξους μεστόν· σπόγγον οὖν μεστὸν τοῦ ὄξους ὑσσώπῳ περιθέντες προσήνεγκαν αὐτοῦ τῷ στόματι.

σκεῦος . . . μεστόν. Nominative subject of ἔκειτο. The adjective μεστόν ("full") stands in the fourth attributive position (see 3:15 on ζωὴν αἰώνιον). This verse is connected to the previous one by asyndeton.

ἔκειτο. Impf mid ind 3rd sg κεῖμαι. This imperfect, which interrupts the main storyline, is used to provide background information about the physical environment of the crucifixion (du Toit, 223).

ὄξους. Genitive complement of μεστόν. ὄξος denotes "sour wine, wine vinegar," which "relieved thirst more effectively than water and, being cheaper than regular wine, . . . was a favorite beverage of the lower ranks of society and of those in moderate circumstances" (BDAG, 715).

σπόγγον . . . μεστόν. Accusative direct object of περιθέντες. μεστόν again stands in the fourth attributive position (see 3:15 on ζωὴν αἰώνιον).

The term σπόγγος ("sponge") is used in the NT only in the crucifixion scene (Matt 27:48; Mark 15:36; John 19:29).

οὖν. Postpositive inferential conjunction and/or transitional particle (see 1:22 and 11:6).

τοῦ ὄξους. Genitive complement of μεστόν. The article is anaphoric, referring to the ὄξους that was introduced in the previous clause.

ὑσσώπῳ. Dative complement of περιθέντες. A Hebrew loan word ὕσσωπος or ὕσσωπον ("hyssop") denotes "a small aromatic bush, the branches of which were often used by the Jews in religious ceremonies" (LN 3.26).

περιθέντες. Aor act ptc masc nom pl περιτίθημι (attendant circumstance). On participles that precede the main verb, see ἐμβλέψας in 1:36.

προσήνεγκαν. Aor act ind 3rd pl προσφέρω. The implied direct object is σπόγγον.

αὐτοῦ. Possessive genitive qualifying στόματι. The preposed pronoun is thematically salient (Levinsohn 2000, 64).

τῷ στόματι. Dative indirect object of προσήνεγκαν.

19:30 ὅτε οὖν ἔλαβεν τὸ ὄξος [ὁ] Ἰησοῦς εἶπεν· τετέλεσται, καὶ κλίνας τὴν κεφαλὴν παρέδωκεν τὸ πνεῦμα.

ὅτε. Introduces a temporal clause, which is fronted as a temporal frame.

οὖν. Postpositive inferential conjunction and/or transitional particle (see 1:22 and 11:6).

ἔλαβεν. Aor act ind 3rd sg λαμβάνω.

τὸ ὄξος. Accusative direct object of ἔλαβεν.

[ὁ] Ἰησοῦς. Nominative subject of ἔλαβεν. The article is omitted in Vaticanus and Washingtonianus and the entire noun phrase in Sinaiticus.

εἶπεν. Aor act ind 3rd sg λέγω.

τετέλεσται. Prf pass ind 3rd sg τελέω (see 19:28).

καί. Coordinating conjunction.

κλίνας. Aor act ptc masc nom sg κλίνω (attendant circumstance). On participles that precede the main verb, see ἐμβλέψας in 1:36.

τὴν κεφαλήν. Accusative direct object of κλίνας. The article is used as a possessive pronoun.

παρέδωκεν. Aor act ind 3rd sg παραδίδωμι.

τὸ πνεῦμα. Accusative direct object of παρέδωκεν. παραδίδωμι τὸ πνεῦμα (lit. "to give over the spirit") is an idiom for "to die, with the possible implication of a willing or voluntary act" (LN 23.110).

John 19:31-37

31Then the Jews, since it was the day of preparation, in order that the bodies may not remain on the cross, for the day of that Sabbath was special, asked Pilate that their legs might be broken and they might be taken away. **32**So the soldiers came and broke the legs of the first and of the other who had been crucified with him. **33**Yet when they came to Jesus, after they saw him already dead, they did not break his legs. **34**But one of the soldiers pierced his side with a spear, and at once blood and water came out. **35**And the one who has seen [it] has testified, and his testimony is true, and he knows that he is telling the truth, so that you also may believe. **36**For these things took place in order that the Scripture may be fulfilled, "Not a bone of his will be broken." **37**And again another Scripture says, "They will look on the one whom they have pierced."

19:31 Οἱ οὖν Ἰουδαῖοι, ἐπεὶ παρασκευὴ ἦν, ἵνα μὴ μείνῃ ἐπὶ τοῦ σταυροῦ τὰ σώματα ἐν τῷ σαββάτῳ, ἦν γὰρ μεγάλη ἡ ἡμέρα ἐκείνου τοῦ σαββάτου, ἠρώτησαν τὸν Πιλᾶτον ἵνα κατεαγῶσιν αὐτῶν τὰ σκέλη καὶ ἀρθῶσιν.

> **Οἱ ... Ἰουδαῖοι.** Nominative subject of ἠρώτησαν.
>
> **οὖν.** Postpositive inferential conjunction and/or transitional particle (see 1:22 and 11:6).
>
> **ἐπεὶ.** Causal conjunction.
>
> **παρασκευὴ.** Nominative subject of ἦν.
>
> **ἦν.** Impf act ind 3rd sg εἰμί. On the function of the imperfect in the FG, see 1:39 on ἦν.
>
> **ἵνα.** Introduces a purpose clause, which is placed before the main clause to which it is related (ἠρώτησαν τὸν Πιλᾶτον).
>
> **μὴ.** Negative particle normally used with non-indicative verbs.
>
> **μείνῃ.** Aor act subj 3rd sg μένω. Subjunctive with ἵνα. Neuter plural subjects typically take singular verbs (see 1:28 on ἐγένετο).
>
> **ἐπὶ τοῦ σταυροῦ.** Locative.
>
> **τὰ σώματα.** Nominative subject of μείνῃ.
>
> **ἐν τῷ σαββάτῳ.** Temporal.
>
> **ἦν.** Impf act ind 3rd sg εἰμί. On the function of the imperfect in the FG, see 1:39 on ἦν.
>
> **γὰρ.** Postpositive conjunction that introduces the explanation of the previous ἵνα clause.
>
> **μεγάλη.** Predicate adjective.
>
> **ἡ ἡμέρα.** Nominative subject of ἦν.

ἐκείνου τοῦ σαββάτου. Epexegetical genitive, clarifying ἡμέρα ("the day, which was that Sabbath"). In this type of genitive construction, the head noun states a large category, "while the genitive names a concrete or specific example that . . . falls *within* that category" (Wallace 1996, 95).

ἠρώτησαν. Aor act ind 3rd pl ἐρωτάω.

τὸν Πιλᾶτον. Accusative direct object of ἠρώτησαν.

ἵνα. Introduces a direct object clause (also known as a "content ἵνα clause") of ἠρώτησαν. "In this usage the direct object often follows a verb of commanding, urging, praying. The ἵνα clause gives the content to the main verb and in this respect answers the question *What?* rather than *Why?*" (Wallace 1996, 475).

κατεαγῶσιν. Aor pass subj 3rd pl κατάγνυμι. Subjunctive with ἵνα.

αὐτῶν. Possessive genitive qualifying σκέλη. The preposed pronoun is thematically salient (Levinsohn 2000, 64).

τὰ σκέλη. Nominative subject of κατεαγῶσιν.

καί. Coordinating conjunction.

ἀρθῶσιν. Aor pass subj 3rd pl αἴρω. Subjunctive with ἵνα. The implied subject of ἀρθῶσιν is τὰ σώματα. Here this neuter plural noun takes a plural verb although earlier in this verse it took singular (μείνῃ).

19:32 ἦλθον οὖν οἱ στρατιῶται καὶ τοῦ μὲν πρώτου κατέαξαν τὰ σκέλη καὶ τοῦ ἄλλου τοῦ συσταυρωθέντος αὐτῷ·

ἦλθον. Aor act ind 3rd pl ἔρχομαι.

οὖν. Postpositive inferential conjunction and/or transitional particle (see 1:22 and 11:6).

οἱ στρατιῶται. Nominative subject of ἦλθον.

καί. Coordinating conjunction.

τοῦ . . . πρώτου. Possessive genitive qualifying τὰ σκέλη. Fronted for emphasis.

μέν. Correlative particle that is usually combined with δέ, but in this instance δέ is omitted. The use of anacoluthic μέν (without correlative δέ) represents "a more or less serious breach of good sentence structure" (BDF §447.3).

κατέαξαν. Aor act ind 3rd pl κατάγνυμι.

τὰ σκέλη. Accusative direct object of κατέαξαν.

καί. Coordinating conjunction.

τοῦ ἄλλου. Possessive genitive qualifying the implied τὰ σκέλη. ἄλλος stands for ἕτερος.

τοῦ συσταυρωθέντος. Aor pass ptc masc gen sg συσταυρόω (attributive). The participle modifies τοῦ ἄλλου, standing in the second attributive position (see 1:29 on ὁ αἴρων).

αὐτῷ. Dative complement of συσταυρωθέντος. The personal pronoun refers to τοῦ ... πρώτου.

19:33 ἐπὶ δὲ τὸν Ἰησοῦν ἐλθόντες, ὡς εἶδον ἤδη αὐτὸν τεθνηκότα, οὐ κατέαξαν αὐτοῦ τὰ σκέλη,

ἐπὶ ... τὸν Ἰησοῦν. Locative, indicating motion in a particular direction ("to, toward"; BDAG, 364.4.b.α).

δὲ. Marker of narrative development with a contrastive nuance.

ἐλθόντες. Aor act ptc masc nom pl ἔρχομαι (temporal). On participles that precede the main verb, see ἐμβλέψας in 1:36.

ὡς. Temporal conjunction (BDAG, 1105.8.a) that "may have almost the force of a causal particle" (Robertson, 963).

εἶδον. Aor act ind 3rd pl ὁράω.

ἤδη. Adverb ("already").

αὐτὸν. Accusative direct object of εἶδον in a double accusative object-complement construction.

τεθνηκότα. Prf act ptc masc acc sg θνῄσκω (predicative). Accusative complement to αὐτὸν in a double accusative object-complement construction.

οὐ ... ἀλλ'. A point/counterpoint set ("not this ... but that") that replaces one action (breaking Jesus' legs) with another action (piercing his side).

κατέαξαν. Aor act ind 3rd pl κατάγνυμι.

αὐτοῦ. Possessive genitive qualifying τὰ σκέλη. The preposed pronoun is thematically salient (Levinsohn 2000, 64).

τὰ σκέλη. Accusative direct object of κατέαξαν.

19:34 ἀλλ' εἷς τῶν στρατιωτῶν λόγχῃ αὐτοῦ τὴν πλευρὰν ἔνυξεν, καὶ ἐξῆλθεν εὐθὺς αἷμα καὶ ὕδωρ.

ἀλλ'. Second element of the οὐ ... ἀλλ' point/counterpoint set that begins in the previous verse.

εἷς. Nominative subject of ἔνυξεν.

τῶν στρατιωτῶν. Partitive genitive qualifying εἷς.

λόγχῃ. Dative of means/instrument. λόγχη refers to "a long weapon with sharpened end used for piercing by thrusting or as a projectile by hurling—'spear'" (LN 6.34).

αὐτοῦ. Possessive genitive qualifying τὴν πλευρὰν.

τὴν πλευρὰν. Accusative direct object of ἔνυξεν. πλευρά denotes "either side of the trunk of the body" (LN 8.41).

ἔνυξεν. Aor act ind 3rd sg νύσσω. νύσσω means "to prick, to pierce" (LN 19.15).

καὶ. Coordinating conjunction.

ἐξῆλθεν. Aor act ind 3rd sg ἐξέρχομαι.

εὐθὺς. Temporal adverb.

αἷμα καὶ ὕδωρ. Compound nominative subject of ἐξῆλθεν. When the verb precedes its two (or more) subjects, as here, it is in the singular, agreeing with the first (BDF §135). Louw and Nida remark that "[t]he real reference of ὕδωρ in Jn 19.34 is to the lymph fluid and not to water as such. It is simply a colorless fluid which was mixed with blood" (LN 8.64).

19:35 καὶ ὁ ἑωρακὼς μεμαρτύρηκεν, καὶ ἀληθινὴ αὐτοῦ ἐστιν ἡ μαρτυρία, καὶ ἐκεῖνος οἶδεν ὅτι ἀληθῆ λέγει, ἵνα καὶ ὑμεῖς πιστεύ[σ]ητε.

καὶ. Coordinating conjunction.

ὁ ἑωρακώς. Prf act ptc masc nom sg ὁράω (substantival). Nominative subject of μεμαρτύρηκεν.

μεμαρτύρηκεν. Prf act ind 3rd sg μαρτυρέω. The clause ὁ ἑωρακὼς μεμαρτύρηκεν refers to an eyewitness testimony.

καὶ. Coordinating conjunction.

ἀληθινή. Predicate adjective. Fronted for emphasis.

αὐτοῦ. Subjective genitive qualifying ἡ μαρτυρία. The preposed pronoun is thematically salient (Levinsohn 2000, 64). The antecedent of αὐτοῦ is ὁ ἑωρακώς.

ἐστιν. Pres act ind 3rd sg εἰμί.

ἡ μαρτυρία. Nominative subject of ἐστιν.

καὶ. Coordinating conjunction.

ἐκεῖνος. Nominative subject of οἶδεν. The demonstrative pronoun refers back to αὐτοῦ, acting as a third-person personal pronoun with a simple anaphoric force (Wallace 1996, 328–29). Some scholars, however, think that ἐκεῖνος must be someone else who is, as Bultmann (678) argues, "in a position to guarantee the truth of the testimony." The candidates include the writer of the FG (who is distinguished from the Beloved Disciple), Jesus himself, and God (Brown, 3:936–37; Barrett, 557–58). The main weakness of these suggestions is that they are not corroborated by the context. Moreover, the anaphoric use of ἐκεῖνος as a third-person pronoun is well attested in the FG (e.g., 1:8; 2:21; 3:30; 4:25; 5:19, 38, 43, 46; 6:29; 7:11; 8:42, 44; 13:25, 30; 16:8, 13, 14; 18:17,

25). It is therefore best to conclude that here ἐκεῖνος also functions in this way.

οἶδεν. Prf act ind 3rd sg οἶδα (see 1:26 on οἴδατε).

ὅτι. Introduces the clausal complement (indirect discourse) of οἶδεν.

ἀληθῆ. Accusative direct object of λέγει. The adjective ἀληθῆ is neuter plural of ἀληθής ("true"), which here functions as a substantive: lit. "what is true" = "the truth."

λέγει. Pres act ind 3rd sg λέγω.

ἵνα. Introduces a purpose clause.

καὶ. Adverbial use (adjunctive).

ὑμεῖς. Nominative subject of πιστεύ[σ]ητε.

πιστεύ[σ]ητε. Aor act subj 2nd pl (with σ) or pres act subj 2nd pl (without σ) πιστεύω. Subjunctive with ἵνα. Campbell (2007, 178) calls this kind of discourse "authorial discourse" because the author addresses the audience directly "as though his were one of the voices of the narrative" (see 20:31 for another example of "authorial discourse"). The letter σ is printed within square brackets because the manuscript evidence for its inclusion (ℵ[1] A D[s] K L N W Γ Δ Θ $f^{1.13}$ 33 565 579 700 892[s] 1241 1424 l844 𝔐) and its omission (ℵ* B Ψ Or) is inconclusive. Traditionally, the aorist subjunctive has been understood as an address to non-Christians, calling them to come to faith, and the present subjunctive as an address to those who already believe, seeking to strengthen their faith (Metzger, 219). From the verbal aspect point of view, the difference between the aorist and present subjunctives is aspectual: the former portrays believing as a complete experience of faith, while the latter portrays it as an ongoing process.

19:36 ἐγένετο γὰρ ταῦτα ἵνα ἡ γραφὴ πληρωθῇ· ὀστοῦν οὐ συντριβήσεται αὐτοῦ.

ἐγένετο. Aor mid ind 3rd sg γίνομαι. Neuter plural subjects typically take singular verbs (see 1:28 on ἐγένετο).

γὰρ. Postpositive conjunction that introduces the explanation of the events described in vv. 33-34.

ταῦτα. Nominative subject of ἐγένετο.

ἵνα ἡ γραφὴ πληρωθῇ. This introductory formula is used nowhere else in the NT except in the FG, where it occurs four times (13:18; 17:12; 19:24, 36). It typically precedes the scriptural quotation, as here.

ἵνα. Introduces a purpose clause.

ἡ γραφὴ. Nominative subject of πληρωθῇ.

πληρωθῇ. Aor pass subj 3rd sg πληρόω. Subjunctive with ἵνα. The verb stands in final, emphatic position.

ὀστοῦν οὐ συντριβήσεται αὐτοῦ. A free quotation based on LXX Exod 12:10 (ὀστοῦν οὐ συντρίψετε ἀπ' αὐτοῦ), 46; Num 9:12 (ὀστοῦν οὐ συντρίψουσιν ἀπ' αὐτοῦ); and/or Ps 33:21 (πάντα τὰ ὀστᾶ αὐτῶν ἓν ἐξ αὐτῶν οὐ συντριβήσεται).

ὀστοῦν. Nominative subject of συντριβήσεται. ὀστοῦν is a contracted form of ὀστέον ("bone"). Fronted for emphasis.

οὐ. Negative particle normally used with indicative verbs.

συντριβήσεται. Fut pass ind 3rd sg συντρίβω.

αὐτοῦ. Possessive genitive qualifying ὀστοῦν.

19:37 καὶ πάλιν ἑτέρα γραφὴ λέγει· ὄψονται εἰς ὃν ἐξεκέντησαν.

καὶ. Coordinating conjunction.

πάλιν. Adverb marking "a discourse or narrative item added to items of a related nature" (BDAG, 752.3).

ἑτέρα γραφὴ. Nominative subject of λέγει. The adjective ἑτέρα stands in the first (anarthrous) attributive position (see 2:6 on λίθιναι ὑδρίαι)

λέγει. Pres act ind 3rd sg λέγω.

ὄψονται εἰς ὃν ἐξεκέντησαν. A quotation of Zech 12:10. The wording of the citation is close to the Hebrew text (וְהִבִּ֥יטוּ אֵלַ֖י אֵ֣ת אֲשֶׁר־דָּקָ֑רוּ), but it does not agree with it completely.

ὄψονται. Fut mid ind 3rd pl ὁράω.

εἰς ὃν. Locative. εἰς ὃν is an ellipsis for εἰς τοῦτον ὃν (Haubeck and von Siebenthal, 604).

ἐξεκέντησαν. Aor act ind 3rd pl ἐκκεντέω.

John 19:38-42

³⁸After these things, Joseph, the one who was from Arimathea, because he was a disciple of Jesus, although secretly for fear of the Jews, asked Pilate that he might take away the body of Jesus, and Pilate gave [him] permission. Then he came and took away his body. ³⁹Also Nicodemus, who at first came to him by night, came bringing a mixture of myrrh and aloes, about a hundred pounds. ⁴⁰So they took the body of Jesus and wrapped it in strips of linen cloth with the aromatic spices, as is the custom of the Jews to prepare for burial. ⁴¹Now in the place where he was crucified there was a garden, and in the garden a new tomb in which no one had yet been laid. ⁴²So there, on account of the Jewish day of preparation, because the tomb was nearby, they laid Jesus.

19:38 Μετὰ δὲ ταῦτα ἠρώτησεν τὸν Πιλᾶτον Ἰωσὴφ [ὁ] ἀπὸ Ἀριμαθαίας, ὢν μαθητὴς τοῦ Ἰησοῦ κεκρυμμένος δὲ διὰ τὸν φόβον τῶν Ἰουδαίων, ἵνα ἄρῃ τὸ σῶμα τοῦ Ἰησοῦ· καὶ ἐπέτρεψεν ὁ Πιλᾶτος. ἦλθεν οὖν καὶ ἦρεν τὸ σῶμα αὐτοῦ.

Μετὰ ... ταῦτα. Temporal. ταῦτα is anaphoric, referring to Jesus' crucifixion and death.

δὲ. Marker of narrative development.

ἠρώτησεν. Aor act ind 3rd sg ἐρωτάω.

τὸν Πιλᾶτον. Accusative direct object of ἠρώτησεν.

Ἰωσὴφ. Nominative subject of ἠρώτησεν.

[ὁ] ἀπὸ Ἀριμαθαίας. The article functions as a nominalizer, changing the PP ἀπὸ Ἀριμαθαίας into the nominative in apposition to Ἰωσήφ. It is printed within square brackets because the external evidence for (א K N W Γ Δ Θ $f^{1.13}$ 𝔐 et al.) and against ($\mathfrak{P}^{66vid}$ A B D^s L Ψ 579) its inclusion is evenly balanced.

ἀπὸ Ἀριμαθαίας. Source. The preposition ἀπό is used here "to indicate someone's local origin" (BDAG, 105.3.b). ἀπό started to replace ἐκ in this sense in Koine Greek (BDF §209.3). Joseph of Arimathea is mentioned in all four Gospels (Mark 15:43; Matt 27:57; Luke 23:51; John 19:38) but nowhere else in the NT.

ὢν. Pres act ptc masc nom sg εἰμί (causal). Many English translations (e.g., NRSV; HCSB; ESV; LEB; NLT) presume that ὢν is attributive, but if this were the case, it would have an article.

μαθητὴς. Predicate nominative.

τοῦ Ἰησοῦ. Genitive of relationship qualifying μαθητής.

κεκρυμμένος. Prf pass ptc masc nom sg κρύπτω (concessive).

δὲ. Marker of narrative development with a contrastive nuance.

διὰ τὸν φόβον. Causal. The PP διὰ τὸν φόβον τῶν Ἰουδαίων is found only in the FG (7:13; 19:38; 20:19).

τῶν Ἰουδαίων. Objective genitive qualifying φόβον (BDF §163).

ἵνα. Introduces a direct object clause (also known as a "content ἵνα clause") of ἠρώτησεν (see 19:31).

ἄρῃ. Aor act subj 3rd sg αἴρω. Subjunctive with ἵνα.

τὸ σῶμα. Accusative direct object of ἄρῃ.

τοῦ Ἰησοῦ. Possessive genitive qualifying σῶμα.

καὶ. Coordinating conjunction.

ἐπέτρεψεν. Aor act ind 3rd sg ἐπιτρέπω.

ὁ Πιλᾶτος. Nominative subject of ἐπέτρεψεν.

ἦλθεν. Aor act ind 3rd sg ἔρχομαι. The implied subject is Joseph of Arimathea.

οὖν. Postpositive inferential conjunction and/or transitional particle (see 1:22 and 11:6).
καὶ. Coordinating conjunction.
ἦρεν. Aor act ind 3rd sg αἴρω.
τὸ σῶμα. Accusative direct object of ἦρεν.
αὐτοῦ. Possessive genitive qualifying σῶμα.

19:39 ἦλθεν δὲ καὶ Νικόδημος, ὁ ἐλθὼν πρὸς αὐτὸν νυκτὸς τὸ πρῶτον, φέρων μίγμα σμύρνης καὶ ἀλόης ὡς λίτρας ἑκατόν.

ἦλθεν. Aor act ind 3rd sg ἔρχομαι.
δὲ. Marker of narrative development.
καὶ. Adverbial use (adjunctive).
Νικόδημος. Nominative subject of ἦλθεν.
ὁ ἐλθὼν. Aor act ptc masc nom sg ἔρχομαι (attributive).
πρὸς αὐτὸν. Spatial (motion toward). αὐτὸν refers to Jesus.
νυκτὸς. Genitive of time (see 3:2).
τὸ πρῶτον. Adverbial accusative indicating time or sequence ("first, in the first place, before, earlier, to begin with" [BDAG, 893.1.a.β]). When used with the article, as here, τὸ πρῶτον means "the first time" (BDAG, 893.1.a.β).
φέρων. Pres act ptc masc nom sg φέρω (manner). On participles that follow the main verb, see βαπτίζων in 1:31.
μίγμα. Accusative direct object of φέρων. μίγμα ("mixture, compound") is a NT *hapax legomenon*. Although the variant ἕλιγμα ("fold, wrapping") is the more difficult reading that has solid textual support (ℵ* B W), the early and diversified attestation of μίγμα (𝔓[66vid] ℵ[2] A D[s] K L N Γ Δ Θ *f*[1.13] 33 565 700 1241 1424 𝔐 sy[h] sa bo) tips the balance in its favor (Metzger, 218).
σμύρνης καὶ ἀλόης. Genitives of material qualifying μίγμα.
ὡς. Particle used with numerals to denote an estimate ("about, approximately").
λίτρας. Accusative in apposition to μίγμα. λίτρα is a loanword from Latin (*libra*) denoting a Roman pound (= 327.45 grams).
ἑκατόν. Indeclinable cardinal number ("one hundred").

19:40 ἔλαβον οὖν τὸ σῶμα τοῦ Ἰησοῦ καὶ ἔδησαν αὐτὸ ὀθονίοις μετὰ τῶν ἀρωμάτων, καθὼς ἔθος ἐστὶν τοῖς Ἰουδαίοις ἐνταφιάζειν.

ἔλαβον. Aor act ind 3rd pl λαμβάνω. The implied subject of the verb is Ἰωσὴφ (v. 38) and Νικόδημος (v. 39).

οὖν. Postpositive inferential conjunction and/or transitional particle (see 1:22 and 11:6).

τὸ σῶμα. Accusative direct object of ἔλαβον.

τοῦ Ἰησοῦ. Possessive genitive qualifying σῶμα.

καὶ. Coordinating conjunction.

ἔδησαν. Aor act ind 3rd pl δέω.

αὐτὸ. Accusative direct object of ἔδησαν. αὐτὸ refers to σῶμα.

ὀθονίοις. Dative of material (Wallace 1996, 169–70). "In the NT ὀθόνιον occurs only in reference to strips of cloth used in preparing a corpse for burial" (LN 6.154).

μετὰ τῶν ἀρωμάτων. Manner.

καθὼς. Introduces a comparative clause.

ἔθος. Nominative subject of ἐστὶν. ἔθος followed by dative denotes "a usual or customary manner of behavior, *habit*" (BDAG, 277.1)

ἐστὶν. Pres act ind 3rd sg εἰμί.

τοῖς Ἰουδαίοις. Dative complement of ἔθος.

ἐνταφιάζειν. Pres act inf ἐνταφιάζω (complementary). ἐνταφιάζω means "to prepare a body for burial" (LN 52.6).

19:41 ἦν δὲ ἐν τῷ τόπῳ ὅπου ἐσταυρώθη κῆπος, καὶ ἐν τῷ κήπῳ μνημεῖον καινὸν ἐν ᾧ οὐδέπω οὐδεὶς ἦν τεθειμένος·

ἦν. Impf act ind 3rd sg εἰμί. On the function of the imperfect in the FG, see 1:39 on ἦν.

δὲ. Marker of narrative development.

ἐν τῷ τόπῳ. Locative.

ὅπου. Marker of a position in space.

ἐσταυρώθη. Aor pass ind 3rd sg σταυρόω.

κῆπος. Nominative subject of ἦν.

καὶ. Coordinating conjunction.

ἐν τῷ κήπῳ. Locative.

μνημεῖον καινὸν. Nominative subject of an implied ἦν. The adjective καινὸν stands in the fourth attributive position (see 3:15 on ζωὴν αἰώνιον).

ἐν ᾧ. Locative. The antecedent of the relative pronoun is μνημεῖον καινὸν.

οὐδέπω. Adverb of time ("not yet").

οὐδεὶς. Nominative subject of ἦν. The two negatives οὐδέπω οὐδεὶς reinforce each other.

ἦν. Impf act ind 3rd sg εἰμί.

τεθειμένος. Prf pass ptc masc nom sg τίθημι (imperfect periphrastic).

19:42 ἐκεῖ οὖν διὰ τὴν παρασκευὴν τῶν Ἰουδαίων, ὅτι ἐγγὺς ἦν τὸ μνημεῖον, ἔθηκαν τὸν Ἰησοῦν.

ἐκεῖ. Adverb of place.

οὖν. Postpositive inferential conjunction and/or transitional particle (see 1:22 and 11:6).

διὰ τὴν παρασκευὴν. Causal.

τῶν Ἰουδαίων. Subjective genitive qualifying παρασκευὴν ("the day of preparation that the Jews celebrate") or attributive genitive ("the Jewish day of preparation").

ὅτι. Introduces a causal clause.

ἐγγὺς. Predicate adverb indicating close spatial proximity (see 2:1 on ἐκεῖ).

ἦν. Impf act ind 3rd sg εἰμί. On the function of the imperfect in the FG, see 1:39 on ἦν.

τὸ μνημεῖον. Nominative subject of ἦν.

ἔθηκαν. Aor act ind 3rd pl τίθημι.

τὸν Ἰησοῦν. Accusative direct object of ἔθηκαν.

John 20:1-10

¹On the first [day] of the week, early in the morning, while it was still dark, Mary Magdalene came to the tomb and saw the stone taken away from the tomb. ²So she ran and came to Simon Peter and to the other disciple, whom Jesus loved, and said to them, "They have taken the Lord out of the tomb, and we do not know where they have put him." ³Then Peter and the other disciple went out and were going to the tomb. ⁴The two were running together, and the other disciple ran ahead, faster than Peter, and came to the tomb first. ⁵And when he bent over to look, he saw the strips of linen cloth lying there, though he did not go in. ⁶Then Simon Peter also came, following him, and went into the tomb and saw the strips of linen cloth lying there ⁷and the face-cloth, which was on his head, not lying with the strips of linen cloth but rolled up in a place by itself. ⁸Thereupon the other disciple who came to the tomb first also went in, and he saw and believed. ⁹For they did not yet know the Scripture that it was necessary for him to rise from the dead. ¹⁰So the disciples went back to their homes.

20:1 Τῇ δὲ μιᾷ τῶν σαββάτων Μαρία ἡ Μαγδαληνὴ ἔρχεται πρωῒ σκοτίας ἔτι οὔσης εἰς τὸ μνημεῖον καὶ βλέπει τὸν λίθον ἠρμένον ἐκ τοῦ μνημείου.

Τῇ . . . μιᾷ. Dative of time. The cardinal number μιᾷ is used for the ordinal number πρώτῃ (BDF §247.1). This elliptical formulation implies the addition of ἡμέρᾳ after μιᾷ: "on the first [day]." Fronted as a temporal frame.

δὲ. Marker of narrative development.

τῶν σαββάτων. Partitive genitive qualifying μιᾷ ("the first [day] of the week" = Sunday). The plural noun refers to "a period of seven days, week" (BDAG, 910.2). In the NT, both singular (Luke 18:12; Mark 16:9; 1 Cor 16:2) and plural (Mark 16:2; Matt 28:1b; Luke 24:1; John 20:1, 19; Acts 20:7) forms of σάββατον can refer to a week (BDAG, 910.2.a-b).

Μαρία. Nominative subject of ἔρχεται.

ἡ Μαγδαληνὴ. Nominative in apposition to Μαρία. On the meaning of Μαγδαληνὴ, see 19:25.

ἔρχεται. Pres mid ind 3rd sg ἔρχομαι. All finite verbs in the first two verses that describe Mary Magdalene's behavior are historical presents, marking a narrative transition from the account of Jesus' burial to the report about the discovery of the empty tomb and giving thematic prominence to her actions (see 1:15 on μαρτυρεῖ). Runge argues that "[t]he repeated use of the HP here has the effect of building to a dramatic peak, yet this should not be construed as the semantic meaning of the HP. Each HP portrays the action as though it were a transition to some new stage of the discourse. The net effect is to slow the discourse flow and build anticipation. Each one also highlights the next event, only to have the resolution deferred by the presence of another HP" (2010, 141).

πρωΐ. Temporal adverb ("early in the morning").

σκοτίας. Genitive subject of οὔσης.

ἔτι. Adverb ("still").

οὔσης. Pres act ptc fem gen sg εἰμί (genitive absolute, temporal).

εἰς τὸ μνημεῖον. Locative (motion toward). Here εἰς is used for πρός (Zerwick §97). The context indicates that Mary Magdalene came to the tomb but did not enter it (see 11:31, 38; 20:3, 4, 8).

καὶ. Coordinating conjunction.

βλέπει. Pres act ind 3rd sg βλέπω. The historical present (see ἔρχεται above).

τὸν λίθον. Accusative direct object of βλέπει in a double accusative object-complement construction.

ἠρμένον. Prf pass ptc masc acc sg αἴρω (predicative). Accusative complement to τὸν λίθον in a double accusative object-complement construction. The stative aspect of the perfect tense calls attention to the position of the stone away from the tomb entrance (see 11:39 on ἄρατε).

ἐκ τοῦ μνημείου. Separation. ἐκ stands for ἀπό (Zerwick and Grosvenor, 344).

20:2 τρέχει οὖν καὶ ἔρχεται πρὸς Σίμωνα Πέτρον καὶ πρὸς τὸν ἄλλον μαθητὴν ὃν ἐφίλει ὁ Ἰησοῦς καὶ λέγει αὐτοῖς· ἦραν τὸν κύριον ἐκ τοῦ μνημείου καὶ οὐκ οἴδαμεν ποῦ ἔθηκαν αὐτόν.

τρέχει. Pres act ind 3rd sg τρέχω. The historical present (see ἔρχεται above).

οὖν. Postpositive inferential conjunction and/or transitional particle (see 1:22 and 11:6).

καί. Coordinating conjunction.

ἔρχεται. Pres mid ind 3rd sg ἔρχομαι. The historical present (see ἔρχεται above).

πρὸς Σίμωνα Πέτρον. Locative (motion toward).

καί. Coordinating conjunction.

πρὸς τὸν ἄλλον μαθητήν. Locative (motion toward). The adjective ἄλλον stands in the first attributive position (see 2:10 on τὸν καλὸν οἶνον). It means "a disciple other than Peter" because "there is no reference to a second 'beloved disciple'" (Barrett, 562).

ὅν. Accusative direct object of ἐφίλει.

ἐφίλει. Impf act ind 3rd sg φιλέω. This is the only instance in the FG that uses the verb φιλέω to identify the Beloved Disciple (see 13:23 on ἠγάπα). There is no difference in meaning between φιλέω and ἀγαπάω (see 21:15).

ὁ Ἰησοῦς. Nominative subject of ἐφίλει.

καί. Coordinating conjunction.

λέγει. Pres act ind 3rd sg λέγω. The historical present (see ἔρχεται above).

αὐτοῖς. Dative indirect object of λέγει.

ἦραν. Aor act ind 3rd pl αἴρω. It is not clear who the implied subject ("they") of the verb is. Since Mary makes the same suggestion to the angels in 20:13 (ἦραν τὸν κύριόν μου), the unexpressed subject of the verb highlights Mary's bewilderment at the disappearance of Jesus' body.

τὸν κύριον. Accusative direct object of ἦραν.

ἐκ τοῦ μνημείου. Separation. In this PP, ἐκ has its standard meaning "out of."

καί. Coordinating conjunction.

οὐκ. Negative particle normally used with indicative verbs.

οἴδαμεν. Prf act ind 1st pl οἶδα (see 1:26 on οἴδατε). The use of the first plural verb is odd, since no other character beside Mary Magdalene is mentioned. This could be a reminiscence of an original story that included several women, as it is transmitted in the synoptic accounts (Barrett, 563), or an Oriental mode of speech with Greek analogies, whereby the first-person plural stands for the first-person singular (Bultmann, 684 n. 1). However, it should be noted that, in the repetition of Mary's words to the angels in 20:13, the verb is in the first-person singular (καὶ οὐκ οἶδα ποῦ ἔθηκαν αὐτόν), which undermines the idea that the first-person plural is a manner of speech.

ποῦ. Indirect interrogative adverb of place.

ἔθηκαν. Aor act ind 3rd pl τίθημι. The implied subject of ἔθηκαν is most likely the same as the implied subject of ἦραν, but the actual referent remains unclear.

αὐτόν. Accusative direct object of ἔθηκαν. The personal pronoun refers to τὸν κύριον.

20:3 Ἐξῆλθεν οὖν ὁ Πέτρος καὶ ὁ ἄλλος μαθητὴς καὶ ἤρχοντο εἰς τὸ μνημεῖον.

Ἐξῆλθεν. Aor act ind 3rd sg ἐξέρχομαι.

οὖν. Postpositive inferential conjunction and/or transitional particle (see 1:22 and 11:6).

ὁ Πέτρος καὶ ὁ ἄλλος μαθητής. Compound nominative subject of Ἐξῆλθεν. When the verb precedes its two (or more) subjects, as here, it is singular, agreeing with the first (BDF §135). The verb that follows the compound subject (ἤρχοντο) is plural. The other disciple, who is identified as the Beloved Disciple in v. 2, is throughout the account of the discovery of the empty tomb consistently referred to as ὁ ἄλλος μαθητὴς (vv. 2, 3, 4, 8).

καί. Coordinating conjunction.

ἤρχοντο. Impf mid ind 3rd pl ἔρχομαι. The imperfective aspect of the verb calls attention to the progressing to the tomb, which is further elaborated in the next verse.

εἰς τὸ μνημεῖον. Locative (motion toward). Here εἰς is used for πρός (Zerwick §97). The disciples were going toward the tomb, but they did not enter it before v. 6 (see 11:31, 38; 20:1, 4, 8).

20:4 ἔτρεχον δὲ οἱ δύο ὁμοῦ· καὶ ὁ ἄλλος μαθητὴς προέδραμεν τάχιον τοῦ Πέτρου καὶ ἦλθεν πρῶτος εἰς τὸ μνημεῖον,

ἔτρεχον. Impf act ind 3rd pl τρέχω. The imperfective aspect portrays the running of Peter and the other disciple as an action in progress.
δὲ. Marker of narrative development.
οἱ δύο. Nominative subject of ἔτρεχον.
ὁμοῦ. Adverb ("together").
καὶ. Coordinating conjunction.
ὁ ἄλλος μαθητὴς. Nominative subject of προέδραμεν (see 2:3 on ὁ Πέτρος καὶ ὁ ἄλλος μαθητὴς).
προέδραμεν. Aor act ind 3rd sg προτρέχω.
τάχιον. Comparative of the adverb ταχέως ("more quickly, faster").
τοῦ Πέτρου. Genitive of comparison.
καὶ. Coordinating conjunction.
ἦλθεν. Aor act ind 3rd sg ἔρχομαι.
πρῶτος. Predicate adjective in relation to ὁ ἄλλος μαθητὴς ("as the first one"); ἦλθεν πρῶτος = "he was the first one to come" (BDAG, 893.1.a.α). Here the superlative πρῶτος is used instead of the comparative πρότερος (Zerwick §151). While in classical Greek the use of πρῶτος indicates that at least three items are compared, the NT authors frequently apply it to only two things/persons (e.g., John 1:15, 30; 1 Tim 2:13; Heb 10:9), as here (Wallace 1996, 303).
εἰς τὸ μνημεῖον. Locative (motion toward). The preposition εἰς is used for πρός (see 11:31, 38; 20:1, 3, 8).

20:5 καὶ παρακύψας βλέπει κείμενα τὰ ὀθόνια, οὐ μέντοι εἰσῆλθεν.

καὶ. Coordinating conjunction.
παρακύψας. Aor act ptc masc nom sg παρακύπτω (temporal). On participles that precede the main verb, see ἐμβλέψας in 1:36. παρακύπτω means "to bend over or stoop down, with the implication of looking into something" (LN 17.31).
βλέπει. Pres act ind 3rd sg βλέπω. The historical present gives prominence to the Beloved Disciple's visual perception of the interior of the tomb.
κείμενα. Pres mid ptc neut acc pl κεῖμαι (predicative). Accusative complement to τὰ ὀθόνια in a double accusative object-complement construction. Fronted for emphasis. When κεῖμαι ("to be in a place so as to be on someth[ing]" [BDAG, 537.2]) is applied to cloths, as here, it is intransitive and means "to lie (there)."

τὰ ὀθόνια. Accusative direct object of βλέπει in a double accusative object-complement construction. This noun is first mentioned in the account of Jesus' burial by Joseph and Nicodemus (19:40).

οὐ. Negative particle normally used with indicative verbs.

μέντοι. Adverbial particle with adversative sense ("though, to be sure, indeed" [BDAG, 630.2])

εἰσῆλθεν. Aor act ind 3rd sg εἰσέρχομαι.

20:6 ἔρχεται οὖν καὶ Σίμων Πέτρος ἀκολουθῶν αὐτῷ καὶ εἰσῆλθεν εἰς τὸ μνημεῖον, καὶ θεωρεῖ τὰ ὀθόνια κείμενα,

ἔρχεται. Pres mid ind 3rd sg ἔρχομαι. The historical present marks the narrative transition to Peter's arrival to the tomb.

οὖν. Postpositive inferential conjunction and/or transitional particle (see 1:22 and 11:6).

καὶ. Adverbial (adjunctive).

Σίμων Πέτρος. Nominative subject of ἔρχεται.

ἀκολουθῶν. Pres act ptc masc nom sg ἀκολουθέω (manner). On participles that follow the main verb, see βαπτίζων in 1:31.

αὐτῷ. Dative complement of ἀκολουθῶν.

καὶ. Coordinating conjunction.

εἰσῆλθεν. Aor act ind 3rd sg εἰσέρχομαι.

εἰς τὸ μνημεῖον. Locative. Unlike the previous occurrences of this PP in the account of the discovery of the empty tomb (vv. 1, 3, 4), here εἰς is used with its proper sense ("inside"), indicating the actual entry into the tomb.

καὶ. Coordinating conjunction.

θεωρεῖ. Pres act ind 3rd sg θεωρέω. The historical present gives prominence to Peter's visual perception of the interior of the tomb (see βλέπει in v. 5). The context does not warrant the supposition that θεωρέω indicates a more penetrating insight than βλέπω (*pace* Harris 2015, 324). θεωρέω is used in 20:12, although Mary does not understand the reason for the angelic presence, and in 20:14, although Mary does not recognize Jesus (Brown, 2:986).

τὰ ὀθόνια. Accusative direct object of θεωρεῖ in a double accusative object-complement construction (see v. 6).

κείμενα. Pres mid ptc neut acc pl κεῖμαι (predicative). Accusative complement to τὰ ὀθόνια in a double accusative object-complement construction (see v. 6).

20:7 καὶ τὸ σουδάριον, ὃ ἦν ἐπὶ τῆς κεφαλῆς αὐτοῦ, οὐ μετὰ τῶν ὀθονίων κείμενον ἀλλὰ χωρὶς ἐντετυλιγμένον εἰς ἕνα τόπον.

καὶ. Coordinating conjunction.

τὸ σουδάριον. Accusative direct object of θεωρεῖ in a double accusative object-complement construction. On the meaning, see 11:44.

ὅ. Nominative subject of ἦν. The antecedent of the relative pronoun is τὸ σουδάριον.

ἦν. Impf act ind 3rd sg εἰμί. On the function of the imperfect in the FG, see 1:39 on ἦν.

ἐπὶ τῆς κεφαλῆς. Locative.

αὐτοῦ. Possessive genitive qualifying κεφαλῆς.

οὐ ... ἀλλὰ. A point/counterpoint set ("not this ... but that") that replaces the incorrect description of the location and condition of the cloth that had been on Jesus' head (lying with the strips of linen cloth) with the correct description of its location and condition (rolled up in a place by itself). Brown (2:986) argues that, since the negative particle οὐ immediately precedes μετὰ τῶν ὀθονίων, it negates only the PP. But the syntax of the οὐ ... ἀλλὰ point/counterpoint set does not support this conclusion because the entire clause between οὐ and ἀλλὰ is repudiated and replaced with the entire clause that comes after ἀλλὰ.

μετὰ τῶν ὀθονίων. Manner (attendant circumstance).

κείμενον. Pres mid ptc neut acc sg κεῖμαι (predicative). Accusative complement to τὸ σουδάριον in a double accusative object-complement construction.

χωρὶς. This is the only place in the NT where χωρὶς is used as an adverb ("separately, by itself"). In all other occurrences it functions as an improper preposition (for the examples in the FG, see 1:3 and 15:5).

ἐντετυλιγμένον. Prf pass ptc neut acc sg ἐντυλίσσω (predicative). Accusative complement to τὸ σουδάριον in a double accusative object-complement construction. While Matt 27:59 and Luke 23:53 use ἐντυλίσσω to describe the wrapping up of Jesus' body in a linen cloth, this verb is used here to describe the condition of the head cover and probably means "that the *soudarion* was rolled up in an oval loop, i.e., the shape it had when it was around the head of the corpse" (Brown, 2:987; cf. LN 79.120).

εἰς ἕνα τόπον. Locative. εἰς stands for ἐν, indicating rest rather than motion (Zerwick §99). If ἕνα means "one," "the σουδάριον was in one place, that is, neatly rolled up (ἐντετυλιγμένον), not simply in a disordered state" (Barrett, 563). If ἕνα stands for the indefinite article "a" (BDAG, 292.3.b), which is more likely, the meaning of the formulation is "in a place by itself." A similar usage can be found in Josephus, *Ant.*

6.125, which contrasts the assembly of the people in one place (εἰς ἕνα τόπον) and the appearance of King Saul and Jonathan in another (κατ' ἄλλο μέρος).

20:8 τότε οὖν εἰσῆλθεν καὶ ὁ ἄλλος μαθητὴς ὁ ἐλθὼν πρῶτος εἰς τὸ μνημεῖον καὶ εἶδεν καὶ ἐπίστευσεν·

τότε οὖν. A combination of the temporal adverb and the postpositive inferential conjunction, in which τότε functions as a connective particle that introduces "a subsequent event, but not one taking place at a definite time ('thereupon,' not 'at that time')" (BDF §459.2). τότε οὖν = "now" (in contrast to the preceding time).

εἰσῆλθεν. Aor act ind 3rd sg εἰσέρχομαι.

καὶ. Adverbial use (adjunctive).

ὁ ἄλλος μαθητὴς. Nominative subject of εἰσῆλθεν.

ὁ ἐλθών. Aor act ptc masc nom sg ἔρχομαι (attributive). The participle modifies ὁ ἄλλος μαθητὴς, standing in the second attributive position (see 1:29 on ὁ αἴρων).

πρῶτος. Predicate adjective in relation to ὁ ἄλλος μαθητὴς (see 20:4).

εἰς τὸ μνημεῖον. Locative (motion toward). The preposition εἰς is used for πρός (see 11:31, 38; 20:1, 3, 4).

καὶ. Coordinating conjunction.

εἶδεν. Aor act ind 3rd sg ὁράω. The object of seeing is not expressed, but the text presumes that the other disciple saw the same things as Peter in v. 7.

καὶ. Coordinating conjunction.

ἐπίστευσεν. Aor act ind 3rd sg πιστεύω. The object of believing is not expressed. Augustine's (*Cons.* 3.24, 69) suggestion that the Beloved Disciple believed Mary's report that the body had been taken from the tomb is, though plausible, nonetheless trivial. It is also unwarranted to interpret the faith of the Beloved Disciple as a mundane faith when in all other instances in the FG in which the verb πιστεύω is used in an absolute sense (1:50; 4:48, 53; 5:44; 6:36, 47, 64; 9:38; 10:25, 26; 11:15, 40; 14:29; 19:35; 20:25, 29), religious faith is in view. Most scholars therefore presume that the Beloved Disciple came to believe that Jesus had been raised from the dead. Yet, even if this interpretation is accepted, the clause καὶ εἶδεν καὶ ἐπίστευσεν suggests that the Beloved Disciple "believed on the basis of what he saw in the tomb, not on the basis of hearing" (Brown, 2:1005). This type of faith therefore does not represent the faith that Jesus praises in 20:29b: μακάριοι οἱ μὴ ἰδόντες καὶ πιστεύσαντες.

20:9 οὐδέπω γὰρ ᾔδεισαν τὴν γραφὴν ὅτι δεῖ αὐτὸν ἐκ νεκρῶν ἀναστῆναι.

οὐδέπω. Adverb of time ("not yet").

γὰρ. Postpositive conjunction that introduces the explanation of the previous verse. The main problem, however, is that this clause describes a situation that is not yet characterized by the proper understanding of Scripture, which forms the basis of the resurrection faith. This verse thus stands in tension with v. 8, which seems to claim that the Beloved Disciple believed that Jesus had risen from the dead. If, however, ἐπίστευσεν in v. 8 refers to an incomplete resurrection faith because it is based on seeing rather than hearing, the explanation in v. 9 becomes intelligible if it describes a fully developed resurrected faith that can only be derived from the correct interpretation of Scripture. The tension with v. 8, however, is thereby not completely resolved because the implied subjects of the γάρ clause are both the Beloved Disciple and Peter (see ᾔδεισαν below), whereas the subject of v. 8 is only the former.

ᾔδεισαν. Plprf act ind 3rd pl οἶδα. The pluperfect tense of οἶδα has the imperfect meaning. Since the verb is plural, the implied subjects are both the Beloved Disciple and Peter.

τὴν γραφὴν. Accusative direct object of ᾔδεισαν. Since no specific passage is quoted, τὴν γραφὴν most likely refers to the entire Jewish Scripture. For similar statements elsewhere in the NT, see Luke 24:25-27, 44-47; 1 Cor 15:3.

ὅτι. Introduces the clausal complement (indirect discourse) of ᾔδεισαν.

δεῖ. Pres act ind 3rd sg δεῖ.

αὐτὸν. Accusative subject of the infinitive ἀναστῆναι. αὐτὸν refers to Jesus.

ἐκ νεκρῶν. Separation. Fronted for emphasis.

ἀναστῆναι. Aor act inf ἀνίστημι (complementary). On the function of the infinitive with δεῖ, see 3:7 on γεννηθῆναι.

20:10 ἀπῆλθον οὖν πάλιν πρὸς αὐτοὺς οἱ μαθηταί.

ἀπῆλθον. Aor act ind 3rd pl ἀπέρχομαι.

οὖν. Postpositive inferential conjunction and/or transitional particle (see 1:22 and 11:6).

πάλιν. Adverb "pert[aining] to return to a position or state" (BDAG, 752.1).

πρὸς αὐτούς. Locative (motion toward). πρὸς αὐτούς stands for πρὸς ἑαυτούς (lit. "to themselves" = "to their homes"; cf. Zerwick and Grosvenor, 344).

οἱ μαθηταί. Nominative subject of ἀπῆλθον.

John 20:11-18

[11]But Mary stood outside near the tomb, weeping. Then, while she was weeping, she bent over to look into the tomb, [12]and she saw two angels in white sitting, one at the head and one at the feet where the body of Jesus had been lying. [13]And they said to her, "Woman, why are you weeping?" She said to them, "They have taken my Lord, and I do not know where they have put him." [14]When she said these things, she turned around and saw Jesus standing there, but she did not know that it was Jesus. [15]Jesus said to her, "Woman, why are you weeping? Whom are you looking for?" She, thinking that he was the gardener, said to him, "Sir, if you have carried him away, tell me where you have put him, and I will take him away." [16]Jesus said to her, "Mary!" She turned and said to him in Aramaic, "Rabbouni!" (which means "Teacher!"). [17]Jesus said to her, "Do not hold on to me, for I have not yet ascended to the Father. But go to my brothers and say to them, 'I am ascending to my Father and your Father and my God and your God.'" [18]Mary Magdalene came, announcing to the disciples, "I have seen the Lord!" and that he had said these things to her.

20:11 Μαρία δὲ εἱστήκει πρὸς τῷ μνημείῳ ἔξω κλαίουσα. ὡς οὖν ἔκλαιεν, παρέκυψεν εἰς τὸ μνημεῖον

Μαρία. Nominative subject of εἱστήκει.

δέ. Marker of narrative development with a contrastive nuance.

εἱστήκει. Plprf act ind 3rd sg ἵστημι. The pluperfect tense of ἵστημι has the imperfect meaning.

πρὸς τῷ μνημείῳ. Locative, indicating spatial proximity (BDAG, 874.2.a).

ἔξω. Adverb ("outside").

κλαίουσα. Pres act ptc fem nom sg κλαίω (manner). In this context, κλαίω means "to weep or lament for the dead" (BDAG, 545.1; cf. 11:31, 33). On participles that follow the main verb, see βαπτίζων in 1:31.

ὡς. Temporal conjunction (BDAG, 1105.8.b; BDF §455.2).

οὖν. Postpositive inferential conjunction and/or transitional particle (see 1:22 and 11:6).

ἔκλαιεν. Impf act ind 3rd sg κλαίω. On the function of the imperfect in the FG, see 1:39 on ἦν.
παρέκυψεν. Aor act ind 3rd sg παρακύπτω (see 20:5).
εἰς τὸ μνημεῖον. Locative. The preposition εἰς is here used with its proper sense, indicating that Mary bent over to look inside the tomb.

20:12 καὶ θεωρεῖ δύο ἀγγέλους ἐν λευκοῖς καθεζομένους, ἕνα πρὸς τῇ κεφαλῇ καὶ ἕνα πρὸς τοῖς ποσίν, ὅπου ἔκειτο τὸ σῶμα τοῦ Ἰησοῦ.

καὶ. Coordinating conjunction.
θεωρεῖ. Pres act ind 3rd sg θεωρέω. The historical present gives prominence to Mary's visual perception of the interior of the tomb (see βλέπει in 20:5 and θεωρεῖ in 20:6).
δύο ἀγγέλους. Accusative direct object of θεωρεῖ in a double accusative object-complement construction.
ἐν λευκοῖς. Manner. The formulation implies the addition of ἱματίοις ("in white [garments]").
καθεζομένους. Pres mid ptc masc acc pl καθέζομαι (predicative). Accusative complement to δύο ἀγγέλους in a double accusative object-complement construction.
ἕνα ... καὶ ἕνα. Accusatives in apposition to δύο ἀγγέλους. ἕνα ... καὶ ἕνα stand for τὸν μὲν ἕτερον ... τὸν δὲ ἕτερον (Zerwick §156).
πρὸς τῇ κεφαλῇ. Locative, indicating spatial proximity (BDAG, 874.2.a).
πρὸς τοῖς ποσίν. Locative, indicating spatial proximity (see above).
ὅπου. Marker of a position in space.
ἔκειτο. Impf mid ind 3rd sg κεῖμαι.
τὸ σῶμα. Nominative subject of ἔκειτο.
τοῦ Ἰησοῦ. Possessive genitive qualifying σῶμα.

20:13 καὶ λέγουσιν αὐτῇ ἐκεῖνοι· γύναι, τί κλαίεις; λέγει αὐτοῖς ὅτι ἦραν τὸν κύριόν μου, καὶ οὐκ οἶδα ποῦ ἔθηκαν αὐτόν.

καὶ. Coordinating conjunction.
λέγουσιν. Pres act ind 3rd pl λέγω. The historical present gives prominence to the angels' question (see 1:15 on μαρτυρεῖ).
αὐτῇ. Dative indirect object of λέγουσιν.
ἐκεῖνοι. Nominative subject of λέγουσιν. The demonstrative pronoun refers to the angels from the previous verse, acting as a third-person personal pronoun with a simple anaphoric force (Wallace 1996, 328–29).
γύναι. Vocative of direct address.
τί. Adverbial use of the interrogative pronoun ("why?").

κλαίεις. Pres act ind 2nd sg κλαίω. On the meaning of the verb, see 20:11 on κλαίουσα. Unlike the synoptic narratives of the empty tomb (Mark 16:1-8; Matt 28:1-8; Luke 24:1-12), the angels in the FG bring no good news to the weeping Mary. They merely ask a question about the cause of her grief.

λέγει. Pres act ind 3rd sg λέγω. The historical present gives prominence to Mary's reply (see 1:15 on μαρτυρεῖ). This clause is connected to the previous one by asyndeton.

αὐτοῖς. Dative indirect object of λέγει.

ὅτι. This is either ὅτι-*recitativum*, introducing the clausal complement (direct discourse) of λέγει, or a causal ὅτι ("because"), introducing Mary's explanation of her weeping.

ἦραν τὸν κύριόν μου, καὶ οὐκ οἶδα ποῦ ἔθηκαν αὐτόν. A slightly revised repetition of 20:2 (ἦραν τὸν κύριον ἐκ τοῦ μνημείου καὶ οὐκ οἴδαμεν ποῦ ἔθηκαν αὐτόν).

ἦραν. Aor act ind 3rd pl αἴρω.

τὸν κύριόν. Accusative direct object of ἦραν. κύριόν, which has an acute accent on the antepenult, acquired an additional accent, the acute, on the ultima from the enclitic μου (Smyth §183; Carson 1985, 48).

μου. Genitive of subordination qualifying κύριόν.

καὶ. Coordinating conjunction.

οὐκ. Negative particle normally used with indicative verbs.

οἶδα. Prf act ind 1st sg οἶδα (see 1:26 on οἴδατε). In 20:2 the verb was in the plural.

ποῦ. Indirect interrogative adverb of place.

ἔθηκαν. Aor act ind 3rd pl τίθημι.

αὐτόν. Accusative direct object of ἔθηκαν.

20:14 Ταῦτα εἰποῦσα ἐστράφη εἰς τὰ ὀπίσω καὶ θεωρεῖ τὸν Ἰησοῦν ἑστῶτα καὶ οὐκ ᾔδει ὅτι Ἰησοῦς ἐστιν.

Ταῦτα. Accusative direct object of εἰποῦσα. The demonstrative pronoun refers to Mary's reply to the angels. This verse is connected to the previous one by asyndeton.

εἰποῦσα. Aor act ptc fem nom sg λέγω (temporal). On participles that precede the main verb, see ἐμβλέψας in 1:36.

ἐστράφη. Aor mid ind 3rd sg στρέφω. Here στρέφω has reflexive sense and means "turn around, turn toward" (BDAG, 948.1.b). On the voice, see "Deponency" in the Series Introduction.

εἰς τὰ ὀπίσω. Locative (lit. "to the things behind" = "backward"). The article functions as a nominalizer, changing the adverb ὀπίσω ("behind") into the object of the preposition εἰς.

καί. Coordinating conjunction.

θεωρεῖ. Pres act ind 3rd sg θεωρέω. The historical present gives prominence to Mary's sight of Jesus (see 1:15 on μαρτυρεῖ).

τὸν Ἰησοῦν. Accusative direct object of θεωρεῖ in a double accusative object-complement construction.

ἑστῶτα. Prf act ptc masc acc sg ἵστημι (predicative). Accusative complement to τὸν Ἰησοῦν in a double accusative object-complement construction.

καί. Coordinating conjunction linking two clauses that stand in adversative relationship (see 1:5).

οὐκ. Negative particle normally used with indicative verbs.

ᾔδει. Plprf act ind 3rd sg οἶδα. The pluperfect tense of οἶδα has the imperfect meaning.

ὅτι. Introduces the clausal complement (indirect discourse) of ᾔδει.

Ἰησοῦς. Predicate nominative. Fronted for emphasis.

ἐστιν. Pres act ind 3rd sg εἰμί. The present tense is retained from the corresponding direct discourse (see 1:39 on μένει).

20:15 λέγει αὐτῇ Ἰησοῦς· γύναι, τί κλαίεις; τίνα ζητεῖς; ἐκείνη δοκοῦσα ὅτι ὁ κηπουρός ἐστιν λέγει αὐτῷ· κύριε, εἰ σὺ ἐβάστασας αὐτόν, εἰπέ μοι ποῦ ἔθηκας αὐτόν, κἀγὼ αὐτὸν ἀρῶ.

λέγει. Pres act ind 3rd sg λέγω. The entire dialogue between the risen Jesus and Mary Magdalene is marked by the historical presents that draw attention to what they say to each other (see 1:15 on μαρτυρεῖ). This verse is connected to the previous one by asyndeton.

αὐτῇ. Dative indirect object of λέγει.

Ἰησοῦς. Nominative subject of λέγει.

γύναι, τί κλαίεις. Jesus' first question is a verbatim repetition of the question of the angels in 20:13.

γύναι. Vocative of direct address.

τί. Adverbial use of the interrogative pronoun ("why?").

κλαίεις. Pres act ind 2nd sg κλαίω. On the meaning of the verb, see 20:11 on κλαίουσα.

τίνα. Accusative direct object of ζητεῖς. Jesus' second question is connected to the previous one by asyndeton.

ζητεῖς. Pres act ind 2nd sg ζητέω.

ἐκείνη. Nominative subject of λέγει. The demonstrative pronoun refers to Mary Magdalene, acting as a third-person personal pronoun with a simple anaphoric force (Wallace 1996, 328–29). This clause is connected to the previous one by asyndeton.

δοκοῦσα. Pres act ptc fem nom sg δοκέω (causal). On participles that precede the main verb, see ἐμβλέψας in 1:36.

ὅτι. Introduces the clausal complement (indirect discourse) of δοκοῦσα.

ὁ κηπουρός. Predicate nominative. A NT *hapax legomenon*.

ἐστιν. Pres act ind 3rd sg εἰμί. The present tense is retained from the corresponding direct discourse (see 1:39 on μένει).

λέγει. Pres act ind 3rd sg λέγω. Historical present (see λέγει above).

αὐτῷ. Dative indirect object of λέγει.

κύριε. Vocative of direct address. κύριε here means "sir."

εἰ. Introduces the protasis of a first-class condition.

σύ. Nominative subject of ἐβάστασας. σύ is emphatic.

ἐβάστασας. Aor act ind 2nd sg βαστάζω. The verb means "to take up and take away" (Barrett, 564).

αὐτόν. Accusative direct object of ἐβάστασας. It is clear from the wider context that αὐτόν refers to Jesus' body, but in the immediate context the closest referent is τίνα. Mary Magdalene does not reply to Jesus' question but continues the conversation as if the identity of the person she is looking for is established.

εἰπέ. Aor act impv 2nd sg λέγω. It marks the beginning of the apodosis of a first-class condition.

μοι. Dative indirect object of εἰπέ.

ποῦ. Indirect interrogative adverb of place.

ἔθηκας. Aor act ind 2nd sg τίθημι.

αὐτόν. Accusative direct object of ἔθηκας.

κἀγώ. Formed by crasis from καὶ ἐγώ. καί is a coordinating conjunction; ἐγώ is the nominative subject of ἀρῶ.

αὐτόν. Accusative direct object of ἀρῶ.

ἀρῶ. Fut act ind 1st sg αἴρω. The verb stands in final, emphatic position.

20:16 λέγει αὐτῇ Ἰησοῦς· Μαριάμ. στραφεῖσα ἐκείνη λέγει αὐτῷ Ἑβραϊστί· ραββουνι, ὃ λέγεται διδάσκαλε

λέγει. Pres act ind 3rd sg λέγω. Historical present (see 20:15 on λέγει). This verse is connected to the previous one by asyndeton.

αὐτῇ. Dative indirect address.

Ἰησοῦς. Nominative subject of λέγει.

Μαριάμ. Vocative of direct address.

στραφεῖσα. Aor mid ptc fem nom sg στρέφω (temporal or attendant circumstance). On participles that precede the main verb, see ἐμβλέψας in 1:36. Like in 20:14, στρέφω has reflexive sense and means "turn around, turn toward" (BDAG, 948.1.b). On the voice, see "Deponency" in the Series Introduction. This clause is connected to the previous one by asyndeton.

ἐκείνη. Nominative subject of λέγει. The demonstrative pronoun refers to Mary Magdalene, acting as a third-person personal pronoun with a simple anaphoric force (Wallace 1996, 328–29).

λέγει. Pres act ind 3rd sg λέγω. Historical present (see 20:15 on λέγει).

αὐτῷ. Dative indirect object of λέγει.

Ἑβραϊστί. Adverb ("in Hebrew/Aramaic" [BDAG, 270]).

ραββουνι. Vocative of direct address. ραββουνι is an indeclinable Aramaic loanword with a first-person suffix (רַבּוּנִי/רְבּוּנִי) that means "my lord, my master" (BDAG, 902). The only other occurrence of this term in the NT is in Mark 10:51.

ὃ λέγεται διδάσκαλε. Parenthetical clause that interrupts the plot of the narrative. The purpose of this editorial gloss is to explain the meaning of the transliterated Aramaic term ραββουνι to the readers/hearers who are not familiar with it. For similar parenthetical comments, see 1:38, 41, 42; 19:17.

ὅ. Nominative subject of λέγεται. The antecedent of the relative pronoun is ραββουνι. ὅ is neuter rather than masculine because in explanatory phrases the neuter is used without much regard to the gender of the word that the phrase explains (Robertson, 411; BDF §132.2).

λέγεται. Pres pass ind 3rd sg λέγω.

διδάσκαλε. Vocative of direct address.

20:17 λέγει αὐτῇ Ἰησοῦς· μή μου ἅπτου, οὔπω γὰρ ἀναβέβηκα πρὸς τὸν πατέρα· πορεύου δὲ πρὸς τοὺς ἀδελφούς μου καὶ εἰπὲ αὐτοῖς· ἀναβαίνω πρὸς τὸν πατέρα μου καὶ πατέρα ὑμῶν καὶ θεόν μου καὶ θεὸν ὑμῶν.

λέγει. Pres act ind 3rd sg λέγω. Historical present (see 20:15 on λέγει). This verse is connected to the previous one by asyndeton.

αὐτῇ. Dative indirect object of λέγει.

Ἰησοῦς. Nominative subject of λέγει.

μή. Negative particle normally used with non-indicative verbs.

μου. Genitive direct object of ἅπτου.

ἅπτου. Pres mid impv 2nd sg ἅπτω. Many scholars suppose that Jesus prohibits the continuation of an action that has already started or has been attempted (Brown, 2:992; Barrett, 565–66; Schnackenburg, 3:318; Talbert, 260; BDF §336.3; Zerwick §247). This assumption is frequently supported by the parallel passage in Matt 28:9, which could have derived from the same tradition as John 20:17. We should keep in mind, however, that whether a prohibition that involves the present imperative refers to the termination of an action that is already in progress depends on the context (Wallace 1996, 716; Porter 1989, 335–61), which is here quite complicated. The explanatory clause that follows does not offer much help except that it indicates that Jesus' ascension to the Father is in progress. The meaning of ἅπτω is disputed (it could mean "touch," "take hold of," or "cling to"), and a comparison between Mary Magdalene, to whom Jesus says μή μου ἅπτου, and Thomas, whom Jesus invites to probe his wounds to verify his identity (20:27), are unhelpful because they refer to different issues. The only conclusion that can be made, all things considered, is that the meaning of the prohibition cannot be determined with the help of the grammar alone but must be based on a coherent interpretation of the entire chapter.

οὔπω. Adverb of time ("not yet"). "The negation οὔπω ... is used for actions that never happened before but are expected to happen, or have already begun but are not yet completed" (Bieringer, 216). Fronted for emphasis.

γάρ. Postpositive conjunction that introduces an explanatory clause that provides a motivation for Jesus' prohibition μή μου ἅπτου. The γάρ clause makes more sense if μή μου ἅπτου means "do not hold on to me" because "[t]he text would be suggesting that Jesus' mode of existence as the risen one is only provisional and transitional" (Bieringer, 210; cf. Theobald, 111–12; for the idea that that the explanatory clause means "do not prevent me from ascending," see Matera, 402–6). An alternative explanation is offered by Zerwick (§476), who suggests that the reason for Jesus' prohibition is not given in the clause that immediately follows γάρ (οὔπω ... ἀναβέβηκα πρὸς τὸν πατέρα) but in the subsequent command to Mary (πορεύου δὲ πρὸς τοὺς ἀδελφούς μου καὶ εἰπὲ αὐτοῖς). In his reconstruction, οὔπω ... ἀναβέβηκα πρὸς τὸν πατέρα functions as a parenthetical statement: "Do not keep hold of me for (I am not yet ascended to my Father) go rather to my brethren and tell them ..." A third possibility, suggested by McGehee, is to understand this γάρ not as a causal conjunction "for" but an anticipatory conjunction "since" that refers to the command that follows. This reading requires putting a full stop after μή μου ἅπτου: "Don't cling to me. Since I have not yet ascended to the Father, go to my brothers and tell them that I am ascending to my Father and your Father and my God and your God" (299; cf. Porter 1989, 356; on anticipatory γάρ in classical Greek, see Smyth §2811). The main weakness of this proposal is that "it seems tautological to say that the reason Mary Magdalene is sent to the brothers to tell them that Jesus is in the process of ascending to the Father is that he has not yet ascended to the Father" (Bieringer, 213). It also leaves Jesus' prohibition to Mary isolated, offering no motivation for Jesus' request (Carson 1991, 642). All things considered, it seems best to me to regard the clause οὔπω γὰρ ἀναβέβηκα πρὸς τὸν πατέρα as providing a reason for the preceding prohibition μή μου ἅπτου.

ἀναβέβηκα. Prf act ind 1st sg ἀναβαίνω. The stative aspect of the perfect tense, along with the adverb οὔπω, indicates that Jesus has not yet attained a state of ascension (Porter 1989, 356).

πρὸς τὸν πατέρα. Locative (motion toward).

πορεύου. Pres mid impv 2nd sg πορεύομαι.

δὲ. Marker of narrative development.

πρὸς τοὺς ἀδελφούς. Locative (motion toward). ἀδελφούς refers to the disciples, not to Jesus' siblings mentioned in 7:5. The term "brothers" is also used for the disciples in Matt 28:10 (ὑπάγετε ἀπαγγείλατε τοῖς ἀδελφοῖς μου).

μου. Genitive of relationship qualifying ἀδελφούς.

καὶ. Coordinating conjunction.

εἰπὲ. Aor act impv 2nd sg λέγω.

αὐτοῖς. Dative indirect object of εἰπὲ.

ἀναβαίνω. Pres act ind 1st sg ἀναβαίνω. The imperfective aspect of the verb indicates that Jesus' ascension is in progress (Porter 1989, 356). It is noteworthy that the message that Mary Magdalene is asked to deliver to the disciples is not the message of the resurrection but the message of the ascension.

πρὸς τὸν πατέρα . . . καὶ πατέρα . . . καὶ θεόν . . . καὶ θεὸν. Locative (motion toward). These four substantives, governed by one article and joined by καί, form a TSKS (article-substantive-καί-substantive) construction. In such formulations, according to the Granville Sharp rule, the single article indicates that all nouns involved have the same referent. This construction also shows, as Wallace helpfully remarks, "that θεός is not a proper noun (from the Greek perspective), for whenever a proper name occurs in Sharp's constructions two persons are in view. Yet, whenever θεός is in this construction, one person is in view" (1996, 274).

μου. Genitive of relationship qualifying the first πατέρα. This and the following three genitive modifiers indicate how Jesus and the disciples relate to God, but they do not suggest that different persons are in view (Wallace 1996, 274).

ὑμῶν. Genitive of relationship qualifying the second πατέρα.

μου. Genitive of relationship qualifying θεόν.

ὑμῶν. Genitive of relationship qualifying θεὸν.

20:18 Ἔρχεται Μαριὰμ ἡ Μαγδαληνὴ ἀγγέλλουσα τοῖς μαθηταῖς ὅτι ἑώρακα τὸν κύριον, καὶ ταῦτα εἶπεν αὐτῇ.

Ἔρχεται. Pres mid ind 3rd sg ἔρχομαι. The historical present marks the narrative transition from Jesus' appearance to Mary to her proclamation of this news to the disciples. This verse is connected to the previous one by asyndeton.

Μαριάμ. Nominative subject of Ἔρχεται.

ἡ Μαγδαληνή. Nominative in apposition to Μαριάμ. On the meaning of Μαγδαληνή, see 19:25.

ἀγγέλλουσα. Pres act ptc fem nom sg ἀγγέλλω (purpose). On participles that follow the main verb, see βαπτίζων in 1:31.

τοῖς μαθηταῖς. Dative indirect object of ἀγγέλλουσα.

ὅτι. This conjunction has a double function, serving as ὅτι-*recitativum* that introduces direct discourse ἑώρακα τὸν κύριον and as declarative ὅτι that introduces indirect discourse ταῦτα εἶπεν αὐτῇ (Zerwick and Grosvenor, 345). Many copyists have tried to improve the grammar by replacing the first-person ἑώρακα with the third-person ἑώρακεν, which presumes that ὅτι introduces only indirect speech (A D K L Γ Δ Θ Ψ 078 $f^{1.13}$ 565 700 1241 1424 *l*855 *l*221 𝔐 it sy$^{p.h}$ sa^{mss} bo^{ms}), but ἑώρακα, which presumes a loose use of ὅτι, is the *lectio difficilior* that has strong external support ($\mathfrak{P}^{66}$ ℵ B N W 892^s a aur vg sy^s sa^{mss} ly pbo bo).

ἑώρακα. Prf act ind 1st sg ὁράω. Porter remarks that "[w]hile seeing the lord is crucial in the resurrection narrative, here the stress seems to fall on Mary as the one who sees and bears witness, particularly crucial in a social context where a woman's testimony was not legally admissible" (1989, 279). The perfect tense of ὁράω + τὸν κύριον is also used in 20:25 to convey the disciples' testimony of the appearance of the risen Jesus. In 1 Cor 9:1 Paul defends his apostleship by asking, οὐχὶ Ἰησοῦν τὸν κύριον ἡμῶν ἑόρακα ("Have I not seen Jesus our Lord?").

τὸν κύριον. Accusative direct object of ἑώρακα.

καί. Coordinating conjunction. The clause that follows is no longer governed by the ὅτι-*recitativum* (see above).

ταῦτα. Accusative direct object of εἶπεν.

εἶπεν. Aor act ind 3rd sg λέγω.

αὐτῇ. Dative indirect object of εἶπεν.

John 20:19-23

[19]Now when it was evening on that day, the first [day] of the week, and the doors had been locked where the disciples were for fear of the Jews, Jesus came and stood in their midst and said to them, "Peace to you."

²⁰And when he had said this, he showed his hands and his side to them. Then the disciples rejoiced when they saw the Lord. ²¹So Jesus said to them again, "Peace to you. As the Father sent me, I also send you." ²²And when he had said this, he breathed on [them] and said to them, "Receive the Holy Spirit. ²³If you forgive the sins of any, they are forgiven them; if you retain [the sins] of any, they are retained."

20:19 Οὔσης οὖν ὀψίας τῇ ἡμέρᾳ ἐκείνῃ τῇ μιᾷ σαββάτων καὶ τῶν θυρῶν κεκλεισμένων ὅπου ἦσαν οἱ μαθηταὶ διὰ τὸν φόβον τῶν Ἰουδαίων, ἦλθεν ὁ Ἰησοῦς καὶ ἔστη εἰς τὸ μέσον καὶ λέγει αὐτοῖς· εἰρήνη ὑμῖν.

Οὔσης. Pres act ptc fem gen sg εἰμί (genitive absolute, temporal).

οὖν. Postpositive inferential conjunction and/or transitional particle (see 1:22 and 11:6).

ὀψίας. Genitive subject of Οὔσης.

τῇ ἡμέρᾳ ἐκείνῃ. Dative of time.

τῇ μιᾷ. Dative in apposition to τῇ ἡμέρᾳ ἐκείνῃ (see 20:1).

σαββάτων. Partitive genitive qualifying μιᾷ (see 20:1).

καὶ. Coordinating conjunction.

τῶν θυρῶν. Genitive subject of κεκλεισμένων.

κεκλεισμένων. Prf pass ptc fem gen pl κλείω (genitive absolute, temporal).

ὅπου. Marker of a position in space.

ἦσαν. Impf act ind 3rd pl εἰμί. On the function of the imperfect in the FG, see 1:39 on ἦν.

οἱ μαθηταὶ. Nominative subject of ἦσαν.

διὰ τὸν φόβον. Causal. This motive for the shut doors is given only in John. Elsewhere in the FG, the PP διὰ τὸν φόβον τῶν Ἰουδαίων is found in 7:13 and 19:38.

τῶν Ἰουδαίων. Objective genitive qualifying φόβον (BDF §163).

ἦλθεν. Aor act ind 3rd sg ἔρχομαι.

ὁ Ἰησοῦς. Nominative subject of ἦλθεν.

καὶ. Coordinating conjunction.

ἔστη. Aor act ind 3rd sg ἵστημι.

εἰς τὸ μέσον. Locative. The adjective μέσον functions as a substantive. Here εἰς does not stand for ἐν because this PP follows the verb of motion ἦλθεν, which is combined with the verb of rest ἔστη, suggesting arrival at the destination (BDAG, 289.1.a.β; Harris 2012, 85; Moule, 68).

καὶ. Coordinating conjunction.

λέγει. Pres act ind 3rd sg λέγω. The historical present gives prominence to Jesus' greeting of his disciples (see 1:15 on μαρτυρεῖ).

αὐτοῖς. Dative indirect object of λέγει.

εἰρήνη. Nominative subject of a verbless clause. Omission of the verb is "normal in formulaic wishes like εἰρήνη ὑμῖν etc." (BDF §128.5). εἰρήνη is here used as a greeting (see also 20:21, 26; cf. 14:27 and 16:33, where εἰρήνη is used as a word of farewell).

ὑμῖν. Dative of advantage.

20:20 καὶ τοῦτο εἰπὼν ἔδειξεν τὰς χεῖρας καὶ τὴν πλευρὰν αὐτοῖς. ἐχάρησαν οὖν οἱ μαθηταὶ ἰδόντες τὸν κύριον.

καὶ. Coordinating conjunction.

τοῦτο. Accusative direct object of εἰπὼν. The anaphoric demonstrative refers to Jesus' greeting in v. 19. Wallace notes that of twenty-two occurrences of the phrase καὶ τοῦτο in the NT, "14 or 15 had a conceptual referent," as here (Wallace 1996, 335 n. 56).

εἰπὼν. Aor act ptc masc nom sg λέγω (temporal). On participles that precede the main verb, see ἐμβλέψας in 1:36.

ἔδειξεν. Aor act ind 3rd sg δείκνυμι.

τὰς χεῖρας. Accusative direct object of ἔδειξεν. The article is used as a possessive pronoun.

καὶ. Coordinating conjunction.

τὴν πλευρὰν. Accusative direct object of ἔδειξεν (see 19:34). The article is used as a possessive pronoun.

αὐτοῖς. Dative indirect object of ἔδειξεν.

ἐχάρησαν. Aor mid ind 3rd pl χαίρω. On the voice, see "Deponency" in the Series Introduction.

οὖν. Postpositive inferential conjunction and/or transitional particle (see 1:22 and 11:6).

οἱ μαθηταὶ. Nominative subject of ἐχάρησαν.

ἰδόντες. Aor act ptc masc nom pl ὁράω (temporal or causal). On participles that follow the main verb, see βαπτίζων in 1:31.

τὸν κύριον. Accusative direct object of ἰδόντες.

20:21 εἶπεν οὖν αὐτοῖς [ὁ Ἰησοῦς] πάλιν· εἰρήνη ὑμῖν· καθὼς ἀπέσταλκέν με ὁ πατήρ, κἀγὼ πέμπω ὑμᾶς.

εἶπεν. Aor act ind 3rd sg λέγω.

οὖν. Postpositive inferential conjunction and/or transitional particle (see 1:22 and 11:6).

αὐτοῖς. Dative indirect object of εἶπεν.

[ὁ Ἰησοῦς]. Nominative subject of εἶπεν. The external evidence for the presence of this noun (A B K N Γ Δ Θ 078 f^{13} 33 700 892^s 1241

1424 𝔐 b f ff² sy^{p.h} sa^{mss}) is somewhat stronger than the evidence for its absence (ℵ D L W Ψ 050 *l*844 lat sy^s sa^{mss} ly pbo bo), but the decision is difficult on internal grounds because ὁ Ἰησοῦς, which is written as a *nomen sacrum* O$\overline{IC}$, could have been accidentally added after AYTOIC by dittography or omitted by haplography (Metzger, 219).

πάλιν. Adverb "pert[aining] to repetition in the same (or similar) manner" (BDAG, 752.2).

εἰρήνη. Nominative subject of a verbless clause (see 20:19).

ὑμῖν. Dative of advantage.

καθὼς ... κἀγώ. A point/counterpoint set ("just as ... also") that compares the Father's sending of Jesus to Jesus' sending of his disciples. κἀγώ is formed by crasis from καὶ ἐγώ. καί is adverbial (adjunctive). ἐγώ is the nominative subject of πέμπω. The closest parallel to this comparative clause is Jesus' petition in 17:18, which also uses the καθὼς ... κἀγώ point/counterpoint set to relate the sending of the Son to the sending of the disciples:

καθὼς ἐμὲ ἀπέστειλας εἰς τὸν κόσμον,	κἀγὼ ἀπέστειλα αὐτοὺς εἰς τὸν κόσμον (17:18)
καθὼς ἀπέσταλκέν με ὁ πατήρ,	κἀγὼ πέμπω ὑμᾶς (20:21)

ἀπέσταλκέν. Prf act ind 3rd sg ἀποστέλλω. ἀπέσταλκέν, which has an acute accent on the antepenult, acquired an additional accent, the acute, on the ultima from the enclitic με (Smyth §183; Carson 1985, 48). The juxtaposition of ἀποστέλλω and πέμπω in this point/counterpoint set indicates that these two verbs are used synonymously, as elsewhere in the FG: the sending of the Son is expressed with ἀποστέλλω in 3:17, 34; 5:36, 38; 6:29, 57; 7:29; 8:42; 10:36; 11:42; 17:3, 8, 18, 21, 23, 25, and with πέμπω in 4:34; 5:23, 24, 30, 37; 6:38, 39; 44; 7:16, 18, 28, 33; 8:16, 18, 26, 29; 9:4; 12:44, 45; 13:20; 14:24; 15:21; 16:5. The perfect-tense ἀπέσταλκέν "indicates that the sending of Jesus ... is regarded not only as an act of the past but as the enduring foundation of the sending of the disciples" (Frey 2018, 81).

με. Accusative direct object of ἀπέσταλκέν.

ὁ πατήρ. Nominative subject of ἀπέσταλκέν.

πέμπω. Pres act ind 1st sg πέμπω. On the synonymous use of πέμπω and ἀποστέλλω, see ἀπέσταλκέν above.

ὑμᾶς. Accusative direct object of πέμπω.

20:22 καὶ τοῦτο εἰπὼν ἐνεφύσησεν καὶ λέγει αὐτοῖς· λάβετε πνεῦμα ἅγιον·

καί. Coordinating conjunction.

τοῦτο. Accusative direct object of εἰπών. The anaphoric demonstrative refers to Jesus' words in the previous verse.

εἰπών. Aor act ptc masc nom sg λέγω (temporal). On participles that precede the main verb, see ἐμβλέψας in 1:36.

ἐνεφύσησεν. Aor act ind 3rd sg ἐμφυσάω. The verb ἐμφυσάω is a NT *hapax legomenon*, but it is used in the Septuagint in Gen 2:7 (ὁ θεὸς ... ἐνεφύσησεν εἰς τὸ πρόσωπον αὐτοῦ πνοὴν ζωῆς καὶ ἐγένετο ὁ ἄνθρωπος εἰς ψυχὴν ζῶσαν ["God ... breathed into his face a breath of life, and the man became a living being"]), Ezek 37:9 (ἐμφύσησον εἰς τοὺς νεκροὺς τούτους καὶ ζησάτωσαν ["blow into these corpses, and they shall live"]), and Wis 15:11 (ἠγνόησεν τὸν πλάσαντα αὐτὸν καὶ τὸν ἐμπνεύσαντα αὐτῷ ψυχὴν ἐνεργοῦσαν καὶ ἐμφυσήσαντα πνεῦμα ζωτικόν ["he did not know the one who molded him and infused him with an active soul and breathed into him a life-giving spirit"]).

καί. Coordinating conjunction.

λέγει. Pres act ind 3rd sg λέγω. The historical present gives prominence to Jesus' words that follow (see 1:15 on μαρτυρεῖ).

αὐτοῖς. Dative indirect object of λέγει and perhaps also dative complement of ἐνεφύσησεν.

λάβετε. Aor act impv 2nd pl λαμβάνω.

πνεῦμα ἅγιον. Accusative direct object of λάβετε. The adjective ἅγιον stands in the fourth attributive position (see 3:15 on ζωὴν αἰώνιον). Although the formulation is anarthrous, it is most likely definite like other anarthrous references to the Holy Spirit in the NT (e.g., Acts 2:4; 8:15, 17, 19; 19:2; cf. Brown, 2:1023).

20:23 ἄν τινων ἀφῆτε τὰς ἁμαρτίας ἀφέωνται αὐτοῖς, ἄν τινων κρατῆτε κεκράτηνται.

ἄν. ἄν stands for ἐάν (BDF §107; Caragounis 2004, 228) and introduces the protasis of a third-class condition (see 13:20). This verse is connected to the previous one by asyndeton.

τινων. Subjective genitive qualifying τὰς ἁμαρτίας ("the sins that certain people have committed").

ἀφῆτε. Aor act subj 2nd pl ἀφίημι.

τὰς ἁμαρτίας. Accusative direct object of ἀφῆτε.

ἀφέωνται. Prf pass ind 3rd pl ἀφίημι. The antecedent of the embedded subject of the verb is τινων ... τὰς ἁμαρτίας. The perfect ἀφέωνται marks the beginning of the apodosis of a third-class condition. Fanning (304) calls it "the proleptic perfect" because it "occurs after a conditional element of some kind which throws the entire statement into the future" (Wallace 1996, 581). The stative aspect of the verb form highlights the state of being forgiven. The primary (ultimate) agent is not expressed, but it is most likely God (Brown, 2:1024). The present-tense variant ἀφίενται (B² K N W Γ Δ Θ 078 33 700 892ˢ 1241 1424 𝔐 sy) and the future-tense variant ἀφεθήσεται (ℵ* q sa ly pbo) are probably "scribal simplifications which weaken the sense" (Metzger, 219).

αὐτοῖς. Dative of advantage. The personal pronoun refers to τινων. Lit. "the sins of certain people are forgiven for them."

ἄν. ἄν stands for ἐάν (BDF §107) and introduces the protasis of a third-class condition (see above).

τινων. Subjective genitive qualifying an implied τὰς ἁμαρτίας.

κρατῆτε. Pres act subj 2nd pl κρατέω. The implied direct object is τὰς ἁμαρτίας. While the aorist subjunctive ἀφῆτε presents forgiveness as a complete event, the imperfective aspect of the present subjunctive κρατῆτε "implies that the state of holding or refusing forgiveness continues" (Brown, 2:1023).

κεκράτηνται. Prf pass ind 3rd pl κρατέω. The antecedent of the embedded subject of the verb is τινων . . . τὰς ἁμαρτίας. κεκράτηνται marks the beginning of the apodosis of a third-class condition. This is another example of the proleptic perfect (see ἀφέωνται above). The stative aspect of the verb form highlights the state of being retained. The primary (ultimate) agent is not expressed, but it is most likely God (Brown, 2:1024; Harris 2015, 331).

John 20:24-29

²⁴But Thomas, one of the Twelve, who was called Didymus, was not with them when Jesus came. ²⁵So the other disciples kept telling him, "We have seen the Lord!" But he said to them, "Unless I see in his hands the mark of the nails, and place my finger into the mark of the nails, and place my hand into his side, I will never believe." ²⁶And after eight days his disciples were again inside, and Thomas [was] with them. Jesus came, although the doors had been locked, and stood in their midst and said, "Peace to you." ²⁷Then he said to Thomas, "Put your finger here and see my hands, and put your hand and place [it] into my side. And do not be unbelieving but believing." ²⁸Thomas answered and said to him, "My Lord and my God!" ²⁹Jesus said to him, "Because you have seen me, have you believed? Blessed [are] those who have not seen and yet have believed."

20:24 Θωμᾶς δὲ εἷς ἐκ τῶν δώδεκα, ὁ λεγόμενος Δίδυμος, οὐκ ἦν μετ' αὐτῶν ὅτε ἦλθεν Ἰησοῦς.

Θωμᾶς. Nominative subject of ἦν (see 11:16).
δέ. Marker of narrative development with a contrastive nuance.
εἷς. Nominative in apposition to Θωμᾶς.
ἐκ τῶν δώδεκα. Replaces the partitive genitive. In the FG, only two disciples are identified as "one of the Twelve": Judas (6:71) and Thomas (here). This is the last of the four references to the Twelve in the FG (6:67, 70, 71; 20:24).
ὁ λεγόμενος. Pres pass ptc masc nom sg λέγω (attributive). The participle modifies Θωμᾶς, standing in the third attributive position (see 1:18 on ὁ ὤν).
Δίδυμος. Nominative complement to Θωμᾶς in a double nominative subject-complement construction (see 11:16).
οὐκ. Negative particle normally used with indicative verbs.
ἦν. Impf act ind 3rd sg εἰμί. On the function of the imperfect in the FG, see 1:39 on ἦν.
μετ' αὐτῶν. Association/accompaniment.
ὅτε. Introduces a temporal clause.
ἦλθεν. Aor act ind 3rd sg ἔρχομαι.
Ἰησοῦς. Nominative subject of ἦλθεν.

20:25 ἔλεγον οὖν αὐτῷ οἱ ἄλλοι μαθηταί· ἑωράκαμεν τὸν κύριον. ὁ δὲ εἶπεν αὐτοῖς· ἐὰν μὴ ἴδω ἐν ταῖς χερσὶν αὐτοῦ τὸν τύπον τῶν ἥλων καὶ βάλω τὸν δάκτυλόν μου εἰς τὸν τύπον τῶν ἥλων καὶ βάλω μου τὴν χεῖρα εἰς τὴν πλευρὰν αὐτοῦ, οὐ μὴ πιστεύσω.

ἔλεγον. Impf act ind 3rd pl λέγω. On the function of the imperfect in the FG, see 1:39 on ἦν.
οὖν. Postpositive inferential conjunction and/or transitional particle (see 1:22 and 11:6).
αὐτῷ. Dative indirect object of ἔλεγον.
οἱ ἄλλοι μαθηταί. Nominative subject of ἔλεγον. The adjective ἄλλοι stands in the first attributive position (see 2:10 on τὸν καλὸν οἶνον).
ἑωράκαμεν. Perf act ind 1st pl ὁράω (see 20:18).
τὸν κύριον. Accusative direct object of ἑωράκαμεν.
ὁ δέ. A construction used in narrative literature to indicate the change of the speaker in a dialogue. The nominative article stands in place of a third-person singular personal pronoun and functions as the subject of εἶπεν.
εἶπεν. Aor act ind 3rd sg λέγω.

αὐτοῖς. Dative indirect object of εἶπεν.

ἐάν. Introduces the protasis of a third-class condition. ἐὰν μὴ can be translated "unless."

μὴ. Negative particle normally used with non-indicative verbs.

ἴδω. Aor act subj 1st sg ὁράω. Subjunctive with ἐάν.

ἐν ταῖς χερσὶν. Locative.

αὐτοῦ. Possessive genitive qualifying χερσὶν.

τὸν τύπον. Accusative direct object of ἴδω. τύπον here denotes "mark, trace" (BDAG, 1019.1).

τῶν ἥλων. Subjective genitive qualifying τύπον.

καὶ. Coordinating conjunction.

βάλω. Aor act subj 1st sg βάλλω. Subjunctive with ἐάν.

τὸν δάκτυλόν. Accusative direct object of βάλω. δάκτυλόν, which has an acute accent on the antepenult, acquired an additional accent, the acute, on the ultima from the enclitic μου (Smyth §183; Carson 1985, 48).

μου. Possessive genitive qualifying δάκτυλόν.

εἰς τὸν τύπον. Locative.

τῶν ἥλων. Subjective genitive qualifying τύπον.

καὶ. Coordinating conjunction.

βάλω. Aor act subj 1st sg βάλλω. Subjunctive with ἐάν.

μου. Possessive genitive qualifying χεῖρα. The preposed pronoun is thematically salient (Levinsohn 2000, 64).

τὴν χεῖρα. Accusative direct object of βάλω.

εἰς τὴν πλευρὰν. Locative (see 19:34).

αὐτοῦ. Possessive genitive qualifying πλευρὰν.

οὐ μὴ. Emphatic negation, which is usually followed by the aorist subjunctive.

πιστεύσω. Aor act subj 1st sg πιστεύω. Used with οὐ μὴ to express emphatic negation.

20:26 Καὶ μεθ' ἡμέρας ὀκτὼ πάλιν ἦσαν ἔσω οἱ μαθηταὶ αὐτοῦ καὶ Θωμᾶς μετ' αὐτῶν. ἔρχεται ὁ Ἰησοῦς τῶν θυρῶν κεκλεισμένων καὶ ἔστη εἰς τὸ μέσον καὶ εἶπεν· εἰρήνη ὑμῖν.

Καὶ. Coordinating conjunction.

μεθ' ἡμέρας ὀκτὼ. Temporal. "After eight days" = "after one week" (by inclusive reckoning).

πάλιν. Adverb "pert[aining] to repetition in the same (or similar) manner" (BDAG, 752.2).

ἦσαν. Impf act ind 3rd pl εἰμί. On the function of the imperfect in the FG, see 1:39 on ἦν.

ἔσω. Adverb of place ("inside" = "in the house"; cf. Harris 2012, 246.).
οἱ μαθηταί. Nominative subject of ἦσαν.
αὐτοῦ. Genitive of relationship qualifying μαθηταί.
καί. Coordinating conjunction.
Θωμᾶς. Nominative subject of an implied ἦν.
μετ' αὐτῶν. Association/accompaniment.
ἔρχεται. Pres mid ind 3rd sg ἔρχομαι. The historical present gives prominence to Jesus' arrival to the house where his disciples gathered. This clause is connected to the previous one by asyndeton.
ὁ Ἰησοῦς. Nominative subject of ἔρχεται.
τῶν θυρῶν. Genitive subject of κεκλεισμένων.
κεκλεισμένων. Prf pass ptc fem gen pl κλείω (genitive absolute, concessive).
καί. Coordinating conjunction.
ἔστη. Aor act ind 3rd sg ἵστημι.
εἰς τὸ μέσον. Locative. The adjective μέσον functions as a substantive. εἰς does not stand for ἐν because ἔστη + εἰς τὸ μέσον is preceded by the verb of motion ἔρχεται, suggesting arrival at the destination (see 20:19).
καί. Coordinating conjunction.
εἶπεν. Aor act ind 3rd sg λέγω.
εἰρήνη. Nominative subject of a verbless clause (see 20:19).
ὑμῖν. Dative of advantage.

20:27 εἶτα λέγει τῷ Θωμᾷ· φέρε τὸν δάκτυλόν σου ὧδε καὶ ἴδε τὰς χεῖράς μου καὶ φέρε τὴν χεῖρά σου καὶ βάλε εἰς τὴν πλευράν μου, καὶ μὴ γίνου ἄπιστος ἀλλὰ πιστός.

εἶτα. Adverb ("then, next").
λέγει. Pres act ind 3rd sg λέγω. The historical present gives prominence to Jesus' words to Thomas (see 1:15 on μαρτυρεῖ).
τῷ Θωμᾷ. Dative indirect object of λέγει.
φέρε. Pres act impv 2nd sg φέρω. The verb here means "to put or place an object by moving it to a particular point—'to put, to place'" (LN 85.42).
τὸν δάκτυλόν. Accusative direct object of φέρε. δάκτυλόν, which has an acute accent on the antepenult, acquired an additional accent, the acute, on the ultima from the enclitic σου (Smyth §183; Carson 1985, 48).
σου. Possessive genitive qualifying δάκτυλόν.
ὧδε. Adverb of place.
καί. Coordinating conjunction.

ἴδε. Aor act impv 2nd sg ὁράω. In this clause, ἴδε does not function as an interjection that is used "when that which is to be observed is in the nom[inative]" (BDAG, 466) but as a second-person singular imperative—a command to Thomas—that requires the direct object in the accusative ("see my hands"). It is therefore misleading to say with Porter (1994, 87) that "ἴδε and ἰδού are always followed by items in the nominative case," but it is also misleading to say with Wallace (1996, 60 n. 88) that this is an exception to the NT usage of ἴδε and ἰδού.

τὰς χεῖράς. Accusative direct object of ἴδε. χεῖράς, which has a circumflex accent on the penult, acquired an additional accent, the acute, on the ultima from the enclitic εἰσιν (Smyth §183; Carson 1985, 48).

μου. Possessive genitive qualifying χεῖράς.

καὶ. Coordinating conjunction.

φέρε. Pres act impv 2nd sg φέρω.

τὴν χεῖρά. Accusative direct object of φέρε. χεῖρά, which has a circumflex accent on the penult, acquired an additional accent, the acute, on the ultima from the enclitic σου (Smyth §183; Carson 1985, 48).

σου. Possessive genitive qualifying χεῖρά.

καὶ. Coordinating conjunction.

βάλε. Aor act impv 2nd sg βάλλω.

εἰς τὴν πλευράν. Locative (see 19:34).

μου. Possessive genitive qualifying πλευράν.

καὶ. Coordinating conjunction.

μὴ ... ἀλλά. A point/counterpoint set ("not this ... but that") that asks Thomas to replace the state of disbelief with that of belief. On the function of ἀλλά in a point/counterpoint set, see 1:8.

γίνου. Pres mid impv 2nd sg γίνομαι. The context indicates that μὴ γίνου ἄπιστος (lit. "do not become unbelieving") forbids the continuation of unbelieving: "[D]o not persist in your disbelief" (Brown, 2:1026).

ἄπιστος. Predicate adjective. This is the only occurrence of this word in the FG.

πιστός. Predicate adjective. This is the only occurrence of this word in the FG.

20:28 ἀπεκρίθη Θωμᾶς καὶ εἶπεν αὐτῷ· ὁ κύριός μου καὶ ὁ θεός μου.

ἀπεκρίθη. Aor mid ind 3rd sg ἀποκρίνομαι. On the voice, see "Deponency" in the Series Introduction. This verse is connected to the previous one by asyndeton.

Θωμᾶς. Nominative subject of ἀπεκρίθη.

καὶ εἶπεν αὐτῷ. Pleonastic clause under Semitic influence, which functions as a redundant quotative frame (see 1:25 on καὶ εἶπαν αὐτῷ).

καί. Coordinating conjunction.

εἶπεν. Aor act ind 3rd sg λέγω.

αὐτῷ. Dative indirect object of εἶπεν.

ὁ κύριός μου καὶ ὁ θεός μου. Since each noun has its own article, this is not an example of the Granville Sharp rule, but the introductory clause (καὶ εἶπεν αὐτῷ) clearly indicates that Thomas addresses Jesus, i.e., that both designations have one referent.

ὁ κύριός. Nominative for vocative. Apart from Matt 27:46, which has θεός in the vocative (twice), in all other instances in the NT God is addressed with the nominative (Wallace 1996, 58). Articular nominative for the vocative is idiomatic in Hebrew and Aramaic usage (Robertson, 451). Another reason for the presence of the article is that "a substantive in the Nominative case used in a vocative sense and followed by a possessive could not be anarthrous" (Moule, 116).

μου. Possessive genitive qualifying κύριός. Wallace explains that "[t]he idea of possession in such expressions is not to be pressed in the sense that the Lord is owned fully by Thomas. But in a broad sense, the Lord belongs to Thomas—now, on this occasion, in a way not true before" (1996, 82).

καί. Coordinating conjunction.

ὁ θεός. Nominative for vocative (see ὁ κύριός above).

μου. Possessive genitive qualifying θεός (see above).

20:29 λέγει αὐτῷ ὁ Ἰησοῦς· ὅτι ἑώρακάς με πεπίστευκας; μακάριοι οἱ μὴ ἰδόντες καὶ πιστεύσαντες.

λέγει. Pres act ind 3rd sg λέγω. The historical present gives prominence to Jesus' words to Thomas (see 1:15 on μαρτυρεῖ). This verse is connected to the previous one by asyndeton.

αὐτῷ. Dative indirect object of λέγει.

ὁ Ἰησοῦς. Nominative subject of λέγει.

ὅτι ἑώρακάς με πεπίστευκας. NA[28]/UBS[5] and SBLGNT punctuate this as a question (supported by many minuscules that include punctuation), but the sentence can also be taken as a statement. Barrett, for example, argues that "in this solemn and impressive pronouncement Jesus does not ask questions, but declares the truth" (573; cf. Brown 2:1027). Schnackenburg interprets the sentence as a reproach of Thomas because "the connection to what follows is . . . better: the statement is followed by the blessing of those who, without seeing, summon up this faith" (3:334).

ὅτι. Introduces a causal clause that is placed before the main clause for emphasis.

ἑώρακας. Prf act ind 2nd sg ὁράω. ἑώρακας, which has an acute accent on the antepenult, acquired an additional accent, the acute, on the ultima from the enclitic με (Smyth §183; Carson 1985, 48). Porter argues that both perfect-tense verbs in this verse, ἑώρακας and πεπίστευκας, refer to the present: "[B]ecause you see me do you believe?" (1989, 265). Excluding any past implication, however, is not completely justified because both events, Thomas' visual recognition of the risen Jesus and his confession of faith, transpired before Jesus spoke to him for the second time. What is probably more important in this context is that the use of the perfect tense gives semantic weight to the acts of seeing and believing, which is further highlighted by the next sentence, in which Jesus praises those who believe without seeing.

με. Accusative direct object of πεπίστευκας.

πεπίστευκας. Prf act ind 2nd sg πιστεύω (see ἑώρακας above).

μακάριοι. Predicate adjective. Fronted for emphasis. This clause is connected to the previous one by asyndeton.

οἱ μὴ ἰδόντες καὶ πιστεύσαντες. Nominative subject of an implied εἰσίν. The Granville Sharp rule is not applicable here because both substantival participles are in the plural. However, the singular article that governs the participles and the contextual markers indicate that this is a plural TSKS construction dealing with two groups that are related to each other (Wallace 1996, 278). Wallace (282) argues that here we have a case of two identical groups, but it is probably more accurate to see the second group as a subset of the first. Since Jesus refers to the future when he will return to the Father, the first group includes virtually everyone, while the second group includes only those who believe apart from sight. This is why many English translations interpret καὶ as adversative (e.g., NRSV: "those who have not seen and yet have come to believe").

μὴ. Negative particle normally used with non-indicative verbs.

ἰδόντες. Aor act ptc masc nom pl ὁράω (substantival).

πιστεύσαντες. Aor act ptc masc nom pl πιστεύω (substantival).

John 20:30-31

³⁰Now Jesus also did many other signs in the presence of his disciples, which are not written down in this book, ³¹but these are written down so that you may believe that Jesus is the Messiah, the Son of God, and that by believing you may have life in his name.

20:30 Πολλὰ μὲν οὖν καὶ ἄλλα σημεῖα ἐποίησεν ὁ Ἰησοῦς ἐνώπιον τῶν μαθητῶν [αὐτοῦ], ἃ οὐκ ἔστιν γεγραμμένα ἐν τῷ βιβλίῳ τούτῳ·

Πολλὰ . . . ἄλλα σημεῖα. Accusative direct object of ἐποίησεν. Both adjectives, Πολλὰ and ἄλλα, stand in the first (anarthrous) attributive position (see 2:6 on λίθιναι ὑδρίαι), but they are separated by the postpositive particles μέν + οὖν and the adverbial καί. Πολλὰ is fronted for emphasis. The use of the term σημεῖα for Jesus' miracles is one of the distinctive features of the FG (see 2:11, 23; 3:2; 4:48, 54; 6:2, 14, 26; 7:31; 9:16; 11:47; 12:18, 37; cf. Barrett, 75–78; Keener, 1:272–79; Thompson, 65–68).

μὲν. Correlative particle that is usually combined with δέ, setting up a contrast between many other signs that are not recorded and those that are recorded (see v. 31). According to Levinsohn, "The presence of μέν not only anticipates a corresponding sentence containing δέ but frequently, in narrative, it also downgrades the importance of the sentence containing μέν. In particular, the information introduced with μέν is often of a secondary importance in comparison with that introduced with δέ" (2000, 170).

οὖν. This postpositive particle is here placed third because the postpositive particle μὲν is placed second. μέν + οὖν could function either as a compound or as a construction in which each word retains its own meaning (Smyth §2901). As a compound, μὲν οὖν could be either resumptive or inferential (Levinsohn 2000, 170; Moule 162). When this combination marks a transition to a new subject, as here, each particle retains its own force: οὖν indicates a shift to a new topic—the signs that Jesus performed—and μέν points ahead to a contrasting counterpart with δέ, underscoring a juxtaposition of signs not written down and signs that have been written down.

καὶ. Adverbial use (adjunctive).

ἐποίησεν. Aor act ind 3rd sg ποιέω.

ὁ Ἰησοῦς. Nominative subject of ἐποίησεν.

ἐνώπιον τῶν μαθητῶν. Locative. ἐνώπιον is an improper preposition (see 1:3 on χωρὶς αὐτοῦ). This is the only occurrence of this preposition in the FG.

[αὐτοῦ]. Genitive of relationship qualifying μαθητῶν. The personal pronoun is printed within square brackets because the external evidence for its inclusion ($\mathfrak{P}^{66}$ ℵ C D L N W Γ Θ Ψ $f^{1.13}$ 33 565 700 892ˢ 1241 1424 𝔐 lat syˢ·ᵖ·ʰ**) and its exclusion (A B K Δ *l*844 *l*2211 f) is evenly balanced.

ἅ. Nominative subject of ἔστιν. The antecedent of the relative pronoun is σημεῖα.

οὐκ. Negative particle normally used with indicative verbs.

ἔστιν. Pres act ind 3rd sg εἰμί. Neuter plural subjects typically take singular verbs (see 1:28 on ἐγένετο). The enclitic ἐστιν is accented ἔστιν when it comes at the beginning of a sentence, when it expresses existence, or when it follows ἀλλ', εἰ, καί, οὐκ, ὅτι, or τοῦτ'. The third condition is fulfilled here.

γεγραμμένα. Prf pass ptc neut nom pl γράφω (perfect periphrastic).

ἐν τῷ βιβλίῳ τούτῳ. Locative.

20:31 ταῦτα δὲ γέγραπται ἵνα πιστεύ[σ]ητε ὅτι Ἰησοῦς ἐστιν ὁ χριστὸς ὁ υἱὸς τοῦ θεοῦ, καὶ ἵνα πιστεύοντες ζωὴν ἔχητε ἐν τῷ ὀνόματι αὐτοῦ.

ταῦτα. Accusative direct object of γέγραπται. The demonstrative pronoun is anaphoric, referring to σημεῖα mentioned in the previous verse (Brown 2:1056).

δέ. Marker of narrative development, introducing the statement that μέν (v. 30) anticipates.

γέγραπται. Prf pass ind 3rd sg γράφω. Neuter plural subjects typically take singular verbs (see 1:28 on ἐγένετο). Runge calls attention to a contrast between the simple perfect γέγραπται in this verse and the copular form ἔστιν γεγραμμένα in the previous verse. In his view, the evangelist's selection of the simple form to express the purpose of his book "suggests that the act of writing is more to the fore than the stative existence of the written form" (2016, 318).

ἵνα. Introduces a purpose clause.

πιστεύ[σ]ητε. Aor act subj 2nd pl (with σ) or pres act subj 2nd pl (without σ) πιστεύω. Subjunctive with ἵνα. Campbell (2007, 42) calls this kind of discourse "authorial discourse" because the evangelist addresses the audience directly rather than through the speech of one of the characters (see 19:35 for another example of "authorial discourse"). The letter σ is printed within square brackets because both its inclusion (ℵ² A C D K L N W Γ Δ Ψ $f^{1.13}$ 33 565 700 1241 1424 *l*844 𝔐) and its exclusion ($\mathfrak{P}^{66vid}$ ℵ* B Θ 892ˢ *l*2211) have good manuscript support. The aorist subjunctive is usually interpreted as an indication that the FG seeks to produce faith in non-Christians ("that you may come to faith"), and the present subjunctive that it seeks to strengthen the faith of those who already believe ("that you keep believing") (Barrett, 575; Brown, 2:1056; Smith, 386–87; Fee 1992, 2193–96). In light of verbal aspect theory, however, this distinction may no longer be tenable. The aorist subjunctive portrays believing as an overall experience, while the present subjunctive portrays it as an ongoing process, but each viewpoint is applicable to both initial and continuing faith. Hence the purpose of the Gospel cannot be based on text-critical arguments and verb tenses because they are inconclusive.

ὅτι. Introduces the clausal complement (indirect discourse) of πιστεύ[σ]ητε.

Ἰησοῦς. Nominative subject of ἐστιν. Carson regards Ἰησοῦς as a predicate nominative, which answers the question, "Who is the Messiah? Who is the Son of God?" (1987, 644). Carson's conclusion is that the FG is primarily an evangelistic document whose purpose is to convince the Jewish audience "that the Christ, the Son of God, is Jesus" (1987, 643; cf. Carson 2005, 693–714; see Jensen, 346–49, for a recent defense of this view). The most substantial critique of Carson's view is offered by Wallace (1996, 44, 46, 47 n. 34; see also Fee 1992), who argues that, in equative clauses that have articular nouns and proper names, the word order may be the determining factor in identifying the subject. He also suggests that when the syntactical evidence is ambiguous, as here, "[e]ither the first noun is S[ubject] or the proper name is S[ubject]" (Wallace 1996, 46). Since Ἰησοῦς is not only the first noun in the clause but also a proper name, it should be regarded as the subject of the verb. In the FG, such a confession is made by Martha in 11:27: ἐγὼ πεπίστευκα ὅτι σὺ εἶ ὁ χριστὸς ὁ υἱὸς τοῦ θεοῦ. Elsewhere in the Johannine literature, similar formulations occur in 1 John 2:22; 4:15; 5:1, 5.

ἐστιν. Pres act ind 3rd sg εἰμί.

ὁ χριστὸς. Predicate nominative. In all equative clauses in the FG that employ this title, ὁ χριστός follows the verb and functions as predicate nominative: ἐγὼ οὐκ εἰμὶ ὁ χριστός (1:20); σὺ οὐκ εἶ ὁ χριστός (1:25); οὐκ εἰμὶ ἐγὼ ὁ Χριστός (3:28); μήτι οὗτός ἐστιν ὁ χριστός (4:29); οὗτός ἐστιν ὁ χριστός (7:26); οὗτός ἐστιν ὁ χριστός (7:41); σὺ εἶ ὁ χριστός (10:24); σὺ εἶ ὁ χριστὸς ὁ υἱὸς τοῦ θεοῦ (11:27).

ὁ υἱὸς. Nominative in apposition to ὁ χριστὸς.

τοῦ θεοῦ. Genitive of relationship qualifying υἱὸς.

καὶ. Coordinating conjunction linking two purpose clauses.

ἵνα. Introduces a purpose clause.

πιστεύοντες. Pres act ptc masc nom pl πιστεύω (means or temporal). On participles that precede the main verb, see ἐμβλέψας in 1:36.

ζωὴν. Accusative direct object of ἔχητε. Fronted for emphasis. The addition of αἰώνιον after ζωὴν (ℵ C(*).1 D L Ψ f^{13} 33 it vg^{mss} sy$^{p.h**}$ sa bo Ir^{lat}) is most likely scribal modification under the influence of 3:15.

ἔχητε. Pres act subj 2nd pl ἔχω. Subjunctive with ἵνα.

ἐν τῷ ὀνόματι. Instrumental. ὄνομα is synecdoche for the whole person ("by his name" = "by the power of his person").

αὐτοῦ. Possessive genitive qualifying ὀνόματι.

John 21:1-14

¹After these things Jesus made himself visible again to the disciples by the Sea of Tiberias. And he made himself visible in this way. ²Simon Peter, and Thomas called Didymus, and Nathanael from Cana in Galilee, and the [sons] of Zebedee, and two others of his disciples were together. ³Simon Peter said to them, "I am going fishing." They said to him, "We also are coming with you." They went out and got into the boat, and during that night they caught nothing. ⁴When it was already early morning, Jesus stood on the beach; yet the disciples did not know that it was Jesus. ⁵So Jesus said to them, "Children, you do not have any fish, do you?" They answered him, "No." ⁶He said to them, "Cast the net to the right side of the boat, and you will find [some]." So they cast [it], and they were no longer able to draw it because of the multitude of fish. ⁷Then that disciple whom Jesus loved said to Peter, "It is the Lord!" So Simon Peter, when he heard that it was the Lord, tucked in his outer garment, for he was [otherwise] naked, and threw himself into the sea. ⁸But the other disciples came in the boat, dragging the net full of fish, for they were not far from the land but [only] about two hundred cubits. ⁹So when they got out on the land, they saw a charcoal fire lying [there], and a fish lying on [it], and bread. ¹⁰Jesus said to them, "Bring [some] of the fish that you have just caught." ¹¹So Simon Peter went up and drew the net to land full of large fish, one hundred and fifty-three; and though there were so many, the net was not torn. ¹²Jesus said to them, "Come, eat breakfast!" But none of the disciples dared to ask him, "Who are you?" because they knew that it was the Lord. ¹³Jesus came, and took the bread, and gave [it] to them, and the fish in the same way. ¹⁴This [was] now the third time Jesus was made visible to his disciples after he had been raised from the dead.

21:1 Μετὰ ταῦτα ἐφανέρωσεν ἑαυτὸν πάλιν ὁ Ἰησοῦς τοῖς μαθηταῖς ἐπὶ τῆς θαλάσσης τῆς Τιβεριάδος· ἐφανέρωσεν δὲ οὕτως.

Μετὰ ταῦτα. Temporal (see 3:22). This verse is connected to the previous one by asyndeton.

ἐφανέρωσεν. Aor act ind 3rd sg φανερόω. Here φανερόω means "to cause to become visible—'to make appear, to make visible, to cause to be seen'" (LN 24.19).

ἑαυτὸν. Accusative direct object of ἐφανέρωσεν.

πάλιν. Adverb "pert[aining] to repetition in the same (or similar) manner" (BDAG, 752.2).

ὁ Ἰησοῦς. Nominative subject of ἐφανέρωσεν.

τοῖς μαθηταῖς. Dative indirect object of ἐφανέρωσεν.

ἐπὶ τῆς θαλάσσης. Locative. Although ἐπί + genitive usually means "upon," it sometimes conveys the idea of vicinity, as here: "on the seashore" and thus "by the sea" (Robertson, 603; LN 83.23).

τῆς Τιβεριάδος. Epexegetical genitive, identifying the city in Galilee—Tiberias—after which the Sea of Galilee is sometimes named (see 6:1).

ἐφανέρωσεν. Aor act ind 3rd sg φανερόω.

δέ. Marker of narrative development.

οὕτως. Adverb of manner ("in this manner, thus, so").

21:2 Ἦσαν ὁμοῦ Σίμων Πέτρος καὶ Θωμᾶς ὁ λεγόμενος Δίδυμος καὶ Ναθαναὴλ ὁ ἀπὸ Κανὰ τῆς Γαλιλαίας καὶ οἱ τοῦ Ζεβεδαίου καὶ ἄλλοι ἐκ τῶν μαθητῶν αὐτοῦ δύο.

Ἦσαν. Impf act ind 3rd pl εἰμί. On the function of the imperfect in the FG, see 1:39 on ἦν. This verse is connected to the previous one by asyndeton.

ὁμοῦ. Adverb ("together").

Σίμων Πέτρος καὶ Θωμᾶς . . . καὶ Ναθαναὴλ . . . καὶ οἱ τοῦ Ζεβεδαίου . . . καὶ ἄλλοι . . . δύο. Compound nominative subject of Ἦσαν.

ὁ λεγόμενος. Pres pass ptc masc nom sg λέγω (attributive). The participle modifies Θωμᾶς, standing in the third attributive position (see 1:18 on ὁ ὤν).

Δίδυμος. Nominative complement to Θωμᾶς in a double nominative subject-complement construction (see 11:16).

ὁ ἀπὸ Κανά. The article functions as an adjectivizer, changing the PP ἀπὸ Κανά into an attributive modifier of Ναθαναήλ.

ἀπὸ Κανά. Source. The preposition ἀπό is used here "to indicate someone's local origin" (BDAG, 105.3.b). ἀπό started to replace ἐκ in this sense in Koine Greek (BDF §209.3).

τῆς Γαλιλαίας. Partitive genitive qualifying Κανά. Galilee denotes the territory within which Cana lies (MHT 3:210).

οἱ. The article functions as a nominalizer, changing the genitive noun τοῦ Ζεβεδαίου into one of the components of the compound nominative subject of Ἦσαν (see above). In this construction, the article + genitive is an ellipsis for filial relationship (see 19:25 on ἡ).

τοῦ Ζεβεδαίου. Genitive of relationship qualifying the implied υἱοί. The is the only reference to the sons of Zebedee in the FG, and even here they are not named. The two sons of Zebedee—James and John—are frequently mentioned in the Synoptic Gospels (Matt 4:21; 10:2; 20:20; 26:37; 27:56; Mark 1:19; 3:17; 10:35; Luke 5:10).

ἐκ τῶν μαθητῶν. Replaces the partitive genitive.
αὐτοῦ. Genitive of relationship qualifying μαθητῶν.

21:3 λέγει αὐτοῖς Σίμων Πέτρος· ὑπάγω ἁλιεύειν. λέγουσιν αὐτῷ· ἐρχόμεθα καὶ ἡμεῖς σὺν σοί. ἐξῆλθον καὶ ἐνέβησαν εἰς τὸ πλοῖον, καὶ ἐν ἐκείνῃ τῇ νυκτὶ ἐπίασαν οὐδέν.

λέγει. Pres act ind 3rd sg λέγω. The historical present gives prominence to Peter's announcement (see 1:15 on μαρτυρεῖ). This verse is connected to the previous one by asyndeton.

αὐτοῖς. Dative indirect object of λέγει.

Σίμων Πέτρος. Nominative subject of λέγει.

ὑπάγω. Pres act ind 1st sg ὑπάγω. This is a futuristic present because the present tense conveys the intention to act, but "both the process and its termination are future" (Fanning, 223).

ἁλιεύειν. Pres act inf ἁλιεύω (purpose). ἁλιεύω means "to catch fish, whether by means of a line or by a net" (LN 44.7). In addition to this occurrence, infinitive of purpose is used in the FG eleven more times (1:33; 4:7 [2x], 9, 10, 15, 38; 6:31, 52; 13:24; 14:2). Much more common is ἵνα + subjunctive.

λέγουσιν. Pres act ind 3rd pl λέγω. The historical present calls attention to the rejoinder of other six disciples. This clause is connected to the previous one by asyndeton.

αὐτῷ. Dative indirect object of λέγουσιν.

ἐρχόμεθα. Pres mid ind 1st pl ἔρχομαι. This is also a futuristic present (see ὑπάγω above).

καί. Adverbial (adjunctive).

ἡμεῖς. Nominative subject of ἐρχόμεθα. The personal pronoun is emphatic.

σὺν σοί. Association (company).

ἐξῆλθον. Aor act ind 3rd pl ἐξέρχομαι. This clause is connected to the previous one by asyndeton.

καί. Coordinating conjunction.

ἐνέβησαν. Aor act ind 3rd pl ἐμβαίνω.

εἰς τὸ πλοῖον. Locative.

καί. Coordinating conjunction.

ἐν ἐκείνῃ τῇ νυκτὶ. Temporal. The preposition ἐν functions as a "marker of a period of time" (BDAG, 329.10).

ἐπίασαν. Aor act ind 3rd pl πιάζω. The verb πιάζω ("to seize, to catch") is here used for catching fish. Elsewhere in the FG, πιάζω is used for arresting a person (7:30, 32, 44; 8:20; 10:39; 11:57).

οὐδέν. Accusative direct object of ἐπίασαν.

21:4 Πρωΐας δὲ ἤδη γενομένης ἔστη Ἰησοῦς εἰς τὸν αἰγιαλόν, οὐ μέντοι ᾔδεισαν οἱ μαθηταὶ ὅτι Ἰησοῦς ἐστιν.

Πρωΐας. Genitive subject of γενομένης. In the NT, πρωΐα (the "early part of the daylight period, [early] morning" [BDAG, 892]) occurs only here and in Matt 27:1.

δὲ. Marker of narrative development.

ἤδη. Adverb ("already").

γενομένης. Aor mid ptc fem gen sg γίνομαι (genitive absolute, temporal).

ἔστη. Aor act ind 3rd sg ἵστημι.

Ἰησοῦς. Nominative subject of ἔστη.

εἰς τὸν αἰγιαλόν. Locative. εἰς is used because a verb of motion is implied (Harris 2012, 85). For the combinations of ἔστη with εἰς that are preceded by verbs of motion, see 20:19 (ἦλθεν ὁ Ἰησοῦς καὶ ἔστη εἰς τὸ μέσον) and 20:26 (ἔρχεται ὁ Ἰησοῦς . . . καὶ ἔστη εἰς τὸ μέσον). Some copyists, however, replaced εἰς (attested in B C K N P Γ Δ ƒ[13] 1 565 1241 1424 𝔐 sy[h]) with the more "correct" ἐπί (ℵ A D L Θ Ψ 33 209 700 892[s] *l*844 *l*2211). Although the variant with ἐπί has good external support, the PP with εἰς is to be preferred because it is the *lectio difficilior*.

οὐ. Negative particle normally used with indicative verbs.

μέντοι. Adverbial particle with adversative sense ("though, to be sure, indeed" [BDAG, 630.2]).

ᾔδεισαν. Plprf act ind 3rd pl οἶδα. The pluperfect tense of οἶδα has the imperfect meaning.

οἱ μαθηταὶ. Nominative subject of ᾔδεισαν.

ὅτι. Introduces the clausal complement (indirect discourse) of ᾔδεισαν.

Ἰησοῦς. Predicate nominative. Fronted for emphasis.

ἐστιν. Pres act ind 3rd sg εἰμί. The present tense is retained from the corresponding direct discourse (see 1:39 on μένει).

21:5 λέγει οὖν αὐτοῖς [ὁ] Ἰησοῦς· παιδία, μή τι προσφάγιον ἔχετε; ἀπεκρίθησαν αὐτῷ· οὔ.

λέγει. Pres act ind 3rd sg λέγω. The historical present gives prominence to Jesus' question that follows (see 1:15 on μαρτυρεῖ).

οὖν. Postpositive inferential conjunction and/or transitional particle (see 1:22 and 11:6).

αὐτοῖς. Dative indirect object of λέγει.

[ὁ] Ἰησοῦς. Nominative subject of λέγει. The article is placed within square brackets because its omission in two major codices—Sinaiticus and Vaticanus—is counterbalanced by its inclusion in A^c C D K L N P Γ Δ Θ Ψ $f^{1.13}$ 33 565 700 𝔐 et al.

παιδία. Vocative of direct address. The term παιδίον ("a child, normally below the age of puberty" [BDAG, 749.1]) is here used "as a form of familiar address on the part of a respected pers[on], who feels himself on terms of fatherly intimacy w[ith] those whom he addresses" (BDAG, 749.3.b). Caragounis, however, argues that παιδία is "a colloquial expression which means 'lads,' 'fellows,' 'guys,' and which is used only in addressing persons of lower social rank or of the same rank by way of familiarity" (2004, 573). Although in the FG this word occurs twice more (4:49; 16:21), this is the only instance when it is used as a form of address. In 13:33, τεκνία is used. Elsewhere in the Johannine literature, παιδία is used as an address in 1 John 2:14, 18.

μή. Negative particle that introduces either a question expecting a negative answer or a cautious assertion (MHT 1:192). NA^{28}/UBS^5 and SBLGNT print μή τι as two separate words, but they could also be written together (μήτι) as in 4:29; 9:22; and 18:35. Since μήτι, like μή, could be used in "questions in which the questioner is in doubt concerning the answer" (BDAG, 649), the shorter or longer form of the particle has no effect on the meaning of the question, which here seems to be hesitating and doubtful (Barrett, 580).

τι προσφάγιον. Accusative direct object of ἔχετε. προσφάγιον ("a relish eaten with bread") is a NT *hapax legomenon*, which in this context refers to fish. If τι is written as a separate word, as in NA^{28}/UBS^5 and SBLGNT, it functions as an indefinite adjective ("some fish").

ἔχετε. Pres act ind 2nd pl ἔχω.

ἀπεκρίθησαν. Aor mid ind 3rd pl ἀποκρίνομαι. On the voice, see "Deponency" in the Series Introduction. This clause is connected to the previous one by asyndeton.

αὐτῷ. Dative indirect object of ἀπεκρίθησαν.

οὔ. When the negative particle is accented, as here, it means "no."

21:6 ὁ δὲ εἶπεν αὐτοῖς· βάλετε εἰς τὰ δεξιὰ μέρη τοῦ πλοίου τὸ δίκτυον, καὶ εὑρήσετε. ἔβαλον οὖν, καὶ οὐκέτι αὐτὸ ἑλκύσαι ἴσχυον ἀπὸ τοῦ πλήθους τῶν ἰχθύων.

ὁ δὲ. A construction used in narrative literature to indicate the change of the speaker in a dialogue. The nominative article stands in place of a third-person singular personal pronoun and functions as the subject of εἶπεν.
εἶπεν. Aor act ind 3rd sg λέγω.
αὐτοῖς. Dative indirect object of εἶπεν.
βάλετε. Aor act impv 2nd pl βάλλω.
εἰς τὰ δεξιὰ μέρη. Locative.
τοῦ πλοίου. Possessive genitive qualifying μέρη.
τὸ δίκτυον. Accusative direct object of βάλετε.
καὶ. Coordinating conjunction.
εὑρήσετε. Fut act ind 2nd pl εὑρίσκω.
ἔβαλον. Aor act ind 3rd pl βάλλω.
οὖν. Postpositive inferential conjunction and/or transitional particle (see 1:22 and 11:6).
καὶ. Coordinating conjunction.
οὐκέτι. Negative adverb of time ("no longer, no further").
αὐτὸ. Accusative direct object of ἑλκύσαι.
ἑλκύσαι. Aor act inf ἕλκω (complementary). ἕλκω means "to pull or drag, requiring force because of the inertia of the object being dragged" (LN 15.212).
ἴσχυον. Impf act ind 3rd pl ἰσχύω.
ἀπὸ τοῦ πλήθους. Causal (MHT 2:461).
τῶν ἰχθύων. Partitive genitive qualifying πλήθους.

21:7 λέγει οὖν ὁ μαθητὴς ἐκεῖνος ὃν ἠγάπα ὁ Ἰησοῦς τῷ Πέτρῳ· ὁ κύριός ἐστιν. Σίμων οὖν Πέτρος ἀκούσας ὅτι ὁ κύριός ἐστιν τὸν ἐπενδύτην διεζώσατο, ἦν γὰρ γυμνός, καὶ ἔβαλεν ἑαυτὸν εἰς τὴν θάλασσαν,

λέγει. Pres act ind 3rd sg λέγω. The historical present gives prominence to the words of the Beloved Disciple (see 1:15 on μαρτυρεῖ).
οὖν. Postpositive inferential conjunction and/or transitional particle (see 1:22 and 11:6).
ὁ μαθητὴς ἐκεῖνος. Nominative subject of λέγει.
ὃν. Accusative direct object of ἠγάπα. The antecedent of ὃν is ὁ μαθητὴς.

ἠγάπα. Impf act ind 3rd sg ἀγαπάω. On the use of ἀγαπάω to identify the Beloved Disciple in the FG, see 13:23.

ὁ Ἰησοῦς. Nominative subject of ἠγάπα.

τῷ Πέτρῳ. Dative indirect object of λέγει.

ὁ κύριός. Predicate nominative. Fronted for emphasis. κύριός, which has an acute accent on the antepenult, acquired an additional accent, the acute, on the ultima from the enclitic ἐστιν (Smyth §183; Carson 1985, 48).

ἐστιν. Pres act ind 3rd sg εἰμί.

Σίμων ... Πέτρος. Nominative subject of διεζώσατο.

οὖν. Postpositive inferential conjunction and/or transitional particle (see 1:22 and 11:6).

ἀκούσας. Aor act ptc masc nom sg ἀκούω (temporal). On participles that precede the main verb, see ἐμβλέψας in 1:36.

ὅτι. Introduces the clausal complement (indirect discourse) of ἀκούσας.

ὁ κύριός. Predicate nominative. κύριός, which has an acute accent on the antepenult, acquired an additional accent, the acute, on the ultima from the enclitic ἐστιν (Smyth §183; Carson 1985, 48).

ἐστιν. Pres act ind 3rd sg εἰμί. The present tense is retained from the direct discourse.

τὸν ἐπενδύτην. Accusative direct object of διεζώσατο. ἐπενδύτης ("outer garment, coat" [BDAG, 361]) is a NT *hapax legomenon*.

διεζώσατο. Aor mid ind 3rd sg διαζώννυμι. The only other occurrence of διαζώννυμι ("tie around" [BDAG, 228]) in the NT is in 13:4-5, where it refers to Jesus' tying a towel around himself. It is usually assumed that in this context the verb refers to putting on some clothes (cf. NRSV; ESV; NASB), suggesting that Peter got dressed before he jumped into the water because he did not want to greet Jesus naked or without an outer garment, if the second meaning of γυμνός is accepted (see below). Barrett defends this interpretation by claiming that "to offer greeting (שאל שלום) was a religious act and could not be performed without clothing" (580). Given the absurdity of the idea of putting clothes on rather than taking them off before swimming, Brown offers a more plausible scenario that makes good sense of διαζώννυμι and the explanatory clause that Peter was γυμνός: "[T]he writer means that Peter was naked underneath the *ependytēs* and that is why he could not take if off before he jumped into the water. Thus we get a more logical picture: clad only in his fisherman's smock, Peter tucks it into his cincture so that he can swim more easily and dives into the water" (2:1072).

ἦν. Impf act ind 3rd sg εἰμί. On the function of the imperfect in the FG, see 1:39 on ἦν.

γάρ. Postpositive conjunction that introduces the explanation of why Peter tied around his coat.

γυμνός. Predicate adjective. γυμνός could refer to "being without covering" ("naked, stripped, bare" [BDAG, 208.1]) or to "being lightly clad" ("without an outer garment" [BDAG, 208.3]).

καί. Coordinating conjunction.

ἔβαλεν. Aor act 3rd sg βάλλω.

ἑαυτόν. Accusative direct object of ἔβαλεν.

εἰς τὴν θάλασσαν. Locative.

21:8 οἱ δὲ ἄλλοι μαθηταὶ τῷ πλοιαρίῳ ἦλθον, οὐ γὰρ ἦσαν μακρὰν ἀπὸ τῆς γῆς ἀλλ' ὡς ἀπὸ πηχῶν διακοσίων, σύροντες τὸ δίκτυον τῶν ἰχθύων.

οἱ ... ἄλλοι μαθηταί. Nominative subject of ἦλθον.

δέ. Marker of narrative development.

τῷ πλοιαρίῳ. Locative dative ("in the boat") or dative of means/instrument ("by boat"). πλοιάριον is a diminutive of πλοῖον ("small ship, boat, skiff").

ἦλθον. Aor act ind 3rd pl ἔρχομαι.

οὐ. Negative particle normally used with indicative verbs.

γάρ. Postpositive conjunction that introduces the clause explaining why the disciples came in the boat.

ἦσαν. Impf act ind 3rd pl εἰμί. On the function of the imperfect in the FG, see 1:39 on ἦν.

μακράν. Adverb of place (BDAG, 612.1.a.α).

ἀπὸ τῆς γῆς. Separation.

ἀλλ'. Marker of contrast.

ὡς. Particle used with numerals to denote an estimate ("about, approximately").

ἀπὸ πηχῶν διακοσίων. Spatial, indicating distance. In this PP, ἀπό is used with the measure of distance "governing not the point from which the distance is measured, but the distance itself" (Zerwick §51). πῆχυς ("cubit") is "traditionally the distance from the elbow to the end of the fingers, about eighteen inches or one-half meter" (LN 81.25). διακόσιοι means "two hundred."

σύροντες. Pres act ptc masc nom pl σύρω (manner). On participles that follow the main verb, see βαπτίζων in 1:31.

τὸ δίκτυον. Accusative direct object of σύροντες.

τῶν ἰχθύων. Genitive of content qualifying δίκτυον (Wallace 1996, 93).

21:9 Ὡς οὖν ἀπέβησαν εἰς τὴν γῆν βλέπουσιν ἀνθρακιὰν κειμένην καὶ ὀψάριον ἐπικείμενον καὶ ἄρτον.

Ὡς. Temporal conjunction (BDAG, 1105.8.a; BDF §455.2).

οὖν. Postpositive inferential conjunction and/or transitional particle (see 1:22 and 11:6).

ἀπέβησαν. Aor act ind 3rd pl ἀποβαίνω.

εἰς τὴν γῆν. Locative.

βλέπουσιν. Pres act ind 3rd pl βλέπω. The historical present marks a transition to the new scene.

ἀνθρακιὰν. The first accusative direct object of βλέπουσιν in a double accusative object-complement construction.

κειμένην. Pres mid ptc fem acc sg κεῖμαι (predicative). Accusative complement to ἀνθρακιὰν in a double accusative object-complement construction. In this context, κεῖμαι means "to be in a place so as to be on someth[ing], lie" (BDAG, 537.2).

καί. Coordinating conjunction linking the first two direct objects of βλέπουσιν.

ὀψάριον. The second accusative direct object of βλέπουσιν in a double accusative object-complement construction. Barrett astutely notes that "[t]o find fish already cooking on the fire before the fish caught by the disciples had been brought is contrary to what might be expected" (581).

ἐπικείμενον. Pres mid ptc neut acc sg ἐπίκειμαι (predicative). Accusative complement to ὀψάριον in a double accusative object-complement construction. ἐπίκειμαι means "to be in a place of something—'to be on, to lie on'" (LN 85.4).

καί. Coordinating conjunction linking the last two direct objects of βλέπουσιν.

ἄρτον. The third accusative direct object of βλέπουσιν.

21:10 λέγει αὐτοῖς ὁ Ἰησοῦς· ἐνέγκατε ἀπὸ τῶν ὀψαρίων ὧν ἐπιάσατε νῦν.

λέγει. Pres act ind 3rd sg λέγω. The historical present gives prominence to Jesus' request (see 1:15 on μαρτυρεῖ). This verse is connected to the previous one by asyndeton.

αὐτοῖς. Dative indirect object of λέγει.

ὁ Ἰησοῦς. Nominative subject of λέγει.

ἐνέγκατε. Aor act impv 2nd pl φέρω. This is the only occurrence of an aorist imperative of φέρω in the NT (see 2:8 on φέρετε).

ἀπὸ τῶν ὀψαρίων. Replaces the partitive genitive (BDF §169). In the first twenty chapters of the FG, ἐκ + genitive was always used to replace the partitive genitive (e.g., 1:35, 40; 3:1, 31; 6:9, 11, 13, 26, 39, 50, 51, 60, 64, 66, 67, 71; 7:19, 25, 31, 40). This is the first and only time in the FG when ἀπό + genitive is used as a partitive PP. ἀπὸ τῶν ὀψαρίων is an ellipsis that presumes addition of τινά, which functions as the implied accusative direct object of ἐνέγκατε: ἐνέγκατε [τινά] ἀπὸ τῶν ὀψαρίων = "Bring [some] of the fish."

ὧν. The relative pronoun ὧν stands for ἅ, serving as the direct object of ἐπιάσατε. It is in the genitive because it is attracted to its antecedent ὀψαρίων.

ἐπιάσατε. Aor act ind 2nd pl πιάζω. In this context, πιάζω means "to catch" animals (BDAG, 812.2.b).

νῦν. Temporal adverb focusing on time shortly before the immediate present (BDAG, 681.1.b).

21:11 ἀνέβη οὖν Σίμων Πέτρος καὶ εἵλκυσεν τὸ δίκτυον εἰς τὴν γῆν μεστὸν ἰχθύων μεγάλων ἑκατὸν πεντήκοντα τριῶν· καὶ τοσούτων ὄντων οὐκ ἐσχίσθη τὸ δίκτυον.

ἀνέβη. Aor act ind 3rd sg ἀναβαίνω.

οὖν. Postpositive inferential conjunction and/or transitional particle (see 1:22 and 11:6).

Σίμων Πέτρος. Nominative subject of ἀνέβη.

καί. Coordinating conjunction.

εἵλκυσεν. Aor act ind 3rd sg ἕλκω. On the meaning of the verb, see 21:6 on ἑλκύσαι.

τὸ δίκτυον. Accusative direct object of εἵλκυσεν in a double accusative object-complement construction.

εἰς τὴν γῆν. Locative.

μεστόν. Accusative complement of τὸ δίκτυον in a double accusative object-complement construction. The adjective μεστός pertains to "a quantity that fills a space beyond expectations or appropriateness" (LN 59.39).

ἰχθύων μεγάλων. Genitive complement of μεστόν. The adjective μεγάλων is in the fourth attributive position (see 3:15 on ζωὴν αἰώνιον).

ἑκατὸν πεντήκοντα τριῶν. Cardinal number functioning as the attributive modifier of ἰχθύων. Given the evangelist's habit of qualifying his numerals with the particle ὡς to denote an estimate (1:39; 4:6; 6:10, 19; 11:18; 19:14, 39; 21:8), the exact number of the fish must be significant, but its purpose remains elusive. For various theories about the symbolic meaning of number 153, see Brown (2:1074–76).

καί. Coordinating conjunction linking two clauses in adversative relationship.

τοσούτων. Genitive subject of ὄντων.

ὄντων. Pres act ptc masc gen pl εἰμί (genitive absolute, concessive).

οὐκ. Negative particle normally used with indicative verbs.

ἐσχίσθη. Aor pass ind 3rd sg σχίζω.

τὸ δίκτυον. Nominative subject of ἐσχίσθη.

21:12 Λέγει αὐτοῖς ὁ Ἰησοῦς· δεῦτε ἀριστήσατε. οὐδεὶς δὲ ἐτόλμα τῶν μαθητῶν ἐξετάσαι αὐτόν· σὺ τίς εἶ; εἰδότες ὅτι ὁ κύριός ἐστιν.

Λέγει. Pres act ind 3rd sg λέγω. The historical present gives prominence to Jesus' invitation to eat breakfast (see 1:15 on μαρτυρεῖ). This verse is connected to the previous one by asyndeton.

αὐτοῖς. Dative indirect object of Λέγει.

ὁ Ἰησοῦς. Nominative subject of Λέγει.

δεῦτε. An adverb ("come here! come on!"), used as hortatory particle followed by the plural (imperative or aorist subjunctive) (BDAG, 220).

ἀριστήσατε. Aor act impv 2nd pl ἀριστάω.

οὐδεὶς. Nominative subject of ἐτόλμα. Fronted for emphasis.

δὲ. Marker of narrative development.

ἐτόλμα. Impf act ind 3rd sg τολμάω. On the function of the imperfect in the FG, see 1:39 on ἦν.

τῶν μαθητῶν. Partitive genitive qualifying οὐδεὶς.

ἐξετάσαι. Aor act inf ἐξετάζω (complementary).

αὐτόν. Accusative direct object of ἐξετάσαι.

σὺ. Nominative subject of εἶ. Fronted for emphasis (BDF §475).

τίς. Interrogative pronoun functioning as the predicate nominative of εἶ.

εἶ. Pres act ind 2nd sg εἰμί.

εἰδότες. Prf act ptc masc nom pl οἶδα (causal). On participles that follow the main verb, see βαπτίζων in 1:31.

ὅτι. Introduces the clausal complement (indirect discourse) of εἰδότες.

ὁ κύριός. Predicate nominative. κύριός, which has an acute accent on the antepenult, acquired an additional accent, the acute, on the ultima from the enclitic ἐστιν (Smyth §183; Carson 1985, 48).

ἐστιν. Pres act ind 3rd sg εἰμί. The present tense is retained from a corresponding direct discourse.

21:13 ἔρχεται Ἰησοῦς καὶ λαμβάνει τὸν ἄρτον καὶ δίδωσιν αὐτοῖς, καὶ τὸ ὀψάριον ὁμοίως.

ἔρχεται. Pres mid ind 3rd sg ἔρχομαι. All three verbs in this verse are the historical presents, highlighting Jesus' actions of coming, taking the bread, and giving it to them. This verse is connected to the previous one by asyndeton.

Ἰησοῦς. Nominative subject of ἔρχεται.

καὶ. Coordinating conjunction.

λαμβάνει. Pres act ind 3rd sg λαμβάνω. Historical present (see ἔρχεται above).

τὸν ἄρτον. Accusative direct object of λαμβάνει.

καὶ. Coordinating conjunction.

δίδωσιν. Pres act ind 3rd sg δίδωμι. Historical present (see ἔρχεται above). The implied direct object of the verb is τὸν ἄρτον.

αὐτοῖς. Dative indirect object of δίδωσιν.

καὶ. Coordinating conjunction.

τὸ ὀψάριον. Accusative direct object of δίδωσιν.

ὁμοίως. Adverb of manner ("likewise, in the same way").

21:14 τοῦτο ἤδη τρίτον ἐφανερώθη Ἰησοῦς τοῖς μαθηταῖς ἐγερθεὶς ἐκ νεκρῶν.

τοῦτο. Nominative subject of an implied ἦν. This verse is connected to the previous one by asyndeton.

ἤδη. Adverb ("now, already"). Fronted for emphasis.

τρίτον. Adverbial accusative ("the third time" [BDAG, 1016.1.b]). Jesus' appearance to Mary Magdalene is apparently not counted, perhaps because she was not considered to be one of Jesus' disciples (Barrett, 582). Fronted for emphasis.

ἐφανερώθη. Aor mid/pass ind 3rd sg φανερόω. The verb could be viewed as either middle (= "pass[ive] w[ith] intr[ansitive] sense" [BDAG, 1048.1.a.β]; see "Deponency" in the Series Introduction) or passive. Since the evangelist uses the active voice of φανερόω in 21:1 (ἐφανέρωσεν ἑαυτὸν . . . ὁ Ἰησοῦς), ἐφανερώθη in this verse is probably passive.

Ἰησοῦς. Nominative subject of ἐφανερώθη.

τοῖς μαθηταῖς. Dative indirect object of ἐφανερώθη.

ἐγερθεὶς. Aor pass ptc masc nom sg ἐγείρω (temporal). On the passive voice of ἐγείρω in reference to Jesus' resurrection, see 2:22 on ἠγέρθη. On participles that follow the main verb, see βαπτίζων in 1:31.

ἐκ νεκρῶν. Separation.

John 21:15-19

¹⁵So when they had eaten breakfast, Jesus said to Simon Peter, "Simon, [son] of John, do you love me more than these?" He said to him, "Yes, Lord, you know that I love you." He said to him, "Feed my lambs." ¹⁶He said to him again a second time, "Simon, [son] of John, do you love me?" He said to him, "Yes, Lord, you know that I love you." He said to him, "Tend my sheep." ¹⁷He said to him the third time, "Simon, [son] of John, do you love me?" Peter was grieved because he said to him the third time, "Do you love me?" and he said to him, "Lord, you know everything; you know that I love you." Jesus said to him, "Feed my sheep. ¹⁸Truly, truly I say to you, when you were young, you used to dress yourself and walk wherever you wanted. But when you grow old, you will stretch out your hands, and another will dress you and carry [you] where you do not want [to go]." ¹⁹Now he said this to indicate by what sort of death he would glorify God. And after he had said this, he said to him, "Follow me!"

21:15 Ὅτε οὖν ἠρίστησαν λέγει τῷ Σίμωνι Πέτρῳ ὁ Ἰησοῦς· Σίμων Ἰωάννου, ἀγαπᾷς με πλέον τούτων; λέγει αὐτῷ· ναὶ κύριε, σὺ οἶδας ὅτι φιλῶ σε. λέγει αὐτῷ· βόσκε τὰ ἀρνία μου.

Ὅτε. Introduces a temporal clause.

οὖν. Postpositive inferential conjunction and/or transitional particle (see 1:22 and 11:6).

ἠρίστησαν. Aor act ind 3rd pl ἀριστάω.

λέγει. Pres act ind 3rd sg λέγω. λέγει is a historical present that in vv. 15-17 introduces each of Jesus' questions, each of Peter's answers, and each of Jesus' replies, giving them rhetorical prominence (see 1:15 on μαρτυρεῖ).

τῷ Σίμωνι Πέτρῳ. Dative indirect object of λέγει.

ὁ Ἰησοῦς. Nominative subject of λέγει.

Σίμων. Vocative of direct address.

Ἰωάννου. Genitive of relationship in an elliptical construction ("[the son] of John"); for similar constructions, see 6:71 and 13:2, 26; see, however, 1:42, which contains the full formulation Σίμων ὁ υἱὸς Ἰωάννου. In the FG, Peter is regularly called Σίμων Πέτρος (6:68; 13:9, 24, 36; 18:10, 15, 25; 20:6; 21:2, 3, 7, 11), but only in Jesus' first conversation with him in 1:42 and in their post-resurrection dialogue in 21:15-17 is Peter identified through his filial relationship. Brown suggests that "by addressing Peter with the patronymic used when they first met (John i 42), Jesus is treating him less familiarly and thus challenging his friendship" (2:1102).

ἀγαπᾷς. Pres act ind 2nd sg ἀγαπάω. The first two of Jesus' questions use the verb ἀγαπάω, while the third uses the verb φιλέω. All three of Peter's answers employ the verb φιλέω.

	Jesus' question	Peter's answer
v. 15	ἀγαπᾷς με πλέον τούτων;	ναὶ κύριε, σὺ οἶδας ὅτι φιλῶ σε.
v. 16	ἀγαπᾷς με;	ναὶ κύριε, σὺ οἶδας ὅτι φιλῶ σε.
v. 17	φιλεῖς με;	κύριε, πάντα σὺ οἶδας, σὺ γινώσκεις ὅτι φιλῶ σε.

It is generally assumed by scholars, both ancient and modern, that this is a stylistic variation with no implications for the meaning of these two verbs. Indeed, the interchangeability of ἀγαπάω and φιλέω in this dialogue indicates that in the FG they are treated as virtual synonyms (LN 25.43; Brown, 2:1102–3; Barrett, 584; Carson 1991, 676–77; Smith, 396; Keener, 2:1235–36; Talbert, 271). Both verbs are used to identify the Beloved Disciple (see 13:23 on ἠγάπα), to express the Father's love for the Son (ἀγαπάω in 3:35; 10:17; 15:9; 17:23, 24, 26; φιλέω in 5:20), to describe Jesus' love for human beings (ἀγαπάω in 11:5; 13:1; 14:21; 15:9; φιλέω in 11:3, 36), and to portray the love of human beings for Jesus (ἀγαπάω in 8:42; 14:15, 21, 23, 24, 28; φιλέω in 16:27). Contextual synonymy of these two verbs in the FG, however, should not be taken as an indication of their semantic synonymy, as Porter rightly warns: "These two verbs, φιλέω and ἀγαπάω, are not true or complete synonyms. One of the differing components in the meanings of these words appears to be related to levels of esteem (a vertical scale) for ἀγαπάω and interpersonal associations (a horizontal scale) for φιλέω. The definition of a true synonym is that the two lexemes are interchangeable in all contexts. That simply is not true for these Greek lexemes: there is a major identifiable pattern of usage that is different" (2015, 299; for a view that φιλέω and ἀγαπάω are semantic synonyms, which should nevertheless be distinguished narrative-critically, see Shepherd, 777–92). Porter suggests that even in John 21:15-17 φιλέω and ἀγαπάω are not complete synonyms because of the logic of the dialogue, in which "Jesus has reduced his first question to a simpler question, and he has received a similarly unsatisfactory answer," which causes him to replace ἀγαπάω with φιλέω in his third question (2015, 300).

με. Accusative direct object of ἀγαπᾷς.

πλέον. Adverbial accusative. πλέον is a comparative from πολύς. The comparative phrase πλέον τούτων appears only in the first of Jesus' three questions to Peter.

τούτων. Genitive of comparison. τούτων (which may be either masculine or neuter plural) is an abbreviated comparison that can stand for (1) ἢ οὗτοι ("more than these men [love me]"), referring to the disciples' love for Jesus (Barrett, 584); (2) ἢ τούτους ("more than [you love] these men"), referring to Peter's love of other disciples; or (3) ἢ ταῦτα ("more than [you love] these things"; see 7:31, where the expression πλείονα σημεῖα ... ὧν corresponds to πλείονα σημεῖα ... ἢ ἅ), referring to nets and fish, i.e., to Peter's career as a fisherman (BDF §185.1; Talbert, 271; Morris, 768) or to this world in general (Ramelli, 336). Since all three options are grammatically valid, the arguments for or against them can only be based on one's assessment of the characterization of Peter in the entire narrative. It should also be noted that Peter's reply does not help resolving the ambiguity of πλέον τούτων because it completely ignores this part of Jesus' question.

λέγει. Pres act ind 3rd sg λέγω. Historical present (see above). This clause is connected to the previous one by asyndeton.

αὐτῷ. Dative indirect object of λέγει.

ναί. Affirmative particle.

κύριε. Vocative of direct address.

σύ. Nominative subject of οἶδας. Fronted for emphasis.

οἶδας. Prf act ind 2nd sg οἶδα (see 1:26 on οἴδατε).

ὅτι. Introduces the clausal complement (indirect discourse) of οἶδας.

φιλῶ. Pres act ind 1st sg φιλέω.

σε. Accusative direct object of φιλῶ.

λέγει. Pres act ind 3rd sg λέγω. Historical present (see above). This clause is connected to the previous one by asyndeton.

αὐτῷ. Dative indirect object of λέγει.

βόσκε. Pres act impv 2nd sg βόσκω. The first (v. 15) and the third (v. 17) replies of Jesus use the verb βόσκω ("feed, tend"), whereas the second reply (v. 16) uses the verb ποιμαίνω ("herd, tend, pasture"). It seems that there is no distinction in meaning of these two verbs (βόσκε = ποίμαινε = βόσκε), which occur nowhere else in the FG except in Jesus' dialogue with Peter.

τὰ ἀρνία. Accusative direct object of βόσκε. ἀρνία ("lambs") occurs only in the first reply of Jesus, whereas πρόβατα ("sheep") occurs the second (v. 16) and the third (v. 17). Given the parallelism between vv. 15, 16, and 17, it appears that both terms are used synonymously (ἀρνία = πρόβατα = πρόβατα).

μου. Possessive genitive qualifying ἀρνία.

21:16 λέγει αὐτῷ πάλιν δεύτερον· Σίμων Ἰωάννου, ἀγαπᾷς με; λέγει αὐτῷ· ναὶ κύριε, σὺ οἶδας ὅτι φιλῶ σε. λέγει αὐτῷ· ποίμαινε τὰ πρόβατά μου.

λέγει. Pres act ind 3rd sg λέγω. Historical present (see 21:15). It is noteworthy that the historical present is used mid-speech, adding extra prominence to the pronouncement that follows. Elsewhere in the NT, the historical present of λέγω is used mid-speech only in Mark 4:13; John 1:51; 21:17 (Runge 2010, 159 n. 38). This verse is connected to the previous one by asyndeton.

αὐτῷ. Dative indirect object of λέγει.

πάλιν. Adverb "pert[aining] to repetition in the same (or similar) manner" (BDAG, 752.2).

δεύτερον. Adverbial accusative ("for the second time" [BDAG, 221.2]). The use of δεύτερον accentuates the repetition of Jesus' question.

Σίμων. Vocative of direct address.

Ἰωάννου. Genitive of relationship in an elliptical construction (see 21:15).

ἀγαπᾷς. Pres act ind 2nd sg ἀγαπάω.

με. Accusative direct object of ἀγαπᾷς.

λέγει. Pres act ind 3rd sg λέγω. Historical present (see 21:15). This clause is connected to the previous one by asyndeton.

αὐτῷ. Dative indirect object of λέγει.

ναί. Affirmative particle.

κύριε. Vocative of direct address.

σύ. Nominative subject of οἶδας. Fronted for emphasis.

οἶδας. Prf act ind 2nd sg οἶδα (see 1:26 on οἴδατε).

ὅτι. Introduces the clausal complement (indirect discourse) of οἶδας.

φιλῶ. Pres act ind 1st sg φιλέω.

σε. Accusative direct object of φιλῶ.

λέγει. Pres act ind 3rd sg λέγω. Historical present (see 21:15). This clause is connected to the previous one by asyndeton.

αὐτῷ. Dative indirect object of λέγει.

ποίμαινε. Pres act impv 2nd sg ποιμαίνω (see 21:15 on βόσκε).

τὰ πρόβατά. Accusative direct object of ποίμαινε (see 21:15 on τὰ ἀρνία). πρόβατά, which has an acute accent on the antepenult, acquired an additional accent, the acute, on the ultima from the enclitic μου (Smyth §183; Carson 1985, 48).

μου. Possessive genitive qualifying πρόβατά.

21:17 λέγει αὐτῷ τὸ τρίτον· Σίμων Ἰωάννου, φιλεῖς με; ἐλυπήθη ὁ Πέτρος ὅτι εἶπεν αὐτῷ τὸ τρίτον· φιλεῖς με; καὶ λέγει αὐτῷ· κύριε, πάντα σὺ οἶδας, σὺ γινώσκεις ὅτι φιλῶ σε. λέγει αὐτῷ [ὁ Ἰησοῦς]· βόσκε τὰ πρόβατά μου.

λέγει. Pres act ind 3rd sg λέγω. Historical present (see 21:15). Like in the previous verse, the historical present is used mid-speech, adding extra prominence to the pronouncement that follows (Runge 2010, 159 n. 38). This verse is connected to the previous one by asyndeton.

αὐτῷ. Dative indirect object of λέγει.

τὸ τρίτον. Adverbial accusative ("the third time" [BDAG, 1016.1.b]). The use of τὸ τρίτον accentuates the repetition of Jesus' question.

Σίμων. Vocative of direct address.

Ἰωάννου. Genitive of relationship in an elliptical construction (see 21:15).

φιλεῖς. Pres act ind 2nd sg φιλέω.

με. Accusative direct object of φιλεῖς.

ἐλυπήθη. Aor pass ind 3rd sg λυπέω. This clause is connected to the previous one by asyndeton.

ὁ Πέτρος. Nominative subject of ἐλυπήθη.

ὅτι. Introduces a causal clause.

εἶπεν. Aor act ind 3rd sg λέγω.

αὐτῷ. Dative indirect object of εἶπεν.

τὸ τρίτον. Adverbial accusative (see above).

φιλεῖς. Pres act ind 2nd sg φιλέω.

με. Accusative direct object of φιλεῖς.

καὶ. Coordinating conjunction.

λέγει. Pres act ind 3rd sg λέγω. Historical present (see 21:15).

αὐτῷ. Dative indirect object of λέγει.

κύριε. Vocative of direct address.

πάντα. Accusative direct object of οἶδας. Fronted for emphasis.

σὺ. Nominative subject of οἶδας.

οἶδας. Prf act ind 2nd sg οἶδα (see 1:26 on οἴδατε).

σὺ. Nominative subject of γινώσκεις. Fronted for emphasis.

γινώσκεις. Pres act ind 2nd sg γινώσκω. Both the correspondence of πάντα σὺ οἶδας and σὺ γινώσκεις ὅτι φιλῶ σε and the parallelism between σὺ γινώσκεις ὅτι φιλῶ σε and σὺ οἶδας ὅτι φιλῶ σε in vv. 15-16 indicate that οἶδας and γινώσκεις are used as synonyms.

ὅτι. Introduces the clausal complement (indirect discourse) of γινώσκεις.

φιλῶ. Pres act ind 1st sg φιλέω.

σε. Accusative direct object of φιλῶ.

λέγει. Pres act ind 3rd sg λέγω. Historical present (see 21:15). This clause is connected to the previous one by asyndeton.

αὐτῷ. Dative indirect object of λέγει.

[ὁ Ἰησοῦς]. Nominative subject of λέγει. It is placed within square brackets because the evidence for its omission (ℵ D W f^1 33 565 lat sy^s pbo bo) is counterbalanced by the evidence for its inclusion (A B C K N Γ Δ Θ Ψ f^{13} 700 892^s 1241 1424 *l*844 𝔐).

βόσκε. Pres act impv 2nd sg βόσκω.

τὰ πρόβατά. Accusative direct object of βόσκε. πρόβατά, which has an acute accent on the antepenult, acquired an additional accent, the acute, on the ultima from the enclitic μου (Smyth §183; Carson 1985, 48).

μου. Possessive genitive qualifying πρόβατά.

21:18 Ἀμὴν ἀμὴν λέγω σοι, ὅτε ἦς νεώτερος, ἐζώννυες σεαυτὸν καὶ περιεπάτεις ὅπου ἤθελες· ὅταν δὲ γηράσῃς, ἐκτενεῖς τὰς χεῖράς σου, καὶ ἄλλος σε ζώσει καὶ οἴσει ὅπου οὐ θέλεις.

Ἀμὴν ἀμὴν λέγω σοι. Metacomment (see 1:51).

Ἀμὴν ἀμὴν. Asseverative particles that mark the beginning of Jesus' solemn declaration (see 1:51). This verse is connected to the previous one by asyndeton.

λέγω. Pres act ind 1st sg λέγω.

σοι. Dative indirect object of λέγω.

ὅτε. Introduces a temporal clause.

ἦς. Impf act ind 2nd sg εἰμί.

νεώτερος. Predicate adjective. νεώτερος is a comparative from νέος, but its sense in this clause it probably positive (BDAG, 669.3.a.β; BDF §244.2).

ἐζώννυες. Impf act ind 2nd sg ζώννυμι. Since in this verse ζώννυμι "involves more than the fastening of one's belt or putting a sash around the waist" (LN 49 n. 3), its sense is "to dress oneself, including the fastening of one's belt as the final act of dressing—'to dress'" (49.8).

σεαυτὸν. Accusative direct object of ἐζώννυες.

καὶ. Coordinating conjunction.

περιεπάτεις. Impf act ind 2nd sg περιπατέω.

ὅπου. Marker of a position in space.

ἤθελες. Impf act ind 2nd sg θέλω.

ὅταν. Introduces an indefinite temporal clause.

δὲ. Marker of narrative development.

γηράσῃς. Aor act subj 2nd sg γηράσκω. Subjunctive with ὅταν. γηράσκω means "to grow old, to become old" (LN 67.105).

ἐκτενεῖς. Fut act ind 2nd sg ἐκτείνω.

τὰς χεῖράς. Accusative direct object of ἐκτενεῖς. χεῖράς, which has a circumflex accent on the penult, acquired an additional accent, the acute, on the ultima from the enclitic σου (Smyth §183; Carson 1985, 48).

σου. Possessive genitive qualifying χεῖράς.
καὶ. Coordinating conjunction.
ἄλλος. Nominative subject of ζώσει. Fronted for emphasis.
σε. Accusative direct object of ζώσει.
ζώσει. Fut act ind 3rd sg ζώννυμι.
καὶ. Coordinating conjunction.
οἴσει. Fut act ind 3rd sg φέρω.
ὅπου. Marker of a position in space.
οὐ. Negative particle normally used with indicative verbs.
θέλεις. Pres act ind 2nd sg θέλω.

21:19 τοῦτο δὲ εἶπεν σημαίνων ποίῳ θανάτῳ δοξάσει τὸν θεόν. καὶ τοῦτο εἰπὼν λέγει αὐτῷ· ἀκολούθει μοι.

τοῦτο. Accusative direct object of εἶπεν. The demonstrative pronoun is anaphoric, referring to Jesus' words in v. 18b.
δὲ. Marker of narrative development.
εἶπεν. Aor act ind 3rd sg λέγω.
σημαίνων. Pres act ptc masc nom sg σημαίνω (purpose). On participles that follow the main verb, see βαπτίζων in 1:31.
ποίῳ θανάτῳ. Dative of manner (see 12:33; 18:32).
δοξάσει. Fut act ind 3rd sg δοξάζω.
τὸν θεόν. Accusative direct object of δοξάσει.
καὶ. Coordinating conjunction.
τοῦτο. Accusative direct object of εἰπών. The referent of τοῦτο is probably the same as of the previous τοῦτο.
εἰπών. Aor act ptc masc nom sg λέγω (temporal). On participles that precede the main verb, see ἐμβλέψας in 1:36.
λέγει. Pres act ind 3rd sg λέγω. Historical present (see 21:15).
αὐτῷ. Dative indirect object of λέγει.
ἀκολούθει. Pres act impv 2nd sg ἀκολουθέω.
μοι. Dative direct object of ἀκολούθει.

John 21:20-23

²¹When Peter turned around, he saw the disciple whom Jesus loved following [them], who also leaned back against his chest at the supper and said, "Lord, who is the one who is going to betray you?" ²¹So when he saw this man, Peter said to Jesus, "Lord, what about this man?" ²²Jesus said to him, "If I want him to remain until I come, what [is that] to you? You follow me!" ²³So this saying went forth among the brothers that that

disciple will not die. But Jesus did not say to him that he would not die but, "If I want him to remain until I come, what [is that] to you?"

21:20 Ἐπιστραφεὶς ὁ Πέτρος βλέπει τὸν μαθητὴν ὃν ἠγάπα ὁ Ἰησοῦς ἀκολουθοῦντα, ὃς καὶ ἀνέπεσεν ἐν τῷ δείπνῳ ἐπὶ τὸ στῆθος αὐτοῦ καὶ εἶπεν· κύριε, τίς ἐστιν ὁ παραδιδούς σε;

Ἐπιστραφεὶς. Aor mid ptc masc nom sg ἐπιστρέφω (temporal). On the voice, see "Deponency" in the Series Introduction (BDAG, 382.2). On participles that precede the main verb, see ἐμβλέψας in 1:36. This verse is connected to the previous one by asyndeton.

ὁ Πέτρος. Nominative subject of βλέπει.

βλέπει. Pres act ind 3rd sg βλέπω. The historical present marks a transition to a new scene (Battle, 128).

τὸν μαθητὴν. Accusative direct object of βλέπει in a double accusative object-complement construction.

ὃν. Accusative direct object of ἠγάπα. The antecedent of the relative pronoun is τὸν μαθητὴν.

ἠγάπα. Impf act ind 3rd sg ἀγαπάω. On the use of ἀγαπάω to identify the Beloved Disciple in the FG, see 13:23.

ὁ Ἰησοῦς. Nominative subject of ἠγάπα.

ἀκολουθοῦντα. Pres act ptc masc acc sg ἀκολουθέω (predicative). Accusative complement to τὸν μαθητὴν in a double accusative object-complement construction.

ὅς. Nominative subject of ἀνέπεσεν. The antecedent of the relative pronoun is τὸν μαθητὴν.

καὶ. Adverbial use (adjunctive).

ἀνέπεσεν. Aor act ind 3rd sg ἀναπίπτω. On the meaning, see 13:12.

ἐν τῷ δείπνῳ. Temporal.

ἐπὶ τὸ στῆθος. Locative (see 13:25).

αὐτοῦ. Possessive genitive qualifying στῆθος.

καὶ. Coordinating conjunction.

εἶπεν. Aor act ind 3rd sg λέγω.

κύριε. Vocative of direct address.

τίς. Predicate nominative. "Interrogatives, by their nature, indicate the unknown component and hence cannot be the subject" (Wallace 1996, 40 n. 12).

ἐστιν. Pres act ind 3rd sg εἰμί.

ὁ παραδιδούς. Pres act ptc masc nom sg παραδίδωμι (substantival). Nominative subject of ἐστιν.

σε. Accusative direct object of παραδιδούς.

21:21 τοῦτον οὖν ἰδὼν ὁ Πέτρος λέγει τῷ Ἰησοῦ· κύριε, οὗτος δὲ τί;

τοῦτον. Accusative direct object of ἰδών. The demonstrative pronoun is anaphoric, referring to the Beloved Disciple from the previous verse.

οὖν. Postpositive inferential conjunction and/or transitional particle (see 1:22 and 11:6).

ἰδών. Aor act ptc masc nom sg ὁράω (temporal). On participles that precede the main verb, see ἐμβλέψας in 1:36.

ὁ Πέτρος. Nominative subject of λέγει.

λέγει. Pres act ind 3rd sg λέγω. The historical present gives prominence to Peter's question that follows (see 1:15 on μαρτυρεῖ).

τῷ Ἰησοῦ. Dative indirect object of λέγει.

κύριε. Vocative of direct address.

οὗτος δὲ τί. An elliptical sentence that literally means "and this man, what?" Its sense in colloquial English is "and what about this man?" (Zerwick and Grosvenor, 348).

οὗτος. Nominative subject of an implied γενήσεται or γίνεται (Schackenburg, 3:369; Harris 2015, 345). Fronted for emphasis.

δὲ. Marker of narrative development.

τί. Predicate nominative (BDF §299.2).

21:22 λέγει αὐτῷ ὁ Ἰησοῦς· ἐὰν αὐτὸν θέλω μένειν ἕως ἔρχομαι, τί πρὸς σέ; σύ μοι ἀκολούθει.

λέγει. Pres act ind 3rd sg λέγω. The historical present gives prominence to Jesus' reply to Peter (see 1:15 on μαρτυρεῖ). This verse is connected to the previous one by asyndeton.

αὐτῷ. Dative indirect object of λέγει.

ὁ Ἰησοῦς. Nominative subject of λέγει.

ἐάν. Introduces the protasis of a third-class condition.

αὐτὸν. Accusative subject of the infinitive μένειν. Fronted for emphasis.

θέλω. Pres act subj 1st sg θέλω. Subjunctive with ἐάν.

μένειν. Pres act inf μένω (complementary).

ἕως. Temporal conjunction.

ἔρχομαι. Pres mid ind 1st sg ἔρχομαι. The verb has the futuristic sense and most likely refers to the return of Christ.

τί πρὸς σέ. An elliptical sentence, whose literal translation is "what to you?"

τί. Nominative subject of an implied ἐστίν (BDF §299.3): "what [is that] to you?" The interrogative pronoun marks the beginning of the apodosis of a third-class condition. Fronted for emphasis.

πρὸς σέ. Reference ("how does it concern you?" [BDAG, 875.3.e.γ]).

σύ. Nominative subject of ἀκολούθει. The fronting of σύ and its placement right after τί πρὸς σέ indicate that it "is in a very emphatic position" (Barrett, 586).

μοι. Dative direct object of ἀκολούθει.

ἀκολούθει. Pres act impv 2nd sg ἀκολουθέω. The verb stands in final, emphatic position.

21:23 ἐξῆλθεν οὖν οὗτος ὁ λόγος εἰς τοὺς ἀδελφοὺς ὅτι ὁ μαθητὴς ἐκεῖνος οὐκ ἀποθνῄσκει· οὐκ εἶπεν δὲ αὐτῷ ὁ Ἰησοῦς ὅτι οὐκ ἀποθνῄσκει ἀλλ᾽· ἐὰν αὐτὸν θέλω μένειν ἕως ἔρχομαι [, τί πρὸς σέ];

ἐξῆλθεν. Aor act ind 3rd sg ἐξέρχομαι.

οὖν. Postpositive inferential conjunction and/or transitional particle (see 1:22 and 11:6).

οὗτος ὁ λόγος. Nominative subject of ἐξῆλθεν. The demonstrative pronoun is cataphoric, anticipating the ὅτι clause that follows.

εἰς τοὺς ἀδελφοὺς. Locative. Robertson (593) notes that the context of many passages in which a verb of motion is combined with εἰς + accusative indicates that εἰς does not of itself mean "into" but could also be translated "among," as here (cf. Luke 6:20).

ὅτι. Introduces a nominal clause that stands in apposition to οὗτος ὁ λόγος (Wallace 1996, 458–59).

ὁ μαθητὴς ἐκεῖνος. Nominative subject of ἀποθνῄσκει (see 21:7).

οὐκ. Negative particle normally used with indicative verbs.

ἀποθνῄσκει. Pres act ind 3rd sg ἀποθνῄσκω. The context indicates that this is a futuristic present.

οὐκ . . . ἀλλ᾽. A point/counterpoint set ("not this . . . but that") that replaces the inaccurate inference that Jesus said that the Beloved Disciple would not die with the actual quotation of Jesus' words. On the function of ἀλλά in a point/counterpoint set, see 1:8.

εἶπεν. Aor act ind 3rd sg λέγω.

δὲ. Marker of narrative development.

αὐτῷ. Dative indirect object of εἶπεν. The antecedent of the personal pronoun is Peter.

ὁ Ἰησοῦς. Nominative subject of εἶπεν.

ὅτι. Introduces the clausal complement (indirect discourse) of εἶπεν.

οὐκ. Negative particle normally used with indicative verbs.

ἀποθνῄσκει. Pres act ind 3rd sg ἀποθνῄσκω. The present tense (referring to a future event) is retained from a corresponding direct discourse.

ἐὰν. Introduces the protasis of a third-class condition.

αὐτὸν. Accusative subject of the infinitive μένειν.

θέλω. Pres act subj 1st sg θέλω. Subjunctive with ἐάν.
μένειν. Pres act inf μένω (complementary).
ἕως. Temporal conjunction.
ἔρχομαι. Pres mid ind 1st sg ἔρχομαι.
[, τί πρὸς σέ]. This clause is omitted in several manuscripts (ℵ* C²ᵛⁱᵈ 565 a e syˢ), but it is included in the majority of witnesses (ℵ¹ A B C* K W Γ Δ Θ Ψ ƒ¹³ 33 700 892ˢ 1241 1424 𝔐 lat syᵖ·ʰ). While the shorter text could be original, it is also possible that some copyists deleted the clause to highlight the main claim that Jesus makes in his reply to Peter (Metzger, 221).
τί. Nominative subject of an implied ἐστίν (see 21:22). It marks the beginning of the apodosis of a third-class condition.
πρὸς σέ. Reference (see 21:22).

John 21:24-25

²⁴This is the disciple who is testifying about these things and who wrote these things, and we know that his testimony is true. ²⁵Now there are also many other things that Jesus did, which—if they were written down one by one, I suppose that not even the world itself could contain the books that would be written.

21:24 Οὗτός ἐστιν ὁ μαθητὴς ὁ μαρτυρῶν περὶ τούτων καὶ ὁ γράψας ταῦτα, καὶ οἴδαμεν ὅτι ἀληθὴς αὐτοῦ ἡ μαρτυρία ἐστίν.

Οὗτός. Nominative subject of ἐστιν. Fronted for emphasis. οὗτός, which has a circumflex accent on the penult, acquired an additional accent, the acute, on the ultima from the enclitic ἐστιν (Smyth §183; Carson 1985, 48). This verse is connected to the previous one by asyndeton.
ἐστιν. Pres act ind 3rd sg εἰμί.
ὁ μαθητὴς. Predicate nominative.
ὁ μαρτυρῶν. Pres act ptc masc nom sg μαρτυρέω (attributive). The participle modifies ὁ μαθητὴς, standing in the second attributive position (see 1:29 on ὁ αἴρων).
περὶ τούτων. Reference. τούτων probably refers to the entire Gospel (Barrett, 588).
καὶ. Coordinating conjunction.
ὁ γράψας. Aor act ptc masc nom sg γράφω (attributive). The participle modifies ὁ μαθητὴς, standing in the second attributive position (see 1:29 on ὁ αἴρων). The most natural meaning of ὁ γράψας is that the Beloved Disciple himself wrote down ταῦτα, but γράφω could also

have a causative sense like in 19:19, suggesting that the Beloved Disciple caused ταῦτα to be written.

ταῦτα. Accusative direct object of γράψας. ταῦτα most likely refers to the Gospel as a whole, with the exception of vv. 24-25, which were added by someone else other than the Beloved Disciple (Barrett, 588).

καὶ. Coordinating conjunction.

οἴδαμεν. Prf act ind 1st pl οἶδα (see 1:26 on οἴδατε). The implied first-person plural subject of the verb ("we") indicates different authorship of this verse and separates it from the previous narrative.

ὅτι. Introduces the clausal complement (indirect discourse) of οἴδαμεν.

ἀληθὴς. Predicate adjective. Fronted for emphasis.

αὐτοῦ. Subjective genitive qualifying μαρτυρία.

ἡ μαρτυρία. Nominative subject of ἐστίν.

ἐστίν. Pres act ind 3rd sg εἰμί.

21:25 Ἔστιν δὲ καὶ ἄλλα πολλὰ ἃ ἐποίησεν ὁ Ἰησοῦς, ἅτινα ἐὰν γράφηται καθ᾽ ἕν, οὐδ᾽ αὐτὸν οἶμαι τὸν κόσμον χωρῆσαι τὰ γραφόμενα βιβλία.

Ἔστιν. Pres act ind 3rd sg εἰμί. Neuter plural subjects typically take singular verbs (see 1:28 on ἐγένετο).

δὲ. Marker of narrative development.

καὶ. Coordinating conjunction.

ἄλλα πολλὰ. Nominative subject of Ἔστιν. The similarity of this expression to Πολλὰ . . . καὶ ἄλλα in 20:30 supports the idea that ch. 21 is an addendum to the FG (Barrett, 588).

ἃ. Accusative direct object of ἐποίησεν. The antecedent of the relative pronoun is ἄλλα πολλὰ.

ἐποίησεν. Aor act ind 3rd sg ποιέω.

ὁ Ἰησοῦς. Nominative subject of ἐποίησεν.

ἅτινα. Nominative subject of an unfinished relative clause that is intertwined with the conditional clause that follows (BDF §294.5). ἅτινα is a combination of the relative pronoun ἃ and the indefinite pronoun τινα, which here probably stands for ἃ because its antecedent (ἄλλα πολλὰ ἃ ἐποίησεν ὁ Ἰησοῦς) is determinate (Zerwick and Grosvenor, 348; Zerwick §216).

ἐὰν. Introduces the protasis of a third-class condition.

γράφηται. Pres pass subj 3rd sg γράφω. Subjunctive with ἐάν.

καθ᾽ ἕν. Distributive ("one at a time, one by one").

οὐδ᾽. A combination of the negative particle οὐ and the marker of narrative development δέ (οὐδ᾽ = οὐδέ). It negates either αὐτὸν . . . τὸν κόσμον ("not even the world itself") or the finite verb οἶμαι ("I do not suppose that the world would contain . . ."), rather than the infinitive χωρῆσαι as it is assumed in some English translations (e.g., NRSV: "I suppose that the world itself could not contain . . ."). οὐδ' marks the beginning of the apodosis of a third-class condition.

αὐτὸν . . . τὸν κόσμον. Accusative subject of the infinitive χωρῆσαι. αὐτὸν functions as an intensive pronoun ("the world itself"). The term κόσμος here denotes the totality of creation.

οἶμαι. Pres mid ind 1st sg οἶμαι. The verb means "to regard something as presumably true, but without particular certainty—'to suppose, to presume, to assume, to imagine, to believe, to think'" (LN 31.29).

χωρῆσαι. Aor act inf χωρέω (indirect discourse). χωρέω means "to be a quantity of space—'to have room for, to be space for, to contain'" (LN 80.4). Fanning argues that "[t]he instances in the NT of aorist infinitives in indirect discourse display a future or potential present sense, rather than an indirect statement about the past" (401).

τὰ . . . βιβλία. Accusative direct object of χωρῆσαι.

γραφόμενα. Pres pass ptc neut acc pl γράφω (attributive). The participle modifies τὰ . . . βιβλία, standing in the first attributive position (see 5:37 on πέμψας).

GLOSSARY

Adjectivizer—An article that transforms a nonadjective into an adjectival modifier. Thus, in the phrase τὴν παρὰ τοῦ μόνου θεοῦ (John 5:44), the article τὴν transforms the prepositional phrase παρὰ τοῦ μόνου θεοῦ into an attributive modifier of δόξαν.

Adjunctive—Providing something additional and supplemental. The term is used in relation to Greek conjunctions, especially καί when it signifies "also."

Anacoluthon—A logical and syntactical break in the flow of a sentence, in which a different idea and corresponding syntax begin without completing what came before.

Anaphoric—Referring back to a word or phrase that is coreferential. In the sentence "Ben went on a drive, and he liked it," the pronoun *he* refers, anaphorically, to *Ben*.

Anarthrous—Not modified by an article.

Antecedent—A word to which another word later in the discourse refers. A relative pronoun's antecedent is the preceding word about which the relative clause will provide further information.

Apodosis—The second element, providing the "then" clause after the protasis in a conditional sentence.

Articular—Modified by an article.

Ascensive—Rising or intensifying. The term is often applied to conjunctions, especially καί when it signifies "even."

Aspect—The depiction of an action, event, or state—either internally, as an unfolding process (e.g., "I am helping"), or externally, as a unified whole (e.g., "I helped").

Asyndeton—The absence of conjunctions connecting one clause to the next, effecting a faster sense of pace or intensity of tone. This is the default mode of connecting sentences in the FG.

Attraction—Rather than taking on the case required by its function within its clause, a relative pronoun occasionally reflects or "attracts" to the case of the antecedent.

Attendant circumstance—A dependent verbal participle that expresses an action that is closely connected to or prepares for the main verb. Although it is a dependent participle in that it does not occur independently of a main verb, it conveys its own verbal sense and may be translated as a finite verb connected to the main verb by *and*. An attendant circumstance participle is typically characterized by five key features: (1) it is aorist in tense, (2) it precedes the main verb in word order and in time of the action or event, (3) the main verb is aorist, (4) the mood of the main verb is indicative or imperative, and (5) it is common in narrative texts and infrequent elsewhere. In John 8:8, the participle κατακύψας in the sentence καὶ πάλιν κατακύψας ἔγραφεν εἰς τὴν γῆν is an attendant circumstance and may be translated "And again *he bent down* and continued writing on the ground."

Background—Information that does not advance the narrative or storyline but, rather, elaborates, supplements, or expands upon a feature of the narrative with supporting detail.

Cataphoric—Referring forward to a word or phrase that is coreferential. In the clauses "I saw her; Jane was running," the pronoun *her* refers, cataphorically, to *Jane*.

Causative—An action or circumstance is produced or initiated by the action of the verbal element.

Clausal complement—A clause that serves as direct object. Frequently this involves the use of ὅτι after verbs of speech; e.g., in the sentence καὶ ὑμεῖς λέγετε ὅτι ἐν Ἱεροσολύμοις ἐστὶν ὁ τόπος ὅπου προσκυνεῖν δεῖ ("you say that in Jerusalem is the place where it is necessary to worship"), the ὅτι clause serves as the clausal complement of λέγετε.

Complement—A clause, phrase, or word required to complete a given expression. This is especially common in double accusative constructions; e.g., in the sentence "Emmet calls turtles frogs," *turtles* is the object, and *frogs* is the complement. Without the complement, the expression is incomplete.

Concessive—An element introducing an idea, action, or circumstance that runs counter to the main clause. Concessive clauses are typically introduced with "although" or "even though."

Constructio ad sensum—A construction that does not correspond to the expected number or gender dictated by normal syntax, because it is responding to something inherent in the *sense* of that word rather than the word itself as a morphosyntactical entity; e.g., "The crowd is hungry and *are* getting restless." The plural *are* results from conceiving the singular crowd in terms of the multiple individuals making up the crowd.

Convertible/subset proposition—Specifies the relationship between subject and predicate in equative clauses. In a convertible proposition both subject and predicate have an identical referent and are interchangeable; e.g., "Christmas is the holiday on December 25." In a subset proposition, the predicate specifies the class of which the subject is an instance; e.g., "Matthew is a doctor."

Copula—The linking verb in an equative or copular clause, connecting a subject and predicate. In the copular clause αὕτη δέ ἐστιν ἡ κρίσις ("and the judgment is this"), the copula is ἐστιν.

Crasis—The formation of a single word from two words by contraction, e.g., κἀγώ for καὶ ἐγώ.

Development—The use of δέ that signals an advance in an argument or narrative but does not convey the overt continuity or discontinuity of a conjunction or adversative.

Deponency—When verbs with middle, passive, or middle/passive morphology were ascribed active meanings, they were labeled "deponent." This view has faced important challenges. Thus, the BHGNT acknowledge that middle morphology involves nuances associated with middle voice that should be taken into consideration. See Series Introduction for more.

Direct discourse—A record of the speech or thought of a character, introduced by an untranslated ὅτι and placed in quotation marks.

Double accusative construction—Some verbs can take two accusatives. In a person-thing double accusative, verbs of teaching, reminding, clothing, or asking can take an accusative direct object (the person) and an object-complement (the thing). Thus, in the sentence, "I taught Eliana the song," *Eliana* is the direct object and *song* is the complement. In an object-complement double accusative, verbs of making, sending, calling, and reckoning take both an object and the object's complement in the accusative. In the clause ἐποίησεν τὸ ὕδωρ οἶνον ("he had made the water wine") τὸ ὕδωρ is the direct object and οἶνον is the complement.

Double nominative subject-complement—Verbs that appear in double accusative object-complement constructions can, in the passive voice, have two nominative nouns functioning in the same manner as the object and complement of the object-complement double accusatives.

Elide/elision—The omission of a letter in a word or of an entire word. In the former case, the closing vowel in certain prepositions or conjunctions may be omitted, as in the α in ἀλλ' ἔγνωκα (John 5:42). In the latter case, an entire word is omitted and must be supplied by reference to context. In John 5:36, a second τῆς μαρτυρίας in the clause Ἐγὼ δὲ ἔχω τὴν μαρτυρίαν μείζω ("But I have a testimony greater than [the testimony] of John.") is elided, leaving only τοῦ Ἰωάννου.

Emphasis—Important information placed in a marked position for greater prominence.

Enclitic—A word that donates its accent to the word directly preceding it, as in πάντοτέ ἐστιν.

Epexegetical—An additional word or group of words that offer greater clarity. Infinitives can function in this way—clarifying or completing words like those relating to duty, ability, expectation, or necessity (e.g., "I hope *to eat*"). Similarly, an epexegetical use of clauses beginning with ἵνα or ὅτι function to clarify or complete an idea. When a head noun is ambiguous, an epexegetical genitive can be used to offer a particular example that clarifies the noun it modifies and may, therefore, be introduced in translation by "namely" or "which is."

Equative verb/clause—Equative clauses link subjects and predicates in constructions of the type "this is that." The verbs that do the linking (typically εἰμί, γίνομαι, or ὑπάρχω) are equative verbs. The sentence αὕτη ἐστὶν ἡ μαρτυρία τοῦ Ἰωάννου ("and the testimony of John is this") is an equative clause, and ἐστὶν is the equative verb.

External evidence—A term from textual criticism, referring to the evidence of manuscripts and versions (e.g., the text-type or antiquity of particular witnesses to a reading) rather than on considerations relating to the content of the text at hand (e.g., the author's style or theology).

First-class conditional—Stipulates the truth of the protasis (by means of εἰ with an indicative verb) for the sake of argument. The apodosis takes any mood and any tense.

Focal/focus—The key piece of information in a clause, frequently highlighted by placement in a marked position.

Foreground—Events that are indispensable to or propel the storyline.

Fronting/fronted—When an element occurs earlier in the sentence than might be expected in standard word order. Typically, this refers to a preverbal location.

Genitive absolute—A dependent clause consisting of a genitive substantive and an anarthrous genitive participle, which is, most of the time, independent of the verb in the main clause. The participle is usually temporal but can perform any of the adverbial functions of participles.

Genitive of . . .—*agency* specifies the agent actually doing the action; *relationship* specifies a social or familial relation; *comparison* usually comes after a comparative adjective and is introduced with "than" (e.g., "greater *than cats*"); *content* specifies what something contains or is full of; *direction* indicates where the head noun is moving; *subordination* specifies what is subordinated under the head noun; *production/producer* specifies what produced the noun to which it relates; *price* specifies the value or price paid; *product* specifies what is produced by the head noun; *purpose* gives the purpose of the head noun; *separation* specifies the point of departure from which the verb or head noun separates; *source* specifies the origin of the head noun; *time* indicates the time within which something happens. Other genitive relationships include *appositional* (specifies or exemplifies an ambiguous or metaphorical head noun by providing a clarifying example), *partitive* (specifies the whole of which the head noun is a part), *attributive* (specifies an attribute of the head noun), *subjective* (the subject of the verbal idea contained in the head noun), *objective* (the direct object of the verbal idea contained in the head noun), *descriptive* (describes the head noun in a broad manner).

Gnomic—A grammatical feature that, when used in reference to tense, expresses timelessness or general truths.

Grammaticalize—Representing semantic features by means of grammatical markers (prefixes, case endings, etc.).

Hapax legomenon—The only instance of a word recorded in a designated body of literature (in this case, the New Testament).

Haplography—The unintentional omission of a segment of text.

Headless relative clause—A relative clause without an antecedent, e.g., "Among you stands [one] *whom you do not know.*"

Hendiadys—Two words linked by καί and expressing one idea.

Historical present—The use of a present-tense verb when a past-tense verb would have been expected, thereby giving prominence to that element of the narrative.

Imperfective (aspect)—The function of present or imperfect tenses when used by a writer or speaker to frame an action or situation as habitual, ongoing, or viewed internally. See, by contrast, *perfective aspect* and *stative aspect*.

Indeclinable—Having no inflected forms; e.g., apart from a preceding article it is impossible to know whether Ναθαναὴλ is nominative, genitive, etc.

Indirect discourse—A record of the content of speech or thought introduced by ὅτι. If someone utters the sentence "I'd like to hold the baby," the indirect discourse would report the content of that utterance but not the utterance itself: "Someone said *he would like to hold the baby.*"

Intermediate agent—The personal or impersonal agent by means of whom/which an action took place, though he/she/it is not the ultimate cause or initiator of the action. The intermediate agent is introduced with διά + the agent in genitive case.

Internally headed relative clause—The relative clause contains the "antecedent" it modifies. In John 6:14, the relative clause ὃ ἐποίησεν σημεῖον contains the "antecedent" (σημεῖον) in the larger construction Οἱ οὖν ἄνθρωποι ἰδόντες ὃ ἐποίησεν σημεῖον ("So when the people saw the sign that he had done").

Intransitive—A verb that does not take a direct object. (Some verbs allow but do not require a direct object and can, therefore, function transitively or intransitively.)

Lectio difficilior—A text-critical principle that states that the more difficult reading is more likely to be original.

Left-dislocation—A sentence-structuring device in which "the next primary topic of the discourse" (Runge 2010 §14.2) is put at the beginning of the sentence and then picked up again with a resumptive pronoun in the main clause; e.g., "*The parents with the new baby*, they need more sleep."

Litotes—Making a statement by negating the opposite idea: "no small feat" = "quite an accomplishment." This kind of understatement typically serves as a means of emphasis.

Marked—When a word departs from standard sentence structure, frequently to highlight or emphasize the element placed in the atypical position. If subjects usually follow verbs in a given language, a subject coming before a verb would be in a "marked" position.

Metacomment—A comment about another comment. A metacomment occurs when speakers "stop saying what they are saying in order to comment on what is going to be said, speaking abstractly about it" (Runge 2010, 101). The pragmatic effect can lend solemnity or slow the pace to emphasize the importance of the subsequent utterance.

Metonymy/metonym—Substituting a word or description closely associated with something for the name/term of the thing itself. "Lend me your *ear*" is metonymy for "Lend me your [auditory] attention." In the expression "For my flesh is true eating" (a wooden rendering of John 6:55), "eating" (βρῶσις) is a metonym for what is eaten; i.e., *food*.

Monadic—Use of the definite article signaling that something is one of a kind.

Nominal clause—A group of words containing a verb and functioning as a noun.

Nominalizer—An article that converts a word, phrase, or clause (frequently adjectives and participial constructions) into substantives.

Paranomasia—A play on words typically involving the use of two or more words with similar forms or sounds.

Parataxis—The juxtaposition of clauses or phrases, which are connected with coordinating rather than subordinating conjunctions.

Parenthesis—A distinct thought connected to but also interrupting the discourse in which it occurs. In John 7:22 the discourse is interrupted with the parenthesis "not that it is from Moses, but from the fathers."

Perfective (aspect)—The function of the aorist tense when used by a writer or speaker to depict an action or situation externally or summarily as a completed whole. See, for contrast, *imperfective aspect*.

Periphrastic construction—The combination of an anarthrous participle and a verb of being functioning together like a finite verb.

Pleonasm/pleonastic—The use of additional words beyond what is strictly necessary. In the FG, pleonasms are a function of Semitic influence; e.g., the addition of καὶ εἶπεν αὐτῷ after ἀπεκρίθη.

Point/counterpoint set—One statement is negated (usually by οὐ or μή) to reject a possible misconception or to establish a key point of contrast and is followed by a positive statement beginning with and emphasized by an introductory ἀλλά (Runge 2010, 92–100).

Predicate nominative/accusative/adjective—The anarthrous element in an equative clause sharing the same case as the subject that it identifies, renames, or describes. In the sentence "Teddie is tough," *tough* is the predicate adjective and would occur in the nominative case.

Prominence—The state of being more significant or highlighted than other elements. In Greek this is regularly achieved by means of word order or the inclusion of words that are not strictly necessary.

Pronominal prolepsis—A pronoun in the main clause that anticipates the subject in a relative clause.

Protasis—The "if" clause in a conditional sentence.

Qal wahomer—Like *a minore ad maius* rhetorical arguments, this rabbinic mode of inference holds that if something is true in a less important matter, it also is true for what is more important.

Redundant quotative frame—Additional verbs introducing direct discourse when a prior verb has already done so; e.g., "And he confessed and did not deny, but confessed, 'I am not the Messiah'" (John 1:20).

Right-dislocation—A structuring device in which grammatically dispensable information is placed outside of the main clause, thus providing post hoc elaboration of something within the main clause; e.g., "They went outside, Zoe and Lee."

Second-class conditional—The "contrary-to-fact conditional," in which the protasis assumes the falsity of a premise for the sake of argument (by means of εἰ and a secondary tense indicative, typically aorist or imperfect). The apodosis typically has ἄν and an indicative secondary tense.

Semitism—Semitic style, idiom, or sentence structure that is not normally found in composition by native speakers/writers of Greek.

Synecdoche—A figure of speech in which one term is used in place of another with which it is associated, specifically involving a part-whole relationship. In the sentence, "Do you have your own *wheels*?" the word "wheels" stands for the entire "vehicle" of which it is a part.

Stative (aspect)—The use of verbs in the perfect and pluperfect tense by a writer or speaker to depict a state of affairs or state of being without reference to unfolding action or process. See, by contrast, *imperfective aspect*.

Third-class conditional—Conveys a logical connection, a hypothetical, or a future eventuality. The protasis uses ἐάν and a subjunctive verb (any tense). The apodosis is in any tense and any mood. A "present general" condition is formed when the apodosis contains a present indicative verb.

Topical frame—A key thematic element is fronted to establish the frame of reference for the following clause. According to Runge, "The two primary uses of topical frames are: to highlight the introduction of a new participant or topic, or to draw attention to a change in topics" (2010, 210).

Ultimate agent—The person ultimately authorizing/initiating and, therefore, bearing final responsibility for an action without necessarily carrying out that action him- or herself. The ultimate agent is conveyed by means of the genitive with ὑπό, ἀπό, or παρά.

Unmarked—Reflects standard usage or word order and, therefore, is not highlighted by the writer or speaker for special prominence.

WORKS CITED

Aubrey, Michael. "Greek Prohibitions." Pages 486–538 in *The Greek Verb Revisited: A Fresh Approach for Biblical Exegesis*. Edited by Steven E. Runge and Christopher J. Fresch. Bellingham, WA: Lexham Press, 2016.

Bakker, Egbert J. "Voice, Aspect and Aktionsart: Middle and Passive in Ancient Greek." Pages 23–47 in *Voice: Form and Function*. Edited by B. A. Fox and P. J. Hopper. Typological Studies in Language 27. Philadelphia: John Benjamins, 1994.

Barackman, Paul F. "The Gospel according to John." *Interpretation* 6 (1952): 63–78.

Barrett, C. K. *The Gospel according to St. John: An Introduction with Commentary and Notes on the Greek Text*. 2nd ed. Philadelphia: Westminster Press, 1978.

Battle, John A. "The Present Indicative in New Testament Exegesis." Th.D. diss., Grace Theological Seminary, 1975.

Beasley-Murray, George R. *John*. WBC 36. Rev. ed. Grand Rapids: Zondervan, 2015.

Bieringer, Reimund. "'I Am Ascending to My Father and Your Father, to My God and Your God' (John 20:17): Resurrection and Ascension in the Gospel of John." Pages 209–35 in *The Resurrection of Jesus in the Gospel of John*. Edited by Craig R. Koester and Reimund Bieringer. WUNT 222. Tübingen: Mohr Siebeck, 2008.

Boring, M. Eugene. *An Introduction to the New Testament: History, Literature, Theology*. Louisville: Westminster John Knox, 2012.

Brown, Raymond E. *The Gospel according to John*. 2 vols. AB 29–29A. Garden City, NY: Doubleday, 1966–70.

Bultmann, Rudolf. *The Gospel of John: A Commentary*. Translated by G. R. Beasley-Murray. Louisville: Westminster John Knox, 1971.

Burkett, Delbert Royce. *The Son of the Man in the Gospel of John*. JSNTSup 56. Sheffield: JSOT Press, 1991.

Burney, Charles Fox. *The Aramaic Origin of the Fourth Gospel*. Oxford: Clarendon, 1922.

Buth, Randall. "Participles as Pragmatic Choice: Where Semantics Meets Pragmatics." Pages 273–306 in *The Greek Verb Revisited: A Fresh Approach for Biblical Exegesis*. Edited by Steven E. Runge and Christopher J. Fresch. Bellingham, WA: Lexham Press, 2016.

———. "Οὖν, Δέ, Καί, and Asyndeton in John's Gospel." Pages 144–61 in *Linguistics and New Testament Interpretation: Essays on Discourse Analysis*. Edited by David Alan Black with Katharine Barnwell and Stephen Levinsohn. Nashville: Broadman & Holman, 1992.

Callow, John C. "The Historic Present in Mark." Paper presented at a seminar at SIL. Horsleys Green, UK, 1996.

Campbell, Constantine R. *Basics of Verbal Aspect in Biblical Greek*. Grand Rapids: Zondervan, 2008.

———. *Verbal Aspect, the Indicative Mood, and Narrative: Soundings in the Greek of the New Testament*. SBG 13. New York: Peter Lang, 2007.

Caragounis, Chrys C. "'Abide in Me': The New Mode of Relationship between Jesus and His Followers as a Basis for Christian Ethics (John 15)." Pages 250–63 in *Rethinking the Ethics of John: "Implicit Ethics" in the Johannine Writings*. Edited by Jan G. van der Watt and Ruben Zimmermann. WUNT 291. Tübingen: Mohr Siebeck, 2012.

———. *The Development of Greek and the New Testament: Morphology, Syntax, Phonology, and Textual Transmission*. WUNT 167. Tübingen: Mohr Siebeck, 2004.

———. "What Did Jesus Mean by τὴν ἀρχήν in John 8:25?" *Novum Testamentum* 49 (2007): 129–47.

Carson, D. A. *The Gospel according to John*. PNTC. Grand Rapids: Eerdmans, 1991.

———. *Greek Accents: A Student Manual*. Grand Rapids: Baker Books, 1985.

———. "The Purpose of the Fourth Gospel: John 20:31 Reconsidered." *Journal of Biblical Literature* 106 (1987): 639–51.

———. "Syntactical and Text-Critical Observations on John 20:30-31: One More Round on the Purpose of the Fourth Gospel." *Journal of Biblical Literature* 124 (2005): 693–714.

Cassirer, H. W. *God's New Covenant: A New Testament Translation*. Grand Rapids: Eerdmans, 1989.

Colwell, Ernest Cadman. "A Definite Rule for the Use of the Article in the Greek New Testament." *Journal of Biblical Literature* 52 (1933): 12–21.

Conrad, Carl W. "New Observations on Voice in the Ancient Greek Verb. November 19, 2002." Online: https://pages.wustl.edu/files/pages/imce/cwconrad/newobsancgrkvc.pdf.

Cooper, Guy L., III. *Attic Greek Prose Syntax*. 2 vols. Ann Arbor: University of Michigan Press, 1998–2002.

Crellin, Robert. "The Semantics of the Perfect in the Greek of the New Testament." Pages 430–57 in *The Greek Verb Revisited: A Fresh Approach for Biblical Exegesis*. Edited by Steven E. Runge and Christopher J. Fresch. Bellingham, WA: Lexham Press, 2016.

Culpepper, R. Alan. *Anatomy of the Fourth Gospel: A Study in Literary Design*. Philadelphia: Fortress Press, 1983.

Culy, Martin M. "The Clue Is in the Case: Distinguishing Adjectival and Adverbial Participles." *Perspectives in Religious Studies* 30 (2003): 441–53.

———. "Double Case Constructions in Koine Greek." *Journal of Greco-Roman Christianity and Judaism* 6 (2009): 82–106.

———. *I, II, III John: A Handbook on the Greek Text*. BHGNT. Waco, TX: Baylor University Press, 2004.

Culy, Martin M., Mikeal C. Parsons, and Joshua J. Stigall. *Luke: A Handbook on the Greek Text*. BHGNT. Waco, TX: Baylor University Press, 2010.

Daise, Michael A. "Quotations with 'Remembrance' Formulae in the Fourth Gospel." Pages 75–91 in *Abiding Words: The Use of Scripture in the Gospel of John*. Edited by Alicia D. Myers and Bruce G. Schuchard. Atlanta: Society of Biblical Literature, 2015.

Daube, David. "Jesus and the Samaritan Woman: The Meaning of συγχράομαι (Jn 4:7ff)." *Journal of Biblical Literature* 69 (1950): 137–47.

Decker, Rodney J. *Temporal Deixis of the Greek Verb in the Gospel of Mark with Reference to Verbal Aspect*. SBG 10. New York: Peter Lang, 2001.

Dennis, John. "Seeking Jesus: Observations on John's Vocabulary of Death." Pages 157–69 in *Repetitions and Variations in the Fourth Gospel: Style, Text, Interpretation*. Edited by G. Van Belle, M. Labahn, and P. Maritz. BETL 223. Leuven: Peeters, 2009.

Dixon, Paul Stephen. "The Significance of the Anarthrous Predicate Nominative in John." Th.M. thesis, Dallas Theological Seminary, 1975.

du Toit, Herman C. "The Function of the Imperfect Tense-Form in the Narrative Discourse of John's Gospel: Some Remarks." *Neotestamentica* 51 (2017): 209–34.

Fanning, Buist M. *Verbal Aspect in New Testament Greek*. Oxford Theological Monographs. Oxford: Clarendon, 1990.

Fee, Gordon D. "On the Text and Meaning of John 20:30-31." Pages 2193–205 in vol. 3 of *The Four Gospels 1992*. 3 vols. Edited by F. van Segbroeck et al. BETL 100. Leuven: Peeters, 1992.

———. "The Use of the Definite Article with Personal Names in the Gospel of John." *New Testament Studies* 17 (1970): 168–83.

Fresch, Christopher J. "Typology, Polysemy, and Prototypes: Situating Nonpast Aorist Indicatives." Pages 379–415 in *The Greek Verb Revisited: A Fresh Approach for Biblical Exegesis*. Edited by Steven E. Runge and Christopher J. Fresch. Bellingham, WA: Lexham Press, 2016.

Frey, Jörg. *The Glory of the Crucified One: Christology and Theology in the Gospel of John*. Translated by Wayne Coppins and Christoph Heilig. BMSEC. Waco, TX: Baylor University Press, 2018.

———. "Love-Relations in the Fourth Gospel." Pages 171–98 in *Repetitions and Variations in the Fourth Gospel: Style, Text, Interpretation*. Edited by G. Van Belle, M. Labahn, and P. Maritz. BETL 223. Leuven: Peeters, 2009.

———. *Die johanneische Eschatologie*. 3 vols. WUNT 96, 110, 117. Tübingen: Mohr Siebeck, 1997–2000.

Goodspeed, Edgar J. *The New Testament: An American Translation*. Chicago: University of Chicago, 1923.

Gundry, Robert H., and Russell W. Howell. "The Sense and Syntax of John 3:14-17 with Special Reference to the Use of ΟΥΤΩΣ . . . ΩΣΤΕ in John 3:16." *Novum Testamentum* 41 (1999): 24–39.

Hagner, Donald A. *The New Testament: A Historical and Theological Introduction*. Grand Rapids: Baker Academic, 2012.

Harner, Philip B. "Qualitative Anarthrous Predicate Nouns: Mark 15:39 and John 1:1." *Journal of Biblical Literature* 92 (1973): 75–87.

Harris, Murray J. *John*. EGGNT. Edited by Andreas J. Köstenberger and Robert Yarbrough. Nashville: B&H Academic, 2015.

———. *Prepositions and Theology in the Greek New Testament: An Essential Reference Resource for Exegesis*. Grand Rapids: Zondervan, 2012.

Haubeck, Wilfrid, and Heinrich von Siebenthal. *Neuer sprachlicher Schlüssel zum griechischen Neuen Testament*. 3rd ed. Giessen: Brunnen Verlag, 2015.

Heckert, Jacob K. *Discourse Function of Conjoiners in the Pastoral Epistles*. Dallas: SIL International, 1996.

James, Patrick. "Imperfects, Aorists, Historic Presents, and Perfects in John 11: A Narrative Test Case." Pages 184–230 in *The Greek Verb Revisited: A Fresh Approach for Biblical Exegesis*. Edited by Steven E. Runge and Christopher J. Fresch. Bellingham, WA: Lexham Press, 2016.

Jensen, Matthew D. "John Is No Exception: Identifying the Subject of εἰμί and Its Implications." *Journal of Biblical Literature* 135 (2016): 341–53.

Johnson, Luke Timothy. "Anti-Judaism and the New Testament." Pages 1609–38 in *Handbook for the Study of the Historical Jesus*. Edited by Tom Holmén and Stanley E. Porter. Leiden: Brill, 2011.

Keck, Leander E. "Derivation as Destiny: 'Of-ness' in Johannine Christology, Anthropology, and Soteriology." Pages 274–88 in *Exploring the Gospel of John: In Honor of D. Moody Smith*. Edited by R. Alan Culpepper and C. Clifton Black. Louisville: Westminster John Knox, 1996.

Keener, Craig S. *The Gospel of John: A Commentary*. 2 vols. Peabody, MA: Hendrickson, 2003.

Kerr, Alan R. *The Temple of Jesus' Body: The Temple Theme in the Gospel of John*. JSNTSup 220. London: Sheffield Academic Press, 2002.

Köstenberger, Andreas. *John*. BECNT. Grand Rapids: Baker Academic, 2004.

Kysar, Robert. *John, the Maverick Gospel*. 3rd ed. Louisville: Westminster John Knox, 2007.

Lappenga, Benjamin J. "Whose Zeal Is It Anyway? The Citation of Psalm 69:9 in John 2:17 as a Double Entendre." Pages 141–59 in *Abiding Words: The Use of Scripture in the Gospel of John*. Edited by Alicia D. Myers and Bruce G. Schuchard. Atlanta: Society of Biblical Literature, 2015.

Leung, Mavis M. "The Narrative Function and Verbal Aspect of the Historical Present in the Fourth Gospel." *Journal of the Evangelical Theological Society* 51 (2008): 703–20.

Levinsohn, Stephen H. *Discourse Features of New Testament Greek: A Coursebook on the Information Structure of New Testament Greek*. 2nd ed. Dallas: SIL International, 2000.

———. "Verb Forms and Grounding in Narrative." Pages 163–83 in *The Greek Verb Revisited: A Fresh Approach for Biblical Exegesis*. Edited by Steven E. Runge and Christopher J. Fresch. Bellingham, WA: Lexham Press, 2016.

Lincoln, Andrew T. *The Gospel according to St. John*. BNTC 4. Peabody, MA: Hendrickson, 2005.

Martyn, J. Louis. *History and Theology in the Fourth Gospel*. 3rd ed. Louisville: Westminster John Knox, 2003.

Mason, Steve. "Jews, Judaeans, Judaizing, Judaism: Problems of Categorization in Ancient History." *Journal for the Study of Judaism* 38 (2007): 457–512.

Matera, Frank J. "John 20:1–18." *Interpretation* 43 (1989): 402–6.

McGaughy, Lane C. *Toward a Descriptive Analysis of EINAI as a Linking Verb in New Testament Greek*. SBLDS 6. Missoula, MT: Society of Biblical Literature, 1972.

McGehee, Michael. "A Less Theological Reading of John 20:17." *Journal of Biblical Literature* 105 (1986): 299–302.

McHugh, John F. *A Critical and Exegetical Commentary on John 1–4*. ICC. London: T&T Clark International, 2009.

McKay, K. L. *A New Syntax of the Verb in New Testament Greek: An Aspectual Approach*. SBG 5. New York: Peter Lang, 1994.

———. "On the Perfect and Other Aspects in New Testament Greek." *Novum Testamentum* 23 (1981): 289–329.

———. "Time and Aspect in New Testament Greek." *Novum Testamentum* 34 (1992): 209–28.

Menken, Maarten J. J. "The Quotation from Isa 40,3 in John 1,23." *Biblica* 66 (1985): 190–205.

Metzger, Bruce M. *A Textual Commentary on the Greek New Testament*. 2nd ed. Stuttgart: German Bible Society, 1994.

Michaels, J. Ramsey. *The Gospel of John*. NICNT. Grand Rapids: Eerdmans, 2010.

Moffatt, James. *The Moffatt Translation of the Bible*. 2nd ed. London: Hodder, 1933.

Morris, Leon. *The Gospel according to John*. NICNT. Grand Rapids: Eerdmans, 1995.

Moule, C. F. D. *An Idiom Book of New Testament Greek*. 2nd ed. Cambridge: Cambridge University Press, 1959.

Moulton, James Hope. *A Grammar of New Testament Greek*. Vol. 1: *Prolegomena*. 3rd ed. Edinburgh: T&T Clark, 1957.

Moulton, James Hope, and Wilbert Francis Howard. *A Grammar of New Testament Greek*. Vol. 2: *Accidence and Word Formation*. Edinburgh: T&T Clark, 1963.

Newman, Barclay M., and Eugene A. Nida. *A Translator's Handbook on the Gospel of John*. Helps for Translators Series. London: United Bible Societies, 1980.

Novakovic, Lidija. *Raised from the Dead according to Scripture: The Role of Israel's Scripture in the Early Christian Interpretations of Jesus' Resurrection*. JCT 12. London: Bloomsbury T&T Clark, 2012.

O'Rourke, John J. "The Historic Present in the Gospel of John." *Journal of Biblical Literature* 93 (1974): 585–90.

Pennington, Jonathan T. "Deponency in Koine Greek: The Grammatical Question and the Lexicographical Dilemma." *Trinity Journal* 24 (2003): 55–76.

Pierce, Madison N., and Benjamin E. Reynolds. "The Perfect Tense-Form and the Son of Man in John 3.13: Developments in Greek Grammar as a Viable Solution to the Timing of the Ascent and Descent." *New Testament Studies* 60 (2014): 149–55.

Porter, Stanley E. *Idioms of the Greek New Testament*. BLG 2. 2nd ed. Sheffield: JSOT, 1994.

———. "In Defence of Verbal Aspect." Pages 26–45 in *Biblical Greek Language and Linguistics: Open Questions in Current Research*. Edited by Stanley E. Porter and D. A. Carson. JSNTSup 80. Sheffield: Sheffield Academic Press, 1993.

———. *Linguistic Analysis of the Greek New Testament: Studies in Tools, Methods, and Practice*. Grand Rapids: Baker Academic, 2015.

———. *Verbal Aspect in the Greek of the New Testament, with Reference to Tense and Mood*. SBG 1. New York: Peter Lang, 1989.

Poythress, Vern S. "The Use of the Intersentence Conjunctions *De, Oun, Kai*, and Asyndeton in the Gospel of John." *Novum Testamentum* 26 (1984): 312–40.

Ramelli, Ilaria. "'Simon Son of John, Do You Love *Me*?' Some Reflections on John 21:15." *Novum Testamentum* 50 (2008): 332–50.

Ridderbos, Herman N. *The Gospel according to John: A Theological Commentary*. Translated by John Vriend. Grand Rapids: Eerdmans, 1997.

Robar, Elizabeth. "The Historical Present in NT Greek: An Exercise in Interpreting Matthew." Pages 329–52 in *The Greek Verb Revisited: A Fresh Approach for Biblical Exegesis*. Edited by Steven E. Runge and Christopher J. Fresch. Bellingham, WA: Lexham Press, 2016.

Robertson, A. T. *A Grammar of the Greek New Testament in the Light of Historical Research*. 3rd ed. Nashville: Broadman, 1934.

Robinson, J. A. T. "The Destination and Purpose of St John's Gospel." *New Testament Studies* 6 (1960): 117–31.

Runge, Steven. "Contrastive Substitution and the Greek Verb: Reassessing Porter's Argument." *Novum Testamentum* 56 (2014): 154–73.
———. *Discourse Grammar of the Greek New Testament: A Practical Introduction for Teaching and Exegesis*. Lexham Bible Reference Series. Peabody, MA: Hendrickson, 2010.
———. "Functions of Copula-Participle Combinations ('Periphrastics')." Pages 307–26 in *The Greek Verb Revisited: A Fresh Approach for Biblical Exegesis*. Edited by Steven E. Runge and Christopher J. Fresch. Bellingham, WA: Lexham Press, 2016.
———. "The Verbal Aspect of the Historical Present Indicative in Narrative." Paper presented at the annual meeting of the Society of Biblical Literature, New Orleans, LA, November 21–24, 2009. Online: http://www.ntdiscourse.org/docs/ReconsideringHP.pdf.
Schnackenburg, Rudolf. *The Gospel according to St. John*. 3 vols. Translated by Kevin Smyth et al. New York: Crossroad, 1968, 1980, 1982.
Shepherd, David. "'Do You Love Me?': A Narrative-Critical Reappraisal of ἀγαπάω and φιλέω in John 21:15-17." *Journal of Biblical Literature* 129 (2010): 777–92.
Smith, D. Moody. *John*. ANTC. Nashville: Abingdon, 1999.
Smyth, H. W. *Greek Grammar*. Revised by G. M. Messing. Cambridge, MA: Harvard University Press, 1956.
Talbert, Charles H. *Reading John: A Literary and Theological Commentary on the Fourth Gospel and the Johannine Epistles*. Rev. ed. Macon: Smyth & Helwys, 2005.
Taylor, Bernard A. "Deponency and Greek Lexicography." Pages 167–76 in *Biblical Greek Language and Lexicography: Essays in Honor of Frederick W. Danker*. Edited by B. A. Taylor et al. Grand Rapids: Eerdmans, 2004.
Theobald, Michael. "Der johanneische Osterglaube und die Grenzen seiner narrative Vermittlung (Joh 20)." Pages 93–123 in *Von Jesus zum Christus: Christologische Studien*. Edited by Rudolf Hoppe and Ulrich Busse. BZNW 93. Berlin: de Gruyter, 1998.
Thomson, Christopher J. "What Is Aspect? Contrasting Definitions in General Linguistics and New Testament Studies." Pages 13–80 in *The Greek Verb Revisited: A Fresh Approach for Biblical Exegesis*. Edited by Steven E. Runge and Christopher J. Fresch. Bellingham, WA: Lexham Press, 2016.
Thompson, Marianne Meye. *John: A Commentary*. The New Testament Library. Louisville: Westminster John Knox, 2015.
Tolmie, D. Francois. "The Ἰουδαῖοι in the Fourth Gospel: A Narratological Perspective." Pages 377–97 in *Theology and Christology in the*

Fourth Gospel: Essays by the Members of the SNTS Johannine Writings Seminar. Leuven: Leuven University Press, 2005.

Torrey, Charles Culter. *Our Translated Gospels: Some of the Evidence.* New York: Harper & Brothers, 1936.

Turner, Nigel. *A Grammar of New Testament Greek.* Vol. 3: *Syntax.* Edited by J. H. Moulton. Edinburgh: T&T Clark, 1963.

———. *Grammatical Insights into the New Testament.* Edinburgh: T&T Clark, 1965.

Van Belle, Gilbert. "Theory of Repetitions and Variations in the Fourth Gospel: A Neglected Field of Research?" Pages 14–32 in *Repetitions and Variations in the Fourth Gospel: Style, Text, Interpretation.* Edited by G. Van Belle, M. Labahn, and P. Maritz. BETL 223. Leuven: Peeters, 2009.

van der Watt, Jan. "*Double Entendre* in the Gospel according to John." Pages 463–81 in *Theology and Christology in the Fourth Gospel: Essays by the Members of the SNTS Johannine Writings Seminar.* Leuven: Leuven University Press, 2005.

———. "Repetition and Functionality in the Gospel according to John: Some Initial Explorations." Pages 87–108 in *Repetitions and Variations in the Fourth Gospel: Style, Text, Interpretation.* Edited by G. Van Belle, M. Labahn, and P. Maritz. BETL 223. Leuven: Peeters, 2009.

von Soden, Hermann Freiherr. *Die Schriften des Neuen Testaments in ihrer ältesten erreichbaren Textgestalt, hergestellt auf Grund ihrer Textgeschichte.* Vol. 1, part 1. 2nd ed. Berlin: Verlag von Arthur Glaue, 1911.

von Wahlde, Urban C. "The Johannine 'Jews': A Critical Survey." *New Testament Studies* 28 (1982): 33–60.

Wallace, Daniel B. *Greek Grammar beyond the Basics: An Exegetical Syntax of the New Testament.* Grand Rapids: Zondervan, 1996.

———. "John 5,2 and the Date of the Fourth Gospel." *Biblica* 71 (1990): 177–205.

Young, Richard A. *Intermediate New Testament Greek: A Linguistic and Exegetical Approach.* Nashville: Broadman & Holman, 1994.

Zerwick, Maximilian. *Biblical Greek: Illustrated by Examples.* English ed. adapted from the Fourth Latin ed. by Joseph Smith. Rome: Pontifical Institute, 1963.

Zerwick, Maximilian, and Mary Grosvenor. *A Grammatical Analysis of the Greek New Testament.* Unabridged, 3rd rev. ed. Rome: Biblical Institute Press, 1988.

AUTHOR INDEX

Bold indicates the volume number.

Aubrey, Michael, **1**.63, 168

Bakker, Egbert J., **1**.xii; **2**.xii
Barackman, Paul F., **1**.xxi; **2**.xxi
Barrett, C. K., **1**.xxi, 13, 35, 60, 61, 71, 74, 75, 85, 87, 96, 100, 122, 124, 142, 146, 162, 168, 182, 189, 198, 217, 230, 246, 253, 274, 279, 285, 302, 317, 326, 327, 332, 341, 358, 359, 366; **2**.xxi, 2, 4, 6, 10, 11, 21, 22, 26, 32, 35, 36, 56, 58, 60, 62, 63, 70, 71, 75, 80, 83, 88, 90, 95, 97, 103, 108, 109, 114, 123, 128, 131, 134, 137, 149, 155, 162, 164, 165, 173, 182, 193, 199, 200, 201, 202, 203, 206, 207, 212, 216, 220, 221, 242, 250, 256, 275, 283, 287, 294, 295, 308, 310, 311, 317, 319, 321, 324, 326, 327, 334, 335, 336, 349
Battle, John A., **1**.29, 110, 324, 387; **2**.28, 111, 234, 332

BDF (Blass, Debrunner, and Funk), **1**.1, 14, 16, 19, 23, 25, 27, 28, 34, 36, 37, 39, 44, 45, 46, 52, 53, 54, 56, 57, 59, 60, 66, 67, 68, 70, 72, 77, 80, 90, 94, 96, 102, 105, 106, 110, 114, 116, 117, 118, 120, 124, 132, 133, 136, 141, 143, 146, 148, 151, 169, 173, 174, 177, 182, 185, 186, 187, 189, 191, 193, 194, 196, 205, 206, 214, 225, 234, 236, 237, 240, 246, 249, 250, 253, 265, 272, 273, 278, 286, 287, 298, 302, 308, 309, 312, 314, 315, 316, 318, 319, 320, 321, 322, 326, 331, 334, 336, 337, 341, 342, 348, 349, 351, 352, 354, 366, 369, 375; **2**.3, 5, 7, 11, 15, 21, 23, 24, 26, 35, 37, 38, 51, 53, 56, 59, 60, 63, 64, 69, 70, 74, 85, 93, 98, 103, 104, 105, 109, 115, 120, 123, 137, 140, 145, 146, 148, 149, 152, 160, 162, 165, 166, 173, 176, 177, 179, 182, 187, 188, 191, 192, 195, 196, 198, 207, 211, 215, 216, 218, 220, 224, 237, 242, 244,

246, 247, 253, 259, 260, 261, 264, 267, 273, 275, 278, 282, 284, 288, 290, 295, 299, 300, 302, 303, 314, 321, 323, 327, 330, 333, 336
Beasley-Murray, George R., **2**.36, 90, 109, 256
Bieringer, Reimund, **2**.296, 297
Boring, M. Eugene, **1**.205
Brown, Raymond E., **1**.2, 13, 16, 29, 33, 69, 84, 86, 87, 101, 103, 112, 117, 123, 246, 258, 266, 268, 287, 297, 343, 358, 359; **2**.6, 44, 61, 63, 88, 90, 109, 110, 114, 115, 118, 127, 147, 149, 153, 159, 170, 171, 172, 173, 182, 189, 191, 205, 206, 212, 216, 219, 238, 241, 249, 255, 256, 259, 264, 268, 275, 286, 287, 288, 295, 302, 303, 307, 308, 311, 319, 322, 325, 326
Bultmann, Rudolf, **1**.14; **2**.52, 90, 114, 170, 171, 172, 208, 275, 284
Burkett, Delbert Royce, **1**.84
Burney, Charles Fox, **1**.xxiii; **2**.xxiii
Buth, Randall, **1**.17, 32, 37, 136

Callow, John C., **1**.14
Campbell, Constantine R., **1**.xi, xxiii, 26, 57, 59, 157, 229, 249, 253, 342; **2**.xi, xxiii, 9, 32, 42, 91, 203, 206, 217, 276, 311
Caragounis, Chrys C., **1**.xiii, 27, 28, 166, 287, 315; **2**.xxiii, 32, 36, 43, 47, 60, 107, 109, 116, 135, 139, 142, 146, 148, 166, 170, 182, 192, 203, 211, 219, 232, 302, 317
Carson, D. A., **1**.15, 16, 30, 34, 35, 49, 50, 65, 78, 79, 122, 128, 131, 132, 135, 137, 152, 153, 154, 157, 165, 170, 174, 176, 178, 189, 198, 200, 201, 206, 207, 208, 211, 214, 216, 220, 221, 222, 225, 226, 231, 235, 242, 248, 249, 251, 255, 257, 261, 265, 283, 290, 293, 295, 298, 301, 304, 306, 316, 320, 321, 322, 325, 327, 329, 330, 334, 335, 338, 339, 343, 356, 358, 365, 366, 367, 369, 373; **2**.7, 29, 30, 31, 55, 58, 64, 77, 79, 81, 93, 95, 98, 102, 108, 111, 112, 118, 121, 123, 125, 126, 130, 131, 135, 136, 139, 141, 147, 150, 155, 159, 163, 168, 171, 175, 176, 177, 178, 182, 183, 185, 191, 193, 194, 195, 196, 198, 200, 205, 209, 211, 212, 213, 220, 222, 239, 240, 252, 253, 267, 292, 297, 301, 305, 306, 307, 309, 312, 319, 323, 326, 328, 330, 335
Cassirer, H. W., **1**.2
Colwell, Ernest Cadman, **1**.2, 3, 12, 49, 167, 231, 317, 328, 347; **2**.264
Conrad, Carl W., **1**.xii, xiii, 312; **2**.xii, xiii
Cooper, Guy L., **1**.312
Crellin, Robert, **1**.179
Culpepper, R. Alan, **1**.40
Culy, Martin M., **1**.19, 20, 29, 37, 42, 48, 79, 80, 91, 109, 125, 189, 312; **2**.5, 12, 36, 148, 151, 192

Daise, Michael A., **2**.55
Daube, David, **1**.112
Dennis, John, **1**.238; **2**.41, 217
Dixon, Paul Stephen, **1**.3
du Toit, Herman C., **1**.xxv, 40, 44, 68, 94, 129; **2**.xxv, 15, 221, 270

Fanning, Buist M., **1**.xxiii, 39, 53, 56, 98, 134, 150, 191, 229, 236, 244, 252, 277, 281, 282, 284, 291, 308, 331, 369; **2**.xxiii, 10, 19, 32, 71, 83, 85, 87, 107, 121, 144, 146, 148, 162, 164, 190, 202, 262, 303, 315, 337
Fee, Gordon D., **1**.157; **2**.311, 312
Fresch, Christopher J., **1**.xxiv; **2**.xxiv
Frey, Jörg, **1**.xxv, 4, 15, 29, 64, 65, 84, 102, 104, 124, 162, 166, 168, 208, 226, 367; **2**.xxv, 62, 80, 107, 135, 167, 172, 174, 190, 200, 222, 301

Goodspeed, Edgar J., **1.**2
Grosvenor, Mary, **1.**81, 96, 124, 206, 228, 234, 267, 276, 288, 303, 338, 368; **2.**57, 115, 123, 132, 140, 142, 150, 151, 159, 160, 187, 213, 244, 262, 283, 290, 298, 333, 336
Gundry, Robert H., **1.**87

Hagner, Donald A., **1.**75
Harner, Philip B., **1.**3
Harris, Murray J., **1.**2, 5, 9, 10, 13, 15, 17, 18, 22, 24, 27, 30, 37, 48, 54, 59, 63, 67, 70, 77, 78, 81, 87, 90, 102, 103, 108, 111, 120, 121, 124, 125, 127, 135, 141, 144, 158, 162, 167, 174, 188, 192, 200, 207, 220, 225, 226, 242, 279, 292, 296, 298, 299, 312, 318, 328, 333, 335, 339, 343, 344, 354, 357, 358, 363, 367, 368, 371, 372; **2.**5, 8, 11, 36, 44, 53, 62, 63, 64, 67, 84, 88, 95, 103, 110, 113, 117, 128, 132, 142, 148, 151, 152, 156, 157, 159, 167, 186, 193, 210, 221, 256, 268, 286, 299, 303, 306, 316, 333
Haubeck, Wilfrid, **1.**9, 24, 37, 48, 172, 173, 177, 200, 219, 250, 344, 347, 351, 363, 367, 372; **2.**41, 48, 65, 66, 116, 140, 148, 151, 193, 246, 277
Heckert, Jacob K., **1.**7
Howell, Russell W., **1.**87

James, Patrick, **1.**368, 369; **2.**3, 7, 9, 10, 15, 26, 27, 28, 35
Jensen, Matthew D., **2.**312
Johnson, Luke Timothy, **1.**66

Keck, Leander E., **2.**203
Keener, Craig S., **1.**17, 60, 71, 74, 142, 146, 182, 189, 198, 253, 326; **2.**35, 44, 56, 71, 310, 326
Kerr, Alan R., **1.**67
Köstenberger, Andreas, **1.**67
Kysar, Robert, **1.**66, 289

Lappenga, Benjamin J., **1.**65
Leung, Mavis M., **1.**14, 15
Levinsohn, Stephen H., **1.**xxv, xxvi, 17, 27, 36, 92, 93, 103, 120, 131, 141, 192, 219, 221, 239, 291, 322, 325, 330, 335, 338; **2.**xxv, xxvi, 24, 54, 64, 73, 78, 82, 87, 88, 93, 114, 138, 153, 169, 181, 191, 195, 243, 246, 271, 273, 274, 275, 305, 310

Martyn, J. Louis, **1.**332; **2.**75, 165
Mason, Steve, **1.**66
Matera, Frank J., **2.**296
McGaughy, Lane C., **1.**2
McGehee, Michael, **2.**296
McHugh, John F., **1.**18, 114, 117
McKay, K. L., **1.**xxiii, 64, 102, 308, 337; **2.**xxiii, 6, 7, 61, 110, 121, 124, 148, 180
Menken, Maarten J. J., **1.**23
Metzger, Bruce M., **1.**4, 5, 18, 20, 22, 26, 35, 41, 62, 85, 87, 96, 102, 104, 112, 114, 133, 144, 147, 148, 149, 171, 174, 199, 206, 215, 218, 222, 230, 232, 238, 260, 269, 273, 279, 296, 298, 302, 310, 313, 316, 341, 343, 351, 354, 358, 359, 360, 364, 366, 374; **2.**13, 23, 24, 37, 43, 46, 49, 55, 67, 74, 83, 84, 90, 97, 103, 107, 115, 117, 118, 119, 125, 126, 129, 137, 147, 149, 167, 173, 181, 182, 186, 191, 196, 200, 208, 211, 215, 231, 257, 263, 266, 276, 279, 301, 303, 335
MHT (Moulton, Howard, and Turner), **1.**10, 14, 22, 25, 27, 42, 52, 55, 90, 108, 144, 145, 219, 255, 339; **2.**36, 43, 48, 58, 73, 74, 85, 93, 104, 124, 147, 160, 169, 226, 228, 238, 249, 264, 267, 314, 317, 318
Michaels, J. Ramsey, **1.**32, 54, 84, 204; **2.**58, 206
Moffatt, James, **1.**2
Morris, Leon, **2.**327

Moule, C. F. D., **1.**5, 6, 23, 87, 90, 110, 286, 328, 338, 363; **2.**70, 140, 143, 146, 159, 201, 212, 299, 308, 310
Moulton, James Hope, **1.**90, 354; **2.**226, 247

Newman, Barclay M., **1.**32
Nida, Eugene A., **1.**3, 10, 32, 112, 118, 132, 277; **2.**14, 18, 52, 127, 154, 275
Novakovic, Lidija, **1.**69

O'Rourke, John J., **1.**14

Parsons, Mikeal C., **1.**19, 79, 189; **2.**5, 36,
Pennington, Jonathan T., **1.**xii, xiii; **2.**xii, xiii
Pierce, Madison N., **1.**85
Porter, Stanley E., **1.**xi, xxiii, xxiv, xxv, 1, 2, 4, 5, 8, 15, 39, 58, 59, 63, 79, 85, 88, 92, 102, 104, 116, 133, 193, 203, 211, 230, 313, 342; **2.**xi, xxiii, xxiv, xxv, 4, 6, 10, 19, 25, 60, 65, 83, 107, 110, 139, 146, 186, 196, 203, 206, 296, 297, 298, 307, 309, 326
Poythress, Vern S., **1.**17, 136

Ramelli, Ilaria, **1.**253; **2.**327
Reynolds, Benjamin E., **1.**85
Ridderbos, Herman N., **1.**84
Robar, Elizabeth, **1.**14
Robertson, A. T., **1.**xii, 1, 2, 3, 4, 11, 16, 36, 39, 55, 59, 66, 68, 70, 80, 85, 98, 123, 128, 148, 211, 273, 302, 317, 333, 336, 339, 349; **2.**xii, 4, 5, 32, 37, 45, 68, 104, 132, 160, 162, 209, 249, 261, 274, 295, 308, 314, 334
Robinson, J. A. T., **2.**58
Runge, Steven, **1.**xi, xxiv, xxvi, 1, 2, 5, 6, 7, 10, 11, 14, 17, 21, 25, 31, 33, 36, 46, 50, 54, 64, 72, 73, 74, 84, 86, 88, 91, 96, 102, 119, 132, 153, 155, 163, 167, 175, 208, 211, 221, 237, 239, 243, 249, 253, 273, 280, 288, 289, 300, 303, 333, 336, 339, 345, 346, 363, 376, 382, 383, 384, 385; **2.**xi, xxiv, xxv, xxvi, 1, 5, 28, 54, 68, 69, 79, 103, 117, 118, 120, 124, 130, 136, 143, 145, 170, 192, 211, 220, 221, 224, 264, 282, 311, 328, 329, 344, 345, 346, 347

Schnackenburg, Rudolf, **1.**85, 87, 148, 268, 359, 374; **2.**52, 88, 90, 114, 119, 155, 170, 182, 205, 250, 268, 295, 308
Shepherd, David, **2.**326
Smith, D. Moody, **2.**57, 311, 326
Smyth, H. W., **1.**15, 16, 26, 30, 34, 35, 49, 50, 54, 65, 78, 79, 98, 122, 128, 131, 132, 135, 137, 152, 153, 154, 157, 165, 170, 174, 176, 178, 189, 192, 198, 200, 201, 206, 207, 208, 211, 214, 216, 217, 220, 221, 222, 225, 226, 231, 235, 242, 248, 249, 251, 255, 257, 261, 265, 283, 290, 292, 293, 295, 298, 301, 304, 306, 316, 320, 321, 322, 325, 327, 329, 330, 334, 335, 338, 339, 343, 356, 358, 365, 366, 367, 369, 373; **2.**7, 29, 30, 31, 58, 64, 77, 79, 81, 93, 95, 98, 102, 108, 111, 112, 118, 121, 123, 125, 126, 130, 131, 135, 136, 139, 141, 147, 150, 152, 155, 159, 163, 168, 171, 175, 176, 177, 178, 182, 183, 185, 191, 193, 194, 195, 196, 198, 200, 205, 209, 211, 212, 213, 220, 222, 225, 239, 240, 252, 253, 254, 267, 292, 296, 301, 305, 306, 307, 309, 310, 319, 323, 328, 330, 335
Stigall, Joshua J., **1.**19, 79, 189; **2.**5, 36

Talbert, Charles H., **1.**84, 367; **2.**90, 295, 326, 327

Taylor, Bernard A., **1**.xii, xiii; **2**.xii, xiii
Theobald, Michael, **2**.296
Thompson, Marianne Meye, **1**.60, 71, 74, 75, 142, 146, 182, 189, 198, 253, 326; **2**.35, 56, 57, 71, 310
Thomson, Christopher J., **1**.230
Tolmie, D. Francois, **1**.55
Torrey, Charles Culter, **1**.xxxiii; **2**.xxiii
Turner, Nigel, **1**.42; **2**.96, 110, 238, 266

Van Belle, Gilbert, **1**.xii; **2**.xii
van der Watt, Jan, **1**.xxii, 260; **2**.xxii
von Siebenthal, Heinrich, **1**.9, 24, 37, 48, 172, 173, 177, 200, 219, 250, 344, 347, 351, 363, 367, 372; **2**.41, 48, 65, 66, 116, 140, 148, 151, 193, 246, 277
von Soden, Hermann Freiherr, **1**.269
von Wahlde, Urban C., **1**.66

Wallace, Daniel B., **1**.x, 2, 3, 5, 6, 8, 11, 12, 14, 18, 19, 22, 23, 27, 29, 34, 36, 39, 41, 45, 46, 51, 52, 53, 54, 55, 57, 58, 59, 63, 66, 67, 68, 72, 74, 75, 77, 78, 79, 81, 85, 87, 88, 91, 94, 100, 103, 106, 109, 110, 111, 113, 114, 115, 116, 117, 120, 121, 122, 123, 124, 126, 127, 131, 133, 135, 136, 140, 141, 146, 148, 150, 151, 152, 155, 162, 164, 165, 167, 168, 171, 173, 175, 176, 180, 181, 196, 200, 205, 214, 223, 227, 231, 237, 239, 251, 256, 264, 267, 272, 280, 281, 288, 293, 297, 299, 302, 312, 313, 315, 321, 322, 323, 331, 334, 337, 339, 341, 342, 347, 348, 349, 351, 352, 353, 354, 365, 369, 371, 372, 373; **2**.x, 3, 7, 8, 10, 14, 16, 21, 26, 28, 33, 37, 53, 56, 58, 60, 65, 66, 67, 68, 73, 74, 80, 82, 84, 86, 93, 102, 105, 106, 107, 109, 110, 113, 120, 129, 133, 136, 140, 142, 144, 147, 148, 151, 154, 159, 162, 163, 169, 170, 172, 174, 176, 178, 179, 185, 193, 194, 198, 204, 208, 210, 211, 213, 221, 224, 225, 226, 227, 229, 230, 232, 236, 239, 246, 247, 249, 250, 251, 255, 256, 258, 261, 262, 264, 273, 275, 280, 285, 291, 293, 295, 296, 297, 300, 303, 307, 308, 309, 312, 320, 332, 334

Young, Richard A., **1**.238; **2**.4, 16, 60, 67, 116, 164

Zerwick, Maximilian, **1**.10, 28, 34, 55, 67, 71, 77, 81, 96, 99, 108, 117, 124, 132, 137, 173, 177, 206, 219, 228, 234, 249, 256, 267, 276, 284, 285, 288, 298, 302, 303, 312, 319, 320, 324, 334, 336, 337, 338, 339, 368, 370; **2**.2, 23, 27, 28, 37, 43, 57, 60, 76, 84, 104, 109, 115, 120, 123, 132, 137, 139, 140, 142, 146, 150, 151, 157, 159, 160, 185, 187, 193, 194, 198, 203, 204, 207, 213, 216, 230, 243, 244, 255, 262, 282, 283, 284, 285, 287, 290, 291, 295, 296, 298, 320, 333, 336

GRAMMAR INDEX

Superscript is used to indicate the number of times a grammatical element appears within a verse.

accusative (adverbial), 1:41; 2:10; 3:4; 4:18, 27; 6:11; 7:51; 8:25; 10:10, 40; 11:29; 12:16; 13:33, 36; 14:19; 15:18, 25; 16:16^2, 17^2, 19^2; 18:13; 19:39; 21:14, 15, 16, 17^2

accusative complement in a double accusative construction, 1:29, 32, 33, 38, 41, 47, 48, 51^3; 2:11, 14, 16; 4:5, 18, 23, 46, 54; 5:6, 11, 15, 18^2, 19, 38; 6:14, 15, 19^2, 30, 62; 7:23; 8:29, 53; 9:22; 10:12, 33, 35; 11:16, 33^2, 54; 14:18; 15:15^2; 16:2, 32; 17:13; 19:7, 12, 13, 17, 18, 26, 33; 20:1, 5, 6, 7^2, 12, 14; 21:9^2, 11, 20

accusative direct object, 1:5, 9, 10, 11, 12^2, 14, 16, 18, 19^2, 21, 22^3, 23, 25, 26, 27, 29, 31, 32^2, 33^3, 36, 38^2, 41^3, 42, 43, 45, 47, 48^3, 50^2, 51^2; 2:3, 5, 7^2, 9^3, 10^3, 11^2, 14^3, 15^6, 16^3, 17, 18^2, 19^2, 20, 22^2, 23^2, 24^2, 25; 3:2^2, 3, 8, 10, 11^3, 12^2, 14, 15, 16^3, 17^2, 19^2, 20^2, 21, 27, 29, 32^2, 33, 34^2, 35^2, 36^2; 4:1, 3, 5, 7, 8, 10^3, 11^2, 12, 14, 15, 16, 17^2, 18^2, 21, 22^2, 23^2, 24, 25, 27^2, 28, 29^3, 31, 32^2, 34^3, 35^2, 36^2, 38, 39^2, 40, 44, 45^3, 46, 47, 48, 50, 52^2, 54; 5:2, 6, 7^2, 8, 9, 10, 11^2, 12, 14, 15, 16^2, 18^4, 19^5, 20^4, 21^2, 22^2, 23^5, 24^3, 26^2, 27^2, 28, 29^2, 30^4, 32, 34^2, 36^5, 37^3, 38^2, 39^2, 40, 41, 42^2, 43^2, 44^2; 6:2^2, 5^2, 6^3, 7, 9^2, 10, 11, 12, 13, 14^3, 15, 19, 21, 23, 24, 25, 26^2, 27^4, 28^2, 29, 30^2, 31^2, 32^2, 33, 34, 36, 37^2, 38^3, 39^3, 40^3, 42^2, 44^3, 46^2, 47, 49, 51, 52, 53^3, 54^4, 56^2, 57^2, 58^2, 59, 61, 62, 63^2, 64, 68, 70, 71; 7:1, 3^2, 4^3, 7^2, 9, 11, 12, 15, 16, 17, 18^3, 19^3, 20^2, 21, 22^2, 23^2, 25, 26, 27, 28^3, 29, 30^2, 31, 32^3, 33, 34^2, 35^2, 36^3, 39^2, 44^2, 45, 49, 51^2; 8:2, 3^2, 5^2, 6^2, 7^2, 10, 11, 12, 15, 16, 18, 19^4, 20^2, 21, 22, 25, 26^4, 28^4, 29^3, 30, 32^2, 34, 36, 37, 38^2, 39, 40^4, 41^2, 42^2, 43^2, 44^2, 45, 46, 47, 48, 49^3, 50, 51^2, 52^2, 53, 54^2, 55^5, 56, 57, 59; 9:1, 2, 4^2, 6^3, 8, 11^2, 13, 14^2, 15^2, 16^2, 17^2, 18, 19, 21^3, 22^3, 23^2, 24^2, 25, 26^2, 28, 30, 31, 32, 33, 34, 35^2, 37, 40, 41; 10:3^2, 4^2, 5, 6^2, 9, 10, 11, 12^3, 14^2, 15^3, 16^2, 17^3, 18^7, 20, 21, 24^2, 25, 27, 28^2, 29, 31^2, 32^2, 33^2, 35, 36, 37, 39, 41^2; 11:2^2, 3, 5^3, 8, 9, 11^2, 17, 19, 22^2, 26, 28^3, 31^2, 32, 33^3, 34, 36, 37, 39, 40, 41^2, 42, 43, 44^2, 45, 46, 47^3, 48^3, 49, 51, 52, 53, 55, 56, 57^2; 12:1, 2, 3^3, 4, 6^3,

7^2, 8^2, 9^2, 10, 13, 14, 16^2, 17^2, 18, 19, 21^2, 24, 25^4, 26, 27^2, 28, 32, 33, 35^2, 36^2, 37, 38, 40^3, 41^2, 43^2, 44, 45^3, 47^3, 48^6, 49^4, 50; $13:1^2$, 2, 3, 4^3, 5^2, 6, 7, 8^3, 9^3, 10^2, 11^2, 12^3, 13, 14^2, 15, 16, 17^2, 18^3, 20^5, 21^2, 23, 26^2, 28, 29^3, 30, 32^2, 33, 34^4, 35, 37, 38^2; 14:2, 3^2, 4, 5, 7^4, 8, 9^4, 10^3, 12^3, 13^2, 14^2, 15^2, 16^2, 17^3, 18, 19^2, 21^6, 22, 23^4, 24^4, 26^6, 27^2, 28, 30^2, 31; $15:2^7$, 3, 4, 5^2, 6, 7, 8, 9^2, 10^2, 11, 12^2, 13^2, 14, 15^5, 16^6, 17^2, 18^2, 19^3, 20^4, 21^3, 22^2, 23^2, 24^5, 25, 26; 16:1, 2^3, 3^3, 4^2, 5^2, 6^2, 7^2, 8, 10, 12, 13^2, 14, 15, 16^2, 17^3, 18^2, 19^3, 21^2, 22^3, 23^4, 24, 25, 26, 27^2, 28, 29, 30^3, 32, 33^4; $17:1^4$, 2^3, 3^2, 4^3, 5, 6^4, 7, 8^3, 11, 12, 13^2, 14^2, 15^2, 17, 18^2, 19, 21, 22^2, 23^3, 24^4, 25^3, 26^2; 18:1, 2^2, 3^2, 4^2, 5^2, 7^3, 8^2, 9^3, 10^4, 11^4, 12^2, 16, 18, 19, 20, 21^4, 22^2, 23, 24, 26^2, 28^2, 29, 30^2, 31^3, 32, 33, 34, 35^2, 38^2, 39^2, 40^2; 19:1, 2^3, 3, 4^2, 5^2, 6^4, 7^2, 8, 9, 10^4, 11^3, 12^3, 13, 15^4, 16^2, 17, 18^3, 19, 20, 22, 23^4, 24^4, 26^3, 27, 29, 30^3, 31, 32, 33^2, 34, 35, 38^3, 39, 40^2, 42; 20:1, 2^3, 5, 6, 7, 9, 12, 13^2, 14^2, 15^4, 18^2, 20^4, 21^2, 22^2, 23, 25^4, 27^3, 29, 30, 31^2; 21:1, 3, 5, 6^2, 7^3, 8, 9^3, 10, 11, 12, 13^2, 15^3, 16^3, 17^5, 18^3, 19^3, 20^3, 21, 24, 25^2

accusative in apposition, 1:14, 41, 45^2; 6:70; 8:40, 41; 9:13; 11:28; 14:17; $17:3^2$; 18:5, 6, 24; 19:13, 23, 39

accusative of reference/respect, 1:15, 45; 4:38; 6:10, 71; 8:25, 27, 54; 9:19, 29; 10:36; 11:44

accusative (predicate), 1:12; 2:9

accusative subject of the infinitive, 1:48; 2:24; 3:14, 30^2; 4:4, 24, 49; 5:39; 6:10; 8:58; 9:4; 10:16; 12:18, 29, 34; 17:5; 18:14; 20:9; 21:22, 23, 25

adjectivizer, 5:44; 12:21; 13:1; 18:16; 21:2

adverbial accusative: *see* accusative (adverbial)

a minore ad maius, 3:12; 13:14

anacoluthon, 6:24

anaphora/anaphoric, 1:2, 4, 21, 30, 33, 34, 37, 38, 41; 2:1, 2, 8, 11, 16, 21, 22^2, 23; 3:2, 8, 10, 16, 26, 30, 32; 4:9, 11, 25, 29, 32, 42, 43, 47, 49, 50; 5:6, 11, 14, 16, 19^2, 28^2, 37, 38, 39, 46, 47; 6:6, 9, 13, 14, 29, 39, 57, 65; 7:11, 17, 18, 22, 29, 40, 45, 51; 8:9, 44; 9:6, 9, 11, 12, 14, 23, 25, 36, 40; 10:1, 6, 25; 11:13, 28, 29, 51; $12:18^2$, 21, 27, 48; 13:11, 25, 26, 28, 30; 14:6, 12, 21, 25, 26; 15:8, 17, 19, 26; 16:1, 3, 4^2, 8, 13, 14, 15, 25, 30, 33; 17:1, 3, 20, 24; 18:1, 16, 17, 21, 25, 38; 19:7, 11, 15, 29, 35, 38; 20:13, 15, 16, 20, 22, 31; 21:19, 21

ἀντί (substitution), 1:16

ἀπό (agency), 5:19, 30; 7:17, 18, 28; 8:28, 42; 10:18; 11:51; 14:10; 15:4; 16:13; 18:34

ἀπό (causal), 21:6

ἀπό (distance), 21:8

ἀπό (locative), 1:33; 7:42; 12:21

ἀπό (partitive), 21:10

ἀπό (separation), 10:5, 18; 11:18; 12:36; 16:22; 18:28; 21:8

ἀπό (source), 1:44, 45; 3:2; 6:38; 11:1; 13:3; 16:30; 19:38; 21:2

ἀπό (starting point), 8:9

ἀπό (temporal), 8:11, 44; 11:53; 13:19; 14:7; 15:27; 19:27

asyndeton, 1:17, 23, 26^2, 28, 29, 35, 39^2, 40, 41, 42, 43, 45, 47, 48, 49, 50; 2:5, 7, 12, 17, 19; 3:2, 3, 4, 5, 6, 7, 8, 9, 10, 11, 12, 18, 22, 27, 28, 29, 30, 31, 32, 33, 35, 36; 4:7, 10, 11, 12, 13, 15, 16^2, 17, 19, 20, 21, 22^2; 24, 25, 26, 30, 31, 34, 35, 36, 38, 47, 49, 50; 5:1, 3, 6, 7, 8^2, 12, 14, 15, 23, 24, 25, 28, 30, 31, 32, 33, 35, 39, 41, 43, 44, 45; 6:1, 7, 8, 9, 10, 22, 26, 27, 29, 31, 35^2, 37,

43, 44, 45, 47, 48, 49, 50, 51², 54, 56, 57, 58, 59, 63, 66, 68, 70; 7:7, 8, 13, 17, 18, 19, 20, 21, 23, 24, 29, 32, 34, 36, 38, 41, 42, 46, 48, 50, 51, 52; 8:4, 12, 14, 15, 18, 20, 26, 27, 30, 33, 34, 37, 38, 39, 41, 42, 43, 44, 46, 47, 48, 49, 51, 53, 54, 56, 58; 9:3, 4², 5, 6, 7, 9, 11², 13, 22, 27⁴, 29, 30, 31, 32, 33, 34, 35, 36, 37, 40, 41²; 10:1, 3, 4, 6, 8, 9², 10, 11², 12, 14, 15, 18, 19, 21, 22, 25, 27, 29, 30, 31, 32, 33, 34, 35, 37; 11:8, 9, 11, 23, 24, 25², 27, 34, 35, 39², 40, 44², 48; 12:12, 16, 19, 22, 24, 25, 26², 27, 28, 30, 31, 35, 36, 41, 46, 48; 13:7, 8², 9, 10, 13, 16, 17, 18², 19, 20, 21, 22, 23, 26, 33², 34, 35, 36², 37², 38²; 14:1², 2, 5, 6³, 7, 8, 9³, 10², 11, 12, 14, 15, 17, 18, 19, 20, 21, 22, 23, 24, 25, 27², 28², 30, 31; 15:1, 2, 3, 4², 5², 6, 7, 8, 9², 10, 11, 12, 13, 14, 15, 16, 17, 18, 19, 20⁵, 22, 23, 24, 26; 16:1, 2, 12, 14, 15, 16, 19, 20², 21, 23, 24², 25², 26, 28², 29, 30², 31, 32, 33²; 17:1², 2, 4, 6², 7, 9, 14, 15, 16, 17², 18, 23, 24; 18:1, 5², 8, 11, 17, 20, 21³, 23, 25, 26, 30, 31, 34, 35³, 36², 37³, 38; 19:6, 7, 10, 11, 12, 15², 22, 28, 29; 20:13, 14, 15³, 16², 17, 18, 23, 26, 28, 29²; 21:1, 2, 3³, 5, 10, 12, 13, 14, 15², 16³, 17³, 18, 20, 22, 24
attraction (dative), 13:5; 17:5, 11, 12
attraction (genitive), 4:14; 7:31; 9:18; 13:38; 15:20; 17:9; 21:10
attributive genitive: *see* genitive (attributive)
αὐτός (intensive), 2:12, 24, 25; 3:28; 4:2, 12, 42, 44, 45, 53; 5:20, 36; 6:6, 15; 7:9; 12:24, 49; 14:11; 16:27; 18:28; 21:25

cataphora/cataphoric, 3:19; 4:37; 5:16, 18, 28; 6:29, 39, 40; 7:22; 8:47; 10:17; 12:18, 39; 15:8, 12, 17; 17:3, 26; 18:37; 21:23
cognate dative: *see* dative (cognate)
conditional sentence (first-class), 1:25; 3:12; 5:47; 7:4, 23; 8:39, 46; 10:24, 35, 37, 38; 11:12; 13:14, 17, 32; 14:7, 11; 15:18, 20²; 18:8, 23²; 20:15
conditional sentence (second-class), 4:10; 5:46; 8:19, 42; 9:41; 11:21, 32; 14:28; 15:19, 22, 24; 18:30, 36; 19:11
conditional sentence (third-class), 3:2, 3, 5, 12, 27; 4:48; 5:19, 31, 43; 6:44, 51, 53, 62, 65; 7:17, 37, 51; 8:14, 16, 24, 31, 36, 51, 52, 54, 55; 9:22, 31; 10:9, 38; 11:9, 10, 25, 40, 48, 57; 12:24², 26², 32, 47; 13:8, 17, 20, 35; 14:3, 14, 15, 23; 15:4², 6, 7, 10, 14; 16:7², 23; 19:12; 20:23², 25; 21:22, 23, 25
constructio ad sensum, 6:2, 9, 22; 7:49, 53; 8:33, 37; 12:12, 13, 18; 17:2
crasis, 1:31, 33, 34; 5:17; 6:44, 54, 56, 57²; 7:28, 29; 8:14, 26, 55; 10:15, 16, 27, 28, 38²; 11:25, 54; 12:32; 14:12, 16, 20, 21; 15:4, 5, 9; 16:32; 17:6, 11, 18, 21, 22, 24, 26; 20:15, 21

dative (cognate), 3:29
dative complement, 3:26, 28, 36; 4:21, 51; 5:10, 18, 24, 33, 38, 46²; 6:30; 7:23; 8:29, 31, 33, 45, 46, 55; 9:9; 10:13, 37, 38²; 11:20, 30, 33, 41, 56; 12:6, 13, 18; 14:11; 18:14, 15², 31, 37; 19:2, 12, 24, 29, 32, 40; 20:6, 22
dative direct object, 1:36, 37, 40, 42, 43; 2:22²; 4:21, 23, 50; 5:47²; 6:2; 8:12; 9:38; 10:4, 5, 27; 11:31; 12:26³, 38; 13:36, 37; 18:15; 21:19, 22

dative in apposition, 1:12; 4:5; 7:37; 20:19

dative indirect object, 1:12; 22², 25, 26, 31, 33, 38², 39, 41, 43, 45, 46², 48², 49, 50², 51²; 2:4, 5², 7, 8², 10, 16, 18², 19, 24; 3:2, 3², 5, 7, 9, 10, 11, 12², 26, 27; 4:5, 7², 9, 10⁴, 11, 12, 13, 14², 15, 16, 17², 19, 21, 25², 26², 28, 29, 32, 33, 34, 35, 42, 50², 52, 53; 5:6, 7, 8, 10, 11², 12, 14, 15, 17, 19², 20², 22, 24, 25, 26, 27, 36; 6:7, 8, 11, 12, 20, 25, 26², 27, 29, 30, 31, 32⁴, 33, 34, 35, 36, 37, 39, 43, 46, 53², 61, 63, 65², 67, 68, 70; 7:4, 6, 16, 19, 21, 22, 26, 45, 47, 52; 8:4, 5, 7, 10, 12, 13, 14, 19, 21, 23, 24, 25³, 27, 28, 34², 39², 40, 41, 42, 48, 51, 52, 58²; 9:7, 10, 11, 12, 15, 17, 24², 26², 27², 29, 30, 34, 37, 40, 41; 10:1, 6², 7, 24², 25², 28, 29, 32², 33, 34; 11:7, 8, 11, 12, 14, 16, 22, 23, 24, 25, 27, 32, 34, 39, 40², 44, 46, 49; 12:5, 22², 23, 24, 29, 34, 35, 38, 49; 13:3, 6, 7, 8², 9, 10, 12, 15, 16, 19, 20, 21, 24, 25, 26², 27, 28, 29², 33², 34, 36², 37, 38; 14:2, 5, 6, 8², 9², 10, 12, 16, 21, 22³, 23, 25, 26, 27³, 28, 29, 31; 15:3, 11, 14, 15, 16, 17, 20, 22, 26; 16:1, 2, 4³, 6, 7, 12, 13, 14, 15, 17, 19, 20, 23², 25³, 26, 31, 33; 17:2³, 4, 6³, 7, 8², 9, 11, 12, 14, 22², 24², 26; 18:4, 5², 6, 8, 9, 11², 16, 17, 20², 21, 22², 23, 25, 30², 31², 33, 34, 35, 36, 37, 38²; 19:3, 4², 5, 6, 7, 9², 10², 11³, 14, 15, 16, 21, 26, 27, 29; 20:2, 12², 13², 15³, 16, 17², 18², 19, 20, 21, 22, 25², 27, 28, 29; 21:1, 3², 5², 6, 7, 10, 12, 13, 14, 15³, 16³, 17⁴, 18, 19, 21, 22, 23

dative (locative), 11:33; 21:8

dative of advantage, 10:3; 11:50; 12:2, 16; 13:12, 15, 26, 35; 14:2, 3, 8; 15:7, 8; 16:7; 18:39²; 19:17, 23; 20:19, 21, 23, 26

dative of agency, 6:13; 18:15; 19:17

dative of disadvantage, 5:14

dative of interest, 5:33; 6:7; 18:37

dative of manner, 3:29; 7:13, 26; 10:24; 11:14, 54; 12:33; 16:25; 18:20, 32; 21:19

dative of means/instrument, 8:6; 11:2, 43, 44²; 12:3, 40²; 13:5; 17:5; 19:34

dative of possession, 1:6; 3:1; 13:35; 15:8; 17:6, 9; 18:10, 39

dative of respect, 6:13; 11:33; 13:21

dative of sphere, 13:21

dative of time, 1:29, 35, 43; 2:1, 20; 6:22, 54; 12:12; 20:1, 19

διά (causal), 1:31; 3:29; 4:39, 41, 42; 5:16, 18; 6:57², 65; 7:13, 22, 43, 45; 8:43, 46, 47; 9:23; 10:17, 19, 32; 11:15, 42; 12:5, 9, 11, 18, 27, 39, 42; 13:11, 37; 14:11; 15:3, 19, 21; 16:15, 21; 19:11, 38, 42; 20:19

διά (instrumental), 15:3

διά (intermediate agency), 1:3, 7, 10, 17²; 3:17; 6:57²; 10:9; 11:4; 14:6

διά (locative/spatial), 4:4; 10:1, 2; 19:23

διά (means), 17:20

διά (purpose), 11:42; 12:30²

double entendre, 1:5; 2:17; 3:3, 31; 4:10; 6:33; 7:39; 8:21; 11:11, 23; 12:16, 23; 13:31, 32; 17:1

ἐγγύς (locative), 3:23; 6:19, 23; 11:18, 54; 19:20

εἰ μή . . . οὐ (point/counterpoint), 9:33

εἰς (in place of ἐν), 9:7; 17:23; 20:7

εἰς (in place of the predicate nominative), 16:20; 17:23

εἰς (in place of πρός), 8:26; 11:31, 38; 20:1, 3, 4, 8

εἰς (goal), 1:12; 2:11, 23; 3:16, 18²; 4:14, 36, 39; 5:29², 45; 6:27, 29, 35, 40; 7:5, 31, 38, 39, 48; 8:30; 9:35, 36; 10:42; 11:25, 26, 45, 48; 12:11, 27, 36, 37, 42, 44³, 46; 14:1², 12; 16:9; 17:20, 23

Grammar Index

εἰς (locative), 1:9, 11, 18, 43; 2:2, 12, 13; 3:4, 5, 13, 17, 19, 22, 24, 36; 4:3, 5, 8, 28, 38, 43, 45², 46, 47, 54; 5:1, 7, 24²; 6:3, 14, 15, 17², 21², 22, 24², 66; 7:3, 8², 10, 14, 35, 53; 8:1, 2, 6, 8; 9:7, 11, 39; 10:1, 36, 40; 11:7, 27, 30, 52, 54², 55, 56; 12:1, 12², 24, 46; 13:2, 3, 5, 22, 27; 15:6, 21; 16:21, 28, 32; 17:1, 18²; 18:1, 6, 11, 15, 28², 33, 37; 19:9, 13, 17, 27, 37; 20:6, 11, 14, 19, 25², 26, 27; 21:3, 4, 6, 7, 9, 11², 23

εἰς (purpose), 1:7; 9:39; 11:52; 12:13, 25; 13:1, 29; 18:37²

εἰς (reference), 6:9

εἰς (result), 4:14, 36; 6:27; 12:25; 13:1

εἰς (temporal), 4:14; 6:51, 58; 8:35², 51, 52; 10:28; 11:26; 12:7, 34; 13:8; 14:16

ἐκ (agency), 1:13; 6:65

ἐκ (causal), 1:13³; 4:6; 6:66; 12:3; 19:12

ἐκ (in place of ἀπό), 18:3²

ἐκ (in place of the partitive genitive), 1:24, 35, 40; 3:1; 6:8, 11, 13, 26, 39, 50, 51, 60, 64, 66, 70, 71; 7:19, 25, 31, 40, 44, 48², 50; 8:46; 9:16, 40; 10:20, 26; 11:19, 37, 45, 46, 49; 12:2, 4, 9, 20, 42; 13:21, 23; 16:5, 17; 17:12; 18:9, 17, 25, 26; 20:24; 21:2

ἐκ (instrumental/impersonal agency), 8:42; 12:3

ἐκ (locative), 1:32

ἐκ (means), 1:13³; 3:34; 9:6

ἐκ (partitive), 3:25

ἐκ (separation), 2:15, 22; 4:30, 47, 54; 5:24; 6:23; 8:59; 10:28, 29, 39; 12:1, 9, 17², 27, 32; 13:1, 4; 15:19; 16:14, 15; 17:6, 15²; 20:1, 2, 9; 21:14

ἐκ (source), 1:13⁴, 16, 19, 44, 46; 2:15; 3:5, 6², 8, 13, 25, 27, 31⁴; 4:7, 12, 13, 14, 22, 39; 6:31, 32², 33, 41, 42, 50, 51, 58; 7:17, 22², 38, 41, 42, 52²; 8:23⁴, 42, 44², 47²; 9:6; 10:16,

32; 11:1, 55; 12:28, 34, 49; 15:19²; 17:14², 16²; 18:36², 37; 19:2, 23

ἐκ (temporal), 9:1, 24, 32; 6:64; 16:4; 19:12

ellipsis/elliptical, 1:8, 21, 22, 32; 3:13; 4:1, 53; 5:2, 7; 6:22, 29, 46, 58, 62, 71; 7:22; 9:3, 36; 12:7; 13:2, 9, 18, 26; 14:2, 11, 31; 15:6, 13, 20, 25; 18:9, 32; 19:24, 37; 20:1; 21:2, 10, 15, 16, 17, 21, 22

ἔμπροσθεν (advantage), 1:15, 30

ἔμπροσθεν (locative), 3:28; 10:4; 12:37

ἐν (agency), 3:21

ἐν (association), 12:35

ἐν (causal), 3:15; 5:35; 8:21, 24²

ἐν (close personal relationship), 3:21

ἐν (instrumental/means), 1:26, 31, 33²; 5:43²; 10:25; 13:35; 14:13, 14, 26; 15:8, 16; 16:23, 24, 26, 30; 17:10, 12, 17; 20:31

ἐν (locative), 1:4, 5, 10, 14, 23, 26, 28, 31, 33, 45, 47; 2:1, 11, 14, 23², 25; 3:14, 21, 23, 35; 4:14, 20², 21², 44, 45², 46; 5:2, 3, 13, 14, 26², 28, 38, 39, 42; 6:10, 31, 45, 49, 53, 59², 61; 7:1², 9, 11, 12, 18, 28, 43; 8:3, 5, 9, 12, 17, 20², 35, 37, 44; 9:3, 5, 16; 10:19, 22, 23², 34; 11:6, 10, 17, 20, 24, 30, 31, 38, 54, 56; 12:20, 25, 35², 46; 13:1, 23, 31, 32², 35; 14:2, 13, 30; 15:4, 7, 11, 24, 25; 16:13, 33; 17:10; 11², 13², 17, 19, 26; 18:20², 26, 38; 19:4, 6, 41³; 20:25, 30

ἐν (manner), 7:4², 10; 12:13; 16:25², 29; 18:20; 20:12

ἐν (reference), 4:37; 9:30

ἐν (state of being), 6:56²; 10:38²; 14:10³, 11², 17, 20³; 15:2, 4³, 5², 6, 7; 16:33; 17:11, 12, 21³, 23², 26

ἐν (state or condition), 4:23, 24; 5:5; 8:21, 24², 31, 44; 9:34; 15:9, 10²

ἐν (temporal), 1:1, 2; 2:19, 20, 23²; 4:31, 45, 52, 53; 5:7, 9, 16, 28; 6:39, 44; 7:11, 22, 23², 37; 9:14; 11:9, 10,

24²; 12:20, 48; 14:20; 16:23, 26; 18:39; 19:31; 21:3, 20
ἐπάνω (advantage), 3:31²
epexegetical genitive: *see* genitive (epexegetical)
ἐπί (locative), 1:32, 33, 51; 3:36; 4:6; 5:2; 6:2, 16, 19, 21; 7:30, 44; 8:7, 59; 9:6, 15; 11:38; 12:14, 15; 13:25; 17:4; 18:4; 19:3, 19, 31, 33; 20:7; 21:1, 20
ἐπί (opposition), 13:18
ἐπί (reference), 12:16; 19:24
ἐπί (temporal), 4:27; 8:3, 4
ἕως (locative), 2:7
ἕως (temporal), 2:10; 5:17; 9:18; 10:24; 13:38; 16:24

first (anarthrous) attributive position, 1:18; 2:6; 6:55²; 8:55; 9:16, 32; 10:32; 12:24; 14:16; 15:13; 18:38; 19:4, 11, 37; 20:30
first attributive position, 2:10; 3:22; 4:23, 42, 44; 5:37, 44, 47; 6:12, 57; 7:8, 16, 37²; 8:16, 18, 31, 51; 10:3; 11:33; 12:49; 14:24; 17:3; 19:5²; 20:2, 25; 21:25
first predicate position, 5:28; 19:18
fourth attributive position, 1:6; 2:6; 3:15, 23; 4:5, 9, 10, 14; 5:2, 5; 6:9; 7:38; 8:3; 9:16; 10:32, 41; 12:3²; 13:34; 15:2, 5, 8; 16:29; 19:11, 13, 29², 41; 20:22; 21:11

genitive absolute (causal), 2:3; 5:13; 6:18
genitive absolute (concessive), 12:37; 20:26; 21:11
genitive absolute (temporal), 2:3; 4:51; 5:13; 6:23; 7:14; 8:30; 13:2²; 18:22; 20:1; 20:19²; 21:4
genitive (attributive), 1:13; 2:6, 13; 5:1; 6:4; 7:2, 23; 12:24; 14:17; 15:26; 16:13; 19:42

genitive complement, 1:14, 27; 2:7; 5:45; 8:6, 52; 11:41, 42; 19:29²; 21:11
genitive (descriptive), 2:16; 6:35, 48, 68; 12:36; 17:12
genitive direct object, 1:37; 3:29; 4:14; 5:25, 28; 6:60; 7:32, 40; 9:31; 10:3, 8, 16, 20, 27; 12:47; 15:20; 16:4, 21; 18:37; 19:13; 20:17
genitive (epexegetical), 2:16, 21; 6:1; 8:1, 12, 44; 9:7; 11:13; 12:24; 13:1; 14:17; 18:1; 19:17, 31; 21:1
genitive in apposition, 4:12; 5:3³; 7:42; 8:44, 53; 9:18; 11:1; 12:38
genitive (objective), 1:4; 2:17; 3:10; 4:42; 5:42, 45; 7:13; 8:12, 34, 50, 54; 9:5; 11:9, 40; 12:7, 31; 14:17; 15:10, 26; 16:13; 17:2, 14, 24; 18:10, 12, 26; 19:14, 38; 20:19
genitive of agency, 6:45; 18:16
genitive of comparison, 1:15, 30, 50; 4:12; 5:20; 7:31; 8:53; 10:29; 13:16²; 14:12, 28; 15:13, 18, 20; 20:4; 21:15
genitive of content, 4:14; 6:13; 7:38; 21:8
genitive of direction, 7:35; 10:7
genitive of material, 12:3; 19:39
genitive of origin, 7:23; 10:37; 11:40
genitive of price, 6:7; 12:5
genitive of producer, 6:33
genitive of product, 4:14; 6:35, 48
genitive of purpose, 2:4; 5:29²; 6:68; 7:30; 8:12, 20; 10:1, 7; 13:1; 16:4, 21
genitive of reference, 7:35; 15:18
genitive of relationship, 1:12, 34, 35, 40, 42, 45, 49, 51; 2:1, 2, 3, 5, 11, 12, 16, 17, 22; 3:4, 13, 14, 18, 22, 25, 29; 4:2, 5, 8, 12², 16, 18, 20, 27, 46, 47, 49, 50, 51, 53; 5:17, 25, 27, 43; 6:3, 8², 12, 16, 22², 24, 27, 31, 32, 40, 42, 49, 53, 60, 61, 62, 66, 69, 71; 7:3², 5, 10, 42; 8:19³, 28, 31, 33, 37, 39², 41, 42, 44², 49, 53, 54, 56; 9:2², 3, 18, 19, 20, 22, 23, 27, 28², 35; 10:18, 25, 29, 36, 37; 11:1,

2, 4, 5, 11, 21, 23, 27, 28, 32, 39, 5;
12:4, 15², 16, 23, 34²; 13:2, 23, 26,
31; 14:2, 7, 20, 21, 23; 15:1, 8, 10,
13, 14, 15, 20, 23, 24; 16:17, 29;
17:1; 18:1², 2, 13, 16, 17, 19, 25,
26; 19:7, 12, 25⁴, 26, 27, 38; 20:17⁵,
26, 30, 31; 21:2², 15, 16, 17
genitive of result, 5:29²
genitive of separation, 5:13
genitive of source, 5:25, 28; 7:16, 42;
10:37; 11:9, 40; 12:3, 24, 43²
genitive of subordination, 1:49; 3:1;
8:54; 10:2; 12:13, 15, 31; 13:16;
14:30; 15:15; 16:11; 17:2; 18:33,
39; 19:3, 14, 15, 19, 21³; 20:13
genitive of time, 3:2; 8:2; 11:9, 49, 51;
12:7; 18:13; 19:39
genitive (partitive), 1:27; 2:1, 11²; 4:5,
39, 46; 5:3; 6:1; 7:37; 8:7; 10:32;
12:3, 11, 13, 21; 13:28; 18:22;
19:20, 21, 34; 20:1, 19; 21:2, 6, 12
genitive (possessive), 1:12, 14², 16,
18, 23², 27², 29², 36, 44, 51; 2:11,
15, 16, 17, 21, 23; 3:4, 8, 10, 18, 29,
35; 4:6, 12, 28, 34, 35, 51, 53; 5:5,
8, 9, 10, 11, 25, 28, 37², 43; 6:33,
51, 52, 53², 54², 55², 56²; 7:18, 38,
51, 53; 8:52; 9:6, 10, 11, 14, 15, 17,
21, 26, 30, 32; 10:3, 4, 5, 11, 12, 15,
16, 17, 21, 23, 24, 25, 27, 28, 29,
34, 39; 11:1, 2², 4, 32, 37, 44, 48;
12:3³, 13, 25², 27, 28, 38, 40², 41;
13:5, 6, 8, 9, 12², 14², 18², 23, 25,
37, 38; 14:1, 2, 13, 14, 24, 26, 27;
15:13, 16, 21, 25; 16:6, 22, 23, 24,
26; 17:1, 6, 11, 12, 26; 18:10², 15,
26², 31, 37; 19:2, 23, 24³, 25, 29,
31, 32², 33, 34, 36, 38², 40; 20:7,
12, 25³, 27⁴, 28², 31; 21:6, 15, 16,
17, 18, 20
genitive (predicate), 4:9
genitive subject, 2:3; 4:51; 5:13; 6:18,
23; 7:14; 8:30; 12:37; 13:2²; 18:22;
20:1, 19², 26; 21:4, 11
genitive (subjective), 1:13, 19, 29;
2:6, 13, 23; 3:3, 5, 11, 19, 20, 21,
32, 33, 34, 36; 4:10, 34², 38, 39, 41;
5:1, 24, 30, 31, 35, 36, 38, 42, 47;
6:4, 28, 29, 38, 39, 40, 51; 7:2, 3, 7,
17; 8:13, 14, 17, 21, 24², 39, 41, 44,
47, 52, 54, 55; 9:3, 4, 31, 41; 10:21,
35, 37; 11:13, 55; 12:38², 43², 47,
48, 50; 14:10, 21, 23, 24²; 15:7, 10⁴,
11, 16, 20, 22; 16:20, 22, 24; 17:6,
20; 18:19, 32; 19:35, 42; 20:23²,
25²; 21:24
Granville-Sharp rule, 5:24; 6:33, 40,
45, 54; 8:50; 9:8; 10:1; 11:2, 26, 45;
12:48; 14:21; 20:17, 28, 29

headless relative clause, 1:3, 26, 33,
45; 3:11², 26², 32, 34; 4:18, 22², 38;
5:19, 21, 38; 6:14, 64; 7:25; 8:25,
26, 38²; 10:29, 36; 11:3, 22, 45, 46;
12:50; 13:7, 26, 27, 29; 15:7, 14,
15, 16; 16:13; 17:3, 24; 18:9, 21²,
26; 19:22
hendiadys, 4:23
historical present, 1:15, 21, 29², 36,
38, 39, 41², 43², 45², 46, 47, 48, 51;
2:3, 4, 5, 7, 8, 9, 10; 3:4; 4:1, 5, 7²,
9, 11, 15, 16, 17, 19, 21, 25, 26, 28,
34, 49, 50; 5:6, 14; 6:5, 8, 12, 19,
20; 7:6, 50; 8:3, 4, 39; 9:12, 13, 17;
11:7, 8, 11, 23, 24, 27, 34, 38, 39²,
40, 44; 12:4, 22⁴, 23; 13:4², 5, 6²,
8, 9, 10, 24, 25, 26³, 27, 31, 36, 37,
38; 14:5, 6, 8, 9, 22; 16:29; 18:3, 4,
5, 17², 26, 28, 29, 38²; 19:4, 5, 6, 9,
10, 14, 15, 26, 27, 28; 20:1², 2³, 5,
6², 12, 13², 14, 15², 16², 17, 18, 19,
22, 26, 27, 29; 21:3², 5, 7, 9, 10, 12,
13³, 15³, 16³, 17³, 19, 20, 21, 22
homoeoteleuton, 13:32
hortatory subjunctive: *see* subjunctive (hortatory)

ἵνα (appositional), 17:3
ἵνα (complementary), 8:56; 9:22;
17:4, 15², 21², 24

ἵνα (direct object), 4:47; 13:2; 19:31, 38
ἵνα (epexegetical), 1:27; 2:25; 5:7; 6:29, 39, 40; 9:39; 11:57; 12:23; 13:1, 34; 15:8, 12, 13, 17; 16:2, 30, 32; 17:2, 3; 18:37, 39
ἵνα (imperatival), 1:22; 13:19, 34; 18:9, 32
ἵνα (purpose), 1:7², 8, 19, 22, 31; 3:15, 17², 20, 21; 4:8, 15; 5:14, 23, 34, 36, 40; 6:5, 12, 15, 28, 30, 38, 50; 7:3, 23, 32; 8:6, 59; 9:3, 36; 10:10², 17, 31, 38; 11:4, 11, 15, 16, 19, 31, 42, 52, 53, 55; 12:7, 9, 10, 20, 35, 36, 38, 42, 46, 47²; 13:15, 18, 19; 14:3, 13, 16, 29, 31; 15:2, 11, 16², 17, 25; 16:1, 4, 24, 33; 17:1, 2, 4, 11, 12, 13, 19, 21, 22, 23², 24, 26; 18:9, 28, 32, 36, 37; 19:4, 16, 24, 28, 31, 35, 36; 20:31²
ἵνα (purpose-result), 3:16; 9:39; 12:40
ἵνα (result), 4:36; 5:20; 6:7, 50; 9:2; 11:37; 17:21
ἵνα (subject), 11:50; 16:7
ἵνα (temporal), 12:23; 16:2, 32
ἵνα (predicate), 4:34
infinitive (cause with διὰ τό), 2:24
infinitive (complementary), 1:43, 46; 3:2, 3, 4³, 5, 7, 9, 14, 27, 30²; 4:4, 20, 24, 33, 47; 5:6, 10, 18, 19, 30, 35, 39, 40, 44; 6:6, 10, 15², 21, 44, 52, 60, 65, 67, 71; 7:1², 4, 7, 17, 19, 20, 25, 30, 34, 35³, 36, 39, 44; 8:5, 21, 22, 26², 37, 40, 43, 44; 9:4², 16, 27², 33; 10:16, 21, 29, 35, 39; 11:8, 37, 44, 51; 12:4, 21, 33, 34, 39; 13:5², 14, 33, 36, 37; 14:5, 17, 22; 15:4, 5; 16:12², 19; 18:8, 31, 32; 19:7, 12, 40; 20:9; 21:6, 12, 22, 23
infinitive (direct object), 5:26; 8:6
infinitive (epexegetical), 1:12; 4:32; 5:27; 10:18²; 13:10; 19:10²
infinitive (indirect discourse), 4:40; 12:18, 29; 16:2; 21:25

infinitive (purpose), 1:33; 4:7², 9, 10, 15, 38; 6:31, 52; 13:24; 14:2; 21:3
infinitive (subject), 18:14
infinitive (temporal with πρίν), 4:49; 8:58; 14:29
infinitive (temporal with πρὸ τοῦ), 1:48; 13:19; 17:5
internally headed relative clause, 6:14; 11:6

καθώς (causal), 17:2
καθώς (comparative), 1:23; 3:14; 5:23, 30; 6:31, 57, 58; 7:38; 8:28; 10:15; 12:14, 50; 14:27; 15:10, 12; 17:11, 14, 16, 21, 22, 23; 19:40
καθώς … καί (point/counterpoint), 13:5, 33, 34; 15:9; 17:18; 20:21
καθώς … οὕτως (point/counterpoint), 14:31; 15:4
καί (adjunctive), 1:31, 32, 33, 34; 2:2; 3:23; 4:45; 5:17, 19, 21, 26, 37, 39; 6:11, 57², 67; 7:3, 10, 47, 52; 8:19, 53; 9:15, 27, 40; 10:16; 11:16, 37; 12:10, 18, 26, 42; 13:14, 32; 14:1, 3, 7, 12, 19; 15:9, 20², 23, 27; 16:22; 17:18, 19, 21, 24; 18:2, 5, 17, 18, 25; 19:19, 23, 35, 39; 20:6, 8, 21, 30; 21:3, 20
καί (ascensive), 1:31, 33, 34; 8:14, 16, 25, 38; 10:38; 11:22, 25; 12:42; 14:12
καί (epexegetical), 1:16; 10:33; 12:13; 14:6
κατά (distributive), 8:9; 10:3; 21:25
κατά (opposition), 18:29; 19:11
κατά (purpose), 2:6
κατά (standard), 7:24; 8:15; 18:31; 19:7

lectio difficilior, 1:24; 6:36; 16:13; 17:24; 20:18; 21:4
left-dislocation, 1:12, 18, 31, 33²; 3:14, 26, 32; 5:11, 19, 21, 26, 37, 38; 6:39², 57; 7:10, 18, 27, 31, 38; 8:26, 28, 45; 10:1, 25; 11:6; 12:16,

48; 13:27; 14:12, 13, 21, 26; 15:2², 5; 17:2², 24; 18:9, 11
litotes, 2:12; 3:34; 6:37

μέν ... δέ (point/counterpoint), 10:41; 16:9, 10, 11, 22
μετά (association/accompaniment), 3:2, 22, 25, 26; 4:27²; 6:3, 33, 66; 7:33; 8:29; 9:37, 40; 11:16, 31, 54, 56; 12:8, 17; 13:8, 33; 14:9, 16, 30; 15:27; 16:4, 19, 32; 17:12, 24; 18:2, 5, 18, 26; 19:18; 20:24; 20:26
μετά (manner), 18:3; 19:40; 20:7
μετά (temporal), 2:12; 3:22; 4:43; 5:1, 14; 6:1; 7:1; 11:7, 11; 13:7; 13:27; 19:28, 38; 20:26; 21:1
metacomment, 1:51; 3:3, 5, 11; 4:35; 5:19, 24, 25; 6:26, 32, 47, 53; 8:34, 51, 58; 10:1, 7; 12:24; 13:16, 20, 21, 38; 14:12; 16:20, 23; 21:18
metonymy, 6:55²
μή (introducing a question expecting a negative answer), 3:4; 4:12, 29, 33; 6:67; 7:31, 35, 41, 47, 48, 51, 52; 8:53; 9:27, 40; 10:21; 18:17, 25; 21:5
μή ... ἀλλά (point/counterpoint), 3:16; 6:27, 39; 7:24; 18:40; 19:21, 24; 20:27
μή μόνον ... ἀλλὰ καί (point/counterpoint), 13:9
μήποτε (introducing a question expecting a negative answer), 7:26
μήτι (introducing a question expecting a negative answer), 8:22; 18:35

neuter plural subject with singular verb, 1:28; 3:9, 19, 20, 21, 23; 5:36; 6:23, 63; 7:7; 9:3; 10:3, 4, 6, 21, 41; 12:16; 15:7; 16:15; 19:28, 31, 36; 20:30, 31; 21:25
nominalizer, 1:29, 35, 43, 45; 4:31; 5:28; 6:22, 62, 66; 7:50; 8:11, 23²,

44; 9:8; 12:12; 18:6, 16; 19:23, 25, 38; 20:14; 21:2
nominative absolute, 19:19, 21
nominative complement in a double nominative construction, 1:41, 42²; 3:2; 4:25; 5:2; 8:4, 9; 9:7, 11; 11:16; 12:46; 19:17; 20:24; 21:2
nominative for vocative, 1:29; 12:15; 13:13²; 19:3; 20:28²
nominative in apposition, 1:18, 23, 27, 40, 42; 3:1, 13; 4:26; 5:29², 36; 6:4, 8², 15, 27, 42, 71; 7:2; 8:56; 10:16; 11:1, 2, 11, 27², 27, 39, 45, 49; 12:4², 13, 14²; 14:22, 26; 15:26; 16:13, 32; 18:2, 5, 16, 17; 19:19², 25², 38; 20:1, 18, 24, 31
nominative of exclamation, 1:29, 36, 47; 19:14, 26, 27
nominative (pendent), 6:39; 7:38; 8:45; 15:2; 17:2; 18:9, 11
nominative (predicate), 1:1², 4, 6, 8, 9, 14, 19², 20, 21², 22, 23, 25³, 33, 34, 40, 42, 49²; 3:1, 6², 10, 19, 28; 4:9, 10, 14, 18, 19, 24, 29, 34; 5:12, 13, 15, 27, 35, 39; 6:10, 14, 22, 29, 33, 35, 39, 40, 41, 42, 48, 50, 51², 55², 58; 6:63³, 64³, 69, 70; 7:18, 25, 26, 36, 40, 41, 49, 50; 8:12, 18, 25, 31, 33, 34, 37, 39², 42, 44³, 48, 54³, 55; 9:5, 8², 9², 14, 17, 19, 20, 24, 25, 27, 28², 36, 37; 10:1², 2, 6, 7, 8², 9, 11, 12², 13, 14, 16, 24, 33, 34, 36; 11:2, 25², 27, 38, 49, 51; 12:2, 6, 24, 34, 36, 42, 50; 13:10, 11, 25, 26, 35; 14:6³, 21; 15:1², 5², 8, 12, 14; 16:17, 18; 17:3, 6, 9, 10, 11, 17, 21, 22²; 18:10, 13², 14, 15, 26, 30, 33, 35, 37², 38, 40; 19:12, 21, 38; 20:14, 15, 31; 21:4, 7², 12², 20, 21, 24
nominative subject, 1:1³, 2, 3³, 4², 5², 6, 7², 8, 9², 10², 11, 12, 13, 14, 15³, 16, 17², 18³, 19⁴, 20, 21², 23², 25, 26³, 27, 28², 30⁴, 31², 32, 33⁴, 34², 35, 37, 38², 39, 40, 41², 42⁴, 43, 44, 45², 46³, 47², 48², 49³, 50; 2:1², 2, 3, 4³, 5, 6, 9³, 10², 11², 12, 13², 17²,

18, 19, 20³, 21, 22², 23, 24, 25²; 3:1, 2⁴, 3², 4², 5², 6², 8², 9², 10², 13², 14, 15, 16², 17², 18², 19⁵, 20², 21², 22, 23², 24, 25, 26⁴, 27², 28², 29³, 31³, 32, 33², 34, 35, 36³; 4:1⁴, 2², 5, 6³, 7², 8, 9², 10³, 11², 12³, 13², 14³, 15, 17², 19², 20³, 21², 22², 23³, 24, 25³, 26², 27², 28, 29², 31, 32², 33², 34², 35³, 36², 37³, 38⁴, 39, 40, 41, 42², 44², 45, 46², 47², 48, 49, 50⁴, 51², 52, 53⁴, 54; 5:1², 2, 3, 5, 6, 7⁴, 8, 9², 10², 11², 12, 13², 14², 15², 16, 17³, 18, 19⁴, 20², 21², 22, 23², 24, 25³, 26, 28², 30², 31², 32², 33, 34², 35², 36⁴, 37², 38², 39², 43², 44, 45³, 46; 6:1, 2, 3, 4, 5³, 7³, 8, 9³, 10³, 11, 12, 13, 14², 15, 16², 17², 18, 20, 21, 22⁵, 23, 24², 26, 27², 29³, 30, 31, 32³, 33, 35⁴, 37², 39, 40³, 41², 42², 43, 44³, 45², 46³, 48, 49, 50², 51⁴, 52², 53, 54², 55², 56², 57⁴, 58³, 60³, 61³, 63⁴, 64⁵, 65, 66, 67², 68, 69², 70³, 71; 7:1², 2, 3², 4², 5, 6³, 7³, 8³, 10², 11², 12³, 13, 14, 15², 16², 17², 18⁴, 19², 20², 21, 22, 23², 25², 26², 27², 28³, 29³, 30², 31³, 32², 33, 34², 35³, 36³, 37², 38³, 39³, 40, 41³, 42³, 43, 44², 45², 46², 47², 48, 49, 50, 51, 52², 53; 8:1, 2, 3, 4², 5², 6, 7, 9, 10², 11³, 12³, 13³, 14⁴, 15², 16³, 17, 18², 19², 20², 21³, 22³, 23⁴, 24, 25², 26², 28³, 29², 30, 31², 32, 33, 34², 35², 36, 37, 38², 39², 40², 41², 42⁴, 44³, 45, 46², 47², 48³, 49³, 50², 51, 52⁴, 53², 54³, 55, 56, 57, 58², 59; 9:2⁴, 3⁴, 4³, 7, 8², 9⁵, 10, 11³, 12, 14, 15, 16⁵, 17, 18, 19², 20², 21², 22³, 23, 24³, 25, 27, 28², 29², 30³, 31², 32, 33, 34², 35², 36, 37², 39⁴, 40, 41²; 10:1², 2, 3², 4, 6², 7², 8³, 9², 10², 11², 12³, 14², 15², 16, 17², 18², 19, 20, 21³, 22², 23, 24², 25⁴, 26, 27², 28², 29², 30, 31, 32, 33², 34², 35², 36², 38², 40, 41⁴, 42; 11:1, 2², 3², 4³, 5, 8², 9³, 10², 11, 12, 13³, 14², 16², 17, 18, 19, 20³, 21², 22, 23², 24, 25³, 26, 27², 28, 29, 30², 31, 32³, 33, 35, 36, 37³, 38², 39², 40, 41, 42², 44², 45, 46², 47², 48², 49², 50², 51, 54, 55², 56, 57²; 12:1³, 2², 3², 4, 5, 7, 9, 10, 11, 12², 13, 14, 15, 16³, 17, 18, 19², 20, 21, 22², 23³, 24, 25², 26⁵, 27, 28, 29³, 30², 31², 32, 34⁵, 35⁴, 36, 38³, 39, 41, 42, 44², 45, 46², 47², 48³, 49², 50³; 13:1², 2, 3, 6, 7³, 8², 9, 10⁴, 11, 13, 14², 15², 16², 18³, 19, 20², 21², 22, 23², 24², 25, 26³, 27², 28, 29³, 30², 31³, 32², 33², 34, 35, 36², 37, 38²; 14:1, 2, 3², 4, 5, 6³, 8, 9², 10⁴, 11², 12⁴, 13, 14, 16, 17², 19⁴, 20⁴, 21⁴, 22², 23³, 24², 26⁴, 27³, 28², 30, 31²; 15:1², 3, 4³, 5⁵, 6², 7, 8, 9², 10, 11², 12, 13², 14², 15², 16⁴, 18, 19³, 20², 23, 24, 25, 26⁴, 27; 16:2², 4², 5, 6, 7³, 8, 11, 13, 14, 15², 17, 18, 19, 20⁴, 21³, 22³, 24, 25, 26, 27³, 29, 30, 31, 32², 33; 17:1³, 3, 4, 5, 7, 8², 9, 10², 11³, 12⁴, 14³, 16, 17, 18, 19², 21⁶, 22², 23⁴, 24², 25⁴, 26²; 18:1³, 2², 3, 4, 5², 6, 8², 9, 10², 11², 12, 13, 14, 15², 16², 17³, 18², 19, 20⁴, 21², 22, 23, 24, 25³, 26³, 27², 29, 30, 31³, 32, 33², 34³, 35³, 36⁵, 37⁶, 38³, 39, 40; 19:1, 2, 4, 5², 6⁴, 7², 8, 9², 10, 11², 12³, 13, 14², 15³, 17, 19, 20³, 21², 22, 23², 24², 25, 26, 27, 28³, 29, 30, 31⁵, 32, 34², 35⁴, 36³, 37, 38², 39, 40, 41³, 42; 20:1, 2, 3, 4², 6, 7, 8, 10, 11, 12, 13, 15⁴, 16³, 17, 18, 19³, 20, 21⁴, 24³, 25, 26⁴, 28, 29², 30², 31; 21:1, 2², 3², 4², 5, 7³, 8, 10, 11², 12³, 13, 14², 15², 16, 17⁴, 18, 20⁴, 21², 22³, 23⁴, 24², 25³

objective genitive: *see* genitive (objective)
ὀπίσω (temporal), 1:15, 27, 30
ὀπίσω (locative), 12:19
ὅπως (purpose), 11:57
ὅταν (temporal), 2:10; 4:25; 5:7; 7:27, 31; 8:28, 44; 9:5; 10:4; 13:19; 14:29; 15:26; 16:4, 13, 21²; 21:18

ὅτε (temporal), 1:19; 2:22; 4:21, 23, 45; 5:25; 6:24; 9:4; 12:6, 17; 13:12, 31; 16:25; 17:12; 19:6, 8, 23, 30; 20:24; 21:15, 18

ὅτι (appositional), 3:21; 5:28; 9:30; 16:19; 21:23

ὅτι (causal), 1:15, 16, 17, 30, 50; 2:25; 3:18, 23; 4:22, 27; 5:16, 18, 27, 28, 30, 38, 39; 6:2, 26², 38, 41; 7:1, 7, 8, 23, 29, 30, 35, 39; 8:14, 16, 20, 22, 29, 37, 43, 44², 45, 47; 9:16, 17, 22; 10:4, 5, 13, 17, 26, 33, 36; 11:9, 10, 47; 12:6, 11, 18, 39, 41, 49; 14:2, 12, 17², 19, 22, 28²; 15:5, 15², 19, 21, 27; 16:3, 4, 6, 9, 10, 11, 14, 17, 21, 27, 32; 17:8, 9, 14, 24; 18:2, 18; 19:7, 20, 42; 20:13, 29; 21:17

ὅτι (clausal complement), 3:7; 4:35; 11:15; 14:28

ὅτι (clausal complement; direct discourse), 1:20, 32; 3:11, 28; 4:17, 35, 37, 39, 42, 52; 5:24, 25; 6:14, 42; 7:12; 8:33, 34, 54; 9:9², 11, 17, 23, 41; 10:7, 34, 36, 41; 11:56; 13:11, 21, 33; 14:2; 16:15, 20; 18:9; 19:21; 20:13, 18

ὅτι (clausal complement; indirect discourse), 1:34, 50; 2:17, 22; 3:2, 28; 4:1², 19, 20, 21, 25, 35, 42, 44, 47, 51, 53; 5:6, 15, 24, 25, 32, 36, 42, 45; 6:5, 15, 22², 24, 36, 46, 61, 65, 69; 7:7, 22, 26, 42, 52; 8:24², 27, 28, 34, 37, 48, 52, 55; 9:8, 18, 19, 20², 24, 25, 29, 31, 35; 10:38; 11:6, 13, 20, 22, 24, 27, 31², 40, 41, 42², 50, 51, 56; 12:9, 12, 16, 19, 34², 50; 13:1, 3², 19, 21, 29, 35; 14:2, 10, 11, 20, 28, 31; 15:18, 25; 16:4, 15, 19, 20, 26, 27, 30²; 17:7, 8², 21, 23, 25; 18:8, 14, 37; 19:4, 10, 28, 35; 20:9, 14, 15, 18, 31; 21:4, 7, 12, 15, 16, 17, 23, 24

ὅτι (consecutive), 14:22

ὅτι (direct object clause), 3:33

ὅτι (epexegetical), 2:18; 3:19; 14:22; 16:9, 10, 11, 21

ὅτι (subject clause), 8:17; 9:32

ὅτι-*recitativum*: *see* ὅτι (clausal complement; direct discourse)

οὐ (introducing a question expecting an affirmative answer), 4:35; 6:45, 70; 7:19, 25, 42; 8:48; 9:8; 10:34; 11:37, 40; 14:10; 18:26

οὐ ... ἀλλά (point/counterpoint), 1:8, 13, 31, 33; 3:17, 28, 36; 4:2; 5:24, 30, 34; 6:22, 26, 32, 38; 7:10, 16, 22, 28; 8:16, 49; 10:33; 11:4, 51; 12:6, 16, 30, 44, 47, 49; 14:24; 15:16, 19; 16:13; 17:9, 15; 19:33, 34; 20:7; 21:23

οὐ ... εἰ μή (point/counterpoint), 6:22, 46; 10:10; 13:10; 19:15

οὐ μή ... ἀλλά (point/counterpoint), 4:14; 10:5

οὐ μόνον ... ἀλλὰ καί (point/counterpoint), 5:18; 11:52; 12:9; 17:20

οὐδέ ... ἀλλά (point/counterpoint), 5:22; 8:42

οὐδείς ... εἰ μή (point/counterpoint), 3:13; 14:6; 17:12

οὐκέτι ... ἀλλά (point/counterpoint), 11:54

οὔτε ... οὔτε ... ἀλλά (point/counterpoint), 9:3

οὐχί (introducing a question expecting an affirmative answer), 11:9

παρά (agency), 1:6; 4:9
παρά (association), 8:38; 17:5²
παρά (locative), 19:25
παρά (source), 1:14, 40; 5:34, 41, 44²; 6:45, 46; 8:38, 40; 9:16, 33; 10:18; 15:15, 26²; 16:27, 28; 17:7, 8
participle (attendant circumstance), 2:15; 8:2, 6, 8, 10; 9:11²; 12:14, 24; 13:25; 18:3²; 19:2, 29, 30; 20:7, 16
participle (attributive), 1:6, 9, 18, 29, 40²; 2:6, 9²; 3:29²; 4:5, 9², 10, 11, 14, 25; 5:2², 5, 12, 13, 23, 35², 37;

6:12, 14, 22, 27², 41, 44, 50, 51²,
57, 58; 7:38, 49, 50; 8:3, 16, 18, 31;
9:7, 11, 40; 11:1, 16, 17, 31², 33,
42, 49, 52, 54; 12:4, 12, 17, 29², 49;
14:24; 15:2, 25; 18:22, 26; 19:13,
17, 24, 32, 39; 20:8, 24; 21:2, 24²,
25

participle (causal), 1:9; 2:3, 23; 4:6,
45, 47; 5:6, 13, 44; 6:14, 15, 18,
61; 11:31, 38, 51; 12:6; 13:1², 3;
17:4; 18:4, 10; 19:28, 38; 20:15, 20;
21:12

participle (concessive), 4:9²; 7:15, 50;
9:25; 10:33; 12:37; 19:38; 20:26;
21:11

participle (conditional), 5:44; 15:2

participle (manner), 1:28, 31; 4:51;
7:15, 28²; 8:9²; 9:7; 11:3, 28, 32;
12:15; 13:22; 17:1; 18:18², 22, 24;
19:5, 17, 39; 20:6, 11; 21:8

participle (means), 17:4; 20:31

participle (imperfect periphrastic),
1:9, 28; 2:6; 3:23; 10:40; 11:1;
13:23; 18:18, 25, 30; 19:41

participle (perfect periphrastic),
2:17; 3:21, 27, 28; 6:31, 45, 65;
10:34, 40; 12:13, 14; 16:24; 17:19,
23; 20:30

participle (pleonastic), 1:15, 26,
32; 4:31; 6:52; 7:37; 8:12; 9:2, 19;
12:21, 23; 18:40; 19:6, 12

participle (pluperfect periphrastic),
1:24; 3:24; 12:16; 13:5; 18:18, 25²;
19:11, 19, 20

participle (predicative), 1:29, 32, 33²,
36, 37, 38, 47, 48, 51³; 2:14; 5:6,
19, 38; 6:19², 62; 7:32; 8:4; 10:12;
11:33², 44; 17:13; 19:26, 33; 20:1,
5, 6, 7², 12, 14; 21:9², 20

participle (present periphrastic),
1:41

participle (purpose), 1:31; 6:6, 24;
8:6; 12:33; 18:32; 20:18; 21:19

participle (result), 5:18

participle (substantival), 1:12, 15,
22, 23, 27, 33²; 2:14, 16; 3:6², 8,
13, 15, 16, 18², 20, 21, 29, 31³, 33,
36²; 4:10, 13, 23, 24, 26, 34, 36³,
37²; 5:3, 7, 10, 11, 13, 15, 23, 24³,
25, 29², 30, 32, 39, 45; 6:2, 11, 13,
33², 35², 37, 38, 39, 40², 45², 46, 47,
54², 56², 57, 58, 63, 64²; 7:16, 18³,
28, 33, 38, 39; 8:12, 18, 26, 29, 34,
47, 50², 54; 9:4, 8³, 18, 32, 37, 39²;
10:1², 2, 12, 21; 11:2², 25, 26², 27,
37, 39, 44, 45²; 12:2, 4, 6, 13, 20,
25², 35, 44², 45², 46, 48³; 13:10, 11,
16, 18, 20³, 28; 14:9, 12, 21⁴, 24;
15:2, 5, 21, 23; 16:2, 5, 13; 17:20;
18:2, 4, 14, 21, 37; 19:11, 12, 35;
20:29²; 21:20

participle (temporal), 1:36, 38³, 42;
2:3, 15, 23; 3:4; 4:39, 47, 51, 54;
5:6², 13, 44; 6:5², 11, 14, 15, 17,
19, 23, 25, 59, 60, 61; 7:9, 14, 28²,
40; 8:2, 3, 9, 10, 20, 30; 9:1, 6, 11²,
25, 35; 11:4, 17, 28, 31, 32, 43, 56;
12:12, 14, 24, 36; 13:1, 2², 4, 21,
26, 30; 14:25; 16:8; 17:1; 18:1, 3,
18, 22, 32, 38; 19:2, 13, 26, 28, 33;
20:1, 5, 14, 16, 19², 20², 22, 31;
21:4, 7, 14, 19, 20, 21

partitive genitive: *see* genitive
(partitive)

pendent nominative: *see* nominative
(pendent)

πέραν (locative), 1:28; 3:26; 6:1, 17,
22, 25; 10:40; 18:1

περί (advantage/representation),
16:26; 17:9³, 20²

περί (reference), 1:7, 8, 15, 22, 47;
2:21, 25; 3:25; 5:31, 32², 36, 37, 39,
46; 6:41, 61; 7:7, 12, 13, 17, 32, 39;
8:13, 14, 18², 26, 46; 9:17, 18, 21;
10:13, 25, 33², 41; 11:13², 19; 12:6,
41; 13:18, 22, 24; 15:22, 26; 16:8³,
9, 10, 11, 19, 25; 18:19², 23, 34;
19:24; 21:24

periphrasis, 5:39

πλησίον (locative), 4:5

possessive genitive: *see* genitive
(possessive)

predicate accusative: *see* accusative (predicate)
predicate adjective, 1:15, 27, 30, 39; 3:19, 33; 4:6, 11, 12, 35, 37³; 5:6, 9, 14², 30, 31, 32²; 6:45, 60; 7:6, 7, 12², 16, 28; 8:7, 13, 14, 16², 17, 26, 33, 36, 53; 9:2, 9, 18, 19, 20, 22, 24, 25, 31, 34, 39, 40, 41; 10:12, 29, 30, 41; 11:39; 13:10, 16², 17; 14:18, 24, 28; 15:3, 20; 16:15, 32; 17:10; 18:15, 18, 26; 19:14, 23², 31, 35; 20:4, 8, 27², 29; 21:7, 18, 24
predicate adverb, 2:1, 13; 3:8, 23; 4:6; 5:5; 6:4, 9, 22, 24, 25; 7:2; 11:55; 18:28; 19:42
predicate nominative: *see* nominative (predicate)
πρός (association), 1:1, 2
πρός (indirect object), 2:3; 3:4; 4:15, 33, 48, 49; 6:5, 28, 34; 7:3, 35, 50; 8:26, 31, 33, 57; 11:21; 12:19; 16:17; 19:24
πρός (motion toward), 1:19, 29, 42, 47; 3:2, 20, 21, 26²; 4:30, 40, 47; 5:33, 40, 45; 6:5, 17, 35, 37², 44, 45, 52, 65, 68; 7:33, 37, 45, 50; 8:2; 9:13; 10:35, 41; 11:3, 15, 19, 29, 32, 45, 46; 12:32; 13:1, 3, 6; 14:3, 6, 12, 18, 23, 28²; 16:5, 7², 10, 17, 28; 17:11, 13; 18:13, 24, 29, 38; 19:3, 39; 20:2², 10, 17³
πρός (purpose), 4:35; 13:28
πρός (reference), 21:22, 23
πρός (result), 11:4
πρός (spatial proximity), 18:16; 20:11, 12²
πρός (temporal), 5:35

redundant quotative frame, 1:20, 25, 48, 50; 2:18, 19; 3:3, 9, 10, 27; 4:7, 13, 17; 5:19; 6:26, 29, 43; 7:16, 21, 52; 8:14, 39, 48; 9:20, 30, 34, 36; 12:30, 44; 13:7, 21; 14:23; 18:25, 30; 20:28

right-dislocation, 1:12, 45; 3:1, 2, 13; 4:26; 6:8², 27; 8:40; 9:13

second (anarthrous) predicate position, 2:6; 9:1
second attributive position, 1:9, 29, 40, 41; 2:9; 3:16, 29²; 4:9, 11; 5:12, 23, 30², 35, 43; 6:13, 14, 22, 27², 32, 38, 41, 44, 50, 51², 58; 7:6², 18, 49; 8:16, 17, 31, 37, 43², 56; 9:11; 10:11², 26; 11:31², 42, 52; 12:12, 17, 26, 29²; 14:15, 26; 15:1, 9, 11, 12, 25; 17:13, 17, 24; 18:10, 16², 35, 36; 19:24, 32; 20:8; 21:24²
second predicate position, 1:29, 32, 33, 36, 47, 51³; 2:14; 5:19, 22, 36, 38; 6:10, 19², 62; 7:32; 8:4; 10:4, 12; 11:44; 12:9, 12; 17:10
subjective genitive: *see* genitive (subjective)
subjunctive (deliberative), 6:5, 28; 12:27, 49²; 18:11, 39; 19:15
subjunctive (hortatory), 11:7, 15, 16; 14:31; 19:24²
subjunctive with ἄν, 1:33; 2:5; 4:14; 5:19; 10:38; 11:22; 14:13
subjunctive with ἐάν, 3:2, 3, 5, 12, 27; 4:48; 5:19, 31, 43; 6:44, 51, 53², 62, 65; 7:17, 37, 51²; 8:14, 16, 24, 31, 36, 51, 54, 55; 9:22, 31²; 10:9; 11:9, 10, 40, 48; 12:24², 26, 32, 47; 13:8, 17, 35; 14:3², 14, 15; 15:4², 6, 7³, 10, 14; 16:7², 23; 19:12; 20:25³; 21:22, 23, 25
subjunctive with ἵνα, 1:7², 8, 19, 22, 27, 31; 2:25; 3:15, 16², 17², 20, 21; 4:8, 15², 34², 36, 47²; 5:7, 14, 20, 23, 34, 36, 40; 6:5, 7, 12, 15, 28, 29, 30², 38, 39², 40, 50²; 7:3, 23, 32; 8:6, 56, 59; 9:2, 3, 22, 36, 39²; 10:10⁵, 17, 31, 38²; 11:4, 11, 15, 16, 19, 31, 37, 42, 50², 52, 53, 55, 57²; 12:7, 9, 10, 20, 23, 35, 36, 38, 40³, 42, 46, 47²; 13:1, 2, 15, 18, 19, 29, 34²; 14:3, 13, 16, 29, 31; 15:2, 8²,

11, 12, 13, 16⁴, 17, 25; 16:1, 2, 4, 7, 24, 30, 32², 33; 17:1, 2, 3, 4, 11, 12, 13, 15², 19, 21³, 22, 23², 24², 26; 18:9, 28², 32, 36, 37, 39; 19:4, 16, 24, 28, 31³, 35, 36, 38; 20:31²
subjunctive with ὅπως, 11:57
subjunctive with ὅταν, 2:10; 4:25; 5:7; 7:27, 31; 8:28, 44; 9:5; 10:4; 13:19; 14:29; 15:26; 16:4, 21²; 21:18
σύν (association/accompaniment), 12:2; 18:1; 21:3
synecdoche, 1:12; 2:23; 3:18; 15:21; 20:31

temporal frame, 1:1, 30, 35, 38, 43, 48; 2:1, 9, 10, 12, 22, 23; 3:2; 4:1, 31, 40, 43, 45; 5:1, 7, 14; 6:1, 12, 22; 7:1, 37; 8:7; 9:5; 10:4; 11:11, 20, 22, 29, 32, 33, 53; 12:1, 12, 16, 27, 31, 36; 13:1, 19, 31; 14:29; 16:5, 13; 17:5, 7, 12, 13; 19:1, 8, 30; 20:1
third attributive position, 1:18; 4:25; 5:2; 7:50; 11:16; 20:24; 21:2
topical frame, 1:1, 2, 3², 4², 5², 10², 11, 14, 15, 17², 18, 19, 21, 24, 25, 26, 28, 30, 31, 33, 34, 38, 39, 42², 45, 49; 2:5, 8, 9, 10, 15, 16, 17, 20, 23, 24; 3:2, 14, 15, 16, 18², 20, 21, 26², 30², 31³, 33, 35, 36²; 4:8, 12, 13, 18, 20, 23, 32, 38, 42², 44², 46; 5:20, 33, 34, 36, 39, 43, 45²; 6:6, 14², 18, 33, 35²; 7:6², 18, 40, 41; 8:7, 12, 21, 35², 38², 44, 47, 49², 50, 53; 9:30, 35; 10:2, 6, 10, 11, 12², 16, 21, 27; 11:4, 10, 11, 19, 20, 22, 25, 26, 27², 31, 32, 33, 37, 41, 42, 43, 45, 46, 49; 12:3, 8², 25², 26, 27, 29, 31, 34, 35, 44, 45, 46², 47, 48; 13:10, 13, 14, 15, 18, 20², 26, 38; 14:9, 10³, 12, 16, 20², 21, 24, 27, 28; 15:20, 23; 16:4, 7, 20, 21; 17:4, 9, 14; 18:20², 35, 36, 37², 38; 19:7, 20

TSKS construction, 5:24; 6:33, 40, 45, 54; 8:50; 9:8; 10:1; 11:2, 26; 12:48; 14:21; 20:17, 29

ὑπέρ (purpose), 11:4
ὑπέρ (reference/respect), 1:30
ὑπέρ (representation), 6:51; 10:11, 15; 15:13; 17:19
ὑπέρ (substitution), 11:50, 51, 52; 13:37, 38; 15:13; 17:19; 18:14
ὑπό (locative), 1:48
ὑπό (ultimate agency), 14:21
ὑποκάτω (locative), 1:50

vocative of direct address, 1:38², 49; 2:4; 3:2, 26; 4:11, 15, 19, 21, 31, 49; 5:7; 6:25, 34, 68; 8:4, 10, 11; 9:2, 36, 38; 11:3, 8, 12, 27, 32, 34, 39, 41, 43; 12:21, 27, 28, 38; 13:6, 9, 25, 33, 36, 37; 14:5, 8, 9, 22; 17:1, 5, 11, 21, 24, 25; 19:26; 20:13, 15², 16³; 21:5, 15², 16², 17², 20, 21

χωρίς (separation), 1:3; 15:5

ὡς (comparative), 1:14, 32; 15:6
ὡς (temporal), 2:9, 23; 4:1, 40; 6:12, 16; 7:10; 8:7; 11:6, 20, 29, 32, 33; 12:35, 36; 18:6; 19:33; 20:11; 21:9
ὥσπερ (comparative), 5:21, 26

www.ingramcontent.com/pod-product-compliance
Lightning Source LLC
Chambersburg PA
CBHW051247300426
44114CB00011B/922